THE CATHOLIC
CATECHISM

Dedicated
with Profound Respect to
POPE PAUL VI

THE CATHOLIC CATECHISM

JOHN A. HARDON, S.J.

DOUBLEDAY & COMPANY, INC.
GARDEN CITY, NEW YORK

Imprimi Potest: Daniel L. Flaherty, S.J.
                     Provincial
                     Chicago Province
                     November 8, 1974
Nihil obstat: Daniel V. Flynn, J.C.D.
                     Censor Librorum
Imprimatur:✝James P. Mahoney, D.D.
                     Vicar General
                     Archdiocese of New York
                     December 13, 1974

The nihil obstat and imprimatur are official declarations that a book or pamphlet is free of doctrinal error. No implication is contained therein that those who have granted the nihil obstat and imprimatur agree with the contents, opinions or statements expressed.

Library of Congress Cataloging in Publication Data

Hardon, John A
The Catholic catechism.

Bibliography: p. 573.
Includes index.
1. Theology, Catholic.   2. Catholic Church—Doctrinal and controversial works—Catholic authors.
I. Title.
BX1751.2.H36   230'.2
ISBN 0-385-08039-5 Trade
0-385-08045-X Paperbound
Library of Congress Catalog Card Number 73–81433

ACKNOWLEDGMENTS

There are too many people to thank for their generous assistance in the writing of this volume to name all of them. But some persons must be mentioned: the members of the hierarchy who encouraged the publication of *The Catholic Catechism* and those who have since given it their warm approval; His Eminence John Cardinal Wright, Prefect of the Sacred Congregation for the Clergy, for his indispensable preface of recommendation; Rev. Joseph T. Mangan, S.J., and Rev. Earl A. Weis, S.J., deans of the graduate and undergraduate departments of theology at Loyola University of Chicago for their careful reading of the manuscript and numerous suggestions; Mr. John J. Delaney, Catholic editor of Doubleday & Company, for his invaluable counsel from the first stages of planning all through the publication of the book; and Mrs. Warren Joyce for her expert secretarial services in preparing the typescript.

CONTENTS

14 CONTENTS

PREFATORY NOTE

When the *General Catechetical Directory* was ordered for publication by Pope Paul VI on April 11, 1971, it faced the urgent need in the Church for sound directives and clear leadership in the world of catechetics, a world that had become beset with mutual contradictions and even chaos. Vatican Council II had introduced many disciplinary changes, and the implementation of these, sometimes pastorally skillful, sometimes irresponsible, required a fresh look at the everyday faith of the Church and its need to be presented in a sound fashion.

In the wake of the Council, and under the aegis of acting in its "spirit" sometimes without reference to what it actually said, not a few aberrations, exaggerations, and deficiencies began to creep into textbooks and classrooms of some parts of the Church's teaching structure. The *Directory* was needed lest tumult break out among believers. In the first place, it offers an authentic guide to the teaching of the updated doctrinal texts issued by the Council. In this capacity it also functions to codify, collect, and direct the thrust of the teaching content of the Council. In response to the confusion in some teaching areas, the *Directory* offered clear, sane guidelines.

But the *Directory* was not intended to be a new universal catechism, like the works that appeared after the Councils of Trent and Vatican I. It was inspired by the need to offer general guidelines that would function like the road signals along any well-marked highway. It gives an indication of just how far the traveler can go before crashing into the ditch. The actual laying out of the roadbed and the paving of the surface are left to those in each land who teach the faith as Captains in Israel and under specific local conditions. The same surface material might not work equally well in Montreal and Lagos, though the same basic orientation of faith prevails, or should, in both.

With this in mind, it devolved upon the various conferences of bishops, teachers of religion, and individuals to prepare catechisms geared to local situations. The *Directory* provides "the basic prin-

ciples of pastoral theology"—principles taken from the magisterium
of the Church and, in a special way, from the Second Vatican
Council. Others are called upon to apply these principles and produce the catechetical texts that will embody them locally and
specifically.

Father Hardon of the Jesuit School of Theology in Chicago has
taken on the task of responsible author of the present book. The
result is a comprehensive work entitled *The Catholic Catechism.*
The work describes itself as a "concise source book on the principal
teachings of the Catholic Church." It offers readings in Catholic
theology on every major segment of the Catholic tradition of faith.

The attempt to present a "source book" has necessarily resulted
in an extensive, though easily read, text with many attractive
features. For instance, the Bible is given special prominence in the
presentation of the doctrine of the faith. The latest insights offered
by the Council are blended with the unchanging dogmas of the
Church to present a clear and logical unfolding of the teaching of
the Catholic Church from the apostles to our own times.

Each group or person who undertakes to do a book of catechesis must choose some outline. And as long as there are alive
two writers, the merits of any one outline can be disputed. No
doubt this is true of the work authored by Father Hardon. There
are, of course, various ways to lay out a highway and different
surface materials to be selected. But as long as the road helps the
traveler reach his goal soundly and safely, the essential purpose of
the highway is satisfied. There is no doubt that the book written by
Father Hardon will not only help the traveler on the road of
catechetical inquiry reach his destination but do so with security
and fidelity.

For today's student of religion, the text offers such topical sections
as The Challenge of Modern Atheism and a balanced explanation
of some of the discussions of Catholic doctrinal development in
times of confusion. One notes particularly the treatment of the
questions of the divinity of Christ and its gradual definition, in
all its aspects, by successive Church councils from Nicea through
Ephesus to Chalcedon. The student will be grateful for the manner
in which this delicate and sometimes confusing discussion is made
intelligible, a quality missing from many discussions, oral and printed.

Another aspect of the work that makes it satisfying is a compre-
hensiveness that takes into account such areas of study as the

theological virtues, Catholic Tradition, and post-conciliar ecumenism. So detailed is the text that one could go on almost indefinitely listing matters of concern within the contemporary Church that form part of the hundreds of pages of this conscientiously thought-out catechetical treatise.

Essentially the question of the merit and value of any catechism boils down to whether it meets the purpose of a book of catechetical instruction. It is an instrument, and as such it must be weighed in the scale of how well it serves the purpose for which it was created. If the instrument works, if it works well and performs the task for which it was invented, then it is a good instrument. Much like the highway system, again, if it gets the traveler to his destination safely and with a minimum of "deviation," then we must call it a good road.

This book has as an obvious recommendation the fact that it does exactly this. It offers itself as a source book on the principal teachings of the Catholic Church. This goal has been accomplished with evident dedication and erudition. For students of the faith and their teachers, this book, *The Catholic Catechism,* will be a warmly welcome tool and, in the midst of confusion, a relief.

JOHN CARDINAL WRIGHT

Vatican City

INTRODUCTION

This volume is intended to meet a widely felt need for an up-to-date and concise source book on the principal teachings of the Catholic Church. Since the close of the Second Vatican Council, there has been such an accumulation of ecclesiastical constitutions and decrees and so many changes they introduced in Catholic practice that few people have been able to keep up with all that has happened. Much less could they be expected to assemble the documents and information in some organized fashion.

At the time of the Council of Trent, a number of manuals were published to capsulize the declarations of that historic council. Among them were the *Catechisms* of Peter Canisius and Robert Bellarmine for popular use, and the authoritative *Roman Catechism,* decreed by the Council for parish priests and teachers to help them explain the faith to the people.

The situation after the Second Vatican Council is somewhat different. Unlike Trent, the twenty-first ecumenical council was not so much struggling to safeguard the faith as to interpret and expand the Church's message of salvation for modern times. As a result, the Vatican documents do not call for the same pastoral editing as was necessary for the definitions and highly technical statements published in the sixteenth century. They are already pastoral in their approach and immediately useful for clergy and laity alike. But they need to be co-ordinated and, as far as possible, synthesized in order to bring out clearly what the Church's hierarchy is saying and what direction the Church is taking as we face the complexities of our communications age. Otherwise the sheer quantity of documentation is liable to confuse or at least obscure the guidance of the Holy Spirit in our day.

The Second Vatican Council presumed on the Church's ageless teaching and built on the declarations of popes and councils, the writings of saints and mystics, and the collective faith of the People of God. This vast tradition represents, along with Sacred Scripture, the revealed wisdom that Catholic Christianity cherishes as its most precious gift from the Father of Lights.

It is not easily accessible to most people, however, and so immense that some synthesis was called for. A parallel purpose of this volume, therefore, is to offer those who use it a handy guidebook of the Catholic tradition, whether formally documented in ecclesiastical sources or implicitly accepted by the faithful under the aegis of the Church's hierarchical leaders. Hopefully it will answer to the desire of many for an expression of their corporate religious convictions, which run deeper than any piece of writing or Church legislation can articulate, since they are born of the invisible grace of God, who is living and active in the hearts of all who believe.

There are three parts to the volume, of unequal length, dealing in sequence with the faith, morality, and ritual of the Catholic Church. While it is impossible, practically, to separate these three levels of doctrine, it is nevertheless useful to do so for reasons of clarity. There will necessarily be overlapping of areas from one level to another, since whatever pertains to belief also affects morality and worship, and so of other relationships. One way to obviate these overlappings was to make sure that cross references were available from belief to morals to worship; yet all the while, each section of the triad has been given its full attention.

Another reason for the threefold division was to help the catechist present the matter in some consistent and pedagogically recognized form. We should be able to distinguish the doctrines we believe on God's revealed word, the actions we practice in response to his manifest will, and the worship of praise and service we give him as our Creator and Lord and the goal of our destiny.

A studied effort was made to concentrate on those aspects of belief, conduct, and ritual that are most significant. This means that a hierarchy of doctrines is not only permissible but recommended. It does not mean that some doctrines are more true than others, since whatever God has revealed is true and whatever we conclude from his revelation is also valid. But some truths are more in the limelight than others, or more immediately pertinent than others, and therefore more pastorally deserving of attention. How does this happen?

In some periods of Christian history, certain features of the Christian faith and order are more severely challenged, or more emphasized because of contemporary needs, or more plainly seen because they answer to people's wants, or more in tune with the changes in culture and more able to satisfy the legitimate expectations of human society. In any case, this adaptation tends to fluctuate and has nothing to do with God's immutable truth. The Trinity of Persons in God and the duality of natures in Christ, the Real Presence of Christ in the Eucharist and the primacy of his vicar on earth are perennially important even while they may differ in the way the Church stresses now one and now another of the Christian mysteries so as to be of best service to mankind. Both continuity and change were given free range in the composition of the book, but each for different reasons. We need a sense of continuity, since we believe that Christ, the invisible head of the Church, is the same yesterday, today, and forever. Hence the attention paid to giving a clear presentation of the basic truths of Christianity. We also need a sense of flexibility since we believe the Church is a living organism that thrives on adaptation. Hence the concern to show the particular value of certain religious principles and practices in the postconciliar age.

The method followed in presenting the Church's doctrine is a combination of history and logic. Doctrines are placed into a historical framework by tracing their origins to the Old and New Testaments and placing their development within the context of persons, places, and times. The doctrine thus becomes more intelligible because it is viewed in the setting of its vital growth over the centuries.

Naturally this attempt to give a historical perspective had to be measured by the page limitations of the book and also by the main focus of what is presented, namely the teachings themselves. The primary aim throughout was to give the doctrines themselves, whether of creed, code, or cult, and to make them plain. Yet without also taking into account their historical background, there was the risk of making the Church's official or accepted teachings seem to be what they are not, a collection of categorical statements produced by ecclesiastical authority and detached from real life.

Some may wonder why we have not had more such compendia of Catholicism published by now, since the Vatican Council finished in the midsixties. The main reason is that there have been three stages to the Council, not commonly adverted to. The first stage was the elaborate preparation, which began in 1959 when Pope John XXIII announced his intention to convoke a general council. During this time extensive studies were made on the basis of an enormous correspondence with all parts of the Catholic world. Out of this period came the agenda for the Council and the preliminary drafts of the future documents.

The second stage was the Council itself, which covered a span of four years. Pope John opened the first assembly, which ran from October 11 to December 8, 1962. Following John's death on June 3, 1963, Paul VI reconvened the Council for the other three sessions, which finally closed on December 8, 1965. The Council prelates issued, with Pope Paul's approval, sixteen distinct documents, i.e., two dogmatic and two pastoral constitutions, nine decrees and three declarations, all of which reflect its pastoral outlook toward renewal and reform in the Catholic Church.

The third stage came after the Council closed, but it depended on what had been decided during the actual sessions. This was to implement many of the conciliar decisions by means of special commissions, working under the Pope. The implementation has taken the form of by now several score "Norms of Application" of the conciliar documents, ranging from new faculties granted to bishops to the directives for mixed marriages. The present compendium of faith and practice could not have been written until a sufficient number of such norms had been officially promulgated as affecting the essential aspects of Catholic living.

In the spirit of the late Council, the Bible is given special prominence in the presentation of what Catholics believe, how they worship, and what their religion means to them. Always kept in view, however, was the fact that, from the Catholic standpoint, the Scriptures are not self-explanatory, that they require the Church's magisterium or teaching authority to explain what the more substantive passages mean and how they are to be lived out by the faithful. The resulting amalgam of biblical passages and ecclesial pronouncements is not strange to one who sees, with St. Peter, that "the interpretation of scriptural prophecy is never a matter for the individual. Why? Because no prophecy ever came from man's initiative. When men spoke for God it was the Holy Spirit that moved them" (2 P. 1:20–21). Catholicism holds that the same Spirit now abides in the Church as a community of believers who are assured of the truth by their agreement among themselves under the guidance of the successors of the apostles united with Peter's successor, the bishop of Rome.

Part of the genius of the Catholic Church, reflected in these pages, is her ability to maintain a careful balance between extremes. Instead of taking one side of a radical "either, or," she remains faithful to God's eternal "and," which spans both sides of what the natural man is inclined to call a contradiction but which the spiritual man knows is simply a mirror of divine mystery.

Christianity is therefore full of paradoxes, or apparent contradictions, which the Holy Spirit has successfully proclaimed for two millennia through the Church, which he animates as the soul of her corporate existence.

As Catholicism looks upon reality it is not monistic, since the universe is not either God or the world; it is God *and* the world. Jesus Christ is not either God or man; he is God *and* man. The head of the Church he founded is not either Christ or the Pope, but Jesus Christ is her invisible head *and* the Pope is Christ's vicar on earth. Man's hope of salvation does not depend on either grace or free will, but on divine grace, which envelops every human action *and* man's free co-operation with the invitation of God. The sacraments we receive are not either pure symbols or sources of God's grace, but they are symbolic rituals *and* causes of divine blessings which they signify. Our conduct is not either all good because everyone is saved or all bad because everyone is depraved, but it is good *and* bad because we can either co-operate with God's will or reject the advances of his love.

Whatever else this catechism is intended to bring out it is the simple complexity of the Christian religion. It is simple in that all, even the least learned, can profess the fullness of faith and grow in that childlike holiness which the Savior expects of his followers. It is also complex, however, in the depth of its revealed mysteries, which defy merely human analysis or the efforts of pure reason to comprehend.

In this sense, a catechism is not like other books. It makes no claim to explain what it contains, except insofar as words need clarification or the terms that are often technical need to be simplified.

The intended reading audience of this Catholic catechism are all those priests, religious, and laity, and above all, parents and teachers, who are looking for a concise statement of the faith they profess, the conduct they practice, and the worship they give to the Lord— not so much for themselves but for others who, under God, have been placed under their care. It is called a catechism, not in the traditional sense of a bare list of questions and answers, but in the modern sense of a manual for catechetical instruction. It presumes that what is here described is already believed, and offers some assistance in communicating to others something of the "breadth and the length, the height and the depth" of the riches hidden in Christ Jesus.

PART ONE

DOCTRINES
OF THE FAITH

I. THE WORD OF GOD

The human spirit has a climate in which it lives, no less than the human body, and in both cases we feel the atmosphere by experience. We know, without being told, whether it is warm or cold or somewhere in between.

In our day, the atmosphere of the spirit is scientific, in the accepted sense that whatever we know has been tested by experiment and proved by factual, even mathematical, demonstration. That is one feature of the age in which we are living, its demand for proof, in size, shape, and numbers, for whatever a person is expected to embrace with his mind. Otherwise, so the argument runs, one would be acting irrationally.

Ironically, though, this same spirit of scientific rationalism has a disarming modesty about it. For all its hard demands to be shown before it accepts anything, it is remarkably slow to claim that what it knows is certainly and, still less, unchangeably true. Theories in the sciences come and go, and the last thing a specialist in any field is supposed to say is "the last word" on whatever subject he has been investigating.

Immersed in the present climate of the scientific age, a believing Christian is pressed on two sides. The world in which one lives keeps asking for evidence, it wants to be shown that what the believer believes is not mere illusion but objectively true. This same world protests that all human knowledge is unstable, that what people know today others will know better and more accurately tomorrow. So the man of faith must defend himself against the charge of dogmatism, as though what he believes now has always been true and will remain essentially unchanged in a universe whose only apparent constant is change.

It would be tempting to try to respond immediately to both levels of criticism in our day. More effective is to look at ourselves and ask what too many Christians have taken for granted: What *do* we believe, and why? This will lead us into pastures that few Catholics, who may be severely orthodox, have ever visited. We are discovering that orthodoxy is no guarantee of perseverance and still less of living up to what the faith demands. Self-knowledge as believers will deepen our loyalty and help evoke generosity, and in the process the commonplace objections will also be satisfactorily answered.

GOD SPEAKS AND MAN LISTENS

Three words are pivotal for a correct understanding of Catholic belief. They are *revelation, faith,* and *reason.* Each has its own long history of conflict and consequent refinement, so that the Church's present insight is deeper and more precise than ever before. We might expect the present challenge from modern science to still further deepen and clarify their meaning.

Divine Revelation. Faith and revelation are related as cause and effect. God reveals himself and, if we respond, we believe. His revelation, therefore, implies God's awareness of the limitations of our mind. The biblical term *apocalypse* (Greek *apocalupsis,* Latin *revelatio*) means an unveiling, so that a revelation discloses what was previously unknown or at least partially hidden from view.

In his goodness and wisdom, God chose to reveal himself and make known to us the hidden designs of his will.[1] His purpose is that, through Christ and with the help of the Holy Spirit, we might have access to the Father and come to share in the divine nature.[2]

Actually God reveals himself on two levels of knowledge. His first witness is in the world of creation, brought into being and kept in existence, as John tells us, through the Word that was with God from the beginning (Jn. 1:1–2). Already in this sense, Christ as God is revealing himself in the universe of created things.

This is sometimes called natural revelation, and the expression is valid if properly understood. It means that, having given us the nature with which we are born (*nati*), God as it were owed us enough access to knowing him and his will as would enable us to reach our human destiny.

St. Paul clearly insists on man's responsibility to praise God arising from his ability to know God from the creatures he has made. He told the recent converts to Christianity that some of their contemporaries were keeping "the truth imprisoned in their wickedness." How so? Because "what can be known about God is perfectly plain to them since God himself has made it plain. Ever since God created the world, his everlasting power and deity—however invisible—have been there for the mind to see in the things he has made. That is why such people are without excuse. They knew God and yet refused to honor him as God or to thank him. Instead, they made nonsense out of logic and their empty minds were darkened. The more they called themselves philosophers, the more stupid they grew, until they exchanged the glory of the immortal God for a worthless imitation" (Rm. 1:18–23).

Nor was that all. Paul told the Romans of every generation of history that failure to give God his due honor cannot be done with impunity. Since they refused to worship the Lord whom their reason could recognize, he in turn "left them to their filthy enjoyments and the practices with which they dishonor their own bodies, since they had given up divine truth for a lie and have worshiped and served creatures instead of the Creator" (Rm. 1:24–25).

As St. Augustine was later to explain in his *Confessions,* there is a grim recompense for man's refusal to acknowledge God as his master. God allows a man's spirit to lose mastery over his own body. Lust is the normal consequence of pride.

Strictly speaking, however, revelation in Judaeo-Christianity refers to God's supernatural manifestation of himself through the patriarchs and prophets of the Old Law, and through Jesus Christ in the New Covenant.

There are two ways that this revelation is (or can be) beyond the natural one already described. In every case it is super- (hence beyond) natural because of the manner in which God discloses himself. It is always somehow miraculous, since God directly inspires the prophet or sacred writer and thus invests him with a share in his own authority. In this kind of disclosure, we assume that our native intellect could arrive at whatever God has kindly revealed. But most people would not acquire this wisdom either adequately or accurately because of our common fallen condition.[3] The Ten Commandments and the immortality of the soul are typical examples.

But revelation can be more sublimely supernatural when what God manifests could not otherwise even be known to exist. Such manifestations are called mysteries, like the Trinity, the Incarnation, and the Real Presence. Moreover, after being revealed, they cannot be fully comprehended by man's reason.

Why should God have shared with us those divine treasures which totally transcend the understanding of the human mind?[4] He did so to offer us the means of reaching our supernatural destiny. Having eternally chosen to make us heirs of heaven and partakers in his own happiness, he gave us the resources for arriving there.

All these resources are summed up in the person of Jesus Christ. After God had spoken in many and varied ways through the prophets, "now at last in these days," he "has spoken to us in his Son" (Heb. 1:1–2). He sent his Son, the eternal Word who enlightens all men, so that he might dwell among men and tell them of the innermost being of God.[5] What makes this revelation unique is that Christ is the physical Incarnation of the Deity. To see Jesus is to see the Father (Jn. 14:9). He speaks as "a man to men." And yet, being God in human form, "he speaks the words of God."[6]

One of the major developments in Catholic doctrine has been the clearer understanding that not only Christ's words but everything about his stay on earth in the first century reveals God to us in our day. Not only what he said, but what he did not say, his silence, is revealing. His signs and wonders, or even his simplest actions, like the tears he shed at Lazarus' grave or his fatigue after a hard day's work are revelatory. But especially his suffering and crucifixion, followed by rising from the dead and the sending of his Spirit of truth, are such historic disclosures of the divinity that the world has been completely changed by them.

We see, then, how radically Christianity differs from other religions of the human race. Its adherents believe that Jesus of Nazareth, a man among men, is Creator of the mother who gave him birth and, as Luke relates, Maker of the angels who announced his coming into the world.[7] Mohammed, the seventh-century founder of Islam, had no doubt who Christians are. The Nasara, followers of the Nazarene, he wrote in the Koran, are those who worship the son of Mary (*Ibn Maryam*) as the Son of God (*Ibn Allah*).[8]

Response of Faith. If anything is clear from the Gospels it is the call to a free response of faith in God's revelation of himself in the person of Christ. How otherwise explain that terrifying passage in the closing verses of Mark where the Master states without reservation that "he who believes and is baptized will be saved; he who does not believe will be condemned" (Mk. 16:16)? Echoing this injunction, the apostle explains why faith is so necessary for salvation. "Only faith," we are told, "can guarantee the blessings that we hope for, or prove the existence of the realities that at present remain unseen." Indeed, "it is impossible to please God without faith" (Heb. 11:1, 6).

St. Paul further identifies faith as a form of obedience, which the First and Second Vatican Councils said "is to be given to God who reveals, an obedience by which man commits his whole self freely to God, offering the full submission of intellect and will to God who reveals," and then freely assenting to the truth communicated by him.[9]

We often apply the term *faith* to the body of truth to be found in the Creeds, the teachings of the Church and, above all, in the words of Sacred Scripture. The terminology is familiar, but we are referring to something else here; namely, our subjective counterpart to God's objective communication of himself to us.

Faith thus understood is the first of the three theological virtues set by St. Paul side by side with hope and charity. They are called theological because they not only go to God, as all virtues do, but they also touch him. They are virtues because they are good habits, as distinct from vices, which are bad habits. They are infused virtues, other than habits we have to acquire by repeated practice, because they are directly infused into (Latin *infusum,* poured into) our souls.

Viewed from another angle, we may say that sanctifying grace vitalizes the human substance and thereupon affects all our faculties of activity. These elevated qualities of action are the infused virtues, from the Latin *virtutes,* meaning "powers," which enable us to act far beyond our natural capacity.

Among these virtues, faith is essentially the power to know God as he has revealed himself; hope makes us trust him as our gracious Father and look forward to joining him; while charity makes us his friends.[10]

As a divinely conferred power of the spirit, the virtue of faith is already present in a newly baptized infant.[11] As a virtue of the intellect, elevated by grace, it responds to the environment in which a child is reared and its development corresponds to the training received from the dawn of psychological influence.

This development of the virtue of faith is the fundamental purpose of Christian education. Once baptized, a person has the conferred right to be gradually introduced to the knowledge of the mystery of salvation, become ever more aware of the gift he has received, learn how to worship in the Christian liturgy, grow in spiritual maturity after the pattern of the Savior, bear witness to the hope that the baptized person has in him, advance the spread of the Gospel and of Christ's Mystical Body, and help in the Christian formation of the world.[12]

If a child has the right to such education, those who brought him into physical existence have the primary responsibility from God to see that the education is received.[13] Thus "it is mainly in the Christian family, enriched by the grace and office of the sacrament of matrimony, that children should be taught from their earliest years (a prima aetate) to have a knowledge of God according to the faith received in baptism, to worship him, and to love their neighbor."[14]

Certainly instruction in the faith and training in virtue should be measured by a child's ability to understand and respond to motivation. But the supernatural power (virtus) is there awaiting development from the moment that divine life was infused into his soul.

Qualities of Faith. As we begin to probe the inner qualities of faith, a bit of history will help to place the matter in context.

The rise of the scientific age introduced, in certain quarters, an extreme distrust of faith as anything but the remnant of an outdated mythology. By the time of Nietzsche's classic work in 1895, *The Antichrist,* those who still believed in Christ and his message were considered intellectual morons. According to Nietzsche, "In Christianity, neither morality nor religion has even a single point of contact with reality. Nothing but imaginary causes (God, soul) . . . nothing but imaginary effects (sin, redemption, grace, punishment, forgiveness of sins)." Logically, then, "This world of pure fiction is vastly inferior to the world of dreams insofar as the latter mirrors reality, whereas the former falsifies, devalues and negates reality."[15]

Not a few Christians, including some Catholics, were embarrassed by this avalanche of criticism. So they opted for a faith without knowledge. Among Catholics, those who held these views came to be called Modernists. They began with the premise that the human mind is entirely restricted to phenomena, the external, sensible properties of things. It has neither the right nor the power to transgress these limits. Consequently, God cannot be the object of true knowledge. He cannot be known by either natural or supernatural revelation.

How does a Christian, in Modernist language, pass from agnosticism in the secular order to faith in the order of religion? He does not. Nothing from outside of man explains faith. It is uniquely from within. In fact, it is part of our nature, "a kind of motion of the heart," hidden and unconscious. It is a natural instinct belonging to the emotions; "a feeling for the divine" that cannot be expressed in words or doctrinal propositions because it has no intellectual content to express. It is an outlook of spirit that all people naturally have but some are more aware of having. There can be no question of revealed truths, which the Church can formulate in precise dogmas. There is only this semiconsciousness of the divine that may be variously stimulated by music or ritual or the sight of a beautiful scene.[16]

Pope St. Pius X dealt at length with the Modernist crisis, to which we shall return. More relevant now is to recall that the First Vatican Council, cut short by the Italian revolution in 1870, anticipated the crisis by analyzing the nature of faith, not so much as a virtue but as an act of responsive obedience to God's revelation.

The Vatican Council said many things about faith, but notably that: Faith is an *assent* of the mind in co-operation with the will under the influence of grace and a *free gift* of God; the *object* or focus of faith is God's revealed word, and once embraced, God will provide that the true faith will be retained *firmly* and faithfully and not denied or brought into positive doubt.

As a sort of preamble to the nature of faith, we are first asked *"Why faith?"* The underlying reason is that "since man depends entirely on God as his Creator and Lord and because created reason is wholly subordinate to uncreated Truth, we are obliged to render by faith a full submission of intellect and will to God when he makes a revelation."[17] Furthermore, since the content of faith (in the mysteries) is beyond the ken of human understanding, "We believe that what God has revealed is true, not because its intrinsic truth is seen with the natural light of reason, but because of the authority of God who reveals it, of God who can neither deceive nor be deceived."[18]

A negative reply to, "What is faith?" says "It is by no means a blind impulse," such as the Modernists were soon to conceive.

Rather, we give "an assent of faith," by which a person is able "to consent to the Gospel preaching."[19] This reflects St. Augustine's famous definition that "Faith is nothing else than thinking with assent."[20]

Faith is a free gift twice over. Once because "no one can consent to the Gospel preaching as he must in order to be saved without the enlightenment and inspiration of the Holy Spirit, who gives all men their joy in assenting to and believing the truth." Consequently, "faith itself is essentially a gift of God, even should it not operate through charity, and the act of faith is a work that pertains to salvation."[21] Thus, without supernatural grace from the Spirit, it is impossible to accept the truth that God has revealed. Moreover, even if a person is in grave sin, he can still believe, and his faith is salvific.

But faith is also a voluntary response on our part. By his act of believing, "man offers to God himself a free obedience, inasmuch as he concurs and co-operates with God's grace, when he could resist it."[22] Our freedom, therefore, meets the divine freedom, and the meeting is divine faith. It is divine because the revelation came from God; it is faith because the liberty of co-operation comes from us.

The next statement promises to be one of the most severely tested teachings of conciliar history. What must a Catholic believe? The answer is disarmingly simple: "By divine and catholic faith everything must be believed that is contained in the written word of God or in tradition, and that is proposed by the Church as a divinely revealed object of belief, either in a solemn decree or in her ordinary, universal magisterium."[23] But there is more to this answer than meets the eye. So many things are said that it will be worth numbering them in sequence.

1. Besides being divine, faith is also to be catholic (lower case), in that a believer is to accept everything that God has revealed. Hence faith should be universal (*catholica*) and not selective of what a person chooses to believe.

2. Through what channels has divine revelation been communicated? Literally "in the written or handed-down word of God." We shall examine the two media later on. Here it may be noted that, while Vatican II further clarified what this means, it repeated its predecessor on the fact that Scripture and Tradition are both sources of God's revealed message to mankind.

3. There is nothing ambiguous about how a Catholic knows what to believe: whatever the Church proposes as having been revealed. Christ, therefore, not only committed *to* the Church the fullness of his word, but *through* the Church he continues to transmit the Gospel of salvation.

4. Then, to remove every shade of ambiguity, Catholics are informed how the Church offers her adherents the word of God. The transmission occurs either by way of occasional, solemn teaching, as in the case of an ecumenical council; or by means of the perennial exercise of the Church's official teaching authority. It is especially this second form of transmission, found in the ordinary and universal teaching of the Catholic hierarchy, that has come under assault by those who want nothing less than solemn definitions as an index of obligation to believe.

What about the duty of a Catholic to remain steadfast in the faith that he professes? The question revolves around the nature of certainty in faith. Four centuries before, the Lateran Council stated the uniform tradition of the Church, that "faith cannot admit any error."[24] Now the problem was more subtle. Would a Catholic ever be justified, because of difficulties against his faith, to doubt or renounce his beliefs? The Council replied by comparing two classes of people, namely Catholics and others. Their respective situations are not the same: "Those who have accepted the faith under the magisterium of the Church can never have any just reason for changing that faith or calling it into doubt."[25] Why not? Because God is never wanting with his grace, and because the evidence for accepting this faith is such that a Catholic does not have objectively valid grounds for doubting or denying what, perhaps subjectively, he finds trouble in believing.[26]

Function of Reason. Inevitably the same Council, which went to such pains to explain the nature of revelation and faith had to cope with the role of human reason in accepting revelation and understanding the faith. Two statements of the Council, one on each level, may first be quoted, then explained:

> In order that the submission of our faith might be consonant with reason, God willed that external proofs of his revelation, namely divine acts and especially miracles and prophecies, should be added to the internal aids of the Holy Spirit.
> If human reason, with faith as its guiding light, inquires earnestly,

devoutly and circumspectly, it reaches, by God's generosity, some understanding of mysteries, and that a most profitable one. It achieves this by the comparison with truths which it knows naturally, and also from the inter-relationship of mysteries with one another and with the final end of man.[27]

There is good warrant in Scripture for saying that our faith should be consonant with reason. St. Paul tells the Romans to worship God "in a way that is worthy of thinking beings" (Rm. 12:1). And the Corinthians are told that "if Christ has not been raised then our preaching is useless and your believing is useless" (1 Co. 15:14). From Peter's Pentecost homily on through the apostolic age, Christ's bodily resurrection was the primary evidence offered to the Mediterranean world that there is no other name than Jesus by which men are to be saved.[28]

In the first century, as in the twentieth, not only prospective but actual believers have been faced with the claims of Christ, and their minds asked for confirmation of these claims. The signs and wonders he performed were, indeed, signs of his wonderful power and goodness by which "he let his glory be seen, and his disciples believed in him" (Jn. 2:11). They are still effective today to strengthen believers in the reasonableness of their faith, and help others come to the Father through the Son since, as unbiased history testifies, no one could have done the marvels that Christ did unless God were in him.[29]

Yet it is not only the miracles worked by Christ during his visible stay on earth, notably his resurrection, that gave rational integrity to the Christian faith. As Catholicism reads the providence of God, he continues working signs and wonders in the Church he established in order to give "external proofs of his revelation," and specifically of his abiding presence in the society that bears his name. We may, therefore, say that Christ's prophecy at the Last Supper is being fulfilled in two ways, when he foretold that "whoever believes in me will perform the same works as I do myself, he will perform even greater works" (Jn. 14:12). Individual Christians have shown forth such wisdom and fortitude, such self-sacrificing generosity as were inspired by the Savior in whom they believed. Mystics and martyrs and heroic sufferers in every culture are witnesses to the power of God's grace in frail human nature and precious testimony to the indwelling Spirit of Christ, which alone could explain their achievements.

Christ's promise, however, has also a social fulfillment in the Church he founded. "The Church herself," so the last two ecumenical councils teach, "because of her marvelous propagation, her exalted sanctity, and her inexhaustible fruitfulness in all that is good, because of her catholic unity and her unshakable stability, is a great and perpetual motive of credibility and an irrefutable proof of her divine mission."[30]

Affirming this in today's chaotic world is already to give some explanation of why so many who had looked to the Catholic Church as "a sign to the nations"[31] have been disappointed. It also explains why the popes have so often pleaded with the Church's leaders to live up to the expectations of their calling, and with those specially consecrated to the Church's service not to fail in their witness of holiness and charity. The logic of the faith has not changed since the time of Christ. Either the people, including present believers, see the zeal and sanctity, the unity and stability that presumably are evidence of Christ's presence in his Church, or the credibility in the Church's divine mission is weakened and, for not a few, has been lost.

Unfortunately, the further function of reason, as an illuminator of mystery, has been overshadowed in some cases by the preoccupation with establishing the credibility of belief. Certainly the latter is of transcendent importance. But it does not exclude the still nobler role of our minds to penetrate, as far as possible with God's grace, into the meaning of what he has revealed.

There is a psychological obstacle, however, that needs to be overcome if this highest activity of man's intellect is to be taken seriously. The obstacle is the prejudice of thinking the mysteries are essentially unintelligible. Most standard lexicons define a "mystery" as something secret, obscure, and unexplained; as that which is beyond human comprehension.

There is a great measure of truth to the definition when applied to the mysteries of Christianity. Among the few anathemas of Vatican I is a sentence against anyone who says that "in divine revelation there are no true mysteries properly so called, but that all the dogmas of faith can be understood and demonstrated from natural principles by a well-trained mind."[32]

Admitting this does not allow us to go to the other extreme and affirm that, because we cannot know everything about mysteries, we cannot know anything about them. Failure here may be put down as one of the main limitations of Christian education in today's questioning age. Rote-memory answers will hardly satisfy the mind. They will surely not prepare the believer to give an intelligent account of his faith, even to himself and less still to the supposedly unbelieving world that wants desperately to hear the word of God and, in its own parlance, "make sense of it."

The Church's formula for "making sense" of revealed mysteries is not complicated. It says that there are three ways they can become profitably intelligible, namely by making three kinds of comparison: between mysteries and the truths known by natural reason, between one mystery and another, and between mysteries and our final destiny. These approaches are not mutually exclusive and, as commentators on the Church's teaching explain, the last of the three methods really includes the other two.

An example of the first comparison would be the resemblance between the mystery of the Incarnation, where the two natures of Christ are united in one divine person, and the manner in which our two components of body and soul are united to form one being. The second would be the resemblance between the mysterious union of divine persons in the Trinity, forming a perfect unity, and the mysterious union among human persons in the Christian community that Christ wants to be patterned on the triune divinity.

The last method of comparison, between Christian mysteries and our final destiny, is actually the whole spectrum of analogies between the natural and the supernatural order. In the former, we have life that we did not confer on ourselves but had to receive from someone else; this life must be nourished from the moment of existence; it must be sheltered, clothed, and cared for; if it is to develop, its powers must be stimulated and its faculties exercised; this life can be weakened through disease and extinguished by death; it is meant to be enjoyed and communicate its joy to others; it has a meaning because it has a purpose, but this goal can only be approximated for the present, since there is a hunger in the human spirit that no earthly food can satisfy; it lives in the hope of a final consummation that will never end.

Transfer these facts and experiences from the natural to the supernatural level, and every manner of insight enlightens the mind that has accepted the mysteries of faith. In the supernatural order, too, we have a divine life, which we did not give ourselves but had to receive it from others, i.e., Christ, the Church, our parents, and all who were instrumental in bringing us into friendship with God; this life of grace has to be nourished by the sacraments and prayer; it must be protected against temptation, clothed in virtue, and put into daily practice; its development depends on the environment that favors its growth and on living out in action what a Christian professes on faith; it can be slackened by sin and destroyed by deliberate rejection of the One by whose indwelling life it lives; as all life, so sharing in God's life is to be thoroughly joyful and much of the happiness comes from a generous love that seeks to give others what others have selflessly given to me; the meaning of this life of grace here is found in the prospect it offers of entering into glory hereafter; and the horizon that faith opens up to the believer is nothing less than heaven, where only God has a right to live.

THE SCRIPTURES AND TRADITION

So far we have seen something of what revelation and faith mean, and how reason is not only enlightened by faith but, under the impulse of grace, can understand something of the mystery by which God wants man to participate in his own being.

Saying this, however, is still not locating the place where such revelation is found. Catholic Christianity, speaking most recently in the Second Vatican Council, identifies this source of revelation as Sacred Scripture and Tradition. Before examining the meaning of each phase of this bifocal source, it will be useful to read the conciliar preamble on the subject. It reflects a new approach to the faith that is one of the best fruits of the modern ecumenical movement. At the same time, it retains all that Catholicism has conceived itself to be.

Divine Revelation Handed On. This preamble, which is more of a *magna charta* of the Catholic faith, comes in three stages. The first stage declares that Christ, who is God's complete revelation, communicated his Gospel to the apostles:

> In his gracious goodness, God has seen to it that what he had revealed for the salvation of all nations would abide perpetually in its full integrity and be handed on to all generations. Therefore Christ the Lord, in whom the full revelation of the supreme God is brought to completion, commissioned the apostles to preach to all men that

Gospel which is the source of all saving truth and moral teaching, and to impart to them heavenly gifts.[33]

This Gospel had been promised in former times through the prophets, and Christ himself had fulfilled it and promulgated it with his lips. This commission was faithfully fufilled by the apostles who, by their oral preaching, by example, and by observances, handed on what they had received from the lips of Christ, from living with him, and from what he did, or what they had learned through the prompting of the Holy Spirit.

The commission was fulfilled, too, by those apostles and apostolic men who, under the inspiration of the same Holy Spirit, committed the message of salvation to writing.[34]

The second stage of Christ's commission is to have provided for the successors of the apostles, the bishops whom they ordained, to receive authority to keep the Gospel intact and vital in Christ's name. Significantly this part of the transmission begins with the word "but."

But in order to keep the Gospel forever whole and alive within the Church, the apostles left bishops as their successors, handing over to them the authority to teach in their own place. This Sacred Tradition, therefore, and Sacred Scripture of both the Old and New Testaments are like a mirror in which the pilgrim Church on earth looks at God, from whom she has received everything, until she is brought finally to see him as he is, face to face.[35]

The last stage of transmitting the word of God involves the Church, in which the hierarchy are the authorized custodians of what they had received—back through the centuries of episcopal ordination—from the apostles who were personally with Christ. Again we may note that the opening word is "therefore." It becomes the conclusion to what had preceded.

Therefore, the apostolic preaching, which is expressed in a special way in the inspired books, was to be preserved by a continuous succession until the end of time. Hence the apostles, handing on what they themselves had received, warn the faithful to hold fast to the traditions which they have learned either by word of mouth or by letter, and to fight in defense of the faith handed on once and for all.[36]

Now what was handed on by the apostles includes everything which contributes toward holiness of life and increase of faith of the people of God. And thus the Church, in her teaching, life and worship, perpetuates and hands on to all generations all that she herself is, all that she believes.[37]

A careful reading of the foregoing statements shows that the operative verb, "to hand on,"—the nearest English equivalent of the Latin *tradere*—has all the nuances of faithfully transmitting to others what one had received as a priceless legacy before him.

Consequently there is a legitimate sense in which Catholics affirm that Christian revelation was "closed" with the apostolic age. The term "closed" should not be jarring. It simply means that since Christ is Truth incarnate, he entrusted the fullness of this truth to men whom he chose as his special witnesses. Perhaps the word "filled" would avoid the impression that what Christ bequeathed to his Church was a static pool. If we are to use figures of speech, a better image would be a bottomless sea.

We must emphasize, however, that the Church is no mere custodian of the Gospel. No doubt, her divinely appointed function is periodically to determine in precise and even technical language what God has revealed, and what his revelation means. But the word of God is also a living voice, ever active and "alive within the Church." Let us remember that the same Christ who revealed himself to the Church as Truth is also the Life who animates the Church he founded and the Way who leads the Church to his heavenly Father.

What Is the Bible? Most people take the Bible for granted. They just assume that it was "always there," without realizing that the history of the Bible gives a fair cross section of the history of God's revelation to the human race. Dates are important, even when some of them have to be approximated because they cover periods that go back several millennia.

Archaeology tells us that, while writing was practiced in very ancient times and by many different people, alphabetical writing or phonetic script originated with the Semites in Mesopotamia about 2000 B.C. This may rightly be called the cultural beginning of the Bible. The development of the alphabet put the capstone on language development. Phoenicians and Hebrews began using symbols with the exclusive phonetic (sound) value of single syllables or consonants. They had dropped the ideographic symbols of nonpicturable things and, of course, pictographic signs altogether. The essence of the alphabet consists in the use of a small number of arbitrary symbols to represent sounds rather than objects or even ideas. Immediately the alphabetic (phonetic) system spread from the Near East to Greece, from there to Rome and, in time, throughout the world, but mainly to Europe and Africa. It went as far east as India. But to this day, the cultures of China and other segments of what we call the Far East are not alphabetical. They are essentially pictographic or ideographic in their written communication.

Among other advantages of the alphabetical form of writing, without which we could not properly speak of the Bible, are that it allows for a maximum of factual and conceptual communication in a minimum area of writing space; it allows for a maximum depth content in the ideas transmitted, with a minimum number of distinct (and easily learned) symbolic expressions; it allows for maximum nuances of meaning, depending on the location of words in a sentence, inflection of words used, and absorption of words from other cultures.

Abraham arrived in Canaan about 1850 B.C., a native of the region where alphabetical writing was born. The Exodus is commonly dated between 1250 and 1230 B.C., during which time Moses received the revelations on Mount Sinai. At least from the beginning of the Christian era, Moses has been credited with the composition of what is known as the Pentateuch (Genesis, Exodus, Leviticus, Numbers, and Deuteronomy); though most scholars now hold that in their present form, these books are made up of various written documents dating from the ninth to the fourth century before Christ. Nevertheless, given the explicit statements of Christ and the apostles about the Mosaic origin of the Pentateuch, the Catholic Church has officially held that the first five books of the Bible are somehow of Mosaic authorship.[38] Moreover, the Church further concedes the existence of pre-Mosaic sources and a gradual growth of the Mosaic laws and historical narratives, due to the social and cultural conditions of later times.[39]

Speaking of the Torah (Hebrew Bible, literally "the Law") as a whole, Vatican II bypassed the cluster of disputed questions about its authorship and gave instead this observation on its indisputable value for Christians:

> The books of the Old Testament, in accordance with the state of mankind before the time of salvation established by Christ, reveal to all men the knowledge of God and of man and the ways by which God, merciful and just, deals with men. Although these books contain some things which are incomplete and temporary, nevertheless they show us a true divine pedagogy. These same books, then, give expression to a lively sense of God, sound wisdom about human life,

and a marvelous treasury of prayers, and in them the mystery of our salvation is present in a hidden way. Christians should receive them with reverence.[40]

The next historic date in the story of the Bible is about the turn of the first century, some thirty years after the destruction of Jerusalem. By that time, a strong rabbinical school had arisen at Jamnia, a dozen miles south of the modern Israeli port of Tel Aviv-Jaffa. It was at Jamnia that the rabbis held, c. A.D. 100, a famous synod at which the canon of the Old Testament was redefined for the people.

The synod laid down four criteria to determine which books should be removed from the Jewish Scriptures as apocryphal. Their first criterion was that the book had to conform to the Pentateuch; besides, it could not have been written after the time of Esdra (c. 400 B.C.), and it had to be written in Hebrew and in Palestine. Since certain books did not meet these requirements, they were rejected. Baruch and the Epistles of Jeremiah were not of Palestinian origin. Ecclesiasticus (Ben Sira) and First Maccabees were written after the time of Esdra. Tobit, along with parts of Daniel and Esther, were originally composed in Aramaic and also probably outside of Palestine, the Book of Judith was probably written in Aramaic, and Wisdom and Second Maccabees were written in Greek. After dropping these books from the Palestinian canon, the latter was closed, and once the contents were fixed, the text was also agreed upon. In their own words, the rabbis "made a fence around it."

They also provided for a new translation into Greek to replace the Septuagint, made in the third century B.C., which the Gentile Christians had appropriated and were using for apologetic purposes —for example, to prove the virginal conception of Christ from the term *parthenos* (virgin) in Isaiah 7:14. The Jewish translator, Aquila, rendered it *neanis* (young woman).

As we come to the New Testament, the present listing of its twenty-seven books, from Matthew to the Apocalypse, corresponds to their sequence in most of the ancient manuscripts. Actually, if we exclude the undatable Hebrew Matthew, the first piece of New Testament writing (all in Greek) was more likely the First Letter of Paul to the Thessalonians (c. A.D. 51), and the last pieces were the three letters of John.

Almost as soon as the present New Testament was written, rival Christian scriptures began to appear. Commonly called the Apocryphal New Testament, its composition spans a period from the end of the first century to the beginning of the fourth.

In spite of their unfamiliarity, the Christian Apocrypha are of capital importance for an understanding of Catholic Christianity. The Koran of Islam, believed to have been revealed to Mohammed, uses the Apocrypha almost exclusively in its extensive presentation of Jesus of Nazareth and the Christian religion. And as early as A.D. 382, Pope Damasus I published a complete list of the canonical (inspired) writings of the Bible in which he decreed "what the universal Catholic church accepts and what it must avoid."[41] He was careful to exclude from the biblical canon all the apocryphal writings that by then had insinuated themselves in some Christian communities of the East. Incidentally, his canon of the Old Testament went back to the Septuagint version, and therefore included what the rabbis at Jamnia had declared were apocryphal Jewish scriptures.

In the midfifteenth century, the Council of Florence (under Pope Eugenius IV), which sought reunion with the Eastern Orthodox, repeated the Roman Catholic canon of the Bible, verbatim as it had been declared by Damasus I a millennium before. But exactly a century later, another General Council, of Trent under Pope Paul III, returned to the same issue. The reason was the challenge of the Protestant Reformers, who preferred the rabbinical Old Testament and dropped several writings of what, by then, was the recognized New Testament. The Council of Trent solemnly restated the teachings of Pope Damasus and the Council of Florence. But it failed to restore complete biblical unity among Christians. By the end of the sixteenth century, it is true, the Protestant New Testament was the same as the Roman Catholic; but the Protestant Old Testament no longer contains the books which the Pharisees at the Council of Jamnia had removed from the Torah.

What Is Tradition?   Much had transpired since the sixteenth century, when the Reformers insisted that the only source of divine revelation was the Bible. To meet this challenge, the Council of Trent began by observing that "Jesus Christ ordered his apostles, who are the source of all saving truth and moral teaching, to preach it to every creature." It went on to add, however, that "this truth and teaching are contained in written books *and* in the unwritten traditions that the apostles received from Christ himself or that were handed on, as it were from hand to hand, from the apostles under the inspiration of the Holy Spirit, and so have come down to us."[42]

Four hundred years later, the Second Vatican Council accepted the teachings of Trent but proceeded to clarify what they meant in a way that reflects an extraordinary development of Catholic doctrine. True, in a basic sense, Catholicism believes that the whole content of God's revealed word is not limited to the biblical page. But it also sees that the Bible and tradition are intimately related, in fact are interdependent:

> There exists a close connection and communication between Sacred Tradition and Sacred Scripture. For both of them, flowing from the same divine wellspring, in a certain way merge into a unity and tend toward the same end. For Sacred Scripture is the word of God inasmuch as it is consigned to writing under the inspiration of the Holy Spirit, while Sacred Tradition takes the word of God entrusted by Christ the Lord and the Holy Spirit to the apostles, and hands it on to their successors in its full purity. Thus, led by the light of the Spirit of truth, they may in proclaiming it preserve this word of God faithfully, explain it, and make it more widely known.
>
> Consequently it is not from Sacred Scripture alone that the Church draws her certainty about everything which has been revealed. Both Sacred Tradition and Sacred Scripture are to be accepted and venerated with the same sense of loyalty and reverence.[43]

The two may not be separated, since "Sacred Tradition and Sacred Scripture form one sacred deposit of the word of God, committed to the Church."[44] Practically speaking, then, they belong together; but theoretically they are distinct. How do they differ?

In the light of Vatican II, we should first cut through the semantic barrier. In the Catholic Church, the Sacred Tradition (always with initial capital letters in the official text) about which the Council speaks is not the mere accumulation of ideas or customs, no matter how sacrosanct they may be. The Friday abstinence and Eucharistic fast from midnight would not qualify as Sacred Tradition.

In positive terms, Tradition and the Bible have much in common. Both are the vehicle for God's revelation; both trace their origin to divine inspiration, to produce the biblical text in one case and the believing community in the other; both ultimately draw on the vision of God incarnate, who gave to the apostles what he came down on earth to teach; so that both are, in that sense, complete and therefore exclude the composition of a new Bible or added Tradition. Moreover, both have been left with the Church and in the Church as a "sacred deposit," which may not be profaned either by adulteration or competition with mere human wisdom.

At the same time, Tradition differs from Scripture. Where the latter is a tangible product, contained in sacred books, the former is a living reality. It is quite correct, in this light, to view the Bible as part of Sacred Tradition. As the vital presence of God's revelation abiding with his Church, we may speak of the main *instruments* or channels by which Tradition has been (and is now) transmitted to the people of God. They are the professions of faith, like the Apostles' and Nicene Creeds; the Church's liturgy and unvarying practices since apostolic times; the writings of the ancient Fathers and archaeological monuments testifying to what Christians believed and how they worshiped over the centuries. Yet, all of these are only instrumental of the *organ* of Tradition in the Catholic Church, which is the Church's teaching authority, or magisterium, namely the bishops as successors of the apostles collegially united among themselves and under the bishop of Rome.

Development of Doctrine.   Intimately related with the nature of revealed Tradition is the fact of its ongoing development. Few aspects of this side of Catholicism are more controverted today, and yet the Church's official teaching is clear enough. It was synthesized in one paragraph of *Dei Verbum:*

> This Tradition, which comes from the apostles, develops in the Church with the help of the Holy Spirit. For there is a growth in the understanding of the realities and the words which have been handed down. This happens through the contemplation and study made by believers, who treasure these things in their hearts; through a penetrating understanding of the spiritual realities which they experience, and through the preaching of those who have received, through episcopal succession, the sure gift of truth. For as the centuries succeed one another, the Church constantly moves forward toward the fullness of divine truth until the words of God reach their consummation in that truth.[45]

What strikes us immediately is the quiet assurance that revealed Tradition is not static but dynamic. It "develops" and "grows," it "moves forward" and it progresses "toward fullness" until all mysteries will cease in the final vision of God.

What is also unquestionable is how the advancement occurs and where. It comes about primarily through the indwelling Spirit of truth, who animates the Church and every member of Christ's Mystical Body. The object of the development is both the revealed mysteries themselves and their human expression in verbalized, symbolic forms. Growth is the result of many converging elements in the Church: prayerful contemplation and theological analysis, personal awareness through faith experience among believers, and the insights of bishops (individually and collectively), whose episcopal office gives special promise of perceiving spiritual truths.

Now we come to the hub of the issue. What exactly does development of doctrine mean or, perhaps more accurately, what does it not mean? Words like "development" and "progress" take on the coloring of the times in which they are used. In today's evolutionary vocabulary, it is necessary to keep our balance. Otherwise the treasures of wisdom implied in doctrinal development can be dissipated, not to say lost.

There is an understandable tendency nowadays to say that terms like "deposit of faith" are echoes of a former age; that this deposit is not a past revelation which the Church preserves. The Church lives in the present, where revelatory-redemptive activity goes on. Until recent years, it is argued, there was an almost exclusive concentration upon the past whenever revelation was discussed. Statements were made that revelation is closed; all the necessary truths are known; there will never be any new truths imposed upon our faith.

On this hypothesis, revelation is not something that can be kept intact. Revelation is what happens between and among persons and exists only as a personal reality. If there is a revelation in the Church today, it can only be in the conscious experience of people.

To speak this way is comprehensible and would be laudable, if only it were balanced with what has already been seen. Undoubtedly the present age of introspection and social communication highlights the fact that God's word, once and for all revealed in Christ, may be better and more deeply appropriated by personal experience and interpersonal relationships among believing Christians. There is only one proviso, but it is of the essence of legitimate doctrinal progress.

The new insights of what some have called continuing revelation cannot, on Catholic principles, contradict anything that the Church teaches has already been revealed.

Two canons of the First Vatican Council are sober reminders that the temptation we are describing is not an illusory one. The canons are definitions that censure the following positions:

> Human sciences (*disciplinae*) can be pursued with such liberty that their assertions may be held as true, even though they are opposed to revealed doctrine, and that they cannot be condemned by the Church.
>
> As knowledge (*scientia*) progresses, it is sometimes possible for dogmas that have been proposed by the Church to receive a different meaning from the one which the Church understood and understands.[46]

The logic of the Catholic stance is very simple. If we admit that Christ bequeathed his revelation to the apostles to be "handed down" by their successors in the episcopacy, progress in faith's grasp of what Christ revealed is presumed. It would be unthinkable, however, for Christ to neglect his Church by allowing what seem to be "new insights" to become disclosures so that the supposed successors of the apostles become impostors who have misled the faithful into believing what, it now turns out, was positive error.

Revelation as History.   There is one more aspect of revelation that needs to be examined in the present context: the problem raised by rationalism and literary criticism about the factual validity of the New Testament and especially the Gospels.

Rationalism as a theory of knowledge claims that unless something can be fully verified by the known laws of nature, it cannot be a valid object of human certitude. On these premises, anything of a supernatural character like miraculous phenomena or supernatural mysteries may, of course, be believed, but the "faith" is unreasonable and should be more accurately termed credulity.

Literary criticism of the Bible has two very different forms. One derives from rationalism and, therefore, excludes on principle such events as the Resurrection on the ostensible grounds that the history of religion is filled with purported "resuscitations" of incarnate deities from the dead. The other form seriously copes with the admitted problem of four versions of the one Gospel of Christ, with numerous variations and sometimes divergent expressions, notably among the Synoptic writers, as also between them and the evangelist John.

There is obviously a close tie-in between Scripture and Tradition, since the plain Gospel narrative about certain events or statements in the Savior's life is not "plain" enough for easy acceptance. It needs verification from outside the biblical text; in a word, it calls for some kind of "tradition." Given the Catholic approach to the Bible, it is not surprising that the Church has repeatedly stepped into the picture since rationalism and literary criticism have come on the scene. The creation in 1902 of the Pontifical Biblical Commission, and its complete reorganization in 1971, give some indication of Rome's desire to stimulate the scientific study of the Bible and insure due respect for the inspired writings. Almost seventy years of experience went into the statement of the Second Vatican Council vouching for the factual character of the canonical Gospels:

> Indeed, after the Ascension of the Lord, the apostles handed on to their hearers what he had said and done. This they did with that clearer understanding which they enjoyed after they had been instructed by the glorious events of Christ's life and taught by the light of the Spirit of truth. The sacred authors wrote the four Gospels, selecting some things from the many which had been handed on by word of mouth or in writing, reducing some of them to a synthesis, explaining some things in view of the situation of their churches, and preserving the form of proclamation. But they always did this in such a fashion that the things they told us about Jesus were true and unreserved (*vera et sincera*).[47]

Both dimensions of the challenge to revealed history were met in this declaration. There is first of all the calm acceptance of the whole sweep of the Gospels with their numerous miracles, prophecies, and preternatural events. No phenomenon is excluded, nor any teaching of Christ. After all, they were means to an end—namely, man's eternal salvation. Granted faith in this destiny, we should expect God incarnate to conduct himself on earth like God incarnate!

Moreover, granting that the apostles were at least honest men, not to say specially chosen by God, we would expect them not to fabricate. Nor would the other evangelists—Mark, the companion of Peter; and Luke, the associate of Paul—have any earthly reason to prevaricate. All they could look forward to, on the promise of the Master, was suffering and persecution for telling the truth; and they were not disappointed.

At the same time, generations of biblical research are reflected in how we now understand the "true and unreserved" facts about Jesus were finally set down by the evangelists. There was the extraordinary clarity with which the apostles finally understood what the Savior had done and said, after the Resurrection and descent of the Holy Spirit. But there were also different men writing, for different churches and affected by the believing communities in which they wrote. They also had various purposes in view, like Matthew to vindicate Christ's fulfillment of the prophets, and Luke to indicate Christ's mission to all mankind. They had to choose among many events and, in choosing, exercised their freedom in dissimilar ways. They culled from numerous witnesses, who would naturally remember different things. Most significantly, they were not composing a bare chronicle of cold data but writing as men who were preaching, what actually took place but also what could not be fully expressed in the narrow limits of, not four, but a hundred Gospels. We get some idea of how the evangelists felt as we read the closing sentence of the last of them, who confessed: "There were many other things that Jesus did. If all were written down, the world itself, I suppose, would not hold all the books that would have to be written" (Jn. 21:25). John the mystic knew. He was not referring so much to the number of facts in Christ's visible stay on earth as to the depth of mystery which these facts implied.

II. THE LIVING GOD

God is the principal focus of revelation. No doubt within this focus are many corollary aspects of his relationship to the world. But always God remains at the center; his attributes of divinity are the main object of man's recognition and worship. By implication, then, since God has shown himself so glorious in majesty and yet so generous in mercy, man should in turn give himself unreservedly to God.

Consistent with this focal theme in the Scriptures, it is not surprising that the Church's tradition reveals the same preoccupation. As a Christian today reviews the history of the Church in the first eight hundred years, the most striking feature of the seven general councils held during that period—what we now call the Patristic Age—is their concern to safeguard the reality of the triune God and man's responsibility to give him the worship he deserves.

Seen in this perspective, it was to be expected that the Christianity which survived the crisis of those times came to call itself Orthodox, which means "right worshiping," since true Christians were presumed to be those who worshiped the right object, the true God, and in the right way, as Christ wanted the Trinity to be adored.

Significantly, too, those first seven councils are the only ones on which the whole believing Christian world today agrees; which indicates both the direction that valid ecumenism must take and the only sure foundation on which it can be built.

While these councils say a great deal about God, their preoccupation is with his truine character. Our principal concern will be with the modern scene, where titanic forces are struggling for mastery of the human mind. The area of analysis will span about one hundred years, from the first Vatican council to the second, and it will revolve around certain issues: the rise of modern atheism, which has occasioned a new realization of the existence and nature of God; and the development of social communications, which has evoked deeper insights into the meaning and relevance of the mystery of the Holy Trinity.

THE NATURE OF GOD

Historians of religion commonly trace the beginnings of modern atheism to the eighteenth century and identify its original form as essentially "political." In their fight against the social and political institutions of their day, the materialist philosophers and encyclopedists came up against a Church which, in their mind, was an aspect of the State and that "sanctioned despotism by divine right." Their labor was described to the people as a struggle to win freedom from tyranny.

The masses were told in scores of books and pamphlets, "It is perfectly clear that the Christian religion runs counter to the political health and well-being of nations." Christianity, therefore, is "the art of making men drunk with ecstasy in order to divert their attention from the evils heaped upon them below by those who govern them."

Apart from Marxism, nineteenth-century atheism was on the whole "scientist." It opposed religion, notably Christianity, as being a prescientific or nonscientific explanation of the world. Its role was to drive from the field all the attempts to contain God in the provisional insufficiencies of knowledge, all the superstitions that nourish the appetite for mystery, the readiness to accept man's impotence and welcome the miraculous.

Marxism, born in the nineteenth century, was (and remains) substantially "humanist." Its learned defenders contend that it starts, not from negation, but from an affirmation. It affirms the autonomy of man and therefore involves the rejection of every attempt to rob man of his creative and, in fact, self-creative power.[1]

Karl Marx denied the Christian interpretation of history as the working out of divine providence. The main difficulty with the Christian view of history, according to Marx, is that it postulates the existence of God who created the world and on whom therefore all of man's development finally depends. More reasonable was the Marxian interpretation, which is economic. The production of the goods and services that support human life, and the exchange of these goods and services, are the real bases of society. Economics is in man's power to control. He does not need to look to any deity beyond his own collective genius to achieve the happiness he desires.[2]

Divine Attributes. Confronted with the growing tide of atheism, whether overt or disguised as humanism, Vatican I issued a unique profession of faith in God. Unlike former credos, which faced the more subtle questions of the trinitarian life of God, this one addressed itself specifically to God's existence and nature. At stake was the faith of all believers and not only of Catholics or Christians, since the opposition denied the validity of the very concept of a supramundane being, whether he is called God or Yahweh or Allah.

> The holy, Catholic, apostolic Roman Church believes and professes that there is one true and living God, the Creator and Lord of heaven and earth. He is almighty, eternal, beyond measure, incomprehensible, and infinite in intellect, will and in every perfection.
> Since he is one unique spiritual substance, entirely simple and unchangeable, he must be declared really and essentially distinct from the world, perfectly happy in himself and by his very nature, and inexpressibly exalted over all things that exist or can be conceived other than himself.[3]

Fifteen internal attributes of God, independent of his role as Creator, are enumerated. These are not mere expressions of piety and still less were they chosen at random. They represent so many affirmations about the Godhead as the genius of unbelief had raised to the surface. In the century since this divine litany was assembled and, more than ever today, it serves as a check list of faith in a being without whose existence no other premise of Christianity has meaning.

God is said to be *one* in the absolute sense that there cannot be another, and in the relative sense that there are not many gods (polytheism), or just one chief god (henotheism), or two gods (Manichaean dualism). Each of these exclusions had been made, some many times, in the previous conciliar history of the Church's defense of the divine unicity.[4]

He is the *true* God and not a figment of the human mind. His existence is objectively verified, and not, as men like Ludwig Feuerbach (1804–72) claimed, that God is a product of the imagination, since religion is simply the mirror of man's own fears and desires.[5] Marx rested his case against theism on the writings of Feuerbach.

He is a *living* God, where life declares animate existence and vitality that belongs to the nature of his existence. He is, therefore, not some impersonal force or cosmic energy, such as certain Moslem philosophers advocated in the early Middle Ages and their European admirers resurrected in the 1800s.

Divine *omnipotence* is attested by all of revelation: "With God all things are possible" (Mt. 19:26). It was described in the Old Covenant by the sacred name El, especially in the composition of El shaddai (God almighty), and says that nothing is impossible to God, except, of course, what would contradict his nature. Thus God cannot change, cannot lie, cannot effect anything that is contradictory in itself. In other words, he cannot disown his own being.

The *eternity* of God is a dogma which asserts that he possesses the divine being without beginning and without end, and without succession in a constant, undivided now. In their conflict with the genealogies of paganism, the ancient Fathers frequently spoke of God's eternity. According to Augustine, "The eternity of God is his essence itself, which has nothing mutable in it. In it there is nothing past, as if it were no longer; nothing future, as if it were not yet. In it there is only 'is,' namely, the present."[6]

God's *immensity* or measurelessness is another way of saying that he is sublime and therefore beyond all spatial dimensions. The term was consecrated by the Fourth Lateran Council in answer to the Albigenses, who restored the Manichaean notion of deities who occupied (and were circumscribed by) the earthly and stellar regions. In the first article of a first-century creed, we read, "For the first thing believe, that there is only one God . . . who encompasses everything, while he alone cannot be encompassed."[7]

His *incomprehensibility,* also borrowed from the Fourth Lateran, is the same as God's immensity, but with the added connotation that his presence is not limited, even in a nonspatial way. Thus the angels, who are created spirits, are not incomprehensible, although they do not occupy local space. God is not confined either in the manner of a body or of a created spirit.

Among the attributes of the Deity, none is more crucial than his *infinity.* On it everything else depends, and against it every form of atheism has been opposed. Three aspects of infinity are specified, "in intellect, will, and in every perfection." The Fathers of the Church furnished the vocabulary for this attribute. They speak of God as infinite, boundless, uncircumscribed. For Gregory of Nyssa (c. 330–

c. 95), "he is in every way without limit."[8] Theologically this goes beyond affirming that God has no limitations. It says that he has within himself the fullness of all perfection, whether knowledge or power or being.

Above his oneness is the divine *uniqueness*. To bring out the significance of this perfection, Church writers since the second century have restated the doctrine in a clear dilemma. Revelation unambiguously teaches that God is the Highest Greatness. It follows, then, that "the Highest Greatness must stand unique and must have no equal, in order not to cease to be the Highest Essence. Since God is the Supreme Essence, our ecclesiastical truth with justice declares: If God is not One, there is no God."[9]

The *spiritual substance* of God may be understood in two different ways, and both are necessary to a sound grasp of the divine nature. Since he is pure spirit, God is therefore immaterial. He has no body or corporeal dimensions. More positively, however, he has a mind and will; in a word, he is personal in the basic sense of possessing what we commonly identify as the basic quality of a person (before we think of anyone as an individual), that he has a mind with which he thinks and a will by which he loves. Moreover, when the First Vatican Council spoke of God as substance (*substantia*), it did not mean that he also had accidental properties. The divine substance is really the divine *being*, a term used already at I Nicea to identify the being (*ousia*) of the first and second persons of the Trinity.

In vernacular language, *simplicity* is an ambiguous word. Doctrinally it means that there are no components or parts in God—say, of body and soul, of bodily members, of substance and accidents, or essence and existence, of nature and person, of power and action, of passivity and activity, or genus and specific difference. In revelation, God's essence simply is equated with his attributes. Christ said of himself, "I *am* the way, the truth and the life," and St. John says that "God *is* love" (Jn. 14:6).

His *unchangeableness* is likewise a matter of faith. The Psalms are filled with references to God's immutability, and more than once the Scriptures bluntly affirm the fact. Speaking of himself, in the prophet Malachi, God says, "I, Yahweh, do not change" (Ml. 3:6), and the apostle James encourages the Christians to confidence in the "Father of all light," with whom "there is no such thing as alteration, no shadow of a change" (Jm. 1:17). Not even the Incarnation effected any change in God. If we analyze more closely why he must be changeless, the reason is that he eternally possesses the fullness of being, whereas all that changes ceases to be what it was and begins to be what it was not. Not so God. When he acts outside of his own being, as in creating the world, he is not performing a new action but entering on a new realization of his eternal will to bring into existence something out of nothing.

The final attributes of God's *transcendence,* as really distinct from the world; of *perfect happiness* in himself and without dependence on any other being for beatitude; and of *sublimity* above whatever exists or could conceivably be—are all relative to creation and follow logically on all that historic Christianity believes about God. But they needed to be brought into the open, because modern atheism, which denies the God of Christianity, has its own substitute for the Deity. What it postulates is not so much a world without God, as a world that is God.

Atheism as Pantheism. Among the satisfying features of the Catholic faith is seeing how providentially, sometimes prophetically, the Church's magisterium anticipates the needs of the future. Who would have thought, as early as 1870, that by 1970 almost one third of the human race would be under the political domination of an ideology that professedly excludes the existence of a personal God? Yet in 1870 the same Council that elaborated the divine attributes to strengthen the faith of believing Christians also evaluated the position of those who, only vaguely then, were devising to supplant the divine majesty.

It can be said without exaggeration that the five anathemas against pantheism stated by Vatican I are the single most sensitive area of the Catholic faith being threatened today. They are here quoted and for the sake of later reference, numbered:

1. Nothing exists except matter.
2. God and all things possess one and the same substance and essence.
3. Finite things, both corporeal and spiritual, or at least spiritual, emanated from the divine substance.
4. The divine essence becomes all things by a manifestation or evolution of itself.
5. God is universal or indefinite being, which by determining itself makes up the universe, which is diversified into genera, species, and individuals.[10]

As one reads these conciliar condemnations, they sound too extreme for anyone but a Hindu Vedantist to take them seriously. Yet, in one form or another, they have entered the stream of Western thought, where they pose a grave crisis in Christian theology.

The Church's doctrine on God is here contradicted to its depths. The adversative positions are far more subtle than the apparently simple declarations of the Council might imply. The subtlety has been one reason for their wide acceptance even in nominally Christian circles.

1. It must seem strange to claim that "nothing exists except matter." The trouble with the word "matter" is that it suggests raw flesh and blood, protoplasm, sense feeling, or the lifeless forces of nature. Actually, materialists can be very cultured people and their philosophy anything but crude. They do not openly deny the existence of what Christians call spirit; they simply claim that "spirit" is a function of matter. It is not as though there were no other reality than the dimensional world; but whatever exists, including the Christian God, must be measured by or considered the product of space and time.

2. To say that "God and all things possess one and the same substance and essence" is only a plain way of affirming what learned philosophers may couch in sophisticated language when they teach pantheism. While pantheistic systems go back to very early times, they were popularized in northern Europe in the late eighteenth and early nineteenth centuries. Another name for pantheism is monism or singularism. It asserts that God and the universe are ultimately identical. Each of three forms of atheistic pantheism was condemned by the Council and identified in the conciliar Acta with the writings of three men, whose influence has been all-pervasive in the twentieth century.

3. Emanational pantheism was propounded by Johann Fichte (1762–1814). He taught that each human being's ego is simply an emergence of the impersonal Absolute Ego in individual consciousness. More simply stated, we are not individual persons really distinct from God but only individual "awarenesses" of God's knowledge of himself or, better, of the absolute's consciousness of itself.

4. Evolutionary pantheism of the unfolding type was taught by Friedrich Schelling (1775–1854). In his theory, the whole universe (including what believers call God) is one great organism whose latent potencies are constantly developing by a "dynamic process."

History is the progressive revelation of the absolute, which animates the world of space and time as its soul.

5. More elaborate and significant was the evolutionary pantheism of Georg Hegel (1770–1831). In the Hegelian system God exists only as the "Idea which is eternally producing itself."[11] Unlike other evolutionists, however, Hegel postulated development through a dialectical process in which one thing (antithesis) succeeds another thing (thesis), and the resulting conflict gives rise to a third thing (synthesis). This progress through conflict has been going on for aeons in the past and will continue into the unpredictable future. Nothing can be said simply to exist; it is still becoming. In this system, God is the universal Idea which, through incessant conflict, becomes ever more perfect. Its growing perfection may be seen in the development of the human race, which is at once a mirror of the evolution of God and a sign that everything is still finite but on its way toward (without reaching) infinity. Marxism has built its notion of God and the universe on Hegelianism.[12]

Responsibility of Christians. By the second half of the twentieth century, loss of faith in God or indifference to his existence had assumed global proportions. Vatican II took stock of the situation in the longest and most elaborate analysis of atheism in the sixteen hundred years of Catholic conciliar history. This fact alone gives some indication of how different are the issues facing the Church to-day from those that threatened its integrity during the days of Arius, Nestorius, and Pelagius.

Typical of the ambiguous meaning of words in modern times, the Council admitted that *atheism* spans a confusing variety of forms.

While God is expressly denied by some, others believe that man can assert absolutely nothing about him. Still others use such a method to scrutinize the question of God as to make it seem devoid of meaning. Many, unduly transgressing the limits of the positive sciences, contend that everything can be explained by this kind of scientific reasoning alone or, by contrast, they disallow that there is any absolute truth. Some praise man so extravagantly that their faith in God lapses into a kind of anemia, though they seem more inclined to affirm man than to deny God. Again some form for themselves such a fallacious idea of God that when they repudiate this figment they are by no means rejecting the God of the Gospel. Some never get to the point of raising questions about God, since they seem to experience no religious stirrings nor do they see why they should trouble themselves about religion.[13]

No less than eight species of atheism are identified to give as complete an array of infidelity as any era of Christianity has ever witnessed. It will be useful to give each of these species a name by which it is commonly identified in contemporary literature. Alongside each name is a label by which those who believe in God are nicknamed, since one of the features of modern infidelity is its uncanny ability to stigmatize the supposed limitations of the Christian faith.

Disbelief correctly describes those who positively deny the existence of God; while they often call believers "credulous" or "gullible" because they blindly accept what is simply unprovable. It is *agnosticism* to assert that we cannot know anything certain either about God's existence or his attributes; whereas believers are, by contrast, "dogmatic" and "closed-minded," since they refuse to raise the possible question that there might not be a God. *Nominalism* is an ancient term, but in today's parlance it applies to people who may discourse learnedly about God yet whose "God language" is only that and nothing more; their faith in the God of the Scriptures is gone, and they charge those who profess to believe with being "deluded" for thinking that he is real. The advances of science have led some into *positivism* or *empiricism,* which says that we cannot penetrate beyond the empirical world of space and time, or know anything (least of all God) for certain beyond the external phenomena that affect our senses; while the faithful are called "unrealists" because they worship a being who lacks dimension and size and cannot be measured in mathematical terms.

We pause for a moment to note that the most common "attribute" of the god of today's atheism is that he has a history, that he partakes of time, that he is therefore changeable and part of the marvelous progress unveiled by modern science.

Although *relativism* has many meanings, in the present context it refers to those who hold that truth is relative and therefore varies from individual to individual, from group to group, and from time to time, having no objective standard. Applied to God, he is not an infinite being who exists apart from the human mind but an idealized concept that different people in different ages variously conjure up to satisfy their unrealized desires or to quiet their unavoidable fears. To the relativist, those who profess their faith in God are "absolutists" because they *reify,* i.e., make real what is only an ideal.

So, too, *humanism* has many noble meanings, but for not a few atheists today it is the deification of man to the exclusion of a transcendent God. The contrasting image for the believing Christian has a litany of labels, like "unsocial" or "irrelevant" or "uninvolved" or "inhuman" because, so the charge goes, he ignores the sublime dignity and pathetic needs of man to spend his energy on the cultic demands of God.

Under siege of so much secularism, it is not surprising that some people have not been properly instructed in the meaning of the one true God; they have acquired a "mythology" that only vaguely resembles the theism of Christianity. As they grow in mental maturity, they wish to be rid of this "faith," which they now discover is mainly fancy. There may be a substratum of real belief underneath the fanciful debris. Properly speaking, they are not so much atheists as searchers who are sincerely looking for the God of their fathers.

There is, last, the *indifference* of millions in nominally Christian cultures for whom God does not "really matter." Lost in the pleasures or problems of the tangible world around them, he is seldom on their minds and so little in their hearts that they fail to experience his presence or taste the joys of intimate, prayerful communion with God. Quite naturally, devoted believers are dismissed as "visionaries" or, more kindly, as "poets" who are living in their dreams.

Not satisfied with identifying the forms of modern atheism, the Second Vatican Council goes on to say that Christians may be partly responsible for the unprecedented rise of unbelief in countries that, until a few years ago, prided themselves on being Christian.

> Believers can have more than a little to do with the birth of atheism. To the extent that they neglect their own training in the faith, or teach erroneous doctrine, or are deficient in their religious, moral or social life, they must be said to conceal rather than reveal the authentic face of God and religion.[14]

This is not so much an indictment of the past as the expression of a hope for the future: that religious education at every age and maturity level be carefully fostered; that what is taught be the true faith and not some spurious or approximate counterpart; that this faith be not merely believed but put into sedulous practice, religiously in private and public worship of God, morally in the conduct of a truly Christian life, and socially in concern for the victims of human injustice or of the mysterious providence of God.

Moreover, unless the faith be thus practiced, it will do more than obscure the image of God for others; it will hide this image from the believer himself. We need to see the effective results of our interior convictions, at the risk of first suspecting and then abandoning these convictions as useless.

THE TRINITY: MYSTERY AND MEANING

Parallel with the hunger for God, of which modern atheism is both a symptom and the sign of a desperate need, has been the growing preoccupation with society and the effort to satisfy another deep-down longing of the human race, namely, its desire for community. In the language of Vatican II, "Every day human interdependence grows more tightly drawn and is spreading by degrees over the whole world."[15] While there are many reasons for this, development of the electronics media, easy transportation, and almost instant intercommunication among the most distant peoples have been paramount.

Running as a theme throughout the documents of the latest ecumenical conclave of the Catholic Church is this awareness that a new era has dawned in the history of humanity: Reciprocal ties and mutual dependencies among people are growing constantly; all nations are coming into ever closer unity; men of different cultures and religions are being brought together in closer relationships; the media of social communication are setting off chain reactions for the widest possible circulation of ideas and feelings; mass migrations are vastly multiplying new ties among individuals; large-scale socialization increases the bonds that unite different people.

At this critical juncture in the development of the human race, Christianity offers believers a reassessment of the mystery of the Trinity which, for too long, they had taken for granted or had failed to apply to the pressing problems of our day. If it seems odd to introduce the Trinity into a discussion of the world's growing sense of community, we should recall Christ's discourse at the Last Supper. He simultaneously proclaimed his new commandment, "that you love one another as I have loved you," and offered the model and motive for this difficult mandate in his revelation of the Trinity.

What Christ taught the night before he died is now being seen in a new light, as the human family is drawing closer together physically and needs to unite spiritually—at the risk of destroying itself because nearness breeds contempt unless animated by charity.

No other single doctrine of the Catholic faith has been more frequently or precisely taught by the Church than the mystery of the Trinity. In the first century, Peter the apostle began his first letter with greetings "to all those living among foreigners . . . who have been chosen by the provident purpose of God the Father, to be made holy by the Spirit, obedient to Jesus Christ and sprinkled with his blood."

As one council after another faced the issue (faith in the triune God), it clarified successive aspects of this belief with increasing sharpness to meet each heresy as it came along. At Nicea I, the focus was on "Jesus Christ, the Son of God, the only-begotten born of the Father, that is, of the substance of the Father."[16] At Constantinople (A.D. 381), the stress was on "the Holy Spirit, the Lord and giver of life, who proceeds from the Father (and the Son), who together with the Father and the Son is adored and glorified, who spoke through the prophets."[17]

Indicative of the seriousness with which the Church has always taken its trinitarian formulations is the rift between Eastern and Western Christianity over the words "and the Son (*Filioque*)," which were not in the original text of the Creed of Constantinople. By the middle of the sixth century, the phrase was inserted in the Spanish liturgy as a sincere effort to avoid certain deviant ideas about the divinity of the Holy Spirit. Gradually the whole West adopted the insertion, eventually approved by Rome. But the Eastern Orthodox to this day object to what they call either a heretical tampering with the Creed or an unjustified exercise of papal authority.

Behind the controversy about the *Filioque* is an article of the undivided Christian faith, that the Holy Spirit proceeds not only from the Father but also from the Son as from a single Principle, through what is called a single Spiration. Thus, according to the Scriptures, the Holy Spirit is indeed the Spirit of the Father, but he is likewise the Spirit of the Son (Mt. 10:20; Ga. 4:6). Moreover, the Holy Spirit receives his knowledge, as Christ declared, from the Son (Jn. 16:13–15). In a word, "all that the Father has, is mine." If the Son, by virtue of his eternal generation from the Father, possesses everything that the Father has except the Fatherhood and not being generated (which are not communicable), then he must also have the power of spiration. Father and Son together are a single Origin of the Holy Spirit.

When the Fathers of the Church came to describe this mystery, they agreed on the doctrine but used different expressions. Hence the roots of the later controversy. The Latin Fathers preferred the co-ordinating formula, "from the Father and from the Son," whereas the Greek favored the subordinating formula, "from the Father through the Son." Why the Greek preference? One reason was to bring out more clearly that the Son, though fully God, is himself generated and in that sense subordinated to the Father.

What complicated the issue was that by the ninth century some Greek Orthodox leaders were saying that the Holy Spirit proceeds from the Father alone. It was therefore understandable why Rome favored the Latin formula, which left no doubt about the perfect equality in divine nature of the three Persons of the Trinity.

While still a sensitive issue among certain Orthodox spokesmen, there is a growing acceptance by their Churches of the *Filioque,* as there is also a reluctance on the part of Rome to press the verbal expression once it is certain that the faith is unimpaired.

The Church has not been satisfied with merely proclaiming the existence of three persons in God; it further declared how the triune Godhead is constituted. Starting from the biblical revelation that the Son proceeds from the Father, and the Holy Spirit from the Father and the Son, it concluded that there are in God three persons who are really distinct from one another. The word "person" referring to God has been defined by the Church several times, and with luminous clarity.[18]

Analyzed theologically, "person" is an intelligent individual sub-stance, that is, single in itself and distinct from others. "Human person" implies that an individual has this body and this soul; they are his own and no one else's.

In God, however, distinctions arise from different relations of origin. Thus the Son is distinct from the Father because he originates from the Father, who is consequently not the Son. And the Holy Spirit is distinct from Father and Son because he originates from them, who are consequently not the Holy Spirit.

Summarizing the teaching of the ages, Pope Paul VI in his *Credo of the People of God* restated the Church's faith in the Trinity for our communitarian times.

We believe in one only God, the Father, Son and Holy Spirit. . . .
We believe that this only God is absolutely one in his infinitely holy essence as also in all his perfections, in his omnipotence, his infinite knowledge, his providence, his will and his love.
"He is he who is," as he revealed to Moses; and he is "Love," as

the Apostle John teaches us. So that these two names, Being and Love, express ineffably the same divine reality of him who wished to make himself known to us.

God alone can give us right and full knowledge of this reality by revealing himself as Father, Son and Holy Spirit, in whose eternal life we are by grace called to share, here below in the obscurity of faith and after death in eternal light.

The mutual bonds which eternally constitute the three persons, who are each one and the same divine being, are the blessed inmost life of God thrice holy, infinitely beyond all that we can conceive in human measure.

We believe then in the Father who eternally begets the Son, in the Son, the Word of God, who is eternally begotten, in the Holy Spirit, the uncreated person who proceeds from the Father and the Son as their eternal love.[19]

In the light of this revealed vision of the eternal society of persons who are the Godhead, it becomes more understandable why Christ should have so insisted on the unity among his followers being patterned after the unity which he and the Father and Holy Spirit possess among themselves. It also becomes more intelligible why the Fathers of the Church saw a foreshadowing of the Trinity in God's statement in Genesis, "Let us make man in our own image, in the likeness of ourselves" (Gn. 1:26). By implication, therefore, mankind is made to the image and likeness of God twice over: once in being like God, and unlike lesser creatures, because we have an immortal spirit, which is able to think and choose; and once again because, like God, we are individual persons, indeed, but capable of living in communion with other persons as a loving society.

Practically speaking, the Trinity affords a sublime lesson to Christians on the meaning of selfless charity. It is all too possible to conceive charity as an external rule imposed from the outside, as though sharing what belongs to us personally were some grudging concession to the demands of social existence. It is possible to think that human fulfillment consists in self-satisfaction, with only so much given to others as the "law," human or divine, requires in order to meet the requirements of communal living.

What a different understanding charity acquires when viewed from the vantage point of the love that obtains among the persons who form the Godhead! God, as we have seen, is the necessary being who cannot not exist, who therefore must be. Since God is triune love, then love cannot not exist, it therefore must be. In God, this necessity is of the essence of his being. The three persons cannot not be joined together in perfect unity. In similar fashion, speaking analogously, this necessity to love belongs to the essence of our created being. Unlike God, we can be so jealous of our individual liberty as not to share what we possess with others in the human family. But then we do violence to our humanity, modeled after the Trinity. So far from being an alien imposition on our nature, what we call the "command" to love our neighbor is actually the profoundest human need. It is a positive hunger of the spirit to exercise its freedom, by freely giving of ourselves, as persons, in order to benefit other persons and, in the process, contribute toward the formation of the earthly counterpart of the triune heavenly community.

III. GOD, MAN, AND THE UNIVERSE

There are two ways of looking at the relationship between God and the world. One is to begin with the world and rise to God; the other is to begin with God and descend to the world.

The first method is proper to philosophy, which investigates the universe of space and time, reflects on the marvelous perfections of man and outside of man, and thus comes to some knowledge of the God who alone can explain the world and rationally account for its existence and the wisdom of its complex activity.

This system is not only valid but, to meet the charge of the Fideists, who minimized the powers of human reason, it was defined by the First Vatican Council, drawing on the teaching of St. Paul already presented. Stated positively, "Holy Mother Church holds and teaches that God, the origin and end of all things, can be known with certainty by the natural light of human reason from the things that he created."[1] Then negatively, no one may claim that "the one and true God, our Creator and Lord, cannot be known with certainty with the natural light of human reason by means of the things that have been made."[2]

Not the least value of recognizing this native capacity of the mind to come to the knowledge of God is that it gives us sound, objective grounds for our faith. Otherwise we would be reduced to arguing in a vicious circle if someone asked us why we believe. We would have to say that we believe in what God revealed because we believe in a God whose existence we cannot intelligibly establish to be true.

The second method of seeing this relationship begins with the assumption that God has, indeed, told us many things not only about himself as Creator and Guardian of the universe but about the whole span of creation in which, we are told, "he himself has made small and great and provides for all alike" (Ws. 6:8).

Within the broad spectrum of all that God has revealed in this matter we can distinguish the two elements covered by the opening article of the Nicene Creed; namely, "We believe in one God, the Father almighty, Creator of heaven and earth," *and* "of all things both visible and invisible." For the sake of convenience we may call the first part the "act of creation," and the second the "fact of creation."

Regarding the act of creation, while there are numerous aspects deserving attention, we shall confine ourselves to those which the Church has most often or most insistently taught, either because of opposition to the doctrine from various quarters or because of the felt need for clarifying the Christian faith at certain periods of salvation history. They answer to the basic questions: How did God bring the world into existence? How is the world governed and preserved by God? Why did God create the world?

AUTHOR OF THE UNIVERSE

Since the dawn of recorded history, men have wondered about the origin of the world, about its myriad forms of activity, and about its purpose of existence, especially of that important component of the universe called the human race.

Left to their own devices, people have arrived at all kinds of answers to these fundamental questions, which explains both the frequency and persistence of God's revelation on the subject. It also accounts for the Church's complete clarity in teaching what is, after all, the bedrock of everything else.

Creation out of Nothing. Nowadays we are so accustomed to use the word "creation" in a variety of senses that its strict doctrinal meaning may be obscured. As Christianity understands it, creation means "the production of material and spiritual things in their whole substance, done by God out of nothing."[3] Accordingly, to create means that a cause (God) produces an effect (the world). Furthermore, the production is such that the whole substance of what God creates is the result of his creative action; so that there is nothing in the created effect which does not depend on the act of the Creator, in contrast with other forms of production, where the cause merely effects some change in what already exists. Finally, God creates out of nothing both because he starts with no pre-existing material and because he parts with nothing of his own being in the act of creation.

That God alone created the world is an article of the Catholic faith, found in all the Christian creeds and solemnly taught by several ecumenical councils, notably, the Fourth Lateran and First Vatican.[4] The basis in revelation for the doctrine spans the whole of Scripture, from Genesis to the writings of St. John.

The two creation narratives in Genesis are in studied contrast with the pagan mythologies of the Babylonians, Egyptians, and Phoenicians, by whom the sons of Abraham were warned not to be contaminated. The *Enuma Elish* of the Babylonians, for example, describes the struggle between chaos and the gods. And all the cosmogonies, except Genesis, depict a plurality of deities that is utterly foreign to the opening book of the Bible. Here the one true God is described as alone creating and adorning the world. The sun and moon, worshiped as divinities by the Babylonians, are simply creations, and so far from having dominion over the human race were made by God for the service of man. So, too, the beasts and birds adored by the Egyptians are the work of God's hands and put by him under the control of man.

This implicit repudiation of polytheism was more effective than would have been any explicit denial, since the Jews knew only too well what their Gentile neighbors held about the origin of the world. In pagan mythology, the gods did not make the chaos out of which the universe was made and, in fact, somehow the world came into being out of the substance of the gods whose existence is not explained.

While the Genesis narrative implies creation out of nothing, this is explicitly taught in the last of the historical books of the Old Testament, where the mother of the seven martyred sons tells her youngest boy, "I implore you, my child, observe heaven and earth, consider all that is in them, and acknowledge that God made them out of what did not exist, and that mankind comes into being the same way" (2 M. 7:28).

In the New Testament, God is said, without qualification, to have created the world. Thus the early Christians prayed in thanksgiving, "Master, it is you who made heaven and earth and sea, and everything in them" (Ac. 4:24). Moreover, since the world is the work of divine wisdom, it was only natural for St. John in the prologue of his Gospel simultaneously to affirm that the Word of God is:

co-eternal with the Father, God himself, and Creator of the universe
(Jn. 1:1-3).

John began his Gospel with conscious awareness of the opening
words of Genesis, "In the beginning was the Word," knowing that
he could not make a stronger affirmation of Christ's divinity than
to identify Christ as the Word of God by whom the world was
made.

Creation in Time. One of the commonplaces of unbelief in every
age is the assumption that the world is eternal. This occurs not
only among those who do not accept the faith of Christianity; it
applies to every culture where faith in a personal God is set aside in
favor of purely human speculation. Some writers, like Thomas
Aquinas, were so impressed by this fact that they held there was
no compelling proof on merely rational grounds against an eternal
creation of the world.[5] The Fathers of the Church, on the other
hand—e.g.—Athanasius, were sure that a creature without a beginning is impossible. Why so? Because the succession involved in a
change constitutes the essence of time. An unchangeable creature,
however, is inconceivable, since changeability necessarily exists with
finite limitations.

Speculation aside, it is revealed truth that the world had a beginning in time. Intimated in the first words of Genesis, it is repeatedly stated in the Old Testament, especially in such biblical
prayers as the Psalms: "Before the mountains were born, before
the earth or the world came to birth, you were God from all eternity
and for ever" (Ps. 90:2). It is reaffirmed by Christ in his own
high-priestly prayer to the Father: "Now, Father, it is time for you
to glorify me with that glory I had with you before ever the world
was" (Jn. 17:4).

By the thirteenth century, the Albigensian heresy became such a
threat to the Church that it was condemned on several counts,
including the claim that the material world is eternal. Parallel with
this assertion and its logical basis was the theory that there were
two ultimate principles of good and evil, spirits deriving from the
good and matter from the bad principle. Reacting to this threat
against the faith, the Fourth Lateran Council defined that "We
firmly believe and profess, without qualification, that there is only
one true God . . . Creator of all things visible and invisible, spiritual and corporeal, who by his almighty power, from the very begin-

ning of time, has created both orders of creatures in the same way out of nothing."[6] The original Latin of the definition brings out what is almost unexpressible in translation. It says *simul ab initio temporis,* which might be rendered, "simultaneously from the beginning of time." The implication is that time began when the world was created. There was no time before creation, since there were no changeable beings whose change could be measured (which is time) until the immutable God brought creatures into existence.

Creation with Perfect Freedom. The question still remains, and it is a burning issue in modern philosophy, whether God was in any sense compelled to create the world. Naturally, those who would settle for a finite god still reaching perfection assume that the "creator" needs the world no less than the world needs him. Evolutionary pantheism, though often veiled under different names, asserts without qualms that the world is as necessary to God as God is necessary to the world.

Clearly, on these premises God is so bound to the world he ostensibly created that we could not speak of his freedom in creation or, for that matter, his freedom anywhere in the world since then.

While such theories were prevalent in every period of the Church's history, they reached a peak of gravity in the nineteenth century, when the idea of universal evolution took hold of the popular imagination. Instead of creation, total evolutionists postulated a process of unfolding from (ultimately) nothing in rising crescendo through countless past aeons into an unpredictably lengthy future. As expressed by a modern proponent, "In evolutionary pattern of thought, there is neither room nor need for supernatural beings. . . . The earth is not created, it evolved."[7]

All that we saw the First Vatican Council said about the various forms of pantheism, including the evolutionary form, applies in this case to God's freedom of creation. For what else does pantheism implicitly deny if not the existence and exercise of divine freedom in creation? There cannot have been liberty in God creating the universe out of nothing if God is literally part of the universe in such a way that both he and it are still in the "process of becoming" whatever they will eventually be.

Not satisfied with proscribing pantheism, the Council also affirmed God's freedom in creation, declaring that "this one and only true God, by his goodness and almighty power and by a completely free decision . . . created both orders of creatures in the same way out of nothing, the spiritual or angelic world and the corporeal or visible universe."[8] Worth noting is that, while quoting the Fourth Lateran Council almost verbatim in this context, the Fathers of the First Vatican Council added the crucial phrase "by a completely free decision" (*liberrimo consilio*), where the word "decision" carries with it the connotation of freedom exercised through wisdom.

More than once in its conciliar history, the Church has defended divine liberty in creation and regularly appealed to the Scriptures and Tradition for its defense. As we analyze this teaching, we discover that it covers different aspects of God's freedom, which may be capsulized in three phrases: freedom of *decision,* freedom of *choice,* and freedom of *blessing.*

By his freedom of decision, God was at complete liberty either to create the world or not to create it. He was not coerced to do so, not even by his love. The contrary position was excluded by I Vatican, against "anyone who says that God created not with a will free from all necessity, but that he created necessarily, just as he necessarily loves himself."[9] Behind this declaration is the outspoken witness of the Bible that "Yahweh's will is sovereign" (Ps. 135:6). He is not constrained by anyone or anything. Or, in Augustine's words, "The cause of all that he created is his will."[10]

Seen from the standpoint of God's absolute self-sufficiency, no other conclusion is possible. Coercion from without or compulsion from within is incompatible with divine independence and infinity. Not even God's goodness may be said to have forced him to create. As far as our minds can comprehend, we can say that the innate desire to communicate oneself, which is inherent in the nature of goodness, is (humanly speaking) satisfied perfectly through the internal divine communications among the persons in the Trinity. No doubt God's goodness is the reason why God communicated his being to creatures outside himself. But he is not compelled to make this communication. If he does, it is a gift made sovereignly free.

By his freedom of choice, God was equally free to create this world or any other. The present universe was not the only one he could have made. If it seems odd to even suppose the opposite, the history of Christian thought records any number of writers who honestly believed that God was obliged to create the best imaginable of all possible worlds which, consequently, ours is. Names like

Peter Abelard (1079–1142), Nicolas Malebranche (1638–1715), and Gottfried Wilhelm Leibnitz (1646–1716) immediately come to mind. Encouraged by St. Bernard of Clairvaux (1091–1153), the provincial Council of Sens (later confirmed by Rome) took issue with the following proposition of Abelard: "God can do only those things which he has done, or leave undone what he has left undone, or in such a way, or at such a time as he has done them, and no other."[11]

Apart from what must be common experience, this kind of optimism is incompatible with God's attributes. Even we can conceive a better possible world. Nor did God owe it to himself to create the best world, because his perfections and happiness cannot be increased by anything he creates, whether it is good or better or the best. If one were to deny God's freedom of choice between this or that world, he would limit his omnipotence, which extends to all that is inherently possible.

By his freedom of blessing, God must be said to have chosen to create a good world, which both he approves, insofar as he created it, and which we must approve as a blessing conferred by the Creator. We will, for the time being, pass over the delicate question of why God's providence permits evil in the world and how he can draw good out of evil.

The Manichaean tendency has plagued the Church from its earliest days. According to the Manichaeans, there is not only one God. There are two gods, of which the good one authored all that is good in the world, and the evil one created all that is bad. Combated by St. Augustine, himself once a Manichaean, the theory never really died, but sporadically has continued to challenge historic Christianity to this day.

In the fifteenth century, the Council of Florence sought to reunite the Jacobites with Rome. It formulated a profession of faith that took cognizance of any latent Manichaeism among these Syrian dissidents, who a millennium before had denied Christ's true humanity, partly on the grounds that God would not unite himself in one divine person with crude, fleshly matter. They also had difficulty with accepting the Old Testament, with its anthropomorphic concepts of God and its noticeably earthbound morality compared with the sublime ethic of the Gospels. Although some of the creed will be repetitious, it should be quoted in full, as a concise summary of the Catholic faith relative to creation and with stress on the universal goodness of all that God has made:

> The Holy Roman Church firmly believes, professes, and preaches, that the one true God, Father Son and Holy Spirit, is the Creator of all things visible and invisible. When God willed, in his goodness he created all creatures both spiritual and corporeal. These creatures are good because they were made by the Supreme Good, but they are changeable because they were made from nothing. The Church asserts that there is no such thing as a nature of evil, because every nature insofar as it is a nature is good.
>
> It professes that one and the same God is the Author of the Old and the New Testament, that is, of the Law, of the Prophets, and of the Gospel, because the holy men of both Testaments have spoken under the inspiration of the same Holy Spirit.[12]

The Florentine Creed, therefore, reaffirms what revelation constantly says, from Genesis where we read that "God saw all that he had made, and indeed it was very good" (Gn. 1:31), to St. Paul's universal statement that "Everything God has created is good" (1 Tm. 4:4). But it also explains why all creatures as proceeding from the hands of God must be good. God could not create a world that was morally bad, since by virtue of his absolute holiness he cannot be the originator of sin. This is the same as disclaiming that God positively chose to create moral evil.

Again, if it seems odd that someone would teach the opposite, the Council of Trent in the sixteenth century had to take issue with an implicit Manichaeism in the predestinarian theories of John Calvin (1509–64). Trent excluded the idea that "it is not man's power to make his ways evil, but that God performs the evil works just as he performs the good, not only permissively but also properly and directly, so that Judas' betrayal no less than Paul's vocation was God's own work."[13]

Without dwelling on the issue, it may be noted that the credo of Florence gives the reason why man is able to "make his ways evil." Having been "made from nothing," man has the inherent capacity to assert his nothingness, as it were, every time he sins. He is by nature changeable because, unlike God, he is not his own reason for existence nor does he possess the fullness of goodness of being.

At the other extreme to the optimism of such men as Abelard and Leibnitz, Arthur Schopenhauer (1788–1860) thought this was the worst imaginable world. Deeply influenced by Buddhism, with its axiom that "to exist is to suffer," Schopenhauer based his unalloyed pessimism on the fact that "human endeavors and desires always delude us by presenting their satisfaction as the final end of will. As soon as we attain them, they no longer appear the same. . . . They are therefore thrown aside as vanished illusions."

Steering a middle course between the two extremes, Christianity professes a world view (and of God's freedom in making the world) that is relative optimism. Admitting the capacity for sin in rational creatures, and the consequent evil resulting from sin, it looks upon the present world as relatively the best since, as the creation of divine wisdom, it corresponds to the aim predetermined for it by God, and unites in wonderful harmony the multitudinous stages of perfection among the creatures that God has made.[14]

This variety in creation is part of the design of God's freedom. Why, then, is there such a profusion of different things in the world? Because, as Aquinas tells us, one solitary creature would not suffice to communicate and show forth divine goodness:

> Therefore he makes creatures many and diverse, that what is wanting in one may be supplied by another. Goodness in God is simple and consistent, in creatures scattered and uneven. He is better represented by the whole universe than by any one thing.
>
> Contrast and oddness come not from chance, not from flaws in the material, not from interference with the divine plan, not from our deserts, but from God's purpose, who wills to impart his perfections to creatures, as much as each can stand.[15]

So far from being an accident, diversity in creation is part of the divine plan and the condition, among human beings, for the exercise of charity. Just because people are so different, it is possible for them to practice patience and kindness toward one another. Diversity is the raw material of social unity.

Keeping the World in Existence. It takes some mental adjustment to see that God's act of creation is an ongoing exercise of his omnipotence. Yet even casual reflection must show that, if the world was made out of nothing, the same almighty power that first brought it into being must continue to keep it from lapsing into the nothingness from which it came.

The Scriptures clearly distinguish this need for divine preservation from the original creation. "You love all that exists," God is told,

"You hold nothing of what you have made in abhorrence, for had you hated anything, you would not have formed it. And how, had you not willed it, could a thing persist, how be conserved if not called forth by you?" (Ws. 11:25–26).

Sacred Tradition echoes the biblical revelation—e.g., in Augustine's strong statement, "The world would not endure for a single moment, if God were to withdraw his governing power from it."[16] Aquinas gives the reason; it is bound up with the radical difference between God and the universe. "Existence," he explains, "is not the nature or essence of anything created, but of God alone. Nothing therefore can remain in existence when the divine activity ceases."[17]

Assuming, then, that God's creative power must be ever present in creation to keep creation in existence, the next question is: What about the activities of creatures? Do these activities not depend just as completely on divine co-operation? Yes, they do, and with an intimacy that beggars description.

In St. Paul's speech before the Council of the Areopagus, he told the Athenians that the unknown God they worshiped was really the God whom he was proclaiming. Paul stressed the fact that this is "the God who made the world and everything in it," and is "himself Lord of heaven and earth," and thus God is absolutely transcendent (Ac. 17:24). At the same time, for all his distance in being, this same God "in fact is not far from any of us, since it is in him that we live, and move, and exist" (Ac. 17:28). He is, therefore, truly immanent.

Historic Christianity is unique among the religions of the world in recognizing on faith what mere human reason tends to see as contradictory: that God is both infinitely distant from us in his essence and intimately close to us by his presence.

This nearness of God to his creatures affects every least spark of their being and every single movement of their activity. In theological terms we speak of God as the *First Cause* co-operating with the action of creatures as *secondary causes*. For all its cold language, the reality that this relationship implies is filled with mystery and profoundly important for the life of prayer and of things of the spirit.

The saints urge the need for reflection on God's manifold benefits to stimulate our love for him. Among the blessings that call for meditation is that "God dwells in creatures: in the elements giving them existence, in man bestowing understanding. So he dwells in me and gives me being, life, sensation, intelligence, and makes a temple of me."[18] In everything I am and in all that I do, God is in a way more present to me than I am to myself since, except for God, I would not even exist let alone be able to do anything.

Awareness of this nearness of God produces great confidence in the believing soul, reverence at being so close to the Infinite, humility at the condescension of the Almighty toward his creatures, prayerfulness in being able to address him in our hearts, a sense of power in knowing that his power is always at hand, and a wholesome fear in realizing that nothing we do or think can possibly escape his eyes.

Divine Providence. God had done more, we know, than brought the world into existence. He sustains it by his almighty power and co-operates, as the First (in the sense of underlying) Cause of all created activity. In saying this, we are careful of course to insure the real existence of creatures and their real creaturely activity. We may not so conceive God's indispensable presence in the world as to deprive the world (including man) of its true and objective reality. That would be to fall into the pantheistic philosophy of Vedanta Hinduism, which considers the world of space and time, and plurality of beings in the world, as *maya* or illusion.

Nor should we ascribe part of the activity to the divine Cause and part to the creature. The action as a whole belongs simultaneously to God and to creatures, with the latter subordinated to God without abrogating their own causality. Christ told his followers, "Look at the birds in the sky. They do not sow or reap or gather into barns; yet your heavenly Father feeds them" (Mt. 6:26). Christ did not mean that birds do not feed themselves, or that their eating is mere fancy. He wished to stress that, while men and animals must, indeed, nourish themselves on real food and drink, God is the unseen and ultimate Agent of their nourishment, even as he is the continued Author of their being.

But there is still more to God's presence in the world he brought out of nothing. He has an all-wise plan for the universe he made; he carries out this plan by his loving rule or governance; and his fulfillment of both plan and governance we call divine providence.

The Church decided recently to solemnly proclaim the fact and nature of God's providence. This seems quite remarkable until we

reflect that Deism, which denies this mystery, is a rather late innovation in the history of religious thought. The names of John
Locke (1632–1704), Voltaire (1694–1778), and Jean-Jacques
Rousseau (1712–78) are typical of what is certainly a modern
ideology. Although professing themselves somehow Christian, Deists
either claim that God is only the Creator with no further interest
in the world; or they admit providence, but only in the material,
not in the moral and spiritual order; or they recognize certain
moral attributes of God, but no future life; or they might accept
all the truths of what they call "natural religion," including a life
to come, but reject supernatural revelation. Modern Unitarians are
professedly Deistic.

First Vatican, however, declared that, "By his providence, God
watches over and governs all the things that he made, reaching from
end to end with might, and disposing all things with gentleness
(Ws. 8:1). For 'all things are naked and open to his eyes' (Heb.
4:13), even those things that are going to occur by the free action
of creatures."[19]

In theological language, providence (from the Latin *providere*
[to see in advance]) is the plan conceived in the mind of God, according to which he directs all creatures to their proper end or
destiny. It may be said to partake of prudence, since it refers
mainly to the means that God chooses with reference to the end
he has in mind. As such, therefore, providence belongs to the
divine mind, but presupposes that he wills the goal or end. Moreover, it logically precedes the divine government of creation, which
is God's practical means of carrying his providence into effect. Thus
God's providence is universal, infallible, and immutable.

Saying that providence is universal is only another way of affirming that all events taking place in this world, even those apparently
fortuitous or casual, are part of God's eternal plan for the universe.
With God there is no such thing as chance. Nothing merely "happens" as far as he is concerned. Everything is meant to serve a
purpose, mysteriously foreseen and foreordained by God.

Providence is infallible because the ultimate plan that God has
for the universe cannot fail. Whatever occurs in the world takes
place within the mosaic of his infinite knowledge and all-embracing
will. In spite of so much ostensible evidence to the contrary, what
God has intended for the world will eventually come about.

Divine providence is also immutable because God himself is unchangeable. His eternal plan is not make-believe, as though he adjusted things as time goes along or unexpected situations arise. Nothing unexpected can ever occur with God, nor can anything take place that would make him change his mind or will about the world he brought into being.

Having said all of this about providence, a host of paradoxes begin to crowd the mind demanding explanation. To mention only a few: Where is human freedom if God has planned everything? What is the value of prayer if God already knows and determines beforehand? How can evil in the world be reconciled with an infinitely good providence?

Human freedom is part of the divine plan. God wills the ultimate effects of all created actions and has provided that they be achieved, some by means of what we call necessary causes (like gravity) and others by means of truly free choices (like obedience). Creatures supply the proximate causes, but God wills the ultimate end.

> With regard to the divine will, remember that it is not like ours. It transcends the system of particular things, of which it is the cause. God's will suffuses the whole of reality and all its shades of variety. Consequently necessity and liberty enter into things from the divine will itself. The distinction applies to events from the nature of their proximate causes. To effects which he wills to be necessary, God provides necessary causes. To effects he wills to be free he provides contingent active causes, that is, causes able to act otherwise. The nature of the proximate cause settles whether an effect should be called necessary or contingent. Yet every effect depends on the divine will as on the First Cause which stands above the system.[20]

We are still left with the insoluble problem of explaining how our actions remain free if they have been eternally willed by God. But at least we have some understanding of the fact that God wills two kinds of activity in the universe: one that is predetermined by its own nature, and another that is "able to act otherwise."

So far from being incompatible with providence, prayer belongs to its essence, since part of the divine plan is that we should obtain many of the things we need only by asking others, and especially the great Other, who is God. What must be noted, however, is that petition is different when addressed to men and when addressed to God.

With human intercession we seek to inform another person of

our wants, and then to sway his will on our behalf. Obviously neither of these considerations applies when we make our petitions to God. Our intention is not to divulge our needs and hopes, for God knows all things: "Lord, all that I long for is known to you, my sighing is no secret from you" (Ps. 38:9). Our Savior told us, "Your heavenly Father knows that you need all these things" (Mt. 6:32). Nor can the divine will be persuaded to alter a decision, for "God is no man that he should lie, no son of Adam to draw back" what he has once decided to do (Nb. 23:19). Prayer is necessary for our sake, to make us reflect on our great needs and arouse our wills to desire what God wishes us to have.

We might add that God has foreseen our prayers from eternity and thus included them in his plan for the universe, to give us (and others) what he knew we would ask for. In fact, there is no higher use we can make of our liberty than freely to choose to pray.

Evil is not so much a problem as a great marvel. The wonderment arises from God's incredible reverence for the natures he created. What bears emphasis is that his permission of evil does not derogate from his goodness.

God does not change the natures of things. He respects them. We may say that the perfection of the universe requires that some things should be indefectible, while others be allowed to change consistent with their nature. If evil were entirely swept away, Providence could not regenerate and restore the integrity of things, and this would be a greater evil than the particular evils they suffer.[21] It is in this sense that the Church speaks of the "happy fault" of Adam, which occasioned the coming of the Savior. It is for this reason, too, that God's mercy is even possible only because there are sins which he can forgive.

On a broader scale, we may say that God permits evils in order that he may bring good out of them. Take away all evil and much good would go with it—e.g., the patience of the just supposes persecution from the unjust; and the charity of those who have, presumes there are others in need.

One of the main targets of egalitarian Marxism is this mysterious design of God, who wants diversity and allows injustice in the world according to the unfathomable dispositions of his will. Having created man free, he will not interfere with this freedom, even when it is used contrary to the will of its Maker.

The Glory of God. There are really two answers to the question: Why did God create the world? One is negative, and the other is positive. The negative reply was occasioned by modern rationalism, which claimed that God made the world out of vanity or pride, to have creatures give him praise. Chafing under this criticism, some theologians shifted the biblical emphasis from God to man. They said that Christianity must subordinate God's glory to the welfare of man, so that human happiness and not the divine praise is the ultimate purpose of creation. The positive answer underscored the ageless wisdom of revelation as to why the universe, which need not exist, was brought into existence by God.

Combining the two answers in one, the First Vatican Council declared that God created the world "in order to manifest his perfection through the benefits which he bestows on creatures, not to intensify his happiness nor to acquire any perfection." It went on to exclude any theory which "denies that the world was made for the glory of God."[22]

Implicit in the attitude of those who would see God intensifying his happiness or acquiring any perfection from his creatures is the persistent lure of pantheism, which cannot reconcile itself to an infinite God; for if he is already perfectly happy because he is infinitely perfect, he cannot acquire anything from anywhere, seeing that infinity means the fullness of being. This was St. Paul's argument to the Greeks when he told them that since God "can never be in need of anything," he certainly is "not dependent on anything that human hands can do. On the contrary, it is he who gives everything, including life and breath, to everyone" (Ac. 17:25).

Therefore, God's purpose in creating was his infinite goodness, yet not to be enriched or acquired but simply to be communicated or shared. In this very purpose, however, he wants to be glorified by his creatures according to the nature and measure of their being.

This "glory" of God, which is essential to a proper understanding of creation, regularly appears in the Scriptures as *kabod* (Old Testament) and *doxa* (New Testament). It always means some manifestation of the divine attributes, whether an extraordinary appearance, or intervention in favor of the Chosen People, or the works of nature or, after the Incarnation, the person and deeds of Christ. On man's part, these manifestations should be responded to by acknowledgment and praise.

Two theological words should be inserted here to bring out something of the wealth of insight contained in the idea of glorifying God. His *internal* glory is the ocean of his goodness, which the persons of the Trinity constantly behold and mutually praise. His *external* glory is the share that creatures have in God's goodness—reflecting his myriad perfections. All creation shares in this possession and, to that extent, glorifies God by mirroring his manifold gifts. But among his creatures, those who have intelligence and will further glorify him by their acknowledgment of what they have received and their praise of the Creator for the goodness that he made so lavishly manifest.

But that is not all. There is a direct relation between our glorifying God and his blessing us, so much so that the word "bless" is often used interchangeably in the Scriptures of the faithful blessing God and of God blessing them. We give to God the glory he deserves by our loyal service and love; he gives us the happiness that only those have a right to expect who glorify his name.

The Psalms are a perfect example of this covenant between God and his faithful ones: True peace and joy are reserved, even in this life, for those who acknowledge the divine majesty and strive to do his will (Ps. 1:1, 19:8, 23:1–2, 119:164–65).

This is also the meaning of that classic phrase, "for the greater glory of God." Behind the comparative degree stands the mystery of our freedom to give more or less glory to the Creator. He is more glorified, other things being equal, the more people acknowledge his goodness and put their acknowledgment into loving service. He is likewise more glorified the more intensely we strive to know him and the more selflessly we do his will. And always God responds in kind. The more generous we show ourselves toward him, the more lavishly he bestows his blessings on us.

THE WORLD OF ANGELS

Although human reason may reasonably conjecture the existence of a created world of spirits, it required divine revelation to establish the fact as certain. Indeed, a fair index of fidelity to supernatural revelation is the acceptance of angels as created by God and now living in two states of being: those in heaven, who also minister to the needs of men; and those in hell, who are demons and bent on seducing the human race from its allegiance to God.

The existence of angels, their spiritual nature, the fact that there
are good and bad angels, the fall of the evil spirits of their own
free will, and the role of the devil in bringing about the fall of man
are doctrines of faith that have at various times been solemnly
proclaimed by the Church.[23]

Sacred Scripture witnesses not only to what the Church has
formally defined but to many features of angelology that are part of
historic Christianity.

But while the entire Bible testifies to belief in angels, there is a
real development of faith as the biblical revelation unfolds. The
early books of the Old Testament speak of angels, but in such a
way as not to encourage the Hebrews' notorious tendency toward
idolatry. This was an ever-present danger in view of the rampant
polytheism among the nations surrounding the Israelites. Before the
exile, therefore, angels are so closely associated with God that
some have mistakenly identified these heavenly spirits with God,
as merely divine attributes or symbols of the divinity. As late as the
time of Christ, the Sadducees (unlike the Pharisees) denied the
existence of all angels or heavenly spirits created by God (Ac. 23:8).

After the Exile, however, the angels appear in their full splendor,
notably in Daniel and Tobit. In Daniel, certain angels are given
names for the first time: Gabriel, who foretold to Daniel the
coming of Christ as the "anointed Prince"; and Michael, "who
mounts guard over your people" (Dn. 12:1). Daniel, too, sees the
vision of God and God's angels, which John the apostle saw again
at Patmos: "A thousand thousand waited on him, ten thousand times
ten thousand stood before him" (Dn. 7:10).

The Book of Tobit, through eight of its fourteen chapters, is
the narrative of the angel Raphael, who delivered Tobias' wife
from demonic obsession, safely led him over a hazardous journey,
cured his father Tobit of blindness, and then delivered a stirring
injunction to "Bless God, utter his praise before all the living for
all the favors he has given you." Finally he identified himself. "I
am Raphael," he said, "one of the seven angels who stand ever
ready to enter the presence of the glory of the Lord" (Tb. 12:6,
15).

In the Gospels, an angel appears to Zachary to foretell the
birth of John the Baptist, and to the Blessed Virgin to announce
the mystery of God becoming man. An angel appears to Joseph to
instruct him about the miraculous conception of Christ and to tell

him of King Herod's death. Angels appear to the shepherds at Bethlehem, saying, "Glory to God in the highest heaven, and peace to men who enjoy his favor" (Lk. 2:14). They minister to Christ after his temptation in the desert, and appear many times to announce his resurrection from the dead. Moreover, according to Christ, there are more than twelve legions of angels in heaven; the angels of little ones continually behold the face of the Father; angels will separate the wicked from the just on the last day, and the children of the resurrection will be equal to the angels.

The Acts of the Apostles describe how an angel of the Lord opened the doors of the prison for them during the night; also an angel who spoke to the deacon Philip, who delivered Peter from his jailers, who struck Herod with a fatal disease, and who stood by St. Paul during the terrible storm at sea.

St. Paul clearly distinguishes several classes of angelic spirits— thrones and dominations, principalities and powers, archangels and powers, to which Christian tradition has added the cherubim and seraphim, from the Old Testament, and the "common" angels. By the time of St. Ambrose (339–97), the present number of nine "choirs" of angels had become established in Christian piety.

More significant in Pauline angelology is the relationship of Christ to the world of spiritual creatures, who are inferior to him, and the role of the good and evil spirits in the economy of salvation. Good spirits are God's ministers to those who receive the inheritance of the saints, while evil spirits are permitted to mislead those who allow themselves to be deceived.

As we reflect on all this revealed truth, certain lines of theological insight become evident. The name "angel" is simply an abbreviation of the Greek *angelos,* meaning "one who is sent" or a "messenger"; as such, the term is sometimes used in Scripture to describe men who are sent on a special mission, as St. John the Baptist or the bishops of the Church in the Apocalypse.

More properly, though, an angel is a spiritual creature naturally superior to man and often commissioned by God for certain duties on earth. "The name 'angel,'" wrote St. Augustine, "belongs to his office, not to his nature. You ask what is the name of his office. He is an angel." This is also the accepted teaching of the Church.[24]

We commonly apply the name "angel" only to the good spirits. But strictly speaking, all spiritual creatures are angels, including the demons who are estranged from God. An angel, therefore, is a purely spiritual created substance, who exists as an individual person with mind and will but, unlike man, has no bodily parts that can be perceived by the senses.

On the basis of revelation, we distinguish between good and evil spirits. Both were originally good when created by God, and both were mysteriously tested in their loyalty to God. Those who remained faithful merited to enter heaven and forever behold the Trinity; those who were disobedient were condemned to eternal punishment.

Guardian Spirits. Basing itself on the teachings of revelation in the Bible and Tradition, the Church bids the faithful to honor the angels whom God has given as guardians of the human race. It is certain that each of the faithful has his own guardian angel, as implied in the Scripture and found in the common understanding of believers. Thus, according to St. Basil (330–79), "No one will deny that an angel is present to every one of the faithful."[25] Reasoning further from the fact that Christ died for all mankind, and that he merited the means of salvation for all, we may say that every human being has a guardian spirit since, in the present dispensation of providence, angelic assistance is part of God's universal salvific will.

Guardian angels are consequently part of God's supernatural providence which, as we know, works through creatures from the higher to the lower. Within the realm of created beings, the angels are most like God because they are pure spirits (having no body), but they are also like us because we too have intelligence and will. They are providential intermediaries between God, whose vision they already enjoy, and mankind, whom they are entrusted to lead to the vision not yet attained.

Not only individuals but societies, whether religious like the Church and institutes of Christian perfection, or secular, like states and local communities, are believed to have special angelic guardians. In the lives of the saints, we see an easy communication with the angelic world that breathes a simple faith in unseen spirits whose love "prompts them to pour out their prayers for those countries over which they are placed, as well as for those whose guardians they are, and whose prayers and tears they present before the throne of God."[26]

Otherwise than the saints who are also intercessors for us before

God, angels are specially appointed to guard and direct their charges on earth. That is one side of their ministry, from God to men, which is properly custodial. The other side is from men to God, and this is intercessory. Catholics are therefore bidden to invoke the angels on both counts, to solicit their continued protection and to ask for their prayers in our regard. As St. Ambrose puts it, "The angels should be entreated for us, who have been given us to guard us." The Church encourages the practice.[27]

While the immediate focus of angelic assistance is spiritual and supernatural, it includes concern for our bodily and earthly affairs, insofar as these pertain to salvation and sanctification.[28] The story of Raphael and Tobias is too plain about this bifocal function to be mistaken.

Temptations of the Devil. All the living religions of the world, including Islam and Mahayana Buddhism, believe in the existence of what Christianity calls the devil. But only in the Christian religion is the evil spirit clearly identified as an integral part of revelation.

Somewhat remarkably, the first and last books of the Bible are most eloquent in describing the devil and his activity. In Genesis, he tempts Eve, who in turn tempts her husband to disobey a command of the Lord. Characteristically, the devil disarms Eve's protestations by assuring her that if she, and Adam, disobey God they will become God. Since then the pattern has not changed; it has only become more sophisticated: Manifest your autonomy, even of God, and thus prove to yourself that in your own way you are a god!

In the Book of Revelation, St. John depicts the evil spirit in the role permitted by God, essentially the same work of envy, only now not on the first progenitors of the human race but on all the followers of Christ. As John saw the sequence, there were four stages in the fallen angels' resistance to God: their primordial disobedience, which drove them into hell; their successful seduction of the first ancestors of man; their assaults on the people of Israel; and their continued opposition to the followers of Christ, typified as offspring of the woman who is the Church or bride of Christ. In this present stage, "the dragon was enraged with the woman and went away to make war on the rest of her children, that is, all who obey God's commandments and bear witness for Jesus" (Rv. 12:17).

The Gospels are filled with descriptive narratives about the activity and strategy of the devil. Time and again Christ drove out demons from persons who were possessed. St. Mark's Gospel is especially detailed in the number of exorcisms performed by the Master, and the effortless ease with which he delivered those who were under the influence of the evil one. Already in the first chapter of Mark, after the Savior cured a demoniac in the synagogue, the people were amazed at Christ's power. "Here is a teaching that is new," they said, "and with authority behind it. He gives orders even to unclean spirits and they obey him" (Mk. 1:27).

Not only are the Gospels explicit about the existence and machinations of the evil spirits, but they also state that their number is "legion," which is a biblical synonym for an immense multitude. Some of the Fathers of the Church go so far as to speak of a "Mystical Body of Satan," animated by Satan and his minions and composed of such human beings as are willfully co-operating in the work of the devil on earth. Their success then takes on superhuman, in the sense of preternatural, proportions.

In the mysterious plan of providence, evil spirits are meant to serve a distinctive function toward mankind. Yet immediately we must distinguish between the purpose that the devil has, and the purpose of God.[29]

The devil's purpose is to seduce. He consciously and deliberately wants to lead people astray from their faithful service of the divine majesty. Consequently his intention is always malicious. Everything he does with respect to man is wantonly evil. His purpose is to harm man, spiritually and supernaturally, and, if possible, eternally.

God's purpose, on the other hand, is always good. He permits the devil to tempt us but not to harm us; rather the divine intention is that, by resisting the evil spirit, we might draw closer to God. God allows us to be tempted in order to try our loyalty by giving us the opportunity to show our faith and trust in God; to test our virtue by giving us the chance to grow because of the struggle that this costs; and to prove our fidelity by resisting the devil's blandishments and thus more generously serving God.

Against this common teaching of the faith, we are in a better position to assess some of the ascetical implications for the spiritual life. In each case, we shall briefly state a principle and then make an appropriate comment.

1. "The devil is never permitted to tempt us beyond our strength." This means that we always have enough grace to overcome the devil which, at root, means that we have the grace to pray for light to recognize the evil spirit and strength to resist his advances.

2. "The devil is a consummate deceiver." Three names for the evil spirit are regularly used in the Bible, and each has a profound revealed meaning. He is Satan (Hebrew, *satan*) because he is an "adversary," especially one who plots against another. He is a demon (Greek, *daimon*) because he is a spiritual being possessed of extraordinary powers. He is a devil (Greek, *diabolos*) because he is a calumniator who then accuses those he had deceived by charging them with the sins they committed. Given his deceptive character, we should expect him to hide his real designs; hence the cardinal importance of shrewdness in identifying what may seem to be a divine inspiration but is actually a demonic instigation. The best protection here, on the witness of such masters as Augustine, is humility of mind, because the devil always poses intelligent reasons for what he urges people to do. Proud persons are no match for the devil.

3. "The devil's strategy is eminently logical." He first approaches us with a suggestion in the imagination; this can grow into a specious reason in the mind; if dwelled on, it influences the will by motivating us to do something that is actually bad but apparently good. Thus deceit, hiding the real evil, falsehood, and cunning are basic to the devil's technique. He never reveals his true intentions, but masks his purpose under various disguises. He adapts himself to people's temperaments and character, even to their tastes. If they are meek and submissive, he tries to seduce them along self-effacive lines. If they are bold and headstrong, he urges them to evil under an aggressive guise. If they are worldly and pleasure-seeking, he will enter their door with temptations of the flesh. If they are prayerful and spiritual-minded, he will appear "as an angel of light." If they tend to be emotional, he adjusts his tactics to where his intended victims give least resistance to their passions. If they are intellectual, he will accommodate himself and tempt them to pride and sins of the mind.

4. "The devil uses human beings and human institutions as agents." Here we must be careful to distinguish different ways in which the evil spirit can operate in or through people on earth.

There are such things as *possession,* when the devil exerts his influence over a person by an inner control of his body; and *obsession,* when he attacks their bodies from the outside. The victim's liberty of soul always remains intact. Although the Church's ritual for exorcism mentions as probable (not certain) signs of possession certain phenomena like speaking or understanding an unknown language or showing strength above one's natural capacity, it warns against concluding hastily that a person is possessed by the devil. Many so-called possessions (or obsessions) are no doubt to be attributed to illusion, hysteria, or fraud. Nevertheless, there is no doubt that these experiences occur.

Completely different from possession or obsession is the devil's capacity to so use people or human institutions that they become, in effect, instruments of a demonic will. Masters of the spiritual life intimate this when they describe how Satan "summons innumerable demons and scatters them, some to one city and some to another, throughout the whole world, so that no province, no state of life, no individual is overlooked. Consider the address he makes to them, how he goads them on to lay snares for men, to seek to chain them. First they are to tempt them to covet riches (as Satan is accustomed to do in most cases) that they may the more easily attain the empty honors of this world, and then come to overweening pride." The devil's strategy by which he can "chain" people to his will is to incite them to riches (whether material or otherwise) in order to obtain honor and human recognition, and thus to induce pride. "From these three steps the evil one leads to all other vices."[30]

This "enchainment" is a form of virtual slavery. Held in the devil's shackles, a person (whether individually or corporately) becomes the unwitting tool of the powers of darkness.

Satanism and demonology have suddenly become popular issues, as mounting literature on the subject testifies. They indicate, in a dramatic way, what Christians have always been told: "Be calm, but vigilant, because your enemy the devil is prowling round like a roaring lion, looking for someone to devour. Stand up to him, strong in faith and in the knowledge that your brothers all over the world are suffering the same things" (1 P. 5:8–9).

The devil is very active in the world today, warns the Church, when she sadly admits that for many people it borders on superstition even to talk about the evil spirit as though he were anything else than a symbol. Yet, in our day as in the apostolic age, the devil is "the treacherous and cunning enchanter, who finds his way into us by way of the senses, the imagination, lust, and utopian logic." Those who take him lightly or smile at his existence are the easiest prey of what the apostle called "the mystery of iniquity."[31]

ORIGIN AND NATURE OF MAN

The history of Christian thought is not a straight line, but a weaving curve, as the mysteries of faith move through time and adjust themselves (without collision) to new discoveries and ideas created by the human mind. Man's origin and his nature are classic examples of such adjustment without compromise of the known data of revelation.

Body of the First Man. Until modern times there were two principal areas of controversy about the origin of Adam's body. One theory required angelic co-operation in the process; the other discussed the question of how precisely God formed the body of the first man, whether in an instant or progressively through different stages of development.

Mentioning the above is important because it clarifies what may still be unknown to some, that the theory of evolution is an ancient one in Catholic theological circles. Charles Darwin (1809–82) undoubtedly sparked a new era in anthropology and allied sciences, but Darwinism as such had only minimal impact on Catholic thought, whereas it struck many believers in evangelical Protestantism like a tornado. The issues raised by latter-day evolutionists directly affected the interpretation of the Bible, notably the first three chapters of Genesis. Christians who had only the biblical text as their guide, and no extrabiblical tradition or less still an authoritative Church, were left with only the literal words of Scripture. It was not enough to cope with the rising tide of criticism from scientific quarters, which made the simple narrative of Genesis look like another cosmological myth.

The First Vatican Council made sure that total evolutionism, which included an evolving god, was condemned as only a more subtle form of pantheism. When it came to define man's origin, it merely repeated what had been declared six centuries earlier against the resurgent Manichaeism of the Albigenses, namely that, after having made the angelic and material world, God "formed the creature man, who in a way belongs to both orders, as he is composed of spirit and body."[32]

There the subject still stands, doctrinally, except for two interventions by Pius XII generated by the controversy among Catholic theologians about the evolution of man's body. The first declaration was made in 1941, when the Pope identified three "elements [that] must be retained as certainly attested by the sacred author [of Genesis], without any possibility of an allegorical interpretation."[33] These are:

1. The essential superiority of man in relation to other animals, by reason of his spiritual soul.

2. The derivation in some way of the first woman from the first man.

3. The impossibility that the immediate father or progenitor of man could have been other than a human being, that is, the impossibility that the first man could have been the son of an animal, generated by the latter in the proper sense of the term. In context, the statement reads, "Only from a man can another man descend, whom he can call father and progenitor."[34] On other questions concerning the origin of man, the Pontiff said, we must wait for more light from science, illumined and guided by revelation. The "other questions" still open for development include the degree in which a lower species may have co-operated in the formulation of the first man, the way in which Eve was formed from Adam, and the age of the human race.

Ten years later, faced with the rise of scientism and historicism, the Holy See expressed itself at length on the controversial subject of evolution. This was the first time in the Church's history that papal authority entered at such length into the issue. It highlighted the growing tension between the findings and speculations of the natural sciences and the presuppositions of faith.

The magisterium of the Church does not forbid that the theory of evolution concerning the origin of the human body as coming from pre-existent and living matter—for the Catholic faith obliges us to hold that human souls are immediately created by God—be investigated and discussed by experts as far as the present state of human science and sacred theology allow.

However, this must be done in such a way that the arguments on both sides, those favorable and those unfavorable to evolution, be weighed and judged with the necessary gravity, moderation and discretion. And let all be prepared to submit to the judgment of the Church to whom Christ has given the mission of interpreting authentically the Sacred Scriptures and of safeguarding the dogmas of faith.

On the other hand, those go too far and trangress this liberty of discussion who act as if the origin of the human body from pre-existing and living matter were already fully demonstrated by the facts discovered up to now and by reasoning on them, and as if there were nothing in the sources of revelation which demands the greatest reserve and caution in this controversy.[35]

What is the position of Genesis on evolution? In the first narrative of human creation, the sacred author clearly excludes materialistic evolution, as though the soul of man derived naturally from the body. But nothing is directly affirmed as to how the body of Adam was formed. The second creation text about Adam, although very anthropomorphic, is too detailed and contrasts too strongly with the origin of other creatures (below man) not to imply that God acted in a special way when he brought the body of the first man into being.

Before modern evolutionary theories were in vogue, the ancient Fathers and later Doctors of the Church, along with theologians, held that some special action of God was operative in the formation of the first man's body; this was distinct from the ordinary co-operation of the First Cause with the physical causes built into created nature. Only two main questions were raised prior to modern evolutionism: whether and to what extent God used above natural agencies, like angelic, in the formation of Adam's body; and whether the "dust from the soil" of Genesis implied a body divinely prepared beforehand to receive a rational soul before actual infusion, or whether the body was predisposed for receiving a spirit in the very act when God "breathed into his nostrils a breath of life and man became a living being" (Gn. 2:7).

But since the theories of evolution have been popularized, theologians have come to agree that transformism, or the evolution of the first man's body from a lower species, is compatible with the faith. Two provisos are added, however: that the soul was immediately created by God out of nothing, and that somehow God exercised a special providence over whatever process preceded the origin of man's body, so that the first man was not literally generated by a brute beast.

Evolutionary Theories. In view of the widespread evolutionary attitude in modern thought, and its impact on the Christian faith, something should be said to clarify this posture and place it into theological perspective. Deriving as it does from experiment and reflection, evolution is one of the main sources of apparent conflict between faith and reason about which the First Vatican Council made a memorable declaration:

> Although faith is above reason, yet there can never be any real disagreement between faith and reason, because it is the same God who reveals mysteries and infuses faith, and has put the light of reason into the human soul. Now God cannot deny himself any more than the truth can ever contradict the truth.
>
> However, the chief source of this merely apparent contradiction lies in the fact that dogmas of faith have not been understood and explained according to the mind of the Church, or that deceptive assertions of opinions are accepted as axioms of reason. Therefore, "We define that every assertion opposed to the enlightened truth of faith is entirely false."[36]

Anyone familiar with the trends of current thought recognizes the need for transparency in this matter of evolution, at the risk of either professing an unenlightened faith or of making unfounded assertions of reason in opposition to the faith.

We may summarily divide evolutionary theories into three categories: those dealing with the origin of the inanimate universe, those referring to the origin of organic life apart from man, and those concerned with the origin of man.

1. For the cosmogonist, there are numerous tentative explanations of how the elements of the material universe came into being. All of them postulate the pre-existence of some kind of material substance out of which, on evolutionary grounds, ever more complex substances evolved. The two most commonly held are the "big bang" and the stellar formation theories. According to the first hypothesis, the elements were formed when some of the neutrons (infinitesimally small uncharged particles) decayed into protons (positively charged particles), which then captured the remaining neutrons to form the heavier elements. This was to have taken place in the first half hour of the universe. According to the second hypothesis, the formation of the elements came about by a synthesis caused by nuclear reactions in the stars that had already been formed.

If one postulates an evolution of the elements, it generally implies the evolution of the stars and galaxies. Galaxies are composed of numerous stars, and stars change in their energy content by radiation. Some lose mass, some burn out, some undergo fission into two or three stars, some capture meteors, but they all lose mass and available energy by what is now called the universal law of entropy. Thus the cosmic energy from the stellar regions (including our sun) is "burning out" in the sense that there is a constant increase of unavailable energy in the universe.

Some scientists have speculated, on admittedly slight evidence, that this "burning out" of the universe is partly balanced by the formation of new stars out of gas and dust and the explosive transformation of unstable stellar bodies. In either case, "evolution" means only the continuous natural history of stellar bodies.

The origin of planets, including the earth, also has a variety of hypothetical explanations, but with one factor in common: The planets are derivatives from the stars. It is fairly agreed that the earth and other planets are about four and a half billion years old, the age of samples of moon rock brought back to the earth. The oldest rocks on earth are estimated at a billion years below that figure.

2. About the origin of life there have been as many theories as about the beginnings of the universe. One is superseded by another. The case for spontaneous generation came to a dramatic close with the experiments of Louis Pasteur (1822–95). The cosmozoic theory claims that life existed from the beginning as minute spores, which were transported throughout the cosmos by way of meteorites. But the intense heat and cold in outer space make it virtually impossible that such spores could survive. The virus theory is based on the paradoxical nature of viruses, which have a simple chemical composition and do not respire; but they can reproduce and metabolize when joined with the host organism upon which they act as parasites. Some therefore argued that the virus must be at an advanced stage in the development of life because it depends on a living organism for its "life" as a parasite and cannot be at the beginning of the process of life's origins. But most scholars, while agreeing that the virus is a unique combination of life and nonlife, concede that this is more of a description of what now strangely exists than of how life originally came into being.

The most commonly held theory among evolutionists is some form of biopoesis (from the Greek *bios* [life] and *poiein* [to make]). It was given prominence by the discovery that certain nucleic acids (DNA and RNA) appear to be the key materials in all terrestrial forms of life. Yet this too is recognized by research scientists to be most hypothetical, as reported to the Darwin Centennial Celebration, by comparison with the mounting evidence in favor of organic evolution below the human species.[37]

3. The origin of man in the evolutionary scheme must be immediately distinguished between two very different theories. One theory among scientists holds that the accumulating evidence for the evolutionary process of plant and animal life has also played its role in the origin of man from the physical or bodily side of his nature. But this theory insists there is equally strong evidence that man's psychological side, his mind and free will, is something new, unique, and of a different order than the products of the evolutionary process.

Another theory believes that the whole of man evolved by a process totally within nature, from lower-animal organisms. Swept along by the converging arguments which suggest that man's physical being is part of the ongoing development of life, those who favor this hypothesis rest their case with Darwin on some variant of his own confession of a difficulty and assertion of an unprovable claim.

> The high standard of our intellectual powers and moral disposition is the greatest difficulty which presents itself, after we have been driven to this conclusion on the origin of man.
> But everyone who admits the principle of evolution must see that the mental powers of the higher animals, which are the same in kind with those of man, though so different in degree, are capable of advancement.[38]

Certainly if we apply, as an axiom of philosophy, the theory of evolution to everything, then it is only a logical deduction that man's body and soul evolved (in Darwin's words) "from a hairy, tailed quadruped, probably arborial in its habits."[39] But even scientific data from cultural anthropology do not support the theory. They rather indicate that man was man, and not a mere animal, from the earliest known archaeological remains that we have. He was capable of thought and had volitional powers completely unlike the purely animal instincts of the irrational species. The bridge between man and animal cannot be crossed by factual evidence. It can only be spanned by evolutionism, which denies that spirit is essentially distinct from matter and must be uniquely created by God.

Unity of the Human Race. Evolutionary thinking has also influenced the attitude toward the unitary origin of the present human race from a single man. There had been scattered speculation in past centuries, like the theory that people had existed before Adam. Present-day human beings are the offspring of these pre-Adamites. But concerted challenges did not arise until Darwinism had taken root in Western thought. Polygenists, as they are called, believe that an evolutionary hypothesis of man's origin requires the parallel belief that transition from the animal to the human body was accomplished not in one man and one woman, but in many.

As must seem immediately clear, there is more at stake than a mere question of historical fact, whether the human race actually descended from one man by natural generation. Nor is the Church concerned to prove anything from paleontology or other scientific data. It is to safeguard certain principles of revealed doctrine.

Thus if we are commonly descended from our first parents, we are brothers and sisters in the flesh, with consequences that affect human relations on every level of society. And, in spite of numerous differences, we not only share the same human nature but are literally bound together by ties of blood, which our native instinct, elevated by grace, makes the basis of social justice and charity.

This in turn lays the ground for the supernatural kinship of spirit, which finds expression in the Mystical Body, where grace sublimates the natural bond of the human family by raising it to communion with God under the headship of Jesus Christ.

From still another point of view, our common descent from Adam affects and explains our inheritance of original sin. It is just because we are naturally the offspring of the first man who sinned that, what he contracted, we receive by paternal generation. Conversely, even as we inherit sin from the father of mankind in the flesh, we are redeemed by the passion and death of Christ because he, too, was a descendant of Adam. The human nature that Christ assumed was not by carnal intercourse, but through Mary it was truly human and therefore like to Adam's and ours in all things but sin. Christ could therefore redeem what Adam had lost, because as man he was grafted into the same human tree, which had become infected by sin.

Sin entered the world through one man, and through sin death. . . . Adam prefigured the One to come, but the gift itself outweighed the fall. If it is certain that through one man's fall so many died, it is even more certain that divine grace, coming through the one man, Jesus Christ, came to so many as an abundant free gift. . . . Again as one man's fall brought condemnation on everyone, so the good act of one man brings everyone life and makes them justified. As by one man's disobedience many were made sinners, so by one man's obedience many will be made righteous (Rm. 5:12, 15, 18–19).

When speculation about man's evolutionary origins reached a peak in the midtwentieth century, Pius XII reminded scholars that theorizing about the descent of man's body from primates was one thing, but questioning whether the first parent of mankind was a single person is something else:

> As regards another theory, however, namely so-called Polygenism, sons of the Church by no means enjoy the same liberty. No Catholic can hold that after Adam there existed on this earth true men who did not take their origin through natural generation from the first parent of all, or that Adam was merely a symbol for a number of first parents. For it is unintelligible how such an opinion can be squared with what the sources of revealed truth and the documents of the magisterium of the Church teach on original sin, which proceeds from sin actually committed by an individual Adam and which, passed on to all by way of generation, is in everyone as his own.[40]

As a matter of historical record, the possibility of evolution of man's body was put forth already in the patristic age; so that evolution properly understood is not a modern innovation. According to Gregory of Nyssa, commenting on Genesis, when "Scripture says that man arose last of all the animated beings," it "is simply giving us a philosophical lesson about souls, seeing the most complete perfection realized in the beings formed last of all, because of a certain necessary succession of order." We are thus being taught that "nature is elevated by degrees as it were, that is, through the varieties of life from the lower stages up to the perfect."[41] There are similar passages in Augustine to the effect that "Adam was made from the earth, but in such a way that in the making, and the growth through the ages, the same periods of time would have been occupied which we now see required by the nature of the human species."[42] Augustine personally favored the idea that Adam came into the world at once in full maturity, but Augustine left quite open the theory that Adam's body could have been the end effect of a long process similar (on a large scale) to the development of an embryo in the womb.[42]

Yet Augustine recognized the datum of revelation about the reality, and not mere symbolism, and the oneness, and not plurality, of the first ancestor of the human family. This suggests that the real irritant regarding the origin of man is not so much Monogenism or Polygenism. It is the mystery of original sin.

Original Justice and the Fall. In many areas of the Christian faith, those who have raised problems about the revealed mysteries have been the occasion for a deeper understanding of what God actually revealed. The same holds true regarding original sin.

Two principal adversative positions have faced this cardinal mystery of the faith. Though separated by more than a millennium, they have much in common, even though the second is only lately making its full impact felt on the believing conscience of Christianity. Pelagianism, named after the British monk Pelagius (c. 360–420), denied that Adam's sin deprived all of Adam's descendants of those gifts which God had intended to pass on to the human race. The stress in Pelagianism was on the strength of our native will to work out the eternal destiny to which we have a natural right, provided we rightly use our liberty in obedience to God's commands. This followed as a logical corollary to the denial of any inherent loss in Adam's progeny or any inherent weakness in human nature brought about by the sin of the ancestor of mankind.

Rationalism is not so much an exaltation of the human will as a canonization of the human mind. When dealing with original sin, it assumes various postures. Before the modern age of science, men like Matthew Tindal (1655–1733) and David Hume (1711–76) in England, Voltaire and Jean-Jacques Rousseau in France, and Friedrich Schleiermacher (1768–1834) and Albrecht Ritschl (1822–89) in Germany gave such "rational" explanations that the essential mystery was dissolved. Original sin was due to the necessary limitations of the universe, or man's native propensity to create myths to explain the unknown.

More recently the rationalist approach has taken on two main forms. The first type considers the Genesis narrative a symbol of the passage of humanity in general or of man individually to the status and experience of maturity. Hence the colorful story of struggle for progress and the loss of infantile happiness. On these premises, original sin is a mythological description of man's perennial conflict in trying to rise above his present condition.

Another approach sees in the Genesis story simply an image

of what occurs in the religious life of every human being once he realizes his radical estrangement from God as a sinner. "Adam" is merely the prototype of Everyman as he looks into his heart and sees the chasm that separates his selfish, sensuous ego from the eternal absolute who is God.

A variant of the latter holds that original sin symbolizes man's condition as a finite being. It is therefore not declarative of an objective fact and still less of a contingent situation that need not have been.[43]

Since the beginnings of Pelagianism and up to the most sophisticated theories of rationalism, the Church has never wavered in her essential doctrine about man's original condition as he left the creative hand of God and of what happened when the first man disobeyed his Creator.

The complete record of how Pelagianism rocked the Church in those days can be read in the writings of St. Augustine, who spent much of his life combating what he considered an incredible audacity. His *Confessions* are a masterpiece of self-disclosure describing his own poignant experience of helplessness under the tyranny of pride and lust until rescued from internal slavery by the grace of Christ.

Augustine's doctrine on original justice, the fall, and original sin was many times confirmed by successive Popes. While the language of the papal teaching was to be greatly refined under later challenges, its main features were clear enough already by the end of the sixth century. Before the fall, Adam was "innocent" and spiritually alive; his body was meant to be immortal, and he enjoyed a certain "freedom of the soul." Once he fell, however, he lost these gifts not only for himself but also for his descendants; so that "it was not only the death of the body which is punishment for sin," but also "sin, the death of the soul, which passed from one man to all the human race."[44]

A thousand years later, the Council of Trent returned to the same subject, this time confronted by the resurgent Pelagianism of some of the Reformers. They admitted the fall of Adam, of course, but since they assumed that he had not been raised to a supernatural state in the first place, when he fell Adam did not so much lose any specially conferred gifts as something of his very nature.

Consequently, the Church's doctrine at Trent becomes more sharply defined. Thus "the first man Adam immediately lost the justice and holiness in which he was constituted when he disobeyed the command of God in the Garden of Paradise."[45] Moreover, our concupiscence or lack of built-in control of the passions, which St. Paul at times calls sin, "the Catholic Church has never understood that it is called sin because there is, in the regenerated, sin in the true and proper sense but only because it is from sin and inclines to sin."[46] The reason for this clarification was to carefully distinguish between two states of man's existence, before and after the fall. Before the fall, Adam enjoyed the gift of integrity, which meant absence of the conflict we now experience between our natural urges and the dictates of right reason. After the fall, Adam lost this gift for himself and his posterity, since even those who have been regenerated in baptism are plagued by an interior struggle with their unruly desires and fears.

So, too, Trent repeated in more explicit terms what earlier councils had taught. Adam was to have remained immortal in body. But once he sinned, "he incurred the death with which God had previously threatened him."[47]

Having said all of this, however, the main question still remains: How did Adam's disobedience affect his descendants? The Pelagians claimed that Adam injured only himself and not the rest of mankind, except in the sense of leaving posterity the bad example of his misdeeds. This position was clearly at variance with the teaching of St. Paul, whose doctrine was resolutely defended by the Church. No one may assert that "Adam's sin was injurious only to Adam and not to his descendants," or that "it was only the death of the body which is punishment for sin, and not the sin, the death of the soul, which passed from one man to all the human race."[48] This was repeated almost verbatim at Trent during the Counter-Reformation.

Modern social consciousness has introduced a new dimension into the fuller meaning of inherited sin. Society, we know, can mold character in two ways: in terms of the past that an individual has inherited, and in terms of the future he is entering and by which he will be profoundly affected. Some writers decided to call this "original sin," but the phrase demands careful explanation.

"Original" here would mean not an inheritance of nature, but the acquisition by a person. He is born as this individual, in the twentieth instead of the first century; in a culture that is Austrian, French, or Italian, instead of Arabian, Fijian, or Indian. And he is born of these parents, just this father and mother who procreated just this child at their age in this city, with these neighbors and friends—and no other of a near infinite number of possibilities.

All the factors that make up a person are original to him, and they are in their way as much inherited as the nature that a child receives from the couple who share with him their humanity.

"Original" in this way means original to man as a person, beyond the inheritance of nature as a human being. The distinction is crucial. All that Christianity has always believed about inherited guilt from Adam and Eve is not changed by this additional insight. This is not a resurgent Pelagianism. It is a sober acknowledgment that socialization and collectivization of modern man have immersed him in other men's values and actions to an unprecedented degree.

THE HUMAN PERSON

The Second Vatican Council covered the same doctrinal ground that had been so carefully tilled through sixteen centuries of conciliar history. All the familiar landmarks that we have seen regarding God's creative act and continued providence, man's origin and fall from grace, and the inherited sinfulness of the human race in need of a Redeemer—everything is to be found in the latest ecumenical gathering of the Catholic Church.

But there is one difference. Unlike any other general council before, this one placed a stress on the human person that can only be called extraordinary. One reason for the emphasis may have been the need to reaffirm the sanctity of the individual, who was fast becoming a cog in the machinery of modern technocracy and almost a stranger in the computerized anonymity of today's society.

In order to concentrate a maximum of the Church's teaching into a minimum of words, it will be useful to review historically the stages of doctrinal development in the Catholic understanding of the human person.

Spiritual Substance. Caught in the logic of their own principles, the early Manichaeans denied that the human person had a spiritual soul, whose substance was similar to the nature of the God who created man to God's own image and likeness. Prior to the formal condemnation of the Manichees by a general council, there had been numerous provincial synods that built on the witness of Scripture and the Fathers to vindicate man's personality as essentially spiritual, i.e., not extended or measurable in time and space and capable of thought (not mere sensation) and of free choice (not mere impulse). When the Fourth Lateran Council declared that "the creature man" is "composed of spirit and body,"[49] it used the word "spirit" as synonymous with "invisible" and "not corporeal." By saying it was invisible, it did not mean "unintelligible," as though the spirit of man could not be "seen" by the eyes of the mind. Its invisibility is relative only to the senses of the body. By saying that the spirit was not corporeal, the Council wished to affirm without equivocation that the human person is basically dual in character; on its bodily side it partakes of the same nature as the ground on which we walk and the air we breathe, but on the spiritual side it partakes of the nature of the angels. In Augustine's phrase, being like the angels we are near to God, being like matter we are near to nothing.[50]

Autonomous Individuality. Much as the Manichaeans had borrowed many of their ideas from oriental pantheism, certain Moslems leaned heavily on the Hellenic notion of monopsychism (from the Greek *monos* [one] and *psyche* [soul]). Their leading light was Averroes (1126–98), the Spanish Islamic philosopher whose commentaries on Aristotle became the vogue at the University of Paris, where they threatened the integrity of the Christian faith. Central to Averroes was the doctrine that only one intellect exists for the human race in which every individual participates. As a consequence, there is no room for personal immortality, personal liberty, and personal responsibility. Catholic Averroists at Paris professed to reconcile their teaching with the dogmas of the Church by the expedient of the double truth, according to which they claimed to believe as theologians what they denied as philosophers. It was with Averroism in mind that St. Thomas Aquinas began his *Summa Contra Gentiles* in 1257.

Supported by Aquinas' writings, the bishop of Paris formally anathematized the Averroist theories in 1270, but they continued to flourish for centuries. Finally, in 1518, at the beginning of the Protestant Reformation, the Fifth Lateran Council defined the Catholic doctrine on the individuality of the human soul in each human person. Those who "claim that the intellectual soul is mortal or that there is a single soul for all men" were condemned. Then, on a positive note, the Council explained that the Church believes:

> The soul is not only truly, of its own nature and essentially, the form of the human body . . . but also it is immortal and, corresponding to the number of bodies in which it is infused, is capable of being multiplied in individuals, is actually multiplied, and must be multiplied.[51]

What this means is that each person has his own soul, that each is personally immortal, that each is divinely multiplied by God's creative act at the time of infusion into the body, and that each is so united with the body it animates that they form together one autonomous, i.e., self-responsible, individual.

Through God's Creative Act. A moment's reflection will tell us that what really determines the uniqueness of each human person is the origin of the soul, which animates his body. Bodies are too obviously generated by our parents to raise any question of faith. But where do our souls come from?

One theory about the soul's origin was probably borrowed from the Hindu belief in reincarnation. Although it took various forms when it penetrated Christian theology, the best known is associated with Origen (c. 185–254), who did not himself fully subscribe to what has come to be known as Origenism. Outlawed by the Church in the sixth century, it claimed that souls pre-existed from eternity, and therefore long before their infusion into bodies.[52] They are "exiled" in bodies for different reasons, including the need to expiate their sins. Any kind of pre-existence of the soul would eliminate the possibility of a true personality, because then the indwelling in a body would be a sort of imprisonment rather than a union of body and spirit to form one substance. But if the preexistence is of the strictly Vedanta variety, then we are back in the monopsychism of Averroes, with one soul for the human race. On these premises there are no persons, plural number; there is only a single "oversoul," which animates the whole rational universe.

A variant of pre-existence is the emanationism of the ancient Gnostics and Manichees, who claimed that souls emanate (flow out) from the substance of God. Augustine's reaction to this was that, if the soul were actually a part of God, "it would be in every respect unchangeable," which it most certainly is not.[53] The emanationist theory was solemnly condemned by the First Vatican Council.[54]

One more theory about the origin of the soul touches on the current struggle of believing Christians to safeguard the rights of the unborn child as a human person. Convinced that the child was a person from the moment of conception, Tertullian in the third and St. Augustine in the fourth and fifth centuries suggested the idea of generationism. In its crude form, it is called traducianism (from *tradux,* a cutting or slip). It holds that the soul is produced immediately from the male sperm, and that children are in a sense "cuttings" from the souls of their parents.

Spiritual generationism recognizes the immaterial nature of the soul, so it postulates a kind of spiritual semen by which parents communicate the souls to their offspring. Augustine hesitated between creationism and this type of generationism, mainly because the Pelagians whom he was refuting on the necessity of grace argued that nothing unclean can come from the hand of God. Therefore, they said, the souls of children, which are directly created by God out of nothing, cannot be tainted with original sin.

The Pelagians were right in restating the Church's historic teaching about creationism, but wrong in arguing from this to the absence of original sin. As Aquinas was later to explain, the essence of original sin is the deprivation of what God would have conferred on all of Adam's descendants if the first man had not sinned.[55] It is not some inherent evil in what God produces.

Whatever God creates is, indeed, clean insofar as it is God's creation. But we cannot separate in practice the soul's creation from its infusion into the body. Sin is not something positive. It is rather the lack of something, in this case that supernatural—i.e., super-added—life of grace to which the soul would have been entitled (in God's eyes) if the father of the human family had not originally disobeyed his Creator. Having lost the title to this possession, Adam's progeny are deprived of it at the moment the soul is united with the body.

On a magisterial level, in the midfourteenth century, Benedict XII set forth a number of propositions for the schismatic Armenians to accept as a condition for their reunion with the Church. Among the propositions was the rejection of the thesis that "the human soul of a son is propagated from the soul of his father, as his body is from the body of his father."[56] By implication, the same theory was to be rejected as applying to daughters.

While never formally defined, the fact of a direct creation of each individual soul belongs to the deposit of the Christian faith. Implicitly taught by the Fifth Lateran Council quoted above, it is part of that vast treasury of revealed truths which are jealously safeguarded by the Church. This was brought to the surface in *Humani Generis,* in 1950, when Pius XII proscribed certain deviations from Catholic orthodoxy touching on human origins. He reminded believers that "the Catholic faith obliges us to hold that the human soul is immediately created by God."[57]

Similarly, the Church has never defined the exact moment when the soul is created and infused into the body to form this unique human person. But the Church's mind on the matter can be deduced from its age-long attitude toward abortion.

There has been a broad range of theories in Catholic circles about the precise time when God creates the soul. Men of the stature of Thomas Aquinas were caught in the speculation, and they assigned various times. But they were always careful to explain that they were merely speculating. Actually and in the practical order, no Christian could treat the fetus otherwise than as a human being. This is confirmed, as we shall see, in the Church's unswerving prohibition of abortion at any stage of pregnancy. It is, therefore, assumed that creation of the soul and its infusion take place at the moment of conception.

Dignity Rooted in Freedom.   Since the rise of modern totalitarianism, the main theme of Catholic teaching about the human person has been the subject of liberty. Individuals have rights because they are persons endowed with freedom to co-operate with God's grace in working out their immortal destiny. Three documents—two papal and one conciliar—stand out in a series of statements that read like a Gospel proclamation in today's world: "You are persons, not pawns! You are free, not slaves! You have rights that no one, under God, may take away!"

In his masterful *Human Liberty,* Leo XIII anticipated the age of martyrs about to dawn in the twentieth century. Basing himself on revelation and recalling apostolic times, he told thousands of faithful who would soon die as victims for Christ that "this honorable freedom of the sons of God, which most nobly protects the dignity of the human person, is greater than any violence or any injustice." Physical death cannot destroy it. "This was the freedom that the apostles claimed with unshaken constancy, that the apologists defended with their writings, and that the martyrs in such numbers consecrated with their blood."[58]

John XXIII wrote *Pacem in Terris* in retrospect over the tragedy, by then, of many victims of misguided zeal to solve the problems of humanity without taking into account the laws the Creator has implanted in the hearts of men. These laws, he said, are in the moral order, which means they are to be obeyed with freedom. All men of good will are seeking peace, after so much bloodshed. "Peace," however, "will be but an empty word unless it is founded on the order . . . founded on truth, built according to justice, animated and integrated by charity" and, most importantly, "put into practice in freedom."[59] Nothing can be coerced, not even world peace.

Last, the Second Vatican Council issued its longest document on the most pressing problem of our times, or rather host of problems besetting mankind as it struggles between two ages of history: the age of individualism, which was centuries in the making; and the new age of communitarianism, which is only now beginning. At its center is the conflict between personal desires and the growing demands of the human community. Two freedoms are confronting each other, of the individual and of society. Both "persons and societies thirst for a full and free life worthy of man; one in which they can subject to their own welfare all that the modern world can offer them so abundantly."[60] Never before has liberty faced such a test, where the physical person is called upon to sacrifice self in order to advance the common good; and the corporate person is called upon to restrain its power against the dignity of the individual.

IV. JESUS CHRIST

The Catholic faith in Jesus Christ is a cluster of beliefs that form a harmonious synthesis. They should first be seen if we are to appreciate the history of the Church's doctrine about the person and work of her Founder. Otherwise the sheer quantity of doctrinal detail may obscure what is really a clear image to those who believe.

Who is Jesus Christ? He is the Second Person of the Trinity whom the Father sent into the world to become man of the Virgin Mary in order to save the world from sin. Having lost God's friendship, mankind of itself could not regain this life of grace, any more than a man who is dead can bring himself to life again.

God could have set a new and purely natural destiny for man, and promised him a natural happiness after death. He could also have reopened heaven without the Incarnation by simply forgiving everything without reparation. But this would have been less in keeping with his perfect justice and with the divine will to manifest his perfect love. He therefore decided to take the most sublime course possible. His only Son was to take on human nature and thus representing all humanity, redeem us through his passion and death.

Perfectly adequate reparation and perfectly satisfactory expiation could only be achieved by a man who was at the same time God.

Christ then is our Mediator because by his death he reconciled an estranged human race with its Creator. He is the one perfect Mediator. Others may share in this mediation either by disposing men's hearts to conversion or by ministering the sacraments which Christ established to confer the grace that unites us with God.

The Man, Christ Jesus (1 Tm. 2:5), is even now the eternal Highpriest who stands between God and sinful human beings. He continues reconciling us with God by his favors and gifts, and offers to the heavenly Father prayers and satisfaction for our misdeeds. It is this enduring priesthood of the Savior that serves as the revealed foundation for the Catholic faith in the Mass.

If we ask more closely, "Why did God become man?" we do not exhaust the reasons by saying it was to redeem us from sin. Indeed, not a few doctors of the Church are ready to claim that God would have taken on our human form even though man had not sinned.

God became man to give us the most demanding object of our faith. All other mysteries either derive from this one or, as in the case of the Trinity, are known to us only because the incarnate Son of God revealed them.

Believing in the Incarnation, we profess with the infallible Church that there are in Christ two really distinct natures, one human and the other divine; yet united in such a way that Christ is one individual and not two, and unchanged in such a way that each nature remains truly and unqualifyingly itself. The human nature is just like ours, except without sin. The divine nature is simply infinite, since God did not become less divine by becoming human. Rather in assuming our nature the divine Person exercises a loving and merciful act of condescension, and in no way is debased or dishonored although the Word (which is infinite) became flesh (which is finite).

Time and again Christ insisted on faith in himself as a condition for salvation. It was no wonder, seeing the sacrifice of our reason what acceptance of his divinity requires of those who believe. They are bidden to adore Jesus of Nazareth, who is man with a history, while knowing that in doing so they worship Jesus of Nazareth, who is God from all eternity.

God became man to give us the strongest support for our hopes. We are by nature creatures of desire who cannot be fully satisfied by anything here below, and yet who find ourselves often pandering to our lower cravings in spite of every reason to the contrary. This is where Christ comes in. What we could not do of ourselves, we are assured can be done with his help.

This means not only salvation from sin but sanctity in the practice of virtue, and not only liberation from passion but achievement of moral perfection. Christ is at once the pattern of holiness and its principal inspiration, as he is also its primary source.

The Incarnation offers the faithful their highest motive for loving God, who became man not because he had to but because he freely chose to in order to show how much he loves the human family and how we are to love others after the example he gave us. On both counts we are inspired to gratitude and, from gratitude, to selfless generosity. All that we know about love tells us it seeks to be united with the object of its affections. So it was with God. His union with man in Christ is the most intimate possible for divine love to achieve. We also know that the language of love is sacrifice. That is the reason why God, who as God is perfectly happy, assumed our mortal nature. He wished to be able to suffer. He could thus experience the weakness of our humanity and share in our own endurance of pain.

But Christ is not only in heaven, where he ascended to the right hand of his Father. He is also on earth in our midst as the Head of his Mystical Body, which is the Church, and in the Holy Eucharist, where he is physically present as the living Center of the Christian community.

The Christ of Catholicism, therefore, is not a mere memory nor only a great historical person whose influence still survives among his followers. He is, in his own words, the Alpha from whom all creation took its beginning and the Omega in whom all who believe in him will find their destiny.

WITNESS OF THE NEW TESTAMENT

Christians imply more by the term "New Testament" than is commonly supposed. They affirm two levels of God's communication to the human race, an early witness that spanned the centuries before the coming of Christ, and a later testimony, which began with the Incarnation but which will continue until the end of time.

Our first stage of analysis traces the witness of the Christian Scriptures—the Synoptic Gospels, St. Paul and St. John—to the person and mission of the Savior. Our purpose will be as much to discover how the prophecies were fulfilled in Jesus Christ as to lay the foundation for a more doctrinal understanding of Christ in the later patristic and conciliar age and up to our own day.

At the outset, two technical terms should be introduced. Christology is not the same as Soteriology, since the one, by definition, is the science (*logos*) of *Christos* (the Messiah); whereas the other is the science of Christ as the Savior (*Soter*). Who Christ was and what are the deeper reaches of the Incarnation are the main concerns of Christology; but Soteriology deals with the work of Christ, namely, the Redemption, and implies that God had become incarnate in order to bring a fallen human family to its heavenly destiny.

By and large, the mainstream of traditional Protestantism stemming from the Reformation agrees with Catholic teaching in basic Christology. But Soteriology, which takes into account man's justification and the priesthood, bristles with differences between Roman Catholicism and the inheritors of Luther and Calvin. In ecumenical language, any progress in Christian unity presumes a better understanding on both sides of the mystery of Redemption.

Whatever else the New Testament was meant to be, its driving intention was to bring men nearer to Christ and for that reason its message is strongly personal. The Good News of salvation comes either as *kerygma* (preaching), directed mainly to the will and seeking to motivate a voluntary response to what is good (*bonum*) in the Christian revelation; or as *didache* (teaching), aimed above all at the mind and wanting to instruct the intellect about what is truth (*verum*) in the "tidings of great joy" announced to the shepherds of Bethlehem.

It is impossible to exaggerate the personalist character of the Christian Scriptures, whose object, in the words of the Lord at the Last Supper, is "everlasting life, that they may know you, the only true God, and him whom you have sent, Jesus Christ." Everything else is either presumed or corollary, so that even theological analysis is justified only on these terms.

SYNOPTIC TRADITION

The Gospels according to Matthew, Mark, and Luke are commonly called synoptic because they give a composite view of the life story of Jesus when set in parallel comparison.

Contrasted with the rest of the New Testament, notably Paul and John, the Synoptics are more archaic in their presentation, and more concrete regarding factual data. They are correspondingly less subtle and abstract, and, to that extent, less theological. Unlike Paul and John, their reflections on the person and work of the Master are less frequent. For these reasons it is well to start with them as we examine the biblical witness to Jesus Christ, with stress on his transcendence, which the faith of the early Church recognized as his divinity and which for centuries to come would provoke a series of Christological controversies that rocked the Catholic Church.

Fulfillment of Prophecy. Too often the person of Jesus is separated from the doctrine he taught, and yet the two are of one piece. If he was the Messiah foretold by the prophets, he would also teach as only the Desired of Nations might be expected to enlighten mankind.

Matthew understood this well. That is why he went to such pains to recall the Sermon on the Mount, with its studied contrast with the ethics of the Old Law or, at least of most Jews at the time of Christ. Jesus began by insisting that he did not come to destroy the Law of the Prophets, but to fulfill. Then he proceeded to lay down a standard of morality that marked for all time the cleavage with former days, and the fulfillment of a long-awaited holy One who would sanctify those who believed in his name.

Writing for the Jews, Matthew synthesized the Master's teachings in the eight Beatitudes and climaxed them in the Lord's Prayer. Taken together, these norms of conduct introduced a new dimension into human culture and, quite alone, warrant the conclusion that Jesus of Nazareth professed to be more than a human legislator.

The logic behind this conclusion is clear. Jesus explicitly raised the demands of the Mosaic law, known to have been given by Yahweh. He thereby equated himself with the Lord of the Old Testament, because in his own name, and without apology, he proclaimed such drastic revision of Judaic morality that even after twenty centuries, the Jewish code does not recognize the change, e.g., in the dissolubility of marriage and the right to remarriage after divorce.

Yet proclaiming a higher standard of conduct would have been meaningless unless those for whom it was intended were assured the moral strength to carry it into effect. At this point, all of Christ's references to himself as the source of grace and moral power come into play—synthesized in the declaration, "Come to me, all you who labor and are overburdened, and I will give you rest. Shoulder my yoke and learn from me, for I am gentle and humble of heart, and you will find rest for your souls. Yes, my yoke is easy, and my burden light" (Mt. 11:28–30).

Christ made his moral doctrine not only possible but, in many ways, prescriptive. He therefore not only described what his followers might aspire to, but, also legislated what they were obliged to do. His parting words to the disciples were that they might teach all "that I have commanded you," and his sanction was that those who would believe and act accordingly would be saved; but those who should refuse to believe, or refuse to live up to their faith, would be lost.

He anticipated that acceptance of him as the Messiah would cost his followers dearly, in terms of friendships betrayed and enemies gained (Mt. 10:34–39).

No one but a charlatan, or a person who speaks with divine authority could seriously pit himself against a man's dearest possessions and demand allegiance above everything else. No Isaiah or Jeremiah would have dared to suggest, let alone require, that loyalty to themselves stood higher than all human love, and that life itself was cheap and to be sacrificed for them.

We see in this teaching of Christ the whole fabric of Christian spirituality, with stress on the sacraments, which the Savior instituted precisely to help the faithful find his yoke easy and his burden light. Without such means of grace, fidelity to his demands would be impossible.

Given this backdrop of elevated messianic teaching, it is no wonder that the Synoptics speak of the Savior simply as Messiah (the Christ) and that Matthew should spend his whole Gospel showing how the prophecies were fulfilled in Jesus of Nazareth.

Matthew is eloquent in quoting the Savior's prediction that believing in the Messiah would bring persecution (Mt. 5:11–12), and Peter makes it plain that the prediction was being fulfilled: The followers of Isaiah's "Suffering Servant" were duplicating his experience as Messianists (Christians).

Son of God and Son of Man. If the prophecies intimated that the "One to come" would have a twofold origin, this duality is reflected in the terms most commonly applied to Jesus in the Synoptic writers, *Son of God* and *Son of Man*. Both are rich in meaning to fill out the biblical portrait of Christ.

In theological language, sonship implies origin of one person from another person, in such a way that the one originated has the same nature as the one originating. This is so true that in the biological sciences a species is often identified by the ability of two mates to reproduce their kind.

The Messiah, therefore, might be expected to profess both types of filiation, of God as divine and of man as human. Yet between the two names, the title "Son of Man" is more revealing in the synoptic tradition than elsewhere in the New Testament.

Various people are called "sons of God" in the Scriptures. All mankind, created to the image and likeness of God, is related to him by the sonship of being like him in the possession of mind and free will. The children of Israel are sons of Yahweh by a special claim, because he chose them as his own and showed them his unswerving care. All the just who are in God's friendship, "who are born not of the will of the flesh, nor of the will of man, but of God," are his sons by supernatural adoption. Their destiny is to be like him in knowing and loving him, as he knows and loves himself.

Although Jesus never said outright, "I am the Son of God," he did better (in view of the ambiguity of the term) by revealing an intimacy between himself and the Father that could only mean an identity of nature with the Father. "Everything," he said, "has been entrusted to me by my Father; and no one knows the Son except the Father, just as no one knows the Father except the Son and those to whom the Son chooses to reveal him" (Mt. 11:27).

This passage is so clear in stating Christ's unique consciousness, one with Yahweh, that critics who believe his divinity was a later development of the Church deny the authenticity of the text and urge that John (or some Hellenist) interpolated the words. But manuscript evidence shows only Matthean origin, and is supported by the whole tenor of the first three Gospels, where Jesus identifies himself as the only son of the parable, compared with the servants (prophets) of the master of the vineyard; where he regularly contrasts "my Father" with "your Father"; and where he distinguishes between his Davidic origin and being David's Lord.

With few exceptions (e.g., Ac. 7:56), the title "Son of Man" is found only in the Gospels and here always on the Savior's lips. Several uses may be classified: the Son of Man is One who is to appear at the Last Judgment "coming with the clouds of heaven" (Mk. 14:62) or sitting on the throne of his glory as judge of the world (Mt. 19:28). These passages derive their meaning from association with Hebrew eschatology. Again, the Son of Man relates to the future sufferings, death and resurrection of the Messiah (Mt. 17:22 and Mk. 8:31); or finally to Jesus as simply an individual speaking in his own name, where parallel texts in another Gospel sometimes have

"I" or "me" instead of the formal term (Mt. 5:11; 10:32 and Lk. 6:22; 12:8).

Implied in this title is a transcendence that should be traced to the prophecy of Daniel, and that Christ appropriated to himself at the dramatic moment when his fate was being decided by the Jewish Sanhedrin. Caiphas the high priest was vexed with the Savior and puzzled by his silence. He questioned Jesus and received an answer (Mt. 26:62–66).

> "I put you on oath by the living God to tell us if you are the Christ, the Son of God." "The words are your own," answered Jesus. "Moreover, I tell you that from this time onward you will see the Son of Man seated at the right hand of the Power and coming on the clouds of heaven."

If the title "Son of Man" is the clearest profession of divine transcendence in the Synoptics, it is also symbolic of Christ's unique dual nature, at once divine and human. It focuses on the uniqueness of the Messiah in the history of world religions.

Outside the Jewish tradition, other religious systems also believe in "incarnations." On closer analysis, however, these *avataras*, as the Hindus call them, are not believed to be literal "enfleshments of the Deity." Neither the oriental "Ground of Being" (*Brahman*) nor the material body of man are held to be what Christianity teaches about both; the one is an impersonal force permeating the universe; the other is an illusion that hides what alone is real in the world, namely, monistic Spirit.

Among the Jews, too, there had been epiphanies (appearances) in their religious history, as with Abraham, Jacob, Moses, and the prophets. But never had Yahweh become human, and much less claimed lineage by carnal generation of an earthly mother. It was this human ancestry especially that was stressed by the title, while including under its concept the possession of suprahuman qualities.

PAULINE CHRISTOLOGY

As we move from the Synoptic Gospels into St. Paul and the early Christian community, the first and strongest impression they leave us is the devotion of the early Christians to the person of Jesus. He dominated their thoughts, determined their ritual customs, inspired their daily practices, and so completely entered every phase of their lives that it is no wonder they were soon given the simple title of "Christians," as followers of one whom they called the Messiah and on whom all their religion centered.

It is impossible to read a single letter of St. Paul without feeling that for him Christianity was Christ. Paul speaks of himself as the servant of Jesus Christ, and tells those to whom he is writing that they belong to Jesus Christ. His preoccupation with the Savior makes him say, "if anyone does not love the Lord, a curse on him." In closing salutations, he writes, "My love is with you all in Christ Jesus" (1 Co. 16:22, 24).

When necessary, he vindicates his authority that he is an apostle, "who has been appointed by Jesus Christ and by God the Father . . ." (Ga. 1:27). In his suffering, he rejoices bearing the marks of the Lord Jesus Christ on his body, and in humility he prays that he only glory in the cross of Christ.

Paul's exhortations were not so much to virtue as to the following of Christ. "In your minds you must be the same as Christ Jesus" (Ph. 2:5). His reproaches are less against vice than against those who seek only their own interests and not those of Jesus. His great hope is to be dissolved, and to be with Christ. By comparison with this treasure, "I believe nothing can happen that will outweigh the supreme advantage of knowing Christ Jesus my Lord. For him I have accepted the loss of everything" (Ph. 3:8).

There is a rarity about Paul's understanding of Christ that sets him apart from the other writers of the New Testament. Most likely he never met the Savior during Christ's visible stay on earth, which gives Pauline Christology an interiority not found in others, even in St. John. Paul thus became the great apostle of the risen Savior and witness to the Lord's invisible Spirit working in the Church.

He was, on his own account, converted suddenly by the grace of Christ; and he would spend the rest of his days testifying to the power of that grace in a way not found in Matthew, Mark, Luke, or John.

In the deepest sense of the term, Paul preached Christ as Savior, and his letters are preoccupied with man's sinfulness, from which he cannot rescue himself unless Jesus comes to his help. If we would distinguish between the two names of the Lord, *Jesus* and *Christ,* Paul gives us a theology of Jesus as Savior, more than the others, who stress the role of Christ as the Messiah come into the world.

While it is impossible to do full justice to Pauline Soteriology, we can profitably approach his writings about the Savior by classifying his main letters and specifying those features in each that best illustrate his concept of the Redeemer.

Christ Our Hope.   The two epistles to the Thessalonians, reputedly the earliest expositions of the New Testament, delineate St. Paul's eschatology in terms of Christ in a way that has added a new dimension to the familiar treatment of the subject in theological manuals before the modern renascence of the Bible. In Paul's view, man's destiny is indeed to possess God in the beatific vision, but God Incarnate, who is beheld at once by the soul in union with its Creator and by the body in the presence of the human Redeemer.

Drawing on language familiar to his readers, the apostle spoke of this destiny from several viewpoints. It was to be a *parousia,* arrival, to signify the coming of Christ when a person dies and Christ's coming at the end of time. It would also be an *apantesis,* meeting, to describe the coming together of Christ and Christian when the arrival takes place. And finally, it will be an *epiphania,* manifestation, wherein Christ reveals the fullness of his beauty and bestows his beatitude on the people who are saved.

Historically the terminology was borrowed from the customary practice of emperors and kings in those days to celebrate their coming to a city or province on a royal visit, at which time they were met by chosen delegates of the citizens, and when the rulers would show their generosity by releasing prisoners, relaxing taxation, or giving alms to the poor.

Paul compares the hapless condition of the pagans who live without hope, with the Christian expectation, and bids the faithful take comfort from this certitude (1 Th. 4:13–18).

Time and again, Paul had to caution the faithful to be patient and not expect the *parousia* soon. They were not to be anxious, and much less cease from labor in the work of the Lord, as though his advent was nigh. About dates and times, he warned them, we need not write to you, "since you know very well that the Day of the Lord is going to come like a thief in the night" (1 Th. 5:2). Or again, about the coming of our Lord Jesus Christ and his gathering of us to himself, he begged the faithful, "please do not get excited too soon or be alarmed by any prediction or rumor, or any letter claiming to come from us, implying that the Day of the Lord has already arrived. Never let anyone deceive you in this way" (2 Th. 2:2–3).

Yet, in a true sense, the *coming of the Lord* was near to every man with the nearness of the person's death, with obvious implications for living the kind of life that believers in Christ's second coming were expected to practice.

This readiness for the Lord meant that a Christian loved his fellow man. Always one to encourage virtue before rebuking vice, St. Paul reminded the Thessalonians that "you have learned from God yourselves to love one another," so that no words from Paul were needed. But there was room for improvement: "However, we do urge you, brothers, to go on making even greater progress" (1 Th. 4:9–10).

And all of this was to be done, not from constraint but joyfully. "Be happy at all times," Christians were told, "pray constantly; and for all things give thanks to God, because this is what God expects you to do in Christ Jesus" (1 Th. 5:17–18).

Life in Christ. Knowing the past history of the Greeks, it was not surprising that the Corinthians were no sooner baptized than they were embroiled in the familiar problem of intellectuals: pride that created factions, and bickering that threatened to end in schism. In fact, a generation after Paul, the Corinthians became so quarrelsome that they evoked the first extant exercise of papal authority outside the Scriptures.

For a people reared in the culture of Hellenism, they were prone to philosophize to the point of endangering the faith. They had to be told that human wisdom is folly by comparison with the saving knowledge of Christ (1 Co. 1:23–24; 2:1–2).

If the creed of a Christian is Christ, the code of morals is self-control. Coupled with pride, the natural man is given to lust. The remedy for both is the same: To overcome pride, man's spirit must be subject in humility to Christ and joined with him in pain; to overcome lust, his body must be united with Christ in the mortification of the sex urge. The practice of chastity marked the true believer and distinguished him from the infidel.

Along with faith and temperance, the Christian religion has its own worship focused on the person of Christ. He is the center of its ritual and the purpose of its cultus—in the Eucharist—in opposition to the pagan mysteries and their mythological gods.

His body and blood in the sacrament are really present, an extension now invisibly of the incarnate presence visibly on earth. His sacrifice is truly enacted—not detracting from the infinite merits of the cross. His memory continues, as he requested before he died; and his grace is conferred by doing what he commanded "in commemoration of me."

Then back to the familiar theme: "Every time you eat this bread and drink this cup, you are proclaiming his death," until he comes (1 Co. 11:26). The relationship is causal, as Christ had said. Those who receive his body and blood will enjoy the *parousia;* those who reject the Eucharist condemn themselves.

The Philippians, no less than the Corinthians, were a factious group. Both had to be spurred to unity by an appeal to Christ. Typically Paul refers the practice of community to having the spirit of humility after the example of the Son of God. How can foolish man refuse to live peaceably with others, through pride, when the Son of Man took on the nature of a slave to redeem mankind? (Ph. 2:5–16).

Unity among Christians is not a function of virtue only, as though it depended exclusively (or even mainly) on their practice of humble charity. It is a leaven of God's re-creation of the human race. Through the merits of his Son and the death he suffered on the cross, mankind who believe in him are already joined with him, and therefore to one another, by grace—quite independent of their practical humility. Their contribution is to conserve what Christ has wrought in the human family and to grow in the bond of mystic unity that forms with him one supernatural body. "Now you together are Christ's body," Christians are reminded, "but each of you is a different part of it" (1 Co. 12:27).

Salvation Through Christ. St. Paul's doctrine of Salvation has become the mainstay of the Church's teaching on the Redemption. Reviewing the sequence of the apostle's thought will help us to follow his teaching.

He takes a cosmic view of mankind, from before the fall of Adam, through its condition under the Old Law (and outside the law among pagans), and now, after Christ, under the new dispensation of grace from the Redeemer.

Before the lapse of our first parents, man was in a state of righteousness with God. Sin entered the world through one man, and through sin, death. Thus man's original condition was sinless, and his privilege was not to die.

The state of sinfulness affected not only Adam, who disobeyed God, but infected Adam's posterity who derived from him. Every phase of man's nature suffered from this fall.

First *reason* was darkened, so that, although naturally attainable, the knowledge of God was obscured by passion (Rm. 1:18–23). Darkened reason led to *irrational urges* that flared up in myriad ways, but notably in lusts of the body (Rm. 1:24–27).

Sex perversion leads to *every kind of vice*. As modern psychology shows, once a person becomes addicted to sex indulgence, nothing is sacred to him. No law is too holy or mandate too binding not to be broken (or breakable) by one who is enslaved by the flesh (Rm. 1:28–32).

Given this picture of man's unregenerate nature, Paul asks how, then, will anyone be saved. It cannot be through the Mosaic law for, as history shows, the law only made matters worse for those who sinned. They sinned once in rejecting the voice of conscience, weakened by the fall; they sinned again by disobeying the law revealed to them on Sinai and interpreted by the prophets.

Only Christ, the second Adam, can save mankind fallen from innocence and estranged from the Creator. Indeed, the redemptive work of Christ more than makes up for the disruptive work of Adam (Rm. 5:15–21).

This note of optimism pervades the writings of Paul and characterizes even those of his disciple Luke. The two go together. Paul should be read in the light of Luke, and Luke in Paul's writings. If the latter gives the theology of man's salvation, the former recounts the history, which has been rightly called the Gospel of Mercy, every chapter of which breathes the universal salvific will of God, and the ease (if only men respond) of salvation through the grace of Christ.

Paul's teaching was not born of speculation. It came as a result of special insight into the conflict that raged in his own being. He struggled in his own person between the antipodes of fallen nature and saving grace, and expressed for all time the inner conflict of every child of Adam.

In fact, this seems to be the rule, that every single time I want to do good it is something evil that comes to hand. In my utmost self I dearly love God's Law, but I can see that my body follows a different law that battles against the law which my reason dictates. This is what makes me a prisoner of that law of sin which lives inside my body.

What a wretched man I am! Who will rescue me from this body doomed to death? Thanks be to God through Jesus Christ our Lord (Rm. 7:21–25).

The Lordship of Christ. Up to this point, Paul's letters reveal the Savior as man's Redeemer and the one hope of reaching his destiny. But there is more to him than serving a contingent function, albeit an important one, to remove what was after all a contingent element in man's history, sinfulness brought on by Adam and deepened by the disobedience of his posterity.

Paul's vision of Christ sees him as the keystone of the cosmos and the Lord of all creation. By natural right, as the Son of God, he is ruler of the universe, to whom all nations belong and under whom everything is subject. And by acquired right, through redemption, he enjoys dominion over the whole earth.

Two letters especially bring out this theme. The Epistles to Colossae and Ephesus are almost duplicates, and were occasioned by the Gnostic speculators who conceived the cosmos as made up of a universe of hierarchical beings, among whom, as a creature, was Jesus Christ. Their theory was consistent with the popular oriental tendency to synthesize the world under one orderly whole, which they called the *pleroma*.

Paul undertook to place Christ where revelation sees him, not inside the world as an aeon or demigod, but as ruler of the universe, of angels and men. To add solemnity to his statement, Paul writes in the form of a hymn whose literary structure is unsurpassed in either Testament. It comes as a diptych to set forth two kinds of primacy of Christ in the world: in the order of natural creation, and then in the order of supernatural re-creation, which is the Redemption (Col. 1:15–17, 18–20).

The whole universe, then, with Christ as ruler, is the true fullness of Christianity. As a result, all things are permeated with the presence of God, and correspondingly the whole world shares, also, the fruits of the Redemption. In Pauline terminology, there are two productive Words of God: one creative, which brought the cosmos into being out of nothing; another redemptive, which rectifies and sanctifies a created world that was separated from its God. Christ is that Word of God in both senses, and so by a double title "Christ the King."

Loyalty to Christ. While the notion of loyalty to Christ pervades all of Paul's correspondence, his letters to Titus and Timothy are patterns in this respect. The two epistles to Timothy are urgent appeals that his disciple might strive energetically against false teachers and engage zealously in organizing the Christian community.

They reflect the final touch in Paul's vision of Christ, that the Savior is, indeed, the invisible head of his body, but Christ also operates through the visible ministry of the apostles and their successors. Christ is in them, and active through them; and salvation comes to men by their ministry. Paul presents a new concept of man's relation to God and dependence on his Son made man; precisely, that Christ might communicate through human instruments the grace that he won on the cross.

Timothy (and Titus) are reminded they have authority from Christ to teach and rule in his name. First to recall they have the power: "That is why I am reminding you how to fan into a flame the gift that God gave you when I laid my hands on you" (2 Tm. 1:6). Then to encourage them not to weaken, but to "Accept the strength, my dear son, that comes from the grace of Christ Jesus" (2 Tm. 2:1). Again to tell them how he, Paul, learned from experience what it means to be an apostle, "so I bear it all for the sake of those who are chosen, so that in the end they may have the salvation that is in Christ Jesus" (2 Tm. 2:10).

All of which is a prelude to the main lesson, that fidelity to Christ for a Christian means obedience to the will of Christ, manifested by those who derive authority from Jesus and teach in his name.

Faith is no subjective fancy, but demands loyalty to what Christ taught his followers. Hence the apostle's concern, "My dear Timothy, take care of all that has been entrusted to you" (1 Tm. 6:20), and to Titus, "It is for you, then, to preach the behavior which goes with healthy doctrine" (Tt. 2:1). And a parting exhortation, "Remember the Good News that I carry, 'Jesus Christ risen from the dead, sprung from the race of David' " (2 Tm. 2:8).

JOANNINE CHRISTOLOGY

The writings of the apostle John are his Gospel, the Book of Revelation, and three letters, all composed toward the end of the first century and therefore reflecting the Church's faith almost two generations after the Savior's Ascension.

The portrayal of Christ in St. John is consequently more developed than anything found elsewhere in the New Testament. It is also unique because it supplements what others had written about the Savior, and complements what Jesus himself had taught during his visible stay on earth. John wrote under the influence of more than half a century of divine guidance by the Spirit of Christ in the infant Church, and he was the recipient of a special communication from Christ, which John embodied in the Apocalypse.

In a sense there are five Gospels; the four commonly called such, and a fifth narrating what the invisible Savior revealed to his beloved disciple (Rv. 1:1–3).

Even if the Gospel was not the last thing he wrote (which is likely), it was certainly colored by a lifetime of mystic communion with the Spirit of Christ. Yet the immediate occasion for writing it was the rise of two errors that were to vex the Church for centuries to come: by Gnostics and others (like the Ebionites), who denied that Christ existed before he was born in the flesh, that he was only the natural son of Mary and Joseph; and by Docetists, who questioned if Jesus had a truly human nature.

The Humanity of Christ. John wanted to be sure that Docetist theorizing would not infect the early Church. As a branch of the Gnostics, the Docetae disclaimed the Incarnation on the premise that since matter was evil, God could not have become man; and since matter and spirit are in eternal conflict, there can be no question of conquest of sin by a composite being like Christ. Salvation, they held, comes only by liberation from matter, not from union of Spirit (in the person of God's Son) with matter.

His Gospel is a mosaic of witnesses to the truly human nature of Jesus. The Word of God became flesh and dwelled among us. He was weary at the well in Samaria. He showed deep emotion at the grave of Lazarus. He could be troubled in spirit. In the passion, he carried his own cross, became thirsty in his agony. And when he died, proof of his death was that blood and water flowed from his open side. After the resurrection, his body showed the marks of the wounds and evoked from the doubting Thomas the profession of faith, "My Lord and my God" (Jn. 20:28).

Like the Synoptics, John used the title "Son of Man" of Jesus;

and like them, he meant to have Christ give testimony to his human ancestry. But unlike the other evangelists, he developed a dialectic between Christ's dual sonship that made clear the relationship of one filiation to the other.

Christ suffered as man, but he was thereby glorified as God. His humanity was a means to an end: to show forth his love for mankind, and thereby win their love for himself as divine in return. The Joannine expression "lifted up" illustrates this purpose: "As Moses lifted up the serpent in the desert," even so must the Son of Man be lifted up, that those who believe in him may not perish, but may have life everlasting (Jn. 3:14; 8:28).

Divinity and Transcendence.   John is so explicit about Christ's oneness with the Father and Christ's transcendent divine nature, that critics of the faith are reduced to dismissing John's writings as Hellenist superimpositions on the simple message of the Synoptics.

John begins the fourth Gospel with a Prologue that leaves nothing to the imagination. His triad is a close-knit testimony to the person of Jesus Christ. The Logos, therefore, is *God;* the Logos became a *human* being; and this Logos as a human being lived among men and was *witnessed* by them. Language cannot be clearer, as John intended to leave no doubt who Jesus Christ really was.

Behind this premise John built the Gospel, the Apocalypse, and his letters. In the Gospel, he quotes the Savior affirming the Savior's oneness with God the Father and gives the natural reaction of the Jewish people.

> The Jews fetched stones to stone him, so Jesus said to them, "I have done many good works for you to see, works from my Father; for which of these are you stoning me?" The Jews answered him, "We are not stoning you for doing a good work but for blasphemy: you are only a man and you claim to be God" (Jn. 10:24–33).

Consistent with this claim, Christ's miracles (says John) are signs that manifest his divinity. Their function is to reveal the presence of God, active in the world and breaking through the laws he himself had made.

Soteriology.   Unlike Paul, who stresses man's sinfulness and need for a deliverer, John emphasizes man's creatureliness and need of a sanctifier. No sooner does he introduce the Logos become flesh, than he must identify the Logos as the life that was the light of men. If the Son of God is divine life, those who believe in him receive a share in this life to become "children of God . . . born not out of human stock or urge of the flesh or will of man but of God himself" (Jn. 1:12–13).

Accordingly, where Paul contrasts two states of man (as sinner and saved), John compares two levels of man's existence (as human and divine). The first he receives from his parents according to the flesh; they give him the physical life of the body. The second he obtains from Christ according to the spirit; who confers on those who believe in him a new life for the soul. Nicodemus had this explained by Christ in a dramatic passage that synthesizes Joannine Soteriology (Jn. 3:3–6, 16–17).

The whole edifice of the supernatural will be built on these grounds: that there are two levels of being, the created and the divine. Man unredeemed has only the finitude of his own contingency, further lessened by reason of Adam's fall and his own personal sins. But man redeemed is raised to a higher order of reality, where he partakes of God's divinity and is destined to enjoy nothing less than the undivided Trinity (1 Jn. 3:1–3).

Everything by comparison pales into insignificance. Thanks to the Incarnation, wherein God became man, man is enabled to become like God with a destiny that parallels the divine. God has eternal life in himself by nature—to enjoy the plenitude of beatitude that makes him God; he became one of us to give us a share in the same happiness through faith in his love. In Joannine terms, nature is what we have as creatures; grace is what we get from Christ as God through Christ as man to possess Christ the God-man in eternity.

TESTIMONY OF THE CHURCH

As we move from the biblical record of Christ's life and redemptive mission to the Church's reflection on the revealed doctrine since the apostolic age, we enter a new and very complex area of Catholic belief.

It is new because previously hidden insights about the person and work of the Savior are disclosed. It is complex because the issues are bewildering in variety and involve the most subtle controversies of the Church's history.

Our purpose is not to review the whole story of the Church's answer to "Who is Christ?" It will be simply to capsulize the main features of Catholic doctrine on the subject. Since its development has occurred in two principal stages, there is practical value in their sequence: first, the teaching of the Church as it faced the speculative theories of oriental Christendom in the four great Councils of Nicea, Constantinople, Ephesus, and Chalcedon; and then the progress in Catholic doctrine up to modern times.

FOUNDATIONS OF ORTHODOXY

It was providential that within a period of less than three hundred years, the Christian world was challenged by a phalanx of ideas that confronted all the basic premises of the New Testament revelation about Christ. In spite of their long and generally unfamiliar names, these theories are important. They have quite exhausted the possible ways that the human mind can react to the Savior's question to his disciples "Who do men say that I am?"—apart from the simple faith expressed by Simon Peter. Some said this and some said that—in the postapostolic age as on the shores of the Lake of Tiberias. Christ's further question, "But you, who do you say that I am?" was also echoed in the corresponding reply of the Church of which Peter in his successors is the visible head.

These theories have come down to us as heresies and, for that reason, might be dismissed as mere historical memories. But they are highly significant. For one thing, they represent the continually recurring tendency of human genius to rationalize, in the sense of explain away, the mystery of Christ. They are therefore as modern as today. Moreover, they served as catalysts to evoke a deeper understanding of the Incarnation.

Each of the four general councils dealing with this vagrant speculation helped to lay the foundation on which the faithful have since built the edifice of their belief in the founder of Christianity. The whole ensemble of conciliar teaching was finally stabilized in the liturgy through what has come to be known as the Nicene Creed.

Consubstantial with the Father. The Council of Nicea (A.D. 325) started a new era in the Catholic Church. This Council began a series of definitions that have continued to the present day, in which the Church passed judgment on a major issue of critical times.

In terms of doctrinal development, we may distinguish a number of levels, under papal leadership, as Christ's exercise of authoritative teaching since the Ascension. There was the use of an adversative position, arising within the Church, as the occasion for determining what truth, among Christian teachings, needs to be singled out for special magisterial presentation to the faithful. There was the careful choice of language to express the doctrine of Christ in clearer and more precise terms than found in the Scriptures.

Concretely at Nicea, the specific truth singled out for doctrinal definition was Christ's relationship with God the Father.

A priest of Alexandria, Arius (b. A.D. 250), was uncomfortable with the plain words of the Gospels that Christ and the Father are one. He soon acquired a large following, and his ideas eventually came to be embodied in a system called Arianism.

As the Arians saw the problem, we find parallel biblical texts in which God is repeatedly spoken of as Father, and others in which Christ is described as God's Son. The question is: How is God the Father related to Christ as his Son?

According to Arian logic, God is absolutely one, in every sense of the term. He is in no sense generated, and in no sense does he generate, as one who communicates his nature. He can only communicate outside of himself, but not within himself. He can only communicate by creation out of nothing.

Consequently, when the Scriptures speak of God as Father, they always mean a created communication: either of a unique being called Logos, or the Word, of whom John says he became flesh in the person of Christ; or of the rest of rational creation below the Word of God.

Given these premises, why must the Word of God, said to have become incarnate, have itself also been created? The reasons form a cluster centering about the meaning of fatherhood and sonship.

Common sense tells us that a son always has a beginning, that he depends on the father as an effect depends upon its cause, that he is necessarily a part of the father with the implication that something of the father is divided or separated to become the son, that by begetting a son the parent is changed because he becomes a father, that a son implies a body derived from his father, and a free decision on the father's part to want to procreate.

On all these counts, said the Arians, God cannot be the Father of a true, natural Son. He can be Father only as Maker. Therefore

Christ is the Son of God only as a unique creature. His sonship is in the character of an adjective to describe derivation from the Creator, but it is not generation whereby God is literally Father to a being who is literally his Son.

Led by St. Athanasius (296–373), bishop of Alexandria, the Council of Nicea stated the Catholic teaching in unambiguous terms. It used seven expressions, now imbedded in the Creed.

> We believe in one God, the Father Almighty, Creator of all things visible and invisible; and in one Lord Jesus Christ, the Son of God, only-begotten of the Father, that is, of the substance of the Father, Son of God, Light of Light, true God of true God, being of the same substance with the Father, by whom all things were made in heaven and in earth, who for us men and for our salvation came down from heaven, was incarnate, was made man, suffered, rose again the third day, ascended into the heavens, and he will come to judge the living and the dead. And in the Holy Spirit.[1]

Behind the repetition of what must seem like the same terms was the Church's intention to make the profession of faith in Christ's divinity unqualifyingly clear, not only in the fourth century but into the distant future.

Christ is, therefore, said to be the "only-begotten of the Father," in order to distinguish his origin of the Father from all other kinds of origin. Thus Christ is absolutely unique in proceeding from the Father, in complete contrast to others, like angels and human persons, who are also called sons of God.

He is of the substance of the Father, which in the original Greek says that he is "out of the being (*ousia*) of the Father." This affirms that, unlike mere creatures, who may be said to be *from* God, his only-begotten Son comes literally out of the Father's own being. Creatures come from God, indeed, because he wills them to exist. Not so the Son of God, who cannot not exist. His existence does not depend on the free will of the Creator.

He is God of God, in the sense that he is as much God as the Father, sharing perfectly in the one and same divine nature. Yet the two are really distinct, because one originates and the other is originated.

He is Light of Light, to bring out the total oneness of essence between Father and Son, in a way similar to how radiation from a light has an identical nature as the light from which it emanates.

He is true God of true God, to avoid any ambiguity of what we believe when we profess that Christ is divine. Since truth means agreement, the Son of God is the perfect mirror of the Father. Both are equally and fully divine, with no compromise or mere approximation of divinity between them.

"He is begotten not made," declares the profoundest mystery of our faith: that within the Godhead a generation has been going on from eternity. Unlike all other generations, this one implies no production of a new being, no change in the generator, no cause-and-effect relationship, no dependence of offspring on parent, and no semblance of decision on the part of the Father to bring the Son into existence.

He is of one substance with the Father. This was the keystone in the arch of orthodoxy, where the terms "of one substance" or "of one being" or "consubstantial with the Father" are English equivalents of what must be the single most famous word in doctrinal history, the Greek *homoousios,* which means having the same (*homo*) being (*ousia*) as the Father. The word was chosen because it expressed in plain language what the sound faith of the people had always proclaimed, that Father and Son were certainly two individuals, but they had only one divine nature (or substance or being). There is a plurality of persons in God, but there is only one God.

This Son of God, together with the Father and the Holy Spirit, is Creator of the universe; but he himself was not made. Everything in the heavens and on earth came into being because the Trinity willed it to. It continues in existence only because of that same will, which is one and the same in the three persons, who always work together whenever they produce anything in the order of nature or of grace. Since the Son of God is Creator, it is obvious that he is not a creature.

It was this eternal Son of God who came down from heaven, not by motion through space but by the descent of humility. He took upon himself our flesh to become incarnate, in order that as man he might suffer, and by suffering might die, and by dying might redeem, and by rising from the dead might become the source of our grace. Having ascended into heaven, he will return to judge the human race, at the end of time. This is only fitting, since Christ is God who made man, and who became man to evoke man's loving response to his Maker.

Immediately after Nicea there was an outcropping of Arian-sponsored councils, at Sirmium, Arles, Milan, Beziers, Rimini, and Seleucia, where the anti-Nicene party triumphed through pressure (including physical violence) from imperial authority dominated by

Arian bishops from the East. At the last two synods, most of the Catholic bishops were induced by fraud and forced to sign a noncommittal symbol of faith, which was then flaunted to the world as an Arian victory. St. Jerome commented on this period that "The whole world sighed as it awoke in wonder to find itself Arian." Actually the Christian world was not Arian, but many of its leaders had been betrayed into leaving that impression.

A sad illustration of the crisis through which the Church was passing is what happened to Pope Liberius (352–66), the first Pontiff to whom the title of "Saint" is not applied, probably because of his lack of courage under trial. He was seized at Rome by the Arian Emperor Constantius for his ardent defense of Athanasius and the Nicene Creed. After years in exile, and under threat of death, Liberius is reported to have signed a compromise formula as the price of restoration to the Roman See. When Constantius died (361), Liberius publicly condemned Arianism.

This fact, plus the circumstances of the case, prove that no breach of infallibility was involved. It is also an unsolved question as to which of three formulas Liberius actually signed, since only one was heretical. His conduct before and after exile was rigidly orthodox; hence the unlikelihood of heresy during exile. He was under duress, so that his acts were not morally valid. Finally, even if what Athanasius said is true, that "Liberius, being exiled, gave way after two years and, in face of threats of death, subscribed his name," there was no intention to proclaim a dogma for acceptance by the universal Church. Nevertheless, Liberius stands as a symbol of the lengths to which convinced zealots were willing to go to change the ancient faith in Christ's divinity.

Our Complete Humanity. Preoccupied with the question "What think you of Christ," Eastern speculators directed their attention from Christ as God (vindicated at Nicea) to Christ as man. They asked themselves: If Christ has two *perfect* natures, human and divine, how is he only one person? If he is only one individual, it seemed that at least one part was perfected by the union. Since it could not be his divinity, it must have been his humanity. Christ had to lack something as man, which his divinity supplied.

Among the answers given, the theory of Apollinaris, who lived somewhere between A.D. 310 and 390, has made history. He was a close friend of Athanasius and a stanch defender of Nicea. In his zeal to refute the Arians, he developed a theology of the Incarnation that created such a stir in Asia Minor that he was finally driven from Laodicea, where he was bishop, after condemnation at Rome (374 to 380) and the Second Ecumenical Council at Constantinople.

Following Plato's theory of three elements that constitute man—body, soul, and spirit—Apollinaris thought he found the key to the problem of Christ's personality by substituting the Logos for the Savior's spirit or rational principle of life. In his system, Jesus was formed of a conjunction of body (material element), soul (principle of animal life), and Logos (the Son of God), who replaced the rational part of Christ's nature.

What added to Apollinaris' conviction that the divinity should substitute for Christ's rationality was the impiety, as he felt, of saying that the Redeemer had a finite principle of moral and intellectual activity. Were this so, he could then be charged with ignorance and the possibility of sin.

As a result, the Apollinarian Christ was, indeed, consubstantial with the Father because he was true God, but not consubstantial with us because he was missing what most makes us human, our intellect and will.

Pope Damasus I (366–84) demanded that Apollinaris subscribe to the doctrine that the Son of God assumed a complete human nature: "body, soul, senses, that is, the whole Adam and, to be still clearer, our complete inherited humanity." When he refused to submit, he broke with the Church.

Not unlike at Nicea, the Emperor entered the controversy, and quite on his own summoned a council at Constantinople in May 381 that was over by July. Originally, 186 bishops, all from the East, assembled for the conclave. But once the Arian party learned in what direction the council would go, 36 bishops left, and the remainder proceeded to publish a series of anathemas, which concluded with "that of the Apollinarians."

Of special significance was Canon 3 of the council, which read: "The Bishop of Constantinople shall have the privileges of honor after the Bishop of Rome, because it is new Rome."[2] This declaration is doubly important. It recognized the Roman primacy, which by then had been exercised so dramatically in defending the revealed doctrine of Christ's divinity. But it also affirmed the new sense of dignity for Constantinople, so named when in A.D. 330

Constantine made it his capital on the site of the Greek city of Byzantium. The town, which soon grew, remained the capital of the Eastern Empire until 1453, when the Moslems made it the center of the Turkish kingdom. For a thousand years, therefore, Constantinople was the political (and later ecclesiastical) rival of Rome, even though dogmatically the First Council of Constantinople acknowledged the primacy of the Roman Pontiff.

The Nicene-Constantinople Creed, usually ascribed to the first two general Councils, actually derived from the original Baptismal Creed of Jerusalem, whose beginnings go back to the time of the apostles. Since the time of the Council of Chalcedon in 451, it has been regarded as the principal creed of the Church.

Hypostatic Union.   It is not difficult to trace the intellectual lineage of Nestorianism, which provoked the Council of Ephesus and advanced the doctrine of the Incarnation beyond Nicea and I Constantinople.

There were two rival schools of biblical interpretation: Antioch in Syria and Alexandria in northern Egypt. Allowing for many exceptions, the stress of the Antiochean school was more historical and favored dependence on Aristotle; it emphasized the literal meaning of Scripture. The Egyptian school of Alexandria preferred a mystical approach to the Bible, with more dependence on Plato; it favored a spiritual understanding of the sacred text. To be noted, however, is that these differences of stress run through the teachings of heretics and orthodox alike; and they are in some way the ancestors of the two main streams in Catholic theology to this day. They also help to explain, as in the case of Nestorianism, how an exaggerated stress in theology can lead to heterodoxy in faith.

Characteristic of the Antiochene school of exegesis, Theodore of Mopsuestia (d. A.D. 428) favored dividing Christ, and sharply distinguished between his two natures, over and against the Alexandrian school, which favored a unification. According to Theodore, the union of the Logos with Christ's human nature consists of an indwelling, not of God's being but of his good pleasure or special approval. God is everywhere and so is his influential power. Hence, absolutely speaking, there is no more of God dwelling in one creature than in another. But his approval or complacency may rest more on one created being than on some other. His love has different influence on different persons—which explains why people are so different in perfection.

What distinguishes Christ, then, is simply that God's love set a much higher approval on the person of Jesus Christ. In that sense, he might even be accorded divine honors as one specially appealing to God.

Moreover, the two natures of Christ thus understood are not literally fused into one thing. They are at most joined together to form a closely co-operative combine. This co-operation began with the first formation of the humanity in Mary's womb, and in later life showed itself in a ready practice of virtue and a determined avoidance of sin. Yet all the whole Christ was two persons joined with one another, and not a united being that forms one individual.

All of this would have passed out of history without notice except for Theodore's disciple Nestorius, who rose steadily from monk, to priest, to patriarch of Constantinople. An able preacher and outspoken critic, he had two faults that led to his conflict with orthodoxy: He was a pliant tool of political authority; and once convinced of something, nothing could change his mind. His accession to the see of Constantinople was a court appointment.

Not long after, Nestorius' chaplain began to preach that Mary was not to be called the Mother of God. "Let no man," he said, "call Mary Theotokos (Mother of God). For Mary was only a woman, and God cannot be born of a woman."

People were scandalized because the title had been accorded Mary for generations. But the chaplain Anastasius denounced the title and appealed to his bishop for support. Nestorius elaborated and gave reasons why Mary cannot be called Mother of God. "They ask," the bishop replied, "whether Mary may be called Theotokos. Has God then a mother? In that case we must excuse the pagans, who spoke of mothers of the gods. Paul is not a liar when he affirms that the Godhead in Christ is without father or mother or genealogy of any kind. Mary did not give birth to God. A creature cannot deliver her Creator, but only a man who is the instrument of the divinity. I honor this garment which he uses, for the sake of him who is hidden within and that cannot be separated from the vesture it wears. I separate the two natures, even while I unite my respect. See what it means. The one who was formed in the womb of Mary was not God himself, but God assumed him, and because of him who assumes, the one assumed is also called God."[3]

A violent controversy broke out, with Nestorius finding himself challenged by the bishop of Alexandria, St. Cyril (d. A.D. 444), whose role in the succeeding events can be compared with that of Athanasius at Nicea. Seeing that nothing could be settled by simple dialogue, both sides appealed to Rome. Among the few surviving statements of Nestorius is his letter to Pope Celestine I, in which he sought to clear himself of the charge of heresy.

On receipt of Nestorius' letter and the complaints against him, Pope Celestine called a council at Rome in August 430, where Nestorianism was condemned. Cyril was commissioned by the Pope to pronounce sentence of deposition against the bishop of Constantinople if he would not retract.

In November of the same year, Cyril took action, and on the seventh of the following month delivered his sentence into Nestorius' hands by legates sent to Constantinople. Meanwhile, Cyril had been in correspondence with Nestorius, and the two patriarchs exchanged a series of letters unique in the annals of the Church. Each tried to convince the other of the error of his ways, and each appealed to the need for preserving the true faith.

The difference in their respective approach was that Cyril based his position on the teachings of the ancient Church, while Nestorius argued from what he called the logic of the faith. Cyril said that dividing the person of Christ undermined the Redemption and cut away the bulwark of Christian Tradition, which always held that Jesus Christ was God incarnate. Nestorius claimed that the opposite was true: God did not become man but only dwelled in the man Jesus, as in a temple.

What sparked the controversy into a conflagration was the strong devotion of the Eastern people to the Blessed Virgin. They instinctively sensed that if Mary was denied the dignity of divine motherhood, their faith was dissolved, and all they believed about her divine Son was in doubt.

These popular sentiments, along with Cyril's insistence that Nestorius be brought to task, led Emperor Theodosius to recommend that a general council be held at Ephesus. St. Augustine had been invited to the council and would almost certainly have presided, but he died after receiving the personal invitation and before he could leave Hippo for Asia Minor.

The doctrine of Ephesus consists mainly of two items, both taken from the writings of St. Cyril and both originally in Cyril's letters to Nestorius in which he tried to dissuade the patriarch from dividing Christ and asserting that in the Savior there were two personalities, one human and the other divine.

Ephesus thereby canonized the positive teaching of Cyril on the Incarnation, as found in his second letter to Nestorius. Its later confirmation by Rome made the epistle part of the Church's official teaching. Two paragraphs illustrate the precision of this Catholic doctrine.

> For we do not say that the nature of the Word became man by undergoing change; nor that it was transformed into a complete man consisting of soul and body. What we say, rather, is that by uniting to himself in his own person a body animated by a rational soul, the Word has become man in an inexpressible and incomprehensible way and has been called the Son of Man; not merely according to will or complacency, but not by merely assuming a person either. And we say that the natures that are brought together into true unity are different; still, from both there is one Christ and Son; not as though the difference between the natures were taken away by their union, but rather both divinity and humanity produce their perfection of our one Lord, Christ and Son, by their inexpressible and mysterious joining into unity. . . . It was not that first an ordinary human being was born of the holy Virgin, and then the Word descended upon that man; but in virtue of the union he is said to have undergone birth according to the flesh from his mother's womb, since he claims as his own birth, the generation of his own flesh. . . .
>
> Thus the holy Fathers of the Church have not hesitated to call the holy Virgin Mother of God.[4]

Cyril and the Council begin by affirming that "Emmanuel is truly God, and the holy Virgin is, therefore, Mother of God, for she gave birth in the flesh to the Word of God made flesh." Behind this statement stands the implication that, since the child born of Mary was a divine person, Mary was mother of the one she bore. Mothers give birth to individuals, i.e., persons, and thereby become bearers of the person to whom they give birth.

More specifically, Mary is truly Mother of God in two ways: She contributed everything to the formation of Christ's human nature that every other mother contributes to the fruit of her womb; and she conceived and bore the second person of the Trinity, not of course according to the divine nature but according to the human nature that the Logos assumed.

On a more technical level, the Church believes that "the Word of

God the Father was hypostatically united to flesh and that Christ is one having his own flesh, that is, one person who is both God and man." The word "hypostatically" became as crucial as *homoousios* at the Council of Nicea. It means that the two natures in Christ are united *personally,* in such a way that while the source *from* which the union was effected was two distinct natures, which remained essentially unchanged, the being in which the union was completed was one individual (in Greek, *hypostasis*), which individual was divine.

An issue that would arise centuries later in the adoration of Christ's humanity and his Sacred Heart, was anticipated in the position of the Nestorians, who insisted on using the prefix "co" every time they spoke of giving Christ divine honors. The Church thought otherwise. We should not say that "the man assumed ought to be coadored with God the Word, and coglorified and conamed God, as one person *in* another—for this is the interpretation that the constant addition of 'co' will lead to." A Catholic must "adore Emmanuel with one adoration and apply to him one doxology, inasmuch as the Word was made flesh." Such bifurcation would mean there was a human personality side by side with the divine.

Another facet of Ephesus was its explanation of the Holy Spirit. The action of the third person on Christ may not be simply equated with his action on other holy men. Hence we cannot say that "the one Lord Jesus Christ was glorified by the Spirit as though through the Spirit Jesus exercised a power not proper to himself, and as though he had received from him the ability to act against unclean spirits, and to work miracles among men." Consequently, believing Christians must affirm that the "Spirit by which he worked the miracles was his very own."

The point here was to clarify the relationship of the second and third persons. The Spirit is Christ's own, for although he proceeds from the Father, he is not alien from the Son. Moreover, since *"all* the Father has" belongs to the Son, the Spirit therefore is also his. Christ worked the miracles because he was united in trinitarian intimacy with Father and Spirit.

Christ's priesthood was also affirmed. According to St. Paul, Christ became the high priest of the new covenant, and offered himself up to God as our sacrifice on the cross (Heb. 3:1). The Nestorians weakened this concept out of existence by urging that not the Word of God in human form but "another man, distinct from him, who was born of woman," made the oblation of Calvary. From another angle, they held that Christ offered the sacrifice of himself not only for our sins but also for his own, claiming that the human nature of Christ (not being hypostatically united with the second person) was sinful and therefore in need of redemption.

Nestorius undercut the salvific work of Christ by denying that his humanity was the channel of redemption. As he put it, "the flesh of the Lord is not life-giving because it does not belong to the very Word of God. Rather it belongs to someone else than God (who is a human person) and who was linked with God by dignity, and in whom the Godhead had a divine indwelling."

Ephesus countered by emphasizing the role of Christ as the great sacrament of the New Law, declaring that his "flesh is life-giving because it was appropriated by the Word who had power to give life to all things." The Savior as God is the creator of supernatural life, and as man (united with the divinity) he is the unique instrument by which this life is communicated to mankind.

Finally, in the Nestorian system only a man suffered and died. Ephesus replied by insisting that "the Word of God suffered in the flesh, and was crucified in the flesh, and experienced death in the flesh, and became the first-born from the dead, inasmuch as he is, as God, both life and the giver of life."

After Ephesus passed judgment, the followers of Nestorius had second thoughts about supporting the bishop of Constantinople. Forty bishops were involved, and Cyril was moved by the spectacle of so many prelates denying an article of faith.

As an effort toward explaining himself more clearly, and bringing the Nestorian sympathizers back to the fold, Cyril wrote his famous *Formula of Union,* a masterpiece of charity joined to theological clarity. Without giving up an iota of what Ephesus defined, he restated the Council's teaching to make it palatable to the unhappy bishops, and found his efforts rewarded by a mass reconciliation. One paragraph of Cyril's correspondence with the reconciled bishops is revealing.

> You must surely clearly understand that almost all our defense of the faith was connected with our declaring that the holy Virgin is Mother of God. But if we say that the holy body of Christ the Savior of us all was from heaven and not of her, how could she be thought of as Mother of God? For whom indeed did she bear, if it is not true that she bore Emmanuel after the flesh?[5]

Cyril's letter is one of the earliest examples of how carefully teachers and churchmen have to distinguish between theological pluralism and doctrinal contradiction. Preoccupation with one aspect of Christ's being—as a composite of two natures—had obscured the Nestorian vision of Christ as a single individual.

True God and True Man. When the moderate Antiochene bishops came to terms with Cyril in A.D. 433, the "compromise" ostensibly settled the controversy, and Ephesus joined Nicea as an expression of the Church's belief on the twofold nature of her founder. Before long, however, the germ of another deviation, latent this time in Alexandrian theology, began to bear fruit. If Alexandria had emphasized Christ's unity against those who would divide him, it also carried the impediment of ambiguous language, which less orthodox Christians would use to their own advantage. The most prominent such exploiter was Eutyches (378–454), head of a large monastery at Constantinople.

Eutyches' keen opposition to Nestorianism led him to maintain that after the divine nature had been united to the human in the person of Christ, his human nature was merged in the divine, so that from the moment of his "incarnation" only a divine nature remained. This theory came to be known as Monophysitism (from the Greek *monos* [one] and *physis* [nature]).

In A.D. 448, when he had been a monk for more than sixty years, Eutyches was accused of Apollinarist tendencies. The patriarch of Constantinople, Flavian, called a synod of some thirty bishops and summoned Eutyches to clear himself. When he finally came, his statements at the Council were too vague to be meaningful, until faced with the direct question: "Do you confess the existence of two natures even after the Incarnation, and that Christ is consubstantial with us?" Eutyches replied, "I confess that before the union [of the second person and human nature] Christ was of two natures, but after the union I confess only one nature."[6]

Pressed to conform to traditional teaching, he protested that for the sake of peace he would agree but that personally he was sure the Church was wrong. He could not find the idea of two distinct natures anywhere in the Bible or the writings of the Fathers. Thereupon he was deposed and excommunicated.

At this point Emperor Theodosius II stepped in. Eutyches appealed to him through a friend, the eunuch Chrysaphius, and set to work placarding the city with signs denouncing Flavian and defending his own Christology. To get more support, he wrote to Alexandria, Jerusalem, Ravenna, and Rome, with special urgency to Pope Leo I that he might decide in his favor.

Leo waited to hear the other side. When Flavian submitted the case against Eutyches, the Pope wrote his classic *Dogmatic Letter to Flavian*, which has made theological history. More popularly called "The Tome of Leo," it confirmed the decision of the bishops under Flavian and condemned Eutyches.

"The Tome of Leo" was accepted at Chalcedon, and is the most prominent (and extensive) papal teaching imbedded in the ecumenical councils recognized by all Christendom. The full text of some ten thousand words is also a fine specimen of the straightforwardness and clarity of the Latin mind—from the facts of faith rather than the speculations of philosophy. Not unnaturally, Leo's doctrine was further expounded in his sermons for the feast of Christmas, which has commonly been more central in Western than in Eastern piety.

The full text of "The Tome" could be quoted in full and without apology. At once a witness to the Church's clear knowledge of the Savior's person and mission, and evidence of the primacy, it was needed in the fifth century to discover the truth in a welter of contradictory opinions, and it is needed today to sift the conflicting ideas of an ecumenical age.

Chalcedon, by any calculation, was the work of Leo I, whom posterity surnamed the Great. Attended by upward of six hundred bishops, it was unsurpassed for grandeur up to the Second Council of the Vatican.

When the Nicene Creed and Leo's "Tome" were read, the assembled prelates exclaimed, "This is the faith of the Fathers. This is the faith of the Apostles. This is the faith of all of us. Peter has spoken through Leo."[7]

Nicea and Leo were enough, but the bishops wanted to reduce Leo's doctrine to a short summary. They wished to vindicate the mystery of the hypostatic union, where two natures remain truly themselves and yet are bound together in a single divine personality.

Following the holy Fathers, therefore, we all with one accord teach the profession of faith in the one identical Son, our Lord Jesus Christ. We declare that he is perfect both in his divinity and in his humanity, truly God and truly man composed of body and rational soul; that he is consubstantial with the Father in his divinity, consubstantial with us in his humanity, like us in every respect except for sin (Heb. 4:15). We declare that in his divinity he was begotten of the Father before time, and in his humanity he was begotten in this last age of Mary the Virgin, the Mother of God, for us and for our salvation. We declare that the one selfsame Christ, only-begotten Son and Lord, must be acknowledged in two natures without any commingling or change or division or separation; that the distinction between the natures is in no way removed by their union but rather that the specific character of each nature is preserved and they are united in one person and one hypostasis. We declare that he is not split or divided into two persons, but that there is one selfsame only begotten Son, God the Word, the Lord Jesus Christ. This the prophets have taught about him from the beginning; this Jesus Christ himself taught us; this the creed of the Fathers has handed down to us.[8]

The doctrine of Chalcedon is the Church's final classic expression of faith on the person of Christ. It placed the capstone on Nicea, Constantinople, and Ephesus. Ever since, all papal and conciliar teaching has merely refined and clarified the dogmatic essentials formulated by the end of the fifth century.

What are these essentials?

– that Christ assumed a real and not just an apparent body. He was born of a woman, from whom he received a truly human nature.

– that in becoming man, he assumed not only a body but also a rational soul, with intellect and will. Christ therefore had a divine and human mind, a divine and human will.

– that the two natures in Christ are united to form one individual. Christ is one person, the second person of the Trinity.

– that in Christ each of the two natures remains unimpaired, they are not confused or changed in their respective properties; nor are they divided or separated, as though merely co-existing side by side.

– that in becoming man, Christ was and remains true God, one in nature with the Father. When St. Paul speaks of God "emptying himself" to become man, this does not mean that God somehow ceased to be God.

– that even as man, Christ is absolutely sinless. He not only did not sin, but he could not sin because he was God. Only in the spurious supposition that Christ has two persons is sin conceivable, since the human person might then commit sin, while the divine person would be perfectly holy. Since Christ was utterly sinless, he was also free from concupiscence or unruly passions, and also free from such effects of concupiscence as positive ignorance or error.

– that the reason for the Incarnation was redemptive. Christ was born into the world "for our salvation," to undergo the meritorious death that, except for this mortality, would have been impossible.

– that Mary is consequently not only Mother of Christ but Mother of God, since he was "born of Mary" in time who is begotten of the Father in eternity.

– that, since the Savior was one person, whatever he did (or does) was (and is) done simultaneously by both natures, although in different ways. When Christ talked and walked and ate and slept and died, it was the God-man who did all these things. When he worked the miracles of healing disease, calming the storm at sea, and raising the dead, it too was the God-man who did all these things. Now at the right hand of his Father, it is the same God-man who is our heavenly high priest and who on the last day will come to judge the living and the dead.

MODERN DEVELOPMENT

The Church's doctrinal teaching about Jesus Christ remained substantially unchallenged in the Christian world for the next thousand years. It is to this day honored and respected not only among Catholics but among the faithful in Eastern Orthodoxy and Protestantism.

No doubt the Church's magisterium spoke often and at length about the salvific work of Christ (Soteriology) since the eighth century and the Second Council of Nicea. These aspects of the Catholic faith are part of the Church's teaching on grace and the sacraments. Our primary concern here is with the two principal issues in Christology that arose within the Church's ranks: from Jansenism in the seventeenth and eighteenth centuries and from Modernism in the nineteenth and twentieth centuries.

Each system ranged broadly across the octaves of Christian belief and practice. We shall look now only at their respective positions on the person of Christ, his adorability, and our access to the knowledge of what modern writers call "the historical Jesus."

Adoration of Christ's Humanity. The Jansenist attitude toward Christ's humanity and the adoration of his Sacred Heart is easy to trace. According to its theory of salvation, when God became man he did not intend to save the whole human race. His will was to save only the predestined, so that all others would be foreordained to damnation. With this limited view of the Redemption, it was not surprising that the leaders of Jansenism, first in France and Holland, and then in northern Italy, challenged the centuries-old devotion to the humanity of the Savior. When this devotion took the special form of adoration of the physical heart of Christ, they claimed that those who practiced it were "heart idolators."

By the end of the eighteenth century, the Church had many times spoken in defense of what the Jansenists called into question, but the issue of defending the adorability of Christ's humanity did not become crucial until Scipione de Ricci (1741–1809) became bishop of the diocese of Pistoia in the Italian duchy of Tuscany.

It is a principle of faith, Ricci said, that very few adults will be saved. Priests must ever keep this fact before the minds of the faithful, in order to draw them away from evil and move them to salutary repentance. Consequently they should not give sacramental absolution to every penitent nor allow most of the people to receive Holy Communion.

The climax of Ricci's effort to reform his diocese was reached at the synod he opened at Pistoia on September 18, 1786. There were 234 participants, including 171 parish priests and 13 religious. After 10 days of session, the synod published its vast decrees.

Although Ricci had the priests of the diocese under his thumb, he was not accepted by most of the Tuscan hierarchy, and the laity finally succeeded in having him resign. With his innovations, historians record, he outraged the most sacred sentiments of the people. They gave full vent to their fury, which did not subside until Ricci had taken flight. When the cathedral chapter joined the popular demonstration, the bishop had no choice but to resign, which he did on June 3, 1791.

Efforts were made to forestall a formal evaluation of the Synod of Pistoia, but Pius VI, "to fulfill his apostolic and pastoral duty," caused 85 statements to be quoted from the records, and each one was to be appraised separately to avoid any misunderstanding. On August 28, 1794, the Pope issued the Constitution *Author of Faith*, incorporating the quoted passages and corresponding censure.

Three of the propositions deal with Christ's humanity and the devotion to the Sacred Heart. The first claims that Christ's humanity may not be adored directly without blasphemy; the second charges that devotion to the heart of Christ, as part of his human body, is at least dangerous if not heretical; and the third rebukes those who worship the heart of the Savior because they confuse a part for the whole and render homage to a creature that should be reserved for God.

1. According to the Jansenists, "directly to adore the humanity of Christ, and above all a part of that humanity, is to give a creature the honor due to God." This proposition was considered by Rome to "be injurious to the praiseworthy devotion that the faithful have rendered and should render to the humanity of Christ."[9]

2. Consistent with the same attitude, the followers of Jansenius branded devotion to the Sacred Heart "erroneous" or a least "dangerous." Not so, declared Pius VI: "If this devotion is understood as the apostolic see has approved it."[10]

3. Finally, still on the subject of devotion to the Sacred Heart, the Synod of Pistoia claimed that those who worship the heart of Jesus are unaware that the sacred flesh of Christ, or even the whole humanity when separated and divided from the divinity, cannot be adored with the worship of adoration. On the contrary, declared the Holy See, "those who adore the heart of Christ adore it as it is. They are worshiping the heart of the person of the Word, to whom it is inseparably united—even as the bloodless body of Christ in the three days of death was adorable in the sepulcher without separation from the divinity."[11]

As one reads the strange concern of the Jansenists to safeguard the divinity of Christ, it is not easily apparent why they should have been so critical of those who worshiped his humanity, and in the humanity his Sacred Heart. The reason lay deep in their concept of the Redemption, as indicated earlier, but with a peculiar logic that carried through on their premises. Once they had bought the notion of selective salvation, it was surely "blasphemous" to claim for Christ's humanity what God never intended it to mean. It was not his will that, by becoming man, all men should be saved, and to worship the heart of Christ as the symbol of his universal love is contrary to the idea that Christ died for all mankind.

The real irritant, therefore, was not that Christ's human nature was wrongly given divine honors. It was the assumed fact that

Christ's divine nature was wrongly given the attributes of merciful love, extending to every human being.

Implicit in the Church's vindication of divine honor to Christ's humanity because it is substantially united to the Word of God was something more than settling a passing controversy with Jansenism. It was the recognition of a constant tradition, based on revelation, that the man Jesus can also be imitated by the faithful in their practice of Christian virtue. Indeed, modeling their lives on the earthly virtues of the Master, they grow in the likeness of God, since Jesus is God.

The Historical Jesus. The latest and still current challenge to the Church's historic faith in Christ started at the turn of the twentieth century and, by its own profession, has been called Modernism. As explained by its founders, Modernism was the effort among Catholic scholars, captivated by contemporary philosophy and science, to modernize the Church by applying to its teachings and practices the principles of Kantian subjectivism. Although the external fabric of ecclesiastical organization and dogmatic terminology was to remain, behind this exterior was to come a reinterpretation of Catholic Christianity in the light of modern needs.

"Revelation," on these terms, "is not an affirmation but an experience." Concretely this means that a person's own subconscious experience is the best interpreter of Catholic doctrine. Dogmas of faith, though solemnly defined by the Church, are really only external stimuli or, from another viewpoint, adaptable and changing guides. Truth, then, is a passing phenomenon that varies with individuals and with different times.

St. Pius X took issue with and denounced this position in a series of propositions he published in 1907, nine of which deal specifically with the person of Christ. The Modernist statements are to be understood as incompatible with the Church's historic faith in her founder.

> The divinity of Jesus Christ is not proved from the Gospels. It is rather a dogma which the Christian conscience has deduced from the notion of a Messiah.
> While exercising his ministry, Jesus did not speak in such a way as to teach that he was the Messiah, nor did his miracles have as their purpose to demonstrate this fact.

It may be legitimately granted that the Christ whom history presents is far inferior to the Christ who is the object of faith.

In all the Gospel texts the name "Son of God" is simply equivalent to the name "Messiah." It certainly does not mean that Christ is the true and natural Son of God.

The doctrine about Christ which is handed down by Paul, John, and the Councils of Nicea, Ephesus, and Chalcedon, is not the same as Jesus taught.

It is impossible to reconcile the natural sense of the Gospel texts with what our theologians teach about the consciousness and infallible knowledge of Jesus Christ.

It is obvious to anyone, who is not hindered by preconceived ideas, that either Jesus professed to be in error about the imminent messianic coming, or the greater part of this doctrine in the synoptic Gospels lacks authenticity of content.

A critic cannot affirm that Christ's knowledge was unrestricted by any limit, except by making a supposition that is historically inconceivable and that contradicts moral sense. The supposition would be that Christ as man had the knowledge of God, but that he did not want to communicate his awareness of so many things with the disciples or with posterity.

Christ did not always have the consciousness of his messianic dignity.[12]

As in its conflict with Jansenism, so here Rome was less concerned with exposing the negative postulates of the Modernists than with preserving the Church's faith in Jesus Christ. There were four principal issues at stake: the divergence between the Jesus of history and the Christ of faith, the extent and inerrancy of Christ's human knowledge, Christ's awareness of his own identity, and the Resurrection as historical fact. Each of these has since developed its own library of theological data.

Basic to the tenets of Christ's critics was their conviction that the Gospel narratives about Jesus are already embellishments of a believing community. The Gospels do not reflect the true picture of who Jesus really was but have added the hopes and aspirations of his first admirers. As a result, the evangelists depict more than actually took place and therefore cannot be trusted to give us an accurate account of the "works and words" of the Savior.

What the first-century believers began in creating the Gospels continued in subsequent centuries. The "Christian consciousness," which means the creative imagination of faith, further adorned the original facts about Jesus until Councils like Nicea and Chalcedon had produced a whole system of ideas about Christ to make him one in being with the Father, the natural Son of God, and one of the Trinity of persons who brought the world into existence out of nothing.

Needless to say, on these premises all that Catholicism teaches about Christ is at best illusory and at worst a distortion of the truth. The Church sensed the challenge, and for half a century encouraged biblical scholars and theologians frankly to investigate the witness of Scripture and the findings of the sciences relative to the person of the Savior. Then in 1965, when the Second Vatican Council published its *Constitution on Divine Revelation,* the document stated in a tone of finality what could not, humanly speaking, have been said without decades of study about the supposed divergence between the real Jesus and the Christ of ecclesiastical fancy.

> Holy Mother the Church has firmly and with absolute constancy held and continues to hold that the four Gospels . . . whose historical character the Church unhesitatingly asserts, faithfully hand on what Jesus Christ, while living among men, really did and taught for their eternal salvation until the day he was taken up into heaven.[13]

Terms like "historical character," "faithfully hand on," "really did and taught," and in a later context "the honest truth about Jesus," had been clarified in a long process of refining.

What about the accuracy of Christ's knowledge? Consistent with their attitude toward the Gospels as a mixture of fact and spurious piety, the Modernists had no trouble isolating evidences of Christ's ignorance, e.g., his mistaken claims of an early Second Coming. Is it any wonder, they asked, that St. Paul and the early Christians were expecting Christ to return to earth and announce the Day of Judgment in the first century? To still claim, in the light of such facts, that Christ was infallible or shared in the limitless knowledge of the Godhead can only be attributed to dogmatic fervor overriding the bounds of reason.

The same scholarship that established the historicity of the Gospels on exegetical and historical grounds was applied to this matter, and Rome passed on the findings to Catholic scholars. There are too many scientifically sound explanations of what the Second Coming meant in the Gospels and the writings of St. Paul to resort to accusations of error on the part of Christ.

More fundamental was the broad charge of ignorance in Christ and the dismissal of Christ's unlimited knowledge, even as man. This touched on the core of the Incarnation and was recognized by the Church as a resurgent Nestorianism.[14] Ten years after Pius X's censure of Modernism, Benedict XV returned to the same theme and specifically on the question of "the knowledge possessed by the soul of Christ," to make sure there was no ambiguity. Three propositions were declared incompatible with the Catholic faith:

> It is not certain that there was in the soul of Christ, during his life among men, the knowledge possessed by the blessed or those in glory.
>
> Equally uncertain is the statement which claims that the soul of Christ was ignorant of nothing, but that from the beginning it knew in the Word all things, past, present, and future; in a word, that it knew all things which God knows by the knowledge of vision.
>
> The position of some recent spokesmen about the limited knowledge of the soul of Christ should be no less acceptable in Catholic schools than the statement of the ancients about its universal knowledge.[15]

Behind this contemporary defense of Christ's human knowledge lay centuries of conflict on the subject, dating to the time of Arius and Nestorius. A high point was reached with the rise of the Agnoetes (Greek *agnoeo,* to be ignorant of) in the sixth century. They attributed ignorance to the human soul of Christ. Their teaching was opposed by many churchmen, notably by Eulogius, patriarch of Alexandria. In the year A.D. 600, Pope Gregory I confirmed the position of Eulogius and decided that the theories of the Agnoetes were heretical.[16]

The basic reason for the impossibility of error in Christ lies in the hypostatic union. Although man, Christ is a divine person. It is therefore irreconcilable with the dignity of a divine person to ascribe to him such imperfections as error or moral deficiency.

In affirming this, the Church does not of course deny that Christ's soul also possessed what is called acquired or experimental knowledge. This is the human knowledge that proceeds from sense experience and that is achieved through the abstracting power of the intellect. Christ had this kind of knowledge because he had a real and complete human nature, since it is connatural for a human being to have sense perception and derive corresponding knowledge from such experience. To deny experiential knowledge in Christ would lead finally to Docetism, namely that his humanity was only make-believe.

The more delicate question of how Luke's statement about Christ's growth in human knowledge should be taken is commonly interpreted to mean two things. On the one hand, real progress in knowledge was not possible either in the Savior's beatific vision or in the spiritual concepts that were immediately and habitually infused in his soul by the Spirit of God. On this level, the only "progress" would be a successive manifestation of the knowledge he had from the beginning. Real progress, however, was possible in Christ's experiential way of knowing, since the knowledge acquired from sense perception could be increased step by step through the activity of his human reason. Nevertheless, he already knew from the beatific vision and supernaturally infused ideas what he learned from sense experience. Consequently, his acquired learning was new, and to that extent can be called progressive, only in the manner in which Christ attained it.

The further claim by Modernists that "Christ did not always have the consciousness of his messianic dignity" followed on their disclaimer that the Gospels can be trusted as authentic history. Certainly the evangelists make it clear that Jesus repeatedly affirmed he was the fulfillment of the prophets, that he was the Messiah they foretold.

There was a deeper reason, however, behind the denial that Christ knew who he was. It was the theory that redefined the meaning of "person" as applied to Jesus Christ. Drawn from the psychological sciences, "person" was identified as "the center of action of finite self-consciousness and of human freedom."

Taken by itself, there would be no problem with saying that personality is self-awareness and the seat of human liberty. The difficulty came when this psychological description was applied to Christ, since it implied that if the Savior had human self-awareness and human freedom, he also had a human personality. This became all the more serious as theologians probed more and more deeply into the character and, as they said, "personality" of Christ. In their laudable effort to preserve the true humanity of Jesus, they risked losing sight of his unique divine personhood.

Pius XII took the occasion of the fifteenth centennial of the Council of Chalcedon (1951) to restate the Church's unqualified doctrine about Christ's humanity, even in our day of psychological terminology.

There is no objection, of course, to having the humanity of Christ more deeply investigated even by psychological norms and methods. In difficult studies of this nature, however, there are some who are too ready to abandon what is already in possession in order to pursue things that are new. As a result they do an injustice to the definition of the Council of Chalcedon while propounding their own theories. They so elevate the status and qualities of Christ's human nature that it seems to become an autonomous subject all by itself, as though it did not subsist in the very person of the Word. But the Council of Chalcedon, in full agreement with that of Ephesus, clearly affirms that each nature of our Redeemer is joined "in one person and subsistence," and it forbids postulating two individuals in Christ, as though some sort of "assumed human being," having his own autonomous individuality, existed side by side with the Word.[17]

This was no academic question. What the Church wishes to reaffirm is that modern science does not change what the Church had defined a millennium and a half ago. Psychologists may use the term *personality* to describe the sum total of all observable reactions of an individual. In this sense, most of Christ's observable reactions were evidently human; he ate and slept and walked and talked and performed all the normal actions of a human being. Yet faith tells the Christian that while Jesus was truly human, he was also truly divine, since he had two natures. But he had only one individuality, which made him one complete person, the second person of the Trinity.

Shrouded in mystery, one of the nearest comparisons to illustrate how this is possible is the union of our own rational soul with the body. We are composed of two distinct elements, spirit and matter. Nevertheless, we are each of us one individual whose personality is that of a rational being; nor do we consider our body somehow "deprived" because its existence depends on the soul. No less should the human nature of Christ be considered inferior because its existence depends on the infinite Word of God.

V. BLESSED VIRGIN MARY

Catholic Christology is unintelligible without knowing the role of Christ's mother in the development of faith from the simple narrative of the Gospels to the elaborate Mariology of modern times.

The synoptics were mainly concerned with tracing Christ's lineage as the Son of Man and, therefore, as Son of Mary—with Matthew (writing for the Jews) stressing Christ's descent from Abraham, and Luke (disciple of the universalist Paul) Christ's origin from Adam, father of the human race. Yet both writers also stressed the celestial origins of the Savior. Matthew was at pains to point out that Mary's Son fulfilled the Isaian prophecy about the Messiah being born of a virgin to become Emmanuel, which he interpreted to mean "God with us." Luke gave a long account of the angel's visit to Mary, to announce to her that "the child will be holy and will be called the Son of God" (Lk. 1:36).

St. John followed the same pattern. He introduced Mary as the mother of Jesus when Jesus began his public life. In deference to her wishes, Christ performed the miracle at Cana, to manifest his transcendence and strengthen the faith of his disciples, while the context reveals nothing more clearly than the warm sympathy of a son responding to the desires of his mother.

Paul said little about Mary. But his one classic statement to the Galatians summarized the whole evangelical teaching: "when the appointed time came, God sent his Son, born of a woman, born a subject of the Law, to redeem the subjects of the Law and to enable us to be adopted as sons" (Ga. 4:4–5). The Son of God is the Son of Mary. Generated eternally by the Father, he came into the world as Mary's child, that we might partake of his divinity as divine sons by adoption.

In the early centuries of the Church's history, the concentration was on the person of Christ. Except for the Council of Ephesus, which declared Mary to be the Mother of God, conciliar theology was only obliquely concerned with Christ's mother. Even modern councils from the Middle Ages to the present day have not treated Mary's person or place in the economy of redemption except parenthetically, where absolutely necessary to bring out some facet of Christology. In fact, the late Vatican Council issued the first ecumenical pronouncement of any length on the Blessed Virgin; although here, too, the context was Mary's relationship to the Church.

HISTORICAL BACKGROUND

Until the nineteenth century, the main issues were Mary's divine maternity and perpetual virginity. And with good reason. Unless Mary could be called Mother of God in a true sense, and not by a shift of language; if her divine maternity meant that she gave birth to a mere man and not to the divine Word incarnate, the hypostatic union is denied and Mary is not the Mother of God because her Son was not also the Son of God.[1]

Mary's perpetual virginity posed no such crucial dilemma, as though Christ could not (absolutely speaking) have been born of a woman who had conceived by natural intercourse. Significantly, however, those who impugned her right to the title Theotokos were often the same who questioned Mary's inviolate celibacy. Augustine hinted at a reason for this when he said, "When God vouchsafed to become Man, it was fitting that he should be born in this way. He who was made of her, had made her what she was: a virgin who conceives, a virgin who gives birth; a virgin with child, a virgin delivered of child—a virgin ever virgin." Given the *fact* of the Incarnation, its *manner* becomes a matter of course.[2] Why should not the Almighty who created his mother have also preserved intact the body of which he would be born? But this kind of appropriateness makes sense only on the hypothesis of Christ being truly God. Any suspicion that he was less than divine removes the only rational grounds for considering Mary more than the mother of a man.

The sinlessness of Christ's mother had been recognized from the beginning, but was little dwelled upon except in the writings of the Greek and Latin Fathers when they described her perfect holiness and compared her with the first woman, Eve. They spoke of her as "holy, innocent, most pure, inviolate, undefiled, immaculate," in a way that left no doubt they considered her absolutely without sin. In general, the patristic attitude before Nicea was to compare Mary with Eve, where the latter brought on the ruin of mankind by disobedience and Mary co-operated with Christ with perfect holiness to bring about man's restoration. After Nicea the preference was for extolling Mary's sanctity and implying that she had never been estranged from God.

After the Fathers and up to the early Middle Ages we find explicit references to Mary's freedom from sin from the first moment of her life. Paschasius Radbertus (ninth century), for example, wrote that she was exempt from sin since the beginning of her existence.[3] As early as the late half of the seventh century, a feast of the Immaculate Conception was celebrated annually in the East under the title "Conception of St. Anne." St. Andrew of Crete (d. A.D. 720) composed a hymn with the inscription: "The Ninth Day of December, Conception of the Grandmother of God, St. Anne."

In the West, the feast of the Immaculate Conception was first observed in Ireland, and by A.D. 840 in Italy and Sicily, no doubt transported from the Orient. As it spread from Italy to England and France, a controversy arose among theologians about the lawfulness of the feast; yet all the while the faithful continued honoring Mary conceived without sin, and not only in the womb of her mother, as John the Baptist was believed to have been freed. No such problem arose in the East.

The root of the problem was a compound of ambiguity about original sin and concupiscence, and of strange notions about conception and animation of the human embryo. Critics of the Immaculate Conception kept stressing, "Was the Blessed Virgin sanctified before or after the infusion of her soul into her body?" It never occurred to some that the soul of Mary might have been sanctified at the moment of its creation.

Why their position? The reason was that, while believing she had to be redeemed like everyone else, they never thought of redemption other than as a cleansing from original sin already contracted. St. Bernard of Clairvaux (writing in A.D. 1140) severely reprimanded those who honored Mary's Immaculate Conception. "If Mary could not be sanctified before her conception, since she did not yet exist, nor in the act of conception itself, on account of the sin (concupiscence) involved therein, it follows she was sanctified in the womb after conception, which, since she was cleansed from sin, made her birth holy and not her conception."[4]

Bernard's preoccupation with active conception (seminal intercourse between husband and wife) made him overlook what the Church really meant as regards Mary, namely, passive conception, or the infusion of soul into a human body. Those who thought as he did also failed to see that Mary might have been redeemed by preservation or prevention. Even St. Thomas missed the point, along with Albertus Magnus and Bonaventure. Albertus leaned on Bernard when he wrote, "We say that the Blessed Virgin was not sanctified before animation, and the affirmative contrary to this is the heresy condemned by St. Bernard in his letter to the canons of Lyons."[5]

Bernard's attitude aroused strong protests, mainly among the Franciscans. But they were not taken seriously until Duns Scotus (A.D. 1264–1308) wrote his commentary on the four books of Peter Lombard. Scotus argued, "He who is the most perfect mediator must have a most perfect act of mediation in regard to some person on whose behalf he exercises the mediatorial office. Now Christ is the most perfect mediator . . . and he had no more exalted relation to any person than to the Blessed Virgin Mary. . . . This could not be if he had not merited for her preservation from original sin."[6]

Scotus solved the objection that Mary was a daughter of Adam before she became an adopted child of God, by admitting that in the order of nature, Mary was a child of Adam before she was justified; but in the order of time, her sanctification coincided with the creation of her soul. He used a now famous simile: "Some have been raised up after they have fallen, but the Virgin Mary was sustained as it were in the very act of falling, and prevented from falling, like the two men who were about to tumble into a pit."[7]

Behind Scotus' analysis stood his concept of preredemption, which he contended is possible, because God can, absolutely speaking, infuse grace without first expelling previously existing sin. He further held that preredemption was a fitting way of preserving the Blessed Virgin because she was the mother of God, and as such could never be at enmity with God, which would have to be said if she had not been kept free from original sin.

Eventually Sixtus IV approved the feast and Mass of the Immaculate Conception in 1476, and seven years later he issued an apostolic constitution, *Grave Nimis,* in which he threatened to excommunicate anyone who dared charge his opponent with heresy on the subject. Trent advanced the cause beyond Sixtus by declaring "it is not the intention of this Synod to include in the decree which treats of original sin the Blessed and Immaculate Virgin Mary, Mother of God."[8] Nevertheless, it renewed the Sixtine prohibition about name-calling on both sides.

The Dominican Pope St. Pius V condemned Baius (1567), predecessor of Jansenism, for holding that "no one but Christ was without original sin, and therefore the Blessed Virgin died in consequence of the sin contracted through Adam, and endured affliction in this life, like the rest of the just, as punishments for actual and original sin."[9] In the following year Pius extended the feast of the Immaculate Conception to the universal Church and made it a holy day of obligation. But three centuries had to elapse before the doctrine was formally defined by Pius IX.

Comparable to the dogmatic history of the Immaculate Conception was the background to belief in Mary's bodily Assumption into heaven. Less explicit than Mary's sinless origin, her assumption into heaven in body and soul can be traced in patristic literature from the sixth century—although the idea was implicit in earlier writers when they spoke of Mary's immunity from sin.

The Eastern Emperor Mauritius (582–602) introduced the feast of the Koimesis (Falling Asleep) of the Virgin and ordered its celebration annually throughout the Byzantine Empire on August 15 where it had not yet been observed. In the West, the earliest extant testimony is the statement of Gregory of Tours (d. 596), that "The Lord commanded the holy body [of Mary after her death] to be borne on a cloud to Paradise, where, reunited to its soul, and rejoicing with the elect, it enjoys the never-ending happiness of eternity."[10] However, the most extensive witness comes from St. Andrew of Crete (d. 720), St. Germanus, patriarch of Byzantium (733), and especially St. John Damascene (d. after 754). Damascene is so definite on the subject and so detailed (with three homilies for the feast of the Assumption) that the faith of the people in the doctrine must have been very strong and widespread by the middle of the eighth century.

Summarizing the patristic tradition, we find that four approaches were used, reasoning on dogmatic grounds to Mary's bodily assumption after death. The most fundamental was her freedom from sin. Since the dissolution of the body is a result of sin, and Mary was sinless, she must have been exempt from the common curse, and therefore her body did not corrupt in the grave. Moreover, she was the Mother of God. So that as Christ's body took its existence from her body (*Caro Jesu est caro Mariae*), she ought to share in his bodily glorification. In present-day language this would mean that the physicomoral relationship of Mary with her Son required special participation in his resurrection before the general resurrection of mankind.

Some argued from her virginity, that as her body was preserved in spotless chastity, it should not be subject to natural dissolution after death. But the most cogent reason, later on adopted by Pius XII, was the participation by Christ's mother in his redemption of the world. She took a most active part in all that he did on earth and thus deserved, as no one else, to share in the full fruits of the redemption, which consists in the glorification of soul as well as body.

Unlike the Immaculate Conception, the Assumption stirred no major controversy in the Church, and its definition in 1950 came as no surprise to the Catholic faithful. Writing early in the twentieth century, manualists agreed that the argument from Tradition is so strong that the formal definition of the Assumption was a matter of time. They rightly expected the Church to avoid defining anything more than the actual Assumption, while leaving Mary's physical death to be taught as a theological conclusion.

MARIAN CENTURY

It is no exaggeration that the hundred years from 1854 to the close of the Second Vatican Council were the most prolific in doctrinal development in Mariology. Nothing like it was seen in any comparable period of Catholic history.

One reason for the sudden upsurge was the reaction against rationalism in modern times. When critics of the faith challenged the foundations of belief in Christ's divinity, the response of the Church would understandably be in defense of Nicea and Chalcedon, with special concern to safeguard the dignity of Mary, Mother of God.

Devotion to Mary also grew apace as the role of women became more prominent in private and professional life, and their unique position was threatened by a rampant secularism that wants to exploit them for its own ends. Writers in every tradition have described the ennobling influence of faith in Mary's dignity on the life and literature of Western thought. What mainly distinguishes an advanced civilization is its reverence for womanhood. By this norm, the honor paid to Mary as the ideal of her sex has done more to elevate the status of women than any other postulate of the Christian religion.

Devotion, however, is not yet doctrine, and Mary's role as the highest symbol of womanhood is significant but, from the Catholic standpoint, valuable only if firmly rooted in Christian revelation.

It was at this juncture of history that a series of Marian doctrines was presented to the Church's faithful to assure them that what they had been practicing was divinely authorized and that their piety was founded on the principles of faith.

IMMACULATE CONCEPTION

Demands for a definition of the Immaculate Conception had been received at Rome long before Pius IX, but with his accession to the papacy these demands were renewed with vigor because of the Pope's known veneration for the Mother of God. Among the less-well-known facts of his life is the cure from epilepsy that John Mary Mastai-Ferretti, the future Pius IX, attributed to the intercession of the Blessed Virgin. He vowed to do everything in his power to advance her cause and make her better known and loved by the people.

Accordingly, on June 1, 1848, at the most critical stage of the Papal States' involvement in the Austrian War, he commissioned a group of twenty theologians to study whether it was feasible to define Mary's immunity from original sin.

From Gaeta, in the folowing year, the Pope issued an encyclical letter addressed to the bishops of the Catholic world. It was an act of papal collegiality in which he asked the prelates to help him decide on the question. Of some six hundred replies, only that of the archbishop of Paris, Sibour, with one or two others, took the line that the belief was not definable. A few more, mainly from Protestant countries, considered it inopportune. The overwhelming majority, better than 90 per cent, were enthusiastic.

Pius IX's proclamation of the Immaculate Conception was issued on December 8, 1854, in the document *Ineffabilis Deus,* whose full text is a masterpiece of theological restraint. It shows none of the effusion of which Pius has been charged by his critics.

In the first of three parts, the Pope examines the testimony of tradition, first in the interpretation of Scripture and then in the teaching of the Church. Without claiming that Scripture reveals the doctrine explicitly, he shows that the most common interpretation of the relevant texts by the ancient Fathers and current theologians sees in these texts an implicit teaching that Mary was conceived without sin.

He begins with the passage in Genesis, where the Lord predicts: "I will make you enemies of each other: you and the woman, your offspring and her offspring. It will crush your head and you will strike its heel" (Gn. 3:15).

The seed of the woman was understood as referring to the Savior (*autos* in the Septaugint), so that the Mother of Christ came to be identified with the woman. As early as the second century, this messianic-marian exegesis was known in Christian tradition, for example, in Ireneus, Epiphanius, Cyprian, and Leo the Great.

The bull *Ineffabilis* approves this interpretation and draws from it the conclusion that Mary, because of her intimate relation to Christ, "with him and through him had eternal enmity toward the evil spirit, triumphed over him completely, and crushed him with her immaculate foot."

More directly appealing to Tradition, Pius recalls all the pertinent titles by which the Fathers called Mary "not only immaculate, but entirely immaculate; not only innocent, but most innocent; not only spotless, but most spotless. They called her holy and completely removed from every stain of sin, all pure and all but the very archtype of purity and innocence . . . who alone and in her entirety has become the dwelling place of all the graces of the Holy Spirit. God alone excepted, she is superior to all."

What the Church writers described was reflected in the liturgy, whose prayers and ritual, feasts and invocations are a tessera of professions of faith in Mary's freedom from sin from the beginning of her existence. This introduces the admission that Rome was asked to define the Immaculate Conception. The initiative came from the bishops and faithful, but the Pope had to speak to make the doctrine irreversible. Pius IX condensed the definition into a single paragraph.

To the honor of the holy and undivided Trinity, to the glory and adornment of the Virgin Mother of God, to the exaltation of the Catholic faith, and the increase of the Catholic religion, We, by the authority of Jesus Christ, Our Lord, of the Blessed Apostles, Peter and Paul and by Our Own, declare, pronounce, and define that the doctrine which holds that the Blessed Virgin Mary, at the first instant of her conception, by a singular privilege and grace of the omnipotent God, in consideration of the merits of Jesus Christ, the Savior of mankind was preserved free from all stain of original sin, has been revealed by God, and therefore is to be firmly and constantly believed by all the faithful.[11]

The doctrine of the Immaculate Conception is synthesized in the statement: "The Blessed Virgin Mary, at the first instant of her conception, by a singular privilege and grace of the omnipotent God, in consideration of the merits of Jesus Christ, the Savior of mankind, was preserved from all stain of original sin." It affirms: (1) this immunity was a special grace from God, (2) through the foreseen merits of Christ, (3) Mary was exempt from original sin contracted by the rest of mankind, and (4) the exemption took place at the first moment of her conception in the womb of her mother.

Exemption from original sin must have been an extraordinary grace because other human beings, except Christ, are conceived with sin on their souls. However, this does not mean that Mary was necessarily exempt from the universal necessity or need of being subject to sin, i.e., "the debt of original sin," where two kinds of debt are to be distinguished. The remote debt (necessity) simply means membership in the human race, derived by ordinary propagation from sexual intercourse. Christ, other than Mary, did not incur this necessity. Mary did, and therefore had to be redeemed. The proximate debt involves inclusion in the willful act by which Adam, as representative of mankind, sinned and thereby implicated human nature in his fall. As stated, the dogma of the Immaculate Conception certainly includes the Blessed Virgin in the remote debt, and probably also in the proximate necessity of contracting original sin, which would have infected Mary's soul had she not been miraculously preserved.

Christ's redemptive merits operated on his mother by anticipation. This preredemption is commonly taught to have consisted in the infusion of sanctifying grace into her soul at the moment of its creation, which was simultaneous with infusion into her body.

Exemption from original sin carried with it two corollary consequences: From the time of her conception, Mary was also free from all motions of concupiscence, and also (on attaining the use of reason) free from every personal sin during the whole of her life.

Like her divine Son, Mary was subject to the ordinary limitations of human nature, except those that involve moral defect. She was therefore free from the effect of inherited sin, which is the unreasoning drive of the appetites (sensual and spiritual), which are irrational precisely because they anticipate the dictate of reason and tend to perdure in spite of reason and free will telling a person that the urge in question is wrong. True, there is no actual sin in concupiscence unless a person consents to an inclination that he knows is morally bad. Nevertheless, concupiscence is incompatible with Mary's fullness of grace because, even without consent, it implies excitation to commit acts that are materially against God's will.

If we ask how Mary could gain merit if she was not subject to concupiscence, the answer is the same as with Christ. Certainly the inner drive is an occasion for merit, but not an indispensable condition. Mary acquired merit not by struggling interiorly against a native irrationality, but by her love of God and a host of other virtues. She always had the option of choosing among various good actions; between action and inaction; and among numerous ways of performing acts of virtue—all of which are free choices and meritorious before God.

Long before Pius IX, the Council of Trent said that Mary "by a special privilege of God" was exempt from all sin, even venial ones, during her whole life. Like the Immaculate Conception, which it presupposes, Mary's personal sinlessness follows from the Church's constant belief in her spotless purity and is founded on her dignity as the Mother of God. Some oriental writers, including Chrysostom, held that Mary was sometimes guilty of such minor defects as vanity, as when she urged Jesus to work the miracle of changing water into wine at Cana. They were misled by the notion of woman as inferior to man, and quite incapable of rising above the petty faults of human nature. Yet even they did not charge her with formal sin.

Was the Blessed Virgin free from stain because she did not offend God, or because she was impeccable and incapable of sin? The latter is common teaching in Catholic Tradition, while distinguishing it from the impeccability enjoyed by Christ. His may be called absolute and derived from the union of his human nature with the divinity. He could not sin because he was God, and God is infinitely holy. Mary could not sin by reason of an inherent quality, which some place midway between the state of souls in the beatific vision and that of our first parents before the fall.

Concretely this quality may be identified with perseverance in grace as regards grave sin, and confirmation in grace for lesser sins. In either case, however, her incapacity for sin differed radically from that of Christ. Where his was based on the fact that he is a divine person, hers was an added prerogative. It was absolutely necessary that he could not sin, since God is sinless. It was a free gift of God's mercy that Mary could not sin, but only because she was protected by divine favor.

ASSUMPTION INTO HEAVEN

Almost as soon as Pius IX defined the dogma of Mary's Immaculate Conception, Rome was beseiged with petitions for defining also her bodily Assumption. It is calculated that from 1870 to 1940, over four hundred bishops, eighty thousand priests and religious, and more than eight million of the laity had formally signed requests asking for the definition.

As a consequence, on May 1, 1946, Pius XII sent the following questionnaire to all the bishops of the Catholic world: "Do you, Venerable Brethren, in view of the wisdom and prudence that is yours, judge that the bodily Assumption of the Blessed Virgin can be proposed and defined as a dogma of faith; and do you, along with your clergy and faithful, desire it?"

Within a few months, the replies received in Rome were "almost unanimous" in favor of definition. The Pope drew the inevitable conclusion from the consent of those whom "the Holy Spirit has placed as bishops to rule the Church of God."

On November 1, 1950, Pius XII answered these requests of the Catholic Hierarchy with a solemn definition that "by the authority of our Lord Jesus Christ, of the Blessed Apostles Peter and Paul, and by Our Own authority, We pronounce, declare, and define as divinely revealed dogma: The Immaculate Mother of God, Mary ever Virgin, after her life on earth, was assumed, body and soul to the glory of heaven."[12]

The spontaneous reaction of the faithful was gratitude for the exalted honor paid to the Mother of God. The Pope's own sentiments were expressed to the bishops gathered in Rome for the occasion when he told them the joy he felt over the proclamation and the assurance it gave him that Mary would obtain the graces of which mankind stood in such dire need. On the level of piety and devotion, therefore, Mary's Assumption was only the climax in a series of definitions to honor the Blessed Virgin, beginning with the divine maternity at Ephesus and terminating in the past century with the doctrine of her Immaculate Conception. But dogmatically the Constitution of *Munificentissimus Deus* has a much deeper meaning.

Pope Pius defined Mary's Assumption as a truth divinely revealed. Of the two sources of revelation, theologians commonly say the Assumption was implicit in Tradition, in spite of the practical absence of documentary evidence before A.D. 300. Yet the Pope finally declared that the doctrine was in revelation. How do we know? On the answer to this question rests a new insight into Christian Tradition that had been gaining momentum since the eighteenth century. Briefly stated, Tradition is coming to be identified more with the Church's magisterium or teaching office and less exclusively as the source along with Scripture, of the truths of salvation. Behind this new emphasis is a development of dogma since the Council of Trent that reveals hidden depths in the Mystical Body of Christ. The Church is not only the guardian of a faith once and for all given to the apostles, but expositor of that faith in every age to the end of time.

In August of the same year that he defined the Assumption, the Pope laid down the principles that guided the marian definition. The Church's teaching authority, he said in *Humani Generis,* is not confined to reflecting or consolidating the past. It is also, and especially, the vital present-day function of an organism animated by the Spirit of God. "Together with the sources of revelation (Scripture and Tradition) God has given to his Church a *living* magisterium to elucidate and explain what is contained in the deposit of faith only obscurely and, as it were, by implication."[13] The degree of obscurity, we may add, is unimportant. Given this faculty by her founder, whose Spirit of truth abides with her at all times, the Church can infallibly discern what belongs to revelation no matter how cryptic the contents may be.

Consequently, when Pius XII defined the Assumption, he did more than propose the doctrine for acceptance by the faithful or give them a new motive for devotion to the Blessed Mother. He indicated the Church's right to authorize a legitimate development in doctrine and piety that scandalizes Protestants and may even surprise believing Catholics. The Assumption thus becomes part of a larger process, along with Catholic Action, the liturgical movement, and even such practical matters as the mitigated Eucharistic fast, in which the current problems of the Church and the present needs of souls are being met by the Holy Spirit. Without the premises inherent in *Munificen-*

tissimus Deus, the Second Vatican Council could not have done its monumental work of updating the Church in modern times.

It was no coincidence that on the day following the Assumption definition, the Pope expressed the hope that this new honor to Mary would introduce "a spirit of penance to replace the prevalent love of pleasure, and a renewal of a family life stabilized where divorce was common and made fruitful where birth control was practiced." If there is one feature that characterizes today's world, it is the cult of the body.

Three years after defining the dogma of the Assumption, Pius XII called on the Catholic world to join in the observance of a Marian Year to commemorate the centenary of Pius IX's definition of the Immaculate Conception. He introduced the Marian Year with the encyclical *Fulgens Corona,* whose doctrinal content went beyond the immediate purpose of proclaiming a season of special prayers to the Mother of God.

According to Pius, the Assumption was a consequence of the Immaculate Conception, not merely in the superficial sense of something suitable, but in the logic of supernatural merit and providence. "These two singular privileges bestowed upon the Mother of God stand out in most splendid light as the beginning and the end of her earthly journey. For the greatest possible glorification of her virgin body is the complement, at once appropriate and marvelous, of the absolute innocence of her soul, which was free from all stain. Just as she took part in the struggle of her only-begotten Son with the serpent of hell, so also she shared in his glorious triumph over sin and its sad consequences."[14]

In the same document the Pope made another association, this time a historical one, not between the first and final mysteries in the life of the Blessed Virgin, but between the Immaculate Conception and the supernatural phenomena at Lourdes. In his judgment the Virgin Mary herself wished to confirm by some special sign the definition that the Vicar of her divine Son had pronounced amid the applause of the whole Church. "Four years had not yet elapsed when, in the French town at the foot of the Pyrenees, the Virgin Mother showed herself to a simple and innocent girl at the grotto of Messabielle and to this same girl, earnestly inquiring the name of her with whose vision she was favored, with eyes raised to heaven and sweetly smiling, she replied, 'I am the Immaculate Conception.'" Following the original visions, thousands of people from every country in the world have made pilgrimages to Lourdes, where "miraculous favors were granted them, which excited the admiration of all and confirmed the Catholic religion as the only one given approval by God."[15]

In the context of the Lourdes apparitions and the constant stream of preternatural wonders there granted by God, this means that what Lourdes stands for is attested as true. The Immaculate Conception is a strict mystery, not even conceivable apart from revelation. Miracles are visible signs of divine intervention that lead the well disposed to believe (or strengthen their belief) in what cannot be seen, on the argument that the same agency producing the phenomena also revealed the doctrine in whose atmosphere the phenomena take place.

DOCTRINE OF THE SECOND VATICAN COUNCIL

If devotion to the Mother of God is an index of Catholic piety, we should expect a Pontiff as charismatic as the late Pope John to have been devoted to the Blessed Virgin. We know that he was, as the definitive biography *Journal of a Soul* reveals on almost every page. His favorite prayer was a marian hymn in twenty-two stanzas, which he recited regularly.

His first words at the solemn opening of the Vatican Council reflected the same spirit. "Mother Church rejoices," he told the assembled prelates, "that by the singular gift of divine providence, the longed-for day has finally dawned when—under the auspices of the Virgin Mother of God, whose maternal dignity is commemorated on this feast—the Second Ecumenical Council is being solemnly opened here beside St. Peter's tomb."

Throughout the Council and up to the time of his death, Pope John called upon the faithful to ask Mary's help and expressed his own conviction that with such aid the conciliar deliberations would bear much fruit. The Pontiff died before the Council finished its work, but it is certain that the Constitution on the Church, which contains the long chapter on Mary, faithfully reflects the mind of John XXIII. His successor, Paul VI, credited him with the spirit that inspired the document.

Some have read into the Constitution a minimizing of "Marianism" in the Catholic Church. They suggest that by relegating Mary to the concluding chapter on the Church, the council put a check on excessive devotion to the Mother of God. Quite the contrary: Mary's place in the economy of salvation and her relationship to Christ and the Church are enhanced by being integrated in the larger perspective of the Mystical Body.

A superficial reading of the Vatican Council's treatise on Mary might disclose nothing new. In a sense that is true. Yet one phase of marian theology shows remarkable growth, mainly under the impact of the ecumenical movement that Pope John had bequeathed to the Vatican Council.

In order to appreciate the significance of the Vatican's Mariology, we must see in it the framework of what is happening in the Protestant and Orthodox world. One of the less-known aspects of ecumenism, the Church's teaching about Mary, is actually the keystone of the world movement for Christian unity.

The reason is obvious. Marian doctrine and practice in the Church focus attention on those crucial areas of Christianity in which Protestants mainly differ from Roman Catholicism, and where the Eastern Orthodox are most nearly like Rome.

Accordingly, the Vatican Council had the delicate task of proclaiming the Church's ancient faith about Mary with two perspectives in mind: Remove as far as possible the misunderstanding under which many Christians labor, and reaffirm as clearly as possible that Catholic belief about the Mother of God is the same as that of Eastern Christendom.

There was no difficulty satisfying the Orthodox that Catholic devotion to Mary was equal to theirs, and that she holds as prominent a place in the Church's faith (if not always in Catholic piety) as obtains among Christians of the East. The real test of ecumenical communication was to so state what Catholics think about the Blessed Virgin that nothing doctrinal is sacrificed, and yet needless misunderstandings are clarified.

Three levels of approach were taken, comparing in each instance the role of Christ as mediator, Redeemer, and source of grace for mankind—and the corresponding but subordinate role of his Mother. There was great wisdom in taking this stand, because the root of most objections to what some have called Mariolatry is that Mary is somehow placed equal to Christ in the scheme of salvation and, if not deified, made so nearly divine that the unique function of Jesus Christ is obscured and almost nullified.

Christ the One Mediator—and Mary. The Council was at special pains to insist that Jesus Christ is the one and only mediator between God and man. All other mediators, including Mary, take their meaning and efficacy from him: "There is but one mediator as we know from the words of the apostle, 'for there is one God and one mediator of God and men, the man Christ Jesus, who gave himself a redemption for all.' "[16] How, then, does Mary fit into this plan and in what sense is she, what the Council calls her, "mediatrix"?

It was the first time in conciliar history that this bone of contention was treated extensively with a view to meet sincere objectors in their search for the true relation between Christ and his Mother, the one mediator and the other mediatrix. To understand the Council's further explanation, we must see what the respective mediations are, as Catholicism understands them.

Technically a mediator (*mesites* in St. Paul) is a person who holds a favorable position between parties at variance, and can therefore interpose between them as the equal friend of each. The history of religion is filled with attempts to bridge the gap between the Deity and man, and in Christianity, the heretical systems of Gnosticism and Arianism were essentially misguided efforts to find this mediator in someone less than Christ. Thus in Gnosticism the aeons or "intermediate beings" were supposed to span the chasm between the Godhead and the material world, which was believed intrinsically evil. In Arianism, the Logos, as the most exalted of creatures and creator of the rest, served the same purpose.

From this standpoint, the main thrust of all the early councils—Nicea, Constantinople, Ephesus, and Chalcedon—was to settle once and for all that no one but the second person of the Trinity become man, is man's mediator with the Almighty. His mediatorship was declared to be both in the order of being (natural or objective) and in the order of action (functional or moral). In the order of being, Christ is our mediator by the fact of his hypostatic union, joining in one person the two natures that need to be mediated: divine, which He has in common with the Father; and human, which he shares with us. In the order of action, Christ alone is our mediator by the fact that his death atoned for man's sins, and his humanity is the channel of grace from God to the human race.

Another way of looking at the two mediations is to say that the Incarnation corresponds to mediation in the order of being, and the

Redemption (remission of sin and conferral of grace) is mediation morally.

This kind of mediation is incommunicable. No one but the Savior unites in himself the divinity, which demands reconciliation, and the humanity, which needs to be reconciled.

Nevertheless, lesser and subordinate mediators are not excluded. The question is what purpose they serve and in what sense do they mediate. They can help the cause of mediation in the only way that human beings (or creatures) can contribute to the work of salvation, namely, by their willing response to grace: either better disposing themselves or others for divine grace, or interceding with God to give his grace, or freely co-operating with grace when conferred.

Everyone who is saved has, in some sense, been such a mediator between himself and God, which the Church assumes by its claim that man's freedom was not extinguished by the fall; that he can (and must) collaborate with God's grace to reach the God for whom he was made.

Moreover, vicarious mediation is also part of the plan of salvation, since we are bidden to concern ourselves about others, and the solidarity of mankind in Christ lays the foundation for helping others save their souls, too.

It is in this context that the Blessed Virgin enters as mediatrix par excellence. We presume that she co-operated fully with the graces she received, to save her own soul. But she mediated for others, as well, by her vicarious assistance to the rest of mankind. She deserves the title mediatrix because she co-operated in a unique way with Christ in his redemptive labors on earth, and because in heaven she continues interceding for those who are still working out their salvation as pilgrims in the Church Militant or souls suffering in purgatory. The Vatican Council takes account of both types of mediation and shows how they depend upon the primary role of Christ, her divine Son.

> The Father of mercies willed that the Incarnation should be preceded by the acceptance of her who was predestined to be the mother of his Son, so that just as woman contributed to death, so also a woman should contribute to life. That is true in outstanding fashion of the mother of Jesus, who gave to the world him who is Life itself and who renews all things and who was enriched by God with the gifts which befit such a role.
>
> Thus Mary, a daughter of Adam, consenting to the divine Word,

became the mother of Jesus, the one and only mediator. Embracing God's salvific will with a full heart and impeded by no sin, she devoted herself totally as a handmaid of the Lord to the person and work of her Son, under him and with him, by the grace of Almighty God, serving the mystery of redemption.[17]

Nor did Mary's consent stop with Christ's entrance into the world. It revealed itself during his life in her womb, at birth in Bethlehem, at the visit of the shepherds and Magi, and flight into Egypt, when she offered him in the temple and twelve years later found him there teaching the scribes and elders. It was shown during his public life at strategic points in the Gospels, notably at the beginning of Christ's miracles in Cana and the dramatic episode when he declared blessed those who, like her, heard the word of God and kept it. She was with him in his passion and stood under the cross at Calvary. She mothered the infant Church of her Son, before Pentecost and afterward, until her departure from this world to be assumed into heaven.

Once entered heaven, she did not cease her mediatorial function in favor of mankind. Terrestrial mediation now became celestial. While co-operating with Christ's redemptive task, by freely consenting to all that he asked of her, when she was still on earth, her mediation was meritorious; she was still a wayfarer, and thus joined in spirit with the earthly side of the Savior's reconciliation of the human race with his Father. After the Assumption she could no longer merit grace for others, but she can still intercede and by her prayers exercise in glory a role comparable to that of other saints in heaven but immeasurably more effective because she is the Mother of the God with whom she pleads. As nearly as it is possible to say, she is mother of mankind in the order of grace:

This maternity of Mary in the order of grace began with the consent which she gave in faith at the Annunciation and which she sustained without wavering beneath the cross, and lasts until the eternal fulfillment of all the elect. Taken up to heaven she did not lay aside this salvific duty but by her constant intercession continued to bring us the gift of eternal salvation. By her maternal charity she cares for the brethren of her Son, who still journey on earth surrounded by dangers and difficulties, until they are led into the happiness of their true home. Therefore, the Blessed Virgin is invoked by the Church under the titles of Advocate, Auxiliatrix, Adjutrix, Mediatrix. This, however, is to be so understood that it neither takes away from nor adds anything to the dignity and efficaciousness of Christ the one mediator.[18]

Although she is mediatrix, Mary remains a mere creature, and "no creature could ever be counted equal with the incarnate Word and Redeemer. Just as the priesthood of Christ is shared in various ways both by the ministers and the faithful, and as the one goodness of God is really communicated in different ways to his creatures, so also the unique mediation of the Redeemer does not exclude but rather gives rise to a manifold co-operation which is but sharing in this one source."[19] Mary's mediation, therefore, is a sheer gift of her Son; it is participated in a way similar to the way all creatures share in the attributes of the Godhead—contingently, not naturally—and no more detracts from Christ's unique mediatorship than parenthood in human beings detracts from the unique fatherhood of the Creator.

The Atonement of Christ—and Mary. When we speak of Christ's mediation and of Mary's subordinate co-operation with him, we are talking abstractly about what the Redemption means concretely. It was through the Redemption that the Savior exercised his mediatorial reconciliation, and that his mother shares in the process.

Yet the redemptive action of Jesus Christ may be conceived from two vantage points: It may be understood negatively in terms of remission from sin, and then it coincides with the atonement; or it may be seen positively, as the bestowal of grace that leads to heaven, which is properly justification through the merits of the Redeemer.

As Catholic Tradition understands it, "atonement" means reparation of any wrong or injury, either material (as the loss of something valuable) or moral (which is an injury or offense). Material harm requires restitution; moral injury calls for satisfaction, which is nothing else than compensation for some wrong done to another.

After man had sinned, he was obliged to repair the injustice committed against God, which God took upon himself to expiate in the person of Jesus Christ. Our interest here is not to recapitulate what the Church has always held, that Christ by his sufferings and death rendered vicarious atonement to God for the sins of men.[20] We wish to see how Vatican II viewed the Mother of Christ in co-operating with the atonement. Most of the difficulties center on this delicate question.

Her supporting role is stated in a single sentence: "The Blessed Virgin advanced in her pilgrimage of faith, and faithfully persevered in her union with her Son unto the cross, where she stood, in keeping with the divine plan, grieving exceedingly with her only-begotten Son, uniting herself with a maternal heart with his sacrifice, and lovingly consenting to the immolation of this victim, which she herself had brought forth."[21]

Mary's title to mediatrix-in-atonement rests on the pain she freely underwent in union with her Son. The sins of men called for suffering from the God-man, and he wished his mother to share in the pain as she was the one whom he loved most and whose sympathy for him was the main source of her own distress.

Christ the Source of All Grace—and Mary. In reality there is no difference between satisfaction and merit, so that Christ's sacrificial death on the cross was at once the perfect atonement for man's sins and the meritorious cause of man's justification before God. Yet we may distinguish between the two and say that atonement presupposes a debt to be remitted, whereas merit implies a debtor who gives a reward.

St. Paul teaches that salvation can be acquired only by the grace merited by Christ, and St. Peter testified before the High Council that "neither is there salvation in any other" than Christ Jesus Our Lord.

Whatever grace anyone receives, therefore, comes to him through the merits of the Savior, whose humanity was capable of reward before God because it was filled with divine grace, which is the principle of supernatural life, much like the soul animates the body as its source of human activity.

Alongside her Son, Mary has become part of this plan by contributing her share to the justification of the human race, beginning with herself and extending to everyone ever justified. Her contribution is part of the mystery of merit, and is no more surprising than how anyone can deserve a reward before God, when the very freedom we exercise is a divine gift and the grace with which we co-operate is another favor from on high. Mary was more instrumental than any other creature in thus "comeriting" with Christ, and subordinate to him as only a creature can be subordinate to its Maker.

What makes her unique is not the altruistic merit she gained by leading a holy life, and now in heaven continues interceding effectively as a reward of her virtue. All the saints did and do as much. Her singularity lies in the exalted sanctity she enjoyed as one full of grace, holier than the angels, and therefore as much more influential with God as the holiest of beings is more pleasing to him than any of his lesser creatures.

To make sure there is no mistake, the Constitution on the Church explains that "all the salvific influence of the Blessed Virgin on men originates, not from some inner necessity, but from the divine pleasure. It flows from the superabundance of the merits of Christ, rests on his mediation, depends entirely upon it and draws all its power from the same. In no way does it impede, but rather does it foster the immediate union of the faithful with Christ."[22] If Mary is called "Mother of divine grace," and "Virgin most powerful," these titles are due her only because Christ made her so exalted in holiness that on earth she merited a high place in heaven, and now in heaven is able to plead our cause with her Son more efficaciously than anyone else among the elect.

Ecumenical Implications. Still the problem remains, because not a few Christians who profess the divinity of Christ without qualification and accept him as Savior, are opposed to giving Mary any value in the economy of salvation. They are willing to call her the Mother of God and the first Christian; to be loved and so lead us to the love of Christ; to be imitated and so lead to the imitation of Christ; to be called happy and blessed among women, and so lead us to the praise of God. But that is all. She may not be invoked as intercessor with God, or honored as our mediatrix with Christ.

Mary's mediation was recognized by the Vatican Council as the crucial issue on which Catholic and other Christian traditions divide. The reason lies hidden in the concept of merit. If in the fall of Adam all men are conceived and born in sin, and later purification merely covers over the depravity of human nature like a cloak, without removing the sin, then the ravages are so deep that freedom is completely destroyed and we have nothing left but the name. Without liberty of choice, merit is impossible; and without merit we cannot speak of saint or degrees of sanctity or, what depends on holiness, intercessory power with God. We are all equally powerless during life to do anything meritorious for heaven and after death to intercede for those who are still living on earth.

In this scheme, the only purpose of having saints would be as models to encourage us with resignation to an immutable fate. There is no question of imitating their virtues nor of asking for their aid. The hierarchy of God's friends whose good works made them, in varying degrees, powerful mediators in heaven, disappears if we reduce everyone to sinful uniformity. Nothing we do has any true merit in the eyes of God; all is exclusively the work of his grace. Even the Mother of Christ would be no exception. She could do no more for us than the least of those who are saved; she would be as much a sinner as they and would now be just as helpless in obtaining the graces that we need.

Among the dramatic changes taking place in wide realms of Christian thought is the admission that merit is not out of the question, and consequently sanctity is a real prospect in spite of the ravages of sin. One result has been that Mary is coming to be more and more honored in Christian Churches of every tradition.

With this in mind, the Council warned Catholics to be on their guard not to muddy the issue by falling into either of two extremes: undercutting their marian piety and thus hindering the Eastern Churches from communion with Rome, or imprudently urging devotion to Mary beyond the limits of sound teaching and so compromising the Church before Protestants.

> Let the faithful remember that true devotion consists neither in sterile or transitory affection, nor in a certain vain credulity, but proceeds from true faith by which we are led to know the excellence of the Mother of God, and we are moved to a filial love toward our mother and to the imitation of her virtues.[23]

Catholics who take their faith in Christ for granted may be surprised to find how sensitive other Christians are to what seems to be a corollary of this faith: devotion to Mary and belief in her influential intercession. The Council's teaching will serve as a welcome corrective, not to be less devoted to her but to grow in a devotion that is strong in its foundations and truly attractive to all who love Christ and therefore wish to grow in the love of his Mother.

VI. THE GRACE OF GOD

Among the mysteries of Catholicism, none is more practically important for our personal and social lives than the doctrine of grace. It is the very heart of Christianity on its human side, since it describes the panorama of God's dealings with each one of us in the depths of our souls. The study of grace corresponds in theology to the science of psychology, but with implications in every aspect of the Christian religion that have no counterpart in merely human philosophy.

All the dogmas of faith take on new meaning from the existence of a supernatural order. The Trinity of persons is meaningful because their eternal communication within the Deity are the source of his gifts outside the divinity. They are the fountainhead of grace from the Father, through his Son, our Lord, in the Spirit who dwells in the souls of the justified.

By the very fact that we believe in things unseen and hope for the promised reward of those who love God, we are witnesses to the action of a superhuman power, which is divine grace operating on the mind and will and enabling us to see and want what the natural man cannot perceive or desire.

We say that the sacraments are seven signs instituted by Christ to confer the grace they signify. And more broadly we hold that the Catholic Church is the great sacrament of the New Law that Christ founded to be the unique channel of grace to all mankind, with special title to those who are baptized and active members of the Mystical Body of Christ. But no matter how conceived, the sacraments are so far significant and membership in the Church so much more appreciated if we see the great mysteries of Christ in their true perspective as visible and human agencies for the transmission of invisible divine blessings to the human race.

As we look to the future prospects of a heavenly reward, it is grace again that gives heaven its only meaning, as a prolongation of the life in God's friendship here on earth. Our faith here becomes vision there, our hope here becomes possession there, and our charity in time the measure of our love of God in eternity—all aspects of the same mysterious reality that completely distinguishes the Christian religion from every other. We might in justice define Christianity as "the religion of grace." Except for Judaism, from which it arose and above which it stands, Christianity is unique among living religions in resting its whole structure on the existence of a supernatural world of which the visible and natural universe is only a feeble analogy.

If the love of God is conditioned on knowledge, the depth of love will be determined by the extent of our knowledge of him, not only as the Creator of nature but as the Author of grace. And since faith is required to recognize this higher operation of divine goodness, we have in the Catholic doctrine on grace the single most powerful motive for the apostolate.

In sending forth his disciples, Christ directed them before all else to teach, make disciples, and thus to convert the world. It is significant that the Gospel terms "teach," "disciple," "master," and "prophet" are so many aspects of the teaching apostolate. The primary function of the minister of the Gospel is to impart knowledge, i.e., revelation, from which arises faith and through which the faithful may obtain grace. If the Church's ultimate purpose is to sanctify the souls of men, this purpose would not be conceivable unless people were first instructed to believe that holiness is necessary and acquirable through the outpouring of grace, notably, in the Mass and sacraments, which God chose to institute and reveal.

Having understood the importance and dignity of grace, the mystics attested to its excellence. Neither the gift of prophecy, nor the working of miracles, nor any speculation, however sublime, is of any value without it. For the gifts of nature are common to the good and bad; but grace is the proper gift of the elect, and they who are adorned with it are esteemed worthy of eternal life.

BIBLICAL ORIGINS

Not the least obstacle to the study of grace is the practical one of meaning. The word "grace" is derived from the Latin *gratia,* used by the Roman translators of the New Testament for the Greek *charis* in the second century, and ever since adopted by the Church in all her official teaching of the faithful.

In order to get behind the scriptural meaning of grace, therefore, we must examine the import of the Greek term *charis,* which is, so to speak, our human link with the concept intended by the Holy Spirit in Christian revelation. Biblical scholars say that the Greek mind has in no other word uttered itself and all that lies at its heart more distinctly than in this disyllable, which the authors of the New Testament chose to epitomize God's merciful love for men.

History of the Term. The great expositor of the meaning of grace was St. Paul, who speaks of it in all his epistles, including the short one to Philemon, which he begins and ends with a prayer for the grace "from" and "of our Lord Jesus Christ." In the Pauline letters, supported by the Acts and St. Peter, the single term *charis* includes all the nuances that the Christian faith partly borrowed from the Greeks but sublimated to a level never found in classic antiquity.

Underlying these meanings, of course, is the basic notion of a benefit freely granted by God to his creatures. The operative word is "freely" or "gratuitously," which is opposed to whatever is due or on which a person has a rightful claim. Broadly speaking, the very elements that constitute our nature, our body and soul, are not due to us but were freely created by the love of God. Yet this kind of gratuity is at best negative, because we had no claim on coming into existence to begin with. God could have not made us. Once we came into existence, however, a variety of other blessings may be called due to us, such as are needed to make our lives purposeful and enable us to reach the perfection proper to our human nature. Yet even these are not strictly by right, but are divine gifts with the same gratuity as the nature on which they finally depend.

Early Christian literature sometimes describes these gifts of nature as graces, and one of the major heresies in the early Church was built on the theory that human freedom was the only or the highest type of grace we receive. But that is not the understanding of the concept in Catholic theology. When the Scriptures, Fathers, or councils of the Church refer to "grace" properly so called, they mean that gift which is the fruit of the blood of Christ, by which we become Christians and children of God, are justified, made holy, and enter into heavenly glory. They often oppose grace to nature, teaching that nature must be repaired, made sound, helped, and saved by grace. We are able to do by grace what the lone powers of nature could never do.

The appropriateness of the term "grace" for this special benefit of divine love becomes evident once the existence of a higher than natural order is recognized. Certainly if the gifts of nature are gratuitous, those of supernature are given gratis to an eminent degree.

In addition, if we examine the meaning of gratuity, we see that graces, other than gifts of nature, are freely conferred with no positive claim on our part to receive. It is not only that we *had* no claim to whatever we possess naturally—how could we, since we did not even exist to press such a claim? But as objects of divine benevolence in the form of grace, we *have* no claim to these benefits, although we exist, and enjoy certain rights to the perfection and destiny of our given, existing humanity.

This divine benevolence that we call grace may be understood concretely as God, viewed in his own trinitarian life, which he communicated to his rational creatures. All three persons of the Trinity are concerned: the Father, who sent his only-begotten Son to redeem us; the Son, who became man and died on the cross to merit the grace of our salvation; and the Holy Spirit, who has been revealed as the term of divine life in our souls through whom the Son, who is generated by the Father, sanctifies those he redeemed.

There are really two gifts involved: one uncreated, which is God communicating himself to his creatures; and the other created, which is the effect he produces in souls by his new presence to us. Both are graces, and both absolutely undeserved, since their function is to make us capable of living a life that is proper to God alone: of knowing and loving him as he knows and loves himself, of possessing him with the happiness that he enjoys by nature and we are privileged to share by the sheer benevolence of grace.

Too often people equate the idea of grace with some special kind of help from God, as though grace were only remedial of human weakness or distress. It is indeed remedial, and to our way of thinking, this may seem to be its main function, as it is certainly the most frequent object of prayer. However, grace is not primarily a help but an elevation, a raising of created nature and faculties to an order of being where only the divinity has the right to abide. Its principal function is to make us partakers of the inner life of the Trinity in the beatific vision, where the divine essence is seen intuitively in a face-to-face vision, with no interposition of any creature between the soul and the triune God.

Accordingly, supernatural grace has two elements that characterize it and distinguish it from everything merely natural: its posi-

tive and absolute gratuity, and its heavenly finality. The first refers to God as efficient cause, who willed to produce a benefit for us
beyond the most extravagant conception of a finite mind; the second
refers to God as final cause, toward whom we are being directed as
our trinitarian end. Taken together, the two elements give us a definition of grace as a supernatural gift that God confers gratuitously on
rational creatures in order to bring them to eternal life.

Communication of Divine Love. An adequate estimate of grace
must see it as a communication of divine love. St. John tells us that
"God is love," meaning that in God reside all the treasures of infinite
goodness, perfectly shared among the three persons, and graciously
communicated to mankind outside the Trinity; first naturally in creation by bringing us out of nothing into existence and endowing us
with the divine image of intellect and will; then supernaturally in the
Incarnation, which is the source of our life of grace and the meritorious cause of our salvation. While admitting, and almost transmitting,
the prior evidence of God's bounty in creating us, St. John says "God's
love for us was revealed when God sent into the world his only Son so
that we could have life through him" (Jn. 4:9).

Among the different forms of grace, the primary type is habitual
or sanctifying, by which we become children of God and heirs of
heaven. All other forms are secondary to this one and take their
meaning from sanctifying grace.

The ultimate purpose of this gift from the side of God is his glory
and that of his divine Son, but from ours everlasting happiness with
the Trinity. The agent of this gift is the merciful God (in the words
of the Council of Trent), "who freely washes and sanctifies, sealing
and anointing us with the Holy Spirit of his promise, who is the
pledge of our inheritance"; the meritorious source is the "beloved
only-begotten Son of God, our Lord Jesus Christ, who, when we
were enemies, by reason of his very great love wherewith he has
loved us, merited justification for us by his own most holy passion on
the wood of the cross, and made satisfaction for us to God the Father."
The instrumental means are the sacrament of baptism, in water or at
least by desire; and the reality that constitutes the grace of divine
friendship is the righteousness, i.e., right orientation to our heavenly
destiny, that we have "as a gift from him and by which we are renewed in the spirit of our mind," since we take on the personality of

Christ to become by adoption what he was by nature, children of God and joint heirs with Christ of his kingdom.

The value of considering grace as a manifestation of God's love is manifold. We thereby recognize the depth of his charity, which is measured by the freedom and generosity of the benefits conferred which, in grace, are consummately free (with not the semblance of creature claim) and generous to the limit of God's bounty in receiving us into his own trinitarian family. We also appreciate what it cost the Son of God to make our supernatural life possible, that we were redeemed not with perishable things, with silver or gold, but with the precious blood of Christ. We see the selectiveness of God's love in calling us to the true faith and giving us the grace of justification as the pledge of our final glorification: "We know that by turning everything to their good God co-operates with all those who love him, with all those that he has called according to his purpose" (Rm. 8:28).

Looking upon grace as an expression of divine charity, we can redefine the providence of God as the constant, solicitous care he has in directing every moment and every detail of our lives to that final goal of union with himself in beatitude. Instead of considering grace as a sporadic assistance or even a static possession, we thus see it as a perpetual outpouring of divine benevolence, channeled through creatures and a dynamic power that God intends to have grow and mature under his providential hand.

Above all, if we identify grace with divine love, we place it in the stream of daily life, where it really belongs. In the last analysis, grace is an invitation; it is not coercive. Actual grace can be resisted, and habitual grace can be lost. They require a loving response on our part to become effective in one case and remain alive in the other. Co-operation with grace, therefore, is our answer to the prior love of God.

SUPERNATURAL LIFE

Since the order of grace is similar to that of nature, we should expect that just as naturally God exercises his goodness toward us in two different ways, by giving us the nature we have as human beings and co-operating with that nature through his providence, so supernaturally he acts in similar fashion: by giving us a supernature which places us into the divine family, and by helping our minds and wills acquire, retain, and grow in the supernatural life to which we have been raised.

The first form of grace was implied in the statement of St. Athanasius "God has not only made us out of nothing; but he gave us freely, by the grace of the Word, a life in correspondence with God"; the second was described by St. Ambrose, "every holy thought is the gift of God, the inspiration of God, the grace of God." In technical terms, the second form is called actual grace, as opposed to primary sanctifying grace, although the terminology is fluid and a variety of synonyms is used for both concepts. Our concern here is with the habitual, supernatural state of soul, as distinct from the transitory assistance received from God, comparable to the principle of rational life, which makes us human as distinguished from the passing divine influence that accompanies our every action.

The most fruitful analogy that revelation gives us for sanctifying grace and the state of righteousness is the concept of life, which the Greek authors of the New Testament regularly rendered by the word *zôê*, in preference to two other terms they might have used, *bios* and *psuche*.

Where English and Latin have only one word, "life" and *vita*, respectively, Greek has three; and the choice of one of these to describe the divine life we receive through grace must be significant. The true antithesis of *zôê* is *thanatos* (death), and means life taken intensively, as contrasted with *bios,* which refers to life extensively, or its duration, and with *psuche,* the breath that in animated beings is a sign of life.

The term *zôê* is used selectively and exclusively to designate the supernatural life that God communicates to us through Christ; indeed, he is our life and its author. Most often the combination *zôê aiônios* (eternal life) is found in the Gospels and St. Paul; yet the same *zôê* that we possess on earth will continue into eternity. This is the divine life that was in the Word from the beginning, "and that life was the light of men" (Col. 3:4; Ac. 3:15; Jn. 1:4). It was also the life that the persons of the Trinity have in common. "For the Father, who is the source of life, has made the Son the source of life" (Jn. 5:26). It is a participation in this life that those who believe in Christ have received.

Nature and Origins. In order to appreciate what our sharing in the divine life means, we should begin by inquiring what life itself is. As explained by St. Thomas, the higher a nature the more intimate what comes from it, for its inwardness of activity corresponds to its rank in being.[1] Inanimate bodies hold the lowest place of all, because nothing emanates from them except by the action of one thing on another.

Above inanimate bodies are plants, in which there is an issuing from within, since they can grow and reproduce themselves. They represent the first degree of life, for living things are those that set themselves into activity, whereas things that are in motion only inasmuch as they are acted upon from the outside are lifeless. This is the index of life in plants, that within them is a principle of motion.

Yet plant life is very imperfect, for though the emanation is from within at the beginning, that which comes forth gradually becomes wholly extraneous in the end. The blossoms change into fruit distinct from the boughs on which they grow, and presently these, when ripe, fall to the ground and become other plants. Scrutiny shows that the principle of this process is extrinsic to the plant.

Above plants there is a higher grade of being, namely that of sensitive things. Other than with plants, their process, though initiated from without, terminates within the animal; and the more perfect the animal, the more interior this result. A sensibly perceptible object impinges on the external senses; the impression goes into the imagination and then deeper into the store of memory. So that what began from the outside is thus worked up within, for the sensitive powers are conscious within themselves. Consequently the vital process in animals is superior to what it is in plants, because of its greater immanence. However, it is not wholly perfect, since the emanation is always from one thing to another.

Only in the mind do we reach the highest and perfect grade of life, where a person reflects on himself and understands himself. Yet there are various degrees of intelligence. At the lowest rung is the human intellect, which can know itself but must start from outside objects and cannot know these without accompanying sense images. Above the human level are angels, or pure spirits, whose mind does not proceed from outside things to know itself, but knows itself by itself, without prior dependence on phenomena outside.

Nevertheless, even angelic knowledge is not the highest form of life, for though the ideas that angels have are deeply immanent, they are not identical with the substance of their minds, since the being and understanding of spiritual creatures are not the same. The highest perfection of life is in God, where activity is not distinct from being, and where knowledge *is* the divine essence.

By his infinite goodness and in a way that eye has not seen nor ear heard, nor has it entered into the heart of man, God has made possible a participation in this divine life by his rational creatures, to be had in faith and hope on earth and through sight and possession in heaven.

Following the basic analogy of grace as a form of life, we find that like other types of life, it has a beginning. There is such a thing as being born into the supernatural life of grace. As our natural life comes to us through generation, so deiform life begins through the spiritual birth of baptism, according to the words of Christ, that unless a man be born again of water and the Holy Spirit, he cannot enter the kingdom of God.

However, baptism is only the normal sacramental agency for conferring the life of grace. It presupposes the profession of faith, personally in adults and vicariously in those responsible for the baptism of infants. This presses the analogy with natural life a stage farther, since no one comes to the Christian faith (except by a miracle) unless someone who already believed had first brought him the message of salvation; just as in the natural order, no one brings himself into the world but depends absolutely on the previous and loving co-operation of others, his parents in the flesh, to make his conception and eventual birth possible.

St. Paul had this law of communication in mind when he told the Romans, "by believing from the heart you are made righteous," i.e., unto supernatural life, which rests on belief in the Lord calling upon his name.

> But they will not ask his help unless they believe in him, and they will not believe in him unless they have heard of him, and they will not hear of him unless they get a preacher, and they will never have a preacher unless one is sent (Rm. 10:14–15).

The duty of communicating the supernatural life to those who do not yet have it rests not only on the successors of the apostles, the bishops and priests of the Church, but on all members of the Mystical Body. "As members of the living Christ," the Second

Vatican Council declared, "incorporated into him and made like to him through baptism, confirmation, and the Eucharist, all the faithful are duty bound to co-operate in the growth and increase of his body, so as to bring it, as soon as possible, to completed growth."[2]

Moreover, since this life of God is eminently vital, it requires proper nourishment, atmosphere, and exercise to remain alive and to grow. The indispensable means for this perseverance and development is grace, which Christ has promised to furnish us by the sacramental system, through prayer, and through the practice of virtue.

Law of Conflict and Struggle. The reason for this necessity of constant prayer is the inevitability of conflict that the supernatural life must face, not unlike the struggle for survival that is common to all living things, from the lowest among the animal species to the physical well-being of man.

There are few things on which Christ was more insistent than the universal visitation of trials to be experienced by those who follow him and live by his Spirit. The Beatitudes are a summary of the difficulties to be overcome by the faithful Christian. He spoke of persecution for the sake of justice; of being brought before the tribunals and put to death for belief in his name; of the inner struggle within men's hearts when they are torn between fidelity to him and to their relatives, friends, and all natural loves; of the need his disciples would have of patience under duress, in which alone they would "possess their souls"; his parable of the seed that fell amid thorns and briars was to stress the conflict with the world, the flesh, and the evil spirit.

Christianity is quite unique in recognizing the element of trial at the heart of man's religion, and that "it seems to have been determined in the designs of God that there would be no salvation for men without struggle and pain." The very redemption of the human race was conditioned on the Lord's becoming man and expiating sin to the last degree; and though Christ might have satisfied the divine justice in other ways, he chose to do so by enduring the worst kind of suffering climaxed in the sacrifice of his life.

> Therefore he has imposed it upon his followers as a law signed with his blood, that their life should be an endless strife with the vices of their age. What made the apostles unconquerable in their

mission of teaching truth to the world? What strengthened our countless martyrs in bearing witness by their blood to the Christian faith? Their more than readiness to obey fearlessly this law. All who have taken heed to live a Christian life and to seek after virtue have trodden the same path. We, too, must walk along this road if we desire to assure our own salvation or that of others.[3]

But man's powers alone are unequal to the responsibility of so many and varied contests. Consequently, "as we must ask God for our daily sustenance of the body, so we must pray to him for strength of soul that we may be sustained in virtue." Hence that universal condition and law of our supernatural life, which is a perpetual warfare; and the correlative indispensability of prayer.

Since the whole of life is a probation, the constancy of prayer for help is a revealed necessity. It ends only with death, which itself should be the special object of supplication, to persevere in God's friendship in spite of the assaults of fallen nature and the enemy of the human race.

Intensity and Variety. We saw that the biblical term for the life of grace communicated to souls is *zôê*, whose characteristic feature is life taken intensively. The principle of analogy with living things in nature allows us to speak of degrees of intensity and variety in the supernatural life, since no two people are equally vibrant with physical energy, and no two are perfectly alike. Even so, there are modes of supernatural vitality and varieties of form that the divine life may take in the soul.

The number of factors that determine the variations of sanctifying grace is myriad. According to the divine will, "everybody has his own particular gifts from God, one with a gift for one thing and another with a gift for the opposite" (1 Co. 7:7). It would be an impertinence to inquire why St. Paul did not have the grace of Peter, why Augustine was not Jerome, or Ignatius not a Francis of Assisi. The best we can say is that God is mysteriously glorified by this diversity, and his infinite perfections more manifest as we see them participated in so many different ways.

But if providence ultimately determines the degree and variety of spiritual vitality, our co-operation with graces offered is also a large determining factor. The supernatural life is capable of increase and depth, depending on the frequency and fervor with which the sacraments are received, on devotion to prayer and, in fact, on the

whole gamut of good works performed, which merit growth in sanctifying grace and advancement in the soul's nearness to God.

It was not a passing remark when the Council of Trent described
justification as a "renovation of the interior man through the *voluntary* reception of grace," since our free wills have much to do with
setting limits to divine generosity.[4] St. Francis de Sales observed that
in the measure to which we divest ourselves of self-love, so that
our heart does not refuse consent to the divine mercy, God "ever
pours forth and ceaselessly spreads his sacred inspirations, which
ever increase and make us increase more and more in heavenly
love." He then asks how it happens that we are not so advanced
in the love of God as some of the saints: "It is because God has not
given us the grace. But why has he not given us the grace? Because
we did not correspond with his inspirations as we should have. And
why did we not correspond? Because being free we have herein
abused our liberty."[5]

Living in grace, therefore, is a vital process from the divine side
and from ours: God is free to confer this life and in the degree that
pleases his unfathomable will, and we are free to receive what he
offers and as much as we choose according to our generosity.

Weakness, Death, and Resurrection.   The natural life of the body is
liable to sickness and debility arising from alien forces or weakness
from within. In similar fashion, the spiritual life of the soul may be
injured and debilitated through conflict with temptations and yield-
ing to what are called venial sins. Furthermore, as the physical body
may be not only ill or suffer injury, but cease to retain its principle of
life, so the soul can lose sanctifying grace through mortal sin and
supernaturally cease to live.

Catholic theology explains the difference between mortal and
venial sin in terms of a soul's proper orientation to its last end,
the triune God, by analogy wih the respective conditions in a human body.

> The degrees of disorder may be marked. One turns the whole or-
> der upside down; the other leaves the principles intact, but mud-
> dles the details and subordinate pattern. The balance of health may
> be so utterly wrecked that life is destroyed; or it may be upset so
> as to cause sickness, but not death. The final purpose of life is the
> key to the moral order. When our acts are so deranged that we
> turn away from our last end, namely God, to whom we should be

united by charity, then the sin is mortal. Short of that, the sin is venial.[6]

This means that a soul in grave sin is spiritually dead because it is no longer united with God, who gives it supernatural life, even as a body is dead on separation from its animating principle, which is the soul. While still on earth, this union with God is both a possession and a movement; we possess him by grace and in faith, and we are moving toward him in the beatific vision of glory. When a man sins mortally, he is dead twice over, once because he loses the gift of divine life he formerly had, and once again because he is no longer moving toward the consummation of that life in heaven.

Theology further compares the two types of sin in terms of their curability. "Bodily death is incurable by nature, but for sickness remedies may be found." The same thing holds true in the supernatural order. "Turn away from your last end, then of itself your sin is mortal and beyond repair, with everlasting penal effects. But venial sin can be repaired, and is undeserving of interminable punishment."[7]

This difference explains why grave sins are called mortal, and light sins venial. The former are not remissible through any power within the soul itself; much as the human body, once dead, cannot be brought back to life except by a special intervention of God. But venial faults are venial (from *venia,* pardon) precisely because the soul still has the vital principle that allows a cure from within, similar to the healing of a sick or diseased body whose source of animation (the soul) is still present to restore the ailing bodily function to health.

Both kinds of sin are detrimental, but in vastly different ways. Deliberate venial guilt is a disease that slackens the spiritual powers, lowers a man's resistance to evil, and causes him to deviate from the path that leads to glory. It places obstacles in the way of virtue and reduces fervor for the things of God. "Can this be of little consequence?" asked Teresa of Avila. Yet the person who sins venially, even through inveterate habit, is supernaturally alive. Not so the man estranged from God. He is spiritually dead, and in patristic literature the restoration is compared to the resuscitation of Lazarus. The exercise of almighty power in either case is the same. "Everyone who sins dies," said St. Augustine. Only the Lord, "by his great grace and great mercy raises souls to life again, that we may not die eternally."[8] It is only the frequency of this wonder that makes people forget the divine love and condescension it implies.

INDWELLING SPIRIT

Few doctrines of the Catholic faith are more personally satisfying than the mystery of divine inhabitation assured us by Christ at the Last Supper. "I shall ask the Father," he said, "and he will give you another advocate to be with you forever, the Spirit of truth whom the world can never receive, since it neither sees nor knows him; but you know him, because he is with you, he is in you" (Jn. 14:16). Then to clarify the trinitarian nature of this indwelling, he added, "If anyone love me, he will keep my word, and my Father will love him, and we shall come to him and make our home with him" (Jn. 14:23).

From the earliest Christian Tradition, the faithful reflected on the love that prompted God to give the souls in grace not only the created gift of supernatural life but the uncreated gift of himself. "We believe in the Holy Spirit," the Credo of Epiphanius read, "who dwells in the saints."[1] St. Augustine summarized the Church's Tradition at the beginning of the fifth century.

> Although God is everywhere wholly present, he does not dwell in everyone. It is not possible to say to all what the Apostle says, "Know you not that you are the temple of God and that the Spirit of God dwells in you?"
>
> He that is everywhere does not dwell in all, and he does not dwell equally in those in whom he does dwell. It is (moreover) remarkable how God dwells in some souls who do not yet know him and does not dwell in others who do. We say, then, that the Holy Spirit dwells in baptized children although they do not know it. They are unconscious of him although he is in them. He is said to dwell in such as these because he works in them secretly that they may be his temple, and he perfects his work in them as they advance in virtue and persevere in their progress.[2]

The Council of Trent made special reference to the indwelling Spirit in speaking of those who fall into mortal sin after having been justified. Their sin is more serious who, "after they have received the gift of the Holy Spirit, have not been afraid to destroy knowingly the temple of God and grieve the Holy Spirit."[3]

Mode of Presence. We begin with the established fact, universally taught by faith, that God is present in a special manner in the justified, other than in sinners, or unbelievers, or the unbaptized. The precise mode of this presence, called inhabitation, has not yet been determined. However, certain features must be verified.

> There is question here of a hidden mystery, which during this earthly exile can only be dimly seen through a veil, and which no human words can express. The divine persons are said to indwell inasmuch as they are present to beings endowed with intelligence in a way that lies beyond human comprehension, and in a unique and very intimate manner, which transcends all created nature, these creatures enter into relationship with them through knowledge and love.[4]

This is one area of the faith where the Church's saints are invaluable guides for explaining something of what this mystery means. They offer such insight as only those can give who have had some experience of the indwelling. Reflecting on their testimony, we can say that the real newness of the indwelling consists in God's presence as the object of a special knowledge and love.

Part of this intimate knowledge of God is an insight into divine truth, which the mind acquires quite without effort and with a clarity that no amount of natural reflection could provide.

What is most distinctive about the knowledge that some would identify with the indwelling is not only its intensity but its span of perception of divine objects, which are now accepted by faith and one day will be seen in vision. No mystical experience is needed to recognize the chasm that separates the believing from the unbelieving mind, the one having the Spirit of truth and the other operating on its own. Mysteries like the Incarnation and the Real Presence, the solidarity of the faithful in the Mystical Body and the Church's power of forgiving sins, doctrines like papal infallibility and the Catholic teaching on marriage and social morality are believed with a conviction that scandalizes those who do not have the light of the abiding Spirit.

This special knowledge is associated with a corresponding love for the things of God. Thus a serial analogy can be made, starting from the general sort of love we have for the "human race," on through the various persons who have more and more intimately entered our lives, until we come to the one person above all others whom we love the most. In comparable fashion, the soul in whom the Trinity dwells has the capacity for loving God in a way that as far exceeds the native power of the will as the supernatural is above nature. Once again, the mystics give us an insight into the extremes of this love, as in the famous passage where Teresa of Avila describes the rapture of having her heart pierced through with a long spear of gold. When the angel of the vision "drew it out, he seemed to draw out my very entrails also, and to leave me all in fire with a great love of God."[5]

As with knowledge, so with the love that comes from the Spirit of God, its experiential character is not limited to certain saints, whose raptures do not prove sanctity. This love is the common experience of all believers, graded from the lowest to the highest, depending on the measure of God's presence in their soul.

As might be expected, the supernatural union that results from the indwelling is also a possession of God. He gives himself personally so that he is not only in the soul but belongs to the soul. The soul possesses him as its property, since "by the gift of sanctifying grace the rational creature becomes capable of enjoying not only the created gift but even the divine person."[6] Our having God is really the same by grace as it will be in glory. In this life the enjoyment is through a mirror, darkly, but in heaven there will be no created medium between the soul and God.

Nevertheless, already by grace God's abiding union with the soul can effect supernatural happiness that faith tells us is a foretaste of final beatitude. "Whoever possesses God is happy," wrote St. Augustine.[7] In the *City of God* he expanded on the principle that underlies this concept of the indwelling as an inchoate beatific vision. There are two kinds of persons: those who seek their happiness in God, and those who look for it in themselves; the first have the Spirit of the Lord within, the second are dwelling alone. "If it is asked why the one are happy, the right answer is, because they cleave to God. If it be asked why the others are miserable, the right answer is, because they do not cleave to God. There is no possession that can make any rational or intellectual creature happy except God."[8]

Accordingly, in the measure that God, who alone can satisfy the heart of man, is present in the soul, and the soul responds to his presence, *true* happiness will result. For there are two kinds of happiness for mortal men: that which is carnal and earthly, and hangs on the changing circumstances of life, and that which is spiritually perfect, which depends on the possession of God.

Appropriation to the Holy Spirit. Although we normally speak of the third person of the Trinity inhabiting the souls of the just, there is a real problem if we take the expression literally. At the Last Supper, when Christ foretold the mystery, he affirmed that all three persons would come and make their abode in the faithful. Interpreted by Tradition, this means that "God the Trinity, Father, Son, and Holy Spirit come to us, as we come to them; they come to assist and we to obey; they to illuminate and we to behold; they to supply and we to receive that vision of them which is not external but deeply within; so that their dwelling in us should not be for time but for ever."[9]

Nevertheless, there is a special fitness if we appropriate the indwelling to the third person in preference to the others. To appropriate, in general, means to apply to one some action that is common to all. Of course, this is not to say that one of the persons is more active in producing a certain effect, since that would destroy their absolute equality of nature. It is simply a human way of saying that some effect outside of God bears a greater resemblance to an operation within God that pertains to one divine person rather than another. In this way goodness may fitly be ascribed to what is proper to the Holy Spirit, who proceeds from the Father because power, as such, is a kind of principle or source, and it is proper to the first person to be the principle of the whole divinity; and by the same token, whatever involves wisdom in creation can be referred to the Son because it is characteristic of him who proceeds from the Father as the Word of God by means of intellectual generation.

Since the manifestations of divine love in the world are comparable to the Holy Spirit who is the personal love, proceeding from the Father and Son, they are rightly attributed to him in the workings of grace consequent on the divine indwelling. Hence the statement of St. Paul, "the love of God has been poured forth into our hearts by the Holy Spirit, which has been given us" (Rm. 5:5).

Moreover, we may speak of the Holy Spirit as in the nature of a personal gift, since love carries the idea of a primary gift through which all other gifts are freely granted. "The Holy Spirit comes forth as the substance of love, and Gift is his name."[10] Among the blessings of divine generosity, none ranks higher than the personal dwelling of the Trinity in the just, which the Church therefore attributes to the Holy Spirit, whom we invoke as "the Giver of gifts" and "the Gift of God most high."

ACTUAL GRACES

Our dependence on God and his supernatural communication affect every aspect of our being. Through sanctifying grace we are given a new life that raises us to the divine family and makes us partakers in the very nature of God. This corresponds to the vital principle in the physical order and enables us to perform actions that are meritorious of heaven. But just as naturally speaking we receive from God both our nature and the constant influx of his divine power, so supernaturally he gives his elect not only the wellspring of deiform vitality but also the special assistance we need to guide the mind and inspire the will in our pathway to glory. Another name for this transitory light and inspiration is actual grace.

The precise term "actual grace" is relatively new, and seems to have been used for the first time, in its technical sense, by the Dominican theologian John Capreolus (1380–1444), whose stout defense of St. Thomas did much to establish Aquinas' reputation in Catholic thought.

If the specific name was a medieval innovation, the concept of actual grace is rooted firmly in the Scriptures. Already in the Psalms we find the recurring theme of God's providential care in giving his light and strength to those who ask him, and of man's corresponding need to pray for this help at the risk of falling prey to man's enemies. "Enlighten my eyes, for I fear to fall asleep in death," the Psalmist begs. "Explain to me how to respect your Law and how to observe it wholeheartedly" (Ps. 119:34).

The evangelist St. John, with his preference for the symbolism of light, tells of how God comes to illumine every man born into this world, and quotes the words of Christ about the divine call to the mind that must precede any following of the Master. " 'No one can come to me unless he is drawn by the Father who sent me' " (Jn. 6:44), so that everyone who has listened to the Father, and has learned, comes to him. And in the same strain, the author of the Acts describes the conversion of Lydia, the seller of purple, who worshiped God and as she listened to the preaching, "the Lord opened her heart to accept what Paul was saying" (Ac. 16:14).

St. John again, in the Apocalypse, pictorially speaks of divine grace operating on the will. Christ orders him in a vision to write to the lukewarm bishop of Laodicea, "I *am* the one who reproves and disciplines all those he loves: so repent in real earnest. Look, I am standing at the door, knocking. If one of you hears me calling and opens the door, I will come in to share his meal, side by side with him" (Rv. 3:19–20). The Corinthians are reminded to the same effect that "I did the planting, Apollos did the watering, but God makes things grow" (1 Co. 3:6). Paul and Apollos are only the external instruments of the Word, who preach the Gospel, but unless the Lord co-operates within by his grace, all their ministrations are in vain.

There was no serious disagreement over this concept of specialized assistance from God until the time of Pelagius. He and his followers changed the meaning of actual grace by their position on the native capacities of man. Having denied his real elevation to the super-natural order, they reduced whatever help he obtains to mere external assistance. They admitted that we may benefit from the life and works of Christ, but not so as to receive internal grace super-naturally infused into our souls. "There was a help to keep the law and doctrine," wrote Pelagius, "already in the time of the prophets. But the help of grace, which is grace properly so called, comes to us from the example of Christ." Its function is "to show us the way we must walk, although we possess in our own free wills the power not to stray from the right path and therefore do not really need any aid outside of ourselves."[1] At most this auxiliary grace was to make the practice of virtue easier; it was not strictly necessary.

In the writings of St. Augustine we have the first detailed exposition of the nature of actual grace. "It is God," he quoted St. Paul, "who of his good pleasure works in you both the will and the performance. Wherein the apostle clearly shows that even our good will is performed in us by the operation of God. Indeed, unless the will have something occur to it by which it is attracted and invited, it can never be moved; this occurrence is not in the power of man" but only of God.[2]

The same limitation applies to the mind. "Let us understand this if we can, that sometimes God so deals even with his holy ones as not to give them either the assured knowledge or the conquering delight for performing a certain good work, to make them realize that they receive what light they need to illumine their darkness not of themselves but from him, and that he is the one who bestows the serenity that causes the earth of their souls to bear fruit. When we plead with him to grant us help to practice and perfect our justice, what else are we asking but to have opened what is closed, and to make pleasant what is not to our taste?"[3]

Church councils further clarified and stamped with authority the teachings of Augustine, Jerome, Prosper, and others who defended the existence and necessity of actual grace. At the Council of Carthage, it was decreed that "knowledge of what we ought to do and love for doing it are both gifts of God."[4] In the catalogue of papal pronouncements, published shortly after the death of Augustine, every kind of naturalism is condemned, since "God so works in the hearts of men and in free will itself that the holy thought, the gentle counsel, and every movement of a good will is from God, because it is through him that we can do any good, and without him we can do nothing."[5]

Still more explicitly, the Council of Orange declared how helpless man is to do anything on the road to salvation without the prior assistance of God, "without the illumination and inspiration of the Holy Spirit."[6] This terminology has since become technical to define actual grace as the internal enlightening of mind and inspiration of will that God supernaturally infuses in the respective faculties.

During the whole patristic period and into the Middle Ages, there was no particular effort to distinguish actual from habitual grace, although the early councils were clear enough about the existence of the two kinds of benefits to the soul. With the advent of Scholasticism, however, the familiar categories of habit and action were impressed into the service of theology, with the result that by the time of St. Thomas the difference between a "habitual gift" and "the divine help for willing and doing well" was fully established.[7] Others then added the terms "habitual" and "actual," which are current today.

Consistent with their ideas of justification, the sixteenth-century Reformers paid little attention to what Catholics called actual grace, since they questioned the existence of a supernatural order that implied an elevation of man above his natural power of being and operation. They allowed for neither habitual nor actual grace, in the

Catholic sense. Sanctifying grace for them meant the merciful favor of God, who imputes (without conferring) the holiness of Christ to the justified. Actual grace would mean a kind of direct assistance that affects the soul, in the absence of true human freedom, and moves it to perform good actions for which God alone is fully responsible.

Since the principal kind of actual grace denied by the Reformers was that which precedes man's justification, the Council of Trent stressed its absolute need and utility. The justification of adults must begin with God's call, by which "God touches the heart of man with the illumination of the Holy Spirit; if a man receives that inspiration, he can also reject it."[8] The same kind of assistance is available after a person has sinned gravely and finds himself urged to repent from salutary fear. This is a "gift of God and an inspiration of the Holy Spirit, not, indeed, as already dwelling in the soul, but as merely giving the impulse that helps the penitent make his way toward justice."[9]

In Catholic circles, the most debated issue about actual grace has been the domestic one of its relation to human conduct, and especially to the free co-operation by man. The long and sometimes acrimonious controversies were partly stimulated by the earlier conflict with Jansenism. If they contributed somewhat to clarifying the meaning of actual grace, they had the practical effect of obscuring the importance of habitual righteousness and the sublimity of the indwelling Trinity. A new impulse to study the implications of God's transitory operation on the faculties has come from the modern interest in applied psychology, notably in the area of motivation and the development (or conquest) of moral habits.

More promising of lasting benefit to the Christian world has been a dramatic rediscovery in our day that more is needed to save human society than ethical principles and activity. Unless God enters history, here and now, to enable man to cope with the demonic forces unleashed in the present generation, they are sure to prevail, and it is quite correct to predict an early post-Christian age.

The term coined to express the new approach is "grace as empowerment to live the moral life." It assumes that we can recognize an obligation without being able to fulfill it. It further assumes that our actual moral experience is to discover a power beyond the self that enables us to make a right moral response.

Such a view of grace as power and not merely mercy has important implications for the ecumenical movement, as Christians of every persuasion challenge the popular theory that we cannot be expected to do what we cannot of ourselves perform. Faith tells believers that God will not, indeed, command the impossible, but the "impossible" is not limited to our own native powers. He offers everyone who asks him the grace to fulfill what he expects of us, not only in the periodic trials of life but constantly in all the circumstances of our pilgrimage back to the Father who made us.

INFUSED VIRTUES AND GIFTS

We commonly speak of "natural goodness" that some people seem to have as part of their native temperament. Yet we know that this is only a figure of speech because so-called natural virtue is not born of nature but comes as a gift of God, who endows some people with qualities of mind and heart that others, after a lifetime of effort, never acquire.

But there is nothing rhetorical in the Catholic belief that part of the divine life we obtain in sanctifying grace is the possession of certain enduring powers, the infused virtues and gifts. Nowhere else does the true character of the supernatural appear more evident than in the endowments of infused virtue.

The soul is what makes a person a human being, and places him into the natural order; sanctifying grace, by analogy, is that quality of the soul which gives a person all that is properly divine and puts him habitually into the family of God. Comparing the two with each other, the soul is the foundation of natural life, as sanctifying grace is the basis of supernatural life.

Yet we know that the soul is not all we have in the body; that the soul itself has various powers through which it operates and by which it gives expression to its rational nature. Even so, by a divine consistency, the "soul of the soul," as sanctifying grace has been called, must have channels for the new life that God pours into the just. These are the virtues, theological and moral, according to their respective purposes; not unlike the native abilities through which mind and will come into contact with the visible world around us, and the world, in turn, comes into contact with us.

Among the infused virtues, however, some are concerned directly with God and operate in a field in which the unaided nature cannot work; they are called theological. Others have as their object not God himself, the final end of all things, but human activities that are subordinate to the final end; they are called moral and, because four of them (prudence, fortitude, temperance, and justice) are primary, are said to be cardinal (Latin *cardo,* hinge) in human conduct.

Moreover, the powers of nature are possessed of certain instincts or impulses, which are natural propensities that incite animals (including man) to the actions essential to their existence, preservation, and development. In like manner, the powers of supernature are endowed with spiritual instincts or gifts by which the Holy Spirit directs souls to follow his inspirations easily and more securely toward the attainment of their heavenly goal.

THEOLOGICAL VIRTUES

Etymologically "virtue" seems to be derived from the same root as the Latin *vis* (power), suggesting that in its primitive sense, virtue implied the possession of such qualities as strength and courage and, in the moral order, of goodness and human perfection.

The Scriptures have several equivalents for the English "virtue," notably, *ischus* (strength or power), *dunamis* (might), and *arethê* (moral excellence or perfection). In the Hebrew Old Testament there is no specific word for virtue, but in the Septuagint *arethê* is used in the books written originally in Greek to mean moral goodness or a particular moral quality.[1] In the New Testament the Greek word for virtue is used only five times: twice to describe the powers of God, twice meaning moral vigor, and only once for moral virtue in particular.[2]

But if the specific term was used only seldom in the New Testament, the concept of a divinely infused power that God confers on the elect appears throughout the letters of St. Paul and in the two epistles of Peter.

The theological virtues are identified as unique possessions conferred specially on the soul by God. "In short, there are three things that last: faith, hope, and love [charity]," St. Paul wrote to the Corinthians, "and the greatest of these is love" (1 Co. 13:13). In

the introduction to his first letter to the Thessalonians, he told them
he was mindful "before God our Father how you have shown your
faith in action, worked for love [charity] and persevered through
hope, in our Lord Jesus Christ" (1 Th. 1:3).

These are not passing favors but permanent endowments, since
those who possess them are urged to "put on faith and love for a
breastplate, and the hope of *salvation* for a *helmet"* (1 Th. 5:8).
The faithful are to use them as their constant weapons in the battle
against evil, and their protection against the wiles of Satan. They are
said to abide, in the manner of enduring principles of action; and
among them, love—charity—never fails, because it continues into
eternity.

Not everyone receives these gifts, but only those who are the
friends of God. "So far then we have seen that, through our Lord
Jesus Christ, by faith we are judged righteous and at peace with
God, since it is by faith and through Jesus that we have entered
this state of grace in which we can boast about looking forward to
God's glory." In spite of tribulations, "hope is not deceptive, because
the love of God has been poured into our hearts by the Holy Spirit"
(Rm. 5:1–6). Faith, hope, and charity, therefore, proceed from the
state of grace, which they manifest and through which the divine life
is made to grow.

In the patristic period, the theological virtues were the object of
frequent writing and, in Pelagian times, of controversy. The commentaries of the Fathers on St. Paul offer a complete treatise on
the subject; and St. Augustine's *Manual of the Christian Religion*
was always referred to by him as "a book on Faith, Hope, and
Charity." For Augustine, therefore, a summary of these virtues was
an epitome of the essentials of Christianity.

Catholic theology defines "virtue" as "a good habit bearing on
activity," or a good faculty-habit. Basic to the concept of virtue,
then, is the element of habit, which stands in a special relation to the
soul, whether in the natural order or elevated to the divine.

The soul is the ultimate source of all our activities; faculties are
the proximate sources built into the soul by nature; habits are still
more immediate sources superadded to the faculties either by personal endeavor or by a supernatural infusion from God.

Habits reside in the faculties as stable dispositions or "hard to
eradicate" qualities that dispose the faculties to act in a certain way,
depending on the type of habit. If the habit is acquired, it gives the

faculty power to act with ease and facility; if it is infused, it procures not readiness in supernatural activity, but the very activity itself. Natural or acquired habits result from repeated acts of some one kind; they give not the power to act, but the power to act readily and with dexterity. Thus in the natural order, the faculty without the habit is simple power to act; the faculty with the habit is power to act with perfection. Since custom is parent to habit, it is called second nature. Faculty is like first nature, and habit the second.

Not every habit is a virtue, but only one that so improves and perfects a faculty as to incline it toward good—good for the faculty, for the will, and for the whole man in terms of his ultimate destiny.

There is a broad sense in which we can speak of the natural dispositions of any of our powers as innate virtues, but this is a loose rendering and leads to confusion. More properly, the infused virtues should be contrasted with the acquired, in which the will of the individual plays the dominant role. My consistent effort to concentrate on a given course of action, repeating the process over a long period of time and in spite of obstacles, gradually develops a tendency to perform the action spontaneously and almost without reflection, yet with a degree of perfection that someone else without the virtue cannot duplicate.

The infused virtues are independent of this process. They are directly produced by God in the faculties of man, and differ mainly from the acquired because they do not assume the human effort that determines the faculty to a particular kind of activity, namely, facility induced by repetition. God himself pours in (*infundere*) the infused virtues, not by compulsion or overriding the free will, but without dependence on us, which, Augustine says, "are produced in us by God without our assistance." They are supernatural gifts, freely conferred through the merits of Christ, and raise the activity of those who possess them to the divine level in the same way that sanctifying grace elevates their nature to a share in the life of God.

Theological virtues supply for the mind and will what neither faculty has of itself: the salutary knowledge, desire, and love of God and his will, without which there could be no supernatural *order,* which means the voluntary choice of suitable means to reach the heavenly goal to which we were elevated. These virtues make us well adjusted to our last end, which is God himself; hence they are called theological, because they not only go out to God—as all virtue worthy of the name must do—but they also reach him. To be well adjusted to our destiny we must know and desire it; the desire demands that we be in love with the object to which we are tending and are confident of obtaining it. Faith makes us know the God to whom we are going, hope makes us look forward to joining him, and charity makes us love him.

Unlike the virtues known to philosophy, faith, hope, and charity are not applications of the golden mean between extremes. In Aristotle's language, a moral virtue is a certain habit of the faculty of choice, consisting of a mean (*mesotes*) suitable to our nature and fixed by reason in the manner which a prudent man would fix it. It is a habit that stands midway between excess and defect. Courage, for example, keeps the balance between cowardice and reckless daring; sincerity, between ironical depreciation and boastfulness; modesty, between shamelessness and bashfulness; and just resentment, between callousness and spitefulness.

But a theological virtue can be measured either by what the virtue demands or by what our capacity allows. Concerning the first, "God himself is the rule and mode of virtue. Our faith is measured by divine truth, our hope by the greatness of his power and faithful affection, our charity by his goodness. His truth, power, and goodness outreach any measure of reason. We can certainly never believe, trust, or love God more than, or even as much as, we should. Extravagance is impossible. Here is no virtuous moderation, no reasonable mean; the more extreme our activity, the better we are."[3]

Nevertheless, there is a valid sense in which even the theological virtues observe a kind of mean, or better a center of gravity to which they tend. As far as God is concerned, he can never be believed in, trusted, or loved too much. But from our viewpoint, we should exercise these virtues according to the measure of our condition. Christian faith goes midway between heretical extremes, for instance between Pelagianism, which dispenses with divine grace, and Jansenism, which denies a free will; Christian hope must choose a path among the numerous prospective means of salvation; and Christian charity must find a balance in the myriad opportunities for loving God.

MORAL VIRTUES

Besides the theological virtues of faith, hope, and charity, a person in sanctifying grace receives an infusion of the moral virtues. Most

Catholic theologians explain both sets of infused virtues as supernatural counterparts of the virtuous habits we can possess naturally. The infused theological virtues, then, correspond to our natural knowledge, trust and love of God. The infused moral virtues are divinely conferred habits that supplement and elevate our naturally acquired prudence, temperance, fortitude, and justice.

In order to understand what the infused moral virtues are, it is useful to see what they mean naturally, since the infusion of these powers does not radically change their natural character but sublimates and raises their capacity to a higher than natural end.

The four cardinal virtues can be considered either the main characteristics of every virtue or special types of virtue. In the patristic tradition, especially of St. Augustine, they are treated as elements of every true virtue: all directing knowledge is prudence, all balanced fairness is justice, all firmness of soul in misfortune is fortitude, and all moderation in the use of earthly values is temperance. Accordingly, no prudence is genuine unless just, courageous, and temperate; no temperance is perfect unless strong, just, and prudent; no courage is complete unless prudent, temperate, and just; and no justice is true unless prudent, strong, and temperate. That there should be four cardinal virtues is a matter of stress, and not, as medieval Scholastics held, because they are specifically different habits dealing with diverse types of objects.

More commonly, however, they are treated as special virtues, each occupied with its own proper type of situation, without denying that they overlap, or that one flows into the other. Thus fortitude is temperate and brave, for a man who can contain his lusts can well control himself in danger of death; and if he can face death unflinchingly, he can also withstand allurements.

Just as there are four faculties that contribute to our moral acts—intellect, will, appetite of desire, and appetite of aversion—so there must be four virtues to keep these faculties straight: prudence for the mind, justice for the will, temperance for the urge to what is pleasant, and fortitude for the instinct away from what is painful. The Latins summarized their function in the words *circumspice* (look around), *age* (act), *abstine* (keep away from), and *sustine* (bear up with).

The existence of supernatural equivalents for the natural moral virtues follows logically on all that the Scriptures say about man's condition in the state of sanctifying grace. The justified are enabled to perform actions beyond the capacity of their native powers because of the new dispositions they received from the indwelling Spirit. These dispositions in the moral order are the infused virtues, directing the justified to a supernatural destiny in the beatific vision.

More than once, St. Paul spoke of various types of these virtues as the special possession of those in the friendship of God. "I implore you therefore to lead a life worthy of your vocation," he told the Ephesians. "Bear with one another charitably, in complete selflessness, gentleness, and patience. Do all you can to preserve the unity of the Spirit by the peace that binds you together" (Ep. 4:1–3). Timothy was reminded, "God's gift was not a spirit of timidity, but the spirit of power, and love, and self-control" (2 Tm. 1:7). In a long exhortation to the Romans, the converts were urged to practice zeal and fervor, patience and perseverance, hospitality and condescension, peaceableness and justice.

The Church's Tradition reflects the same idea, that the souls of the just are graced with infused moral powers beyond the reach of acquired virtue. Early in the thirteenth century, Innocent III censured the Albigensian speculators for saying that "faith or charity or the other virtues are not infused in children since children do not give their consent."[4] At the Council of Trent, the justified were said to advance from virtue to virtue by mortifying the members of their flesh, showing them as weapons of justice unto sanctification by observing the precepts of God and the Church.

In his letter on true and false Americanism, Leo XIII singled out the infused moral virtues as specially potent in the spiritual life because they imply the operations of divine grace. He took issue with those who underrated these supernatural powers. "It is hard to understand," he said, "how those who are imbued with Christian principles can place the natural ahead of the supernatural virtues, and attribute to them greater power and fecundity." At most the latter lead to human perfection, but only the former direct us to God. "For as the nature of man, because of our common misfortune, fell into vice and dishonor, yet by the assistance of grace is lifted up and borne onward with new honor and strength; so also the virtues which are exercised not by the unaided powers of nature, but by the help of the same grace, are made productive of supernatural beatitude."[5]

Here, if anywhere, the familiar dictum that "grace does not destroy but builds upon nature" is eminently true. All that we say about these virtues as naturally acquired qualities holds good for the infused, but much more. With reason enlightened by faith, the scope of virtuous operation is extended to immeasurably wider horizons. Faith furnishes motives of which reason would never dream, and theological charity offers inspiration that surpasses anything found in nature.

GIFTS OF THE HOLY SPIRIT

Along with the infused theological and moral virtues, sanctifying grace also includes the gifts of the Holy Spirit, which were anticipated in the prophetic text of Isaiah. "A shoot springs from the stock of Jesse, a scion thrusts from his roots: on him the spirit of Yahweh rests, a spirit of wisdom and insight . . . of counsel and power . . . of knowledge and of the fear of Yahweh" (Is. 11:1–2).

The gifts, although directly attributed to the Messiah, are implicitly the common possession of all Christians in God's friendship, since Christ received them as the Second Adam to be dispensed to all who come under his influence and receive from the fullness of his grace.

A parallel text familiar to the Fathers was the passage that "Everyone moved by the Spirit is a son of God" (Rm. 8:14). They argued that for the sons of God to act supernaturally, they must be directed by a higher than natural disposition that operates on a level commensurate with their divine dignity. This disposition is assured permanence by the infused gifts of the Holy Spirit, who disposes the souls of the just to be moved according to his will.

If we would define the exact difference between the virtues and gifts, it lies in the need for having a supernatural counterpart for the natural instincts of mind and will. Even the infused virtues are not enough. They do not, by themselves, so perfect a man on the road to heaven that he has no further need of being moved by the yet higher promptings of the Holy Spirit. For whether we consider human reason and will in their natural powers alone, or as elevated by the theological virtues, they are still very fallible and require help: wisdom against folly, understanding against dullness, counsel against rashness, fortitude against fears, knowledge against ignorance, piety against hardness of heart, and fear of God against pride. The gifts of the Holy Spirit supply this help by giving us remedies against these defects and making us amenable to the promptings of his grace.

It follows, then, that the gifts, no less than the virtues, are necessary for salvation, at least to meet those critical situations when the mind and will, though elevated by ordinary grace, cannot cope with the problem or difficulty but require assistance, which is ready at hand in the gifts. Moreover, according to the present economy of salvation, the special help we need to persevere in God's friendship includes immediate illuminations and impulses from the Holy Spirit. The infused gifts further furnish us with the readiness to answer these divine invitations and thereby save our souls.

The function of the gifts cannot be understood without reflecting that God acts upon the soul in two different ways. In one case he accommodates himself to the human mode of action. He gives light to see the best means available to perform a good work and strength of will to carry it out; yet we are left to take the initiative on the basis of reason enlightened by faith. We are thus acting, through the virtues, under the impulse of grace.

At other times, however, God takes the initiative himself, before we have a chance to reflect on a course of action, by sending illuminations and inspirations that call for immediate response. His movements affect us, as it were from the outside, although deep in the soul and never without our consent. Hence the call for a supernatural responsiveness to these visitations; where the habitual disposition to react favorably and easily is one of the gifts of the Holy Spirit. They are in the nature of supernatural reflexes, or reactive instincts, that spontaneously answer to the divine impulses almost without reflection but always with full consent.

Wisdom, the first of the gifts, is also the highest in dignity, since it makes the soul responsive to the Holy Spirit in the contemplation of divine things and in the use, so to speak, of God's ideas for evaluating every contingency in the secular and spiritual order. Often the word is used to describe a fullness of knowledge possessed by a man through study and acuteness of mind; but this is far removed from the gift, which implies fullness of knowledge, derived from an affinity to divine things, as when a person learns to know the passion of Christ through suffering or the joys of virtue by personal experience.

Where faith is a simple knowledge of the articles of belief that Christianity proposes, wisdom goes on to a certain divine contemplation of the truths that the articles contain, that faith accepts without further development. Built into wisdom is the element of love, which inspires contemplative reflection on these dogmas of belief, rejoices in dwelling upon them, and directs the mind to judge all things according to their principles.

The gift of understanding is a supernatural enlightenment given to the mind for grasping revealed truths easily and profoundly. It differs from faith because it gives insight into the meaning of what a person believes, whereas faith, as such, merely assents to what God has revealed.

Ascetical writers since Augustine have said that understanding characterizes the clean of heart, following the teaching of Christ, "Happy the pure in heart: They shall see God" (Mt. 5:8). This Beatitude, they explain, contains two clauses: One refers to merit, namely, cleanness of heart; the other to reward, namely, seeing God. Both in a sense correspond to the gift of understanding.[6]

Sometimes called "the science of the saints," the gift of knowledge enables us, through some form of relish and warmth of charity, to judge everything from a supernatural viewpoint by means of lesser causes. Closely tied in with this gift is the lesson of past experience, after a person has learned the emptiness of things created and the hollowness of sin.

Thus the function of knowledge is to help us pass judgment on creatures, which can be the occasion for our turning away from God. Sorrow for past mistakes answers to the gift of knowledge; then comes consolation when creatures are accepted as God would have us do. So that knowledge corresponds to the third Beatitude, "Happy those who mourn: They shall be comforted" (Mt. 5:5). Mourning is by way of merit, comfort by way of reward. In the measure that a person knows the vanity of this world, his comfort begins already now and is destined to reach fruition in heaven, when all things on earth will pass away.

Counsel is a special gift that assists the mind and perfects the virtue of prudence by enlightening a man on how to decide and command individual supernatural acts. It refers primarily to prudent conduct in one's own case, and only secondly in favor of others. Its proper object is the right ordering of particular actions, after the gifts of knowledge and understanding furnish the general principles. Enlightened by the Spirit, a person learns what to do in a specific case and what advice to give when consulted or command to make if he is in authority.

Implicit in this gift is the native inability of reason, left to itself, to grasp all the facets of a concrete situation and see at a glance all the circumstances. It needs the help of God, who comprehends all things and who acts in the capacity of counselor to the humble soul, just as in human affairs we consult others who have more experience or knowledge than we. Speaking of this interior guide, St. Augustine says that, in the last analysis, it is not external teachers who instruct us, "but Truth that presides within, over the mind itself; though it may have been words that prompted us to make such consultation. The One consulted, who dwells in the inner man, he it is who teaches, Christ, the unchangeable Power of God and everlasting Wisdom. No doubt every rational soul consults this Wisdom, but to each one only so much is shown as he is able to receive because of his own good or bad will."[7]

Hence the importance of nearness to God and personal holiness in those whose position requires them to direct other people. The interior Counselor will advise them on how to advise others in virtue of their office, but the greater their sanctity, the more claim they have on this divine consultation. Patristic tradition further associates counsel with the Beatitude "Happy the merciful: They shall have mercy shown them" (Mt. 5:7). The reason is that among the virtues that counselors need, none stands higher than mercy, which knows how to be compassionate and forbearing under provocation, and communicates this spirit to those who come for advice. "The only remedy for great evils, the only way of plucking them out is to forgive and to give."[8] When persons come for help, no matter what their problems may be, two things they always need and that the counselor should offer by word and example are forgiveness of injuries (real or imagined) and great generosity, both covered by the concept of mercy.

Piety as a gift of the Holy Spirit aids and supplements the virtue of justice by disposing us to show reverence for God as a most loving Father and for men as the sons of God. We respect and serve our parents through the virtue of piety, which is therefore analogous to the gift that prompts us to offer worship and service to the divine Parent of our souls in the natural and supernatural order.

Consistent with the same analogy, as the virtue of piety urges us to serve everyone related to us by the bonds of blood, the gift makes us ready not only to worship God but also to honor his children. "The saints are honored, misery is relieved, the Holy Scriptures are not contradicted, whether they be understood or not."[9] In a word, whatever is connected with God as the Author of nature and of grace comes within the scope of piety.

The characteristic feature of this gift is a filial attitude toward God and a fraternal attitude toward our neighbor, which it engenders in the soul, with special reference to our spiritual regeneration and incorporation in the Mystical Body of Christ. It makes us look upon God not only as Lord and Master but as the Originator of our being, naturally by creation and supernaturally by grace; and upon our fellow men not as competitors in the struggle of life but co-equals under God as our common Maker and brothers in Christ through the saving merits of his passion.

Fortitude as a gift goes beyond fortitude as a virtue by carrying to a successful conclusion even the most difficult tasks in the service of God. "This is beyond human power, for sometimes we are not strong enough to win through and override all evils and perils, which press us down to death. The Holy Spirit leads us to eternal life, which is the final achievement of all we do, the escaping from all ills and dangers."[10]

Two forms of courage are implied in the gift of fortitude: to undertake arduous tasks and to endure long and trying difficulties for the divine glory. The two are quite distinct. There is a type of courage that anticipates grave obstacles while entering on a course of action, a state of life, or a new venture in the spiritual life or the apostolate, but the obstacles are faced with a quiet trust in providence that inspires willingness to suffer in the prosecution of the plan. Fortitude of this kind is characterized by a dauntless spirit of resolution, firmness of mind, and an indomitable will.

Another form of courage does not pioneer in God's service but finds itself tried by unexpected trials, sickness, persecution, and external failure. Nevertheless, it perseveres in the practice of virtue and unflinchingly carries on in spite of oppressive odds.

Both types of courage are necessary for salvation, at least to the extent that perseverance in grace over a long period of time will call upon the deepest resources of courage. Not the least strength a man needs is to live up to his ideals in spite of the criticism and, perhaps, opposition he meets from those who should encourage him in the struggle for perfection. "When any Christian has begun to live well, to be fervent in good works, and to despise the world; in this newness of his life he is exposed to the condemnations and contradictions of cold Christians. But if he perseveres, and gets the better of them by his endurance, and faints not in good works, those very same persons who before hindered will now respect him."[11] His strength of character, born of the Spirit, will become a grace of attraction for others to follow his example.

The seventh of the gifts, and yet first in the rising scale of value, is the fear of the Lord, which confirms the virtue of hope and impels a man to a profound respect for the majesty of God. Its correlative effects are protection from sin through dread of offending the Lord, and a strong confidence in the power of his help.

Unlike wordly or servile fear, the gift of fear is filial because based on the selfless love of God, whom it dreads to offend. In servile fear, the evil dreaded is punishment; in filial, it is the fear of offending God. Both kinds may proceed from the love of God, but filial fear is par excellence inspired by perfect charity and, in that sense, inseparable from divine love. When I dread the loss of heaven and the pains of hell, my fear, though servile, is basically motivated by the love of God, whom I am afraid of losing by my sins, since heaven is the possession of God, and hell is the loss of him for eternity. To that extent, even servile fear cannot be separated from supernatural charity. On a higher plane, however, when the object of my fear is not personal loss, though it be heaven, but injury to the divine majesty, then the motive is not only an implicit love of God, but also love to a sublime degree. And this is the scope of the infused gift of the fear of the Lord.

Consequently, the gift of fear gives us the power to sublimate all lesser fears, including the salutary and much-needed dread of God's justice. In the measure that this gift becomes active through generous co-operation, a person comes closer to realizing the ideal of the Christian life, that charity casts out fear. His love of God becomes so intense that gradually the dominant disposition is to fear losing the least spark of God's friendship; and as he grows in charity, the dread of God's punishments flows into a calm assurance of ultimate salvation, and even a strong desire, like St. Paul's, to be dissolved and to be with Christ.

VII. THE CHURCH

There is a true sense in which we can say that the Church began with the birth of human society. Even if these beginnings were only anticipations of what the Church was eventually to become, they were nevertheless important. They stem from the fact that, in the designs of providence, "it has not been God's resolve to sanctify and save men individually with no regard for their mutual relationship. Rather he wants to establish them as a people who would give him recognition in truth and service in holiness."[1] The Church, therefore, corresponds on the level of grace to our social existence on the level of nature.

Whatever may be said about the foreshadowing of the Church before the call of Abraham, the covenant that God made with the patriarch marked the origin of that Chosen People to whom the Church of Christ would always refer as its spiritual ancestor. Yahweh chose Israel as his very own, on whom he promised to lavish extraordinary blessings provided they remained faithful to him. Step by step, he taught and prepared the children of Abraham by sending them prophets to reveal himself and the decrees of his will, in order to make them holy.

FORMATION OF THE CHURCH

Then came the Incarnation, and with it the shadow gave way to substance. "At various times in the past and in different ways," we are told, "God spoke to our ancestors through the prophets; but in our own time, the last days, he has spoken to us through his Son, the Son that he has appointed to inherit everything and through whom he made everything there is" (Heb. 1:1–2).

With the advent of Christ, we can distinguish three stages in the actual establishment of the Church: The Redeemer "began building the mystical temple of the Church when by his preaching he made known his precepts; he completed it when he hung glorified on the cross; and he manifested and proclaimed it when he sent the Holy Spirit as Paraclete in visible form on his disciples."[2] Preaching, suffering, and promulgation would aptly summarize the three stages.

Faithful to the mission he had received from the Father, he chose twelve apostles and sent them, as he had been sent, to teach and to govern, to serve and to sanctify the assembly of believers. He appointed their head and his vicar on earth. He made known to them all things whatsoever he had heard from the Father. He also determined that through baptism those who would believe would be incorporated in the body of the Church and, when he came to the close of his life, he instituted at the Last Supper the wonderful sacrifice and sacrament of the Eucharist.

It is the unanimous teaching of the ancient Fathers that the Church was born from the side of the Savior on the cross like a new Eve, mother of all the living. As we look behind the imagery, we see what this means. By Christ's death the New Testament replaced the Old Law, which had been abolished. The Law of Christ, with its mysteries, enactments, institutions, and sacred rites, was thereby ratified for the whole world in the blood of the Redeemer. It was no coincidence, according to Leo the Great, that the veil of the temple was torn at the moment Christ died. "To such an extent," he explained, "was there effected a transfer from the Law to the Gospel, from the Synagogue to the Church, from many sacrifices to one Victim, that, as our Lord expired, the mystical veil which shut off the innermost part of the temple and its sacred secret was rent violently from top to bottom."[3]

If we probe still deeper, we learn that by his death on the cross, Christ merited human salvation, he made it possible for those before and since to receive the grace they need to reach heaven. Comparatively speaking, he opened the treasures of his bounty to the faithful who believe in him in a way and to a degree never available before. Also by comparison, while he became the second head of the human family already in the womb of the Virgin Mary, it was only by the power of the cross that he began to exercise fully his office as head of the Church, which is his Mystical Body.

The Catholic faith associates Christ's Resurrection with the crucifixion as forming one indissoluble unity. Unlike his death, the Resurrection does not, of course, merit our redemption. It is, however, an integral part of the economy of salvation as its victorious consummation. Humanly speaking, the Resurrection meant the beginning of justification, even as the crucifixion meant the end of our estrangement from God. And on our part, faith in Christ's Resurrection is a condition for benefiting from the Redemption. Like Abraham, whose faith justified him, "Our faith too will be 'considered' if we believe in him who raised Jesus our Lord from the dead, Jesus who was put to death for our sins and raised to life to justify us" (Rm. 4:24-25). This mystery takes on startling implications once we realize that it is the risen Christ, who will die no more, who is the invisible head of his Church and by whom the faithful are constantly taught, governed, and sanctified.

Having founded the Church by his blood, Christ strengthened it on Pentecost and inspired it with its sense of mission to preach the Good News to all nations. "He wished to make known and proclaim his spouse through the visible coming of the Holy Spirit with the sound of a mighty wind and tongues of fire. For just as he himself, when he began to preach, was made known by his eternal Father through the Holy Spirit descending and remaining on him in the form of a dove, so likewise, as the apostles were about to enter on their ministry of preaching, Christ our Lord sent the Holy Spirit down from heaven, to touch them with tongues of fire and to point out, as by the finger of God, the supernatural mission and office of the Church."[4]

Thus the cycle of the Church's formation was finished as it started, with the Holy Spirit. He overshadowed Mary at Nazareth "and the Word was made flesh." He descended on the disciples at Jerusalem and "that very day about three thousand were added to their number."

BIBLICAL IMAGES

Since the Church is a mystery, the biblical writers resorted to a litany of images to bring out something of its inner meaning. We recall that all the books of the New Testament were written after the descent of the Holy Spirit and therefore under his guiding influence, even when narrating events or discourses that took place before Pentecost. The terms the sacred authors used to describe the Church, therefore, are part of their understanding of her mystery through the help of the Spirit.

The most frequent title occurs in the Gospel narratives where

Christ regularly speaks of the *basileia* or kingdom. All that he taught about the society he came to found was somehow identified with the kingdom, from the opening of his public life when he began to preach repentance, "for the kingdom of heaven is close at hand," to his dying profession before Pilate that "mine is not a kingdom of this world." Christ used the word "Church" only twice, which the evangelists identified with *ekklesia,* corresponding to the Hebrew term *quhal,* meaning a congregation or assembly of the faithful.

Evidently Christ spoke of two kinds of kingdom: an earthly and a heavenly one. When he compared it to a grain of mustard seed that a man cast into his garden, then it grew and became a large tree, this referred to an earthly kingdom that grows and develops in membership and influence. Again when he said the kingdom of heaven is like a net cast into the sea that gathers in fish of every kind, the good and bad, which are later sorted out and the bad thrown away, this cannot mean the kingdom after death. The parable illustrates what will happen at the end of the world when the angels separate the wicked from the just. On the other hand, Jesus also spoke of a kingdom reserved for those who have carried their cross with patience to the end, of the reward in store for those who during life had fed the hungry and clothed the naked in his name.

These two kingdoms are related as condition and consequence. Between them stands the easily missed "if," which Christ was at pains to apply to the New Covenant. The kingdom in heaven will be reached if his kingdom on earth has been faithfully lived up to.

The Church of Christ is also a sheepfold, whose unique and indispensable entrance is the Savior. In more simple terms, the Church is the flock, and God himself proclaimed beforehand that he would be its shepherd. Its sheep, while herded by human shepherds, are unfailingly guided and fed by Christ, the Good Shepherd, Chief Shepherd, who has laid down his life for the sheep.

Moreover, the Church is God's tillage or field. This is the field where the ancient olive grows; the patriarchs were its consecrated root. On this tree Jew and Gentile were and will be reconciled. There are two other levels to this tree imagery: the vineyard and the vine. As the choice vineyard, it was planted by the heavenly vinedresser. As the true vine, it is Christ who gives life and abundance to us, the branches; we abide in him through the Church, since apart from him we can do nothing.

In the New Testament outside the Gospels, the Church is frequently called God's building. Christ compared himself to the stone that the builders rejected, yet it became the head of the corner. Paul went on to explain that this is the foundation on which the apostles built and from which the Church receives her steadiness and cohesion. She is, therefore, God's household because in her lives his family, the "dwelling place of God in the Spirit" and "God's dwelling among men." She is the consecrated temple that has inspired the creation of the great works of Christian art and architecture over the centuries.

From still another viewpoint, the Church is the unblemished bride of the unblemished lamb. She is the bride whom Christ loved and gave himself up for her, that he might sanctify her. The covenant by which he has tied himself to her is indissoluble. He wants her to be cleansed and close to him, lovingly and loyally submissive. He has loaded her forever with the good things of heaven, to enable us to know what surpasses human knowledge, the love of God and Christ for us. Thus the Church on earth is away from the Lord, as it were in exile, waiting for the day of his return, when she will appear in glory with her bridegroom.

For St. Paul, the most descriptive figure of the Church is Christ's body. Almost everything he says about the Church fits into this category. Why are we baptized? In order to mold us to Christ's likeness, "for by one Spirit we were all baptized into one body" (1 Co. 12:13). Why do we receive the Eucharist? In order that, by sharing the Lord's physical body, we might be raised to fellowship with him and with one another, "Because there is one bread, we who are many are one body, for we all partake of the one bread" (1 Co. 10:17).

The relation of the faithful with Christ is like that of the members and the human body. There may be a great number of them, but the body they form is one. In the structure of the body of Christ, too, there is a diversity of members and functions. How so? The Spirit is one, and he dispenses his gifts in variety, for the Church's benefit, according to the wealth and requirements of the Church's ministry. Among these gifts the foremost is taken by the grace of the apostles, for the Spirit himself makes even those with spiritual gifts, like miracles or prophecy, subject to their authority. In virtue of the same Spirit, the myriad parts of the body are interconnected through the charity he diffuses among the Church's members. Consequently, if one member suffers, all suffer together, and if one member is honored, all rejoice together.

The head of this body, Paul never tires of repeating, is Christ. By Christ's mighty power he has dominion over heaven and earth. His pre-eminent perfection and deeply interior activity enable him to fill the whole body with the wealth of his glory.

All the members of the Church are to be molded to his likeness until Christ be formed in them. This is the reason we are caught up in the mysteries of his life, made like to him, sharing his death and Resurrection, until we shall share his reign. Making our pilgrimage on earth until that time, we follow his footsteps through trial and persecution. Our association with his sufferings, then, is essential to our membership in his body. We not only share his pain in order to share his joy, but belonging to his Church means reflecting in our lives what he experienced in his—the cross, which leads to glory.[5]

ESSENTIAL ATTRIBUTES AND MEMBERSHIP

With the close of the apostolic age, the Church's leaders were soon called to reflect upon what the Church is and who belongs to her. They had no choice. There were challenges from within and opposition from without. People were claiming to be followers of Christ, yet acting in ways that contradicted the Gospels, or, out of fear, not professing what the plain teachings of the Savior required of those who were truly his disciples.

Unity of Faith and Communion. It was clear enough from the writing of St. Paul that all members of the Church should inwardly believe the truths of faith proposed by the apostles and their successors, and outwardly confess what they believe. "By believing from the heart," he wrote, "you are made righteous; by confessing with your lips, you are saved" (Rm. 10:10). Paul described the unity of the Church by picturing her as a house, and again as a human body. He expressly enjoins internal and outward unity among the followers of Christ (Ep. 4:3–6).

Already in the second century, however, this unity was tested by the inroads of heresy. Gnosticism was the principal solvent of the true faith, with its claims to personal insight apart from the teaching hierarchy. In order to insure this unity of faith, by the year A.D. 150, converts to the Church were expected to memorize (besides the Lord's Prayer) and adequately understand certain formulations of doctrine called creeds. Two stages are traceable in the development of these baptismal creeds: a simple affirmation of the outstanding articles of faith; and a carefully structured formula that aims at touching on the four major areas of Christian belief, namely, God the Father and creation, God the Son and redemption, God the Holy Spirit and sanctification, and the Catholic Church and final resurrection. Our present Apostles' Creed, though supported in every article by New Testament evidence, can be traced by manuscript sources in its present form only from the last decades of the second century.

The terms "heresy" and "schism" derive from the earliest patristic writings. They have always been considered ruptures in Christian unity, where heresy means a breach of faith and schism a failure in charity. In practice, of course, it has been difficult to remain long in schism without also lapsing into heresy on some doctrine of belief. Significantly the first major patristic writing dealing with both forms of disunion, Ireneus' *Against Heresies,* isolated the root of all heresy (from within the Church) as a refusal to accept the Church's teaching authority as centered in the bishop of Rome. This was echoed seventeen hundred years later by the First Vatican Council when it declared, speaking of Christ, "In order that the whole assembly of the faithful may remain in unity of faith and communion, he placed St. Peter over the other apostles and instituted in him both a perpetual principle of unity and a visible foundation."[6]

There are, therefore, two forms of unity in the Church: of faith and of communion. By their union of faith, those who belong to the Church believe the same faith proposed to them by the Church for acceptance. By their unity of communion, the faithful are submissive to the authority of the bishops and the Roman Pontiff, which is sometimes called hierarchical unity. Communion also describes the mutual bond among the members themselves because they are joined together socially on their participation in the same sacraments and forms of worship as channels of grace, which may be called liturgical unity.

As we compare the Church's teaching on her own unity, say a thousand years ago, with her teaching in modern times, there has been no essential change of doctrine; but there is a difference in attitude. When Vatican II came to define the Church founded by Christ, and identify her presence in the world today, it said, "This Church, constituted and organized in the world as a society, sub-sists in the Catholic Church, which is governed by the successor of Peter and by the bishops in communion with him. Nevertheless, there are many elements of sanctification and truth found outside of her structure. These elements, as gifts belonging to the Church of Christ, are forces impelling toward Catholic unity."[7]

There is only one Church established by Christ; not only one but uniquely one. What, then, about the many "Churches" that we see in contemporary Christianity? Is the Roman Catholic Church only a Christian denomination, one of many branches of the Church, each of whom shares in a partial possession of Christ's revealed truth and its own equally valid and effective means of sanctification?

For the first time in conciliar history, this issue was squarely faced and answered. The issue in question was not *whether* the Church is one. No believer in Christ would say otherwise. The issue was *where* this one Church of Christ can be found. The Second Vatican Council's answer is unequivocal. That which constitutes the one true Church—its churchness, so to speak—not merely exists but it subsists in the Catholic Church, which is governed by the successor of Peter and by the bishops in communion with him. Behind the carefully chosen verb "subsists" stands the affirmation that the ob-jective fullness of Christ's heritage to the Church—totality of his revelation, totality of his sacraments, and totality of authority to rule the people of God in his name—resides in the Catholic Church, of which the bishop of Rome is the visible head.

Other Christian bodies participate, in greater or less measure, of those elements of sanctification and truth that exist in their divinely ordained fullness (hence subsist) in the Roman Catholic Church.

It was to clarify this crucial point of the Church's identity that eight years after the Council Pope Paul VI issued the document *Mystery of the Church,* in which he restated in the most explicit terms that the true Church already exists. It is not, as some patrons of ecumenism were saying, yet to come about as the result of reuni-fication among Christians. The faithful, he said, "are not free to hold that Christ's Church nowhere yet really subsists today; so that the Church is considered only as an end which all Churches and ecclesial communities must strive to attain."[8]

Holiness in Purpose, Means, and Fruitfulness. What is reputed to be the earliest extant creed, the *Letter of the Apostles* in five articles, professes belief "in the holy Church." And ever since, every creed of the faith has affirmed the same.

Needless to say, the Church is holy by reason of her founder, Christ the Lord, and we should expect what he established to be holy too. Yet immediately we must recall that he was holy because he was God, whereas the Church can be holy only because of her relationship or attachment to God. Her sanctity derives from him, or leads to him, or is the effect of his divine presence in those who possess him.

As deriving from Christ, there is doubt what purpose he had in founding the Church on earth as prelude and condition for the Church in heaven. Speaking to husbands and wives, and exhorting them to sanctity through their marriage bond, St. Paul told them to imitate Christ, who "loved the Church and sacrificed himself for her to make her holy. He made her clean by washing her in water with a form of words, so that when he took her to himself she would be glorious, with no speck or wrinkle or anything like that, but holy and faultless" (Ep. 5:25–26).

More critical, and more often challenged in the Church's history, is the means the Church provides to sanctify those who belong to her. They are the doctrine of faith and morals, the Mass and sacraments, the directives of those in ecclesiastical authority, and that communication of merits that the creeds describe as the communion of saints among the justified on earth or between those in glory and the members of the pilgrim Church below. At the center of these means of holiness and their ultimate source is the indwelling Spirit of Christ, which animates the Mystical Body.

They are available to everyone, so that "all the faithful of Christ, of whatever rank or status, are called to the fullness of the Christian life and the perfection of charity." This assumes, however, that one other means must be used, namely, one's own free will in co-operation with the channels of grace offered by the Church. Consequently, "in order that the faithful may reach this perfection, they must use their strength according to the measure they have received it as a gift of Christ. They must follow in his footsteps and conform themselves to his image by seeking the will of the Father in all things. They must devote themselves with all their being to the glory of God and the service of their neighbor."[9] This conciliar exhortation actually spells the difference between reaching sanctity or failing to do so. The channels of grace are abundantly present and open to all, but not all co-operate with the graces offered or with complete generosity.

The Church is finally holy in the fruitfulness of sanctity, which those who use the means are sure to attain. As far back as Aristides (A.D. 140), Christian apologists in their defensive struggle with paganism pointed to the moral reformation that the religion of Christ effected in those who gave themselves to the Church's guidance. "The communities of God," wrote Origen, "to which Christ has become teacher and guide are, in comparison with communities of the pagan people among whom they live as strangers, like heavenly lights in the world."[10]

Since catacomb days, members of the Church gave evidence of above-ordinary sanctity, not only in contrast to their non-Christian contemporaries but also within their own ranks. Those who suffered death at the hands of the persecutors were the first to be venerated, as we know from the first-century custom of celebrating Mass over the tombs of the martyrs. Besides the actual martyrs, those who had survived their sufferings (confessors of the faith) were also paid special honors, and their power of intercession after death asserted, e.g., by St. Cyprian. Origen was apparently the first of the Fathers to give veneration of saints an express theological foundation. He placed it within the doctrine of the communion of saints and taught that the prayer of the saints is efficacious insofar as the faithful follow in their footsteps.

From the fourth century, devotion to the saints spread rapidly. St. Cyril of Jerusalem (315–86) distinguished the saints commemorated at the Eucharistic sacrifice who offer our prayer to God from the ordinary dead who would be benefited by the sacrifice. At about the same time, the ranks of those accounted saints were enlarged by the addition of confessors and virgins, on the ground that a life of renunciation and holiness might equal the devotion of those who had died for Christ. Thus ascetics such as St. Anthony of Egypt (251–356) and bishops such as St. Athanasius and St. John Chrysostom were soon venerated in the East and West. St. Augustine was honored as a saint at Carthage before A.D. 475.

Two Roman Pontiffs laid the doctrinal position of the Church on extraordinary sanctity. St. Leo I affirmed that saints are special intercessors who obtain for us the mercy of God by their prayers; St.

Gregory the Great urged the faithful to place themselves under the protection of the saints in order to overcome the devil and the seductions of the world.

All the while that ecclesiastical writers and Popes were extolling the Church's holiness, they were careful to avoid the other extreme of claiming that members who are not holy cease to belong to the Church. Not even mortal sinners are thereby excluded from the Mystical Body.

The Donatists of northern Africa in the fourth and fifth centuries broke with Catholic unity because they insisted that the Church of the saints cannot harbor former apostates. Such people had to be rebaptized and reordained; otherwise, the sacraments they administered were invalid. A series of regional councils, supported by Rome, condemned the Donatists.[11] St. Augustine wrote strenuously against them. Yet their schism persisted until the divided African Church was destroyed by the Saracens in the seventh and eighth centuries.

Similar theories of ecclesiastical Puritanism rocked the Church at other periods of its history. Each time, the papal and conciliar reaction was the same. Innocent III answered the Waldenses (1208) by declaring that "the wickedness of a bishop or priest does no harm to the baptism of an infant, nor to consecrating the Eucharist, nor to the other ecclesiastical offices exercised for subjects."[12] The Council of Constance (1415), confirmed by Martin V, condemned John Wycliffe and John Hus for denying sinful Popes, bishops, and priests the power to administer the sacraments, and for withdrawing the duty of obedience to civil rulers "in mortal sin."[13] The Jansenists were censured by Clement XI for postulating a Church composed only of the predestined saints. Who belongs to the Church on these premises? Jansenism gave two answers, both alike:

> The Church or the whole Christ has the Incarnate Word as head, but all the saints as members.
> There is nothing more spacious than the Church of God; because all the elect and the just of all ages comprise it.[14]

In recent times, Pius XII applied these perennial principles to the contemporary scene and made some important distinctions. "Schism, heresy, or apostasy are such of their very nature that they sever a man from the body of the Church. But not every sin, even the most grievous, is of such a kind."[15] This calls for some explanation.

As commonly understood by the Church, "If a person, after receiving baptism and retaining the Christian name, pertinaciously denies any of the truths which are to be believed with divine and Catholic faith, or if he doubts the same, he is a heretic. If he departs entirely from the Christian faith, he is an apostate. If finally he will not be subject to the Supreme Pontiff or refuses to associate with members of the Church subject to him, he is a schismatic."[16] In each case, the assumption is that the person acts knowingly and culpably, which excludes all baptized non-Catholics in good faith who may be, as we say, materially but not formally (or sinfully) heretical, apostate, or schismatic.

What, then, is meant by saying that culpable heresy, schism, or apostasy severs a man "from the Body of the Church?" It means just that. He cuts himself off from the visible part of the Church, which includes the right to receive the sacraments (until he repents), to public recognition as a Catholic, and to those numerous benefits of fraternal acceptance among the faithful that the professed members of the Church may claim. This is not severance from that irremovable bond of the baptismal character, which remains in spite of any infidelity.

Short of such sins, however, even grave crimes like murder and adultery do not separate a Catholic from the body of the Church. His sinful condition certainly deprives him of the life of grace in his soul and, if he dies in that condition, he will not be saved. Nevertheless, he remains a member of the Church, although a sinful member, on the assumption that the Church of Christ is a visible society which a person enters by the visible rite of baptism and in which he remains by the profession of faith and communion with the body of the Church's believers.

Universality of Catholicism. Literally, the word "Catholic" (Greek, *katholike*) means "general" or "universal." The title was first used in A.D. 107, by St. Ignatius of Antioch in his letter to the Smyrneans, "Where Jesus Christ is, there is the Catholic Church."[17] By the end of the second century, it had acquired the two meanings now mainly associated with the term: "universal" in the sense of extended throughout the world, and "orthodox" or faithful to the teachings of Christ. The two concepts are closely related.

The Gospels clearly show that Christ intended his Church not only for a chosen few, as among the Jews before the Messiah came, but for all mankind. "This Good News of the kingdom," he foretold, "will be proclaimed to the whole world as a witness to all the nations. And then the end will come" (Mt. 24:14).

Some have interpreted this to mean that once the Gospel had been preached everywhere, the end of the world will come. The more logical interpretation is that the apostles would begin to proclaim the Gospel and establish the Church among the nations—that is, beyond the confines of Jewish Palestine—before the destruction of Jerusalem. The city was destroyed by the Romans after a four-year siege, A.D. 66 to 70. By the end of the first century, over one hundred dioceses had been founded throughout the Mediterranean world.

Responding to this mandate of the Savior, Christian missionaries since the time of St. Paul labored to make this intentional catholicity also actual. They succeeded to such a degree that, since apostolic times, the faithful have professed in the liturgy their belief "in the holy catholic Church," where the original Greek is never capitalized. The custom of using the separate title "Catholic Church" (initial capital letters) can be certainly traced to the time of the Eastern Schism, finalized in 1054, when oriental Christians isolated the term "Orthodox Church" to identify themselves as distinct both from the Nestorians and Monophysites. Consistent with this approach, the Council of Florence (1445) speaks of the "holy Roman Church," to emphasize acceptance of Rome as a condition for complete unity.

The realization of the Church's catholicity is an ongoing process and goes beyond the mere preaching of the Gospel or the token establishment of the Church in representative parts of the world. Hence the close connection between "catholic" and "missionary," where the latter is the means of extending the former. There is such a thing as becoming more and more catholic, in the sense of more widely diffused among nations and intensively established in the hearts of the people "through the grace and love of the Holy Spirit."[18]

Catholicity also means unity amidst diversity, on several counts. The Church has never been a respecter of persons. Poor and rich alike, the learned and unlearned are equally welcome. All cultures and every stratum of society belong to the Church, and where this is not verified, the fault lies with those who have failed to combine "both the universality of the Church and the diversity of the world's nations" in their preaching of the Gospel.[19] Also within the Catholic

Church are numerous rites, or different liturgical families that have flourished since the fourth century. Besides ritual differences, these families also reflect numerous cultural adaptations that the "postconciliar" Church is encouraging as part of modern evangelization.

As a mark of orthodoxy, the Church's catholicity is part of that mysterious paradox whereby the same essential faith and worship are held and practiced by a bewildering variety of peoples, separated geographically across the globe, culturally across the range of mankind, and historically across the centuries. This is absolutely unique among world religions, which seem incapable of transcending regional or even political interests. In fact, one of the lessons of Christian history is the inevitable rise of national churches whenever they separate from Roman Catholicism.

The glory of the Catholic Church but also her most difficult task is to maintain a balance between what seem to be irreconcilable extremes: continuity and openness to change. Pope John stressed this in his opening message to the Second Vatican Council. On one side, he insisted, "under no circumstances may the Church turn away from the sacred patrimony handed down by our ancestors." On the other side, "it is also necessary to keep the present times in view, to see what new situations they disclose, what new ways of living and new paths for the Catholic apostolate they may show."[20] A synonym for "catholicity" would be "adaptability," but without sacrifice of one's divinely conferred identity.

Apostolic Collegiality. The Church's apostolicity says many things: that her origin goes back to the apostles; that her teaching has remained faithful to what the apostles received from Christ; that the Church's pastors, the Pope and bishops, are directly connected with the apostles by the succession of their office; and that this succession witnesses to the organic oneness of the Church of the apostles with the Roman Catholic Church of our day.

But a new dimension has entered the picture in the past century, or rather an always present dimension received new emphasis and raises some new, even startling, implications for the future. Collegiality must now be seen as an aspect of apostolicity. It is the Church's apostolicity seen from the standpoint of her social or collective, hence collegial, character.

Christ conferred on the apostles the threefold office he had received from the Father. Thus he told them to "make disciples of all nations" (Mt. 28:19). He gave them such authority that "whatever you bind on earth shall be considered bound in heaven; whatever you loose on earth shall be considered loosed in heaven" (Mt. 18:18). He communicated to them, among other gifts, the ability to re-enact what he had done at the Last Supper, "Do this as a memorial of me" (Lk. 22:19); and the power of remitting sins, "As the Father sent me, so I am sending you. . . . For those whose sins you forgive, they are forgiven; for those whose sins you retain, they are retained" (Jn. 20:21–23).

These apostolic prerogatives were not merely functional but inherent in the sacramental powers they received from Christ. The apostles were not only commissioned to carry on his work; they were consecrated to do so. Their right to teach, govern, and sanctify was rooted in their ordination to a share in Christ's priesthood, which took place at the first Lord's Supper. In virtue of this ordination, they received all the graces necessary to exercise their apostolate effectively for the people of God.

They were also empowered by Christ to transmit the essentials of this threefold office to their successors by the laying on of hands. This is the basis, as defined by the Council of Trent and restated by Vatican II, for the historical episcopate and presbyterate and the fundamental reason why the Catholic Church of today is called apostolic.[21]

Having said all this, however, is not to say everything; for the apostles were not only called individually by Christ and sent as individuals into the world in his name, they were also a collegial community, bound together by their common loyalty to him and intended by him to work, under Peter, as the nucleus of his Church.

We see them acting as a body during the novena of waiting for the Spirit after Christ's Ascension, when, on Peter's initiative, they chose Matthias to replace Judas. We see them doing the same at the council in Jerusalem to settle the thorny problem of whether Christian converts had to follow the Jewish laws.

By the end of the apostolic age, the bishops of the Catholic world began meeting together periodically on a regional basis; and before the year 100 we have record of the bishop of Rome writing to the contentious Corinthians about the solidarity in love that Christ bequeathed to the apostles and their successors. Epistolary collegiality was practiced by the apostles, including Peter, as seen in the letters that bear their names. As the Church expanded, so did the number and frequency of the meetings and correspondence. We know that whenever matters of greater import arose and major decisions had to be made, the bishop of Rome was consulted, and his judgment was crucial. Thus the date of Easter in Asia Minor, the rebaptism controversy in North Africa, and the threat of Gnosticism almost everywhere—all involved collective episcopal action co-ordinated with deference to Rome as final arbiter.

With the first ecumenical council at Nicea in 325, this co-operative activity reached worldwide proportions. The very name "ecumenical council" describes the two elements that have since become associated with collegiality: a council because the bishops meet for united deliberation and decision, and ecumenical because their meeting represents the whole Christian world in union with the see of Peter.

For more than sixteen centuries, these forms of collegiality-in-practice were commonplace in the Church, yet the doctrine itself was only partially realized until the midtwentieth century and formalized under John XXIII and Paul VI. Several reasons may account for this, but one contributing factor was the dawn of the communications age and the rise of the secular state.

The modern means of rapid transportation within countries and between continents, and of almost instant thought communication around the globe, made it increasingly clear that the bishops of a country or, for that matter, of the world can now be in contact with one another and with the bishop of Rome in a way never dreamed possible before. The new situation, therefore, called for an in-depth appraisal of the doctrinal basis of their intercommunication, which is only another phrase for collegiality.

At the same time the specter of national churches, where princes would support bishops who claimed their autonomy of Rome, became decreasingly likely with the secularization of so many civil governments. Caesaro-Papalism, as it is called, assumes that "Caesar" is sufficiently religious to want to establish his own state-church independent of papal authority. Exceptions to this rule, as in Maoist China, are only apparent because there the "nationalization" of the Church was actually its total dechristianization.

The Vatican Council's description of collegiality is simple enough. "By the Lord's establishment," it says, "St. Peter and the other Apostles constitute a single apostolic college. In like manner, the Roman Pontiff, Peter's successor, and the bishops, successors of the apostles, are linked together."[22] This is the essence of the doctrine and, as such, would have required no special elaboration.

But it did require extensive and carefully nuanced explanation because of the psychological climate in which the doctrine was offered. It demanded, while developing the legitimate rights of bishops, that the authority of the Pope was not diminished. Collegiality is basically a relationship among bishops, which causes no great problem, and between bishops and the Pope, which can present a problem.

The relationship of the bishops with the Pope is not a mere juridical dependence on the bishop of Rome and less still a human construct devised for reasons of order or efficiency. It was created by Christ himself and belongs by divine right to the essential nature of the Church he founded.

When the bishop is consecrated, he receives, in virtue of his consecration, the fullness of the sacrament of orders. He receives the fullness of episcopal power, which is called the high priesthood. But consecration alone does not make him a member of the community that succeeds the apostolic college. He must also be received as confrere by the other members of the Catholic episcopate. While his consecration makes him bishop, it must be supplemented with acceptance by the episcopate under its papal head to incorporate him into the episcopal college. He must, of course, also intend to accept his fellow bishops under the Pope.

In order to clarify the matter still further, the council distinguished the three powers inherent in the episcopacy. The first is the power of administering the sacraments, including the consecration of other men as bishops. The second is the office of teaching authoritatively and sharing in the Church's divine guidance of communicating revealed truth. The third is the right to govern and direct the people of God according to norms of worship and conduct that are binding on the consciences of the faithful.

The first of these three comes to a bishop through his ordination. It belongs to him as a man who has received the plenitude of Christ's priesthood. He should not exercise its powers except with the approval of the bishop of Rome. But if he does, he acts validly, and the sacraments he confers (including episcopal consecration) take their effect as soon as the sacrament is received.

It is quite otherwise as regards teaching authority and pastoral government. Certainly they are rooted in the sacramental consecration of a bishop. But this consecration confers only the virtual capacity, not its actual realization. One sentence in the *Constitution on the Church* sets the matter in perspective. No doubt, "episcopal consecration confers the offices of teaching and ruling." Having these offices, though, is not enough. "Of their nature, however, they *can only* be exercised in hierarchical communion with the head and members of the college."[23]

What are the implications of this doctrine? Episcopal collegiality becomes operative only if a bishop, or group of bishops, is in actual communion with Rome and the rest of the hierarchy united with the Pope. Apart from such communion, any episcopal action has no assurance of divine approval, no matter how many prelates may agree among themselves.

There is also an obverse side to this relationship. Bishops depend on Rome for the actualization of their authority, whether as individuals with respect to the people under their immediate care or as a college with responsibility to the whole Church of God. Not so with the Pope. Nothing the Second Vatican Council said about collegiality undermines what the First Vatican Council said about the papal primacy. Two statements must, therefore, be made:

1. "The college or body of bishops has no authority unless it is understood together with the Roman Pontiff, the successor of Peter as its head." Consequently union with the Vicar of Christ determines whether and how much authority the bishops actually exercise.

2. The Pope, however, is not determined by a corresponding approval from the bishops. Collegiality notwithstanding, "the Pope's power of primacy over all, both pastors and faithful, remains whole and intact. In virtue of his office, that is, as Vicar of Christ and pastor of the whole Church, the Roman Pontiff has full, supreme, and universal power over the Church. And he is always free to exercise this power."[24]

Few aspects of the Church's apostolic character are more promising for the future than its collegiality. Its function is to give internal cohesion within the hierarchy and, through them, to all the faithful. Beyond that, however, it will evoke among the bishops a new sense of responsibility not only for their own dioceses but for all the people of Christendom.

INFALLIBILITY IN BELIEF AND DOCTRINE

Briefly defined, infallibility is immunity from error, excluding not only its existence but even its possibility. Strictly speaking, only persons can be infallible, as only they are fallible; but the term may also be applied to expressions of the mind in the form of speech or the written word. While the immediate effect of infallibility is negative because it keeps a person from making a mistake, the actual preservation from error is due to a very positive influx of divine grace, which enlightens the mind and, if need be, strengthens the will in order to insure inerrancy.

Infallibility does not mean preservation from sin, which is impeccability. In apostolic times, St. Peter was infallible in the exercise of his office. But, unlike the Blessed Virgin, he was not impeccable, although it is commonly held that all the apostles were confirmed in grace on the day of Pentecost and thus preserved from losing the friendship of God. Moreover, since the transmission of truth involves a speaker and a listener, infallibility is both communicative and receptive.

Also, infallibility must be distinguished from revelation. When a revelation occurs, God directly and internally enlightens the human mind which, in relation to the divine light, humbly acknowledges what he reveals as a truth that is somehow new. Infallibility, on the other hand, presupposes an existing revelation that needs to be preserved. Unlike what happens in revelation, divine providence in the case of infallibility is, so to speak, external to the mind. God, as it were, stands ready to prevent error from creeping into the mind and erroneous judgments pertaining to revelation from being declared.

Infallibility is not inspiration. Inspiration implies that God is the principal author of the word or work inspired, although using a human instrument; whereas infallibility is a providential aid, so that the human being who was helped (and not God) is the immediate author of an infallible statement.

Summarily, we can say that in revelation, God speaks his divine word; in inspiration, he projects it; and by the assistance of infallibility, he safeguards what was spoken and produced. Peter's declaration before the Sanhedrin illustrates the various differences. "Of all the names in the world given to men," he said, "this is the only one by which we can be saved" (Ac. 4:12). The salvation of the world by Jesus Christ is a matter of revelation; the instinct to protest against the injustice of the Jews and proclaim the name of Christ, we are told by St. Luke, was a divine inspiration, since Peter was "filled with the Holy Spirit," and in writing this episode, the author of the Acts was supernaturally inspired. But when Peter spoke as the Vicar of Christ to "rulers, elders, and scribes," he was divinely assisted by the gift of infallibility.

Integrity and Influence of the Faithful. A major development in the Catholic doctrine of infallibility is the clarification of the respective roles played by the faithful who belong to the Church, and by the hierarchy who direct the lives of the faithful.

Since the same term "infallibility" is used for both, it may be useful to distinguish their different meanings by referring to the faithful as having integrity and influence in matters of revelation, and to the hierarchy in union with the Pope as having decisive authority to pass judgment on what has been revealed.

We begin by noting that God, who is absolutely infallible, deigned to bestow on his new people—the Church—a certain shared infallibility, but within three carefully restricted limits: (1) in matters of faith and morals; (2) when the whole people of God unhesitatingly hold a point of doctrine pertaining to these matters; and (3) always dependent on the wise providence and anointing of the grace of the Holy Spirit, who leads the Church into all truth until the glorious coming of its Lord.[25] Vatican II identified this form of infallibility as a prelude to the more familiar kind associated with the bishops and the papacy.

> The university of the faithful, whom the holy One has anointed, is incapable of error in belief. This is a property which belongs to the people as a whole; a supernatural discernment of faith is the means by which they make this property manifest, when, "from bishops to the most obscure layman," they show their universal agreement in matters of faith and morals.
>
> This discernment of faith, which is roused and maintained by the Spirit of truth, is the cause of the unfailing adherence of the people of God to the faith that was once and for all delivered to the saints (Jude 3). It is the cause, too, of the deeper entry that it makes into the faith by right judgment and of a more complete application of the faith to life.

This all takes place under the guidance of the sacred magisterium, when the people of God, in loyal submission to it, accepts not the word of man but what really is the word of God (1 Th. 2:13).[26]

We are told that "the university of the faithful" (*universitas fidelium*) cannot err in belief; and they manifest their supernatural discernment when the faithful "show their universal agreement" (*universalem consensum*) in matters of faith and morals.

At first sight, these expressions seem either unintelligible or unrealistic. What does "university of the faithful" mean? And when in the history of the Church has there been universal agreement in matters of faith and morals?

The trouble is not with the terms but with our mechanistic culture, which has drastically affected the meaning of words. In its original and still basic definition, the adjective "universal" means "turned into one" or "combined into one," with the assumption that different persons are united in thought and aspirations or joined together in some common enterprise. It does not principally mean what our mathematical society takes it to mean, "including or covering the whole or all, either collectively or distributively." "Universal," therefore, has reference primarily to the unity of those who are joined together, and it is in this sense that the Church understands "universality" in the present context.

What, then, is intended by saying that the university of the faithful is infallible in belief? It affirms the age-old conviction that the faithful of Christ are joined together by their unerring belief in the mysteries of revelation. They are united by their common allegiance to the faith. They are united in a believing society by the truth; they cannot be joined together by falsehood. They form a university of the faithful, since there could only be a conflict or, to coin a word, a "controversity" of unbelievers. Truth unites, error divides. This is the verdict of twenty centuries of Christianity. Those who believe, and insofar as they believe, are one community not only or mainly because they subjectively believe but because what they believe is objectively true, indeed is the Truth that became man and dwelled among us.

Against this background, it is easier to see what universal agreement among the faithful must mean. They are faithful insofar as they are agreed on the truth, where the source of their agreement is not a semantic use of the name "Christian" or "Catholic," but the deeply interior adherence to what God has revealed. Consequently, whether they realize it or not, all who agree on the revealed truth, under the guidance of the sacred magisterium, belong to the faithful. Their agreement on the truth and allegiance to the magisterium gives them universality, i.e., spiritual unity. The truth interiorly possessed gives them consensus, and not the other way around, as though their consensus on some doctrine made it true!

In more than one critical period since apostolic times, it was this rugged collectivism of orthodoxy among the faithful that carried the Church successfully through its crisis. The stout defense by the laity of Mary as Mother of God when this was denied by Nestorius is only the best-known example of how "God's people, sustained by the Spirit of truth, clings without fail to the faith."[27]

Given their possession of revealed truth, the faithful may be said to share, in their own way, in Christ's prophetic office. They contribute to the Church's deeper understanding both of the events and words of revelation by their reflective study of what God has revealed when, like Mary, they ponder these truths in their hearts; by their more profound experienced penetration of spiritual matters when they live out in practice what they believe in principle; and by their transmission of what they learn when they listen to the preaching of those who have received with the episcopal succession an assured spiritual gift of truth.[28]

Inerrancy of the Magisterium. All the preceding infallibility of the faithful depends on the existence of the divine institution of the magisterium, which is vested exclusively in the successors of Peter and the other apostles. There can be no inversion of functions here.

> No matter how much the sacred magisterium avails itself of the contemplation, life, and study of the faithful, its office is not reduced merely to ratifying the assent already expressed by the latter. Indeed, in the interpretation and explanation of the written or transmitted word of God, the magisterium can anticipate or demand their assent. The people of God has particular need of the intervention and assistance of the magisterium when internal disagreements arise and spread concerning a doctrine that must be believed or held, lest it lose the communion of the one faith in the one body of the Lord.[29]

While the exercise of such decision-making infallibility can be traced to New Testament days, the Church's clearer understanding of what this means came only gradually as circumstances required.

The first significant clarification came in the early fifth century, when Nestorius sought the support of Emperor Theodosius II, who was urged to call a council in defense of Nestorius and against Pope Celestine I. At the Council of Ephesus, the papal legate read the statement that was later to be incorporated into the text of the First Vatican Council's definition of papal infallibility. "There is no doubt," said the legate, "and in fact it has been known in all ages, that the holy and most blessed Peter, prince and head of the Apostles, pillar of the faith and foundation of the Catholic Church, received the keys of the kingdom from our Lord Jesus Christ, the Savior and Redeemer of the human race. To him was given the power of loosing and binding sins, who even at this time and always, lives and judges in his successors."[30] The legate went on to point out that, since Pope Celestine is Peter's successor and holds his place, in his name the condemnation of Nestorius is thereby confirmed by papal authority. The implication was that the Council of Ephesus, convoked by the Emperor and composed of bishops, required such papal approval to be authentic.

Further clarification was occasioned by the position of the Protestant Reformers who claimed that all the faithful are priests and therefore the hierarchy is no more divinely authorized to teach infallibly than other baptized Christians. The Council of Trent insisted that the Catholic Church holds otherwise. Specifically, she teaches that the hierarchy has been divinely instituted, and the bishops who have succeeded the apostles belong in a special way to the hierarchical order, since "they have been placed by the Holy Spirit to rule the Church of God" (Ac. 20:29). Their authority to rule, moreover, is rooted in their sacred ordination. To place everyone in the Church on the same footing would be equivalent to contradicting St. Paul and saying that all are apostles, all prophets, all evangelists, all pastors, all teachers.[31]

In the nineteenth century, the theory of Gallicanism asserted the more or less complete freedom of the Catholic Church from the ecclesiastical authority of the bishop of Rome. As a result there was widespread confusion among the faithful, especially in the realm of doctrine, where the Pope had for centuries exercised supreme teaching authority in full accord, it was assumed, with the premises of revelation.

When the First Vatican Council met in 1869, Gallicanism was answered in a way that left no doubt about the main issues under controversy, namely, who possesses the gift of infallibility, when is it exercised, and what is the scope of infallible teaching.

> It is a dogma divinely revealed: that the Roman Pontiff when he speaks *ex cathedra,* that is, when acting in the office of shepherd and teacher of all Christians, he defines, by virtue of his supreme apostolic authority, doctrine concerning faith and morals to be held by the universal Church, possesses through the divine assistance promised to him in the person of St. Peter, the infallibility with which the divine Redeemer willed his Church to be endowed in defining doctrine concerning faith or morals; and that such definitions are therefore irreformable of themselves, and not from the consent of the Church.[32]

It is necessary to consult the proceedings of the Council to see how it answered the three main questions that the definition settled:

1. Who is infallible? The Pope is personally infallible, yet in a very particular sense. His infallibility is personal because it belongs to the Roman Pontiff, not to the Church in Rome or to the Roman See. It is personal insofar as it belongs to each legitimate occupant of this See. It is not personal, however, in belonging to the Pope as a private theologian and much less as a private individual. Although we attribute the gift of infallibility to the person of the Roman Pontiff, it belongs to him as a public person, the head of the Church in his relation to the Church universal. Nor is he infallible simply as Pope, but as subject to the divine assistance guiding him. As Pope he is always the supreme judge in faith and morals, and the father and teacher of all Christians; but he enjoys the unique grace to protect him from error only when he actually and specifically exercises the office of supreme judge in controversies of faith and of teacher of the universal Church.

2. How is the Pope infallible? His infallibility is unique and distinctive because it is founded on the special promise of Christ and on the special grace of the Holy Spirit, which is not the same as that enjoyed by the whole body of the teaching Church joined with its visible head. Having said this, however, we may not go on to separate the Pope from his divinely ordained conjunction with the Church. He is infallible only when, as teacher of all Christians and intending to speak for the whole Church, he judges and defines what is to

be believed or rejected by all the faithful. He can no more be separated from the Church than a foundation can be separated from the building it supports.

Furthermore, we do not separate the Pope teaching infallibly from the co-operation of the Church, at least in the sense that we do not exclude such co-operation. In the first place, the very issue or problem on which infallible pronouncement is solicited arises within the Church, and referred by her to the Holy See for settlement or decision. Then in view of the gravity of the matter, the Pope is bound by his office to take suitable means for ascertaining the truth before defining it. Such means are regional and ecumenical councils, episcopal synods, or the counsel of bishops, cardinals, and theologians. The means differ in various cases and, although the Pope could define infallibly without these instruments, they are the ordinary means provided by Christ to assist the Pontiff in arriving at an infallible judgment.

We also do not separate the Pope actively teaching from the Church responsively consenting to his doctrine, provided we do not make this consent a condition for papal infallibility either before or after a definition is made. Juridically, therefore, the Pope's decision does not require approval from the bishops or the body of the faithful in order to take effect. But actually this consent of the Church will not be withheld, for as we believe that the Pope is objectively infallible by divine assistance, we also believe that the Holy Spirit insures that the subjective assent of the Church will not be wanting. This is another way of saying that God will not permit the whole Catholic hierarchy to be separated from their visible head nor allow the universal Church to fail.

3. What is the scope of papal infallibility? As explained by the Vatican Council, the function of infallibility is to "preserve the flock of Christ from the poison of error." Since error can occur in two areas of human life—in knowledge as such and in knowledge pertaining to conduct—infallibility covers both forms of cognition. Hence the expression, which may at first seem odd, "doctrine concerning faith or morals." The infallible pronouncement is said to be doctrine (Latin *docere,* to teach) because it is taught by the Church. The doctrine, however, may deal either with something that is to be simply accepted by the mind as true, e.g., Mary's Immaculate Conception, and then it pertains to faith; or it may deal with

something that is also to be acted upon by the will as good, e.g., the indissolubility of Christian marriage, and then it pertains to morals.

The papal infallibility defined by the Church refers not only to the occasional exercise of the Pope's prerogative to proclaim such dogmas as the bodily Assumption into heaven of the Blessed Virgin, or such dogmatic facts as the canonization of saints. It spans the entire spectrum of solemn teaching authority in all ages and in every contingency, notably the confirmation of ecumenical councils and, on rare occasion, of certain decisions of regional councils affecting the universal Church. A dramatic instance of papal selectivity in confirming an ecumenical council involved the Council of Constance, which successfully healed the Western Schism when there were three claimants to the papacy. Among the Council's decrees, however, was one drawn up by a minority of the bishops which stated that "all persons of whatever dignity, even the Pope himself, are bound to obey the council in all that regards the faith." Pope Martin V deliberately excluded this decree from his approbation.

Within the ambit of papal infallibility are not only truths immediately revealed by God, like Christ's divinity or the Real Presence, but also those that are somehow connected with the revelation in Scripture and sacred Tradition. They are needed either to safeguard the deposit of revealed truth, or rightly to explain it, or efficaciously to carry it into practice.

The truths of revelation are included directly and immediately in the Vatican definition as the primary objects of the infallible magisterium. As regards the secondary objects or truths, not formally revealed but connected with revelation, a careful explanation should be made because it was precisely this area of infallibility that the Jansenists questioned and later developed into Gallicanism. Our guides in this matter are the official proceedings of the Council and specifically the theological commission that drew up the definition.

The focal question that the Council asked itself was: Do we wish to define the Pope's infallibility to include both revealed truths and such nonrevealed truths as philosophical principles and dogmatic facts? Their intention was a simple affirmative: "The infallibility of the Church in such definitions," the bishops were told before they voted, "while not directly asserted, is nevertheless implicitly declared. For the opinion which denies the obligation of mental assent in this type of definition is proved to be false from the Church's infallibility not only in truths that are immediately (per se) revealed, but also in those which are somehow connected with the former." In setting up the definition of infallibility, the commission consciously chose the expression "when he defines doctrine to be held," and not "doctrine to be held by divine faith."[33] Had the Council intended to limit infallibility to what is directly and explicitly revealed, the phrase "by divine faith" or its equivalent would have been essential. The Council Fathers were informed that any such limiting term was deliberately omitted in order to extend papal infallibility beyond immediate revelation to include whatever is related to the revealed content of the Bible and Tradition.

When papal infallibility was defined a century earlier, the Council had stated that the Pope's inerrancy partakes of the indefectibility with which Christ willed his Church to be endowed. Concretely, therefore, once the notion of collegiality was unraveled it was only a logical step to affirm that, besides papal infallibility properly so called, there is also such a thing as collegial infallibility. The Second Vatican Council took this logical step, and its statement in that direction marks a turning point in doctrinal history.

> Individual bishops do not enjoy the prerogative of infallibility. Nevertheless, when, in the course of their authentic teaching on faith or morals, they agree on one position to be held as definitive, they are proclaiming infallibly the teaching of Christ. This happens when, though scattered throughout the world, they observe the bond of fellowship tying them to each other and to Peter's successor. This occurs more obviously when, united in an ecumenical council, they are the teachers and judges of faith and morals for the universal Church, and an obedient adherence must be given to their definitions of faith.[34]

Several elements in this conciliar statement are of capital importance:

1. Unlike the apostles, their successors are not individually infallible. Yet, like the apostles, they are infallibe when they concur on some one position of faith and morals. Needless to say, their agreement does not make the doctrine inerrantly true; their concurrence manifests what is already and therefore objectively true. Thus the operation of the Spirit of truth depends on the collegial co-operation of the hierarchy in union with the successor of Peter.

2. This concurrence among the bishops may be either vertical,

as reflected in the historic continuity of teaching, or horizontal, as seen in their agreement at any given period of the Church's life and worship. The implication is that we need not be able to trace historically through ecclesiastical documents the Church's hierarchical teaching on some matter of faith and morals. It is enough if the combined Catholic episcopate, united with the bishop of Rome, show such agreement. The dogma of Mary's Assumption was finally defined by the Pope on the strength of this horizontal consensus.

3. The evidence of collegial infallibility is most obvious when the bishops meet in ecumenical gatherings, as they have from A.D. 325 to the Second Vatican Council, which closed in 1965. What this means is more than may have been heretofore supposed. Ecumenical councils are not merely consultative gatherings of the hierarchy at which discussions occur and the results casually passed on to the Pope for him to do with as he arbitrarily pleases. It is not as though the *council* is simply a collective *counsel,* which the Pope may treat with indifference since, it might be said, he is personally infallible anyway. Not at all. Assuming that the bishops leave the final decision up to the Roman Pontiff, yet their conciliar deliberations partake of the charism of infallibility; their conciliar insights are under the direct influence of the Spirit of wisdom; and their conciliar agreement is a divinely given sign that God is enlightening the Church through their decisions.

4. Always it is assumed that what the bishops agree upon among themselves has also been approved by the bishop of Rome. The manner of this approval will depend on the situation and, as the Church's history more than once testifies, it cannot be just taken for granted. It must be either explicit or so abundantly clear from the circumstances that the faithful can have no doubt that their bishops are in full agreement with the Vicar of Christ.

5. The scope of collegial infallibility extends to the whole range of doctrine on faith and morals, comparable to what the First Vatican Council had defined regarding the Pope. Accordingly, the freedom from error is not limited to matters of strict revelation, but covers also whatever is in any way connected with revealed truth and on which the bishops of the Catholic world agree in their authentic teaching, i.e., in their official capacity as shepherds of the flock of Christ. In the moral order, the Church's teaching on contraception exemplifies this kind of inerrancy.

SACRAMENT OF SALVATION

The Catholic Church makes claims about herself that are easily misunderstood, especially in the modern atmosphere of pluralism and ecumenism. Among these claims, the most fundamental is the doctrine of the Church's necessity for salvation. Not unlike other dogmas of the faith, this one has seen some remarkable development, and the dogmatic progress has been especially marked since the definition of papal infallibility. It seems that as the Church further clarified her own identity as regards the papacy and collegiality, she also deepened (without changing) her self-understanding as the mediator of salvation to mankind.

The New Testament makes it plain that Christ founded the Church to be a society for the salvation of all men. The ancient Fathers held the unanimous conviction that salvation cannot be achieved outside the Church. St. Ireneus taught that "where the Church is, there is the spirit of God, and where the spirit of God is, there is the Church and all grace."[35] Origen simply declared, "Outside the Church nobody will be saved."[36] And the favorite simile in patristic literature for the Church's absolute need to be saved is the Ark of Noah, outside of which there is no prospect of deliverance from the deluge of sin.

Alongside this strong insistence on the need for belonging to the Church was another Tradition from the earliest times that is less well known. It was understandable that the early Christian writers would emphasize what is part of revelation, that Christ founded "the Catholic Church which alone retains true worship. This is the fountain of truth; this, the home of faith; this, the temple of God."[37] They were combating defections from Catholic unity and refuting the heresies that divided Christianity in the Mediterranean world and paved the way for the rise of Islam in the seventh century.

But they also had the biblical narrative of the "pagan" Cornelius who, the Acts tell us, was "an upright and God-fearing man" even before baptism. Gradually, therefore, as it became clear that there were "God-fearing" people outside the Christian fold, and that some were deprived of their Catholic heritage without fault on their part, the parallel Tradition arose of considering such people open to salvation, although they were not professed Catholics or even necessarily baptized. Ambrose and Augustine paved the way for making these distinctions. By the twelfth century, it was widely assumed that a person can be saved if some "invincible obstacle stands in the way" of his baptism and entrance into the Church.

Thomas Aquinas restated the constant teaching about the general necessity of the Church. But he also conceded that a person may be saved extra sacramentally by a baptism of desire and therefore without actual membership by reason of his at least implicit desire to belong to the Church.

It would be inaccurate, however, to look upon these two traditions as in opposition. They represent the single mystery of the Church as universal sacrament of salvation, which the Church's magisterium has explained in such a way that what seems to be a contradiction is really a paradox.

Since the Fourth Lateran Council in 1215 defined that "The universal Church of the faithful is one, outside of which no one is saved," there have been two solemn definitions of the same doctrine, by Pope Boniface VIII in 1302 and at the Council of Florence in 1442. At the Council of Trent, which is commonly looked upon as a symbol of Catholic unwillingness to compromise, the now familiar dogma of baptism by desire was solemnly defined; and it was this Tridentine teaching that supported all subsequent recognition that actual membership in the Church is not required to reach one's eternal destiny.

At the Second Council of the Vatican, both streams of doctrine were delicately welded into a composite whole:

> [The Council] relies on sacred Scripture and Tradition in teaching that this pilgrim Church is necessary for salvation. Christ alone is the mediator of salvation and the way of salvation. He presents himself to us in his Body, which is the Church. When he insisted expressly on the necessity for faith and baptism, he asserted at the same time the necessity for the Church which men would enter by the gateway of baptism. This means that it would be impossible for men to be saved if they refused to enter or to remain in the Catholic Church, unless they were unaware that her foundation by God through Jesus Christ made it a necessity.
>
> Full incorporation in the society of the Church belongs to those who are in possession of the Holy Spirit, accept its order in its entirety with all its established means of salvation, and are united to Christ, who rules it by the agency of the Supreme Pontiff and the bishops, within its visible framework. The bonds of their union are

the profession of faith, the sacraments, ecclesiastical government and fellowship. Despite incorporation in the Church, that man is not saved who fails to persevere in charity, and remains in the bosom of the Church "with his body" but not "with his heart." All the Church's children must be sure to ascribe their distinguished rank to Christ's special grace and not to their own deserts. If they fail to correspond with that grace in thought, word and deed, so far from being saved, their judgment will be the more severe.[88]

Using this conciliar doctrine as guide, we see that the Church is (in its way) as indispensable as Christ for man's salvation. The reason is that, since his ascension and the descent of the Spirit, the Church is Christ active on earth performing the salvific work for which he was sent into the world by the Father. Accordingly, the Church is necessary not only as a matter of precept but as a divinely instituted means, provided a person knows that he must use this means to be saved.

Actual incorporation into the Church takes place by baptism of water. Those who are not actually baptized may, nevertheless, be saved through the Church according to their faith in whatever historical revelation they come to know and in their adequate cooperation with the internal graces of the Spirit they receive.

On both counts, however, whoever is saved owes his salvation to the one Catholic Church founded by Christ. It is to this Church alone that Christ entrusted the truths of revelation which have by now, though often dimly, penetrated all the cultures of mankind. It is this Church alone that communicates the merits won for the whole world on the cross.

Those who are privileged to share in the fullness of the Church's riches of revealed wisdom, sacramental power, divinely assured guidance, and blessings of community life cannot pride themselves on having deserved what they possess. Rather they should humbly recognize their chosen position and gratefully live up to the covenant to which they have been called. Otherwise what began as a sign of God's special favor on earth may end as a witness to his justice in the life to come.

MISSION TO THE WORLD

There are few words in the Catholic vocabulary that have more meanings than "mission." The term can refer to the mission that

Christ received from his Father when he came into the world to redeem the fallen human race; or the Church's mission from Christ to carry on his work until the end of time; or the sense of mission that all the faithful should have to bring others to a knowledge and love of Christ; or the mission enterprises in which certain persons leave their home and fatherland to preach the Gospel to distant peoples; or the mission sponsored in a locality or diocese to arouse the people to a greater fidelity in the practice of religion. "Mission" is also used to describe the appointments that men and women religious receive from their superiors, and it commonly refers to the smaller or outlying groups of believers who are not yet large enough to form a parish but homogeneous enough to have the regular services of a priest ministering to their needs.

Extension of the Incarnation. Underlying these and similar uses of the term is a fundamental concept that touches on the essence of the Church as an extension of the Incarnation of the Son of God. It is not a new concept, but today's age of communications has given it such apostolic implications as were only vaguely surmised even a century ago.

From the beginning of his public life, Christ called to himself those whom he desired, and they came to him. He appointed twelve to be with him in a special way, and he sent them out to preach even while he was still among them before his passion and death. Thus the apostles were the seed of the new Israel and at the same time the origin of a sacred hierarchy. After his resurrection from the dead and receiving, as he said, all power in heaven and on earth, he founded his Church as the sacrament of salvation and sent the apostles into the whole world, just as he had been sent by the Father. In doing so he gave them a mandate, "Go therefore and make disciples of all nations, baptizing them in the name of the Father and of the Son and of the Holy Spirit, teaching them to observe all that I have commanded you" (Mt. 28:19–20); and again, "Go into all the world and preach the Gospel to the whole creation. He who believes and is baptized will be saved; but he who does not believe will be condemned" (Mk. 16:15–16).

These words of Christ place a double responsibility twice over on his followers. They have the duty to propagate both the true faith in Christ and the merited salvation by Christ; and their duty arises not only from the Savior's command but in virtue of the divine life that he pours into his members.

It follows, then, that in its most basic sense the Church has a mission, because all who believe in Christ are to share with others what he has freely bestowed on them. What this means can now be capsulized in two sentences of Catholic doctrine:

> The mission of the Church is fulfilled by that activity whereby, in obedience to Christ's mandate and moved by the grace and charity of the Holy Spirit, she becomes fully and actively present to all men or nations, in order to lead them to faith in Christ, to his freedom and his peace, by living example and preaching, by the sacraments and other means of grace, so that a clear and reliable way may be opened to them toward full participation in the mystery of Christ.

> Because this mission is a continuation and, through the course of history, an unfolding of the mission of Christ himself, who was sent to preach the Gospel to the poor, the Church, prompted by the Spirit of Christ, must proceed along the same way that Christ followed, i.e., the way of poverty, obedience, service, and self-sacrifice even to death.[39]

Practical Implications. One of the features of modern thought is the way religious writers speak of various persons or cultures in their relationship to Christianity. Nuances have entered the language that were quite absent not many generations ago. Thus we speak of the non-Christian religions like Hinduism and Buddhism because their adherents are, de facto, not Christians and their religious ancestry, as among the Hindus, may reach back several millennia before Christ. We speak of other people as behaving in un-Christian ways or having un-Christian morals because their conduct is contrary to the Christian spirit or principles; they may be Christian in name, but their lives are contrary to what they profess to be. When a whole segment of society seems to betray this kind of departure from Christian values, we say it is post-Christian or has become de-Christianized. And when organized forces of power are actively engaged in opposition to Christians as a people or their religion as a way of life, we call them anti-Christian in character.

Each of these four strata of human society is a valid object of the Church's mission enterprise in a way and to an extent that was either not so apparent or necessary or possible before what we call the present age.

Addressing herself to the non-Christian cultures of mankind, "the Catholic Church rejects nothing that is true and holy in these religions. She regards with sincere reverence those ways of conduct and of life, those precepts and teachings which, though differing in many respects from the ones she holds and sets forth, nonetheless reflect a ray of that Truth which enlightens all men."

Admission of this, however, only indicates that salvation is possible for non-Christians because grace is not denied them. But the Church's mission is to lead all men to a complete sharing in the mystery of Christ. Her duty, therefore, is to proclaim, and "she must ever proclaim Christ the way, the truth, and the life, in whom men may find the fullness of religious life, in whom God has reconciled all things to himself."[40]

The operative word in the evangelization of non-Christian peoples is "fullness," by which is meant that through the Gospel they have access to a plenitude of divine gifts that would otherwise not be obtainable.

Un-Christian behavior among those who profess the Christian name has deeper significance than merely saying that they misbehave. For a large number of still nominal believers, it means that not only their conduct but their principles have become de-Christianized. Their condition may be the result of a long process of spiritual regression in the society into which they were born, to such a degree that "though they belong to the Church, they have in fact never given a true personal adherence to the message of revelation." Technically speaking, the mission efforts directed toward such persons are rather catechesis than evangelization; showing that, according to circumstances, evangelization can precede or accompany catechesis.[41] This means that conversion is an essential part of teaching the faith, whether as catechesis to those who have already been baptized or as evangelization to those who have not yet been actually incorporated into the Mystical Body. Conversion, in turn, is that deeply sensed commitment by which a person gives himself freely and from inner conviction to Christ in the Catholic Church.

The mission work of the Church is intended not only for individuals but for societies; and not only to Christianize those who so far have been only lightly touched by the Gospel, but those too who need to be re-Christianized after having lapsed from their corporate allegiance to the Savior. Between the two apostolates, experience shows that to reconvert a society is often more difficult than original evangelization. Apathy and indifference, coupled with self-righteous immersion in the things of this world, are formidable obstacles to conversion.

Although seldom thought of in these terms, the Church's mission includes proclaiming the Gospel to those who are actively engaged in opposing the followers of Christ. Since the opposition has become so massive and internationally organized, this kind of evangelization takes on historic importance. This is only gradually coming to be appreciated, but it has a noble heritage, dating from the first missions of the Church, in apostolic and postapostolic times. They were productive of untold converts to Christianity; but they were also the ages of great persecution.

St. Paul spoke in this vein when he told the Corinthians that "we have been persecuted, but never deserted; knocked down, but never killed. Always, wherever we may be, we carry with us in our body the death of Jesus, so that the life of Jesus, too, may always be seen in our body" (2 Co. 4:9–10). His endurance was his effective witness to Christ.

At the canonization ceremonies for the forty martyrs of England and Wales, Paul VI drew on the experience of history and quoted from the Second Vatican Council, which he confirmed to bring out the single greatest need for the Church's mission to the world:

> The Church of Christ was born from the sacrifice of Christ on the cross, and she continues to grow and develop in virtue of the heroic love of her most authentic sons and daughters. "The blood of martyrs is the seed of Christians." Like the shedding of Christ's blood, so the martyrs' oblation of their lives becomes, in virtue of their union with Christ's sacrifice, a source of life and spiritual fertility for the Church and for the whole world. "Martyrdom makes the disciple like his Master in his unconstrained acceptance of death for the world's salvation. The Church values it as the choice gift, the highest test of charity."[42]

Seeing the extent of this "choice gift" in so many parts of today's Christian world offers great promise of "spiritual fertility for the Church" into the future.

CATHOLIC ECUMENISM

History tells us that already during the first century there was evidence of Christian disunity and corresponding efforts to heal such breaches. One particular rift elicited an ecumenical document by Pope Clement I. "Do we not have one God, one Christ, and one Spirit of grace poured out upon us? And is there not one calling in Christ?"

he asked the Corinthians.[43] Why, then, should there be divisions in the Church of Christ?

As the rifts became more extensive and the divisions more permanent, the Catholic Church increased its efforts to reunite what Christ was so plain in saying should be his one flock. Looked at from the vantage point of our day, these Catholic efforts may appear to have been one-sided—always the insistence on the acceptance of Rome's authority and always the Church's claim to possessing the fullness of God's revelation. But in this sense Catholic ecumenism has not changed, even with and since Vatican II. What the Council did, however, was to enter a movement that had been generations in the making, mainly among the Protestant bodies of the world—initiated by the heirs of the Reformation. Their leaders reminded them that it was impossible to give the non-Christian world a united witness of Christ as long as Christians were divided into so many competing denominations.

A little-known document was authorized by St. Pius X, though sent by the bishop of Cremona, to the Protestant-sponsored international conference at Edinburgh in 1910, which inaugurated the present ecumenical movement. "The elements of faith in which you all agree are numerous and are common to the various Christian bodies, and then can serve as a point of departure for your discussion." Indeed, "this is a work in which we in our day may well cooperate."[44]

Benedict XV and Pius XI followed the growth of ecumenical interest closely. But they also cautioned against hasty expectations. When Pius XI issued the Church's first encyclical on ecumenism, many were disappointed. Authentic unity, according to the Pope, "can be born of but one single authority, one sole rule of faith, and one identical Christian belief."[45]

Protestant historians have since admitted that the warning was timely and saved the cause of unity from lapsing into a vague sort of fellowship that ignored the grave issues which divide the Churches of Christendom.

Pius XII returned to the same theme, expressing his keen interest in the unification efforts in Europe and North America, but he also stressed that the Church must remain "inflexible before all that could have even the appearance of a compromise, or of an adjustment of the Catholic Faith with other confessions."[46] His successor, John XXIII, though commonly credited with giving Christian unity its principal impetus among Catholics, was equally explicit when it came to the essentials of doctrine. He foresaw the Council he had convoked as "an admirable spectacle of truth, unity, and charity. We have confidence that such a manifestation will be for Christians separated from Rome a gentle invitation to seek and find that unity for which Christ offered to his Father such an ardent prayer."[47]

Under Paul VI, the *Decree on Ecumenism* of the Second Vatican Council represents the first formal statement by a general council on the doctrinal principles for reuniting a dismembered Christianity.

The Second Vatican Council began by noting that there had been divisions among Christians from the beginning and, as these became ecclesiastically structured, many persons were born into churches now separated from visible unity with the successors of the apostles under Peter. But they cannot now be charged with sin for being separated. They are, in fact, embraced by the Catholic Church as brethren and should be treated with respect and affection.

Such persons are Christians as long as they have been truly baptized and believe in Christ. They are consequently "established in a fellowship with the Catholic Church, even if the fellowship be incomplete." Moreover, "they are incorporated in Christ," and they possess "a number of the important elements or gifts from which the Church derives her structure and life." Thus they have "the written word of God, the life of grace, faith, hope, and charity, and other inward gifts and visible elements from the Holy Spirit."[48]

They also perform certain ritual actions that are sources of grace for themselves and those to whom they minister. "Christ's Spirit," therefore, "has not refused to employ them as means of salvation," so that their "churches and communities," though deficient by Catholic standards, pertain to the mystery of redemption.

Catholicism then adds one inevitable limitation. These Christians are not blessed with the unity that Christ wants his followers to possess. They also lack the fullness of those benefits of the New Covenant that Christ entrusted "to the apostolic college over which Peter presides."

As a conclusion to these premises, the function of ecumenism becomes very clear. It is something inspired by God, which comprehends "all the activities and attempts that are initiated and coordinated for the purpose of encouraging the unity of Christians; they vary with the needs of the Church and the moments of opportunity."

On the practical level, this means that Catholics should avoid any words, judgments, or actions that do not correspond to what other Christians believe or do. Positively, they should engage in dialogue with separated brethren through discussion, co-operative action, and corporate prayer. Such dialogue presumes study and the desires to learn how the Orthodox, Anglicans, and Protestants worship, what they believe, and how their allegiance to Christ has affected their lives.

More important than anything else, however, is "spiritual ecumenism," which can best be seen as reversing in the future what had been done in the past. One of the main reasons historically for Christian disunity was the disloyalty to Christ among those who called themselves Catholic. Their religious descendants today cannot do better to advance the cause of unity than to follow the Savior with great generosity, notably in the love of his cross, in order to contribute to the "daily cleansing and renewal of the Church, which carries the lowly and dying state of Jesus in its body, until Christ shall summon it into his presence in all its beauty" at the end of time.[49]

CHURCH AND STATE

The doctrine on Church and State and their mutual relationship is as old as Christianity. It arose with the advent of Christ, because in ancient times the public authority had equal competence in the field of religion and the secular domain. With the coming of Christianity, however, an essential change was introduced by its founder, who transferred to the Church the sphere of religion and the whole moral direction of mankind independent of the power of the State.

Our immediate purpose is to see the development of this relationship between these two separate societies. As we go through the doctrinal issues, they will be seen to fall into two categories: those that are immutable because they flow from divine law and by God's divine revelation; and others, which are adaptable to different times and which even in the same period may vary according to different circumstances.

Duties of Citizenship in the New Testament. Significantly, the classic statement of Christ on the relationship of his kingdom to the civil power was provoked by religionists who had no sympathy with the secular authority to which they were subject. The Pharisees sought to trap Jesus by asking him if it was lawful to render tribute to Caesar, where the word "tribute" embraced all kinds of taxes payable to state officials. Pharisees and Herodians had long since adjusted their conscience to the payment. But they hoped to force Christ to compromise himself no matter how he answered. If he advised nonpayment, as they expected, he became indictable to Rome. The pseudo-Messiah, Judas the Galilean, had perished for this very cause some twenty years before. Should he advise payment, he would lose his Messianic hold on the people for whom Messianism meant complete independence of foreign domination.

Instead of falling into the trap set for him, Jesus forced his enemies to convict themselves by asking for a coin with Caesar's image, and then declaring that, since the coin had come from Caesar, justice requires that it be returned to him. "Give back to Caesar," he said, "what belongs to Caesar—and to God what belongs to God" (Lk. 20:25). Civil transactions like the payment of taxes are on one plane, the rights of God on another. There is no inevitable clash unless, as happened in the relationship of Rome to the Jewish people, the civil authority hinders a man's duties to God.

In the apostolic Church, Peter implemented the teaching of his Master by urging Christians to accept the established form of government and submit to those in authority "for the sake of the Lord," i.e., for Christ. "Accept the authority of every social institution: the Emperor, as the supreme authority, and the governors as commissioned by him. . . . God wants you to be good citizens, so as to silence what fools are saying in their ignorance." And he concluded, "fear God and honor the Emperor" (1 P. 2:13-17).

As in the case of Christ, so here the injunction to be subject to the Emperor takes on added significance when the Emperor is identified as Nero, and the motive indicated is the will of God.

However, St. Paul again was the more elaborate exponent of Church and State relations in early Christianity. His exhortation to the Romans remains to this day an epitome of the obedience that a Christian owes to civil rulers. "You must all obey the governing authorities," he enjoins, "since all government comes from God, the civil authorities were appointed by God, and so anyone who resists authority is rebelling against God's decision, and such an act is bound to be punished." Yet the ultimate reason for submission is not the physical punishment that follows on disobedience. Rather, "You must obey, therefore, not only because you are afraid of being punished, but also [and primarily] for conscience' sake." Again, "This is also the reason why you must pay taxes, since all government officials are God's officers" (Rm. 13:1–6).

All subsequent teaching on the duties of Christian citizens has appealed to this dictum of St. Paul, that there exists no authority, including the civil, except from God, and those who possess it have been authorized by God.

The early Christians clearly distinguished between the spiritual allegiance they owed the Church and the civic loyalty that was due to the State. Where the latter encroached on the former, it could not be obeyed; but within the limits of due authority the State had a right to perfect obedience and a title to Christian prayer, that the Lord might direct the rulers in their government and assist their temporal reign.

From Established Religion to Separate Powers. Not long after the Edict of Constantine, Catholicism had become so widely recognized that the civil authorities found in religious unity their strongest support for political solidarity.

Before the end of the fifth century, we have a statement of the Holy See on the relative status of ecclesiastical and civil power, which to this day is the most succinct expression of the Church's mind on the subject. It was occasioned by the attitude of the Eastern Emperor, Anastasius I, who presumed to favor the schismatic patriarchs of Constantinople, particularly with regard to the Monophysite heresy condemned by Rome. Pope Gelasius I (492–96) wrote to the Emperor to point out to him the illegality of his interference in Church affairs. His letter included an exposition of the Gelasian thesis that the spiritual and secular authorities are each independent in their own realm, with which the other must not interfere:

> There are two powers by which this world is chiefly ruled: the sacred authority of the Popes and the royal power. Of these, the priestly power is much more important, because it has to render account for the Kings of men themselves at the divine tribunal. For you know that although you have the highest place in dignity over the human race, yet you must submit yourself faithfully to those who have charge of divine things, and look to them for the means of your salvation . . . For if in matters pertaining to the administration of public discipline, the bishops of the Church, knowing that

the Empire has been conferred on you by divine instrumentality, are themselves obedient to your laws, lest in purely material affairs contrary opinions may seem to be voiced, with what willingness, I ask you, should you obey those to whom is assigned the administration of divine mysteries?[50]

Gelasius adds that if the hearts of the faithful should be submissive to all who have ecclesiastical authority, how much more to him who presides over that see which God himself had placed over the whole Catholic priesthood.

Gelasius' document was chronologically the beginning of a long line of similar papal reactions to Caesaro-Papalism. Basically the attitude was not different than Peter's during the Neronian persecution, except that now the Church could protest against political intrusion instead of merely exhorting the Christians to bear the injustice with patience. However, as in Peter so in Gelasius, the sovereign rights of the State are forcefully recognized, even to the point of obedience among ecclesiastics when "purely secular interests are involved."

As the Church converted Europe to the faith, the Pope gained an ascendancy even in the political sphere that was simply unique. It was an experience that has not been repeated since. Given the turbulent times, it was quite natural for the people to look upon the bishop of Rome as the one unifying force, not only in things of the spirit, but in civil affairs as well.

The most controversial figure in this period of Church and State relations was Pope Boniface VIII, and his Bull *Unam Sanctam*, issued in 1302, was the high point of the controversy. Certainly no statement of the Holy See on this subject has been more roundly criticized or considered more embarrassing to Catholics.

The immediate occasion of the document was a long and heated conflict between the Pope and the King of France, Philip IV, called "the Fair." Philip insisted on deriving his authority in the tradition of Charlemagne and was reluctant to admit any principle of subordination to the papacy in secular matters. When the King imposed a heavy tax on the French clergy without previous agreement with Rome, Boniface took this as an infringement of ecclesiastical rights, and after protracted study of the principles involved, published the statement that was to sum up the plenitude of papal power over all the Christian community, including France and her King.

After declaring that there is only one holy, Catholic, and apostolic Church over which Christ placed only one head, "not two heads, as if it were a monster," Boniface explains the relation of the secular power to the spiritual:

> We are taught by the words of the Gospel that in this Church and in its power there are two swords, namely, a spiritual and a temporal. Both are in the power of the Church; the one, indeed, to be wielded for the Church, and the other by the Church. The former by the priest, the latter by the hands of kings and knights, but by the bidding and consent of the priesthood. It is necessary that one sword should be under the other, and that temporal authority be subjected to the spiritual. For, the truth bearing witness, the spiritual power should instruct the temporal power and judge it, if it be not good. . . . Hence we declare, affirm, define and pronounce that *it is altogether necessary for the salvation of every creature to be subject to the Roman Pontiff.*[51]

We must immediately distinguish between defined doctrine and ordinary papal teaching. Only the final sentence, as italicized, was solemnly defined and represents traditional Catholic dogma on the Church's necessity for salvation.

But how are we to understand the preceding statements on the subordination of State to Church, that the temporal sword is wielded "by the bidding and consent of the priesthood"? Those who say that Boniface VIII meant that the whole sphere of temporal jurisdiction is directly subject to the Church do the Pope an injustice against which he himself protested after the bull was published. Followers of Philip the Fair inserted into the document the spurious phrase, "We wish you (the King) to know that you hold your kingdom from us," adding that anyone who denied the proposition was a heretic. In a solemn consistory, Boniface denounced the forgery. "For forty years we have studied law, and we know that there are two powers appointed by God. Who should, then, or can, believe that we entertain, or have entertained, such stupid absurdity? We declare that in no way do we wish to usurp the jurisdiction of the King. . . . And yet, neither the King nor anyone else of the faithful can deny that he is subject to us where a question of sin is involved."[52]

The Pope's phrase "question of sin" has since become the standard norm to judge when and to what extent the Church may use its spiritual authority to intervene in the secular affairs of State. It may do so when an otherwise temporal affair (like civil divorce or legalized abortion) affects the religious interests of the faithful by placing an unwarranted burden on their conscience, exposing them to sin or otherwise conflicting with that spiritual welfare over which the Church alone has ultimate jurisdiction by the mandate of its founder. Of course, it takes courage for the Church's leaders to "intervene," and the history of men like Thomas à Becket or, in our times, of Faulhaber and Mindszenty tells how heroic the intervention can be.

In the next five hundred years, the Catholic Church experienced more than sporadic conflicts with oppressive political power. This period saw the rise of the secular State, with its claims to complete independence of the Church and its use, at times, of the most repressive measures to coerce conformity with its political will.

This naturally changed the tone of the Church's doctrinal defense of her rights over the consciences of the faithful, but it did not alter the principles that had been enunciated since the days of Constantine.

Separation of Church and State. Up to the Second Vatican Council, the writings of Leo XIII were the most incisive papal documentation on the relation of Church and State. Pope Leo recognized two kinds of Church and State separation, and they are radically different. The first he called separation as anti-Christianity, and the second was separation in which the Catholic Church did not enjoy preferential status before the civil law.

Speaking of the "vast conspiracy that certain men have formed for the annihilation of Christianity," the Pope denounced their boasted separation of Church and State as "equivalent to the separation of human laws from Christian and divine legislation. For as soon as the State refuses to give to God what belongs to God, by necessary consequences it refuses to give to citizens what as human beings they have a right to receive. The reason is that the rights of man derive from his duties toward God." Any separation built on these premises is a practical denial of the Church's right to existence. It is another name for political atheism.

More than a score of papal documents, of Pius X and Benedict XV, Pius XI and XII, John XXIII and Paul VI, returned to the same theme. As Marxism swept its way across Europe and Asia and found entrance in Africa and the two Americas, it became obvious that a titanic struggle was under way with an ideology that considered religion, especially the Christian religion, an opiate of the people and therefore to be either crushed or absorbed out of existence.

Pius XI stigmatized the Marxist state as atheistic in principle, utopian in plan, and inhuman in its means of subordinating all other values to the dream of a new civilization built on blind evolutionary forces culminating in a humanity without God.[53]

Thirty years later, Vatican II could look back on a generation of experience with Marxian utopianism. It was an era of social destruction. Consequently, "it is right to reject the disastrous doctrine which strives to construct society without taking any account of religion, and which impugns the religious liberty of citizens and destroys it."[54] The record of thousands of Christians who shed their blood in witness of their faith was evidence of how ruthless in its exercise of power is a system whose social engineers deny liberty to anyone who will not submit to their scheme.

A less obvious and more delicate situation faces the Church where she has the free exercise of education and worship but without the priority she objectively deserves as the only true religion.

The Church sets forth the ideal situation, where "States are governed by the principles of the Gospels." As an ideal, it represents "the immutable law" of religious history, that "when civil power and the priesthood are in agreement, the world is well governed and the Church flourishes and develops. But when they disagree, not only smaller interests suffer but even things of greatest moment fall into miserable decay."[55] In spite of cupidity and human ambition, for centuries civil governments were built on a Christian foundation, with consequent benefits to themselves and posterity that only a prejudiced mind will deny. Then came the "lamentable rage for innovation that reached a climax in the sixteenth century" and is the acknowledged source of modern indifference toward the true religion.

Facing the issue realistically, we should admit that in many countries the government is not openly hostile to the Catholic Church but equates her with every religious denomination, with no preferential status before the law. "As a matter of principle," therefore, "the Church regards it unlawful to place various forms of divine worship on the same footing as the true religion." Nevertheless, "she does not, on that account, condemn those rulers who for the sake of securing some greater good, or of hindering some great evil, allow in practice that these various forms of religion have a place in the State. And in fact the Church is most careful not to have any one forced to embrace the Catholic faith against his will, for, as St. Augustine wisely reminds us, 'Man cannot believe except of his own free will.' "[56]

Religious Liberty. Successive Roman Pontiffs addressed themselves more than once to the same theme: the status of the Catholic Church in countries where the civil laws professed a separation of Church and State while recognizing the legitimacy of religious bodies and giving them protection or a degree of assistance from the State. But as time went on, it became more and more obvious that at heart was no mere question of expediency; that the real issue for the Catholic Church was to vindicate her unique position in the world of religion even where the State did not validate this position in political or legislative terms.

What is this unique position? Catholicism believes that "the Church is the spiritual authority set up by Christ the Lord with the duty, imposed by divine command, of going out into the whole world and preaching the Gospel to every creature." The result is that the Church claims two kinds of freedom, one social and the other personal. On the social level, "the Church claims her right to freedom in every human society and before every public authority." No State and no organized power on earth has the right to interfere with what the Church considers to be a mandate of the Son of God. On the personal level, "the Church also claims her right of freedom as being a society of men who enjoy the right to live in civil society according to the tenets of the Christian faith."

These two freedoms differ in that the Church is first of all a hierarchical society whose divinely instituted authorities have the right to teach, govern, and sanctify the faithful in "the things that pertain to God." But the Church is also composed of individual persons who have the correlative right to be taught, governed, and sanctified according to what faith tells them is the will of God.

Separation of Church and State, therefore, cannot mean subordination of Church to State. Too often verbal recognition or legal safeguards of the Church's freedom are only minimally implemented in practice. What the Church wants, and demands, is not only juridical but real liberty.

Only then does the Church possess by right and in practice stable conditions for the independence necessary in fulfilling her divine mission. Church authorities have been insisting with increasing urgency on this right in society. Christians also have the same civil rights as other men to be free in conducting their lives according to their consciences. Thus there exists no contradiction between the Church's liberty and that religious liberty which must be recognized as a right of all men and all communities, and given safeguards in the external legal order.[57]

As commonplace as these statements may sound, they reflect a major development in the doctrinal teaching of the Church on her relationship to the State. Out of numerous and largely unresolved conflicts between the Church's rights and the interests of State, three things had become clear.

1. Civil authorities have to be convinced that what the Church is asking is not exceptional. No doubt from the viewpoint of the Church, her position in the world is unique. But that is a matter of faith for those who believe in Catholic Christianity. Yet, concretely the freedom that Catholics request and expect are, in their way, no more exotic than those demanded by other societies within the State. Since societies have a moral personality all their own, they have the right to remain themselves and pursue their proper goals, provided this does not conflict with the legitimate rights of the State. So far from conflicting with the welfare of civil authority, the Church's existence and goals foster this welfare.

2. In language that everyone can understand, the Church's new stance on liberty is an appeal to conscience, of the people who compose the Church and of those who direct the destiny of States. In words that echo a previous era of persecution, the ecumenical council that spoke for the persecuted Church of today urged the faithful not to have their claims dismissed without a hearing. In equivalent terms, the modern State is asked: "Why do you suspect that what the Church teaches is hostile to the State? Why not give the faithful as much liberty to follow their consciences as you obviously grant others to follow theirs?"

3. In the light of its own fuller understanding of the Church as comprising all the baptized who accept Jesus Christ, Catholicism now speaks of the religious liberty not only of professed Catholics but of all Christians. They share a common bond in their allegiance to the Savior; and since the turn of the twentieth century they have shared in great measure a common suffering for this allegiance at the hands of those who mistakenly suppose that somehow good Christians cannot be good citizens.

Freedom of Education. No single area of Church and State relations has been more critical than that of education. This has been especially true since the "knowledge explosion" that began in the late nineteenth century.

As the years went by, two things became increasingly clear: that the modern expansion in knowledge of the material and psychological universe evoked an extraordinary desire for education in every country of the world, and that this legitimate hunger for learning was being supported by civil authorities. It all depended on how the authorities viewed the acquisition of knowledge. If they saw it mainly as an instrument for achieving temporal goals, they would shape the schools and curriculum accordingly. They would concentrate on one freedom: the State's to decide on what education, for how long, and in what schools best suited the people. The freedom of Christian parents to give their children the education they wanted, or of Christian students to learn what they desired, would be ignored.

At this juncture, the conciliar document consciously dealt with Christian, and not only Catholic, education. It was meant to be a beacon for all Christians, equally pressed by the State to defend their educational liberties. Moreover, its focus was on the corresponding freedom of parents and teachers to balance the already recognized academic freedom of the teacher.

Two kinds of freedom were being defended: the individual freedom of each parent and student, and the collective freedom of the institutions of education under the aegis of the Church.

> Parents have the primary and inalienable duty of educating their children, and must enjoy true freedom in choosing schools. Public authority, therefore, whose part it is to watch over and defend the liberties of its citizens, should, in the interest of distributive justice, take care that public assistance is dispensed in a way that enables parents to choose schools for their children according to their conscience, with genuine freedom.
>
> It is for the State, however, to see to it that all its citizens have the possibility of access to a due share in culture, and are given the necessary preparation for exercising their civil duties and rights. . . . In all this the State should have in view the principle of subsidiary function, excluding, therefore, any monopoly of schools; for this is hostile to the natural right of the human person, to the progress and spread of culture itself, and to the peaceful association of citizens and the pluralism that now has force in many societies.[58]

Before this magna charta of Christian education was proclaimed, the Holy See had many times defended the primary rights of the Church to educate the faithful, since the Church was established by Christ to teach all nations what he had first taught the apostles. So, too, the rights of parents were vindicated, as prior to those of the State because, unlike the State, father and mother are the natural teachers of the children they brought into the world.

While both priorities, of Church and parents over the State, called for restatement, it was especially the rights of parents that had to be defended in the face of a rising statism that sought to control the minds of its citizens by controlling schools. Everyone, whether Catholic or not, or even whether Christian or not, could appreciate the danger when the Second Vatican Council came to the defense of parental freedom in education.

There was a difference, however, between the freedom of all parents to have their children taught in schools under teachers of their own preference, and the freedom of Christian and Catholic parents to insure an authentically Christian education for their offspring.

The freedom of parents in general is the liberty from coercion, not to be forced by civil sanctions to send their children to institutions that contradict the parents' deepest natural convictions. After all, the child belongs to the parents before he or she becomes a citizen of the State. The parents gave the child being, not the State: existence does not come from the State, but from the parents.

The freedom of Christian and Catholic parents is not merely liberty from coercion; it is also the liberty of communication. And it is not only rooted in reason but has its foundation in faith. What does this mean? It means that parents who believe they have been given the fullness of God's revelation and have access to the plenitude of sacramental grace have a right twice over to see that those whom they procreated are also properly educated: once the right not to be compelled to let the State (or its agencies) substitute for their parental privilege to reproduce themselves in their children both physically and mentally; and once again the right to communicate to their children the supernatural treasures of faith that God through the Church had so generously bestowed on them.

VIII. HUMAN DESTINY

Human destiny is a principal preoccupation of the Scriptures and Sacred Tradition. We expect this from the revelation whose main concern is that we serve God faithfully in the present life in order to be happy with him in the life to come. What may be less obvious is that Catholic Christianity has a calm assurance about what this destiny is and how it is to be attained, and builds the whole edifice of the faith on its eschatology (from the Greek *eschata,* meaning "last things"). This is only logical. Depending on how we view what happens at bodily death and what we expect after we die, everything else follows. Since the Church believes that God has revealed very clearly that we do not die at death but merely change, and that our earthly habitation is to be exchanged for a heavenly one, all the rest is simply a means to an end. Indeed, what we are prone to call the end, because it seems to finish what our senses call real, on these premises is not the end but the beginning. But this beginning to which we are looking forward becomes the end, i.e., purpose, to which all our strivings on earth are supposed to tend. This is what the inspired writer had in mind when he counseled, "In everything you do, remember your end, and you will never sin" (Si. 7:40).

Although the customary last things are said to be death, judgment, heaven, and hell, they are to be taken in the exclusive sense that there are only two sets of ultimates for human existence. At the close of each person's life, we are told "men die only once, and after that comes judgment" (Heb. 9:27). There is no endless cycle of reincarnations. At the close of the present world, there will be a final retribution, of happiness or of misery.

Before the end of time, however, Catholicism believes there is still the prospect for expiation (not repentance) called purgatory because its function is to purify those who die in God's friendship but are not fully cleansed of the effects of their sins.

There is a stark realism in all of this, as the Church's teaching never fails to point out. Why fear death, the faithful are told, since it is the most beautiful adventure in life? So it is, but only to those who believe that this adventure is part of God's unfailing revelation to mankind.

AFTER DEATH COMES JUDGMENT

Christianity believes in two final destinies, one for man individually and the other for humanity as a whole. Our concern is mainly with the first, but in reflecting on personal death we may see in it a symbol and prelude of the end point of the universe itself. Often in the Bible the two destinies are so closely intertwined that it is not easy to distinguish whether the one or the other or both are being spoken about.

End of Probation. Not all parts of the Old Testament are equally clear about the future life or, in this case, about life as the time of probation during which a person can freely obey or disobey God. The classic passages occur in those books that belong to the Alexandrian Canon, i.e., accepted by the ancient Jews outside of Palestine. Among the most explicit are those that warn about worrying over loss or gain during life; it is the account to be given at the moment of death that counts (Si. 11:22–30).

The New Testament is so clear on the subject of death and its aftermath that the Gospels are almost thematic on the need for serving God faithfully in this life, because after death there is no chance of repentance. Christ's parable about Lazarus and the rich man is unmistakable. When the rich man begged Abraham for some relief from his sufferings, the man was told, "My son, remember that during your life good things came your way, just as bad things came the way of Lazarus. Now he is being comforted here while you are in agony. But that is not all: between us and you a great gulf has been fixed, to stop anyone, if he wanted to, crossing from our side to yours, and to stop any crossing from your side to ours" (Lk. 16:25–26).

St. Paul merely confirmed what Christ had taught. He spoke of our pilgrimage away from the Lord as long as we are in the body. Once the body is shed, we are able to possess the Lord. He said he was looking forward to death, so that he might be with the Lord and receive the crown of justice prepared not only for him but for all who have kept the faith until death. All of which indicates that, immediately after death, we receive the judgment of our works, either reward or retribution. In a rare outburst of expectation, Paul could say, "We are full of confidence, and actually want to be exiled from the body and make our home with the Lord. Whether we are living in the body or exiled from it, we are intent on pleasing him. For all the truth about us will be brought out in the law court of Christ, and each of us will get what he deserves for the things he did in the body, good or bad" (2 Co. 5:9–10).

In the history of Christian belief, there have not been many who challenged this doctrine: that the state of wayfarer or time of probation in God's service closes with death, and that immediately after death the eternal condition of the soul is determined by particular judgment, whose outcome is promptly carried into effect. One exception was the Origenists, claiming to follow in the footsteps of Origen. They were condemned by the Church in the middle of the sixth century for holding that "The punishments of devils and wicked men is temporary and will eventually cease, that is to say, that devils or the ungodly will be completely restored to their original state."[1]

Fortunately for the sharpest clarity on this subject, there occurred an incident during the Middle Ages that will also illustrate the role of the believing Church in maintaining the revealed faith.

John XXII (1249–1334) was one of the Avignon Popes whose exile from Rome later precipitated the Western Schism. As Pope he often preached in the churches at Avignon. In the course of a sermon delivered on All Saints' Day 1331, he said that the souls of the blessed do not enjoy the full sight of God until after the general judgment. The Pope's political enemies denounced him as a heretic. The University of Paris was disturbed; the King of France and the Emperor of Germany were invoked and sought to pacify the people. At first Pope John was adamant and defended himself by appealing to a few scattered passages in some of the Fathers. Then he called an assembly of cardinals and theologians, who convinced him he was mistaken. Soon after, on his deathbed (December 4, 1334), he publicly retracted the theory of "suspended judgment," while explaining that he had spoken not as head of the Church but simply as a private person.

Within a year of his elevation to the papacy, John's successor, Benedict XII (d. 1342), issued the famous *Constitution on the Last Things*. Its main intent was to settle once and for all the immediacy of divine judgment passed on those who die, and remove forever any suspicion raised by the Avignon Pope's "indiscreet" statements.

The Benedictine constitution states that "We, with our apostolic authority, make the following definition," and then goes on to declare that the souls of the just, who die in God's friendship, "soon after death and, in the case of those who need it, after purification, have been, are, and will be in heaven." Similarly, "the souls of those who die in actual mortal sin go down into hell soon after their death."[2] The operative word in this doctrine is usually translated "soon," i.e., *mox* in Latin, and it is understood to mean "promptly."

Meaning of Death. Few mysteries of the faith are more frequently kept before the eyes of the people than the mystery of death. Every Eucharistic liturgy is a sacramental memorial of Christ's death on the cross and of ours in union with him. Every sign of the cross is a symbolic reminder of the same truth, every Hail Mary is a prayer for a happy death.

In its preaching about death, the Church has been careful to avoid two extremes; either so concentrate on the moment of death and the transitory character of earthly things as to undervalue the importance of this life; or so ignore the sublimity of death as to canonize the goods of this world and distract the faithful from the pursuit of holiness.

Christ's words about the supreme importance of being ready when he calls us, as a thief in the night, and his stress on the passing worth of riches and honor in comparison with the grace of God remain as valid today as when he first spoke them in Palestine. It is possible, however, for someone looking at just this aspect of the faith to "accuse Christianity of being an enemy of temporal values and incapable of appreciating the present life." But the Church does not sanction this narrow view. She recognizes the values "that make the goods of creation, of nature, of human achievement, and of the present age, worthy of esteem."

Christianity is not pessimistic. The work of God, and the work of man, are objects of great importance in the Christian economy. But when man's life on earth is measured by time and by the standard of moral value, then some careful reassessment needs to be made. Measured by time, this life is short, whereas eternity is long. Measured by moral standards this life should be seen in all its terrifying, and exciting, potential for deciding our immortal destiny.

This concept of human life is certainly not fashionable. Everything today conspires to make us forget it. People live with an attitude that is fixed on the present moment only, as if this were permanent and not inevitably swept away by the following moment.

Thus we live in a twofold illusion, as if we were masters of time, and as if we could live on a plane of moral indifference, without duties based on a norm that is independent of our wills and autonomous conscience.[3]

Reflection on death helps to remove both illusions, as the lives of the saintly men and women of the Church testify. They asked themselves, with Augustine, whether to call their stay on earth a living death or a dying life. But in either case, they reached the same conclusion, that what most matters in life is to die commending their souls into the hands of God.

Death also offers the Christian the prospect of dying after the example of Christ. Faith teaches that all the actions of Christ are somehow exemplary for us, not excluding his death on the cross. By his death, he left us a perfect pattern of virtue, or rather a litany of virtues, notably of charity in laying down his life for others, of fortitude in courageously accepting death at the hands of his enemies and with the stigma of crime attached to his name, of patience in dying with calm resignation and with pardon for those who plotted his death, and of perfect obedience to the will of his Father.

The General Judgment. Belief in a general judgment on the last day is imbedded in the Apostles' Creed and the Nicene Creed, which affirm that Christ now "sits at the right hand of God the Father almighty, from there he shall come to judge the living and the dead."

The Savior's discourse before the passion about his return in glory is well known, but it contains too many profound mysteries of the faith to be taken for granted. It was preceded by a series of parables to bring out the importance of being alert, "So stay awake because you do not know the day when your master is coming." One parable compares the conduct of a faithful and an unjust steward, and praises the former, who typifies all the loyal disciples of Christ. The parable of the ten bridesmaids also compares five that were foolish and five that were sensible. Again the same moral from their respective conduct, negligence, and alertness, and then the warning, "So stay awake, because you do not know either the day or the hour" (Mt. 25:13). Then the long parable about the talents: five talents, two talents, and one talent given respectively to three different servants. Two were praised and the last was condemned, but again not for positive wickedness but for negligence, for "you should have deposited my money with the bankers, and on my return I would have recovered my capital with interest" (Mt. 25:27).

The parable on the last judgment foretells how the Son of Man will come in majesty, escorted by all the angels. Then he will take his seat on his throne of glory. "All the nations will be assembled before him and he will separate men from one another as the shepherd separates sheep from goats. He will place the sheep on his right hand and the goats on his left" (Mt. 25:32–33). The basis of his judgment will be how generously people had responded to the needs they met among those who entered their lives. Christ will identify these human needs with himself. To those on his right he will say, "I was hungry and you gave me food; I was thirsty and you gave me drink; I was a stranger and you made me welcome; naked and you clothed me, sick and you visited me, in prison and you came to see me" (Mt. 25:35–36). When "the virtuous" ask him when they saw him hungry or thirsty and ministered to him, he will tell them, "insofar as you did this to one of the least of these brothers of mine, you did it to me" (Mt. 25:40). Those on the left will be rejected for not having responded to the same wants.

The final judgment, therefore, is a social judgment because it will answer to the social side of humanity. We are to be judged not only as individuals but as members of society, to reveal to the world God's justice in those he condemns and his mercy in those who are saved.

But there is a deeper reason for the final judgment, arising from the nature of human actions. Their full import cannot be gauged the moment they are done, or even at the end of the life of a person who does them.

Things in a process of change are not fit subjects for judgment before they have come to a stop. No action can be fully assessed before it is finished and its results are evident. What may seem to be profitable at first may turn out to be damaging.

All the same, though a person's career ends with death, his life still goes on in a sense, and is affected by what happens afterward. He lives on in people's memories, and his reputation, good or bad, may not correspond to his real character. He lives on also in his children who are, so to speak, part of their parents.

But most important, a person survives in the results of his actions. Unkindness does not stop with an act of impatience or spite; its effects continue in a never-ending spiral long after the sin was committed. Charity does not cease with the love-inspired word of encouragement or the selfless sharing of pain; it starts a chain reaction of generosity that goes on for centuries after the one who began the reaction has died.

All these are submitted to divine scrutiny the moment a person enters eternity, but a full and public verdict cannot be pronounced while time rolls on its course. Only on the last day, when everything we have done will have reached its end result, can a truly final judgment be made. The manifestation would not be complete otherwise, since virtue is to be judged not only by the generosity that prompts it, but by the good effects it produces; and vice can be known not only by the selfishness that induces sin, but also by the harm that sinful actions bring.

LIFE EVERLASTING

Few doctrines of the faith have more practical importance for the believing Christian than the existence and nature of heavenly beatitude. It is at once the goal of all human effort and the motive for earthly achievement. The very name of a supernatural order takes its meaning from the end to which it is directed, and grace is only the means required to reach what is unattainable by any created being without elevation to the family of God.

When we speak of heavenly happiness, we really mean there are two sources of final beatitude. One is the possession of God, as seen, loved, and enjoyed by those whom he beatifies; and the other is a happiness that comes from the knowledge and love of creatures who are possessed along with God. No doubt the first is what makes heaven what the Creed professes it will be, everlasting life; but in heaven we shall also enjoy what on earth we know can be so attractive, and this, too, belongs to our future destiny.

Beatific Vision. The biblical teaching about heaven stresses what most needs to be said, namely, that eternal happiness is the reward for earthly fidelity to God's will and generous co-operation with grace. "The kingdom of heaven," Jesus taught, "may be compared to a King who gave a feast for his son's wedding. He sent his servants to call those who had been invited, but they would not come" (Mt. 22:1–2). So the King sent out a second invitation, and then a third. Finally there was a response, but even then one of the guests came to the feast not wearing a wedding garment. He was thrown out "into the dark." Christ's final observation was that many are called but few are chosen. No matter how interpreted, the implication is that heaven has to be striven after and only those who strive will attain.

It was left to the apostles to try to describe, without explaining, what the essential joy of heaven is like. Mysteriously, it consists in the immediate vision of God. "My dear people," the aged John told the Christians, "we are already the children of God, but what we are to be in the future has not yet been revealed; all we know is, that when it is revealed we shall be like him because we shall see him as he really is" (1 Jn. 3:2). St. Paul also compared the belief in God we have in this life with the experience that awaits us. "Now we are seeing a dim reflection in a mirror; but then we shall be seeing face to face. The knowledge that I have now is imperfect; but then I shall know as fully as I am known" (1 Co. 13:12).

There was no need for any formal statement of the Church on the beatific vision until the crisis arose in the Middle Ages, which provoked the *Constitution* of Benedict XII. His series of definitions remains the most authoritative teaching of the Catholic faith on the joys of heaven.

> We define that, since the passion and death of the Lord Jesus Christ, they (the souls in heaven) have seen and do see the divine essence with an intuitive and even face-to-face vision, without interposition of any creature in the function of the object seen. Rather, the divine essence immediately manifests itself to them plainly, clearly, openly.
>
> We also define that those who see the divine essence in this way receive great joy from it, and that because of this vision and enjoyment the souls of those who have already died are truly blessed and possess life and eternal rest.
>
> We further define that the souls of those who die hereafter will see the same divine essence and will enjoy it before the general judgment.

We define that this vision of the divine essence and the enjoyment of it do away with the acts of faith and hope of those souls, insofar as faith and hope are theological virtues in the proper sense.

And we define that after this intuitive and face-to-face vision has or will have begun for these souls, the same vision and enjoyment remains continuously without any interruption or abolition of the vision and enjoyment, and will remain up till the final judgment and from then on forever.[4]

Unequivocally, therefore, the essential object of heavenly happiness is God. He is the foundation and fulfillment of the joy of the blessed, in whom their souls find perfect rest.

But if God is the source of their beatitude, how is he seen? The Church teaches that he is seen by an intuitive vision, which means several things:

— It is intuition because the knowledge is not derived from reflection or a process of human reasoning.

— It is face-to-face vision to emphasize that nothing less than God stands between the soul and the divine essence, or rather that nothing stands between the human spirit and its Creator.

— It is perception without the interposition of any creature acting as medium through which God is beheld.

— It is an immediate manifestation, to express the indescribable intimacy between the soul and God, comparable to the nearness of the ego to a man's knowledge of himself. All created media are excluded.

— It reveals the Godhead plainly, openly, and clearly, because the meaning of the mysteries is disclosed. God is seen as he is in himself and not (as in this life) reflected only in his creatures. He reveals to the just his very being and not simply the products or finite beings he has made.

At the reunion Council of Florence, the Church added another dimension to the foregoing by defining that the souls of those who have not committed any sin after baptism, and those who have committed sin but have been cleansed either while in the body or afterward "are promptly taken up into heaven and see clearly the triune God, just as he is, some more perfectly than others according to their respective merits."[5]

Accordingly, it is God as the Trinity who is seen, the God of mystery and not of mere nature. This important qualification was occasioned by the strong trinitarian spirit of the Eastern Christians. Moreover, God will be seen "as he is," which not only incorporates the words of St. John but emphasizes that our present knowledge of God is, by comparison, a negative sublimation. We say that God is uncreated and infinite and immortal since the best we can do this side of heaven is to affirm that God is not what we know of creatures, which are created and finite and mortal. But in heaven, no more negation. God will show himself in himself as he really is.

Although the same God will be viewed by all and enjoyed by all, not everyone will have the same degree of happiness. The depth of beatitude will depend on the merits with which a person enters heaven.

Knowledge and Love of Creatures. Catholic Tradition holds that, besides the immediate vision of God, the joys of heaven also include the enjoyment of creatures. This may seem strange at first, since we would suppose that the vision of God is enough. How can creatures add to the beatitude conferred by the Creator?

A bit of reflection tells us, however, that all the happiness of heaven is from God. But not all comes from God in the same way. The essence of this happines comes, indeed, from the beatific vision. But there is also what the Church calls accessory happiness. This comes ultimately from God but immediately from other possessions along with God, not unlike the joys on earth.

Towering above all these heavenly possessions and common to all the blessed is the company and mutual love of the glorified Christ, the Virgin Mary, the angels and saints. Biblical comparisons liken heaven to a wedding feast; the good thief is promised paradise with Christ; and in heaven Christ said there were many mansions, which he went ahead to prepare for his followers. Heaven is described by St. John as a new city, of which Christ is the light and where those who served him will share in his victory.

One kind of created celestial joy pertains more directly to the spiritual powers of man, his mind and will; another form of created possession pertains to the body and presumes the general resurrection on the last day.

In the intellect of the blessed will remain those supernatural gifts that are not incompatible with their state of vision, excluding faith and hope, which imply limitations. Faith will be replaced by sight, and hope by attainment.

Knowledge acquired during one's life on earth is commonly said to carry into glory, as well as memory of past experiences, but always presupposing that such knowledge is beatifying.

Since there is communication of minds in heaven, knowledge is acquired from this interchange; otherwise the very purpose of companionship would be missing. The constant reference in Scripture to the societal character of heaven implies a society of communicating, intelligent beings.

It also seems necessary to postulate that those minds which on earth were unable to grow to normal perfection, like infants and others, are endowed in eternity with what is wanting to them. In the same way, after the resurrection of the body there will be new horizons of experience coming from that source, adding to the store of knowledge already acquired or infused before the last day.

The will of those in heavenly glory is freed from every sorrow and filled with every joy. Though clothed in symbolic language, the prophetic passages in the Apocalypse indicate something of this satisfaction of human desire:

These are the people who have been through the great persecution, and because they have washed their robes white again in the blood of the Lamb, they now stand in front of God's throne and serve him day and night in his sanctuary; and the One who sits on the throne will spread his tent over them. They will never hunger or thirst again; neither the sun nor scorching wind will ever plague them, because the Lamb who is at the throne will be their shepherd and will lead them to springs of living water; and God will wipe away all tears from their eyes (Rv. 7:14–17).

The blessed love everyone and everything ordinately, in God and for him. There can be no sadness over past sins, their own or that of others, nor regret over past mistakes and lost opportunities. Chrysostom summarized the Church's faith in this felicity in one of his homilies on the Letter to the Hebrews. "That will be true rest," he explained, "where all sorrow, sadness, and grief have passed away; where no more cares or labor, anguish or fears of mind are present, but only the wish to please God is filled with every joy. In heaven are all peace, pleasure, happiness, goodness, meekness, justice, and charity; no longer any competitive spirit or envy, no sickness or death of body, no prospect of death of soul, no darkness or night of spirit, but all is endless day and light and serenity. In heaven we shall never weary and never get bored, but be always on the alert for more."[6]

After the resurrection, the bodies of the blessed will be gifted with those properties of which St. Paul wrote to the Corinthians. After noting that there are differences in beauty between sun and moon, and one star differs from another, he said we can expect God who created these differences to also change the bodies that rise from the grave.

> It is the same with the resurrection of the dead. The thing that is sown is perishable but what is raised is imperishable. The thing that is sown is contemptible but what is raised is glorious. The thing that is sown is weak but what is raised is powerful. When it is sown it embodies the soul, when it is raised it embodies the spirit (1 Co. 15:42–44).

Since the Council of Trent, four terms have been officially used to identify the qualities of the risen body: impassibility, or immunity from death and pain; subtility, or freedom from restraint by matter; agility, or obedience to spirit with relation to movement and space; and clarity, or refulgent beauty of the soul manifested in the body.[7]

The common teaching is that, while in one sense we shall be drastically changed at the resurrection, we shall nevertheless still be essentially the same persons we were before. In heaven we shall not lose our identity.

Among mortal human beings, the generative impulse intends a kind of immortality. But when God restores man's nature on the last day, God's intention goes beyond this instinct. The resurrection is not designed to perpetuate the human species, which could be saved by continuous interminable generation. Its purpose is to perpetuate the individual.

What needs to be stressed, and what Christ was at pains to prove to the disciples after his resurrection, is that change from mortality to immortality means no specific change or numerical increase. Risen persons are still of the same human species and still the same individuals they were on earth. The word "mortal" designates no essential property of human nature; it merely denotes a liability to undergo change. When we say that the glorified body is no longer mortal, we do not imply that it ceases to be a body. It becomes, of course, a spiritualized body; but it does not lose its corporeity. It remains truly human, though with an immortality coming from the divine strength, which enables the soul to so dominate the body that corruption can no longer enter what had formerly been subject to decay.

Social Joys of Heaven.   Revelation constantly speaks of heaven as a kingdom or a city, and the Church considers souls in glory as belonging to the triumphant Mystical Body of Christ. The social dimension of eternal happiness, then, is part of the Christian faith.

Tradition further amplifies this idea by suggesting the joys of the blessed when they meet and recognize one another, not only in the intuitive vision of God but also by direct mutual intercourse. To deny such communication would be to deny them the legitimate exercise of their faculties and contradict the very concept of beatitude, which is the perfection of every human power and satisfaction of every legitimate desire.

Since Christianity differs from such oriental religions as Hinduism and Buddhism precisely in believing that man retains his identity in a future life, it is essential to the Christian notion of heaven that its inhabitants live together as distinct persons, knowing and being known by their fellow citizens in the New Jerusalem, and living in the company of those they had known and loved on earth.

A prominent feature of this "city on high," implicit in the doctrine of perfect charity, is that happiness will be increased by the absence of envy. St. Anselm makes much of this.

> If anyone else whom you love as much as yourself possessed the same blessedness, your joy would be doubled because you would rejoice as much for him as for yourself. If two or many more have the same joy, you would rejoice as much for each one as for yourself, if you love each as yourself. Thus in that perfect love of innumerable angels and sainted men where none will love another less than himself, everyone will rejoice for each of the others as for himself.
>
> If the heart of man will scarcely contain his joy over his own great good, how will it contain so many great joys? Because everyone rejoices as much in another's good as he loves the other, it follows that, as in perfect happiness each one undoubtedly will love God beyond comparison and more than himself and all the others with himself, so he will rejoice beyond measure in the happiness of God, more than in his own and that of all the others with him.[8]

Few aspects of the faith are more satisfying to the believing soul than the realization that, besides the vision of God, heaven means interpersonal relationship among the blessed, and that ties of blood and friendship begun on earth will somehow continue into eternity.

Communion of Saints. The Second Vatican Council placed great emphasis on the communion that exists between the faithful on earth and the blessed in heaven, and wants this doctrine explained and developed as it had not been before. To some people it may seem odd to speak of the "Eschatological Nature of the Pilgrim Church and its Union with the Church in Heaven"—which is the title of a whole chapter of Vatican II's *Constitution on the Church.* Yet this doctrine is the foundation of the Catholic practice of invoking the saints, and is the basis for canonization. It is at the heart of much of the Church's liturgy.

The Old Testment as well as the New Testament witness to the Christian vision of a life beyond the present one and distinguish three states of existence in union with God and therefore of communion among the saints: the pilgrim Church on earth, the suffering Church in purification, and the Church in Heaven.

> Therefore, the union of wayfarers with the brethren who have gone to sleep in the peace of Christ is not in the least weakened or interrupted, but on the contrary, according to the perpetual faith of the Church, is strengthened by a communication of spiritual goods.
>
> For by reason of the fact that those in heaven are more closely united with Christ, they establish the whole Church more firmly in holiness, lend nobility to the worship which the Church offers to God here on earth, and in many ways contribute to its greater edification.
>
> They shared our humanity while their lives were more perfectly transformed into the image of Christ. God vividly manifests his presence in them and his face to men. He speaks to us in them, and gives us a sign of his kingdom, to which we are strongly drawn, having so great a cloud of witnesses over us (Heb. 12:2) and such testimony to the truth of the Gospel.[9]

Catholic worship and piety in future generations will be deeply affected by this renewed stress on the continuum between the Church in pilgrimage and the Church in its destiny. Certainly Eastern Orthodoxy is colored by this emphasis, which might also neutralize the secularism—in the sense of this-worldism—of certain features of Western civilization.

ETERNAL LOSS

There are few doctrines of Christianity that cause more scandal to those who do not share the Christian faith than the mystery of hell. Also among the faithful, belief in eternal punishment places a heavy burden on their minds, since it seems to run so counter to all that revelation tells us about the goodness and mercy of God.

The existence of hell is a mystery, which means that even after the fact has been revealed, we are still unable to understand why it must be so or how the attribute of God's justice, which stands behind the mystery, can be reconciled with his infinite love.

Yet the fact is revealed, and the Catholic Church has never flinched in communicating this truth from Christ along with the Savior's assuring promise that his words would never fail. It would be a mistake to blame the Church for certain graphic descriptions of hell that seem incompatible with man's condition after death. Dante's *Inferno* assumes the Church's doctrine and builds around it an elaborate theme. But Dante is not the Church.

The discomfort that people sometimes feel at the thought of eternal pain may be due to the imagination dwelling on certain aspects of the subject while overlooking the simple teaching of the Gospel.

Angelo Roncalli as a youth memorized a quatrain that became a motto for the rest of his life. It was entitled *Four Future Things:*

Death, than which nothing is more certain.
Judgment, than which nothing is more strict.
Hell, than which nothing is more terrible.
Paradise, than which nothing is more delightful.[10]

This attitude of the future John XXIII is also the balanced attitude of the Church toward what the believing Christian recognizes is part of the same message of salvation as the promise of eternal life, "than which nothing is more delightful." The prospect of losing heaven is what makes the thought of hell so terrible.

The Catholic Tradition. The Church bases its teaching about the existence of eternal punishment on the words of Christ. In view of its importance, a brief explanation should be given of the two terms found in the New Testament for the perpetuity of hell. They are *aionios* (eternal) and *eis aionas aionon* (for ages and ages). The context and interpretation of the Church indicated that they mean eternity in the strict sense, or duration without end.

The classic passage is in Christ's prediction of the last judgment, when he compares the sentence of the just with the condemnation of the wicked. Christ as judge will first say, "Come, you whom my Father has blessed, take for your heritage the kingdom prepared for you since the foundation of the world." But to the unjust, "Go away from me, with your curse upon you, to the eternal fire prepared for the devil and his angels" (Mt. 25:34, 41).

What is so plain about this prophecy is that Christ recapitulates the two judgments with a conclusion, speaking first of the lost and then of the saved, "And they will go into eternal (*aionios*) punishment, and the virtuous to eternal (*aionios*) life" (Mt. 25:46). Since there is no question about the endless duration of heaven, we must say the same about hell.

The word "eternal" is used in the New Testament over seventy times, mainly concerning God but also, as in the prediction of the last day, regarding eternal life. In all these places the meaning is duration without end, which requires the conclusion that elsewhere the concept is the same. St. John is absolutely clear about this, when he exhorts the faithful to remain strong in their obedience to God's will and loyalty to Christ. Speaking of the wicked, he says, "the smoke of their torture will go up for ever and ever." Then the moral: "This is why there must be constancy in the saints who keep the commandments of God and faith in Jesus" (Rv. 14:11–12).

Besides the term "eternal," the New Testament often describes the pains of hell, where either the termination of pain is excluded or its endlessness is affirmed. Speaking of removing obstacles on the way to heaven, Christ says, "If your hand or your foot should cause you to sin, cut it off and throw it away. It is better for you to enter into life crippled or lame, than to have two hands or two feet and be thrown into eternal fire" (Mt. 18:8). The parallel version about the same drastic means says, "It is better for you to enter into life crippled, than to have two hands and go to hell, into the fire that cannot be put out" (Mk. 9:43).

In looking at the patristic tradition, three stages should be kept in mind: before the third century, when the Origenist controversy had not yet arisen; from the time of the controversy to the fifth century and St. Augustine; and since the condemnation of Origenism, about the end of the fifth century, to the present time.

Before Origenism, the Fathers clearly asserted the eternity of the pains of hell. Ignatius of Antioch, Justin, Ireneus, and Hippolytus are explicit. We read in St. Ignatius that anyone who corrupts the faith of a Christian believer "will go into inextinguishable fire."[11] According to Ireneus, "the pains of those who do not believe the Word of God and contemn his coming and revert to their former way of life are increased, not only temporally but eternally."[12]

Origen then came on the scene. He had been misled by Platonic philosophy, especially regarding the pre-existence of souls. He therefore held the theory that all the angels, except perhaps Satan, and mankind would finally return to God after suffering their lot of punishment.

Two obscure names that stand out among the followers of Origen who doubted the eternity of hell are Pamphylus (240–309) and Didymus (313–98). Gregory of Nyssa (330–95) was also less than certain on the subject. However, these and others were either dubious about their position and changed their mind, or they were strongly opposed by their Eastern contemporaries, like Sts. Methodius (d. 311), and Epiphanius, who branded any mitigation of eternal punishment as foreign to the mind of the Church.

Traces of Origenism appeared in the West, as in the younger Jerome, before 394, when he suggested a possible repentance for all mankind. Soon, however, he retracted this position and strenuously fought against the self-styled *Misericordes* (Mercifuls), who opted for universal salvation. Even Ambrose for a while was tainted with Origenism, where he seems to imply an eventual salvation for the faithful departed, namely those who died in the true faith but who were estranged from God because of other sins than infidelity.

There were many opponents of Origenism among the early Fathers, notably St. Augustine, who pointed out that the words of Christ about the last judgment are unequivocal about the eternity of heaven and hell. His best-known defense of the Catholic faith on this critical mystery occurs in *The City of God,* written in his mature years and expressing the common faith of the Church in the midst of the Origenist controversy:

> Why has the Church been so intolerant with those who defend the view that, however greatly and however long, the devil is to be

punished, he can be promised ultimately that all will be purged or pardoned? Certainly, it is not because so many of the Church's saints and biblical scholars have begrudged the devil and his angels a final cleansing and the beatitude of the kingdom of heaven. Nor is it because of any lack of feeling for so many and such high angels that must suffer such great and enduring pain. This is not a matter of feeling, but of fact.

The fact is there is no way of waiving or weakening the words which the Lord has told us he will pronounce at the last judgment: "Depart from me, accursed ones, into the everlasting fire which was prepared for the devil and his angels." In this way he showed plainly that it is an eternal fire in which the devil and his angels are to burn.

And since this is true of the devil, how can men—whether all or some—be promised an escape, after some indefinitely long period, from this eternity of pain, without at once weakening our faith in the unending torment of the devils.

Can we suppose that God's sentence will hold for angels but not for men? Yes, but only if men's imagination has more weight than God's words! Since this is quite impossible, all those who desire to escape eternal punishment should desist from arguing against God and rather bow in obedience, while yet there is time, to the command of God.

Besides, what kind of fancy is this, to take eternal punishment to mean long-continued punishment and, at the same time, believe that eternal life is endless, seeing that Christ spoke of both as eternal in the same place and in one and the same sentence: "And these will go into everlasting punishment, but the just into everlasting life."[13]

The Church's magisterium would understandably not be silent in a matter of such grave significance. In what has come to be known as the Athanasian Creed, written before 428, the opening article introduces the most important truths of revelation and reads: "Whoever wishes to be saved must, above all, keep the Catholic faith; for unless a person keeps this faith whole and entire he will undoubtedly be lost forever." The closing article referring to Christ's second advent affirms: "At his coming, all men are to arise with their own bodies; and they are to give an account of their lives. Those who have done good deeds will go into eternal life; those who have done evil will go into everlasting fire."[14]

In the early thirteenth century, the Fourth Lateran Council condemned the Albigenses, whose theory about the transmigration of souls affected the doctrine of final retribution. The Council therefore declared that Christ "will come at the end of the world. He will judge the living and the dead; and he will reward all, both the lost and the elect, according to their works. And all these will rise with their own bodies which they now have so that they may receive according to their works, whether good or bad; the wicked, a perpetual punishment with the devil; the good, eternal glory with Christ."[15] A century later, Benedict XII's definitions about human destiny stated that the beatific vision is "unto eternity," and distinguished this reward for the just from the "pains of hell" for those who die "in actual mortal sin."[16] The Council of Trent assumed the doctrine throughout its teaching. Thus when speaking of penitential satisfaction, it explained that this is not "for eternal punishment, which is remitted with guilt." It further declared that the justified person who practices virtue does not merit "eternal punishment," and defended the practice of imperfect contrition, which is fostered "by meditating on the eternal damnation incurred" by the commission of grave sin.[17]

Spiritual Motivation. Implicit in the Christian belief in hell is the belief that human beings are free to either serve God and be rewarded by him or refuse to serve him and suffer the consequences. His mercy is unmeasurable, and his willingness to forgive has no bounds. Yet Christ was also clear about the possibility of rejecting God's mercy and thus, in effect, condemning oneself for turning back on infinite love.

The Catholic faith, therefore, obliges one to admit that human destiny can have a tragic ending, that a vocation can suffer ultimate ruin. This possibility can have a restraining effect on uncontrolled passions. It can also, surprisingly, become the basis for high sanctity.

In his discourse on the last judgment, Christ was offering powerful motives to his followers in foretelling how different will be the lot of those who had loved others and of those who had loved only themselves. He was appealing to human freedom to choose what is right and reject what is wrong, mainly and finally because of love for him. But he also knew the human capacity for selfishness and greed, and so appealed to the desire for fulfillment, which is the possession of God, and the dread of ultimate failure, which is the loss of God.

Actually Jesus promised two kinds of fulfillment, as he also predicted two possible kinds of failure. To the just he will say, "Come, you whom my Father has blessed, take for your heritage the kingdom." To the wicked he will say, "Go away from me, with your curse upon you, to the eternal fire." The two kinds of fulfillment are the familiar rewards of heaven in possessing God and being rewarded with the enjoyment of creatures. The two kinds of failure are the punishments of hell in losing God and being subjected to pain from creatures.

We need both forms of motivation, even as we recognize that the highest reason for service is the selfless love of God. Christ, who knew what is in man, did not hesitate to remind us of the reward we could hope for and the suffering we should fear, even while he told us to give ourselves unreservedly to God. The Church continues to teach us the same thing today.

> Since we know not the day nor the hour, on our Lord's advice we must be constantly vigilant so that, having finished the course of our earthly life, we may merit to enter into the marriage feast with him and to be numbered among the blessed and that we may not be ordered to go into eternal fire like the wicked and slothful servant.[18]

This kind of inspiration is timeless. It is more than ever necessary in our ethically sensitive world, which knows the difference between the meaning of values and the actual practice of virtue. God became man to teach us this difference between understanding or even respecting moral goodness and being morally good.

PURIFICATION AND INTERCESSION

God created man that man might possess his Creator in the beatific vision. Those who die in the state of enmity toward God are deprived of this happiness. Between these extremes are people who are neither estranged from God nor wholly dedicated to him when they die. What will be their lot after death?

The reason of faith is that nothing defiled can enter heaven, and therefore anyone less than perfect must first be purified before he can be admitted to the vision of God. In more concrete terms, which have been carved out of centuries of the Church's reflection on revelation, there exists purgatory, in which the souls of the just who die with the stains of sins are cleansed by expiation before they are admitted to heaven. They can be helped, however, by the intercession of the faithful on earth.

Who are the souls of the just? They are those that leave the body in the state of sanctifying grace and are therefore destined by right to enter heavenly glory. Their particular judgment was favorable, although conditional. They must first be cleansed before they can see the face of God. The condition is always fulfilled.

When we speak of "stains of sins," the expression is consciously ambivalent. It first means the temporal punishment due to venial or mortal sins already forgiven as to guilt but not fully remitted as to penalty when a person dies. It may also mean the venial sins themselves, not forgiven either as to guilt or punishment before death. The Church has never pronounced on this second matter, i.e., whether venial sins are strictly speaking remitted after death and, if they are, how remission takes place. Some would hold that the guilt of venial sins is always removed in this life through grace of final perseverance, even without an act of contrition, while others more commonly say that venial sins are remitted at the moment of death, through the fervor of a person's love of God and sorrow for his sins; for although a soul on leaving the body can no longer merit or make real satisfaction, it can retract its sinful past. We transmit this disputed question and concern ourselves only with temporal punishment still due when a person enters eternity.

We should also distinguish between expiatory penalties and satisfaction strictly so called. The former are really atoning pains, because the souls in purgatory cannot, properly speaking, make satisfaction for their sins. They cannot freely offer anything as compensation for either the guilt of sin or the obligation of punishment due to sin. Satisfaction as merit can be given only during one's lifetime on earth. There is no true merit after death.

A term coined to express what the poor souls endure is to call it satispassion, according to the demands of divine justice. In this sense, sufferings are purely expiatory; they do not gain for those who undergo them any increase in heavenly glory, even though their sufferings are accepted willingly. We might compare satispassion with satisfaction by saying that the latter means "cleansing oneself," whereas the former means "being cleansed."

In spite of some popular notions to the contrary, the Church has never passed judgment as to whether purgatory is a place or in a determined space where the souls are cleansed. It simply understands the expression to mean the state or condition under which the faithful departed undergo purification.

The Catholic practice of making intercession for the poor souls is described as offering suffrages (from the Latin *suffragium,* meaning supplication). Behind the practice stands the Church's faith in the communion of saints and the capacity for mutual assistance between members of the Mystical Body, whether still on earth or already in the life beyond the grave.

Who are the "faithful" who can pray effectively for the poor souls? They are primarily all baptized Christians, but may be anyone who is in the state of grace; at least the state of grace is probably necessary to gain indulgences for the dead. Can the angels and saints in heaven help the souls in purgatory and obtain a mitigation of their pains? Yes, but when they do so, the process is not by way of merit or satisfaction, but only through petition. A study of the Church's liturgical prayers reveals that saints and angels are often invoked for the Church Suffering, but always to intercede and never otherwise.

Sacred Scripture. In its definition on the existence of purgatory, the Church appealed to "Sacred Scripture and the ancient Tradition of the Fathers." The Scripture evidence for purgatory, therefore, is part of the Catholic Tradition, whether the biblical teaching appears in formal documents of the magisterium or, more frequently, as part of the sacred liturgy.

From the Old Testament, the most commonly quoted passage that has been used in Masses for the faithful departed occurs in one of the books of Maccabees. Judas Maccabeus (d. 161 B.C.) was a leader of the Jews in opposition to Syrian dominance and Hellenizing tendencies among his people. He resisted the Syrian army and renewed religious life by rededicating the Temple. To this day the Jewish Feast of Hanukkah annually commemorates this event.

Judas had just completed a successful battle against the Edomites and was directing the gathering up of the bodies of the Jews who had fallen in battle. As the bodies were picked up, it was found that every one of the deceased had, under his shirt, amulets of the idols of Jamnia, which the law forbade the Jews to wear. Judas and his men concluded that this was a divine judgment against the fallen, who had died because they had committed this sin.

All then blessed the ways of the Lord, the just judge who brings hidden things to light, and gave themselves to prayer, begging that the sin committed might be fully blotted out. Next, the valiant Judas urged the people to keep themselves free from all sin, having seen with their own eyes the effect of the sin of those who had fallen.

After this he took a collection from them individually, amounting to nearly two thousand drachmae, and sent it to Jerusalem to have a sacrifice for sin offered, an altogether fine and noble action, in which he took full account of the resurrection. For if he had not expected the fallen to rise again it would have been superfluous and foolish to pray for the dead. Whereas if he had in view the splendid recompense for those who make a pious end, the thought was holy and devout. This is why he had this atonement sacrifice offered for the dead, so that they might be released from their sin (2 M. 12:41–45).

The description of what happened and the sacred writer's commentary on its meaning show that the Jewish priests and people believed that those who died in peace could be helped by prayers and sacrifices offered by the living. Not coincidentally, the Orthodox Christians who also accept the two books of Maccabees as inspired, have a strong devotion to the souls in purgatory. Apart from its inspired character, though, this teaching of the Old Testament gives us an authentic witness to Jewish faith in a state of purgation after death and the ability to help the faithful departed by prayers of intercession on their behalf. Judaic orthodox tradition since the time of Christ supports this ancient belief.

The New Testament evidence in favor of purgatory can best be seen in the context of a letter sent by Innocent IV (1243–54) to the Christians in Greece, prior to the ecumenical Council of Lyons, which sought to reunite the Eastern and Western segments of the Church. The Council later placed the doctrine on purgatory into a formal creed, to which both sides were to subscribe.

"In the Gospel," the letter read, "the Truth declares that whoever speaks blasphemy against the Holy Spirit, it will not be forgiven him either in this world or in the world to come (Mt. 12:32). By this it is to be understood that certain faults are pardoned in this life, and certain others in the life to come. Moreover, the Apostle says that 'the fire will assay the quality of everyone's work,' and 'if his work burns he will lose his reward, but himself will be saved, yet as through fire'" (1 Co. 3:13, 15). Since the Greek Christians believe in purgation after death and the prospect of helping the poor souls by our prayers, there should be no problem seeing in these passages of the Scripture a reflection of the common faith.[19]

Teaching of the Church. Twenty years after Pope Innocent's letter, the Second Council of Lyons in 1274 made a formal declaration of the Catholic doctrine. It was part of the proposed reunification creed, which covered all the substantials from the Trinity to human destiny. But it included a statement on purgatory because of a tension between the East and West. The issue was not whether persons not fully cleansed at death are purified, but rather what the purification consists in and what it purifies. The Churches of the East objected to the concept of a material fire in purgatory, and they were uncomfortable with the distinction between guilt and pain.

As a result, the Council of Lyons confined itself to the two main issues of the existence of purgatory and the usefulness of prayer and pious works offered for the departed:

> If those who are truly repentant die in charity before they have done sufficient penance for their sins of omission and commission, their souls are cleansed after death in purgatorial or cleansing punishments.
> The suffrages of the faithful on earth can be of great help in relieving these punishments, as, for instance, the Sacrifice of the Mass, prayers, almsgiving, and other religious deeds which, in the manner of the Church, the faithful are accustomed to offer for others of the faithful.[20]

Two hundred years later, at another reunion council with the Eastern Churches, held in Florence, the same doctrine was repeated verbatim. It also recalled the earlier teaching about the disparity of happiness in heaven and of suffering in hell, depending on the merits of virtue or the degree of estrangement from God when a person completes his course of life on earth.[21]

The most elaborate exposition however, came in the sixteenth century, when the very concept of merit was challenged and with it even the possibility of some people being destined for heaven, indeed, but having to expiate the penalty for their willful failings after death.

After recalling the constant teaching of the Church about expiation after death and the value of prayers, especially of the Mass, offered for the poor souls, the Council of Trent literally ordered "the bishops to be diligently on guard that the true doctrine about purgatory be preached everywhere, and that Christians be instructed in it, believe it, and adhere to it." At the same time, they should not permit anything that is uncertain to be preached. Moreover, they should forbid as scandalous "whatever is characterized by a kind of curiosity and superstition, or is prompted by motives of dishonorable gain."[22] The final indictment was against the abuse of traffic in indulgences and the practice in some places of favoring wealthy families who could afford Mass endowments for the dead while neglecting to offer the Sacrifice for the souls of the poor.

Most recently the Second Vatican Council made a profession of belief in the Church Suffering, saying it "accepts with great devotion this venerable faith of our ancestors regarding this vital fellowship with our brethren who are in heavenly glory or who, having died, are still being purified." Then in the same spirit as Trent, it urged all concerned, "if any abuses, excesses, or defects have crept in here or there, to do all in their power to remove or correct them, and to restore all things to a fuller praise of Christ and of God."[23]

The wisdom of this pastoral warning can be appreciated from the devastating effects in the sixteenth century of exploiting the natural sympathy of the people through "motives of dishonorable gain." One provision issued during the late Council and authorized by Paul VI highlighted the issue. "Pastors of souls" were told that they "shall work with prudence and charity so that, in the liturgical services and, more especially, in the celebration of Mass and the administration of sacraments and sacramentals, the equality of the faithful shall be evident outwardly and that, further, all appearance of money-seeking be avoided."[24]

In the hierarchy of revealed doctrines, purgatory does not rank as high as the Trinity or the Incarnation. But in the daily living of the faith, it can have more serious practical implications, if for no other reason than at least because the bereaved faithful have a deep sense of kinship with their departed loved ones.

Pain, Joy, and Invocation. Although not defined doctrine, it is commonly held that the essential pain in purgatory is the pain of loss, because the souls are temporarily deprived of the beatific vision.

Their suffering is intense on two counts: (1) the more something is desired, the more painful its absence, and the faithful departed intensely desire to possess God now that they are freed from temporal cares and no longer held down by the inertia of the body; (2)

they clearly see that their deprivation was personally blameworthy and might have been avoided if only they had prayed and done enough penance during life.

However, there is no comparison between this suffering and the pains of hell. It is temporary and therefore includes the assured hope of one day seeing the face of God; it is borne with patience, since the souls realize that purification is necessary, and they do not wish to have it otherwise; and it is accepted generously, out of love for God and with perfect submission to his will.

Moreover, purgatory includes the pain of sense. Some theologians say that not every soul is punished with this further pain, on the premise that it may be God's will to chastise certain people with the pain of loss only.

Theologically there is less clarity about the nature of this pain of sense. Writers in the Latin tradition are quite unanimous that the fire of purgatory is real and not metaphorical. They argue from the common teaching of the Latin Fathers, of some Greek Fathers, and certain papal statements like that of Innocent IV, who spoke of "a transitory fire."

Nevertheless, at the union Council of Florence, the Greeks were not required to abandon the opposite opinion, that the fire of purgatory is not a physical reality.

We do not know for certain how intense are the pains in purgatory. Thomas Aquinas held that the least pain in purgatory was greater than the worst in this life. Bonaventure said the worst suffering after death was greater than the worst on earth, but the same could not be said regarding the least purgatorial suffering.

Most Catholic theologians hold, with Bellarmine, that in some way the pains of purgatory are greater than those on earth. At least objectively the loss of the beatific vision, after death, is worse than its nonpossession now. But on the subjective side, it is an open question. Probably the pains in purgatory are gradually diminished, so that in the latter stages we could not compare sufferings on earth with the state of a soul approaching the vision of God.

Parallel with their sufferings, the souls also experience intense spiritual joy. Among the mystics, Catherine of Genoa wrote, "It seems to me there is no joy comparable to that of the pure souls in purgatory, except the joy of heavenly beatitude." There are many reasons for this happiness. The souls are absolutely sure of their sal-

vation. They have faith, hope, and great charity. They know themselves to be in divine friendship, confirmed in grace, and no longer
able to offend God.

Although the souls in purgatory cannot merit, since they are no
longer in the state of wayfarers, they are able to pray and obtain the
fruit of prayer. Moreover, the efficacy of their prayers depends on
their sanctity. This means that most probably they can obtain a
relaxation of their own (certainly of other souls') sufferings. They
do this not directly but indirectly in obtaining from God the favor that
people might pray for them and that suffrages made by the faithful
might be applied to them.

However, it is not probable but certain that they can pray and
obtain blessings for those living on earth. They are united, as the
Second Vatican Council teaches, with the pilgrim Church in the Communion of Saints. We are therefore encouraged to invoke their aid,
with the confidence of being heard by those who understand our
needs so well from their own experience and who are grateful for
the prayers and sacrifices we offer on their behalf.

PART TWO

MORALITY AND
THE SPIRITUAL LIFE

IX. NORMS AND POSTULATES

In order to understand the meaning of Christian morality, it is useful to know something of its vocabulary as this has developed over the generations of the Church's ethical history. In many ways the vocabulary is commonplace; certainly the words are not strange. But they have taken on nuances of meaning that are peculiar to the Christian understanding of man's response to the ethical demands of the Gospel.

This becomes all the more important in view of the rapid changes in the modern world, where the same words no longer say the same thing they said even a few years ago. If the faithful are to appreciate the basic constancy of their faith as affecting their moral behavior, they need to have some hold on the language that the Church's writers use when they speak of such things as virtue and law, conscience and love, guilt and responsibility. The very term "morality" means different things to different people. But its meaning according to the teachings of faith should be perfectly clear to the follower of Christ.

Determinants of Morality. Whatever else Christian morality deals with, its main interests are *human actions* performed knowingly and freely, and not through physical necessity, inadvertence, or instinctive spontaneity. The latter are sometimes (and not too happily) called *acts of man,* on the assumption that truly human activity proceeds from antecedent reflection and free choice of will, whereas anything else is man's, indeed, but not strictly human. Between the two is the essential difference that some actions, like metabolism or the circulation of the blood, are not under our control. So, too, when a person talks in his sleep or under the influence of drugs, he is not exercising his autonomy. But writing a letter or eating a meal, in spite of distractions or preoccupations, may be done deliberately and is therefore subject to dominion by the will.

However, just because an act is human does not tell us whether it is morally good or bad. The moral quality of our actions derives from three different sources, each so closely connected with the other that unless all three are simultaneously good, the action performed is morally bad.

First of all, the *object* of the act must be good, meaning that the immediate thing with which an action is essentially concerned should conform to the moral law. We should note that the object is not only the physical makeup of an action, like taking what belongs to someone else, but taking it with (or without) his permission. Only in the second case is there any question of theft.

Along with what I do are the attending *circumstances* of my action, which are at once distinct from its object and yet may change or completely alter its moral tone. Circumstances can make an otherwise good action evil, as when a man deliberately goes to sleep while on night watchman duty. Sleep by itself is morally indifferent, but taken at a time when a person has contracted to keep awake, it becomes morally objectionable. Or they can aggravate the guilt, as when a son strikes his mother; or minimize guilt, as a sudden burst of anger under violent provocation; or multiply guilt, as when money is stolen from a person to whom I owe a special debt of gratitude.

Finally the *end or purpose,* beyond the act itself and its circumstances, also affects the moral situation. If the motive is sinful, the whole action is vitiated. Thus for a gangster to give money to charity in order to divert attention from his crime is doing wrong even though (incidentally) people may profit from his philanthropy.

The motive element is of great importance in Christian morality. Some actions, like stealing and blasphemy, are always wrong and may never be done without culpability. But other actions may be either good or bad, depending on why we do them. Although it is generally wrong to kill another person, we may defend ourselves against unjust aggressors and are not forbidden to kill in legitimate self-defense. Many other things we do, like walking, speaking, driving, or reading, may be directed to good or evil ends, and they become good or evil according to the purpose intended—even though the immediate work performed is morally colorless.

If we analyze this motivation more closely, we see it corresponds to the reason a person has in mind when he undertakes a course of action. Other elements enter the picture only as a means to the end, like steps on a ladder or a bridge that spans a chasm.

In order that a person's act be good, his intention must be honorable, and no amount of pious moralizing will change the fact; e.g., it would be criminal to show kindness to a prospective victim of lust. Of course, good intentions alone are not enough, as though we could do moral good by using evil means. This is the error that the end justifies the means. We may never do evil to attain an otherwise good end. Murder, theft, and deception are wrong, and they cannot be done on the pretext that these are desirable because the intention behind them is good. If this principle seems theoretical, it is actually one of the most practical in the field of ethics, because people are so prone to justify their actions on the score of the good they will do (for themselves or others) by untruth, intrigue, bribery, or racial or creedal discrimination.

Writers sometimes illustrate the relationship among object, circumstances, and intention by means of a diagram in which the morally good act is represented by the bull's eye of a target, while the three determinants are the arrow: object=arrowhead; circumstances= arrow shaft; and intention=directing arrow tail. Any defect in any part of the arrow will prevent the missile from reaching its target, as any deflection in moral rectitude in what we do, or how, or why, deflects from moral goodness in the action that results.

Degrees of Imputability.   Christianity is unlike other religions in many things, not the least of which is its concept of moral responsibility. Built into the Christian consciousness is respect for the person who performs an action, either to praise and reward him if he does well or blame and punish if he sins. This implies that not all human actions are equally imputable and, when evil, partake of greater or lesser guilt according to the person's larger or smaller degree of responsibility.

The two foci around which imputability revolves are knowledge and freedom; when both faculties are fully operative, the responsibility is complete; but when either is somehow inhibited, the resulting imputability is lessened. Thus ignorance, emotion, or passion, fear, past habits, and external violence inhibit the activity of the mind and free will, and, therefore, limit human guilt or (on occasion) may remove it altogether.

The word "ignorance" is ambiguous. Too often it is taken to mean merely the absence of knowledge, and it may be equated with being unlettered, uninstructed, unlearned, or simply uninformed. Properly speaking, however, ignorance implies the absence of knowledge that somehow should be present, and then, depending on whether the absence is culpable or not, the ignorance is said to be vincible or invincible.

Ignorance is invincible (from the Latin meaning "unconquerable") when it is present indeed but there is no reasonable way, here and now, of dispelling it so that the person cannot be held responsible for doing what he does not know is wrong. He may not even suspect his ignorance, as when a child uses profane or obscene language that was learned from adults, and in all such cases there is no imputability. Or a man may vaguely suspect his ignorance on a point of moral obligation but, under the circumstances, feels it is practically impossible to acquire the knowledge required. A prosecuting attorney may fully suspect that certain individuals are racketeering and tries to get factual information from victims of the "shakedown." But they refuse to talk for fear of reprisals. The attorney's ignorance of the crime is invincible at least until some other legal way is open to secure the evidence desired.

Vincible ignorance can be cleared up if only a person wants to do so. The measure of his negligence to learn the truth determines his guilt when he does something wrong through lack of sufficient knowledge. At one extreme is slight neglect, as when a doctor fails to study a case as thoroughly as he might and thereby causes harm to one of his patients; at the other extreme is an affected ignorance that a person deliberately encourages to avoid what he suspects will be unwelcome knowledge, as the man who is practically certain the woman he is courting is married and yet fails to make sure for fear of learning the truth.

Emotions are powerful inhibitors of clear thinking and free choice, as common experience teaches, and their influence is generally to lessen and (in rare cases) entirely to erase culpability. According to the emergency theory, emotions are stirred-up conditions in which the body is prepared for strenuous effort; in another theory, emotions are the awareness of such physiological conditions as ensue upon certain perceptions; and in popular terminology, any departure from the calm and normal conditions of an organism is emotional. But whatever the explanation, we know that people under emotional stress are not themselves and therefore should not be held as accountable for their actions (or reactions) as when their feelings are not strongly aroused. The Church is aware of this fact, and Catholic morality in the future will take into account the emotional side of human conduct more than had been done in the past.

People in a panic have been known to fight their way to a hopeful exit and to have been oblivious of their cruelty to anyone who stands in the way. A husband who sees his wife in the arms of another man may suddenly kill one or both of them and later confess that he scarcely remembers anything except a burst of white anger. Actions performed under such circumstances are human only by courtesy, and their moral responsibility is minimal or nonexistent.

However, these are examples of what is called antecedent emotion, where the feelings are aroused before any chance for deliberation. Their general effect is to diminish guilt or absolve from it completely. On the other hand, it is possible to foster certain emotions willfully. People are known to work themselves up to an emotional pitch of anger, lust, envy, or hurt pride, and so far from reducing imputability, such arousal normally increases it. Nursing a grudge over some real or apparent injury is familiar; and unless a person takes means to keep the mind free from such hateful thoughts, negative sentiments gradually dominate one's whole personality and expose their victim to taking revenge at any cost.

In a class by itself is the emotion of *fear,* which follows the same general pattern but deserves special attention because of its pervasive influence in human conduct. Psychologically, fear is an intense, primitive response to danger. It is a condition during which the body is being prepared to run, to elude detection by "freezing," or to fight. In broader terms, fear is mental anxiety because of an impending evil. It may be grave or slight, depending on whether the threatening harm is great or small; it may be external or inherent, according to whether its cause is within or outside the person fearing, as the fear of death is interior, while the fear of another person is external. A unique species is the reverential fear we have to offend someone to whom we owe respect, as a parent or person in authority.

Regardless of its species, fear seldom is so great as to deprive a person of all responsibility for actions performed. Consequently, actions done through fear are normally culpable (if bad) and meritorious (if good), as when one student so fears examinations that he cheats and another that he studies hard. The fear that accompanies many of our actions, without inspiring them, clearly has no direct bearing on moral value. It is too common an experience to affect responsibility either way.

Concepts and Kinds of Law. Popularly conceived, law is a rule of action, and in terms of human legislation is an effective and promulgated command of reason made for the common good by one in charge of a complete society like the family, State, or ecclesiastical entity.

In order to have a full picture, we must begin with the law residing in God, where it is the eternal divine decree which commands that the order of nature and grace be preserved. By this law he directs all creatures in all their activities: the angelic spirits by the ordinations that govern the purely spiritual world; the physical universe (including the acts of men) by myriad laws of nature that are rarely supplemented by miraculous intervention; and the multitude of human acts by means of the natural law (recognized in conscience) and supplemented in the family by precepts of parents, guardians, or those taking the place of either; in the State by civil positive law (whether of sovereign nations or international associations); and in the Church by divine mandates that were directly revealed by God or that have been implemented under legitimate ecclesiastical authority.

A correct understanding of law is so necessary that some attention must be paid to a familiar objection raised against the whole idea of Christian ethics. There are some who claim that law has no place at all in the Christian scheme of things, saying that Christ never legislated and quoting St. Paul's words, "We are not under the law but under grace." It is asserted that by grace we receive the gift of love, which enables us to dispense entirely with laws and regulations. St. Augustine's well-known epigram is cited in proof of this: "Love, and do what you like."

Actually, the writings of St. Paul are the best evidence that Christianity includes legislation. The apostle was engaged in a life-and-death struggle with the Jewish law and legalism. In the course of time the Jewish leaders had developed a system of justification by works that were to be calculated by the oppressive directives of rabbinic casuistry. Christ repudiated this nomism by drawing a clear distinction between law and legalism. He defined legalism as a subordination of the spirit of the law to its crude letter, as in the case of the rabbinical interpretation of the Sabbath observance. According to the Pharisees, although a man was allowed to pull his ox or donkey out of the ditch into which it may have fallen, he was forbidden to pull a man out of an illness (except a grave sickness) on the Sabbath day. Time and time again, Christ insisted that he did not come to destroy the law and the prophets. On the contrary, he came to fulfill and perfect them.

The same with St. Paul. He also held that the law was good. "Is the law sin?" he asked, and answered, "God forbid." In fact, "the law is holy, and the commandment holy and just and good." When he contraposed law and grace, it was the law of Moses in contrast with its fulfillment, the law of Christ; or the pseudolaw of Jewish Talmudists in comparison with the laws of Christian charity. While stressing the liberating features of the faith, he spoke of himself as "not free from God's law, but under the law of Christ" (1 Co. 9:21).

Three objections are commonly raised against laws in the Christian economy of salvation. It is said that Christian morality is positive, whereas laws are negative; that Christian morality is internal, while laws are external; and that Christian morals are based on principles with no reference to laws.

If we read the Gospels carefully, we find that Christ repeatedly urged the observance of the Ten Commandments. He never said or intimated that "these precepts are now obsolete, so far as you are concerned. You have passed beyond them. Do as you please." When pointedly asked by the Jewish lawyer who came to inquire what he should do to enter eternal life, Christ told him to keep the commandments. And when the young man admitted keeping these from his youth, the Master "looking upon him was moved with love [*agape*] toward him." Love is the capacity to put oneself into another's place. Christ did so on that occasion, and then explained to his questioner that, while the law is essential, if he wished to go beyond the law in greater generosity, he should go sell what he had, give it to the poor, and come follow the Savior. The law, therefore, is indispensable, but for those who have the will and the grace, in addition to keeping the law, they can follow the counsels that are not binding under sin but go beyond the call of duty.

Accordingly, Christians never outgrow the need for negatively framed laws, let alone laws of any kind. The Decalogue is not out of date, nor is there a syllable in the New Testament that suggests the contrary. What is true is that the fullness of Christian living cannot be expressed in negative terms, but requires positive dedication as its underlying motive and offers positive supererogation for those who wish to signalize themselves in the divine service.

The objection that laws are external but Christian morals are internal may be similarly answered. Perhaps the root of the difficulty is a faulty conception of the divine law, whether natural or revealed. Man-made laws are imposed from the outside. But God's laws are not like the laws of men. They arise from deep within the human mind, inspired by faith or enlightened by reason, in which the divine mind is teaching what we should do on the road to salvation. True, the laws of God are spelled out in human legislation and interpreted for the Christian by the Church, but the genesis of the law itself and its fundamental binding force on the will come from the divine legislator himself.

There is finally the objection that Christian morals are based on broad principles and not upon laws. But what is a principle? It is the starting point of being or action. Viewed in this light, laws are essential principles of Christianity, since they assume that man has a free will with which he can choose to follow Christ or reject him, and that, unless he chooses to follow, his profession of the Christian name is a misnomer. But choosing to follow the Redeemer is nothing if not acceptance of his teachings in the humility of faith and carrying out his precepts in ready obedience. Words could not be clearer than the warning of Christ: "It is not those who say to me, 'Lord, Lord' who will enter the kingdom of heaven, but the person who does the will of my Father in heaven" (Mt. 7:21).

A sobering reminder is the countercriticism of those who know that Christianity makes heavy demands on its followers and yet see Christians not living up to the obligations of their profession. No sincere Christian can read Marx's statement of condemnation without remorse. "The social principles of Christianity," Marx charged, "have justified ancient slavery, glorified medieval serfdom, and they now recognize the need for approving the oppression of the proletariat—with, of course, a slightly contrite air." If ever Christians forget that their faith requires subscription to laws, beginning with the laws of justice and charity, those who are not Christian know their history too well to make the same mistake.

Conscience in Christianity.   If law is the basis of human conduct, conscience is the means by which the moral law is apprehended and interpreted. Different authors have differently defined conscience. Some hold that conscience is the mind of man governed by rule. For others, "There is a superior principle of reflexion, or conscience, in every man, which distinguishes between the internal principles of his heart as well as his external actions, which passes judgment on himself and them." But the classic definition in the Catholic Church is that of Thomas Aquinas, for whom "conscience is the mind of man passing moral judgments."

Aquinas further recognized two aspects of conscience, which are essential to a correct understanding of its meaning. There is first of all the permanent, inborn disposition of the mind to think of general and broad truths of moral conduct that become the principles from which a man may reason in directing his own moral activities. St. Jerome in the fifth century seems to have coined the term in Christian usage as the equivalent of "a spark of conscience," and Aquinas described it as a habitual quality of the intellect, enabling it to know the basic principles of practical reasoning. He never confused this faculty with conscience proper.

Conscience in the strict sense, however, is the action of the practical intellect deciding whether a particular, proposed operation is good or bad, here and now. It is the conclusion at which reason arrives after duly applying the principles of morality to a specific course of action.

Some writers, when they refer to conscience at all, tend to regard it as heavily if not mainly emotional. Thus they define it as "any emotionally toned experience in which a tendency to act is inhibited by a recognition, socially conditioned, that suffering evil consequences is likely to result from action on the impulse to act."

No doubt one reason why people inject emotions into the idea of conscience is that the operation of our moral guide may be charged with emotional overtones. Conscience is often restrictive. It can tell us, "Thou shalt not," and whenever our actions are suddenly checkmated, feelings are aroused. A good example is fear. In the same way, conscience may lay certain burdens on our love of ease, expose our reputation to the risk of loss, demand endurance of trial and even physical pain. We dread the consequences of these moral imperatives and naturally experience the reactions of a body-and-soul combination that forms the human person.

Yet we cannot reduce conscience to an emotional state without emptying it of all authority. Evidently one feeling cannot have authority over another. If conscience were only emotional, it becomes (as moral relativists claim) a matter of personal taste, where one person's moral preference is no better than anyone else's.

On the contrary, conscience is imbedded in the intellect, so that the human mind has not only the right but the duty to pass moral judgments, and in doing so is inviolable. No dictum is more firmly entrenched in Christian morality than this: Conscience must always be obeyed. For all practical purposes, this is a Christian innovation, and, though it was foreshadowed in the Old Testament and the ancient Greeks, it is built on the infinite worth of every human soul in the sight of God as taught by Christ on every page of the Gospels: "Why, every hair on your head has been counted. So there is no need to be afraid; you are worth more than hundreds of sparrows" (Mt. 10:30).

In the ancient world, outside the Judaeo-Christian stream, it was not the individual but the tribe or nation or society in general that mattered; the individual was of small account.

It is remarkable that when the authority of God is obscured or denied, mankind falls back rapidly upon a totalitarianism that runs roughshod over the claims of individual conscience.

But if conscience is the mind of man passing moral judgments and is inviolable, it is not infallible. It may be in any one of four states of certitude: subjectively *certain,* because a man has no doubt about the morality of the way he should act in a given case; or subjectively *doubtful,* because a person is undecided as to the morality of the action now before him. On the objective plane, his conscience is *correct* when its judgment reveals the true moral appraisal of a situation, and *false* when it erroneously tells a man that this present evil action is good or good action is bad.

The matter of following one's conscience is crucial. What responsibility do we have to follow what our conscience dictates? Everything depends on the degree of sincere certitude we have in facing a moral decision. We are obliged always to act on the dictates of a conscience that is certain. It must be obeyed even though objectively it may be false, because conscience is the nearest available norm we have for knowing what is right and wrong, and the criterion by which God will judge the human soul. On the other hand, we may never act with a doubtful conscience. So that unless the mind clearly says that a prospective action is permissible, we may not do it. Otherwise we should be saying equivalently, "This may be good or bad, offensive or pleasing to God. But I do not care, and will do it anyway."

If the mind is in doubt, therefore, we must either refrain from taking action or resolve the doubt. Information should be sought;

books and other sources consulted; and above all, one must pray for divine guidance.

Parallel with our duty to obey conscience is the obligation to educate it. Otherwise, if we do wrong in ignorance, we may not be free from blame. True, the conscience is not infallible, but, like other faculties of the spirit, it requires development and careful training as a delicate instrument for knowing the laws of God. Ignored and deliberately disobeyed, it becomes insensitive and gradually so dulled that not even the sanctions of civil authority may convince a criminal that he is wrong.

Fidelity to conscience, then, cannot be separated in practice from sincerity in wanting to learn the truth. Human nature is uncanny in the evasions to which it may resort in order not to be convinced that something enjoyable is morally bad, or that something unpleasant should be done. The readiness of a Catholic to listen to the Church is a safe index of his good will, as the opposite gives grounds for suspicion of insincerity.

Objective Principles.   Catholic morality presumes there are objective norms of conduct. Certain actions are good and others bad, certain forms of behavior are virtuous and others sinful, always and everywhere and for everyone who knows what he is doing and does so with sufficient reflection and freedom of assent.

The Church has had to defend this moral objectivity in modern times, whenever subjectivism threatened the foundations of Christian morality. Variously called situation ethics or the new morality, its basic premise is that the ultimate standard of human conduct is "not an objective norm found outside of man and independent of his subjective persuasion." It is an "immediate internal illumination and judgment" of each person for himself. In a formal instruction from the Holy See, it was declared that this subjectivist theory "deviates far from the Catholic teaching handed down through the ages."[1] Right and wrong do not exist only subjectively in the mind.

The most practical implication of the Church's historic teaching concerns the nature of grievous sin. God is the one who makes known, through reason and revelation, what constitutes a grave sin. Those who with full deliberation and consent commit adultery, murder, perjury and similar crimes estrange themselves from God. He sets down the conditions for their estrangement, not they. It is not up to man to decide subjectively whether a deliberate serious sin, like

294   MORALITY AND THE SPIRITUAL LIFE

direct abortion, is also a mortal sin which deprives him of God's friendship. The sinner cannot excuse himself of mortal sin by the clever distinction that psychologically "I do not really want to reject God. I only intend to do what I know God forbids as a serious violation of his law." God alone has the right to determine what separates a sinner from his Creator; a creature does not have the right to stand in judgment on God and tell him what constitutes a mortal sin.

The Church's basic position on mortal sin, therefore, has not changed. Subjectively a person is guilty of mortal sin when he *fully* consents with his will to do what he realizes is a serious offense against God. Otherwise, although the matter is grave, if only partial consent was given then only venial sin was committed. But the object of this consent is what God, and not man, determines is gravely wrong.

Consequently a venial sin is committed either when the matter (misdeed) is not objectively serious, and the circumstances do not make it serious; or when the matter is serious but full consent is not given by the free will.

When Paul VI approved the *General Catechetical Directory,* "confirmed it by his authority and ordered it to be published," this matter of objectivity was identified as central to the Christian way of life. Indeed, the principles of Christian morality are objective several times over.

1. They are objective in being independent of the subjective judgments of the human mind. "Accordingly, the conscience of the faithful, even when informed by the virtue of prudence, must be subject to the magisterium of the Church, whose duty it is to explain the whole moral law authoritatively, in order that it may rightly and correctly express the objective moral order."

2. They are also objective because their validity is not conditioned by changing circumstances or times. Consequently, "the conscience itself of Christians must be taught that there are norms which are absolute, that is, which bind in every case and on all people."

3. They are finally objective in their capacity to evoke great moral courage and generosity. The Church honors men and women of principle only because they have had objective principles to follow and, if need be, to die for. "That is why the saints confessed Christ through the practice of heroic virtues," and "the martyrs suffered

even torture and death rather than deny Christ."[2] They did not become saints in pursuing their own fancy nor die as martyrs for some product of their own minds. They responded to something real, in fact the Reality of God who became man to invite their self-sacrificing charity.

X. COMMANDMENTS OF GOD

FIRST COMMANDMENT

The First Commandment is generally given in abbreviated form, "I am the Lord your God. You shall not have strange gods before me." But the full message that Moses received from the Lord on Sinai is very detailed.

> I am Yahweh your God who brought you out of the land of Egypt, out of the house of slavery.
> You shall have no gods except me.
> You shall not make yourself a carved image or any likeness of anything in heaven or on earth or in the waters under the earth; you shall not bow down to them or serve them. For I, Yahweh your God, am a jealous God and I punish the father's fault in the sons, the grandsons, and the great-grandsons of those who hate me; but I show kindness to thousands of those who love me and keep my commandments (Ex. 20:1–6).

In the Church's understanding of this commandment, it is simultaneously a positive precept and a negative prohibition. Positively it prescribes the practice of the virtue of religion, and negatively it forbids all sins that are contrary to religion.

What is the virtue of religion that opens God's Decalogue to the human race? It is the moral virtue by which we are disposed to render to God the worship he deserves. It is sometimes identified with the virtue of justice toward God, and the idea is correct enough, provided we keep in mind that justice with respect to God is in a category essentially higher than being just toward our fellow man. The rights of God are rooted in his complete dominion over us; the rights of our fellow man derive from his claims to respect as a human being who is created for an eternal destiny. Again, religion is often described as a composite of all the virtues that arise from our relationship to God as the author of our being, even as love is a cluster of all the virtues arising from our response to God as the destiny of our being. Both religion and love are part of God's demand on us, and both are part of his imperative will: religion because he is the alpha of our existence, and love because he is the omega for whom we exist and in whom alone our hearts can find rest.

Concretely, however, we assume that the piety is genuine and, in general, associate religion with the worship of God, which is put into practice by adoration, prayer, and sacrifice; these are covered by the First Commandment of the Decalogue. Or the worship can be shown by vow or by oath, with which the Second Commandment is positively concerned. Or the worship is public and social, manifested in the observance of prescribed festivals, which is the object of the third mandate of God.

ADORATION, PRAYER, AND SACRIFICE

The Catholic Church carefully distinguishes the worship of adoration given to God and the worship of veneration offered to the angels and saints. Only God may be adored, since no one else can claim the entire subjection of his creatures who acknowledge his infinite majesty. Such absolute worship may be offered to no one else, since he alone is Creator, he alone is Lord, he alone is the Most High.

This is completely different from the veneration offered to the angels and saints, no matter how exalted. They deserve to be honored because of their nearness to God. Even the Blessed Virgin, though honored with pre-eminent veneration by the faithful, is nevertheless a creature. She is worshiped as the greatest of the saints and the Queen of Angels, but she is not adored.

The prayer prescribed by the First Commandment is especially the humble recognition of God's majesty and of our lowly creaturehood and entire dependence on the Lord. For our purpose it may be defined as the request of whatever is worthy to ask for from God. Morally speaking, we must pray because otherwise we shall not receive the graces we need for salvation. The depth of our felt need to pray is a fair index of how earnestly we pray. After all, we are told that Christ in the Agony prayed the more earnestly the more bitter became his struggle.

Regarding the required attention at prayer, though we generally refer this to a quality of the mind, it is more correctly an attitude of our affections and will. Provided my intention is to remain somehow united with God, I am praying with substantial attention, since I am aware either of what I am saying (verbal attention) or why I am speaking (spiritual attention) or with whom I am conversing (personal attention). These distinctions are particularly valuable for assessing our distractions in vocal prayer, where we use someone else's formulation in what we are saying, whereas in mental prayer (which may be vocalized) we use our own words to communicate with God. The important thing in any form of prayer, however, is an awareness of whom we are talking with and in whose presence we are; it is far less important to be literally conscious of the phrases we pronounce and less still of the meaning of the words we express.

Sacrifice as a fulfillment of the first precept of the Lord partakes of adoration because it means the acknowledgment of God's majesty; it partakes of prayer because it expresses man's dependence on the Creator. But it goes beyond both expressions of honor in the way acknowledgment and dependence are shown. In sacrifice we use something that is visible or sensibly preceptible as the vehicle of our prayerful adoration and either actually or symbolically "offer it up" by surrendering it to God. The surrender must, of course, be profoundly internal to be genuine. But it qualifies as sacrifice if besides the interior giving up of something precious we also deprive ourselves of its possession or enjoyment or use. The surrender may be a trifle, like some delicacy in food, or it may be great, as when a martyr sacrifices his life. What makes an oblation sacrificial is the willingness to surrender what I like in order to please God.

One feature of Catholic piety that reflects the most ancient practice of the Church is the veneration of the angels and saints, and the cultus of their statues and images. This, too, has been challenged more than once and correspondingly defended by the Church's authoritative teaching.

In historical sequence, the defense of sacred images and relics came earlier and was occasioned by the rise of iconoclasm in the Byzantine Empire. With the spread of Islam in the seventh and eighth centuries, the Christian Eastern rulers were pressured to conform to the Moslem exclusion of icons from religious worship as a form of idolatry. At that time the ecumenical Council Nicea II defined the Catholic doctrine by stating that the veneration of images of "our Lord God and Savior Jesus Christ, of our unstained Lady the holy Mother of God, of the honorable angels, of all the saints and saintly persons" is not only pleasing to God but highly commendable to the practice of the faithful. By such veneration the people are more readily inspired to preserve the memory of the ancients and desire to be like them. Nevertheless, the respect and honor the people pay to them is not the absolute adoration that according to faith may be given only to the divine nature.

Nicea went on to include among the legitimate objects of Catholic worship "precious and lifelike figures of the cross, the holy Gospels, sacred relics and monuments, the use of incense and lights," and in general whatever has been the pious custom since our first forebears. There is no question here of idolatry. Rather "the honor paid to the image passes on to the one who is represented, so that the person who venerates an image venerates the living reality whom the image depicts."[1]

Seven centuries later, the Council of Trent had to return to the same issue, except now not only to defend the use of statues, pictures, incense, and relics, but the veneration of angels and saints themselves. Building on the same traditions as Nicea and invoking the authority of the Council, Trent declared that the saints, reigning together with Christ, offer their prayers to God for men. It is therefore "good and profitable suppliantly to invoke them and betake oneself to their prayers and their helpful assistance because of the benefits they obtain from God through his Son Jesus Christ our Lord, who alone is our Redeemer and Savior."[2]

By the time of the Second Council of the Vatican, the Church quietly assumed that "every genuine show of love on our part for those in heaven has of its nature Christ for its aim, and reaches its conclusion in Christ, who is 'the crown of all the saints'; through him it reaches God, who is to be marveled at in the saints and is called great among them."[3]

DISHONOR TO GOD

A person can sin against the First Commandment by deliberate omission of the duties that this precept enjoins, when he refuses to pay attention to God by conscious acts of adoration or to pray for the assistance that the Lord has a right to confer in answer to humble prayer or to sacrifice as an expression of one's acknowledgment of the divine majesty.

But there are two categories of sins commonly associated with this mandate that are more than failures to do what the commandment prescribes. One category of sins against religion is committed by excess, the other occurs by defect. Both have a long history of prohibition and analysis in the Church's moral teaching.

Superstition. A person sins against the virtue of religion by excess when he gives to God a false or superfluous honor, or when he gives to a creature the honor that belongs to God alone. Properly speaking, only the first is superstition, whereas the latter is idolatry.

Thus, by Catholic standards, it would be superstitious for one of the faithful to worship God by a ritual that formally belongs to a non-Christian religion. But more commonly, the Church warns its members about placing unwarranted trust in a precise number of prayers, genuflections, or lighted candles, when the person relies on the number alone, like the revolutions of the praying wheel in Buddhism.

Aware of the delicate balance that needs to be kept, the Church's magisterium repeatedly urges bishops and leaders "to take the necessary steps to restrain or correct any abuses, by excess or defect, which may have made inroads in places." Especially as regards the veneration of saints, "they must teach the faithful that the authentic cult of the saints consists not so much in the multiplication of exterior acts, as in the intense activity of our love, which makes us aim at our own, and the Church's, greater good by seeking the example of the saints in our way of life, their partnership in our fellowship, and their support by our prayer."[4]

Closely related to superstition but actually distinct is vain observance, by trying to obtain some abnormal effect beyond the powers of nature through implicitly invoking a creature as though that creature were divine. The varieties and forms of vain observance are numerous, but the best-known to Catholic moral science are divination, magic, sorcery, and satanism.

Divination is the religious investigation of the occult by methods wholly disproportionate to the results expected, and is expressly forbidden either in the Bible or in Catholic moral tradition. Augury, the horoscope, chiromancy, necromancy, oracles, and dream omens are typical forms of divination. Crystal gazing is a relatively late import into many Western countries for prying into the past or the future, or into someone else's secrets. So, too, spiritualism has taken on the status of an organized religion in places like America. Speaking of spiritualism, the Holy See was asked "whether it is permissible, either through a medium, as he is called, or without a medium, either using hypnotism or not, to attend spiritualistic locutions or manifestations, even though having all the appearance of honesty and piety; and whether it is permitted at these séances either to question the souls or spirits, or listen to their answers, or even just to look on, even while tacitly or expressly protesting that a person wants to have nothing to do with evil spirits." Rome's answer, which was confirmed by the Pope, was "negative on all counts."[5]

The term "magic" is ambiguous. It may mean simply sleight-of-hand artistry and, as such, has no moral implications. It may also refer to the practices of tribal peoples whose "medicine men" possess specialized knowledge of the healing qualities of certain herbs or lotions, and which in many cases are no more than a primitive kind of folk medicine. But magic can be what the ancient Greeks called *mageia* and against which the first-century manual of Christian practice, the *Teaching of the Twelve Apostles,* warned the Christian faithful. The magician claims to possess preternatural powers, and his magical arts are said to be effective because he invokes some tribal spirit.

There are two different types of magic, and their moral evaluation is also different. In sorcery, the practitioner makes no claims to any preternatural power, but he is supposed to have preternatural knowledge. Using this knowledge with the correct incantations or amulets or ritual movements, he can produce extraordinary effects. In witchcraft the practitioner is in league with some tribal deity or mana, so that his intention alone is sufficient to achieve what could not naturally be done. It is the indwelling spirit that performs the deed, and the history of religions testifies that some prodigies can be truly astonishing.

The Church's condemnation of magic is not on the grounds that people are being duped or victims of suggestion, but that miraculous results are expected (even demanded) of created powers, over which God alone has sovereignty. Moreover, evidence shows that the devil sometimes has a hand in magic. This is particularly true in some mission lands where the native tribes find it hard to wean themselves from magical practices, or lapse into them again after being evangelized.

Satanism was once a rare occurrence, where the devil is deliberately invoked. But the practice is becoming more common, with

"Churches of Satan" being established as legal denominations. Invocation of the devil is a grave sin against God, since it avows that the evil spirit can act independently of God. It is also a blasphemous communication with the enemy of God and of the human race. Among the non-Christian religions, "devil worship" is more often a ritual method of appeasing one or other of the evil deities; whereas satanism properly so called is practiced by those who know who the devil is and invoke him notwithstanding. Quite often the result is possession by the devil, for which the Church provides the rite of exorcism.

Idolatry is giving divine honors to a creature. As such it would seem to be limited to non-Christian polytheists who worship the sun, moon, and elements of nature. And the history of early Christianity witnesses to the courage of the martyrs in refusing to worship idols, even externally, and their readiness to die rather than sin against the First Commandment by adoring a creature in place of God. Practical idolatry, however, is almost synonymous with secularism, which, like Israel castigated by the prophets, substitutes the idols of its own creation for the uncreated God and worships them instead of him.

Its proponents maintain that "it gives man freedom to be an end unto himself, the sole artisan and creator of his own history. They claim that such freedom cannot be reconciled with the affirmation of a Lord who is author and purpose of all things, or at least that this freedom makes such an affirmation altogether superfluous."[6] While other factors have also been operative, modern technical progress has nourished this idolatrous theory of self-sufficiency.

Irreligion. The word "irreligion" is a poor vernacular translation of the Latin *irreligiositas,* which regularly appears in the Church's teaching since patristic times to identify three sins against the First Commandment by defect: tempting God, sacrilege, and simony.

Tempting God might better be rendered "testing God," since it means in essence that a person says or does something that experiments to find out if God is all-wise, powerful, merciful, or has some other divine attribute. The sin is explicit if such a trial is made directly, as by one who challenges God to work a miracle if he can; it is implicit when, for example, a man needlessly exposes his life to grave danger on the casual assurance that God will protect him.

The term "sacrilege" is commonly used to describe any profanation of what is sacred, e.g., perjury or blasphemy. But strictly speaking, a sacrilege is the violation or contemptuous treatment of a person, place, or thing publicly dedicated to the worship or service of God. Thus a sacrilege is personal when directed against a person in holy orders or a religious, e.g., ill treatment or sins against chastity. It is local when committed in a holy place, as willful homicide in church; and it is called real when committed against a sacred object, e.g., treating the Blessed Sacrament irreverently or administering or receiving the Eucharist in a state of mortal sin. One of the clearest allusions to such irreverent treatment of the Eucharist occurs in St. Paul, when he warned that "a person who eats and drinks without recognizing the body (of the Lord) is eating and drinking his own condemnation. In fact, that is why many of you are weak and ill and some of you have died" (1 Co. 11:29–30). Paul considered the sickness and death of some Corinthians to have been a punishment for irreverence to "the body and blood of the Lord."

Simony is the word derived from Simon Magus, described by Luke in the Acts of the Apostles. Simon had been a practitioner in the magical arts who astounded the Samaritan people with his exploits. Converted by Philip the apostle, Simon discovered that by their imposition of hands the apostles communicated the Spirit to the faithful with marvelous effects that he also wanted to possess. So he approached the apostles and offered them some money: "Give me the same power," he said, "so that anyone I lay my hands on will receive the Holy Spirit." Peter rebuked him: "May your silver be lost forever, and you with it, for thinking that money could buy what God has given for nothing" (Ac. 8:18–20). Simon Magus repented of his misdeed, but ever since, his name has been attached to the sin that denotes the purchase or sale of spiritual things.

The legislation of the early councils shows that simony became frequent in the Church after the age of persecution. The Council of Chalcedon (451) forbade ordination to any order for money. St. Gregory the Great later vigorously denounced the same evil. It came to be widespread in the Middle Ages, especially in the form of traffic in ecclesiastical preferment, condemned many times by the Holy See and most explicitly by the Third Lateran Council (1179). Since this was one of the contributing causes of the Reformation, the Council of Trent published a special decree on the subject.

The Church has ever been conscious of the temptation to simony, to which the clergy and laity are prone, especially when there is too close a relationship between Church and State or between those in ecclesiastical authority and the secular powers, whether political or economic. One passage in the Second Vatican Council illustrates what must be called the close of an era when, in some countries, the appointment of bishops was still partly determined by the State:

> Since the apostolic office of bishop was instituted by Christ our Lord, and pursues a spiritual and supernatural end, the sacred ecumenical council declares that the right of nominating and appointing bishops is proper, peculiar, and of itself exclusive right belonging to the competent ecclesiastical authority.
>
> Therefore, to safeguard the Church's freedom, and for the better, unimpeded promotion of the good of the faithful, the sacred council desires that in future no right or privileges be any more granted to civil authorities of election, nomination, presentation, or designation to the office of bishop.[7]

A grave problem exists, of course, in countries under Marxist rule where the State directly interferes in every phase of the episcopal office. But the more subtle possibility of interference with the Church's freedom through simoniacal means in other countries was hereby recognized, where bishops are somehow selected by the temporal powers.

On a more immediately practical level, the Church has more than once affirmed the licitness of nominal fees for various services rendered, such as the granting of marriage dispensations, since the purpose of the fee is to defray the clerical expenses involved. So too with stipends for Masses, which is not considered simony because the money is given for the support of the priest and not in payment for the Mass, and the stipend helps to defray the expenses of the materials used at Mass. At the same time, priests are cautioned to give spiritual ministration without regard to the financial remuneration they receive from the people. More than once those were strongly reprimanded "who would deny sacramental absolution to the faithful who are unwilling to pay their collection dues," assuming the person were otherwise disposed for absolution.[8]

Mindful of the exhortation of James not to try to combine faith in Jesus Christ with "making distinction between classes of people," Catholic priests are told that, while they are the "servants of all," they must take special pains to serve the poor and lowly, because Our Lord was especially devoted to them.[9] Simony is the failure to share one's spiritual gifts or possessions except for a price, whereas

Christ entrusted his grace to the Church to be communicated freely and without looking for mercenary gain.

SECOND COMMANDMENT

Both in Exodus and Deuteronomy, the wording of the Second Commandment is the same: "You shall not utter the name of Yahweh your God to misuse it, for Yahweh will not leave unpunished the man who utters his name to misuse it" (Ex. 20:7; Dt. 5:6). The implication is that the name of God may and should be used, but not misused; otherwise he will punish those who disobey.

Although given as a prohibition, this commandment first of all prescribes the lawful use of the holy name of God—aside from formal prayer, and only then forbids abuse. As a precept, Catholic tradition associates the making of vows and the taking of oaths with the second mandate of the Decalogue. And while vows and oaths are closely related to one another, they are quite distinct. They are, moreover, distinctively Roman Catholic in the Church's new interpretation of what had already been customary under the Old Covenant, and especially in their dependence on the Church's authority as pertaining to all the faithful, but in particular to the clergy and those living in what are called states of perfection.

VOWS

In the Old Testament vows were sometimes explicitly dependent on the performance of certain favors by Yahweh, e.g., the libation of Jacob at Bethel and Hannah's dedication of Samuel. Others appear to have been made unconditionally, as in the anniversary hymn of the Psalms (Ps. 132:1–5).

The obligation to fulfill a vow could be very solemn, as appears in the case of Jephthah, who promised to sacrifice the first person he would meet coming from the door of his house if the Lord gave him victory over the Ammonites. The first person happened to be Mispah, his daughter and only child. It is uncertain whether the sacrifice meant death or perpetual virginity; what is certain is that Jephthah regretted the rash promise he had made. But he kept it (Jg. 11:29–40).

By the fifth century before Christ, a system was elaborated among the Jews whereby persons under vows might replace a direct offering of themselves with the payment of a fixed sum (Nb. 8:10–16). Thus things vowed might be redeemed by the payment of their value together with an extra sum in compensation.

In the New Testament, Christ condemned the rabbinic rule that enabled a man to escape his duty to his parents on the pretext of a vow. The lesson he wished to bring home was that for a vow to be acceptable, the matter of the vow must itself be pleasing to God. St. Paul is recorded to have been on one occasion under a vow (Ac. 18:18), and on another to have aided others to fulfill one (Ac. 21:23–26). Vows of virginity were taken from a very early date, following the example of Christ and his Mother Mary, and extolled by St. Paul in his first letter to the Corinthians.

The word "vow" is derived from the Latin *votum,* which means "to be willed," implying that when a person makes a vow he decisively wills to do something. As understood by Catholic Christianity, a vow is the deliberate promise made to God to do something that is possible, morally good, and, in fact, better than would be its voluntary omission or its contrary.

The Catholic Church recognizes a broad variety of vows that a person may take. A vow is said to be public when made in the name of the Church and received by a legitimate ecclesiastical superior; otherwise it is private. Solemn vows are those so designated by the Church, where the solemnity refers to such features as the gravity of obligation and the rarity of dispensation; vows that are not solemn are called simple. Most vows are "personal," since they concern the actions or conduct of the person who makes them. They are said to be "real" when some physical object (Latin *res,* thing) is promised to God, like a sum of money.

One of the surprises of Catholic morality is that the Church holds that anyone who has reached the age of reason, about seven years, is capable of making a vow. There are certainly ecclesiastical laws that require, for example, a certain age for pronouncing vows in a religious institute; but they do not touch the basic fact that the Church recognizes an early capacity for generous decision in the service of God. Behind this attitude stands the belief in the operations of grace in children to give them maturity of judgment far beyond their physical age.

What is the difference between a mere promise and a vow? They differ mainly in the fact that a vow is not only a promise, made to oneself or another person, but is consciously and with full deliberation made to God. Implicit in a vow, therefore, is both the desire to consecrate a promise by dedicating it to God, and the confident hope in his supernatural assistance to remain faithful to what has been promised.

A vow binds under pain of sin, grave or slight, according to the intention of the one taking the vow, always conditioned by the Church's teaching on such vows as celibacy for priests and those of poverty, chastity, and obedience for religious—which are considered to be grave obligations.

Catholics are often asked why vows are morally virtuous, and on the answer depends a correct understanding of the Church's concept of human freedom and of divine grace. Vows "better" our actions because they unite the person to God by a new bond of religion. Consequently, what is done under vow, besides being good in itself, becomes an act of the virtue of religion. Moreover, those who make a vow surrender to God the moral freedom of acting otherwise, like one who not only gives at times from the fruit of a tree but also gives up the tree itself. Vows also forestall human weakness, since they do not leave matters of spiritual importance to the indecision (or whim) of the moment.

OATHS

Typical of the need for clarity in using ordinary words accurately when speaking of religious or moral matters is the confusion surrounding such words as "swearing," "cursing," "profanity," and "perjury," all of which are somehow connected with oaths but obviously not all meaning the same thing.

The Second Commandment forbids the misuse of God's name, but it assumes that his name should be used reverently. An oath is the reverent use of God's name, who is invoked to witness to the truth of what I say. As such it is an act of divine worship and pleasing to God, and the Church has been careful to defend the practice, although some Protestant denominations forbid it. The Catholic position is based on the Church's long-standing interpretation of the passages in Scripture dealing with oaths.

> You have learned how it was said to our ancestors: You must not break your oath, but must fulfil your oaths to the Lord. But I say to you: do not swear at all, either by heaven, since that is God's throne; or by the earth, since that is his footstool; or by Jerusalem, since that is the city of the great king. Do not swear by your own head either, since you cannot turn a single hair white or black. All you need say is "Yes" if you mean yes, "No" if you mean no; anything more than this comes from the evil one (Mt. 5:33–37).

The Old Testament forbade perjury and infidelity to solemn vows made to the Lord. This was good so far as it went, but Christ wished to teach that such external vehemence should be unnecessary in the new regime of inward sincerity of mind and honesty of purpose. Henceforth, extreme care should be used not to imitate the ancient custom lest it involve a disrespect for God's name amounting to a usurpation of what belongs to God. The disrespect is no less if the name be legalistically avoided, as when the Pharisees swore by heaven and by the Temple. They even sustained the validity of oaths made to the detriment of justice, as when, e.g., a husband vowed to deprive his wife of conjugal rights. This last practice was so common that it may account for Christ speaking of divorce and oaths in the same context of the Sermon on the Mount. Moreover, man has no right to pledge what is God's. He must not swear even by his own body, for over this, too, God has dominion, not man. The youth cannot by an act of the will make his dark hair gray, nor the old man his white hair black.

The Savior asks for simplicity of speech that reflects the Christian spirit, of which the apostle James also warned the faithful. Extravagant vehemence proceeds from a disordered state of human relations; it comes "from the evil one." It has no place in the new order established by Christ.

At the same time, Catholicism explains that Jesus was giving a general rule of Christian life; and his clear-cut phrases must be interpreted with the finesse that all aphorisms demand. Thus, for example, it was no less clear to him than it is to us that some answers cannot be "Yes" or "No," without misleading. Thus, also, he was not opposing juridical procedure in which oaths are calmly and respectfully taken. Yet even here the need for such oaths issues from a defect which, though characteristic of human societies, should (as far as possible) be absent from the kingdom whose charter was being defined by the Savior.

The formula for a lawful oath was given by the prophet Jeremiah, who told the people: "If you swear, 'As Yahweh lives!' truthfully, justly, honestly, the nations will bless themselves by you" (Jr. 4:2).

An oath must first of all be truthful. This excludes lying and reasonable doubt, but does not exclude invincible error or legitimate mental reservations. Truth requires that we should be morally certain of what we are asserting or, in the case of a promise, sincerely intend to keep it. Oaths should also be just, which means that they call for prudence, reverence, and discretion and ought not to be taken without a proportionately grave cause. A reasonably serious purpose for taking an oath is sufficient. The honesty of an oath is its moral integrity, which differs between promissory and assertive oaths. In the promissory kind, the promise made must be about something morally lawful though not necessarily morally better, which would make the oath a vow. In the assertive kind, the affirmation may not refer to anything sinful, such as would be a boastful assertion under oath of some past misdeed, or to strengthen a detraction or calumny.

Immediately we see the difference between perjury, properly so called, and illicit oaths. Perjury is an illicit oath that involves deliberate falsehood (for assertions) or insincerity (for promises); otherwise the swearing would be morally wrong but not necessarily a form of perjury.

In certain countries, the civil law permits people merely to make an affirmation, e.g., on their honor, instead of taking an oath. By itself this would create no problem, except that in practice the two forms of confirming one's testimony tend to be equated. The result is that people who testify in court may consider an oath only a legal formalism since the law places it on a par with "testifying on one's honor." In either case, then, the intent of the law is to evoke a solemn declaration that the truth will be told. Witnesses are thus expected to be more careful to avoid lies during the court proceedings through fear of the heavy penalties prescribed by the law for perjury.

There is one type of sacred invocation which is so common that its special efficacy and significance may be overlooked. It is called adjuration, and it means the use of the name of God or a saint, or the mention of a holy thing, in order to strengthen a command or request. The high priest told Jesus at his trial, "I put you on oath (adjure you) by the living God to tell us if you are the Christ, the Son of God" (Mt. 26:63). Many of the liturgical prayers of the Church close with an adjuration, e.g., "through Jesus Christ, your Son, our Lord." Such adjurations are commendable provided they are made in the name of the true God, in order to obtain some lawful object, and the circumstances warrant this kind of solemn invocation. Among the adjurations with a long Catholic history are those whose object is to expel evil spirits. They are called exorcisms (from the Greek *ex* [out] and *horkizein* [to bind by an oath]).

BLASPHEMY AND CURSING

A particularly virulent kind of profanation of God's name is blasphemy, which literally means "to damage one's reputation." Any speech, thought, or action that manifests contempt for God is blasphemous. It may be directed either immediately against God or mediately against the Church or the saints and, in moral theology, is the classic example of a grave sin that is evil by its very nature. In the Old Testament it was punished by stoning, and it was the principal accusation made against Jesus by the religious leaders of Israel. They charged him with blasphemy because, though obviously a man, he considered himself equal to God.

A revealing aspect of moral sensitivity is the gradual elimination of "blasphemy laws" from the statutes of Christian societies. As late as the ninth century there was a death penalty for blasphemy in western Germany; and in post-Reformation England, blasphemy laws were passed in 1558 and reinforced in 1698. From the time of the Enlightenment the secular authorities in most countries have regarded blasphemy as no longer a crime against God but, at most, an offense against society.

Aside from the subjective dispositions, like passionate anger or despair, which prompt blasphemous speech or conduct, blasphemy is essentially a combination of two factors: religious awareness of God or his saints, and scorn or abuse of what is recognized to be sacred. That is why formal blasphemy is more likely in believing cultures than in societies where Christianity is not yet (or no longer) deeply rooted in the prevalent mores of the people.

Cursing has become a generic name for so many things that it needs to be technically defined. To curse is to call down evil on someone or something. It is therefore not swearing, which means taking an oath; nor blasphemy, which is an expressed contempt of God; nor irreverent use of God's name, which means to use it without good reason and proper respect; nor just profanity, which covers every form of irreverent speech; nor vulgar or obscene language, which pertains to good manners or chastity.

The biblical references to cursing are numerous and instructive. One of the notable changes in Israel as it broke with its pagan ancestry was that people came to attribute the efficacy of a curse no longer to the words themselves but to the power of Yahweh, which controlled the words. That is why the curse often became a prayer of imprecation. The Israelite was fully convinced that he could not constrain the Almighty but only move him by prayer. Unlike the magical incantations of their neighbors, the Jews believed that Yahweh can remove a curse by his blessing, preserve the pious man from a curse he does not deserve, change the blessing of an unworthy priest into a curse, and turn aside a curse from a humble man because of his meekness; in general, the intended evil of a curse takes effect only when the just God wills it.

Also in the Old Testament, wicked people were distinguished from the good by their different attitude toward enemies. Wicked persons curse those they dislike, whereas the good do not curse their enemies, though they do not hesitate to ask the curse of a just God to strike their persecutors, as Jeremiah more than once prayed to the Lord: "Let my persecutors be confounded, not I, let them, not me, be terrified. On them bring the day of disaster, destroy them, destroy them twice over!" (Jr. 17:18).

Christians are sometimes scandalized, e.g., at what are known as imprecatory psalms, in which the psalmist pronounces a curse over the enemies of God and God's people. Several things should be kept in mind in evaluating these hymns, which seem so foreign to the spirit of the Gospel. We must first remember that the revelation of the Old Law was a preparation for the New, and to that extent imperfect. Again in appraising the psalms, we are dealing with the ardent temperament and vivid imagination of the oriental mind, which means that we are prone to take literally what may have been intended symbolically or even mystically. But most important, recognizing that the sacred writer was under divine inspiration, we can say that what he expressed was not only (or mainly) his own desire, i.e., asking God to punish evildoers, but in prophetic terms foretold the divine intention, i.e., what God was going to do to those who resisted his will.

In the New Testament the cursing of persecutors or enemies is strictly forbidden by the word and example of Jesus. He commanded his followers to love their enemies, to be reconciled with their adversaries, and to forgive injuries. In this way they would be like their heavenly Father, who curses no one on earth but causes his sun to rise on the good and the evil; they should be as all-embracing in their charity as the Father, whose very title Abba (Father) signifies merciful love for sinners.

Nevertheless, St. Paul did not hesitate to curse anyone who having known, does not love Christ, or who dared to preach a gospel different from the Gospel he was commissioned by the Savior to preach to the nations. And on one dramatic occasion, he was so deeply moved with love for the people that he could wish for their sake to become accursed and to be separated from Christ, so that they might become more ready to accept the faith.

Catholic morality distinguishes between cursing inanimate objects or living things that are not human and cursing persons. To curse anything less than man is more or less wrong, but only because of the uncontrolled anger or impatience. To curse people by wishing them moral evil is always sinful, depending on how seriously a person intends that some spiritual harm should befall the one cursed. To call down physical evil, like sickness or loss of some kind, is also sinful unless the evil hoped for is sincerely desired as a means for the person's own spiritual good or the greater benefit of others. On the other hand, maliciously to wish someone physical evil for its own sake—say, out of revenge or envy or jealousy—is morally wrong, and the gravity of the sin depends on the seriousness of the harm intended.

St. James aptly synthesized the responsibility of Christians on this easily overlooked subject of cursing by comparing what a person does who wishes evil on his fellow man with what he does when he prays. The tongue, he exclaimed, "is a pest that will not keep still, full of deadly poison. We use it to bless the Lord and Father, but we also use it to curse men who are made in God's image: the blessing and the curse come out of the same mouth" (Jm. 3:8–9). The apostle thus not only laid bare the inconsistency of such conduct but recalled to the faithful the teaching of the Lord's Prayer, that if we expect our prayers for benefits from God to be favorably answered, we must avoid any semblance of cursing our neighbor by wishing evil to befall him. Praying for others, therefore, is the reverse of cursing them and is also the condition for having God bless us when we ask him.

THIRD COMMANDMENT

It is impossible to appreciate adequately the spiritual implications of the Third Commandment without seeing something of what it meant to the Israelites who first received it from Yahweh on Mount Sinai. Both accounts of this precept are alike in prescribing the Sabbath as a day of rest, but they differ in assigning the reason why the people should rest from labor on that day.

> Remember the sabbath day and keep it holy. For six days you shall labor and do all your work, but the seventh day is a sabbath for Yahweh your God. You shall do no work on that day, neither you nor your son nor your daughter nor your servants, men or women, nor your animals nor the stranger who lives with you. For in six days Yahweh made the heavens and the earth and the sea and all that these hold, but on the seventh day he rested; that is why Yahweh has blessed the sabbath day and made it sacred (Ex. 20:8–11).
>
> Remember that you were a servant in the land of Egypt, and that Yahweh your God brought you out from there with mighty hand and outstretched arm; because of this, Yahweh your God has commanded you to keep the sabbath day (Dt. 5:15).

There was never any doubt among the Jews that the Sabbath was divinely ordained, with the double accent on being "ordained" and therefore mandatory; and of being "divinely" communicated and therefore specially revealed by God. The Catholic Church has built the same interpretation of this commandment into its moral tradition by making attendance at Mass and abstention from unnecessary work the first of what are called "Precepts of the Church."

Among the Israelites, the Sabbath was the main focus of their ritual attention. Their weeks of seven days could be described as starting from level ground when each Sabbath ended at sundown and rising to a crescendo until they reached a peak when the next Sabbath began six days later. The Sabbath unified Judaism and symbolized its distinctive features as no other visible expression of the pre-Christian faith.

In New Testament times, Sunday replaced the Jewish Sabbath. St. Paul and the Christians of Troas assembled on the first day of the week "to break bread" (Ac. 20:7), and the apostle bade his converts put by their alms on this day (1 Co. 16:2). St. John called it "the Lord's Day," which the Western Church later translated *Dominica,* the title still used for Sunday in official ecclesiastical Latin.

The immediate reason for the substitution of Sunday for the Sabbath was to commemorate the Resurrection of Christ from the dead on the first day of the week. St. Ignatius of Antioch, at the beginning of the second century, referred to the drastic change that took place with the coming of Christ when "those who walked in ancient customs came to a new hope, no longer sabbathing but living the Lord's Day, on which we came to life through him and through his death."[10] Sunday was to be a day of rejoicing, with no fasting or corporal penance.

Before the year A.D. 100, we already have record of the Sunday practice of assisting at Mass in the *Teaching of the Twelve Apostles.* It is expressed in mandatory form.[11]

In the middle of the second century, Justin the Martyr left a detailed account of how the faithful gathered together for the celebration of the sacred mysteries. He also explained why Sunday was observed among Christians.

> Sunday is the day on which we all gather in a common assembly, because it is the first day, the day on which God, changing darkness and matter, created the world; and it is the day on which Jesus Christ our Savior rose from the dead.[12]

By the time of St. Isidore of Seville (560–636), the Church's tradition recognized a third reason for celebrating Sunday: the descent of the Holy Spirit on Pentecost.

Since the patristic age, Christianity saw in Sunday a weekly commemoration of the new creation—hence the close connection that the Fathers made between Sunday and baptism, and especially between Sunday and the Eucharist, so that St. Augustine in one place uses the word "sacrament" for Sunday, as the one day on which the faithful come into closest contact with the mysteries of Redemption.

It is not surprising that gradually the Church came to legislate attendance at Mass on all Sundays of the year, partly arising from neglect of revealed expectations by the people on the Lord's Day. From the sixth to the thirteenth centuries, ecclesiastical regulation became very explicit, and in some countries was supported by the civil authorities, e.g., by the Anglo-Saxon king, Ine, and by Alfred the Great.

While participation in the Eucharist has always been considered the primary Christian responsibility on Sunday, the earliest ecclesiastical and civil laws prescribed the observance of Sunday as a day of rest consecrated especially to the service of God. It was enjoined by the Council of Elvira in Spain (306), and by the Emperor Constantine in a law promulgated in 321, commanding abstention from work, including legal business, for townspeople, permitting farm labor.

From the fifteenth through the early twentieth centuries, numerous Pontiffs and the Council of Trent passed a variety of decrees dealing with Sunday observance, and in 1918 the Code of Canon Law set down in explicit terms that each Sunday of the year was a "holy day of obligation," which meant that "Mass must be heard; and one must abstain from servile work, from judicial proceedings, and also, unless legitimate custom or special indults permit them, from public trafficking, public gathering of buyers and sellers, and all other public buying and selling."[13]

The current threat to the sanctification of Sunday posed the pastoral problem of how to keep holy the Lord's Day in heavily industrialized and increasingly secularized cultures. When the Second Council of the Vatican faced this problem, it decided to "make the following orders" regarding the observance of this central day of the Christian year:

> Following the apostolic tradition that originated on the very day of Christ's resurrection, the Church celebrates the paschal mystery every seventh day, which day is, therefore, rightly called the Lord's Day or Sunday. On this day, Christians must gather together to hear the word of God, to partake of the Eucharist, and, in this way, to call to mind the passion, resurrection, and glory of the Lord Jesus, giving thanks to God by whom they "have been born

again to a living hope through the resurrection of Jesus Christ from the dead" (1 P. 1:3). Therefore, Sunday is the first of all feast days, to be presented to and urged upon the faithful as such, so that it may also become a day of gladness and rest from work. Other celebrations, unless they are really of the very greatest importance, should not take its place, since it is the foundation and nucleus of the whole liturgical year.[14]

The imperative "must gather together" indicates the gravity with which this conciliar declaration was intended to be taken. It summarily states that the primary duty for Sunday is a communal hearing of the word of God (hence the responsibility of the priest to preach the homily), partaking of the Eucharist (by attendance at Mass *and* receiving Holy Communion), and thus commemorating the mysteries of salvation and giving thanks to God. At the same time, pastors are to teach and exhort the faithful to make sure that Sunday is a day of joy (*laetitia,* interior gladness) and of rest from work (*vacatio ab opere,* taking off from arduous labor).

One of the less familiar aspects of Sunday observance is that it serves as a fair barometer of the intensity of Christian faith in a given society. John XXIII appealed to this fact in his most famous encyclical *Mater et Magistra,* where he pointed out that religion, moral teaching, and care of health require that relaxation be had at regular times. That is why "the Catholic Church for many centuries has decreed that Christians observe this day of rest on Sunday, and that they be present on the same day at the eucharistic sacrifice." Yet he saw with deep sorrow how widely this precept is ignored and, in many countries, made very difficult to keep because rulers of State and leaders in commerce and industry are too preoccupied with the things of this world. He therefore pleaded, "in the words of God," that all men, but especially public officials and the heads of management and industry, "observe this command of God himself and of the Catholic Church, and judge in their souls that they have a heavy responsibility to God and to society in this regard."[15]

His concern was exceptional for a man who seldom expressed himself in such forceful terms. But he shared the concern of Catholic Christianity, which sees in the faithful observance of Sunday the principal corporate means of showing gratitude to God as the sovereign Creator of the universe and the merciful Redeemer of mankind. In both activities God exercised his loving freedom, since he was not compelled to do either. On both counts believing Christians are to respond with loving freedom: to the first by their rest from work, which is the original meaning of the "Sabbath"; and to the second by their participation in the Eucharist, whose original meaning is "to give thanks."

FOURTH COMMANDMENT

The Fourth Commandment is stark in its simplicity. "Honor your father and your mother so that you may have a long life in the land that Yahweh your God has given to you" (Ex. 20:12). Deuteronomy adds two phrases: honor your father and your mother, "as Yahweh your God has commanded you"; do this so that you may have long life "and may prosper" in the land that Yahweh your God gives to you (Dt. 5:16).

This precept synthesizes the whole spectrum of moral obligations growing out of the natural bonds of family life, elevated to the religious sphere by divine revelation through the ancient patriarchs and prophets of the Chosen People.

The Torah expands on the duties of children toward their parents in more than twenty contexts of the Old Testament, spanning a dozen inspired writings and exquisitely detailed in their expectations.

Children are reminded that their honor of father and mother is not only a moral responsibility. It is a heavenly command. Moreover, although the father had the greater authority in the family, yet the mother had a like claim to honor and obedience from the children. The proverb poets insist that she be respected no less than the father. Rising up against one's parents was a crime deserving death. It was the height of ingratitude. The child who by a dissolute life brought grief to his parents and disgrace upon the family sinned grievously.

Children were repeatedly told they should be grateful to their parents, since without them they would have no existence. What hardships every mother suffers as she carries a child in her womb! God himself is the source of parental rights, and therefore children are, in duty, bound to obey the instructions of their parents. When parents become old and feeble, children must provide for them in a kindly way; they sin grievously if they refuse them the needs of live-lihood. God rewards piety toward one's parents (Si. 3:3–11).

The biblical writers left no doubt what retribution awaits those who fail in due honor to their parents: "The eye which looks jeer-ingly on a father, and scornfully on an aging mother, shall be pecked out by the ravens of the valley, and eaten by the vultures" (Pr. 30:17). Conversely, they promised every kind of good to those who respect their father and mother.

At the same time, parents were told they had certain God-given rights and duties toward their children. Since marriage is a divine bond and children a gift from God, the family is a spiritual com-munity. It was the parents' responsibility to keep this community together by their loving care, and see that this was a *spiritual* com-munity bound together by family prayer, family sacrifice, family liturgy, and the family pilgrimage.

Parents were reminded to be an example to their children. They were obliged to nourish them and train them to live God-fearing lives. Time and again, father and mother are identified as the di-vinely chosen teachers of their offspring. Among the commandments they were to teach their children to observe, the most important was to love Yahweh with their whole heart by knowing of his greatness and by serving him as he wants. As the Psalmist saw this parental precept, it was in the nature of a spiritual genealogy, where each successive generation would not only reproduce itself in body but, far more important, procreate itself in spirit (Ps. 78:1–7).

Religious training was to begin in infancy, and the children from their earliest years were to be accustomed to a moral way of life. Strict parents were considered a special blessing. Those who train their children well will be gladdened by them, will be praised by all who know them, and even when dead, their instruction will con-tinue to produce good results; but parents who are remiss will suffer grief. The classic example was the conduct of the priest Eli, whose children the Bible calls "scoundrels," who "cared nothing for Yah-weh" because their father had not corrected his sons when he was fully aware of their wicked deeds.

In the New Testament, Christ accepted and confirmed the Fourth Commandment of the Decalogue when the rich young man came to ask him what he should do to gain eternal life. But it was left to St. Paul to expound the broader implications of obedience in his letters to the Ephesians.

FAMILIAL HONOR IN THE NEW TESTAMENT

The background of St. Paul's teaching on familial honor was the premise he laid down for Christians, to "try to imitate God, as children of his that he loves, and follow Christ by loving as he loved you." Without this as its foundation, the obedience of children toward their parents, and the submission of employees toward their masters cannot be understood. In each case, the basis for what a secular mind would regard as "subjection" is loving affection for those whom God places into our lives as somehow representing his presence in that nucleus of society called the family, meaning a household of "familiars" who live and work together under authority for the common good.

There are two forms of this honor prescribed by St. Paul, after his introductory exhortation, which sounds strange to modern ears: "Give way to one another in obedience to Christ." Let go of self-love, out of love for Christ, in order to build up the Christian community (Ep. 6:1–9).

In her now centuries of commentary on this passage in Ephesians, the Church takes the biblical term "honor" to mean three duties of children toward their parents. They are to love father and mother as the authors of their existence; they are to respect parents as elders on whom they depend for so much of their well-being; and they are to obey them, as long as they are under parental care, in everything that pertains to their divinely authorized right to command.

We see, then, that the duty to honor one's father and mother never ceases in the love and respect they deserve, no matter how old the children may be or even whether the parents are still living or already dead. There is such a thing as love and respect for those who are no longer in this mortal life, because the memory of them survives.

The promise attached to keeping this commandment was mainly understood in the Old Law of temporal blessings, symbolized by "prosperity" and a "long life in the land." In the Christian dispensation, earthly blessings are not excluded; but they are mainly in the spiritual order and in the gifts of grace.

St. Paul's injunction that children obey their parents "in the Lord" sets down the right motive for obedience; it should be to please

God even when, as often happens, what they command may be displeasing to human nature. But it also describes the scope of their obedience. This refers particularly to such major decisions as embracing the Catholic faith, contracting marriage, and entering the religious life.

Children may embrace the Catholic faith once they reach the age of reason, and the Church has defended their right to do so as testified, for example, in times of persecution. Regarding marriage, parents may not exert absolute control over the marriages of their children by imposing or forbidding either marriage in general or a particular marriage, because children are not thus subject in the choice of a state of life, and because the right transferred in marriage is intimately personal. Yet those who are still legally under parental authority even in this matter should consult their parents about a prospective marriage and follow their reasonable wishes. Moreover, parents may not coerce their children to enter the religious state nor prevent them from doing so.

Parents may command their children either under pain of sin or otherwise. Besides the seriousness of the matter they prescribe, their intention determines whether the order they give is sinfully binding. Do they have to explicitly demand obedience or explicitly intend to so bind their children? Not necessarily. God has given them a right to demand obedience, and the extent of the child's obligation depends on how much the parent wishes to be obeyed. Children instinctively sense this when they ask, "Do I *have* to do this?"

Parents have their obligations, too, which St. Paul specifies in three verbs: "to bring up," "to guide," and "to correct." Each term has a variety of moral consequences.

Children are properly brought up when they are cared for in their temporal and spiritual needs. Thus parents are obliged to provide their offspring with suitable food, clothing, and other necessities of life. They must carefully watch over their children's lives and health and protect them against what would be injurious. This duty continues until children can provide for themselves. And always it is presupposed that what parents can do will depend upon their incomes; hence the familiar proviso that they care for their children "to the best of their ability." When children are physically or mentally handicapped, this can place a severe burden on the family, and the State should assist the parents, but the responsibility nevertheless remains the parents'.

Parents are also under a serious obligation to look after the spiritual instruction and training of their children. They should have their children baptized soon after birth and see to it that in due time they receive the sacraments of penance, the Eucharist, and confirmation. In a word, they are to lead them to the channels of sacramental grace, since the children have a supernatural life that requires infusion, sustenance, and strengthening by the means established by Christ.

St. Paul actually subordinates two nouns to the one verb, "bring up," in the original Greek, bidding parents educate their children "by instruction (*paideia*) and admonition (*nouthesia*)." Both are therefore the divinely revealed means by which father and mother are told to rear the offspring God has entrusted to them.

Instruction can mean many things, but essentially it is the imparting of knowledge, more or less methodically, in order to motivate a person to learn or be able to do something. In biblical language it is a type of pedagogy and suggests that parents are to be preceptors to their children, teaching them the truths they need for time and eternity, advising them as needs arise, and counseling them to form a correct conscience in the moral conduct of their lives. The focus is on the mind, which has been made for truth, because unless the mind be rightly trained, the will and affections are left without purpose or direction. Both parents are told by the apostle to share in this sublime *paideia,* each in their own way and each indispensable to a balanced development of the child. Each, too, should give the guidance by word and example; not by word alone, because children need to know not only what to do but how, and not by example alone, because they also want to know why.

Admonition, again in its biblical roots, is mainly directed to the mind. It is a *re-minder* to the growing child of certain truths that either native intelligence or the infused virtue of faith tell him are to be embraced. He therefore embraces them not precisely because mother or father have said so but because the child sees that they are commendable from within his own divinely conferred powers of recognizing right from wrong. The point is that he must have these truths recalled to mind by prudent warning, especially when the child has obviously ignored what by then he knows he should do.

Paul would not have been Paul if he did not imply in this need for correction by admonition what he spent so much time telling the Romans was the common lot of mankind, from infancy, because of

the fall of Adam. We are a fallen human race, with terrible tendencies to do what we will not and to will what we should not, and
no parental training of their children is truly Christian unless it
takes into account this primordial fact of revelation.

While telling parents what they must do, he also warns them what
to avoid: "Never drive your children to resentment." This is the
Pauline balance to pedagogy by instruction and reminder, with overtones of another Pauline expression, "in a way that is worthy of
thinking beings." Without compromise on principle, parents are to
watch their policy. They should strive to so train their children,
which includes giving correction and, when necessary, also punishment (implied by the biblical term), that their children are not
justly indignant because of something they regard as a wrong or an
insult. There is such a thing as being angry without sinning, or having a temper without losing it, reproving another without debasing
his character or making him feel that the reproof was given out of
passion or ill will and not rather out of love.

MASTERS AND SERVANTS

Not a few commentators on Paul's letter to the Ephesians have
been embarrassed by his casual and lengthy treatment of the obedience that slaves owe their masters; and by the further attention he
pays to how masters should treat their slaves. Indeed, he wrote a
whole letter, to Philemon, on this mutual relationship. Without first
disposing of the problem this poses, the inspired lessons intended not
only for first-century Ephesus but for all times and places may be
lost.

"Slavery" as a word is laden with meaning. Basically it is a state
of servitude by which one person is the property of another. As
such, the institution of slavery has been known in all quarters of the
globe and in all cultures. Generally, the ownership of human beings
has been a form of private property, but there have been examples
of public slavery, e.g., temple slaves in ancient Babylon. Slavery
was already well established before the first recorded days of history
in Mesopotamia and Egypt. A large part of the Greek city-states, in
the Golden Age of Plato and Aristotle, were servile. In Roman
times, as in the age of St. Paul, arose a new type of servitude, what

might be called the "plantation slavery," though there continued to be many house and personal slaves.

When Christianity entered the world, slavery was an integral part of the social system whose sudden abolition would have reduced the Roman Empire to chaos. There is no explicit teaching on the subject in the Gospels. But the spiritual equality of men as children of the same Father, together with the Golden Rule—"So always treat others as you would like them to treat you" (Mt. 7:12)—and Christ's affection for the poor and oppressed, provided the principles that were slowly to penetrate the nascent Christian society.

These principles were formulated by St. Paul, though he did not condemn slavery but rather strove to imbue both masters and slaves with the new Christian spirit of charity, which was finally to abolish the institution itself. This is most conspicuous in the passage we are examining.

Once we thus set the matter in perspective, what he teaches about masters and slaves has profound significance for our own times.

He tells slaves to obey their masters as they would Christ. Why? Because they are slaves of Christ and therefore should be earnestly ready to do his will which, in this case, means working hard and willingly "for the sake of the Lord." Before God there is no difference between master and slave; each will be judged for whatever work he has done well. Paul tells masters to treat their slaves "in the same manner"! What can he mean? Since both are servants of the same Master, earthly masters should deal justly and even kindly with those whom a pagan society calls slaves.

The lesson is not lost on those who know that Christ came to redeem man from within, to deliver him in the depths of his soul from the slavery of his passions of greed, envy, and lust. Only as this interior deliverance gradually took place inside of man's spirit did human society, also gradually, become emancipated of such institutions as slavery. But this deliverance is not irreversible. Where men ignore Christ or, having known him, return to their own conceits, we have such spectacles of enslavement as under Marxism or under affluent secularism. They simply prove what St. Paul was at such pains to tell the early Christians: Unless the heart of man is captive to the love of Christ, men will be enslaved by their fellow men in every age, no matter what social system prevails.

FIFTH COMMANDMENT

Within the few words of the Fifth Commandment, "You shall not kill," are contained a history of human morality. Long before the Decalogue was given, the Chosen People had been forcefully instructed to respect human life and avoid willful killing.

Already in Genesis, they heard the story of Cain and Abel, how Abel became a shepherd and kept flocks, while Cain tilled the soil. Time passed, and eventually Cain brought some of the produce of the field as an offering to Yahweh, whereas Abel brought the firstborn of his flock and some of their fat as well. Yahweh looked with favor on Abel's offering, but he was not pleased with Cain's. As a result, "Cain was very angry and downcast." Then followed the dialogue that narrates the first murder and God's estimate of the crime:

> Yahweh asked Cain, "Why are you angry and downcast? If you are well disposed, ought you not to lift up your head? But if you are ill disposed, is not sin at the door like a crouching beast hungering for you, which you must master?" Cain said to his brother Abel, "Let us go out"; and while they were in the open country, Cain set on his brother Abel and killed him.
>
> Yahweh asked Cain, "Where is your brother Abel?" "I do not know," he replied. "Am I my brother's guardian?" "What have you done?" Yahweh asked. "Listen to the sound of your brother's blood, crying out to me from the ground. Now be accursed and driven from the ground that has opened its mouth to receive your brother's blood at your hands" (Gn. 4:6–11).

Far from being a simplistic commandment, the divine mandate is against unjust killing, such as proceeds from human malice or passion, as illustrated in the Genesis story of Cain and Abel.

TEACHING OF CHRIST

In his Sermon on the Mount, Christ made sure that he clarified his role as a legislator who was superior to Moses. It was clear by then to his contemporaries that he was inaugurating a new religious movement; but it was not yet plain in what sense the movement was new and how it related to the Mosaic law.

His opening pronouncement, therefore, had a solemnity that he intended to be impressive. "Do not imagine," he said, "that I have come to abolish the Law or the Prophets. I have come not to abolish but to complete them" (Mt. 5:17). So far from abrogating the covenant demands of God from his people, Christ came to intensify the moral imperatives by bringing them to perfection, i.e., to reveal the full intention of the divine lawgiver.

What is the full intention of the divine lawgiver? It is first of all not the death of the moral order revealed to the Jews, but its rise to a new life, infused with a new spirit. Christ emphasizes this essential continuity. "I tell you solemnly, till heaven and earth disappear," he explains, "not one dot, not one little stroke, shall disappear from the law until its purpose is achieved" (Mt. 5:18). Not until the end of the world shall any essential part, even the smallest, of the law be abrogated. It will be perfected but emphatically not done away with.

The Mosaic law, before the advent of Christ, could control at best only external acts. The New Law, imbued with the Spirit of Christ, reaches down to the innermost part of man, and its sanctions are of the spiritual order. This double truth is expressed in Semitic fashion by our Lord in three parallel and synonymous sentences, without crescendo but with cumulative effect. For internal anger or a sharp, angry word, man is to be accountable before the tribunal of God and thus liable to divine punishment. The tribunals mentioned, the court and the Sanhedrin, are terms that symbolize God's judgment as the last sanction (hell-fire) and the context requires.

Thus where the Mosaic code forbade murder, the Christian code does also, but more. Jesus forbids even the least deliberate indulgence of anger and its manifestations in abusive speech (Mt. 5:21–22).

It may seem extreme that Christ should threaten eternal punishment for internal sins of anger. But the shock is lessened if we remember he is simply saying in striking language that the smallest faults of enmity are matter for accusation before a divine tribunal in whose competence lies even the right to condemn to hell. Naturally, the tribunal will judge whether the sin was greater or less. Nevertheless, Christ wished to bring home the fact that even interior feelings of hatred can be murderous and therefore of mortal guilt.

THE CATHOLIC TRADITION

It soon became apparent to the early Christians that their religion placed demands on their observance of what began as the Fifth Commandment beyond anything expected of their pagan contemporaries, since the Gospel morality surpassed even the ethics of the Jews. No writer of antiquity has better expressed what this meant than the anonymous author of the Letter to Diognetus, a non-Christian dignitary among the Romans (c. A.D. 125):

> The difference between Christians and the rest of men is neither in country, nor in language, nor in custom. . . . They obey the established laws, and in their private lives they surpass the laws.
> They love all men; and by all they are persecuted. They are unknown and they are condemned. . . . They are dishonored, and in their dishonor they are made glorious. They are defamed, but they are vindicated. They are reviled, and they bless; they are insulted, and they pay homage.[16]

In a word, the followers of Christ became striking witnesses of the Gospel teaching that, so far from doing injury to others, Christians patiently accept injury from others.

It would be a mistake, though, to suppose that Christians were a passive lot, or that they did not have to be constantly reminded by their leaders to live up to the expectations of their Master, or that the Church did not have to periodically formulate legislation to curb such excesses as St. Paul already rebuked among the Galatians and Ephesians.

In the course of its history, the Church's moral teaching on respect for one's own life and integrity, and that of one's fellow man, has become enshrined in numerous statements of the magisterium and in countless volumes approved by the highest ecclesiastical authority. While the principles underlying this teaching have remained faithful to the biblical revelation, their application has varied.

Certain issues are specially relevant in the modern world, and they will be given corresponding attention. Whenever appropriate, the pertinent documents of the Church will be quoted.

It should be stressed, however, that the relatively fewer statements of the Church on moral matters, by comparison with the vast documentation in matters of faith, merely indicate that dogmatic issues are infinitely more varied and consequently numerous. They have also more frequently been challenged by intellectuals, notably from within the Church. Both factors account for the large attention given, say, by the Council of Trent to the subject of grace and justification, in contrast to such moral matters as marriage and divorce. Moreover, it is perhaps too obvious to mention that if the dogmatic foundations of faith are not safeguarded, the moral implications of Catholic dogma are likewise threatened.

On the other hand, Vatican II has taken stock of the crisis of our day, which is heavily on the behavioral side of man, and devoted more documentary space to moral questions than any other conclave in conciliar history. Accordingly, we have an extraordinarily rich source of the Church's mind on the practice of the last six commandments of God in the teachings of the twenty-first ecumenical council.

PRESERVATION OF LIFE AND BODILY INTEGRITY

Christians are obliged to use ordinary means to preserve their life. Since God gave us a living body, he intended that this body be kept alive and well. Otherwise, why should he have bestowed this gift, or how would we show our gratitude for his goodness if not by appreciating, i.e., respecting what we had received?

Catholic morality agrees that we must use ordinary means to preserve our life. There is consequently no general obligation to use extraordinary means to keep alive. Why not? God would then be demanding from us what is beyond the ordinary power of most people to fulfill. This would be the same as saying that if we had to employ very difficult means to preserve our lives, we would be obliged to a rule of conduct that exceeds the normal strength of human beings.

Having said this, however, we must also admit there may be times when a person is bound in charity to use even extraordinary means. Such would be the case where a person's life is very necessary to one's family or society. But even in this case, it is assumed that the success in using the extraordinary means is very probable.

More difficult to determine in practice is when the means are ordinary and when they are extraordinary. Proper food, sleep, clothing, and shelter are obviously ordinary means. So also are readily available remedies in case of sickness or injury, and medical attention when needed. But already on this level, and without considering the advances of science, it is clear that what may be very ordinary means in an affluent culture like America can be quite beyond the ordinary in some of the underdeveloped regions of Asia.

It may be said, as a general rule, that the less affluent and scientifically advanced a society, the fewer means it will afford to people in that society for sustaining their health and life. Correspondingly, the more wealthy a nation and the more sophisticated its medical (and other) facilities, the more numerous and varied the means it offers for maintaining its citizens' bodily welfare and physical lifespan.

What, then, has the progress of medical science done to the basic principle just stated, that ordinary means must be used to preserve one's life? Nothing. The principle is as valid today as it was a millennium ago. What about the meaning of the term "ordinary," as applied to these necessary means? This, too, has not changed in the absolute sense that for each person those means are ordinary that *are* ordinary! They are ordinary if they are commonly accepted as such or, from another viewpoint, if they are readily available to that person in the time, place, and circumstances in which he finds himself.

Medical development has broadened the range of ordinary means while, at the same time, it has introduced a variety of extraordinary means that were simply unknown until recent years and are still unknown in large parts of the world.

Practically speaking, extraordinary means of preserving life are those that cannot be obtained or used without extreme difficulty in terms of pain, expense, or other burdening factors. The burden applies either to the person whose life is at stake or to those on whom his welfare depends. In addition, means should be considered extraordinary if, when used, they do not offer a reasonable hope of benefit to the one for whom they are intended.

Assumed in this matter of preserving life is the sincere desire to remain alive, or to keep another person alive, according to the dispositions of God's providence. There is no question of directly intending to terminate one's own or another's earthly existence. No doubt all must die "at the hands of God," so to speak. When this is to take place depends on the fact that some mortal disease or injury has occurred *and* on the fact that extraordinary means would have to be resorted to in order to sustain life. We exclude the exceptional case of someone who is very necessary to his family, the Church, or society; in this case, extraordinary means may be morally obligatory.

What about consciously shortening one's own life? Catholic moralists immediately distinguish between two different situations: one in which a person does something with the avowed purpose of shortening his life, and another where he regrets that his life will be lessened because of some action that he more or less reluctantly performs.

It is sinful to directly intend to shorten one's life. Such would be the case of a person who deliberately chose to work in a sulphur mine in order to shorten his life. The gravity of the sin will depend mainly on the degree of harm intended. Thus it would be gravely wrong to fatally shoot oneself or another, even though death were imminent from sickness, injury, or some other cause.

This is not the same as merely allowing one's life to be shortened for some proportionally good reason. Certain types of work may be seriously injurious to health and reduce one's length of life; or they may involve grave risks of fatal injury, or exposure to contagious diseases. Provided there is a proportionately serious motive, such work may be done and, at times, may be an exercise of heroic generosity.

EUTHANASIA

Until a few decades ago, euthanasia (easy death) was scarcely understood even as a word, let alone discussed except in a small circle of social theorizers. Many people still think of it in terms originally defined by the Euthanasia Society of America as "the termination of human life by painless means for the purpose of ending severe physical suffering."

But much has happened since the Euthanasia Society was organized, and those concerned with the future of society have suddenly awakened to the implications of so-called "mercy killing." These implications strike at the most cardinal premises of biblical revelation. They affect every facet of personal and social existence, and they emphasize with stark clarity the need for sound Christian principles if the very foundations of human civilization are to remain intact.

Science has freed man from subjection to many of the forces of nature and, in large measure, brought them under his control. One effect has been to give man a sense of mastery of the universe, which he never enjoyed before. This includes mastery over human life, from planning conception to determining who shall live and for how long. Another effect has been to immerse man in the satisfaction of this world, which his own genius has discovered, with corresponding indifference to whatever lies beyond the experience of man's life on earth.

Couple these two effects and you have some explanation of why such a practice as euthanasia should have come to the surface in our day, and why its proponents are so logically persuasive in defending what the faith that created civilized human culture considers murder.

It is perfectly reasonable, on secularist grounds, to argue that helpless invalids, bedridden cripples, and the unproductive aged should be quietly but firmly phased out of existence. Why not? They are, on the principles we are examining, useless members of society: useless to themselves, since all they may have facing them is the pain and disability of the future; and useless to others, since what can they contribute to the welfare of society, which measures a person's value by his utility to increase the physical well-being of mankind?

In 1940, the Holy See was asked about the morality of euthanasia. The occasion for the question was the growing specter of legalized murders of those whom the Communists and Nazis considered undesirable.

"Is it permissible," Rome was asked, "upon the mandate of public authority, directly to kill those who, although they have committed no crime deserving of death, are yet, because of psychic or physical defects, unable to be useful to the nation, but rather are considered a burden to its vigor and strength?" The reply was to be expected: "No, because it is contrary to the natural and the divine positive law."[17]

Moral Evaluation. Why does Catholic Christianity condemn euthanasia? Because, no matter what sentimentalists or social engineers may say, it is a grave crime against justice, both human and divine. God alone has the ownership of human life. Those who practice euthanasia assume the right of ownership over life. Therefore the sin committed is either murder or suicide.

There is a built-in respect for human life in the biblical tradition that has created the Judaeo-Christian culture. "You shall not kill" is not only a mandate of the Decalogue. It is the expression of reverence for a human person, no matter how young or old, how strong or weak, and irrespective of his physical, mental, or emotional condition.

What would genocide, under the semantic cloak of euthanasia, do to this reverence for life? It would reduce it to a pious irrelevance and remove it from effective influence on the mores of the people.

Implicit in the Christian value system is the realization that human life is sacred, of and by itself, apart from any profitable function it may serve as a tool of "productivity." A mother who cares for her child, cares in two deeply meaningful ways. She cares because she loves and, out of a mother's love that Scripture cites to symbolize selfless dedication, she cares for the needs of the offspring of her womb. So, too, a devoted son or daughter cares for an aged parent, first in the basic sense that the parent is loved, and then in the consequent sense that, out of love, the parent is provided with whatever he or she may need.

Hidden in the revealed mystery of love is the capacity of the human heart to give itself to another person for the sake of that person, to please him, and without thought as to "What will I get out of it?" or "What good will it do for me?"

After all, what do we mean when we speak of the dignity of human life? Do we not mean that a human being is worthy (hence he has the dignity) of being loved just because he is human, no matter how otherwise lacking in dignity he may seem to be, made to the image and likeness of God, redeemed by the blood of Christ, and destined to be with God in heaven for eternity? No wonder the Catholic Church looks upon euthanasia as "infamous, harmful to civilization, and dishonorable to the Creator."[18]

Not only does man have intrinsic dignity, but God has inalienable rights. The divine lordship over human life is an article of the Catholic faith, namely, "I believe in God the Father almighty, Creator of heaven and earth." As a creature of God, to whom man owes every element of his being, man is entrusted only with the stewardship of his earthly existence. He is bound to accept the life that God gave him, with its limitations and powers; to preserve this life as the first condition of his dependence on the Creator; and not deliberately curtail his time of probation on earth, during which he is to work out and thereby merit the happiness of his final destiny.

Another reason why Catholicism reprobates euthanasia is founded on what may be called the principle of "the total good." This postulates a belief in the total and not merely partial reality of human existence. Unless those to whom the care of human beings is confided, believe that man is more than mere animal; unless they further believe that life is not limited to the short span of time between conception and the grave; and unless they believe that man participates marvelously in the very life of God—inevitably their disbelief (or presuppositions) will find expression in what *they* consider "good" for a person.

As the Catholic Church views man's earthly sojourn, it is just that: a pilgrimage on which he has been placed by God during which he is to co-operate with the divine will in order to attain a greater or lesser share in God's infinite beatitude.

The totality of what constitutes man, on Catholic premises, is not body alone, but mortal body joined with immortal spirit. It is not earthly life alone, but a continuum of that life that begins as soon as a child is conceived and bridges the moment called death into eternity. It is not even human life alone, of body and soul, but human life elevated to participation in God's life because God became man in the person of Jesus Christ.

Essential to this view of totality is the value of human liberty, by which a person can freely collaborate with divine grace and thus give glory to God, although lying in bed as a "helpless" invalid; the value of enduring the cross by patiently accepting, in oneself and in others, the ravages of disease or the heavy demands of old age; and the value of loving mercy, which does not ask why, but like Christ, sacrifices self for others just because they are others, and knows that the self-oblation is pleasing to God.

Allied Issues. Given the premise that only God has absolute mastery of human life, only he may take away what he originally conferred, whenever and under whatever circumstances he wills. Ours is not mastery but only ministry, of our own lives as of the lives of others. We may not, without grave injustice to God, deliberately terminate innocent human life.

The first qualification, then, is that the divine commandment not to kill applies to all innocent persons, whether born or unborn. Disqualified from the precept are those who are judged (by rightful civil authority) to be a grave menace to society—such as criminals; unjust aggressors from whom we may protect ourselves and others, or the equivalent of unjust aggressors in prosecuting a just war.

Assuming that a person is innocent, not only may we not deliberately take away his life, but we may not even intend to do so. That is one side of the issue.

The other side is that which matters most here, the person's intention. Even in the case of innocent persons, situations can arise where there is no intent to have someone die. Just the opposite. The desire is that he or she might live. But the death of an innocent person may be permitted, in the sense of tolerated, if again (just as in the example of an individual risking his life for the common good) it is in the pursuit of a proportionately good end. Thus where radical surgery is urgently necessary to save a mother's life, a diseased organ like the uterus may be removed although it contains a nonviable fetus that will certainly die as an unwanted side effect of the hysterectomy.

Precise words on this matter are critical. Something is *directly* intended when it is the immediate object of a human act, when it is the specific motive for my action, when it is the guiding purpose I have in view.

We now shift focus from the negative prohibition, that innocent life may not be deliberately terminated, to the positive injunction that man has an obligation to sustain his own life and the life of those who depend on him.

It is at this point that the developments of modern science, notably of medicine, enter the picture. The discovery of vitamins, hormones, antibiotics, sulfa drugs, penicillin; of genes and chromosomes as hereditary transmitters; of the continuity of germ plasm and the laws of genetic mutation—have all been made by men whose lives spanned the last and present centuries, and whose contributions to longevity have no parallel since the origin of man.

For our purpose, the moral axiom remains that we must use ordinary means to sustain life, and that extraordinary means, as we have seen, are not obligatory except in rare circumstances. What is changing, of course, is the range of possibilities for extending the human lifespan, in some countries by almost 50 per cent since the turn of the century. As a result, what used to be extraordinary may become ordinary means of maintaining life, with prospects for a longer stay on earth for a larger number of people. Christianity views this progress with approval, and the Church encourages its advancement for the service of man. But it must be "man in his entirety, with attention to his material needs and his intellectual, moral, and spiritual demands in the proper order."[19] Viewed in this light, euthanasia is a misnomer. It should be called "lugrothanasia," i.e., unhappy death, because it deprives a person who could live longer of the prospect of giving greater glory to God and of gaining more happiness in the life to come.

One aspect of euthanasia seldom referred to in popular writing is its possible connection with the transplanting of vital human organs. It was not by chance that the Catholic hierarchy has issued directives for hospital facilities indicating that a transplant may be done provided the loss of such organ(s) does not deprive the donor of life itself. As specialists in the field are careful to explain, two questions hover like clouds over the transplanting of vital organs. One is to know precisely, on scientific grounds, when a person is dead. The other is how effective a transplant can be if a vital organ, like the heart, is transferred from an authentically dead body. The medical temptation is to anticipate actual death in order to insure an effective transplant.

ABORTION

The Roman Empire into which Christianity was born practiced abortion and infanticide on a wide scale. Chronologically, the exposure of unwanted infants came earlier, and was sanctioned by Roman law. By the first century B.C., Romans were gradually getting away from exposure, while abortions were on the increase. The distinction they made between infanticide and abortion was due to the difference between the emotional reactions to what they must see and what they could avoid seeing.[20]

From the outset, therefore, the Christian religion was confronted with a society in which abortion was the rule rather than the exception. The Church reacted immediately and vigorously. The *Didache* (composed before A.D. 80) told the faithful what they must not do: "You shall not procure abortion. You shall not destroy a newborn child."[21]

Before the year A.D. 138, the epistle of Barnabas was equally explicit, placing the crime of abortion among the actions of those who walk the Way of Darkness. "There are two Ways of instruction," Christians were told, "as there are two powers, that of Light and that of Darkness. And there is a great difference between the Two Ways. The one is controlled by God's light-bearing angels, the other by the angels of Satan. And as the latter is the Ruler of the present era of lawlessness, so the former is Lord from eternity to eternity." Among the precepts of the Way of Light is this: "Do not murder a child by abortion, or commit infanticide."[22] Significantly, the two operative words in the prohibition are explicitly "murder" (Greek *phoneuō*, bloody slaughter) and "child" (*teknon*).

As the Christian attitude toward abortion began to penetrate Roman society, Christian believers were challenged by the prevalent Stoic theory of human life beginning only at actual birth of the fully developed infant. This would mean that there could be no destruction of a child by abortion. The faithful were therefore reminded that this was not true; rather that the life begun at conception continued essentially unchanged during its whole period of development. Induced abortion at any stage was a homicide.[23]

Two distinctions should be kept in mind regarding this matter: between Catholic morality and canonical penalties, and between the official teaching of the Church and ecclesiastical writers, no matter how celebrated. Clarification here will help dissipate what has become a gray area for many Catholics in today's animated controversy over abortion.

The Moral Issue.   On the level of morality, Roman Catholicism has always held that the direct attack on an unborn fetus, at any time after conception, is a grave sin. The history of this teaching has been consistent and continuous, beginning with the earliest times and up to the present.

The Church's teaching on abortion is just that; it is doctrine the Church proclaims on the prior assumption that the magisterium is empowered by Christ to proscribe and prescribe in any area of human conduct that touches on the commandments of God, whether derived from nature or from supernatural revelation. Arguments may be given and reasons offered to support the Church's teaching; but the ultimate "reason" why Catholics obey this teaching is the authority given the Church to command obedience in Christ's name. If this seems like "arguments made by an external judge," the

Catholic faithful will answer, "We must put aside all judgment of our own, and keep the mind ever ready and prompt to obey in all things the true spouse of Christ our Lord, our holy Mother, the hierarchical Church."[24]

Once this is admitted, that for a Catholic the Church's moral teaching partakes of faith in the Church, it is quite secondary and, in fact, irrelevant, that the doctrine should also be expressed in juridical terms. As a visible society that believes it has the right from God to make laws for its members, the Church encourages what has come to be known as Canon Law. But Canon Law is only an attempt to organize and systematize for prudential reasons the external aspects of what is essentially not juridical: the will of God in its demands on the will of man. It would be a mistake, therefore, to suppose that the Catholic teaching on abortion uses arguments that are based on a juridical model. Quite the contrary. The juridical model is not the basis of Catholic morality; rather, juridical norms are only as valid as they are based on the faith principles of the Church's moral doctrine.

The term "abortion" as understood in Catholic morality means expelling an immature fetus from the mother's womb. The fetus must, first of all, be living; if it is certainly dead, its removal is not only permissible but ordinarily necessary. Moreover, the fetus must be immature or nonviable, by which is meant that it cannot live outside the womb even with the most extraordinary medical care. In ordinary circumstances a fetus is considered viable by the end of the twenty-eighth week of pregnancy, allowing for two or so weeks earlier if the child is to have special medical assistance like an incubator.

Since the modern legalization of abortion, however, the same term is used medically to describe what is more properly a form of feticide, where the living fetus is directly killed by a variety of now sophisticated physical or chemical means. In moral language, this too is abortion, but with the added malice of a direct assault on human life within the womb.

More important, though, from the moral standpoint is the intention that motivates an abortion. Although the same word "abortion" is used, it has a totally different moral meaning—depending on whether the motive is to directly attack the fetus, no matter what purpose is alleged to excuse the attack; or whether the motive is to save the life of a pregnant mother and, in the process, the unborn child is reluctantly permitted to die.

Consequently, even though pregnancy is involved, it is lawful to extract from the mother a womb that is dangerously diseased (e.g., cancerous). This is not the same as direct abortion, and Catholic morality allows this kind of increasingly rare surgery according to what has come to be known as the principle of the double effect. To be licitly applied, the principle must observe four limiting norms:

1. The action (removal of the diseased womb) is good; it consists in excising an infected part of the human body.

2. The good effect (saving the mother's life) is not obtained by means of the evil effect (death of the fetus). It would be just the opposite, e.g., if the fetus were killed in order to save the reputation of an unwed mother.

3. There is sufficient reason for permitting the unsought evil effect that unavoidably follows. Here the Church's guidance is essential in judging that there is sufficient reason.

4. The evil effect is not intended in itself, but is merely allowed as a necessary consequence of the good effect.

Summarily, then, the womb belongs to the mother just as completely after a pregnancy as before. It she were not pregnant, she would clearly be justified to save her life by removing a diseased organ that was threatening her life. The presence of the fetus does not deprive her of this fundamental right.

With the development of modern science, these so-called therapeutic abortions, where the mother's life is in immediate danger, are becoming increasingly rare. The point has now been reached that more and more doctors come to reject the idea of therapeutic abortion entirely.

In actual practice, of course, numerous abortions had been performed for "therapeutic reasons" that were far removed from any immediate danger to the mother's life, long before one country after another legalized abortion. Legalizing abortion whenever there is risk "that the continuance of the pregnancy would gravely impair the physical or mental health of the mother, or that the child would be born with grave physical or mental defect" is equivalent to abortion on demand. The "mental health of the mother" is a euphemism to cover every contingency where a woman has an unwanted pregnancy that she is willing to terminate to be relieved of the anxiety of having a child.

Wherein lies the essential sinfulness of abortion? It consists in the homicidal intent to kill innocent life. This factor of intent or willingness to destroy innocent human life is of paramount importance in making a correct assessment of the Catholic attitude toward abortion. It places the controverted question as to precisely when human life begins, outside the ambit of the moral issue; as it also makes the now commonly held Catholic position that human life begins at conception equally outside the heart of the Church's teaching about the grave sinfulness of abortion.

The exact time when the fetus becomes "animated" has no practical significance as far as the morality of abortion is concerned. By any theory of "animation," abortion is gravely wrong. Why so? Because every direct abortion is a sin of murder by intent. It is, to say the least, probable that every developing fetus is a human being. To deliberately kill what is probably human is murder.

If a person does not know for certain that his action is not killing another human being, he must accept the responsibility for doing so. Anyone who is willing to kill what may be human is, by his intention, willing to kill what is human. Consequently, the one who performs or consents to abortion inescapably assumes the guilt of voluntary homicide.

Furthermore, regardless of when the fetus is animated, to directly destroy it is to usurp a right that belongs solely to God, the right over the fruit of man's reproductive act. Man may not interfere with God's rights without seriously offending the Creator.

Already in the early Church the faithful were warned against those who sought to justify their misconduct by resorting to sophistries about "formed" and "unformed" life in the womb. St. Basil the Great, writing in A.D. 375, stated categorically: "A woman who deliberately destroys a fetus is answerable for murder. And any fine distinction as to its being formed or unformed is not admissible among us."[25] If some jurists later on invoked the distinction to assess different canonical penalties, based on the accepted civil codes of their day, the Catholic Church itself never altered its permanent moral judgment that direct abortion is always gravely offensive to God because it is willingly homicidal in intention.

Teaching of the Church. As might be expected, the Church's hierarchy had to condemn the practice of abortion from the earliest years, and it has continued to do so unremittingly to the present day. The reason is twofold. The faithful had to be warned about the prevalent practices of unbelievers among whom they lived, and they needed motivation as Christians to resist their naturally selfish impulses to destroy unborn human life.

Literally hundreds of documents from the first through the present century testify to the same moral doctrine, with such nuances as time, place, and circumstances indicated. Only a few representative of these statements of the magisterium will be cited, and only in partial quotation or paraphrase. Two features that are common to all of this teaching are that abortion is a grave crime and that it is sinful because of its homicidal intent. One other feature that stands out is the frequent association of three sins in the same context: abortion, contraception, and sterilization, with such implications as the documents themselves clearly reveal.

The acceptance by the hierarchy of the *Didache,* which in the first century condemned abortion along with infanticide, made it the earliest extant authoritative witness to the Church's proscription of taking unborn life.

From the second through the fifth centuries, one after another of the Fathers of the Church condemned abortion in the most stringent language.

The apologist Athenagoras, writing to the Emperor Marcus Aurelius in A.D. 177, said that "all who use abortifacients are homicides and will account to God for their abortions as for the killing of men."[26] Clement of Alexandria, in his work *The Teacher,* attacked abortion on the dual ground that it destroyed what God had created and, in the destruction of the fetus, was an offense to a necessary love of one's neighbor.

Origen directed his words at women who call themselves believers but actually conform to the pagan unbelief around them. "There are some women," he said, "of rank and great wealth, so-called believers, who began by taking drugs to make themselves sterile; and then they bound themselves tightly to procure an abortion because they do not want to have a child born of a slave father or of a man of lower station."[27] Abortion was therefore added to contraceptive sterilization to make absolutely certain that, if pregnant, they would not give birth to an unwanted child.

Epiphanius, bishop of Salamis, published a similar work, *Refutation of All Heresies,* in which he traced the malpractices of some Christians to their infection by pagan ideas. He included the practice of contraception among immoral actions that spring from the erroneous belief that conjugal relations may be indulged without reference to their God-given purpose. Then, if contraceptives fail, abortion is resorted to.[28]

St. Jerome wrote in a similar vein during the fourth century, but about unmarried women who found the Church's teaching on chastity too demanding. First he cites those who have intercourse out of wedlock, but make sure they do not conceive by taking appropriate drugs. Others become pregnant and then commit abortion to avoid exposure of their guilt.

> It becomes wearisome to tell how many virgins fall daily. [They] drink potions to ensure sterility and are guilty of murdering a human being not yet conceived. Some, when they learn they are with child through sin, practice abortion by the use of drugs. Frequently they die themselves and are brought before the rulers of the lower world guilty of three crimes: suicide, adultery against Christ, and murder of an unborn child.[29]

The reference to murder of a human being not yet conceived is typical of the Catholic tradition, which sees in the contraceptive mentality a homicidal willingness to destroy in the womb what attempted sterilization did not prevent. The proscription of adultery against Christ assumes that Christian virginity is somehow consecrated to the Lord.

As we get into the fifth and sixth centuries, the testimony of John Chrysostom and Augustine, of Cyril of Alexandria and Caesarius of Arles merely confirms what, by then, was assumed to be part of the Catholic faith.

Although there was ecclesiastical legislation at an earlier date, the first well-known laws with prescribed penalities for both contraception and abortion were drafted in Spain (A.D. 527), by St. Martin of Braga, at the council of bishops over which he presided.[30]

In this historic legislation, three sins are joined together as of equal gravity, i.e., infanticide, abortion, and contraception. When the law stated that formerly such persons were not to receive Communion even at death, this did not mean that they were not absolved of their sin; but to stress the seriousness of their crime, the early Church in some parts of the Catholic world saw fit to withhold the added privilege of Holy Communion.

In the light of all this, it is not surprising that Post-Reformation Popes like Sixtus V, Gregory XVI, and Innocent XI, and the modern Pontiffs were so outspoken in condemning abortion, and appealed to the unbroken Catholic teaching in support of their condemnation. Pius XI called it a "very serious crime," which attacks the life of the offspring hidden in the mother's womb. He not only stigmatized the sin but also isolated the complicity in crime practiced by those in public office who condone the practice or even promote its legalization.

> Some wish it [abortion] to be allowed and left to the will of the father or the mother; others say it is unlawful unless there are weighty reasons, which they call by the name of medical, social, or eugenic "indication." Because this matter falls under the penal laws of the State by which the destruction of the offspring begotten but unborn is forbidden, these people demand that the "indication," which in one form or another they defend, be recognized as such by the public law and in no way be penalized. There are those, moreover, who ask that the public authorities provide aid for these death-dealing operations.[31]

Pius XII returned to the sophism that the Church prefers the life of the child over that of the mother. That is not true. "Never and in no case has the Church taught that the life of the child must be preferred to that of the mother. It is erroneous to put the question with this alternative: either the life of the child or that of the mother. No, neither the life of the mother nor that of the child can be subjected to an act of direct suppression. In the one case as in the other, there can be but one obligation: to make every effort to save the lives of both, of the mother and the child."[32]

John XXIII carried forward the same principles, with special insistence on the evil effects of legalized abortion on the whole of society, once its leaders approve the slaying of the unborn. "Human life," he wrote, "is sacred; from its very inception the creative action of God is directly operative. By violating his laws, the divine majesty is offended, the individuals themselves and humanity are degraded, and the bonds by which members of society are united are enervated."[33]

When the Second Vatican Council, in its Constitution regarding today's world, declared that "Life from its very conception must be guarded with the greatest care," and that "Abortion and infanticide are abominable crimes," it rested its case on almost two millennia of Catholic faith and doctrine. Paul VI confirmed this teaching with a special declaration in the clearest possible terms. "Respect for human life," he wrote, "is called for from the time that the process of generation begins. From the time that the ovum is fertilized, a life is begun which is neither that of the father nor of the mother; it is rather the life of a new human being with his own growth. It would never be made human if it were not human already." Consequently, "Divine law and natural reason exclude all right to the direct killing of an innocent human being."[34]

STERILIZATION

While sterilization has been practiced since time immemorial, it has taken on new and more serious implications with the rise of various theories about improving the standard of living and the quality of the human race. This in turn has created different forms of sterilization, which have one thing in common: to deprive the body of the power of either begetting or of bearing children. It consists in rendering the faculties of generation unfruitful.

The differences come from the varied purpose for which a person is sterilized. Their moral evaluation differs immensely. As a therapeutic procedure, its purpose is to relieve a patient of some pathological condition. As a preventive procedure, its function is to inhibit the conception and development of undesired offspring, for the satisfaction of a person's own wishes and/or for the relief of an economic or social need. As a eugenic procedure, it is aimed at assuring the elimination of offspring having allegedly undesirable traits and to develop an environment more advantageous for humans having allegedly desirable traits. And as a legally authorized procedure, besides the legalization of any of the foregoing, sterilization is a legislative enactment either to punish certain crimes or to deter a person from committing further crimes. These are commonly called therapeutic, contraceptive, eugenic, and penal sterilizations.

Before entering on an analysis of each of these procedures, the general moral attitude of the Catholic Church may be stated. It is based on the premise that while man does not have sovereign dominion over the use of his bodily faculties and therefore may not mutilate his body, he does have the right to sacrifice members (or functions) of his body for the well-being of the whole body. The most obvious cases are those in which death would result unless an amputation or operation were performed. Lesser reasons than danger of death also justify mutilation. Consequently, if a serious pathological condition can be removed by radical surgery, this is justified, even though there is no danger of death; always provided that the loss sustained is in proportion to the seriousness of the surgery and that the success of the operation is reasonably certain.

One more distinction is stated by Catholic moralists. The organ removed or its function suppressed need not itself be diseased to warrant removal. In some cases an otherwise healthy organ can stimulate the growth, e.g., of cancerous tissue, and it may be removed or its function suppressed in order to check the growth of the disease.

In appraising the morality of the different procedures with application to these norms, it must always be kept in mind that a new dimension has entered the scene. What was mainly a speculative issue, even at midcentury, is no longer so. The State in one country after another has entered the field of sterilization on an unprecedented scale.

We might add in passing that, while the operation that sterilizes a person (especially the male) is slight, the loss of procreative power is great, and generally speaking it may be considered irreversible. Also well to keep in mind is that, on moral grounds, sterilization is direct if it is done in order to take away the power of reproduction; it is indirect if it is permitted while seeking to remedy some pathological condition.

1. The morality of therapeutic sterilization is already implied in evaluating the ethics of mutilation. Any grave physical condition which, in the judgment of a competent and conscientious physician, would be cured or at least notably relieved by sterilization warrants the procedure on Catholic principles. It is important, however, for the doctor not to allow himself to be swayed by the urging of others and without sufficient regard for what is medically necessary. Contraceptive intentions are so prevalent that they can easily enter the motives behind a requested sterilization. One fair index of real need is whether the same physical condition could not be remedied by less drastic means than depriving a person of procreative powers.

Various drugs have been developed that render a woman temporarily sterile. The use of such drugs should be judged on the same principles. If they are used in order to avoid pregnancy, this becomes direct (although temporary) sterilization and is wrong. But if they are used to cure a pathological condition, and there is a proportionate reason for allowing temporary infertility, this may licitly be done.

Among the least adverted to consequences of sterilization is the effect this has on the sex impulse and sexual satisfaction. Most writers minimize the effect, and the results vary somewhat with different persons. But in general the reduced libidinal experience is considerable and should be taken into account when evaluating the "proportionate reasons" favoring sterilization, since for married persons this unfavorable effect can be of decisive importance.

2. Contraceptive sterilization is self-explanatory and its morality falls under the same category as contraception. In fact, the two practices can be simply one practice under two names. Where sterilization describes what is done, contraception tells why it is done.

A clear affirmation should be made, however, regarding the Church's uniform teaching on the subject. Direct contraceptive sterilization may not be performed either as an end or even as a means toward some otherwise good purpose. This applies whether the sterilization is permanent or temporary, whether of the man or of the woman.

3. The most explosive area of sterilization today is in the field of eugenics, lately associated with ecology or improving the human environment. As a social theory, eugenics studies methods to improve the human race physically and mentally through control of mating and heredity. It is directed toward discouraging propagation by the unfit and encouraging it in those who are considered superior persons. Its goal is genetic improvement, and its method is a more or less coercive control of reproduction by those who hold the reins of power in a society.

Since the very term "eugenics" was first coined by Francis Galton (1822–1911), cousin of Charles Darwin and his great admirer, it is not surprising that the Church's declarations on the morality of eugenic sterilization are correspondingly recent. The first extensive treatment of this subject was given by Pius XI. He first distinguished between legitimate concern for a sound offspring and the "pernicious practice" that tries to legislate a eugenic, i.e., well-born society.

The proponents of these draconian measures, he explained, invert the right order established by God and want to reduce citizens to pawns of an omnicompetent civil power.

> Those who act in this way are wrong in losing sight of the fact that the family is more sacred than the State and that men are begotten not for the earth and for time, but for heaven and eternity. Although often these individuals are to be dissuaded from entering matrimony, certainly it is wrong to brand them with the stigma of crime because they contract marriage, on the ground that, despite the fact that they are in every respect capable of matrimony, they will give birth only to defective children, even though they use all care and diligence.

Behind the Church's teaching on this matter stands the Christian principle that "public magistrates have no direct power over the bodies of their subjects. Therefore, where no crime has taken place and there is no cause for grave punishment, they can never directly harm or tamper with the integrity of the body, either for reasons of eugenics or for any other reason."[35]

One area of eugenic sterilization with which the hierarchies of several nations have taken public issue concerns the mentally retarded, often rudely classified as "feebleminded." Like legalized abortion, it deeply affects those agencies and institutions under Catholic auspices that serve the needs of this segment of the population. Church authorities point out that, in addition to the bad morality of sterilizing the feebleminded, it is also bad social science. First of all, many of the cases of feeblemindedness arise from non-hereditary causes, so that a large per cent would not be affected by sterilization; the remainder may be attributed to hereditary causes. But then feebleminded offspring come from two sources: from feebleminded parents and from normal parents who are carriers of feeblemindedness. If all the feebleminded parents were sterilized, the procreation of mentally retarded children by normal parents who are carriers would not be affected.

Only a small fraction of congenital retardations come by inheritance from feebleminded parents. To sterilize this fraction would not appreciably reduce feeblemindedness in future generations. Thus it is estimated that if the entire feebleminded segment of society were sterilized, it would take more than a thousand years of constant sterilization to reduce feeblemindedness from a proportion of one per thousand to one per ten thousand.

4. Where penal sterilization is approved by the civil laws, the Church's attitude is one of great reserve. She teaches that in the case of criminals the State has indeed the right to inflict such punishment. This follows from the prior right of the State over the life and death of justly tried and convicted criminals. Capital punishment is part of the acknowledged Christian tradition, illustrated by St. Paul's statement that, "The State is there to serve God for your benefit. If you break the law, however, you may well have fear; the bearing of the sword has its significance. The authorities are there to serve God; they carry out God's revenge by punishing wrongdoers" (Rm. 13:4).

Certainly if capital punishment is morally justified, punitive sterilization is also legitimate on principle. But there is the further question of its reasonableness on two counts: Is penal sterilization a real punishment? Is it a real preventative? On both counts, Catholic moralists commonly reply in the negative.

Penal sterilization is not a real punishment because it does not effectively deprive the convicted person of anything precious in his eyes. He retains his criminal sexual tendencies and, if he is turned loose on the community, he still remains a danger to society. If he is kept in prison, there is no need for sterilization.

For the same reasons penal sterilization is not a real preventative to deter would-be criminals from sexual crimes. They have nothing grave to fear if they assault others sexually and are threatened with the loss of reproductive fertility. In fact their sterilized condition may even encourage them to promiscuity.

WAR AND PEACE

It should only be expected of the Church whose founder is called the Prince of Peace and who called peacemakers blessed, to have spoken often and clearly on the subject of war and peace.

There are, in fact, so many passages in the New Testament dealing with peaceful tranquillity among men that Christianity may seem to be opposed to all war on principle and that pacifism is a Gospel mandate.

In reality, though, the Church has been careful to distinguish between the sinful passions that give rise to war, and the permissibility for Christians to engage in a just war.

It must be admitted that in a world wholly governed by Christian principles, war would be ruled out as at variance with the moral teaching of Christ, especially as contained in the Sermon on the Mount. But since Christians also are citizens of a secular order in which the exercise of force is sometimes necessary to maintain the authority of the law, the Catholic Church has held that the method of war and the active participation of Christians in it are on occasion morally defensible and may even be praiseworthy.

Three documents from the early Church are sometimes cited to prove that the Church was at first pacifist and only later on changed its mind to sanction military conflict and permit military service for the faithful. There is a collection of the Canons of Hippolytus, a regulation from the Council of Nicea, and a work of Tertullian called *The Soldier's Crown*. But the canons of Hippolytus, though attributed to the antipope of that name (170–236), were not compiled until about the year 500. The regulation in Canon 12 of Nicea in the year 325 was directed against Christian soldiers who served in armed forces where their faith was in grave jeopardy. And by the time Tertullian wrote his famous treatise on pacifism, he had ceased to be a Roman Catholic and became a Montanist.

What was the attitude of the early Church toward the bearing of arms? More truly citizens of the earthly fatherland than has sometimes been thought, Christians similarly did not hesitate to become soldiers, charged with their country's defense and perhaps extension. Accordingly, we find numbers of them in the Roman armies at a time when military service was obligatory only for the sons of veterans or in the infrequent cases of extraordinary levies. The fact that Emperor Galerius on the threshold of the fourth century had to "purge" the armed forces because they had too many Christians is the best proof that, from the end of the second century to the beginning of the fourth, "conscientious objection" was not felt by the majority.

It existed, however, and even spread, mainly because of the intransigence of Tertullian, who was supported in this by Origen. Tertullian's argument was that military service is absolutely incompatible with the profession of Christianity, in view of the obligation to use the sword. This was equivalent to forbidding Christians to enter the army.

In spite of the exhortations of Tertullian, along with Origen and Lactantius, it is striking that these were never more than isolated cases. Most Christians, and certainly their leaders, exhorted the pacifists to return to a different frame of mind by putting before them the examples of their Christian comrades. The reasoning of Tertullian and Origen, which the Church's magisterium did not adopt as its own, did not therefore have a far-reaching effect. Those who answered the pacifists argued that Christians are to become a substantial part of a nation and should wish to bring, if possible, all its people to the faith. If this is true, then as citizens of the State the faithful are obliged to serve the essential interests of the State, which at times will include military service. The option would be to reduce Christianity to a minority sect, or to impose the ideal of perfection on all believers, whereas the monastic life is not meant for all but only for those who are specially called. If ever monasticism became normative of the whole human race, the days of mankind would be numbered.

They further appealed to the words of St. Paul, bidding the faithful, "Let everyone stay as he was at the time of his call" (1 Co. 7:20). And they also quoted St. Luke's passage on the preaching of John the Baptist: "Some soldiers asked him in their turn, 'What about us? What must we do?' He said to them, 'No intimidation! No extortion! Be content with your pay!' " (Lk. 3:14).

Tolerance of Warfare. From the time of Constantine, the Church has consistently deplored the fact of conflict between nations, but it has not condemned war as intrinsically wrong. St. Augustine defended it when undertaken for the good of society, and after the Middle Ages Catholics had laid before them the principles of a just war by moralists such as St. Thomas Aquinas. His three conditions are now classic. In order for a war to be just, it must be on the authority of the sovereign; the cause must be just; and the belligerents should have a rightful intention. In the sixteenth century a fourth condition was added, namely, that the war must be waged by "proper means."

More recently the second of these conditions, that the cause must be just, has been further refined. The assumption, of course, is that the act of waging war is in itself morally indifferent, so that the evils resulting are merely permitted for a proportionally good reason.

1. The nation's rights, e.g., its sovereign independence or possession of vital natural resources needed, are unjustly violated. The attack on these national rights must either be actually under way or at least imminent.

2. Other means of preventing the aggression have been tried and failed. Such would be diplomatic measures, trade embargoes, and economic sanctions. Even if these other means have not been tried, but it is clearly foreseen that they would be useless, there is no strict obligation to try them since there is no duty to attempt what is certain to fail.

3. There has to be a proportion between the foreseen evils of conflict and the hoped-for benefits of engaging in war. Therefore a war would not be justified if greater harm than good would result from the armed conflict.

While these calm principles of a just war are easy enough to state in print, they become excruciatingly difficult to put into practice. Not only are the relationships among nations far more complex, but the weapons of modern warfare are so destructive that there is perhaps no moral problem today causing greater uneasiness for Christians who value the dignity of human life as a divine mandate. Hence the value in reading the mind of the first ecumenical council of the Catholic Church since the dawn of the atomic age:

> The increase of scientific weapons has increased the horror and wickedness of war immensely. Action carried out with these weapons can cause vast and indiscriminate destruction which goes far beyond the limits of legitimate defense.
>
> All this forces us to examine war in an entirely new frame of mind. Our contemporaries should know that they will have to give a very serious account of their waging war. The future will hang very largely on their present decisions.
>
> Bearing this in mind, the Council makes its own, the condemnation of total war already issued by recent Popes and declares: All warfare which tends indiscriminately to the destruction of entire cities or wide areas with their inhabitants is a crime against God and man, to be firmly and unhesitatingly condemned.[36]

Because of the totally different situation today, the Church therefore is far more reserved in recognizing the conditions of a just war. Catholic moralists agree, for example, that although nuclear war might be defended in theory, it is next to impossible to justify it in practice.

Also in reviewing papal and conciliar statements, along with declarations of various hierarchies, certain duties are agreed to pertain to citizens during time of war. Thus, during a just war a citizen must aid his country to gain victory, but he may not voluntarily provide help if his nation's cause is evidently unjust. Moreover, those conscripted or in military service when war is declared may, if they doubt the justice of the war, assume that their nation is right and so engage in the conflict. The reason is that they do not have complete knowledge of the facts to warrant making a contrary judgment. Volunteers, on the other hand, should seriously investigate whether or not their country's cause is a just one. Since a volunteer freely chooses to enter battle, he must himself make sure that he is on the right side and that he can with a good conscience pursue the enemy. This means that an objector must follow his sincere conscience. He should make an honest effort to find out the merits of the situation and, if he cannot persuade himself that the war is licit, he must abstain from active military participation.

Pursuit of Peace. While recognizing that "insofar as men are sinners the danger of war hangs over them and will hang over them till the coming of Christ," the Church has never been more insistent in pleading for peace and in offering nations the means for peace. Four such means have become thematic in the Church's teaching in our day.

1. To establish peace, there is need above all to "root out the causes of dissensions among men, on which war thrives, and especially injustices." Some of these come from excessive economic inequalities and from delay in applying suitable remedies. "Others come from the desire to dominate and from contempt for persons and, if we ask for deeper reasons, from human envy, mistrust, pride and other selfish passions."[37] It is remarkable that these are almost the exact sentiments of the first papal document on dissension in the first century. Clement I told the Corinthians what history teaches, that from pride sprang "jealousy and envy, strife and sedition, persecution and anarchy, war and captivity. Then the dishonored rose up against the honored, the ignoble against the highly esteemed, the foolish against the wise, the young against their elders." Christians are no exception. Among them, too, "piety and peace are far removed" once they abandon "the fear of God and have lost the clear vision which faith affords and nobody regulates his conduct by the norms of his commandments or tries to make his life worthy of Christ."[38]

2. Peace is possible only on the grounds of a social order based on justice and charity, but one that also recognizes that perfect happiness is not possible until the world to come. To achieve peace, therefore, Christians must not succumb to ideologies that consider "religion the opiate of the people because the principles of religion, which speak of a life beyond the grave, dissuade the proletariat from the dream of a Communistic paradise which is of this world."[39]

3. What is true of persons is also true of societies. Although material prosperity alone is no guarantee of peace, nevertheless a sound economic base is an important condition for peaceful co-existence among nations, especially since in our days a serious gap has developed between prosperous and materially undeveloped nations. "The present unity of the human race demands greater international co-

operation in the economic field." This means that "the citizens of every country must be prepared by education and professional training to face various duties of social and economic life." It also means that "if the developing nations are to be given material aid, the habits of present-day world trade will have to change profoundly."[40] Otherwise, all the inequalities that tend to stir up dissension among persons will be aroused among nations.

4. If peace is to be achieved among nations, they must set up institutions for international co-operation on every level of human enterprise (not only economic) and actively support (and improve) such global institutions already in existence. In this endeavor, the "Church should certainly be present in the community of nations to foster and stimulate co-operation among men. And this not only by means of her public institutions but also through the full and sincere collaboration of all Christians, given with the sole motive of service."[41] The opportunity to practice the Beatitude of peacemakers on a cosmic scale has never been more open to the followers of Christ.

SIXTH AND NINTH COMMANDMENTS

It has been customary since apostolic times to relate the Sixth and Ninth Commandments of God as two aspects of the same divine mandate. They forbid respectively the external and internal sins against chastity.

Immediately, however, a distinction should be made between the Jewish understanding of the meaning of these commandments and the attitude of Christ. No other single element of human behavior brings out more clearly how the Savior elevated the law or, as he said, brought it to fulfillment.

Since the Mosaic code allowed divorce and remarriage, and even polygamy, adultery in the Old Testament was essentially a sin against justice. Once a man married, his wife had a right to him in the same way as he had a right to her; so that intercourse with someone else than one's spouse was an act of injustice toward the married partner. This is brought out dramatically in the Ninth Commandment, which occurs as part of a longer prohibition: "You shall not covet your neighbor's wife, you shall not set your heart on his house, his field, his servant—man or woman—his ox, his donkey or anything that is his" (Dt. 5:21). The assumption was that, no less than depriving one's neighbor of anything else that belongs to him, it is forbidden to alienate another person's spouse since she (or he) too is one's property.

Christ raised the commandment to hitherto unknown heights. The new lawgiver thus demanded a response immeasurably higher from his followers than Yahweh expected of the Jews.

> You have learned how it was said: You must not commit adultery. But I say this to you: if a man looks at a woman lustfully, he has already committed adultery with her in his heart. If your right eye should cause you to sin, tear it out and throw it away; for it will do you less harm to lose one part of you than to have your whole body thrown into hell. And if your right hand should cause you to sin, cut it off and throw it away; for it will do you less harm to lose one part of you than to have your whole body go to hell (Mt. 5:27–30).

Also, Christ did more than stress the need for internal mastery of one's passions to be his disciple. He identified adultery as a sin against chastity and thereby changed the whole focus of the virtue with which the Sixth and Ninth Commandments were thereafter to be mainly concerned.

It was no longer merely a question of justice by keeping one's hands, so to speak, off what belongs to someone else, or even not to covet what belongs to another. It was now to be a practice of charity in which the object of virtue is really a form of self-sacrifice. This, the faithful were being taught, is characteristic of those who love Christ.

As Catholic tradition was gradually to unfold the meaning of chastity, it was indeed a form of temperance with regard to sexual pleasure. So that a chaste person is one who tempers, in the sense of restrains, the desire for venereal satisfaction by not having the experience except within the divinely ordained precincts of marriage. Within these bounds, it is a sacred enjoyment that God has associated with the responsibilities of Christian marriage. But for those who follow Christ, beyond this there must be sacrifice.

At the heart of the virtue, therefore, is the notion of surrender of what we like, namely sexual gratification, in order to please God, for whose sake we make the oblation. Writing to the Corinthians,

St. Paul made clear what this meant. "Keep away from fornication," he told them. "Your body, you know, is the temple of the Holy Spirit, who is in you since you received him from God. You are not your own property; you have been bought and paid for. That is why you should use your body for the glory of God" (1 Co. 6:18–20). A Christian is to be chaste because his body does not belong exclusively to him, not only in the natural sense that it was created by God but in the supernatural sense that it has been elevated by grace to be the dwelling place of the Holy Spirit wherein he abides as in his home. Chastity, then, in the Christian hierarchy of values recognizes the sacredness of our reproductive powers, sacred twice over: because by using them we can co-operate in the procreative work of God to bring another human being into the world, and because by sacrificing their use we can prove our love for that infinite Other who is pleased with our willing surrender of what he knows is so pleasing to us.

SEXUAL PLEASURE

In order to understand the Church's teaching on the morality of sexual pleasure, it will be useful to briefly state some of the normative principles that underlie this teaching. They are always implicit in what the Catholic teaching authority tells the faithful they must do in order to live up to the Christian expectations of the Sixth and Ninth Commandments of the Decalogue.

First of all, sexual organs are good and beautiful because they have been given to men and women by God for a most noble purpose, the continuation of the human race. In the first chapter of the first book of the Bible, we are told: "God created man in the image of himself, in the image of God he created him, male and female he created them. God blessed them, saying to them, 'Be fruitful, multiply, fill the earth and conquer it'" (Gn. 1:27–28).

Second, the sexual act in marriage is also good and beautiful because of its twofold God-given purpose: for the generation of children, and as an expression of true mutual love between the spouses.

Third, sex among Christians is essentially unselfish because it is to be directed toward others, ultimately to the offspring that God may give husband and wife and proximately to one's marriage partner.

The fourth norm is that when sex is used for selfish purposes it is disoriented by Christian standards. The disorientation may be done in various ways: when its ultimate purpose is deliberately frustrated by contraception; or when intercourse is had in circumstances where the children would be brought into the world without proper care for their upbringing and education, as in adultery and fornication; or when sexual union is sought merely to satisfy one's own selfish desires without regard for the fatigue or illness of the other partner.

The fifth principle indicates that there must be a morally good reason for any action that brings about sexual stimulation, whether the stimulation is primary, e.g., by touch, or secondary, e.g., through the other senses. Direct sexual actions, whose immediate and exclusive intention is to arouse or encourage sexual pleasure, are the privilege only of married partners between themselves. They are forbidden to the unmarried, because such conduct would be contrary to the virute of chastity. Indirect sexual actions are those whose purpose is not to arouse sexual stimulation but some other good reason. If there is such a reason, the actions are not sinful, provided a person neither intends the sexual pleasure nor consents if it spontaneously arises.

Lest there be any misunderstanding about the Church's attitude toward sexual experience between married spouses, we should recall the teaching of the Second Vatican Council: "The sexual activity by which married people are intimately and chastely united is honorable and worthy and, if done in a truly human fashion, it signifies and fosters the self-giving by which the couple gladly and gratefully enrich each other."[42] It is unfortunate that words like "impurity" and "unchastity" have taken on nuances that suggest there is something wrong with the sexual experience. It is sacred, and its very sacredness is the reason why indulgence outside of marriage becomes profanation of a holy thing.

Catholic moralists have always given due attention to sexual experiences outside of marriage that are called "unnatural," notably masturbation and homosexuality. But their increase in certain affluent cultures has led some people to wonder if, perhaps, they are all that sinful. What can be so wrong about "relieving emotional pressure" or, in the case of homosexuals, about two men or two women "being in love"?

Writers who defend the practices generally follow the expedient of reducing the morality of human acts to the intention. How a person enjoys sexual pleasure is unimportant; what matters is the reason why. Self-abuse then becomes sex release, and the sin that St. Paul said excluded one from the kingdom of heaven is described as a form of gaiety.

The Church has consistently proscribed homosexuality and masturbation as objectively contrary to the will of God.[43] At the same time, she recognizes that the subjective responsibility of the persons involved is greatly affected by the culture in which they live.

As a society's attitudes change toward sexual activity outside of marriage, it becomes increasingly difficult for men and women to maintain their Christian convictions and accept the Church's teaching. Accordingly, manuals in moral theology now give special counsel to confessors and spiritual directors about helping their penitents come to grips with the problems that underlie self-indulgence. Pastoral psychologists have found a remarkable correlation between the urge to masturbation and physical or emotional fatigue, insecurity, or lack of acceptance by others. They have also connected homosexuality with disoriented relations between child and parents, and with imbalanced sense of guilt, exorbitant malice, and inner depression.

More than ever, the Church is becoming aware of the need for probing beneath the surface of not only what a person is doing but why he is doing it. Impulses and tendencies that well up from the subconscious (or unconscious) are seen as contributing to overt actions that reflect the behavioral pattern of the environment, even while they contradict the deepest values in which a person believes. He may have an unexplainable desire and feel the desire persist in spite of conscious reasons to the contrary; he may experience an unaccountable inner drive without apparent cause in his conscious life; or he may experience an unclear sense of fear or attraction for which there is no assignable cause.

That is one reason why religious instruction, especially of adolescents, should take into account their tendency to identify with surrounding customs as an expression of personal autonomy. "From this kind of autonomy there arises what can be called a 'temptation to naturalism,' which makes adolescents tend to perform their actions and to seek their salvation by their own powers. The bolder the personality, the stronger will be an inclination of this sort."[44]

Hence the importance of sound pastoral care and the Church's insistence that her priests and teachers not only present the moral doctrine to the faithful, without dilution and with perfect candor, but also help the people to cope with their moral problems and train them to Christian maturity.

This Christian maturity is a new term in the Catholic vocabulary. It corresponds to the achievement of a fully developed personality, one of whose features is a balanced control of the sex impulses and a harmonious unity of all the experiences of one's personal, social, and spiritual life. What must be kept in mind, however, is that such maturity is not some starry ideal but an attainable reality. Of course, this means self-mastery, with the help of divine grace. "If we wish, we can keep our body and spirit chaste. The Master, who speaks with great severity in this matter (Mt. 5:28), does not propose an impossible thing. We Christians, regenerated in baptism, though we are not freed from this kind of weakness, are given the grace to overcome it with relative facility."[45] We have the promise that "since the Spirit is our life," we shall be "directed by the Spirit," which means that we shall not be victims of our "self-indulgent passions and desires" (Ga. 5:24–25).

DIVORCE

When Christ was questioned by the Pharisees about divorce, they did so with the intention of trapping him. There were then two schools of thought among the Jews divided on the matter of sufficient motive for divorce in the full sense of separation and the right to remarry. The followers of Rabbi Shammai allowed complete divorce only on the grounds of adultery. Those of Hillel, Shammai's pre-Christian contemporary, allowed it for less serious, even trivial reasons.

By the first century of the Christian era, the school of Hillel was becoming less acceptable, at least among ordinary people, and divorce with remarriage was more common in the upper classes. The Pharisees' question, therefore, was equivalent to: "Is Hillel right? Can divorce for any cause whatsoever be permitted?" If the Savior sided with Hillel, he would estrange himself from the ordinary folk in Palestine. If he sided with Shammai, he would turn off the leaders of the people.

To their embarrassment, Christ pronounced for neither school but went straight to the original act and word of God. Having created man and woman, Yahweh declared through the inspired writer that their union was closer even than ties of blood. It produced, as it were, a new single and indivisible person—"one flesh." The Savior implied that no human authority, either Hillel or Shammai, has the right to interfere with the will of God. When they objected, he told them why the Mosaic "bill of divorce" made the best of an existing situation by demanding a formality that restrained hasty action and that safeguarded the divorced wife from recall at her divorcing husband's whim. In the process, Christ restored the stability of the primeval institution on his own authority, with the implicit assurance of his grace to remain faithful to his teaching.

> They said to him, "Then why did Moses command that a writ of dismissal should be given in cases of divorce?" "It was because you were so unteachable," he said, "that Moses allowed you to divorce your wives, but it was not like this from the beginning. Now I say to you: the man who divorces his wife—I am not speaking of fornication—and marries another, is guilty of adultery" (Mt. 19:7–9).

He had already taught, in the Sermon on the Mount, that "anyone who marries a divorced woman commits adultery" (Mt. 5:32). And the evangelist Mark, writing for non-Jewish converts among whom women had the right to divorce their husbands, recalled the Master's saying that "if a woman divorces her husband and marries another she is guilty of adultery too" (Mk. 10:12).

The Catholic Church has interpreted these passages in the Gospels to mean that two baptized people who contract a valid marriage and have consummated their union by intercourse after marriage cannot be allowed to remarry during the lifetime of their Christian spouse. What some have called an "exceptive clause," where Christ says he is not speaking of fornication, the Church does not consider an exception, as though Christian spouses could not only separate for such reasons as infidelity (which separation Christ permits) but also remarry. Besides the logic of the situation, which would have Christ reversing his uncompromising position with casual parentheses, we know that neither Mark nor Luke nor Paul, who report the Savior's teaching on the indissolubility of marriage, give any hint of an exception.

Building on the uninterrupted tradition of the past, the Council of Trent defined that the Church teaches the truth when it reaffirms what Christ and the apostles taught:

> The bond of matrimony cannot be dissolved because of adultery of one of the married persons. [Consequently] both, or even the innocent party who has given no occasion for adultery, cannot during

the lifetime of the other contract another marriage. [So that] he, who after the dismissal of the adulteress shall marry another, is guilty of adultery, and she also, who after the dismissal of the adulterer shall marry another.[46]

Since it is the teaching of Christ that marriage is indissoluble even on account of adultery, it follows that any lesser grounds are equally intolerable according to the mind of the Savior.

It might be asked whether only Christian marriage is indissoluble. The Catholic position is that a permanent bond, until death, partakes of the essence of every true marriage, even among persons who are not baptized believers. This is very pertinent to the question of whether the State has a right to dissolve the validly contracted marriages that are not sacramental, since it is clearly outside the scope of civil authority to give Christians the moral right to remarry. The answer is unequivocal.

> Although the sacramental element may be absent from a marriage, as is the case among unbelievers, still in such a marriage, inasmuch as it is a true marriage, there must remain and indeed there does remain that perpetual bond which by divine right is so bound up with matrimony from its first institution that it is not subject to any civil power.[47]

As Catholicism views every marriage, therefore, either it is so contracted that it is really a true marriage, in which case it carries with it that enduring bond which by divine right is inherent in every true marriage; or it is thought to be contracted without that perpetual bond, and in that case there is no marriage.

But does not the Church dissolve marriages, even between baptized persons and, in fact, Catholics? The best way to answer this question is first to make a general statement: The Church does not dissolve and does not believe that any earthly authority has the right to dissolve a marriage with the right to remarry while the other spouse is still living where (1) both partners were validly baptized before marriage, (2) they entered into a valid marital contract, and (3) they consummated their marriage by natural intercourse after the sacrament of matrimony was received.

All cases in which the Church, through lawful ecclesiastical authority, actually or apparently dissolved a marriage were those in which one or more of these conditions for an absolutely undissolvable marriage were proved to be missing.

1. The Church's warrant for permitting a previously unbaptized convert of the faith to remarry, with ecclesiastical approval, rests on what has come to be known as the Pauline Privilege. This is the privilege conceded by St. Paul in his letter to the Corinthians:

> If a brother has a wife who is an unbeliever, and she is content to live with him, he must not send her away; and if a woman has an unbeliever for a husband, and he is content to live with her, she must not leave him.
>
> However, if the unbelieving partner does not consent, they may separate; in these circumstances, the brother or sister is not tied; God has called you to a life of peace. If you are a wife, it may be your part to save your husband for all you know; if a husband, for all you know, it may be your part to save your wife (1 Co. 7:12–16).

Attested to from the earliest times, e.g., by St. John Chrysostom, the exercise of the Pauline Privilege assumes that a "natural marriage," which is not a sacrament, does not carry with it the absolute indissolubility inherent in Christian matrimony. It may be dissolved, on apostolic authority, when the unbelieving partner would seriously interfere with the practice of the Catholic faith.

In recent years, the Church has applied the same basic doctrine to the dissolution of a marriage in which one partner was a Christian at the time of marriage, and the other was not baptized. Consistent with the Church's understanding of the Pauline Privilege, the underlying principle was extended to the solution of a "natural bond," on the presumption that unless both partners to a marital contract are baptized, neither one receives the sacrament of matrimony.

Admitting this, however, does not say that the Church is not extremely careful in applying the Pauline Privilege. Particularly important is the need of making sure of St. Paul's proviso, "if the unbelieving partner does not consent" to live peaceably with the Catholic. Unless this is assured, the Church believes it cannot touch the case, since the apostle expressly tells the believer to remain with the unbelieving partner if the latter wishes to live in marital peace. The hope is that a believing wife may save her infidel husband, and a believing husband his non-Christian wife. St. Augustine, whose mother Monica was a model of patient kindness toward her dissolute husband, later wrote about the providential role we may serve in the economy of grace by seeing ourselves as the means of winning the salvation of those who cause us the most suffering.

2. Since marriage is a bilateral covenant, it is valid only when both parties make it with adequate knowledge and freedom of will. If either positive error or lack of freedom are proved to have been present when the marriage was entered, the Church may declare the contract invalid from the beginning. And though people sometimes speak of this as dissolving a marriage or annulling it, more accurately the Church makes a declaration of nullity, saying in effect that what was thought to be a matrimonial union really was not.

Catholic morality distinguishes various levels of possible ignorance and error that may invalidate matrimony, notably the nature of marriage and its properties. Matrimonial consent consists essentially in giving and accepting the permanent and exclusive right to the body, i.e., the right to such actions as are suitable for the propagation of the human race. One does not marry validly if he or she refuses to give the matrimonial right or to accept its corresponding obligations.

Among the properties of marriage that appear in the Church's marriage decisions, unity and indissolubility are very prominent, where unity refers to one husband with one wife, and indissolubility concerns the permanence of marriage until the death of one of the parties. A basic distinction must be inserted, however, on which the Church is adamant in its handling of proposed nullity proceedings. The distinction is between simple error and a positive act of the will in which error finds expression.

Thus a simple or theoretical error regarding the unity or indissolubility or sacramental character of marriage does not nullify the marital consent. Such an error occurs when the mistake is only in the mind and does not positively move the will. Non-Catholics who think that marriage is a soluble contract marry validly, even though they would not marry if they knew the truth. Error is presumed to be merely theoretical until the contrary is proved.

On the other hand, when the error positively influences the will, it invalidates marriage. Hence marriage would be invalid in the case of one who expressly stated that he or she intended to contract a dissoluble union, or that they would renounce marriage rather than receive a sacrament.

This has grave implications for mixed marriages, where a Catholic enters matrimony with a person whose education and background may tell him that marriage is not indissoluble. The usual approach by the Holy See in deciding on nullity cases presented to it for judgment has been to say that such unions were valid even though the party concerned would not have contracted marriage had he known the opposite, i.e., had he known that marriage is by its nature a lifelong union. On the other hand, the contract is considered null, when one or both parties said, in effect, "I wish to contract marriage, but I do not wish to transfer to my partner a permanent right." So there would be two conflicting wills: one general (to marry), the other specific, to exclude what pertains to the essence of marriage; and the latter, because specific, prevailed over the former, which was general.

Since marriage cannot be contracted without free consent, violence or grave fear would invalidate the contract. Suppose a person is physically forced, e.g., to nod the head as a sign of consent while not agreeing interiorly to the marriage. Then it is null whether between Christians or nonbaptized persons.

More frequently the Church has been asked to declare a marriage void because of grave fear. A distinction to keep in mind here is the difference between marrying *with* fear and marrying *out of* fear. Only the latter invalidates the contract. Through generations of handling such cases, the Church has laid down certain qualities of fear that must be present in order to vitiate the marital consent. Fear voids a marriage that is contracted under the influence of a fear that is grave, and unjustly caused by an external agent, and from which one can free himself only by choosing marriage. In such cases, the marriage is invalid and ecclesiastical tribunals may declare it null, although there was interior consent. This presumes, of course, that the party who entered marriage out of fear has not since then decided to willingly marry the other person.

3. There is not too much to say about intercourse after marriage consummating the union and making it, if sacramental, absolutely indissoluble. This has been the Church's tradition from time immemorial, as testified, for example, by the declarations of dissolution and permission to remarry where it could be certainly proved that the marriage had not been consummated.

With the rise of modern contraceptive cultures, however, a new dimension has entered the Church's understanding of what consummation means. Thus one of the instructive features of not a few decisions by Rome is the Church's willingness to say that a marriage was invalid if there were proved intention to have only contraceptive coitus. Some analysts of Rome's attitude argue that these are cases of nonconsummation. Others reason that the contract itself is vitiated. The noteworthy aspect of this is that natural intercourse has a sacred character that Catholic Christianity looks upon as the seal of matrimony and its sign of irrevocability.

POLYGAMY

There is some value in reflecting on the Church's teaching about polygamy. For one thing, polygamous marriages are not uncommon in non-Christian societies. Among others, Islam allows a man to have four wives and believes that the permission is part of Allah's revelation to Mohammed. With over five hundred million Moslems in the world, not to mention adherents of other religious systems that legitimize polygamy, the Catholic position on plural marriages directly affects its work of evangelization.

Then, too, it is common knowledge that besides permitting divorce with the right to remarry, the Jewish people practiced polygamy, and the Old Testament more than once quite casually mentions that some great personage had so many wives.

All that Jesus taught regarding divorce may be understood implicitly regarding polygamy; for if he forbade remarriage after divorce, even when the grounds were adultery, then even more certainly he forbade polygamy to his followers. The absence of any specific precept on the matter in the Gospels is explained by the fact that, though allowed in principle, the practice of polygamy had grown so infrequent in later Judaism that monogamy (allowing for successive marriage) was taken for granted.

As Christianity spread throughout the Empire, Church writers were more often, as with Augustine, compelled to explain how it was that a man could have more than one wife under the Old Law and forbidden even to remarry after divorcing his wife in the new dispensation. Their main approach was to resolve the question in terms of greater grace being available with the coming of Christ; with more grace, the faithful are capable of making greater sacrifices; and among the sacrifices they are called upon to make, out of love for Christ, is surrendering the Mosaic concession of polygamy and, indeed, for those who have the gift, even sacrificing the privilege of one marriage.

The Council of Trent, which declared in favor of the permanence of Christian marriage also defined monogamy, pronouncing anathema on anyone who says that "it is lawful for Christians to have several wives at the same time, and that it is not forbidden by any divine law."[48] One reason for the definition was the speculation (reduced to practice) by some who argued that there is no essential difference between Mosaic and Christian morality as regards marriage; and that if the ancient worthies of Israel were permitted more than one wife, the same privilege should be allowed to Christians.

At various times, the Popes returned to the same theme, especially when overzealous missioners felt that some leeway should be given prospective converts from polygamous cultures to become Christians without giving up all their wives save one. It was argued that this would place too great a hardship on the neophytes, or show a lack of regard for their native culture, or disturb the social order in which they lived.

Pius XI is the most eloquent witness to the Church's constant teaching on perfect monogamy and its prohibition of plural marriages:

> Conjugal faith demands in the first place the complete unity of matrimony which the Creator himself laid down in the marriage of our first parents when he wished it to be not otherwise than between one man and one woman. And, although afterward this primeval law was relaxed to some extent by God, the supreme lawgiver, there is no doubt that the law of the Gospel fully restored that original and perfect unity, and abrogated all dispensations, as the words of Christ and the constant teaching and action of the Church show plainly. With reason, therefore, does the sacred Council of Trent solemnly declare: "Christ our Lord very clearly taught that in this bond two persons only are to be united and joined together when he said, 'Therefore they are no longer two, but one flesh.' "[49]

One of the least-known features of the Christian faith is the impact that its moral imperatives have had on non-Christian cultures, particularly in the matter of polygamy. Islam, for example, has long considered polygamy a divinely revealed privilege. But under the influence of monogamous Christian living, the best minds in Islam are now seriously talking about monogamy as objectively and in principle preferable to polygamy. They are suggesting that Moslems rethink what for too long has been (they claim) mistakenly identified with the name of Mohammed. The Koran, we know, permits polygamy but prescribes that all the wives be treated with equal justice. Moslem writers are now saying that the term "justice" ('adl) in the Koran means not only equality of treatment in the matter of lodging, clothing, and other domestic necessities, but also as far as possible complete equality in love, affection, and esteem. This kind of equality, they insist, especially in affection, is impossible; so that what for so long had looked like a permission was in reality a prohibition.

These are not isolated sentiments but the growing attitude of Moslem leaders, notably those who have come to know and admire the Christian position on monogamy. Islamic writers are increasingly saying that polygamy was allowed by Mohammed only for abnormal times, as during a period of war to solve urgent social problems.

FIDELITY

While not minimizing the sin of adultery, Christ insisted that there is such a thing as "adultery in the heart," and a man's lustful looks make him guilty first of injustice toward the man whose wife he seduces and to his own wife if he is married. But second (and mainly), he is guilty of infidelity toward God, who requires as a mark of loyalty to him that a man restrain his wanton passion.

The notion of infidelity not only to a human being but to God is clearly brought out by St. Paul where he tells the Corinthians and Thessalonians that adultery is a violation of the divine will. Among others who "will not inherit the kingdom of God" are adulterers. St. Peter calls them self-willed people "with eyes always looking for adultery, men with an infinite capacity for sinning, they will seduce any soul which is unstable" (2 P. 2:11, 14).

Besides elevating fidelity in marriage to a religious sphere as an expression of loyalty to God, the Gospel also placed it within the larger framework of the Christian mandate to love.

This is concisely summarized in the closing epilogue of the letter to the Hebrews. The faithful are told that there is a rising inflection of duty to love, first strangers, then those in physical or social need, and finally (mainly) one's marriage partner, with no discrimination between the loyalty expected of each spouse:

> Continue to love each other like brothers, and remember always to welcome strangers, for by doing this, some people have entertained angels without knowing it. Keep in mind those who are in prison, as though you were in prison with them; and those who are being badly treated, since you too are in the one body. Marriage is to be honored by all, and marriages are to be kept undefiled, because fornicators and adulterers will come under God's judgment (Heb. 13:1–4).

The joint indictment of fornicators and adulterers in reference to fidelity in marriage is better understood if the generic term "fornicators" is taken to mean harlotry, so that two forms of marital infidelity are condemned: with another person for hire, and with another person than one's spouse but without pay.

Throughout its history, the Catholic Church has not failed to repeat and re-enforce the Gospel and apostolic teaching that fidelity in Christian marriage is loyalty based on love. St. Augustine called it "the faith of chastity," by which he meant that another name for marital fidelity is marital chastity. Husband and wife are to so love one another that, outside their own marital embrace, they preserve themselves chaste from alien sex experience and even from alien affections. Matrimonial faith, according to Augustine, demands that husband and wife be joined in an especially holy and pure love, not as adulterers love one another, but as Christ loved the Church.

By this the Catholic Church implies that spouses are to become so faithful that the underlying motive of their fidelity is complete devotion to one another, and infidelity would become a failure in selfless love:

> The love, then, of which we are speaking is not that based on the passing lust of the moment, nor does it consist in pleasing words only, but in the deep attachment of the heart which is expressed in action, since love is proved by deeds. This outward expression of love in the home demands not only mutual help but must go further. It must have as its primary purpose that man and wife help each other day by day in forming and perfecting themselves in the interior life, so that through their partnership in life they may advance ever more and more in virtue, and above all that they may grow in true love toward God and their neighbor on which indeed "depends the whole law and the prophets."[50]

The essence of marital fidelity, by Catholic standards, is the practice of dedicated love. This dedication seeks the welfare of the one loved; of the husband seeking the best interests of his wife, and the wife of her husband. These interests are certainly the physical and social well-being of one's spouse; but they are especially the spiritual well-being of the one whom I marry in order to help him (or her) reach with me that eternal destiny where, as Christ tells us, there will no longer be any marrying or giving in marriage.

Throughout the New Testament, the single prohibition of adultery (from the Old Testament) is expanded to cover a multitude of sins against chastity. So extensive is the Christian understanding of this virtue that a series of different terms are used in the biblical text to identify what the faithful are expected to avoid. They must avoid licentiousness (*aselgeia*), with its implication of wanton and dissolute behavior. They are forbidden to give in to unnatural sexual conduct, to which St. Paul gave the generic name of uncleanness (*akatharsia*), such as was rampant among the pagans in Rome, Corinth, and Ephesus. They may not give in to unlawful sexual intercourse (*porneia*), including fornication, incest, and prostitution. And as previously stated, they must avoid adultery (*moicheia*), which to a Christian meant more than a sin of injustice; it was a crime of disloyalty to Christ, since the bodies of the faithful are temples of the Holy Spirit.

Of special importance for dealing with today's problems of sexual morality is the apostolic concern to protect the faithful from the sins of impurity to which they were exposed in their day. The language of St. Paul is clear enough to know that he meant to include what today we could call masturbation and homosexuality. He spoke of those who "dishonor their own bodies," of women who "have turned from natural intercourse to unnatural practices," and of men who "have given up natural intercourse to be consumed with passion for each other" (Rm. 1:24–27).

The immediate commentators on the New Testament in the first and second centuries made it still more plain what this forbidden impurity meant. It included all the sexual indulgence that the poets and playwrights of Greece and Rome praised to the skies and of which the gods and goddesses of the Empire gave the sorry example to the people.

Moreover, the early Christians were duly warned that the practice of purity was more than avoidance of moral evils; it was also the following of revealed truth. The sexual immorality of the pagans was intimately connected with error in matters of belief. It was not only that the pure of heart would see God, but that purity was an expression of truth, even as impurity was living a falsehood.

CONTRACEPTION

Anthropological studies show that contraception is a social practice of much greater antiquity and cultural universality than was commonly supposed by medical and social historians. Medical papyri describing contraceptive methods are extant from 2700 B.C. in China, and from 1850 B.C. in Egypt.

As might be expected, Christians were faced from the beginning with the option of following the more difficult teaching of the Church on procreative love or of conforming to their pagan environment. What this environment was may be inferred from the extensive treatise of the Ephesian gynecologist Soranos (A.D. 98–138), who described no less than seventeen medically approved methods of contraception (Greek *atokion,* means used to not have a child). He went to such lengths to offer contraceptive methods on the premise that it is safer, medically speaking, for the mother "to prevent conception from taking place than to destroy the fetus" already conceived.

Christian Tradition. Given the widespread contraceptive practice of the first century of the Christian era, euphemistically referred to as "using magic" and "using drugs," it is logical to see in the New Testament prohibition of *mageia* and *pharmakeia* an implicit condemnation of contraception. This is especially true when the contexts (Ga. 5:20 and Rev. 21:8, 22:15) refer to sins against chastity.

The *Didache,* which explicitly condemned abortion, also implicitly condemned contraception. The early Christians were told in four successive precepts: "You shall not use magic. You shall not use drugs. You shall not procure abortion. You shall not destroy a newborn child."[51] Records from the practices of those times tell us that the people would first try some magical rites or resort to sorcery to avoid conception. If this failed, they would use one or another of the medical contraceptives elaborately described by Soranos. If notwithstanding a woman became pregnant, she would try to abort. And if even this failed, there was always the Roman law that permitted infanticide.

Before the end of the second century, Clement of Alexandria wrote the masterful catechetical treatise *Paidagogos,* which synthesized the pattern of Christian education in the East and in North Africa in the first generation after the apostles. It also reflects a very balanced attitude toward marriage. On the one hand, Clement defended marriage and marital intercourse as good and holy. Thus he said that marital "love tends toward sexual relations by its very nature," and "sometimes nature denies them (husband and wife) the opportunity to perform the marriage act so that it may be all the more desirable because it is delayed."

On the other hand, he said the Church is adamant on the right use of conjugal relations: "To indulge in intercourse without intending children is to outrage nature, whom we should take as our instructor."[52]

In succeeding decades, Justin the Martyr and Origen, Lactantius and Epiphanius, Ambrose and Jerome, John Chrysostom and Augustine repeated the Church's stand on contraception. It was wrong because it imitated the malpractice of the pagans; it placed carnal pleasure before the love that wants children; it profaned the generative act, which is sacred; it was indifferent to God's intention to create a soul as the normal aftermath to intercourse; it denied that God's grace will sustain a married couple who practice continence; it made those who practice it willing to commit murder by abortion if contraception fails; it was like the idolatry of those who offer up human semen to their obscene gods; it debauched the human person by making it subject to unnatural lust; it was an act of ingratitude to God, who offers the gift of human life; it was an injustice against the laws of God; and it was irrational to have sexual intercourse while excluding the desire to have children.

It is noteworthy that up to the beginning of the fifth century, most of the Church's spokesmen on the sinfulness of contraception were writing from Near Eastern and North African Christian communities. They were mainly not from what has since become known as the "juridical West." And in many cases they wrote so strenuously against contraception not only because it was a moral aberration but because, by then, it had become part of a heretical mind-set that had infected Christian circles.

Not the least of these heresies was Manichaeism. As such, it made a devastating distinction between marriage as an institution and sexual intercourse as a legitimate bodily action to which people are irresistibly driven by the Deity who reigns over the material world.

St. Augustine was the great Father of the Church who exposed the errors of Manichaeism. It was Augustine, too, who wrote most extensively against the practice of contraception, which those who were influenced by Manichaeism had come to defend on ideological grounds.

Among the best-known passages of Augustine on the subject of contraception is the one quoted by Pius XI in his *Encyclical on Christian Marriage,* where the African bishop is commenting on St. Paul's cryptic phrase, "If they cannot control the sexual urges, they should get married" (1 Co. 7:9). Augustine did not see this passage addressed to Christians in general, but specifically to those who have trouble with sexual control. With St. Paul, he tells them not to evade the responsibilities of marriage. "It is better to be married," he paraphrased Paul, "than to burn with unbridled passion." But Augustine did not mean, no more than St. Paul, to have this taken universally, as though marriage was only a remedy for passion, or as though persons cannot enter the sacred state of matrimony for very noble reasons that have nothing to do with merely bridling one's passions.

St. Augustine then went on to tell these same people, whose passions are so strong, not to suppose that even marriage is an infallible means of self-control. Married people, too, can give in to their unruly passions, no less than the unmarried—the latter by committing fornication and the former by resorting to contraception. The unmarried who do not control their sex impulses run the risk of "begetting children in disgrace or avoid having offspring by a degraded form of intercourse." But the married, too, may be "lawfully wedded spouses who resort to this last; for intercourse with one's legitimate wife is unlawful and wicked whenever the conception of offspring is prevented."

It was on this occasion that Augustine concluded with the now memorized statement that "the procreation of children is itself the primary, natural, legitimate purpose of marriage."[53] It is primary in the sense that married people may not deliberately frustrate this purpose for any other reason whatsoever; it is natural because human nature provides in the institution of marriage the kind of care and nurture that children require for their balanced and happy future; and it is legitimate because one of the main reasons why people have the moral right to enter marriage is in order to procreate offspring and rear them as the physical but spiritual image of themselves.

Church's Teaching Authority. As in other areas of faith and morals, the Church's formal condemnation of contraception became more or less prominent as the practice of interfering with conception was more or less prevalent among the faithful.

While the teaching was always there, and already there, before some explicit pronouncement on the subject was made, the magisterium expressed itself with vigor whenever the need arose because Catholics were being pressed by contrary reasons to abandon the Church's authorized doctrine.

The list of such declarations would be interminable. In country after country and in every century, bishops and councils forbid "contraceptive potions," "herbs or other agents so you will not have children," "spilling the seed in coitus," "coitus interruptus," "poisons of sterility," "avoiding children by evil acts," "putting material things in the vagina," and "causing temporary or permanent sterility." These and similar statements occur in ecclesiastical documents before the end of the thirteenth century.

One document out of many is worth noting because it is so concise and states in clearly distinct terms what has always been the Church's mind. The Decretals of Pope Gregory IX (1148–1241) are a summary of the Church's legislation in the lifetime of Thomas Aquinas. Like the *Summa Theologica*, the Decretals summarize the Church's whole moral tradition.

Three things are specially significant about the decree on contraception. It unambiguously identifies contraception with any action taken to prevent generation, conception, or birth; it distinguishes between taking a drug out of lust (instead of abstaining from intercourse) and taking a drug from hostile motives; and it calls all of these actions homicidal, in the technical sense of intending to destroy life at any stage of the vital process.[54]

In the late sixteenth century, Sixtus V passed a series of laws to curb the immorality of his day. Among these laws solemnly promulgated by the Pope was one that simultaneously covered abortion and contraception.[55]

Coming closer to our day, during the pontificate of Pius IX (1846–78), at least five decisions were handed down by the Holy See with

regard to contraception. One of these was made by the Holy Office
and approved by the Pope. It touches on one type of contraception
(withdrawal), but in doing so it clarified two facts: that onanism
is against the natural law, and that confessors have a duty to inquire about contraception if they have good reason to suppose that
it is being done.[56]

The foregoing included a quotation from Innocent XI's censure
of the theory that sexual immorality belongs only to divine positive
law (i.e., God wills it, but not to divine natural law) that is
crucially important. If contraception were not wrong because it
contradicts human nature, some could argue (as they do) that
changed circumstances might justify what was formerly wrong. But
no circumstances can justify what is against the very nature of man;
so that wherever you have human beings you have the prohibition of
certain conduct, like contraception, abortion, and infanticide.

By the time of Pius XI, promoters of contraception had successfully crossed the barrier of keeping the subject from the open forum.
In one country after another the clandestine practice became public
knowledge. The first international birth-control congress was held at
Paris in 1900, and by 1930 the first official teaching of a Christian
denomination in favor of contraception was issued by the Lambeth
Conference of the Anglican churches of the world.

The Pope began by sadly admitting that many nowadays have
the effrontery to call children a troublesome burden of wedlock.
"They urge married people carefully to avoid this burden, not by
means of virtuous continence, which is permissible even in marriage
with the consent of both parties, but by vitiating the act of nature."
He then made two statements that have since made Catholic moral
history: one on the essential sinfulness of contraception; and the other
on the Church's right, in modern times as over the centuries, to pronounce on the morality of human behavior.

> No reason whatever, even the gravest, can make what is intrinsi-
> cally against nature become conformable with nature and morally
> good. The conjugal act is of its very nature designed for the procrea-
> tion of offspring. Therefore, those who in performing it deliberately
> deprive it of its natural power and efficacy, act against nature and do
> something which is shameful and intrinsically immoral.

Pius XI added nothing new to the constant tradition of the Catholic
Church "to whom God has committed the task of teaching and
preserving morals."[57] But he did bring to the surface what some

were challenging, that contraception is "intrinsically immoral," so that no situation could objectively change what is sinful into something morally indifferent.

Humanae Vitae. There would be no need for more than a passing reference to the most dramatic papal statement on contraception, *Humanae Vitae* of Paul VI, except for the circumstances that accompanied the document and the implications it has since had for a better understanding of the Catholic Church's authority to teach the moral law.

Before this now historic document was published, a series of issues had risen in the world to ask once more the question of whether, in spite of these changes, contraception was still prohibited. There was a rapid demographic development, with fear being expressed on all sides, that the world population is growing more rapidly than the available resources. Working and living conditions, coupled with increased pressures in the economic and educational fields, made the rearing of a large family more difficult than it used to be. The status of woman was changing, with a new recognition of her place in society; the fostering of mutual love in marriage and the meaning of conjugal acts in relation to that love came to be more deeply appreciated. But most importantly, man's progress in dominating the forces of nature gave him a new sense of power to regulate the transmission of life.

All of this was brought to a head under John XXIII, who in 1963 formed a Commission on Population and Family Life, which was promptly confirmed by his successor. This commission was broad-based, with persons invited to participate who were known to be either pro or con on the subject of contraception. Its function was to be advisory, as with all such commissions.

Some publicity has been given to the effect that Pope Paul ignored the dominant attitude of this advisory council. However, as the Pope explained, even "the conclusions of the commission could not be considered by us definitive, nor dispense us from a personal examination of this serious question," especially when "certain criteria for resolving the question emerged which departed from the moral teaching on marriage proposed with constant firmness by the magisterium of the Church."[58]

Between his accession to the papacy and the publication in 1968 of *Humanae Vitae,* Pope Paul spoke and wrote several times on family planning. He made it clear that the Church was in no doubt about the doctrine but that he was studying its application to concrete situations today. The long delay in making a formal pronouncement was due to the amount of data involved and the conflicting information from specialists in the field of medicine and allied sciences.

When *Humanae Vitae* was issued, it became the most discussed papal document of modern times. In carefully chosen words, after reviewing the Church's continuous past history on the subject, the Pope synthesized in two paragraphs the essential teaching of Catholic morality on contraception:

> In conformity with these landmarks in the human and Christian view of marriage, we must again declare that the direct interruption of the generative process already begun and, above all, directly willed and procured abortion, even if for therapeutic reasons, are to be absolutely excluded as licit means of regulating birth.
>
> Equally to be excluded, as the teaching authority of the Church has frequently declared, is direct sterilization, whether permanent or temporary, whether of the man or of the woman. Similarly excluded is every action which, either in anticipation of the conjugal act, or in its accomplishment, or in the development of its natural consequences, proposes, whether as an end or as a means, to render procreation impossible.[59]

Every form of anticonception was simply proscribed, where the human will directly intends to interfere with, before, during, or after the life process, what the Author of nature has built into the reproductive faculties of the human organism. Consistent with the Church's two millennia of teaching, *Humanae Vitae* also placed together the practices of contraception, sterilization, and abortion. In the Catholic understanding of contraception, therefore, it is inseparable on a moral plane from either abortion or sterilization. All three are directed against the generative powers over which man has merely the stewardship, but God alone the sovereignty.

But *Humanae Vitae* did more than restate the perennial doctrine. It made an in-depth analysis of this doctrine in a way that had never been done so explicitly. Building on the teaching of Vatican II, it clarified the scope of the Church's inerrant magisterium; and it identified the moral center of the Church's stand on contraception.

1. In order to appreciate the doctrinal development on the Church's teaching authority that *Humanae Vitae* represents, it is necessary to recall that there were two previous stages to this development. The

first came when the First Vatican Council defined papal infallibility; the second came when the next ecumenical council declared that there is also such a thing as collegial infallibility, when the bishops in union with Rome agree on some doctrine of faith or morals.

Paul VI in *Humanae Vitae* carried this teaching a step farther, to the natural law. Does their inerrancy extend also to matters that belong to the natural law, such as the right use of conjugal relations in marriage? The answer is affirmative:

> No believer will wish to deny that the teaching authority of the Church is competent to interpret even the natural moral law. It is, in fact, indisputable, as our predecessors have many times declared, that Jesus Christ, when communicating to Peter and to the Apostles his divine authority and sending them to teach all nations his commandments, constituted them guardians and authentic interpreters of all the moral law, not only, that is, of the law of the Gospel, but also of the natural law, which is also an expression of the will of God, the faithful fulfillment of which is equally necessary for salvation.[60]

What the Pope did was transmit the disputed question of whether and in what sense contraception is forbidden by "the law of the Gospel." He affirmed the Church's right to pass final judgment on "all the moral law," including the natural law "illuminated and enriched by divine revelation."

2. The phrase "illuminated and enriched by divine revelation" was no rhetorical flourish. It added a whole new dimension to the Christian view of marriage and, as a consequence, to the Christian reason why contraception is morally wrong.

To illustrate what this means, we can take a straightforward issue like obedience to legitimate authority. The natural law founded on reason would tell a man that such obedience is good and disobedience is bad because otherwise human society, on every level from the family to the nation, would be unlivable, even unthinkable. But Christian revelation adds new insights to the concept of obedience: A Christian should be obedient because by this virtue he can expiate the sins of disobedience; thus he should be obedient after the example of Jesus, who was obedient even to the death on the cross; and by being obedient he merits divine grace for himself and others, even as Christ's obedience merited the salvation of mankind.

So, too, contraception is fundamentally contrary to the natural law because it deliberately interferes with the divinely ordained purpose of marital intercourse. But Christian revelation illuminates the gravity of the sin by enriching the concept of marital intercourse beyond anything conceivable by the unaided reason. The key factor in this enrichment is the Christian understanding of love.

Even though Christianity looks at marital intercourse as a practice always motivated by love, the question immediately arises, "Whose love and for whom?" The love that moves a partner in marriage to have intercourse with his (or her) spouse can be self love, each selfishly seeking his (or her) own interests while using the other as a means to heighten one's own satisfaction. Or the love can be altruistic, where the spouse honestly wants to please his (or her) partner. This altruism may not be reciprocated, and then we have a one-sided relationship, where the wife (or husband) generously wishes to give of self but the spouse selfishly holds back and refuses to give complete affection in return. Or the altruism is reciprocated, and then we have the ideal relationship, where the love is truly mutual because it is truly self-giving on both sides.

In the Christian estimate of marriage, intercourse is one of the finest means of showing and growing in mutual love between the spouses. Their marital relations are intended by the Creator to be unitive because, when selflessly practiced, they foster that unity of spirit of which their bodily union is both a sign and a sacrament; a sign because it manifests their generous affection for one another, and a sacrament because it serves to increase and deepen the affection already had. But the affection in view is always selfless affection, the kind that Christ said is willing to give without receiving in return and that is willing, if need be, even to lay down one's life for the person loved.

That is one purpose of marital intercourse. It is sacred and highly praised by the Church in the Church's teaching of the faithful. It mysteriously associates the human with the divine; the human that the spouses give one another in their physical embrace, and the divine in what God confers on them by his grace. It is the unitive aspect of conjugal relations.

But the Christian faith looks upon intercourse as also procreative. The love element here is no longer only the affection between husband and wife, as holy and desirable as this may be. Love in marriage "also wants to go beyond the communion between husband and wife; it wants to raise up new lives." There are, therefore, not one but two love functions that intercourse is to serve: the unitive and the procreative. In the unitive, love is fostered *between* husband *and* wife: in the procreative, love is communicated *from* husband-with-wife *to* their potential offspring.

Is it possible to be selfish in marriage by "holding back" on the procreative purpose of intercourse? Indeed, no less than by "holding back" on its unitive function. The only difference is that in the first case the selfishness is mutual, whereas in the second case it is individual.

What is the Church saying? She affirms the duty of selfless love in conjugal relations between husband and wife to one another, and selfless love from them (together) toward the children whom God may wish to give them.

Why, then, is contraception sinful? Because it tries to separate these two built-in qualities of marital intercourse, claiming that one (children) can be deliberately prevented while the other (mutual love) is being retained. Not so, says the Church. Either you admit both or you lose both. Love is one. You cannot successfully divide in practice what God has placed together in principle, as by now the results of a contraceptive mentality on the institution of marriage are beginning to testify.

One question still remains, however: How does the Gospel understanding of love illuminate the Catholic attitude toward contraception? It does so by revealing the depths of selfless generosity that husband and wife are called upon to practice when they engage in the marital embrace.

As Christ made it plain throughout his public life but especially at the Last Supper, love is always self-giving, self-sacrificing, and self-effacing. So essential are these qualities in Christian love that, without them, love itself is destroyed. Conjugal love, therefore, is authentically Christian only if it is truly selfless and self-giving. It either contains within itself the element of self-oblation or it merely simulates what Christ told his followers they must do if they wish to be his disciples. They are to love others not only as they love themselves, which is already the high ethic of the Mosaic law, they are also to love others as he, the God-man, loved and still loves them—which is as far above the Mosaic code as Christ's offering of himself on the cross was greater than any oblation known to ancient Israel.

Underlying this exalted concept of love is the belief in Christ's divinity. When he told his followers to love others as he loved them, he was telling them to love their fellow men as he, who is God, loves the world he created and then became man to redeem. God's love is boundless and totally generous. It is not coerced but utterly free. It is not self-seeking but looks only to benefit the creatures whom God lovingly brought out of nothing to communicate to them, not yet existing, a share in his own infinitely happy being. The same God, with the same freedom and generosity, took on man's humanity—not to enrich himself, since it meant suffering and the cross—in order to give of his goodness and (as God) receive no profit from man in return.

This is the kind of love that Christ, through his Church, expects the married faithful to practice not only between themselves but from themselves (as one flesh) toward the yet unborn and unconceived children whom providence wants to entrust to their care. The realism of this love is intelligible only where the faith on which it is based is strong and ready to give testimony of what it believes. Hence the new-found role of matrimony as a sacrament by which Christian married couples are "strengthened and, actually, consecrated for the faithful accomplishment of their proper duties, for living out their proper vocation even to perfection, and giving their own Christian witness before the whole world. To them the Lord entrusts the task of making visible to men the holiness and sweetness of the law which joins the mutual love of husband and wife to their co-operation with the love of God who is the author of human life."[61] The secret of such Christian witness lies in *making visible* to the world Christ's law of love by a twofold visibility: by their marital fidelity, which testifies to their unitive love of each other; and by their marital generosity, which testifies to their procreative love of the children whom they bear.

Periodic Continence. Although the practice of *rhythm* or periodic abstinence from intercourse has received extraordinary publicity since the turn of the century, its basic elements were recognized already in biblical times. St. Paul wrote on the subject, as he told the Corinthians, in answer to "the questions about which you wrote." He had been asked about it by some who had the mistaken notion that, since celibacy was honored among Christians, married couples would be more perfect it they avoided intercourse or at least had conjugal relations only seldom. His reply is fundamental to a balanced understanding of what the Church has always taken to be licit but what must be understood in the full context of Christian morality:

> The wife has no rights over her own body; it is the husband who has them. In the same way, the husband has no rights over his body; the wife has them. Do not refuse each other except by mutual consent, and then only for an agreed time, to leave yourselves free for prayer; then come together again in case Satan should take advantage of your weakness to tempt you (1 Co. 7:1, 4–5).

Since biblical times, then, it was assumed that a couple could lawfully abstain from marital relations for any worthy reason, symbolized in the Pauline expression "to leave yourselves free for prayer."

But now a new situation has appeared. As the problem of rearing a family in contraceptive cultures became more acute, periodic abstinence took a deeper meaning. As a result, the Church has many times addressed itself to the twofold issue that the ancient practice poses. Under what circumstances is it lawful or may even be commended, and how can further scientific developments in predicting ovulation assist Catholics to limit the number of offspring according to the moral principles of their faith?

When Pius XI restated the Church's prohibition of direct interference with the life process, he was careful to add that, "Those are not considered as acting against nature who in the married state use their right in the proper manner, although on account of natural reasons either of time or of certain defects new life cannot be brought forth."[62]

His immediate successor returned to the same theme on several occasions, referring to a couple who make use of their matrimonial rights on the days of natural sterility besides the days when conception is possible. This is perfectly licit, "for by so doing they neither hinder nor injure in any way the consummation of the natural act and its further natural consequences."[63]

When Paul VI published *Humanae Vitae,* he assumed all of this teaching on periodic continence. He took the occasion, however, to defend what by then had become a focus of critical attention. Medical discoveries opened up prospects to control procreation. "Is it not reasonable in many circumstances to have recourse to artificial birth control if, thereby, we secure harmony and peace in the family and improve conditions for the education of children already born?" To this question, he said, it is necessary to answer with clarity: "The Church is the first to praise and recommend the intervention of intelligence in a function which so closely associates the rational creature with his Creator, but it affirms that this must be done with respect for the order established by God."

What about intercourse during the sterile periods? Science has become an ally of morality in explaining the function of the ovulatory cycle. It confirms the Church's teaching that "if there are serious motives to space out births, which derive from physical or psychological conditions of husband or wife, or from external conditions, it is licit to take account of the natural rhythms inherent in the generative functions."

But is this consistent with the uncompromising position on contraception? Does it not seem like a dodge?

Not at all. There are essential differences between the two practices. In the use of rhythm, "the married couple make legitimate use of a natural disposition." In contraception, "they impede the development of natural processes." But are they not excluding children in both cases? Yes, but the morality of excluding children must be judged by the means employed to achieve this purpose. Married people who practice rhythm merely "renounce the use of marriage during the fertile periods when, for just motives, procreation is not desirable. They make use of it during the sterile periods to manifest their affection and to safeguard their mutual fidelity. By so doing, they give proof of a truly and fully praiseworthy love."[64]

The Church is not impassive to the difficulties, sometimes approaching heroism, that Catholics face in trying to rear a family in today's contraceptive atmosphere. This calls for deep conviction in husbands and wives "concerning the true values of life and the family." It demands growth in "self-mastery." It means that societies must take measures to "create a climate favorable to education in chastity." It mainly requires a deepening of virtue through prayer and the frequent use of the sacraments.

Scientists, too, can make a great contribution "if, by pooling their efforts, they labor to explain more thoroughly the various conditions favoring a proper regulation of births." Although reliable in many ways, the value of the rhythm method depends on the accuracy of prediction of a sterile period. Consequently, "it is particularly desirable that medical science succeed in providing a sufficiently secure basis for a regulation of birth, founded on the observance of natural rhythms." In this way, the Church's teaching will be vindicated that "a true contradiction cannot exist between the divine laws pertaining to the transmission of life and those which foster authentic conjugal love."[65]

Problems of Conscience. Any reflection on the morality of contraception would be incomplete without taking stock of the conflict between ecclesiastical authority and personal conscience that the publication of *Humanae Vitae* brought to the surface.

There is no question of resolving the conflict by unsaying what is too obvious, that the Church's constant teaching has excluded interference with the life process at any stage from conception to birth. There is some value, however, in recalling a parallel tradition in which the Church respects the voice of conscience in each person and bids him respond to it with Christian fidelity. This means that to have one's conscience as guide is not only a good thing, it is our duty. Anyone who acts contrary to his conscience is no longer on the right path. But conscience is not the arbiter of moral values. Its role is to apply the principles of morality, not to create them. Hence the importance of not only following one's conscience, but of educating it according to the mind of the Church, indeed, of continually forming it by intimate converse with God and openness to his grace in prayer.

A few days after Pope Paul issued *Humanae Vitae,* he made a remarkable public statement that sheds considerable light on the issue. "How many times," he confessed, "humanly speaking, have we felt the inadequacy of our poor person to cope with the formidable apostolic obligation of having to make a pronouncement on this matter! How many times have we trembled before the alternatives of an easy condescension to current opinions, or of a decision that modern society would find difficult to accept, or that might be arbitrarily too burdensome for married life."

Finally, he concluded, "after imploring the light of the Holy Spirit, we placed our conscience at the free and full disposal of the voice of truth," until "we had no doubt about our duty to give our decision in the terms expressed in the present encyclical."[66]

Without exception, all the statements of episcopal conferences reacting to *Humanae Vitae* brought up the matter of conscience. This in itself was a commentary on the age, where personalism and individual rights are so typical of modern culture.

Not unlike the Pope's attitude, the bishops showed genuine concern for married couples in today's society. They explained that *Humanae Vitae* does not undertake to judge the consciences of individuals but to set forth the authentic teaching of the Church, which Catholics believe interprets the divine law to which conscience should be conformed.

Those who have resorted to artificial contraception were urged never to lose heart but to continue to take full advantage of the strength that comes from the sacrament of penance, and the grace, healing, and peace of the Eucharist.

PREMARITAL RELATIONS

Premarital relations have become so common in some segments of Western society that the Church's teaching on their sinfulness is a scandal to some defendants of contemporary morality. Like contraception, however, fornication as the voluntary sexual intercourse between unmarried persons was forbidden to the followers of Christ since the origins of Christianity.

The Savior himself distinguished between adultery and fornication when he castigated the Pharisees for their hypocrisy of insisting on external ritual like washing of hands but neglecting the interior movements of the heart, from which come such evil things as adultery and fornication. But the most elaborate attention to chastity outside of marriage was given by St. Paul in several of his letters, and especially in writing to the Corinthians, who had great difficulty adjusting themselves to the demands of Christian morality.

St. John in his Apocalypse warned the bishops of his day against compromising the faith by tolerating the errors of such Gnostic sectarians as the Nicolaitans, who considered themselves at liberty to fornicate. John's reproach was the same as Paul's, that Christians who were told they could return to such pagan practices as fornication were on their way to estrangement from Christ, since abstinence from sexual activity outside of marriage is one of the marks of a true Christian.

As the Church's moral teaching was formulated in canonical prescriptions or codified in specific laws, the sin of fornication was always considered a serious deviation from the divine will. On occasion, this teaching found expression in documents of the Holy See and of ecumenical councils. Thus Tertullian, after becoming a Montanist, charged Pope St. Callistus I with laxity because he, "the bishop of bishops, declares: 'I forgive the sins of adultery and fornication to those who have performed the penance.' "[67]

The thirteenth ecumenical council, held at Lyons in France (1245), answered the challenge raised by some Eastern Christians influenced by Moslem morality. "Concerning fornication," it declared, "which an unmarried man commits with an unmarried woman, there must not be any doubt at all that it is a mortal sin, since the Apostle declares that 'fornicators and adulterers are cast out of the kingdom of God' (1 Co. 6:9)." A century later, the ecumenical Council of Vienne (1311–12) condemned the Beghards and Beguines for claiming that sexual intercourse outside of marriage is not wrong, "since nature inclines to this." In the seventeenth century, Pope Alexander VII censured the theory that a penitent "who had intercourse with an unmarried woman satisfies the precept of confession by saying, 'I committed a grievous sin against chastity with an unmarried woman,' without mentioning the intercourse." And before the end of the same century, Innocent XI condemned the idea that, since premarital intercourse injures no one and may be engaged in from sentiments of love, it is not contrary to the natural law. In the language of those who defended the practice, "Fornication by its nature involves no malice; it is an evil only because it is forbidden."[68]

The same teaching on premarital relations continues in the Catholic moral doctrine of today. But the Church is painfully conscious of the climate of sensual hedonism with which the Christian believer is everywhere surrounded. Hence the urgent need for parents to train their sons and daughters in the practice of what has been called "the difficult commandment." More than ever, "Young people need suitable and timely instruction in the dignity of marriage, its responsibilities, in its practical side. They must learn to reverence chastity so that having practiced it during their engagement they may, at a suitable age, pass on to marriage."[69]

Part of this instruction is to be convinced that the Church's wisdom is also human wisdom; that chastity before marriage is the best preparation for fidelity in marriage; and that the selfless love that is cultivated between the man and woman who plan to marry is the only love that can sustain them through life after they are married.

SEVENTH AND TENTH COMMANDMENTS

The Old Testament had a deep sense of justice. In one simple imperative, the Decalogue commands, "You shall not steal," which is supported by the prohibition of interior greed: "You shall not covet your neighbor's house . . . or his servant . . . his ox, or his donkey, or anything that is his." In Deuteronomy, the word "covet" is made more explicit: "You shall not set your heart on" anything that belongs to another.

Not satisfied with the general precept, the Pentateuch forbids thievery, robbery, unjust acquisition of goods (e.g., through usury or fraud), and all wanton destruction. There are special enactments against embezzlement, false weights and measures, changing landmarks, and profiteering on hired help.

To insure the observance of these prescriptions, the Mosaic law provided for carefully determined restitution. As a general rule, this had to be greater than the damage caused. When money or precious objects were stolen, the thief was obliged to restore twice the value; and the same applied for stolen animals, provided the same animals could be returned. If the stolen animals were already slaughtered or sold, the restitution had to be five oxen for one ox stolen, four sheep for one sheep stolen. The sevenfold restitution mentioned in Proverbs shows a later strengthening of the laws governing private property. Yet this legislation was relatively mild compared with the Babylonian and Hittite laws, which demanded a much higher indemnity and in not a few cases the death penalty for stealing. The only resemblance to such severity among the Jews was the case of a householder who could kill a burglar with impunity when the latter broke into his house at night, and in the case of kidnaping, to which the death penalty was attached by law. The gravity of the law against kidnaping was no doubt due to the fact that persons stolen would then be sold as slaves.

Theft is condemned outright as a serious sin, and even to steal through necessity was considered sinful, although viewed more leniently the more certainly a person took what belonged to someone else because he himself was in real and not neglectful need. In one outspoken paragraph, Jeremiah quotes Yahweh's denunciation of stealing, and places the crime alongside other sins that God urges his people to avoid if they expect his blessings (Jr. 7:4–11).

Again we see that the worship of Yahweh was to be closely associated with the practice of justice toward one's fellow man. It was not enough, and worse than insufficient, for a proclaimed believer in God to pray in the Temple if he defrauded his neighbor outside the Temple. So true was this that a simple, if inadequate, summation of the ancient covenant was that God would be gracious to his people if they respected the possessions of one another.

With the advent of Christ, there was no diminution of the precept against dishonesty. Matthew, Mark, and Luke all record the words of the Savior to the rich young man who asked what he should do to gain eternal life. Among other precepts, he was told, "You must not steal."

Immediately, though, Christ added what some have considered the most distinctively evangelical attitude toward worldly possessions. Having told the young man not to steal or defraud, and invited him to "go sell everything you own, and give the money to the poor," and then, "come, follow me," Jesus made a commentary on the man's declining the invitation. "How hard it is," he sadly observed, "for those who have riches to enter the kingdom of God!" The disciples were astonished at this remark, which Christ then repeated, now adding that "It is easier for a camel to pass through the eye of a needle than for a rich man to enter the kingdom of God" (Mk. 10:19–27).

Christ does not say that the rich cannot be saved; but he does say it will not be easy. The saying is all the more surprising after he had made the distinction between the moral precept "keep the commandments" and the counsel of poverty "if you wish to be perfect." Evidently he is speaking not of impossibility but of difficulty. Nor does he condemn the rich young man, but he illustrates from this case how riches can grip and even suffocate the heart. Indeed, for merely human reason it is inconceivable that those whose heart is possessed by riches should enter heaven. Our Lord expresses this with a slight adaptation of the Jewish proverb that "a man even in his dreams does not see an elephant pass through a needle's eye." He thus deliberately provoked the astonishment of the disciples in order to impress on them the spiritual menace of riches. If possessions are such an obstacle—and there are few who have no possessions—who can be saved? Jesus explains that divine grace can achieve the humanly impossible. Grace may leave the riches, for those who are not called to evangelical poverty, but loosen their grip on the heart.

In the spirit of Christ, St. Paul excoriated those who steal from others to enrich themselves. Thieves, usurers, and swindlers will never inherit the kingdom of God. Those who before their conversion had been dishonest must amend their ways: "Anyone who was a thief must stop stealing; he should try to find some useful manual work instead, and be able to do some good by helping others that are in need" (Ep. 4:28). Thus he will fulfill the teaching of the Master that his followers are not only not to deprive others by stealing but, if possible, deprive themselves to help others who are in want.

St. Peter took the occasion of seeing pagans imprisoned in punishment for their crimes to instruct the faithful that they, too, would be expected to suffer now that they had come to love Christ. But what a difference!

> None of you should ever deserve to suffer for being a murderer, a thief, a criminal or an informer. But if anyone of you should suffer for being a Christian, then he is not to be ashamed of it; he should thank God that he has been called one (1 P. 5:15–16).

This studied contrast between suffering for thievery and suffering for the truth found its most eloquent expression on Calvary, when one of the two thieves rebuked the other who had been abusing the Savior. "Have you no fear of God at all?" he asked. "You got the same sentence as he did, but in our case we deserved it; we are paying for what we did. But this man has done nothing wrong. 'Jesus,' he said, 'remember me when you come into your kingdom.' 'Indeed, I promise you,' he replied, 'today you will be with me in paradise'" (Lk. 23:40–43).

Christ chose to die between two "robbers who were crucified with him." One of them was forgiven because he repented, to symbolize the New Law of mercy toward sinners without minimizing the gravity of their sin.

JUSTICE IN CATHOLIC MORALITY

As important as the virtue of charity is in the Christian moral order, the Church has constantly stressed the prior importance of practicing justice in external conduct (the Seventh Commandment) and internal desires (the Tenth Commandment). The justice with which these two commandments are directly concerned is the right to ownership of property.

As a human right, property is the moral power that a person has to dispose of a thing and its utility according to his will, independently of others, provided there is no infringement on the correlative rights of others. Nowadays it is especially well to recall that our right to acquire and possess permanent property is divinely approved, since the contrary theory of Marxism denies that people have a right to private ownership of anything.

What God forbids must be founded on divine sanction. Yet the Decalogue forbids theft, which would be meaningless unless ownership were a prior and natural right that was approved by the author of nature. Moreover, as experience teaches, the natural law has bestowed on us the threefold right of providing for the preservation of our own life, of perfecting ourselves mentally and spiritually, and of developing ourselves through the labor that we do. None of these would be possible, humanly speaking, without the right to private ownership.

From apostolic to modern times, the Church has sedulously defended the right to ownership, even while reminding the faithful that justice is a two-edged sword. It obligates others to respect the property of an individual and condemns anyone who takes what does not belong to him as stealing. At the same time, it obligates the one who possesses to recognize that justice is not only commutative, between man and man, whether as a physical person (single individual) or moral person (group of individuals); there must also be such a thing as social justice, which regulates the mutual relations between man and society and vice versa. Each of us has grave obligations to society as a whole, even as society has duties toward the individual.

Pressed on the one side by the evils of unbridled ownership and on the other by the theory that private property leads to abuses and therefore all ownership belongs to the State, the Church in our day has had to steer a clear course between two extremes. It has defended ownership and denounced theft as sinful; but it has also insisted on the rights of society and decried selfish greed as morally wrong.

Individual and Social Character of Ownership. Sovereign Pontiffs and now an ecumenical council have regularly taught that ownership of material goods has a twofold character, usually called individual or social as it regards either separate persons or the common good. They have always maintained that nature—in fact, the Creator himself—has given man the right to private ownership not only that individuals may be able to provide for themselves and their families, but also that the goods which the Creator has destined for the entire family of mankind may through this institution truly serve this purpose. All this can be achieved, the Church holds, only through the maintenance of a certain and definite order.

What is this order? It is keeping a balance between two rocks of possible shipwreck. Just as a ruin follows if "individualism" is canonized by denying or minimizing the social and public character of the right of property, so by rejecting or minimizing the private and individual character of this same right, one inevitably runs into "collectivism" or at least risks espousing a collectivist theory of morality.

Immediately we see that two very different, although complementary, duties face the Christian who wishes to steer a middle course between the two extremes. He must respect private ownership as divinely ordained, a right inherent in the human person, which means that the Seventh and Tenth Commandments are still as valid as they were when first revealed on Sinai. And he must realize that ownership is not an absolute, but that society too has rights for which the author of man's social nature equally demands recognition.

We begin by affirming that the right of property is distinct from its use. Thus commutative justice commands sacred respect for the division of possessions and forbids invasion of others' rights through exceeding limit of one's own property. "But the duty of owners to use their property only in a right way does not come under this type of justice. Rather it belongs to other virtues, whose obligations cannot be enforced by legal action. Therefore, they are in error who assert that ownership and its right use are limited by the same boundaries. And it is much farther still from the truth to hold that a right to property is destroyed or lost by reason of abuse or nonuse."[70]

Concretely this means that the Catholic Church has always so stressed the right to property as a natural right that, even when abused, the right does not disappear; no more than the abuse of drink warrants the legal prohibition of all alcoholic beverages to everyone.

But in saying this the Church does not deny—in fact, it insists on—

the rights of society, which are equally binding on the individual to respect. As the faithful were increasingly challenged by a collectivist mentality to explain themselves, the latest ecumenical council and subsequent papal teaching set down certain guidelines for them to follow.

Action to Be Taken. Not satisfied with affirming general principles, the Church has spoken very definitely on the responsibility of Christians in today's world of growing abundance and, in many cases, of growing inequity in the sharing of this abundance.

The magisterium began by quoting the passage from Genesis, "Fill the earth and subdue it," as a clear statement that God entrusted the whole of creation to man's stewardship. It is his responsibility to develop it by intelligent effort and by means of his labor to perfect it for his use.

From this it follows that if the world is made to furnish each individual with the means of livelihood and the instruments for his growth and progress, each man has therefore the right to find in the world what is necessary for himself. "God intended the earth and all it contains for the use of all men and peoples, so created goods should flow fairly to all, regulated by justice and accompanied by charity."[71] All other rights whatsoever, including those of property and of free enterprise, are to be subordinated to this principle. They are not to be denied but fostered, but always with the understanding that people have a grave and urgent social duty to redirect them to their primary finality—which is the common good.

> "If someone who has the riches of this world sees his brother in need and closes his heart to him, how does the love of God abide in him?" (1 Jn. 3:17). It is well known how strong were the words used by the Fathers of the Church to describe the proper attitude of persons who possess anything toward persons in need. To quote St. Ambrose: "You are not making a gift of your possessions to the poor person. You are handing over to him what is his. For what has been given in common for the use of all, you have arrogated to yourself. The world is given to all, and not only to the rich." That is, private property does not constitute for anyone an absolute and unconditioned right. No one is justified in keeping for his exclusive use what he does not need, when others lack necessities. In a word, according to the traditional doctrine as found in the Fathers of the Church and the great theologians, the right to property must never be exercised to the detriment of the common good. If there should

arise a conflict between acquired private rights and primary community needs, it is the responsibility of public authorities to look for a solution, with the active participation of individuals and social groups.

Then to come down to even more specific issues, such as arise in many sectors of the world where there exists a massive disproportion between the very rich and very poor, the Church does not hesitate to use strong language to see that justice is observed:

> If certain landed estates impede the general prosperity because they are extensive, unused, or poorly used, or because they bring hardship to peoples or are detrimental to the interests of the country, the common good sometimes demands expropriation. While giving a clear statement of this, the Council recalled no less clearly that the available revenue is not to be used in accordance with mere whim, and that no place must be given to selfish speculation.

What applies to landed holdings is also applicable to incomes from resources and business in a given country. Those who make such earnings may not "transfer a considerable part of this income abroad purely for their own advantage, without care for the manifest wrong they inflict on their own country by doing this."[72]

The Church's stand is firm on social justice: Charity is required. And once the principle is recognized, it has manifold implications in every aspect of human living. It is also the best answer to such theories of collectivization as would erase all rights to private ownership, and corresponding incentive to private initiative, on the grounds that the collectivity, i.e., the State, is mysteriously exempt from the common temptation to greed.

THEFT AND RETRIBUTION

It is a popular fallacy that only a few people steal, or that ordinary people are not even tempted to take something belonging to another person against his presumed and reasonable wish. No doubt larceny, robbery, extortion, and usury are exotic crimes that the average Christian reads about but seldom, if ever, commits. But there are many ways of offending against the Seventh and Tenth Commandments, and in most cases the offender will not even be recognized, let alone liable to prosecution.

Direct thievery is so obviously sinful that no believing Christian will question the fact. He also knows that restitution of what was stolen is an essential part of a firm purpose of amendment, without which true contrition is impossible and forgiveness before God not to be expected. If restitution is postponed, even indefinitely, because urgent personal needs must be met, the principle still remains. Unless the one who stole sincerely intends to return the stolen object or its equivalent, he stands morally guilty until this attitude of mind is changed.

But there are more subtle forms of stealing that may seduce the unwary and gradually dull their conscience to the wrongness of what they are doing.

Lost and found articles are familiar ground. Some people imagine that just because they found some money, jewelry, or personal belongings, the items belong to them, and the common saying, "Finders keepers," reflects this strange notion of dishonesty. No one but the true owner has a right to undisputed possession and the moral phrase that an "object seeks its owner" illustrates this principle of Christian ethics.

If I find something of value and if I know to whom it belongs, I am obliged in conscience to return it, and the sooner I do it the better, even at some inconvenience to myself. In most cases I will not know who the owner is, and then my first duty is to safeguard what I have found by using the ordinary means at my disposal. I must also make a reasonable effort to discover the owner, with emphasis on the word "reasonable." Articles of moderate value, like a medium-priced watch, might bind me to checking through the lost-and-found columns of the newspaper or perhaps running an ad of my own. But if the object is very costly, like an expensive diamond ring, it would be well to consult the civil law on the point and abide by its provisions. These differ in various places, but the general idea is to specify how long an object must be kept in sincere possession before it becomes the property of the finder.

Businessmen and merchants have their own duties in the matter of honesty. All substantial defects of what I am selling must be revealed to a prospective buyer, where a substantial defect would render the object useless or substantially inhibit its use for what is the presumed purpose of the buyer. For example if a man buys a machine for a certain type of work, and I know that the machine cannot meet his needs, I may not remain silent and suppose that I am innocent of fraud if I knew beforehand that (except for my silence) the machine would not have been bought. Minor defects that do not substantially detract from what something is good for or worth do not have to be revealed unless the customer inquires about them. But in this case the price should be adjusted accordingly.

Catholic moralists further explain that no injustice is committed, provided no fraud or deceit is practiced, to charge a higher price for articles that are rare or that are mere luxuries to the buyer; to dispose of something at a currently high price, without reminding the customer that the price will soon fall; and to ask for a higher price on something that may not be intrinsically valuable but that means a great deal to me personally. On the other hand, it would be wrong to raise the current price because I know the buyer has special need of what I sell. Though not uncommon, this practice is profiteering; it is also forbidden because the purchaser's special need is not my affair but his. It is his property, so to speak, that I cannot presume to "sell."

Abuses in business practice are common enough, and, in the competition of the modern world, become a constant temptation to those who would follow their conscience. Contractors may not do work in such a way that repairs will soon be needed, or use inferior materials at a higher price, or use expensive materials that are not necessary because of a percentage "cut," or put in time not required for the job at hand, or sublet the work to firms that are known for their sharp practices, or pretend that one's material or work is superior and charge accordingly when the facts do not warrant such claims, or use machines and apparatus that are known to endanger the life or health of one's employees, or be satisfied with slipshod work from the employees and yet charge a price that deserves first-class workmanship.

Graft in politics is defined as the acquisition of money, position, or property by dishonest or questionable means, as by taking advantage of one's official status in the administration of justice or government. As normally posed, the question is asked whether it is wrong for a politician to accept a gift from a person for whom he had done a favor in his political capacity. A man may have been appointed to the police force, a firm given a contract to build for the city, or a woman chosen to a prominent post with the board of education.

First we must distinguish a sincere gift from graft proper. There is nothing wrong if a person who has been done a favor wants to show his gratitude, and gives the benefactor a token appreciation. The trouble is that often this gift is suspect.

In practice, the difference between gift and graft is not hard to recognize. Equity requires that the best persons be chosen for a given post, without denying the right of preference for those with whom the man in public office is more familiar and friendly. But if an appointment is made in consideration of a sum of money or other benefit donated by the appointee, this is stealing under disguise, and restitution should be made.

It is not enough to abstain from graft or from dishonest practices when the persons in question have been duly elected or appointed to positions of public trust. They are to behave in such a way that the people's trust in their integrity is not jeopardized.

LABOR AND MANAGEMENT

There are few subjects in the area of social justice on which the Church has spoken more extensively and in greater detail than labor and management. As teacher of nations, the Church took upon herself the task of studying the problems of an industrial society and periodically sharing her insights with the faithful and with all who were willing to listen. Each successive Pope from the First through the Second Vatican Council wrote at length about the Christian view of justice (supported by charity) in the reciprocal relations between labor and management. *Rerum Novarum* of Leo XIII, *Quadragesimo Anno* of Pius XI, and *Mater et Magistra* of John XXIII are only the best-known documents published before *Lumen Gentium,* the conciliar Constitution on the Church in the Modern World, which soon had its own commentary in *Populorum Progressio* of Paul VI.

Many of the issues raised and clarified by this teaching touch on the delicate but crucial matter of justice on both sides quite directly. They have since been interpreted and applied by those who are responsive to the Church's mind on contemporary morals, and without apology for intruding in things that are purely secular. Experience has shown that good morality is also good economics and makes for a good society, so that Christians who seriously implement these principles "have much to contribute to prosperity and peace."[73]

There is such a thing today as the labor movement, which can mean many things, but especially the recognized right of workers to organize. In the teeth of much opposition, the Catholic Church took the lead in this matter. Already in the nineteenth century, the Holy See "encouraged Christian workers to found mutual associations according to their various occupations, taught them how to do so, and resolutely confirmed in the path of duty a goodly number of those whom socialist organizations strongly attracted by claiming to be the sole defenders and champions of the lowly and oppressed."[74]

What are the functions of labor unions? They are mainly two: to protect the rights of working people by insuring just wages, reasonable hours of labor, and conditions of work that are consonant with human dignity; and to secure benefits for employees that are not strictly obligatory but that the management may be legitimately asked to give. Other functions of labor unions are peripheral to these two, e.g., setting up housing and educational programs.

Moral specialists hold that working people must first use the ordinary means of bargaining with the management before they have recourse to the drastic means of striking. Moreover, the strike itself must be conducted in a just and equitable way. Above all, deliberate use of violence and physical force must be avoided.

Correspondingly, Christian defenders of labor are reminding their leaders to caution the rank-and-file members to give a fair day's work for a fair day's pay and warn them not to abuse the well-deserved benefits that the unions have been able to negotiate with their employers. The organized labor movement, it is pointed out, has reached maturity, and the average union member should readily accept reasonable and constructive advice from his leaders about the necessity of increased efficiency and the importance of respecting the rights of employers and consumers.

On their side, employers have the duty of controlling their own organizations and of bringing moral pressure to bear upon those of their associates who may be guilty of harassing the labor movement or of impeding necessary progress in the field of labor-management relations or in the field of legislation. Employers were reminded of the heavy charge imposed upon them by Pius XII, when he addressed an international conference on human relations in industry.

> One expects to find in the employer an intense desire for true social progress. Many people show no lack of good will, but it must be observed at times that an overwhelming attachment to economic advantages tends more or less to blind men to a perception of the

want of equity and justice in certain living conditions. Your Christian instincts will urge you to overcome this obstacle and to exercise your authority in a manner conformable to the ideals set forth in the Gospel.[75]

Needless to say, these ideals involve not only justice but also charity; they call upon motivation that springs not only from equity and giving every man his due, but also from love for one's fellow man as a child of God and heir of heaven.

The Church's principles governing the right relations between employers and those who labor for them are based on a Christian concept of work. As the Church sees it, work is not something to be shunned as demeaning; it is not an evil to be avoided as though leisure were more worthy of man's dignity. In the Christian view of providence, work ennobles man's character as a person and assimilates him to the Savior.

> Whether done independently or managed by others, work proceeds directly from a person, who puts his seal on the things of nature and submits them to his will. By his work, man normally maintains his life and the lives of those dependent on him, is united with his fellow men and serves them, can exercise charity to the full and associate himself with perfecting the divine creation. Indeed, we hold that by his labor, man is associated with the redemptive work of Christ, who conferred surpassing dignity on labor by working with his own hands at Nazareth. Hence arises an obligation for each to work loyally, and also a right to work.

Given these premises, it is not surprising that the Church now recommends a re-examination of the disjunctive roles of employers and workers. Discarding the Marxist idea that capital and labor must be in conflict, Roman Catholicism favors a participation in management by labor, with results that experience shows are of great benefit to the whole of society. "So long," therefore, "as unity of direction is assured, a suitable share in management should be aimed at for everybody—proprietors, employers, management, and workers. Moreover, since economic and social conditions, and hence the future of workers and their children, often depend not on the firm they work for but on higher-level institutions, workers should have a share in these too, either directly or through their freely elected delegates."[76]

Perhaps nowhere else is it more true that justice cannot stand alone and hope to restrain man's inveterate avarice and envy—avarice to obtain what he does not have and envy over the possessions of those who have. It must be strengthened by Christian generosity and animated by the spirit of giving without asking for return. A single problem like the living wage in today's economy includes issues that call upon more than strict equity to solve. When families in some countries have shrunk to a minimum, those who would rear the children God wants to send them are faced with the hard dilemma of compromising with conscience or going along with the tide. Unless those in government and management recognize the dilemma and are willing to help solve it, they become partners in the sins of others because they failed to rise beyond the bare demands of the law, which tends to be shaped by those in power. The law alone can be cruel and, unless tempered by love, can be unjust.

Sometimes the sin of injustice arises from causing damage to another person's possessions or property. A secretary may accidentally spill a bottle of ink on a sheaf of papers she is typing and then have to retype the whole lot while being paid by the company. A workman carelessly fails to check the machine he is inspecting, and several thousand dollars' loss in damaged product is the result. A watchman sleeps while on duty, and thieves take away the complete shipment of refrigerators he was supposed to be guarding. These are typical of the myriad situations where damage or loss is caused by someone other than the owner and where difficult cases of conscience therefore demand a solution.

Restitution or repair of the damage done becomes obligatory only if actual harm is caused. Neglect or even deliberate intention to harm someone would not obligate to restoration until (or unless) the owner suffered actual loss. Also, it must have been my own action that caused the injury, not someone else's. As a lawyer I give my client a certain set of directives on how to proceed in a legal problem, and I get paid for my services. Later on I find that the person did not really follow my advice, or misunderstood it, and as a result lost a considerable sum of money. I am not required to make good the loss sustained by my client, because it was his mistaken action and not my advice that directly caused the damage. And most importantly, I must have been morally responsible and guilty in causing the injury before any duty of restitution will arise. Accidentally breaking a window, or getting into an automobile accident with somebody else's car, or losing another person's book or watch do not, in themselves, obligate to restitution—unless other factors enter the case.

One factor that may enter is a provision of the civil law or the decree of a judge in court which specifies that damages must be paid even though the action that caused damage was not deliberate or morally responsible. The reason behind this provision is to insure public order and the common good, and to prevent irresponsible conduct among the citizens. If there was no risk that my negligence may cause another man serious harm, many people would become utterly reckless in the use of state and public property and in taking care of what does not belong to them.

BETTING AND GAMBLING

Gambling may be defined as the staking of money or other valuables on a future event, chance, or contingency that is unknown or uncertain to the participants.

As commonly understood, the essential feature of gambling is wagering, or the act of staking or hazarding as such. In gambling, the future event is the outcome of a game of chance, or of mixed chance and skill. To the extent to which the outcome can be predicted by knowledge of the strength, skill, and dexterity of the contestants, the element of pure chance is normally increased by odds in favor of, or by handicaps against, the probable winner.

Gambling, however, is more inclusive than gaming because wagers may be placed on any uncertain social or physical contingency, like the outcome of an election or a ball game, or the amount of precipitation during a given month or season. The lottery is one form of gambling in which prizes are distributed by lot or chance among persons who have paid for the chance to win.

Moralists distinguish gambling from other forms of speculation and insurance in that the latter perform useful social services by stabilizing the market and by shifting the incidence of loss or gain due to economic changes that would take place in any event, whereas the former increases instability, creates risks that serve no corresponding economic needs, and adds losses to some and equivalent gains to others that would not occur in the absence of the gambling transaction itself. Nevertheless, speculative transactions may become a form of gambling when the intention of the parties is that no deliveries of commodites or securities shall ever be made, and that the whole price shall never be paid, but that the difference in value shall be ascertained at some future date and the excess or difference shall be paid directly from one party to the other.

Gambling has a long and eventful history. Ancient civilizations in the East and West, and the highest cultures of Greece and Rome, show that the gambling instinct is inveterate in human nature. In analyzing why men gamble, perhaps the best answer is: They enjoy it. They gamble because it gives them amusement, a certain amount of recreation, coming from the thrill (as they see it) of getting something for little or nothing. They do it because for many people life is drab and they want an outlet for their pent-up feelings of weariness and distress.

In some countries, certain groups of religionists who considered gambling essentially evil managed to have the government pass stringent laws against the practice. Catholic moral theology carefully distinguishes among betting, lotteries, and gambling. And though the basic principles governing each are not different, their application is not the same.

Betting may be described as a sort of agreement in which two or more people contract to give a prize to whichever one correctly guesses some future fact or event. Betting on race horses is well known. Given that betting is not illicit in itself, it may become so if certain conditions are not fulfilled. All parties to the contract must clearly understand the conditions of agreement in the same way; they must be sincerely uncertain about the outcome of what is to take place; they honestly want to pay (and can do so) in case they lose the bet; and the bet cannot be an encouragement to do something evil or sinful, like taking a chance on driving at sixty miles per hour through a crowded downtown street, or insulting a prominent person to his face.

While there is nothing wrong with betting done in moderation, it is not easy to control oneself and avoid the "betting urge," with grave consequences to personal integrity and the welfare of those who depend for their livelihood on the gambling addict.

Some critics of gambling say it inevitably produces an un-Christian outlook on life. It is directly in contrast to the Christian view, which believes that the universe is controlled by the loving providence of Almighty God, our heavenly Father. The first duty of man is therefore to learn what is God's will and to be obedient to it. Anything that suggests that our lives are controlled by "luck" is therefore an evil thing, for it undermines man's faith in God and teaches that obedience to God's laws does not matter.

The Catholic attitude is not so uncompromising. The Church has consistently called for moderation. It has never condemned gambling outright, any more than the theater, for all its transgressions, or the screen or television, for all their portential follies, or sports, with their threat of overindulgence. Even playing the stock market is not considered in itself wrong. Like gambling, however, it may easily lead one to squander large sums that are necessary for one's family expenses or for the payment of one's debts in the hope of becoming wealthy with little effort and without long delay. Moreover, when a nation suffers harm through abuses in this area of public conduct, it may be argued that the harm has come more frequently from unwise investments than from gamesters at a table or betters at a race track.

Gambling, therefore, may become a sin, and even a serious sin, when it goes to an excess that would destroy personal honesty, or expose a man to loss so great as to jeopardize society, and above all, his family dependents. Sound Christian morals follow the rule of reason, not condemning outright what is not evil in itself, yet strongly reprobating the abuse of an otherwise good (or at least indifferent) thing.

Unfortunately, the same balanced judgment cannot be attributed to the record of civil governments in dealing with betting: There are inconsistencies among states, and within a single state; sanctioning one form of betting and outlawing others; admitting on principle that betting is licit, yet denying the use of this right for millions who consider it lawful; leaving huge loopholes in the law for government officials to profit from people's aleatory instinct, while imposing huge fines on those who break the letter of the law.

Lotteries are in the same category morally as betting. Some distinction should be made between lotteries sponsored for a charitable cause, where only a small fraction of total receipts comes to the winner, and standard lotteries run professionally or by the government. In any case, however, they are permissible if there is no deception and if some proportion exists between the hope of winning and the amount each contributor pays. It would be less than honest if a home worth ten thousand dollars were raffled off, at ten dollars a chance, and the number of tickets sold amounted to fifty or more thousand. But if the lottery is sponsored for some social benefit or to finance a worthy charity, participants understand there is little chance of winning and their contribution is more like a donation, no matter how many tickets are sold.

Gambling is also permissible by Catholic moral standards, provided the one who gambles with the stakes really owns them, if there is no fraud involved, and if all who participate have the same basic chance of winning or losing. The last item is specially important because of its practical value. Normally an amateur poker player, for instance, may not be licitly invited to join a game with an expert, where considerable stakes are involved and where there is no equality of risk. But if the amateur knows whom he is taking on, and still wants to play the game, he implicitly passes up one of the conditions required for legitimate gambling.

Professional gamblers may take a share of the "earnings" from their customers, and people who frequent gambling houses practically waive their right to equality of opportunity between themselves and the house. But it is hard to defend those who gamble regularly. When respectable citizens encourage gambling institutions by attending them, they scandalize others who do not have the same self-control, and they help foster one phase of recreation that is closely tied in with gangsterism and other social crimes. Where gambling is prevalent, the moral tone of a community is generally lowered and the door easily opened to racketeering and civil corruption.

EIGHTH COMMANDMENT

The Eighth Commandment of the Decalogue, worded identically in Exodus and Deuteronomy, declares: "You shall not bear false witness against your neighbor." As such it simply forbids telling the untruth about another person, on the prior assumption that people do not tell lies against themselves, whether the untruth is told in a court of law or in personal matters.

A false statement in court may cost the life of the defendant in a criminal process. In civil suits it may involve great financial loss, or loss of liberty. And in both cases it means the loss of status in the community. Therefore the Covenant Code of the Old Testament obliged witnesses to speak only the absolute truth, and judges to pronounce sentence only in accordance with right and justice based on truth.

Neither witnesses nor judges were allowed to receive bribes or be moved by false compassion. When the death sentence was imposed, the witnesses were required to cast the first stone upon the guilty, and thus assume full responsibility for the decision. If their statements were proven false during the hearings or after the trial, they incurred the same kind of penalty as was (or was to be) meted out to the person found guilty. As a precaution, the Mosiac law was not satisfied with one witness under any circumstances. "A single witness," it was held, "cannot suffice to convict a man of a crime or offense of any kind; whatever the misdemeanor, the evidence of two witnesses or three is required to sustain the charge" (Dt. 19:15).

But the intent of the commandment was not to protect the accused in a court of law. Throughout the ancient Covenant, all lying was severely condemned:

> Lips that tell the truth abide firm forever, the tongue that lies lasts only for a moment. Lips that lie are abhorrent to Yahweh; dear to him those who speak the truth (Pr. 12:19, 22).
> Lying is an ugly blot on a man, and ever on the lips of the ignorant. A thief is preferable to an inveterate liar, but both are heading for ruin. Lying is an abominable habit, so that disgrace is the liar's forever (Si. 20:24–28).

While all lying was forbidden, there were grades of malice in telling the untruth. In an unforgettable passage of Ben Sira, the inspired writer identified four levels of sins with the tongue:

> There are three things my heart dreads, and a fourth which terrifies me: slander by a whole town, the gathering of a mob, and a false accusation—these are all worse than death; but a woman jealous of a woman means heartbreak and sorrow, and all this is the scourge of the tongue (Si. 26:5–9).

Behind these biblical judgments on lying was the profound respect for truth that the revelation of the Old Law wished to communicate to the Chosen People.

The basic idea of truth (Hebrew, *emet*) among the Jews was the idea of being firm, steady, reliable, trustworthy, and faithful. What was true, therefore, was that which one could trust in, rely on, and according to which he could direct his actions. A "man of truth" was a man who could be depended on, even as a "road of truth" was the right road; it really went to the place where it was supposed to go.

So, too, "peace of truth" was a genuine, lasting peace; and a "judgment of truth" was a decision based on the facts, which thus gave clarity and assurance instead of doubt or uncertainty. Always the essential point of the concept of truth lay in the guarantee of practical certitude that it gave.

As we enter the New Testament, the same idea prevails. The Greek term *alētheia* (truth) universally used by the sacred authors carries the nuance of practicality. It implies that those who speak the truth can be believed, that what they say can confidently be followed, that their statements produce conviction, and that their friendship brings peace.

There is, moreover, a note of objectivity about truthfulness in the Sacred Scriptures that may seem a bit strange until its full import is examined. Telling the truth is not merely saying what is on one's mind, which is still subjective. In biblical parlance it means communicating what is real, what actually exists, or what actually took place. The implication is that we do have access to reality, either by reason or revelation; so that when we speak the truth, our sharing with others is what we have ourselves experienced: the objective world of real persons and events and, with emphasis, the objective world of spirit and of God.

Seen from this perspective, what began as the Eighth of the Ten Commandments becomes, by the end of the last book of the Bible, the universal commandment to use our speech according to the will of God, who is the Truth. Conversely, then, all sins of the tongue are ultimately sins of untruth. They contradict the proper use of human language whenever it is animated by injustice toward the neighbor or infidelity toward God.

That is why Christ placed such a stress on bridling the tongue. That is also why the apostle James, after sadly admitting, "after all, every one of us does something wrong over and over again," confidently added, "the only man who could reach perfection would be someone who would never say anything wrong—he would be able to control every part of himself" (Jm. 3:12). Once the tongue is duly restrained, mastery has been achieved over the heart.

LYING AND MENTAL RESERVATION

It is doubtful if any single aspect of Christian morality has been as minutely analyzed by the Church's writers as the subject of truthfulness in speech and its opposite vice of lying. One reason is that nothing in the moral order is more pervasive than verbal or written communication between or among people. We would therefore expect those who wished to foster Christian solidarity to be specially concerned about truthful communication, without which there cannot be a community.

St. Augustine wrote two lengthy treatises on lying, where he gave what has since become the classic definition: "That man lies who has one thing on his mind and utters something else either in words or by any kind of signs."[77] Since Augustine's day, the concept has been carefully refined. Lying means speaking deliberately contrary to what is on a person's mind.

Evidently the speaking need not be in words. There is such a thing as nonverbal communication. The important factor is that some other person be the intended object of what is communicated. Thus we cannot, strictly speaking, tell a lie to ourselves.

Also what is said must be recognized for what it is. A distraught or distracted person may utter all sorts of mistaken statements, but they are not lies unless he is sufficiently aware of what he says and intends to say it.

Above all, the one who lies must say something he knows is contrary to what is on his mind; there must be opposition between what he says and what he thinks. It all depends on what I think; so that I would be lying if I actually told the truth but thought that my statement was false. And I would not lie if what I said was actually false but I believed it was true.

Circumstances are an integral part of human speech; such circumstances are the time, place, tone of voice, and the persons addressed. Thus what may verbally be contrary to fact, like telling children about Santa Claus, is not lying. Hyperboles are not lies, such as the closing words of the fourth Gospel: "There were many other things that Jesus did; if all were written down, the world itself, I suppose, would not hold all the books that would have to be written" (Jn. 21:25). Similarly, ironical expressions are not necessarily lies. In exasperation, a father might tell his son, who just disobeyed him, how respectful he was to his parents. It may be imprudent to say this, but the meaning was plain. Writers of fiction fabricate all kinds of unreal narratives, but they are not telling lies. In the same category are jokes, which are not lies provided the evident humor of the situation or other circumstances makes it clear that what was said should not be taken seriously. This is not to justify careless storytelling, and other virtues need to be considered, notably, charity; but fictionalized humorous conversation is not lying. A jocose lie, however, is not the same as a joke and becomes sinful when the speaker fails to make it evident that his words are not be taken literally.

Catholic morality traditionally holds that lies, of themselves, are venial sins. They may, of course, become grave under extraordinary circumstances, such as telling a lie under oath or denying one's religion as a Catholic.

Mental Reservation. From time immemorial, while it was commonly recognized that we may never tell a lie, it was also apparent that sometimes we are bound in conscience to veil the truth. Secrets are to be kept, and people's reputation can be injured by revealing what is true but unwarranted. Silence is often possible, but not always; in fact, by saying nothing we may betray the very secret we are trying to hide.

How to escape the dilemma? The best-known way is by means of a mental reservation, which may be of two kinds. In both, the speaker limits the common and obvious sense of his words to a particular meaning. If he limits the meaning and gives no clue, this is a strict mental reservation. But if he limits the meaning while leaving a reasonable clue to the sense intended, this is called a broad mental reservation.

Strict mental reservations are actually lies. There is no way the listener can read the speaker's mind when he says, for example, "I made a trip around the world," when he means that he had a dream to that effect.

In a broad mental reservation, however, there is a clue to the meaning of what is intended, either in the words used or the circumstances under which they are spoken. Provided a person has sufficient reason, he may invoke this kind of reservation by saying one thing and intending something else. Thus in answering the telephone, to say that someone is not at home leaves open the reasonable conclusion that the person is at home physically but not available. When a person who knows he is guilty of a crime nevertheless pleads not guilty, circumstances indicate that the innocence alleged is merely legal and not moral.

What are some sufficient reasons for using a broad mental reservation? The main reason is the need for preserving secrecy, where the value to the common good is greater than would be the manifestation of something that is sure to cause harm.

Evidently such reservations must be used with prudence, at the risk of creating suspicion and mistrust if people cannot be sure that what they are being told is what they hear or what they are supposed to figure out from the situation in which they hear it. They are not expected to be always on the lookout for some "hidden meaning" in what is heard or read.

The gravity of these extenuating reasons must be proportionate to the gravity of the situation in which a broad mental reservation is invoked. In a court of law there would have to be extraordinarily grave reasons for a witness to say implicitly, "I will not tell a lie, but I will tell the truth only insofar as the civil law obliges me to, and beyond that I will use reservations."

SECRETS

An important part of practicing the virtues of the tongue is to keep secrets which, barring the seal of sacramental confession, are forms of hidden knowledge that may not be revealed unless some higher right prevails.

Three types of secrets are generally distinguished, each with a different level of confidentiality. Natural secrets are those that common sense (right reason) tells us are to be kept confidential. From another viewpoint, the natural law binds the one who knows the secret to keep it hidden. Such secrets are the most common. They can be recognized by each person asking himself: Would I want this hidden failing, or defect, or sin, or mistake, or human limitation of mine revealed to others? Christian charity goes a step higher in asking not only whether I would want this secret revealed about me, but whether telling the secret will help or harm the person about whom it is told—quite apart from how I personally feel about it.

Promised secrets are those that a person has promised to keep after having received or come upon the confidential knowledge. Of course, the promise may be either expressed or implied. These secrets assume that the information precedes the promise, as when I find out something embarrassing about another person and then he asks me not to divulge it.

The most rigorous are the entrusted (or committed) secrets that must be kept hidden because of an agreement reached before the confidential information was given. Such an agreement again may be explicit or implicit, namely that the secret is confided on condition that it be kept hidden. To this class belong professional secrets to which one is obliged by virtue of his office or position in society, as physicians, lawyers, civil magistrates, and counselors. The same duty applies to those who work for such officials, e.g., secretaries.

What is the basic reason why secrets should be kept? Because each person is an individual who has exclusive rights to the fruits of his own ideas and ingenuity or, if the confidential matter pertains to his reputation, the right to his good name. Secrets, then, are part of each one's personality. They belong to him and, unless proportionate reasons intervene, may not be alienated any more than other property he owns.

How seriously, then, are secrets to be respected or, from another angle, under what conditions may they be revealed? Each of the three levels of confidentiality has its own normative principles, which have been worked out through fifteen hundred years of Catholic moral tradition.

1. Natural secrets are held to be binding, either in justice or charity: in justice if the unlawful revelation of the secret would cause objective damage to the person or persons concerned; and in charity if the disclosure caused subjective sadness or embarrassment. If the damage done or the offense caused is grave, the violation of the secret is correspondingly grave; otherwise the sin is venial.

As a preliminary observation, relative to all types of secrets, if the guarded knowledge has already become public property (even though illicitly), then the duty to keep the matter confidential ceases. In the same way, the obligation to keep a secret does not bind if it may be reasonably presumed that the person concerned would allow the confidence to be divulged. Such permission, however, should not be easily presumed, particularly in the case of entrusted secrets.

With regard to natural secrets, the obligation of confidentiality ceases whenever keeping the hidden information would involve grave injury or cause serious difficulty to any one of the following: the person who knows the secret; the one who shares the secret; an innocent third party; the Church; the State; the community.

This concession to revealing what is known secretly has been recognized by the Church in numerous ways, notably in the formal request before marriage or before ordination to make known to proper authorities if any grave impediment is known why the couple should not be married or the man not be elevated to sacred orders.

2. Promised secrets are binding according to the wishes of the one who agreed to keep the information confidential. The gravity of the promise, and hence of the sin if the promise is violated, depends mainly on whether the matter itself is grave; and then the same norms apply as in the case of natural secrets. In exceptional cases a person might want to bind himself gravely, not because the secret is that important but because it means so much to the one who shared the confidence.

Revealing promised secrets follows the same principles as those concerning natural confidences. One exception would be if I expressly agree to guard a secret even at grave inconvenience to myself alone. In that instance, I must abide by my agreement, although even here the difficulty caused must refer only to me and not to an innocent third party or to the community.

3. Entrusted secrets are the most sacred. The common good requires that persons in professional positions should be able to receive confidential information and keep it. The least suspicion that people's confidences are not respected or that what they told secretly later became public knowledge would do great injury to society. A single violation can destroy the trustfulness that is essential for social well-being, whether in the Church or in secular communities.

Before dealing with entrusted secrets in general, some observations should be made about the sacramental seal of confession.

By the seal of confession the Church understands the strict obligation to maintain silence concerning what is disclosed in sacramental confession. The origin of the obligation is based on the natural law, the positive divine law derived from revelation, and the Canon Law of the Church.

The obligation applies only to what was told in a sacramental confession, whether the confession was finished or not, whether it was worthy or sacrilegious, and whether absolution was given or refused. Consequently, no such obligation arises from a "confession" made to someone who is not a priest, nor from a mock confession, nor from a conversation with a priest without the explicit intention of confessing, as when a person is seeking advice.

The priest's obligation to absolute secrecy applies to all persons, including the penitent outside of confession. With the permission of the penitent, the priest may speak of sacramental matters with the penitent himself and with others, even outside of confession. Such permission can be given, for instance, so that the confessor may consult someone more experienced in a difficult case of conscience. Presumed permission is never sufficient, and even when asked, the request should be made without the slightest coercion.

No exception is ever to be made, not even to save one's life or for the common welfare. Among the solemn declarations of the Church on the seal of confession was the following declaration of the Fourth Lateran Council referring to confessors:

> Let him constantly take care, lest by word or sign or any other way whatsoever he may at any time betray a sinner. But if he should need more prudent counsel, he should seek it cautiously without any mention of the person, since he who shall presume to reveal a sin entrusted to him in confession, we decree not only must be deposed from priestly office but must also be thrust into a strict monastery to do perpetual penance.[78]

Not only is the confessor bound by the seal of confession, but also anyone who inadvertently or in exercising his office obtains knowledge of confessional matter. Among other famous cases of martyrs for confessional secrecy was St. John Nepomucene (1340–93), who was drowned in the Moldau River by order of King Wenceslas IV of Bohemia for refusing to betray the Queen by revealing what she had told him in confession.

Apart from sacramental secrecy, however, entrusted secrets may be revealed only to avert great imminent harm, to the Church, State, or society in general, to an innocent third party, to the one who received the confidence or even to the person whose secret it is. If disclosure were not licit in such extreme circumstances, professional people would refuse to accept confidential matter for fear of grave injury to them, with immense detriment to the common good. Thus a doctor unjustly accused of malpractice by one of his clients may defend himself by revealing (if necessary) some confidential matter told him by the accuser.

In a class by itself is the reading of another person's letters or other personal writing, like notes or diaries. To read such private matters is sinful unless permission has been given by the owner of the writing, or it may reasonably be presumed he would not mind. On the other hand, letters and similar written confidences may be read if it is considered necessary to prevent grave harm to the writer, to oneself, or to society. Thus mail may be censored in time of war;

a mother may read a child's letter if she thinks it necessary; a wife may read her husband's letter if she has very good reason to suspect it is from another woman trying to alienate her husband's affections.

The sinfulness of reading letters or other private writing without permission or to avert great harm will depend on the importance of the secret information acquired.

DETRACTION AND CALUMNY

The immediate focus of the Eighth Commandment is falsehood that does injury to one's neighbor. Harm to another person's reputation, therefore, is the special prohibition of this divine mandate.

A person's reputation may be injured in various ways, notably by detraction and calumny or slander. Detraction is the unjust violation of the good reputation of another by revealing something true about him. Calumny or slander differs from detraction in that what is said or imputed about a person is not true.

A good reputation is the esteem that one person has formed and entertains about another. It may regard his moral qualities, such as honesty, chastity, or truthfulness; it may regard physical and mental qualities or attainments. In either case, reputation is the object of an acquired right, and consequently to take it away or lower it becomes an act of injustice. Not only the living but also the dead have a right to good esteem. During life we wish to remain in the grateful memory of mankind, and such an expectation can lead us to great exploits.

What needs to be stressed, however, is that a person's good name is something he cherishes even though we may not think he deserves it. No matter; it is his good name, not ours. We may, if we wish, forfeit our good name provided no harm is done to others. But another person's good reputation belongs to him, and we may not do it injury by revealing, without proportionately grave reason, what we know is true about him.

Detraction is consequently a sin against justice because it deprives a man or woman of what they ordinarily value more than riches. Socrates' statement that the way to gain a good reputation is to endeavor to be what you desire to appear highlights the effort required to acquire a good name. All of this, more even than accumulated wealth, can be destroyed by a single criminal act of detraction.

The seriousness of the sin committed will mainly derive from the gravity of the fault or limitation disclosed. But it will also depend on the dignity of the person detracted and the harm done to him and others by revealing something that is hidden and whose disclosure lowers (if it does not ruin) his standing in the public eye.

Not unlike the restitution called for in stealing, detraction demands reparation as far as possible to the injured person's reputation. Often such reparation is next to impossible to make, either because of the number of people informed or the complexity of the situation. But this merely emphasizes the warning of Scripture to "Be careful of your reputation, for it will last you longer than a thousand hoards of gold. A good life lasts a certain number of days, but a good reputation lasts forever" (Si. 41:12–16).

The essence of detraction is the unwarranted disclosure of a hidden failing, which implies that there are occasions when the disclosure can and even should be made.

When the revelation of another person's fault is necessary or very useful, as in defense of self or of others, no injustice is done in revealing it. This would be the case when the failing or defect is made known to parents, or superiors, or for the purpose of seeking counsel or help, or to prevent harm to others, though again, there must be adequate proportion between the lessening of a person's reputation (which is not intended) and the good to be achieved by the disclosure (which is intended). This would cover such contingencies as anticipating unjust harm to oneself in the law courts, or even seeking consolation of a trusted friend by revealing the injustice done.

It is also not detraction to make known what has become juridically notorious, since the culprit has lost his right to esteem in the matter. It is conducive to public security that criminals should be known for what they are. However, since one's reputation may reflect upon a group like an organization or class of people, criminal acts of a single member of that group should not be widely disclosed so as not to jeopardize the reputation of all the persons with whom this one individual is commonly identified. Indiscriminate disclosure of this kind is the seedbed of class prejudice.

All that we said about detraction applies to calumny, with the added malice of falsehood. Moreover, since an untruth was told about another person, reparation is more urgent and mandatory. Somehow the slanderer must not only undo the harm done to his victim's reputation, but he must also correct the falsehood he spoke; it may be with considerable embarrassment to himself.

Excusing factors that might release either the detractor or the calumniator from the duty of repairing the injury inflicted would be, e.g., that the injury no longer exists, or reparation is physically or mortally impossible, or the person defamed excuses his detractor or calumniator at least by an implicit condonation, or (most commonly) reparation would cause the defamer a far greater injury than the one he inflicted.

Closely connected with detraction and calumny are rash judgments, where we entertain an unquestioning conviction about another person's bad conduct without adequate grounds for our judgment. This is not the same thing as seeing someone act in a certain way that is obviously wrong, and spontaneously saying to ourselves, "That is not right." We may be perfectly correct in our assessment of the action and, in fact, would be stultifying our intelligence if we thought otherwise. A sudden outburst of anger that we witness, or a gross failure in justice, or a glaring exhibition of vanity are objectively wrong, and we cannot reasonably deny the obvious.

Where the rash judgment begins is at the point where we go beyond the evidence available to judge the culpability of the action, attribute evil motives, and decide against the character or moral integrity of the person whose conduct we observed.

The sinfulness of rashly judging people, therefore, arises from two sources: the hasty imprudence with which a critical judgment is reached, and the loss of reputation that the person suffers in our estimation because we have judged him adversely.

Hasty imprudence in passing judgment on others is an innate tendency of fallen human nature. We are prone to generalize, without adequate premises, where others are concerned and draw sweeping conclusions about their weaknesses and limitations. It is just the opposite where we are concerned, where the tendency is to excuse and minimize, often in the face of overwhelming evidence to the contrary. Christ's pointed contrast between these two tendencies brings out the difference:

> Why do you observe the splinter in your brother's eye and never notice the plank in your own? How dare you say to your brother, "Let me take the splinter out of your eye," when all the time there is a plank in your own? Hypocrite! Take the plank out of your own eye first, and then you will see clearly enough to take the splinter out of your brother's eye (Mt. 7:3–5).

Besides the hastiness to make sweeping conclusions about other people, rash judgments are sinful because everyone has a right to the good esteem of his fellow men. Even if what he has done is conclusive proof of culpability or of defective character, charity forbids our despising a person or, what comes to the same thing, thinking ourselves superior because we are not like him, as St. Paul told the early Christians:

> True, my conscience does not reproach me at all, but that does not prove that I have been acquitted: the Lord alone is my judge. There must be no passing of premature judgment. Leave that until the Lord comes. He will light up all that is hidden in the dark and reveal the secret intentions of men's hearts. Then will be the time for each one to have whatever praise he deserves, from God (1 Co. 4:4–5).

In order to control this inveterate tendency to praise ourselves and blame others, it is necessary to leave both ourselves and others in God's hands and trust that, in the final judgment, the truth will then appear. Those who deserve to be rewarded will receive the merit they had earned; those who are to be punished will be visited by their just deserts. In the meantime, i.e., during our mortal stay on earth, all definitive judgments about people, whether ourselves or others, are premature. Only God at the end of time has the right to decide conclusively about the human heart.

SOCIAL COMMUNICATIONS

A completely new dimension has been added to the morality of truthful speech since the turn of the twentieth century. With the development of the electronic media—the telephone and telegraph, radio and television, radar and computer, photography and film and their derivatives—every aspect of communicating human thought and feeling is affected with hitherto undreamed-of implications. Simultaneously, millions of persons find themselves equally involved in seeing, hearing, and feeling the influence of a single man or woman with whom they establish instant rapport. This is one side of their involvement. Instinctively they also sense that unseen multitudes of others are equally captivated by the same experience, which now takes on cosmic proportions.

Never before has so much power been so easily available for

elevating or degrading the human spirit, depending on the principles and integrity of those in control. This now includes the printed word, since the modern press after some reluctance has become an enthusiastic partner in the media.

It was inevitable that the Second Vatican Council should address itself to the deep moral issues that these discoveries in communication raise. The decree *Inter Mirifica* dealt exclusively with the means of social communication, and eight years later, the Holy See published a lengthy pastoral instruction to implement the decree. These two documents are the most authoritative teaching of the Catholic Church on the far-reaching practical questions that face the Christian world as it enters the electronics age.

Right to Information.   The first of these practical questions has to do with information, as it is called, or the search for and reporting of news. No one doubts that this has become a most useful instrument of progress in the contemporary world and at times a necessary link of unity that binds the members of human society.

What corollaries follow on this now almost instantaneous publication of news? It implies what until lately we scarcely adverted to, that there resides in society a right to information concerning both individuals and the community of mankind. It further implies that, in exercising this right, the news communicated should be always true and, within the limits of justice and charity, complete.

Society on all levels requires information if it is to make the right decisions. The community needs well-informed citizens. Consequently, the right to information is not only a privilege of private individuals; it is essential to the common good.

Saying this, however, only brings to the surface the heavy responsibility of those who gather, evaluate, and pass on the news to the public.

There is the matter of selectivity. Journalists deal with what has just happened and with what is of present interest. They therefore select what they judge to be the significant facts that will appeal to the audience. So it can happen that the news reported is only part of the whole and does not convey what is of real importance. Prudence and balanced judgment in choosing what is both salient and salesworthy are the first moral requisites of those in charge of mass communication.

Once the raw news has been filtered, communicators must give the information quickly and with easy comprehensibility. Outdated news is a contradiction in terms. As a result the initiative often passes to men who are less responsible and less well-informed but who are more willing to oblige. Competition is keen. If the competitor is unscrupulous, this places a heavy temptation in the path of the communicator who wishes to remain faithful to the truth.

The temptation is obvious. Communicators must hold the wandering attention of a harried public by vivid reporting. Yet they must resist the urge to make the news sensational in such a way that they distort it by taking things out of context or by exaggerating facts out of proportion.

But all the responsibility is not on the side of those who transmit the news. Recipients have their duty, too. And one of the major developments in the Catholic approach to the media is to stress the real obligation the public has to react to what they are being told by the newscasters.

> They should not look for a superhuman perfection in the communicators. What they do have right and duty to expect, however, is that a rapid and clear correction should follow any mistake or misrepresentation that has found its way into a report.
>
> They are to protest whenever omissions or distortions occur. They are to protest whenever events have been reported out of context or in a biased manner. They are to protest whenever the significance of events has been wildly exaggerated or underplayed.
>
> This right should be guaranteed for recipients by agreement among the communicators themselves and, if this cannot be got, then by national law or international convention.[79]

As basic as is the right to information, it is not limitless but must be reconciled with other existing rights. There is the right of privacy, which only in recent years has become recognized but which protects the private life of families, societies, and individuals. There is the right of secrecy that seriously binds in conscience when necessity or professional duty or the good of society requires.

Moreover, the right to information demands another limitation. No one denies that violence and brutality are part of human existence, nowadays perhaps more than ever. But it is one thing to delineate violence in such a way that people will recoil from it, and something else when acts of savagery are too realistically described or too frequently dwelled upon. There is a danger of perverting the image of human life. It is also possible, as specialists in the social sciences admit, that such descriptions may generate first an attitude of mind and then a positive psychosis that escape the power of rational control. In time, people may come to accept violence as the accepted way of resolving conflict.

Education, Culture, and Leisure.   The scope of the communications media for teaching people is literally without boundaries, whether geographically or psychologically. In many places audiovisual aids, sound and video cassettes, and the regular use of radio and television have become accepted teaching instruments. So also has the rapid multiplication of the printed word, now available quickly and in quantity.

Parallel with education, the media are already conspicuous elements in daily life, bringing artistic and cultural achievements within the orbit of a great part of the human race. And so perhaps they will do the same for the whole of mankind.

With increased affluence in many societies, people spend a growing part of their time in reading, seeing, and listening to programs expressly geared to meet the needs of the leisure age.

Each of these factors, however, poses its own moral imperatives. Easily accessible educational media should be exploited by the faithful in the interests of the Gospel and to disseminate the truth. The people of God are urged by the Church's highest authority "to use effectively and at once the means of social communication, zealously availing themselves of them for apostolic purposes."[80]

That is one side of the imperative: to use the providential means available for communicating the truth, indeed Truth himself, among the faithful and beyond them to every corner of the globe.

The other side is more subtle. It is not enough to languidly receive the ideas that others communicate in order to educate. The reception, paradoxically, should be active. The faithful are expected to "exercise personal reflection" and "exchange their views with others." Without personal reflection and communal discussion, the media can become means of passive indoctrination.

"Culture" is an ambiguous term. It may be high or low and, what is more important, it may be Christian or un-Christian in the elementary sense of conformable or alien to Christian values. The problem with the media is their massive audience. They often play for the applause of the lowest cultural levels of their audience, according to the pontifical commission for social communication. The economic factors loom too large for producers to ignore, and popularity ratings of radio and television programs are geared mainly to the number of listeners or viewers, not to their norms of morality. Truth in speech is now seen as also truth in color and sound, and the biblical command not to deceive can be as well broken by a private person as by the media communicator. The individual is expected to tell what is on his mind, when he decides to speak, and to seek to elevate or inspire his listener, certainly not to degrade him. The media too are expected to tell what is on the mind of the culture, i.e., of that part of the culture that is truly formative of the people, when they decide to communicate and to elevate their audience, certainly not to debase them.

The right use of leisure is at once an oppportunity and a challenge. It is one of the mixed blessings of "developed peoples" that they have an increasing amount of sheer time on their hands. Yet the Gospel precept remains that we shall be held accountable for every idle word we speak, and how much more for every idle hour we have squandered.

This is not to say that recreation is bad or that entertainment is contrary to Christian morality, even to Christian perfection. But the faithful must recall some basic principles of their faith:

> Simple entertainment has a value of its own. It lightens the burden of daily problems and it occupies man's leisure. The wide variety of productions that the media offer for these hours of leisure is in fact a remarkable service to mankind.
>
> But recipients should exercise self-control. They must not allow themselves to be so beguiled by the charms of the media's products or by the curiosity that these arouse that they neglect urgent duties or simply waste time.
>
> Moreover, because they—the media—take so much of modern man's time, they can easily divert him from higher and more profitable cultural pursuits.[81]

It is almost as though the Eighth Commandment were directed not only to the one who speaks but to the one who listens. The modern believer is told to speak the truth, whether as individual or as media communicator. He is also told to listen to the truth, which means discernment and self-control, lest his mind become filled with unreality and his time for legitimate entertainment be dissipated by being spent beyond objective needs.

Advertising. The role of advertising in today's world is well established. Its function is to announce publicly in the sense of calling public attention to something by emphasizing its desirable qualities in order to arouse a desire to purchase or invest in what is advertised.

It makes its presence felt everywhere, and its influence is unavoidable. It offers real social benefits. It tells buyers, investors, or contributors of the goods and services available. It thus encourages the widest distribution of products and services and, in doing this, it helps industry and commercial enterprises to develop and benefit the population. All this is to the good as long as the prospective buyer's liberty of choice is respected and the truth is not obscured or concealed.

Symbolic of the changing times, the faithful are now being counseled by the Church on the ethics of advertising, both those who are actively promoting a product or service to the public, and those who are the object of the advertisers' zeal.

If harmful or utterly useless goods are touted to the public, if false assertions are made about the goods for sale, if less admirable human tendencies are exploited, those responsible for such advertising harm society and forfeit their good name and credibility.

More than this, unremitting pressure to buy articles of luxury can arouse false wants that hurt both individuals and families by making them ignore what they really need. And those forms of advertising which, without shame, exploit the sexual instincts simply to make money or which seek to penetrate into the subconscious recesses of the mind in a way that threatens the freedom of the individual, those forms of advertising must be shunned.

It is therefore desirable that advertisers make definite rules for themselves lest their sales methods affront human dignity or harm the community.[82]

Such vast sums are being spent for advertising that the very foundations of the mass media are being threatened. People can get the idea that the means of communication exist to stimulate our desires, which need to be satisfied by the acquisition of what has been advertised. Moreover, because of economic demands and pressure, the essential freedom of the media is at stake. Since revenue from advertising is vital for these media, only those can finally survive that receive the largest share of advertising outlays. This leaves the door open for monopolies that impede the people's right to receive and the communicator's right to give information. Therefore, "a variety of independent means of social communication must be carefully safeguarded even if this requires legislative action."[83]

Anyone familiar with the situation in countries where monopolies exist will recognize in this call to media independence the most urgent need of modern man for access to the truth.

Public Opinion. Long before the electronic media were discovered, public opinion was an essential expression of human nature organized in a society. Philosophers explained its formation as the result of an innate disposition in all of us to give vent to ideas, attitudes, and emotions in order to reach a general acceptance on convictions and customs. Pius XII described it as "the natural echo of actual events and situations as reflected more or less spontaneously in the minds and judgments of men."[84] Freedom of speech is therefore a normal factor in the growth of public opinion, which expresses the ideas and reactions of the more influential circles in a society defined by geography, culture, and history.

Freedom to express and publish one's opinions, within the bounds of morality and the common welfare, was defended by the Second Vatican Council as indispensable in any age of human history, but never more so than today. People must be able to assess and compare differing views that seem to have weight and validity.

Communicators of the mass media have a vital role to play in the formation of public opinion, as the outcome of this free interplay of ideas and attitudes. They are to gather up the different views and compare them before transmitting them so that the people can understand and make a proper decision. But for that very reason, they are obliged to observe certain norms of morality:

1. They should recognize the rights of the leaders of society, whether by reason of office, talent, or experience, to help in forming public opinion. This means giving these leaders the freedom that their potential for influence requires. "The greater their quality of leadership, the greater is their responsibility to exert it in this way." But they must be afforded the liberty to exert their providential responsibility.

2. The process of promoting public opinion, by what is called propaganda, is justified when it serves the truth, when its objectives and methods accord with the dignity of man, and when it promotes causes that are in the public interest. These three conditions are not ideals to be striven after but principles to be adhered to, especially the first one—serving the truth—which undergirds the other two.

But where is truth to be found? Here the faithful are reminded that "the Catholic Church has been established to bring salvation to all men," through preaching the Gospel of truth by all the means at its disposal in any given age. For those who believe, to propagate the truth is not to propagandize; it is to "proclaim the message of salvation by using, among other means, the mass media." Indeed, "the Church has a duty to instruct men in their proper use."[85]

3. Some types of "propaganda" are inadmissible. While their number and variety are legion, certain forms stand out immediately as contrary to right reason and the moral law:

> These include those which harm the public interest or allow of no public reply. Any propaganda that deliberately misrepresents the real situation, or that distorts men's minds with half-truths by selective reporting or serious omissions, or that diminishes man's legitimate freedom of decision—this should be rejected.[86]

It is becoming increasingly necessary to stress this and to educate the faithful in what is happening. Otherwise, the simple declaration of the Bible to always tell the truth and never tell a lie becomes next to impossible to observe, if the very words that people use have been invested with meanings that the Catholic faith disavows.

Christians are also being taught that not every opinion given publicity should be taken as a true expression of the public opinion that is held by a significant number of people. Even the opinion of the majority is not necessarily the best or the nearest to the truth.

We return, therefore, to the biblical understanding of truth as more than conformity of speech with our thoughts, and more than sincerity in what is said. It is the agreement of what enters the human mind with the eternal mind of God, whose wisdom had been spoken at various times, but in our own time has been given to us through his Son. Those who believe in him also believe that he continues to speak through his Church, which gives them a sure guide to judge public opinion and help them to shape it according to the will of God.

XI. GROWTH IN HOLINESS

UNIVERSAL CALL TO SANCTITY

While there are different ways of life among the faithful and different duties, says the Second Vatican Council, "it is one holiness which is cultivated by all who are led by the Spirit of God." Saying this, however, simply reaffirms what the Church has always taught: All Christians are called to grow in the likeness of Christ, who is one, but they have different vocations to become holy in different ways and according to various degrees of sanctity.

Bishops should be outstanding in holiness. Their loyalty to the pastoral office, through "promptness, humility, and courage in carrying out their service" in the care of souls will be an excellent means of sanctifying themselves. Their zeal must be such that "they must not be afraid to lay down their life for their flock," as so many bishops have done in witness of the faith and defense of the people entrusted to their charge.

Priests make up, in the words of Ignatius of Antioch, the bishops' spiritual crown. They share in the grace of the episcopal office through Christ and, "after the fashion of the episcopal order, they must grow in love of God and their neighbor by means of their daily performance of duty. They must safeguard the bond of priestly fellowship, must overflow in all spiritual good, must present all men with a living witness of God, must rival the priests who in the course of the centuries have bequeathed a glorious pattern of holiness in a service which was frequently lowly and hidden." All of these are imperatives in the Church's expectations of her priests.

Married people and parents have their own road of sanctity to follow. "With a love that is loyal they must give each other support in grace throughout their lives. They must steep in Christian teaching and the virtues of the Gospel, the children they have lovingly received from God." Those who are widowed and those who are living single lives in the world often have to work hard. "They should use their human occupations to bring themselves to perfection" by laboring in the apostolate and striving to improve the condition of the whole of society.

Finally, the Church's holiness is fostered in a special way by the numerous counsels that Christ proposed for the observance of his disciples, beyond the precepts necessary for salvation. Among these counsels, God gives the grace to some "to facilitate the devotion of their undivided heart to him alone in the state of virginity or celibacy." He also calls some to witness to the Savior's charity and humility "by accepting poverty with the freedom that belongs to the sons of God and by renunciation of their own will" through obedience.

The Church distinguishes, therefore, between what the faithful must do to gain eternal life and what they should do so that their love of God "may be more complete." Holiness belongs to the second level, and in this sense "all Christ's faithful have an invitation, which is binding, to the pursuit of holiness and perfection in their own station in life. They must all make it their aim to keep a due control over their passions to avoid being impeded in their pursuit of perfect charity by a use of worldly possessions and an attachment to wealth which conflicts with the spirit of Gospel poverty." The Church paraphrases the warning of St. Paul, which is meant for Christians in every age: "Those who deal with the world must not take their stand on it, for the form of this world is passing away."[1] Worldliness and holiness, the Church believes, are contradictories.

STATES OF PERFECTION

Within the Catholic Church since earliest times there has been recognized a way of life whose primary purpose is the pursuit of holiness. Variously called monasticism, consecrated life, religious life and, most comprehensively, states of perfection, its history reaches to the Christian hermits and anchorites of the second and third centuries. St. Pachomius (290–346) of Egypt is considered the founder of coenobitic (community) religious life as distinct from the eremetic (solitary) religious life in the Church. Most religious in the Roman Catholic world follow the coenobitic pattern.

The term "states of perfection" is now commonly applied to two groups of persons: those technically called religious and those belonging to secular institutes. How are they the same and how do they differ?

Four elements make up the religious state: a fixed or stable manner of life, lived in common, in which the evangelical counsels are observed by means of the vows of obedience, chastity, and poverty.

Stability or permanency belongs to the very nature of a state of life. Thus a person who enters a state of life is no longer morally free to abandon it, or move in and out of the state to which he belongs. Such are the married state, entered by sacramental marriage and indissoluble except by the death of one of the spouses; the clerical state, entered by sacred orders and, for those who receive at least the diaconate, objectively indissoluble even when (on occasion) the Holy Father dispenses a deacon or priest from active clerical service and his obligation of celibacy; and the religious state, which a person enters by pronouncing vows that (when final) are binding until death unless for grave reasons the religious was released from them by special permission of the Church.

The common life means especially two things: the religious is a member of a society that enjoys moral personality under a determined superior and a definite rule or way of life, and the religious live together with other members of the same society. The second feature, namely, living together, is the general rule, with exceptions allowed for certain good reasons.

Observance of the evangelical counsels of poverty, chastity, and obedience does not mean that religious already have reached perfection in these areas. They are striving to attain such perfection, and they do so by their effort to master the three main concupiscences of human nature: possession, sexual pleasure, and personal autonomy.

By professing the vows of poverty, chastity, and obedience, religious give firmness to their observance of the counsels. They are bonds that bind the person striving after perfection to the lifelong observance of the three counsels, and thus they provide for the permanency required in the religious state.

The Second Vatican Council clarified what constitutes the essence of the religious life as distinct from other states of life in which Christians are also expected to grow in holiness. That essence is the voluntary profession by which the religious freely vows to follow Christ by imitating his example of dedication to God by a triple totality: a totality of sacrifice in giving up the right to the use of material goods through poverty, of marital privileges through chastity, and of autonomous disposition of one's own time and talents through obedience to superiors; a totality of duration in intending to make the sacrifice lifelong; and a totality of service in consecrating one's labors wholly to the needs of the Church through obedience to hierarchical authority.

Secular institutes, no less than religious communities, may have members who are either clerics or persons not sacramentally ordained. These institutes, which are relatively new in the Catholic Church, may be defined as societies—whether clerical or lay—whose members profess the evangelical counsels in the world in order to attain Christian perfection and to exercise the apostolate fully. They, therefore, are like religious institutes in their observances of the counsels and their profession of poverty, chastity, and obedience under vows. Their profession of vows, however, is not public but private, so that they are not generally recognizable as members of a religious institute. Nor do they obligate themselves to living community life. They are called *secular* institutes because their proper and specific character is to have the members live and work in the world, outside of cloister and common life.

Yet both religious and secular institutes agree on being states of perfection, i.e., permanent ways of life whose primary purpose is to grow in holiness by following in the footsteps of the Master by their intense love of God and complete service to the needs of others. Their primary purpose, then, is the pursuit of sanctity, and they thus become witnesses of transcendence in the midst of a fleeting world: "The profession of the evangelical counsels is seen to be like a sign which has the power of effectively attracting all the Church's members to a lively performance of the duties of the Christian vocation. It must do so."[2] That closing injunction is also the mandate for their existence.

One of the most painful aspects of Catholic life in modern times is that so many priests and religious in certain countries have abandoned their lifetime commitments. The problem is compounded by the fact that not a few religious left their communities because they found them, as they said, secularized. While many reasons can be given for the phenomenon, somewhere near the central cause is the intrusion of alien ideas. The result has been "a habit of mind which wrongly claims that a person should rashly conform to the profound transformations by which our age is being violently shaken." This has "led some people to decide that the distinctive elements of the religious life are destined to die."[3]

The Church's answer to this inversion of Catholic spirituality is to insist that a life of perfection is as possible today as it ever was. Those who have the vocation receive the moral power to be conformed, not to the world, but "to that kind of life of virginity and poverty which Christ the Lord chose for himself and which his virgin mother also embraced."

Some indication of the Church's unchanging respect for a life of sacrifice is the solemn definition of the Council of Trent when priestly celibacy and consecrated virginity were under severe criticism. A Catholic may not say that "the married state is to be preferred to the state of virginity or celibacy."[4] This is not to claim that those living a celibate life are necessarily more holy than the married. It does, however, affirm the Church's constant teaching of how God is pleased with our conformity to the virginal life of his divine Son, who was born of the virgin Mary.

MASTERS OF THE SPIRITUAL LIFE

Not unlike the message of the New Testament, the principal scope of the Church's teaching and guidance since apostolic times has been to lead the faithful on the paths of holiness. This may seem surprising if we think of all the doctrinal statements of Popes and councils about the Trinity, the Incarnation, faith, and revelation; and all the documentation dealing with hierarchical structure, laws, and ecclesiastical regulations.

Nevertheless, the fact remains that in and through all these highly erudite teachings and beyond the external details, the Church's ultimate desire is that of St. Paul addressing the first Christians, that the Lord "may so confirm your hearts in holiness that you may be blameless in the sight of our God and Father when our Lord Jesus Christ comes with all his saints" (1 Th. 3:13).

In fulfilling this task of sanctifying the faithful, the Church has produced an impressive library of doctrine on the meaning of sanctity, its importance for the well-being of the Mystical Body of Christ, and the widely available means at the people's disposal for not only believing in holiness but becoming holy.

Moreover, Catholicism does not stop with doctrine and exhortation. It goes on to offer the example and directives of those who in their own lives have reached high degrees of sanctity. It equivalently says: "Here are models for you to imitate. If you do what they did, according to your ability, and listen to their counsel, what they achieved you can achieve also."

This is one of the main reasons for the Church's ageless custom of venerating saints. They are not only intercessors in heaven but also patterns of virtue for the faithful on earth.

> When we fix our gaze on the life of those who have followed Christ faithfully, we have an extraordinary motive that impels us to seek the city which is to come. At the same time we receive instruction in the safest route whereby we may arrive at perfect union with Christ, which is perfect holiness, a route through the diversity the world offers, a route which suits each person in their own condition and their own circumstance.
>
> In the life of those who share our human nature, yet become more completely changed into the likeness of Christ, God makes his presence, his countenance, vividly manifest to men. In their person he addresses us, he offers us the standard of his kingdom, and we who are surrounded by so great a cloud of witnesses, such a proof of the Gospel's truth, are powerfully attracted to it.[5]

In its canonization process, the Church wants to make sure that those who are raised to the honors of the altar had either suffered martyrdom or, during life, had practiced such heroic virtue that they are worthy of emulation by the faithful. Among other qualities of heroic virtue are such features as cheerful endurance of great suffering, unflinching confidence in God in spite of all human expectations, and a selfless love of others in the face of trial and persecution.

That is one side of the Church's teaching on holiness. It is by now a vast library of hagiography. The printed life and letters of a single canonized saint may run to ten and more volumes in a modern edition. Besides this, however, another large body of writing on the spiritual life has been published under Catholic auspices, weaving the experience of the saints with the Church's revealed wisdom on the imitation of Christ. Most of this literature, by the saints and about sanctity, has been eminently practical and consciously directed to inform the faithful not only what holiness is but how it can be attained.

THE WAY OF THE SAINTS

It is not difficult to isolate the principal features of spiritual methodology in the Catholic tradition as capsulized in the writings of the great teachers of sanctity approved and recommended by the Church. They have varied at different periods of the Church's history only in accidentals since patristic times, when men like Sts. Basil and Gregory of Nyssa, Augustine and Jerome wrote letters of direction and extensive treatises on Christian asceticism and progress in the love of God.

Four elements stand out prominently and may be taken as pivotal in the Catholic understanding of how the faithful who are willing may grow in perfection and, with God's help, rise even to the heights of sanctity:

1. *The plan of God* for mankind in general and "for me" in particular must become deeply impressed on the consciousness of the believer.

2. *Self-knowledge* of one's sinfulness and weakness, as well as of virtue and strength, must be acquired at no matter what cost to pride and complacency, or to sloth and natural timidity.

3. *Practical decisions* must be made that affect one's personal and social behavior, and future commitment in the following of Christ.

4. *A program of life* must be adopted that will differ according to circumstances of person, time, and opportunity; but it should have about it a definite form and content, and a certain pattern of consistency.

On each of these aspects, ascetical and mystical masters have written a library, and the lives of the saints are the best commentary. Their ideas and experiences have become the patrimony of Catholic Christianity in its task of sanctifying the people of God.

DEEP AWARENESS OF THE PLAN OF GOD

The foundation of sanctity is the realization of God's plan for the human race, and then focusing this realization on myself. Without this prior conviction born of faith, the will and emotions are left to the chance impressions that cross the mind; but with this conviction, the pursuit of holiness is the most reasonable thing in the world.

> Man is created to praise, reverence, and serve God our Lord, and by this means to save his soul. The other things on the face of the earth are created for man to help him in attaining the end for which he is created.
> Hence, man is to make use of them in as far as they help him in the attainment of his end, and he must rid himself of them in as far as they prove a hindrance to him.
> Therefore, we must make ourselves indifferent to all created things, as far as we are allowed free choice and are not under any prohibition. Consequently, as far as we are concerned, we should not prefer health to sickness, riches to poverty, honor to dishonor, a long life to a short life. This same holds for all other things.
> Our one desire and choice should be what is more conducive to the end for which we are created.[6]

There should be no doubt that this plan of God is no mere construct of reason but rests on the premises of the Christian faith. Recognizing that man has a "bias" in the direction of things naturally pleasing, but not necessarily conducive to his last end, implies the existence of a fallen human nature, which is clearly a supernatural concept. Accordingly, the salvation of one's soul means the beatific vision; the praise and service of God involve the whole body of Christian faith and morals; "all the creatures of this earth," which are to assist man, include supernatural realities like the Church and the sacraments; and the acquisition of indifference requires the help of divine grace.

Internal Freedom. Of critical importance for sanctity is the acquisition of internal freedom, sometimes called "indifference," which means liberation from internal constraint, caused by an inordinate love or fear of created things. The immediate source of this internal pressure is concupiscence, both carnal and spiritual. In carnal concupiscence, where the sense appetite does not fully submit to the rational will, the latter inclines to embrace whatever pleases and shun whatever gives pain to the senses independently of right reason. In spiritual concupiscence the disorder is the same, except that here the will tends to seek whatever pleases and avoid whatever pains the spiritual faculties, the mind and will, independently of right reason and the teachings of faith. However, the final explanation of this conflict between subjective desire and objective good lies deeper than original sin, which deprived man of the gift of integrity; it is mysteriously bound up with man's condition in the state of probation, where he has the power of choice between moral good and evil.

There are two kinds of constraint that militate against freedom and, on occasion, may suppress it completely: the external coercion of physical force, of which there is no question here; and the internal compulsion of natural tendencies that desire satisfaction without subordination to higher values. The Church recognizes the power of these internal desires and therefore urges their habitual control as the *sine qua non* of Christian perfection. In proportion as a man frees himself from their tyranny, he enjoys indifference or liberty to follow what his mind, enlightened by revelation, tells him is most conducive to the end for which he was created.

Perfection of the "More." The comparative *more*, or its equivalent, lies at the heart of Christian perfection. It occurred in Christ's reminder that "Anyone who prefers father or mother to me is not worthy of me" (Mt. 10:37). It occurred again in the question of the rich young man who asked the Savior, after saying that he kept the Commandments, "What more do I need to do?" (Mt. 19:20). And it occurred again in the question asked by Jesus of Peter after the Resurrection, "Simon, son of John, do you love me more than these others do?" (Jn. 21:15).

As regards the quest for holiness, this expression so envisions our indifference that we choose and desire those things that lead us more to attain the end of our creation. It may be described as a statement of the perfection of indifference, following the doctrine of St. Thomas that "A man's soul is so much the more perfectly drawn to God as it is more detached from affection for temporal things." This is the end product of Christian spirituality, since "all the counsels by which we are invited to perfection have this end in view: that being detached from the love of earthly goods, our souls may tend more freely to God."[7]

Substitute "devotion" for "indifference" and you have the same doctrine expressed from another viewpoint. True devotion like true indifference is not mere passivity in the presence of creatures, allowing them to pound the will with opposition, nor mere stoicism, which resists their seductive attraction with no supernatural end in view. It is an active dynamism that positively seeks out those creatures that the mind, illumined by faith, determines are more conducive to the beatific vision. This implies that there are degrees of efficiency among creatures as instruments of sanctification, and that consequently it behooves us to train the mind for recognizing which are the more efficacious and to develop the will habitually to embrace them.

EFFECTIVE SELF-KNOWLEDGE

Honest and effective self-knowledge is not easy to acquire but, once achieved, it is a precious possession. The Gospels are filled with narratives and parables that remind us of how important sound self-appraisal is in the following of Christ, and what an insurmountable obstacle to perfection is the misjudgment on one's limitations or capacities.

Simon Peter presumed on his loyalty to Christ and, in spite of warning, went on to deny the Master; the prodigal son miscalculated his strength to cope with the temptations of the world, and ended up by dissipating his inheritance and becoming a wastrel; those who heard Christ's promise of the Eucharist underestimated their ability to accept his teaching, and ceased to be his disciples; the wicked and lazy servant in the parable of the talents went off and hid the money entrusted to him because he wrongly feared that he could not earn the interest that his master expected of him.

Progress in holiness begins with the realization that God has a providential plan for all mankind and a special vocation for me. I must be convinced that this plan is practicable and that somehow I am called upon to fulfill a place in that plan.

But that is not enough. No matter how attractive the prospect may be, I will not seriously undertake the road to sanctity until I have come to grips with myself on the two profoundest levels of my being; knowledge of where I presently stand with respect to creatures that stand between me and my God, and knowledge of how far I am willing to go in giving myself to God.

Self-Love and Detachment. Assuming that the object I possess is not inherently sinful, I can still be unduly attached to it, as may be recognized by certain signs. Some of these are external, and others can only be experienced internally.

The standard hierarchy of values—supernatural, spiritual, intellectual, and material—may be applied here. So that if, for example, I am more concerned with an intellectual project than with my spiritual obligations to the evident detriment of the latter, I ought to suspect undue affection for the former.

If I find myself habitually taking complacence in some possession, to the point where I tend to contemn or pity others for lacking what I have, this is a sign of inordinate self-love.

If I often lose peace of mind from definable or undefinable causes, on account of what I have or do, I am too attached to the object, person, or practice, since ordinate affection, being orderly, produces tranquillity of mind, which is the essence of peace.

If I am always afraid of losing or being hindered in the use of some gift or possession, or if I feel dissatisfied with what I have, whether its amount, quality, or perfection, I am too enamored of the object because the right kind of affection precludes such anxiety.

If I regularly talk about my achievement along certain lines or advertise what I have for no better reason than the pleasure I get from being recognized, this is a sign of disorder in the appetitive faculties.

If I am inclined to envy others for some kind of talent, production, or property that I feel outshines or obscures my own, this is a danger signal pointing to the need for greater self-control.

If I tend to be jealous of what I have, slow to share it with others, or fearful that others may acquire the same, I am overly in love with the creature, no matter how lawfully acquired or how holy the thing may be in itself.

The masters of Christian asceticism state without exception that the test of true detachment is the willingness either to keep or to put away a creature to which a person has become strongly attracted. Why, we ask, should this be so?

Whenever a creature produces an undue attraction, the fault must not be sought in the object as such, but rather in me, precisely because the same creature may be safely possessed by someone else without detriment or even with positive benefit to his spiritual life. Perhaps I have not received the grace necessary both to keep physically and spiritually to profit from the disturbing creature. Or I may be lacking, culpably or otherwise, in those qualities of mind and temperament needed to overcome the natural seductiveness of what disturbs my peace of mind. Or most certainly, the state of life to which God has called me makes demands on my generosity and self-sacrifice that cannot be properly fulfilled except at the cost of being freed of certain inordinate affections. In any case, there is no objective assurance of becoming volitionally detached unless I remove what stimulates the attachment, namely, the object itself. There is a limit to my ability to be exposed to the stimulus and to remain ordinately attached. And even this limit is unpredictable, undefinable, and uncertain. To make sure I am delivered of a troublesome affection, I must remove its stimulating source. The degree of my readiness to do this determines my sincerity.

Degrees of Generosity. Effective self-knowledge goes beyond the awareness of inordinate attachments and then taking resolute measures to cure them. There is the further need to look into one's generosity toward God, in order to test and inspire the will for complete dedication to the service of God.

Different saints in writing on the subject use different terms. Some speak of grades of friendship, others of intensity of love, others of humility, others of levels of generosity.

The first type of generosity means that quality of submission to the divine majesty that makes the will ready to sacrifice any created good, even life itself, rather than disobey a commandment of God binding under mortal sin. In terms of indifference, it requires habitual detachment at least from those creatures that may not be enjoyed without loss of sanctifying grace.

Another level of generosity is essentially higher. It presupposes the first and goes beyond it with a readiness to sacrifice anything rather than offend God by venial sin. Like the first, it also requires detachment from creatures, and not only from those which are sinful but to a certain extent also from such as may legitimately be used without sin. This doctrine is in full accord with Catholic tradition, that our fallen human nature requires not a few practices that are not strictly obligatory, hence of counsel, if we are to avoid mortal sin, and a fortiori venial offenses against God.

Is there a still more generous response to God's will? Or does holiness stop with merely avoiding sin? Christian holiness aspires to nothing less than the willingness to suffer out of love for Christ.

The essence of this ideal of sanctity consists in preferring what is difficult. This is done simply out of love for Christ, in order to be more like him in poverty, humiliation, and the cross. Unlike the lesser degrees of generosity, the reasonableness of my attitude here is not so apparent, and except for the light of faith it would be quite unintelligible.

Subjectively the motive for practicing this kind of generosity is sheer love. This is expressed in the desire to be conformed to Christ, the spouse of an ardent soul. No other reason is sought and none is demanded. But objectively there is a deep reason why an earnest follower of Christ should wish to imitate him in want and ignominy. It is the purpose of all pain and suffering, which is reparative and expiatory: reparative in restoring the honor that is owing to God's offended majesty, and expiatory in removing the stain of guilt and debt of punishment that the sinner has incurred.

If I am looking for a reason to prefer poverty to riches and contempt to honor, I have it in my love for Christ. Love is by nature assimilable; it desires to be like the one loved. If I ask further why Christ "for the joy set before him chose the cross," I find it in the mystery of the Redemption. It was the will of his heavenly Father that the world should be redeemed not only by the Incarnation, but in the historical atmosphere of suffering and pain. In obedience to his Father, Christ chose to save the human race by enduring poverty, rejection, opposition, and finally the disgrace of crucifixion although, absolutely speaking, the Redemption might have been accomplished without pain. That Christ preferred this method of saving the world shows his wisdom in proving how much he loves us and how much we mean to him; it also invites us to follow his example and prove our love for him in return.

But the imitation of Christ in his suffering implies more than a way of proving our love for him. It releases an energy that promotes the salvation of the world. The fact is a matter of faith; the explanation must be sought in the doctrine of the Mystical Body. For although the earthly life of Christ and his death more than sufficiently atoned for the sins of mankind, nevertheless by a "marvelous disposition of divine wisdom, we may complete those things that are wanting in the sufferings of Christ in our own flesh, for his body, which is the Church." The mystical identification of Christ with his members makes possible the application of his merits, gained by tribulation, to individual souls, beginning with our own and extending to all humanity, not only on earth but also in purgatory; and not only in the

Church but also outside the Mystical Body. It was on this basis that Pius XI placed the effectiveness of reparation to the Sacred Heart. "In the degree to which our oblation and sacrifice more perfectly correspond to the sacrifice of our Lord; that is, to the extent to which we have immolated love of self and our passions and crucified our flesh in that mystical crucifixion of which the Apostle writes, so much the more plentiful fruits of propitiation and expiation will be gained for ourselves and for others."[8]

The same idea was expressed from another viewpoint by Pius XII, in urging the imitation of Christ suffering for the benefit of the Mystical Body and the salvation of the modern world. Although Christ's passion and death merited for the Church an infinite treasure of mercy, "God's inscrutable providence has decreed that these abundant graces should not be granted us all at once; and the amount of grace to be given depends in no small part also on our good deeds. They draw to the souls of men this ready flow of heavenly gifts granted by God. These heavenly gifts will surely flow more abundantly if we not only pray fervently to God . . . but if we also set our hearts on eternal treasures rather than the passing things of this world, restrain this mortal body by voluntary mortification, denying it what is forbidden, forcing it to do what is hard and distasteful, and finally accept as from God's hands the burdens and sorrows of this present life." If there was never a time when the salvation of souls did not oblige us to associate our sufferings with those of the Redeemer, "that duty is clearer than ever today when a cosmic struggle has set almost the whole world on fire," and only Christ in his members can save it.[9]

PRACTICAL DECISIONS

The logic of Christian spirituality is very simple. Knowledge of God and of self give the bases for an intelligent decision to love God according to his manifest will. Depending on how strongly a person is convinced, he has the ground for a clear and generous choice to give himself to the service of the divine majesty.

While the role of decision-making in the spiritual life has been recognized since New Testament times, it became more prominent since the sixteenth century, and today it is assumed in all Catholic writing on Christian perfection. One reason for the renewed emphasis was no doubt the challenge of the Reformation, when the Church was constrained to face the critical question of human freedom in relation to divine grace.

In the Catholic tradition, holiness has always been mainly and pre-eminently the result of God's gracious mercy. "You have not chosen me but I have chosen you" is written large across the portals of the Church's history of sanctity. Nevertheless, though divine grace is prior and paramount, it is not isolated from man's free response and much less coercive of his deeply personal liberty. No doubt Christ called the apostles to follow him, but they had to decide to follow him. Their commitment was the answer to his vocation. And the tasks to which he called them became their mission from him to the world they were to evangelize in his name.

PROGRAM OF LIFE

Holiness can be many things, but those who wished to serve God with true devotion always decided on some program of life that gave their resolution a form of permanency and was characterized by a certain degree of constancy and even regularity.

This is easier to see in the case of those who either choose to enter the religious state or resolve to be more faithful in living out its demanding self-sacrifice. The very term "regular life" implies certain rules (*regulae*) that those who enter a religious institute bind themselves to practice. And the less familiar Rule when referring to the Rules of Sts. Augustine, Benedict, Dominic, or Francis says what is common knowledge, that each of these religious families has a mode of life that is particularized by certain requirements affecting the forms of prayer, life style, and works in the apostolate. Schools of spirituality, e.g., Benedictine or Franciscan, are also historically derived from these varied Rules of the great founders and foundresses of religious communities.

Less obvious is the need of something similar for persons striving after Christian perfection in the world.

It is here that Francis de Sales' contribution to Catholic life and piety has been so great. He foresaw, with the gradual urbanization that tends to alienate individuals and fragment their families, the need for each believer's personal decision to put some definable form into his service of God while living in the amorphous civilization of modern society.

Early in his *Introduction to a Devout Life,* he made it plain that devotion (or holiness) is not only compatible with every vocation and profession but is within the reach of every Christian who is willing to make the effort, which in practice often means is willing to take the time.

> True devotion does no harm whatever, but rather gives perfection to all things. But when it goes contrary to our lawful vocation, then without doubt it is false.
>
> It is an error, or rather a heresy, to try to banish the devout life from the ranks of the armed forces, the shop of the mechanic, the halls of secular rulers, or the homes of married people. It is true that a purely contemplative, monastic, and religious devotion cannot be practiced in these walks of life. But besides these, there are other forms that are suited to bring to perfection those who live in the secular state.

After recalling such figures as Abraham, Isaac, Jacob, David, Sarah, Rebecca, and Judith in the Old Testament, and the numerous lay persons mentioned by St. Paul, Francis de Sales concludes, "It has even happened that some have prospered among the multitude, which seems so unfavorable to holiness, better than in solitude." The secret is to do God's will, since "wherever we are, we can and should aspire to a life of perfection."[10]

Regular Prayer. Daily prayer at regular times is paramount. All Catholic writers on the spiritual life agree that there should be daily mental prayer, if only for a few minutes, at certain times when a person is sure of being freed from other duties, and there ought to be some system to prayer, particularly for beginners. Most writers recommend various simplified forms of meditation. They tend to reduce all prayer to a consideration of our Lord, either by thinking of him in one of his mysteries, or by speaking with him simply in meditation on the Gospels or the mysteries of faith, or by a simple repose in God, sharing with him whatever is on our minds and conversing with him as a child would talk with a loving father or mother.

The saints placed great emphasis on frequent short prayers to God during the day. "Admire his beauty, invoke his aid, cast yourself in spirit at the foot of his cross, adore his goodness, often inquire of him concerning your salvation; a thousand times in the day offer your soul to him, fix your inward eyes on his kindness, hold out your hand to him as a child to its Father." Then anticipating objections from busy people, we are told, "Such prayers may be interwoven with all our business and occupations without hindering them in the slightest degree. Indeed, our spiritual pursuits are rather helped than hindered by such pauses in spirit and short devotions of the soul."[11] Pious aspirations are a form of true meditative prayer. Without them we cannot live a contemplative life really well, and we make but a poor business of the active life.

Examens of Conscience. A cursory reading of what spiritual masters say about examination of conscience reveals a number of simple facts. They recommend two kinds of examen, a general and particular. Where the general examen covers all our defects or potential virtues, the particular concentrates on one fault or virtue for a definite length of time.

Modern psychology emphasizes the need for specifying the act of will for maximum volitional activity. As a general rule, the more definite a prospective course of action, the more effectively will it be put into execution. The lag and discrepancy between resolution and achievement are common experience. How to make the real more closely approach the ideal? Superficially, it would seem that the more earnest our resolutions, the better results we can expect. Yet, without minimizing the importance of energetic beginnings, the main factor is sustained motivation, whether I resolve on a series of actions like the practice of charitable speech, or a single act like the acceptance of a grave humiliation. In either case, what I need at the time the performance is due are clear motives in the shape of strong convictions that this should be done and this is the way to do it. Here the examination of conscience becomes indispensable. If I have resolutely decided on avoiding sharp criticism whenever I am crossed, this judgment becomes a thought pattern in my life, which I re-enforce every time I make an internal review. There comes an occasion that provokes my patience, and immediately I recall the decision to control myself and keep my tongue—supported by all the motives that I have placed behind the resolution.

However, the previous examination of future acts does more than guarantee motivation for the will. It also supplies planning for the mind. If I have carefully thought through a specific action I want to perform, when the time comes for doing it, I know what I am supposed to do. Being charitable to a difficult person may involve more than biting my tongue. It may require diplomacy to avoid needless exposure to irritating situations; it may call for speaking kindly to the very man who would normally provoke me; it will always require some adaptation to circumstances that I can wisely anticipate and master because of my anticipation.

It may come as a surprise that the daily examination of conscience is so highly regarded by the Church as an instrument of sanctification for all classes of people in every station of life.

Priests and clerics in general are urged to make a daily examination of conscience, which Pius XII called "the most efficacious means we have for taking account of our spiritual life during the day, for removing the obstacles which hinder our spiritual life or retard one's progress in virtue, and for determining on the most suitable means to assure to our ministry greater fruitfulness and to implore from the heavenly Father indulgence upon so many of our deeds wretchedly done."[12] The Second Vatican Council underlined the importance of this practice.

Religious institutes of men and women universally provide an appointed time each day for examination of conscience. Some of the most practical directives left by the founders elaborated on the merits of this practice.

Less familiar is the practice of regular examination of conscience among the laity. "It is a spiritual and ascetic practice of supreme importance, which we will do well to hold in honor."[13]

One important observation, however, on the areas of self-reflection that people ought to make. We should always give preference to those virtues that are most incumbent on us, and not on those that are most agreeable to our inclinations. Every station in life imposes some peculiar obligations: different virtues are incumbent on a priest, a religious, an employer, an employee. Parents have their duties, and children theirs, and although all should practice every virtue, still each should seek chiefly to advance in those required by the state of life to which God has called him. Growth in Christian perfection means first of all fidelity to the duties of one's position in life. To neglect these duties in favor of something more appealing or more showy is to expose Christian piety to ridicule and defeat the Gospel role of sanctity as a witness light to the world.

As the faithful grow spiritually according to their respective states of life, they become correspondingly effective in bringing Christ to others. This is especially true of the laity, to whom the latest ecumenical council addressed the most extensive document in conciliar history on their responsibility in the apostolate:

> In the Church there is a diversity of ministry but oneness of mission. Christ conferred on the Apostles and their successors the duty of teaching, sanctifying, and ruling in his name and power. But the laity, made sharers in the priestly, prophetic, and royal office of Christ, discharge their own roles in the mission of the whole people of God in the Church and in the world. They carry out this apostolic work by their efforts to evangelize and sanctify mankind. They carry it out as they labor to infuse the whole range of things belonging to this world with the spirit of the Gospel.[14]

Since infusing others assumes that the apostle himself is imbued with the spirit of the Gospel, the more holy are the faithful, the more successfully will they sanctify the world in which they live.

PART THREE

RITUAL AND WORSHIP

XII. THE LITURGY

Few aspects of contemporary Catholic life are more prominent than the sacred liturgy. This is partly due to the numerous changes introduced into liturgical practice by the Second Vatican Council. But it is mainly the result of a growing awareness of the importance of the liturgy in the Catholic Church. People are coming to realize that orthodoxy should truly mean "right worship." Fidelity to Christ and his teachings is therefore assured if believers remain faithful in the worship of God that the Savior bequeathed, through the apostles, to the Church he founded.

The Council's extensive doctrine on the liturgy marks a turning point in the history of Roman Catholicism. It is a courageous response to the expectations created by an evolutionary age, and a timely answer to the demands for increased light and strength in the communitarian age. On both counts, the liturgy offers great promise to help the Church progress, according to God's designs, and to preserve the Church, in Christ's words, as a kingdom that is not of this world.

NATURE OF THE LITURGY

The original Greek term *leitourgia* (from *leōs* [people] and *ergon* [work]) was used of any public duty or service. But by the time of the Greek translation of the Old Testament in the third century before Christ, it had come to apply particularly to the services in the Temple. Liturgy in present-day usage refers to the official public worship of the Church, and is thus distinguished from private devotion. Within this ambit of the Church's service, it is the special title of the Eucharist and the administration of the sacraments with the annexed use of the sacramentals.

The clearest way to understand the liturgy is to see it as the exercise now on earth of Christ's priestly office, as distinct from the Church's teaching, which is Jesus continuing his prophetic ministry, and the Church's rule and moral guidance, by which the Savior lives among his people as Christ the King. Since the priestly work of Christ concerns itself with worship and man's sanctification, we should expect the liturgy to be specially directed toward giving due honor to God and making the faithful more holy and pleasing to God.

These two aspects of the liturgy are inseparable. Worship denotes a kind of honor, which in turn is a sign of esteem given a person for his excellence. But in religious matters, worship adds to honor or esteem the sense of one's own inferiority and subjection with respect to the person honored. Since God is the Supreme Being and the Absolute Lord of the universe, to him is due worship in the highest degree. The technical name for the worship of God is adoration or latreutic worship (from the ancient Greek word *latreia,* which meant the service given to the gods). The lesser form of veneration given to the angels and saints that Catholicism recognizes has the theological name of dulia (from the Greek term *douleia,* which means the respect shown to a master by his servant). The Blessed Virgin is said to be honored with hyperdulia, i.e., a higher form of what is essentially the same veneration paid to other creatures among the saints but in essence unlike the adoration given only to God.

How are worship and the liturgy related? They are related in the sense that the ultimate purpose of the liturgy is to glorify God by giving him the honor to which he has a right as man's Creator and final destiny. Consequently, whether the liturgical worship is one of adoration or thanksgiving, of contrition or love, or even of petition, the heart of the liturgy is God-centered and God-directed. When we adore him, we acknowledge his infinity and all-perfection; when we thank him, we are grateful for benefits received; when we are contrite, we are sorry for having offended him; when we love him, we acknowledge his goodness and seek to please him; and when we ask for blessings, we are declaring his sovereign dominion and our complete dependence for the least favor from his hands. In all of these responses we are worshiping God.

The correlative side of worship is sanctification. Since the essence of holiness consists of union with God, worship is already a form of holiness, because through it we freely unite ourselves with God, conversing with him and being in contact, as only spirit can touch Spirit, with the author of our being and the final goal of all our desires.

But holiness is also God's coming to man with his grace, with that supernatural presence of the divinity that penetrates the human person and makes it, as the Gospels and St. Paul tell us, like unto God. This is also an essential function of the liturgy, and the word "function" is helpful in order to distinguish it from the foundation of the liturgy, which is the worship of God.

Having covered these preliminaries, we are now in a better position to see how the Church understands the liturgy when analyzed in its principal components. What is the liturgy? "The sacred liturgy is the public worship which our Redeemer as head of the Church renders to the Father as well as the worship which the community of the faithful renders to its Founder, and through him to the heavenly Father. It is, in short, the worship rendered by the Mystical Body of Christ in the entirety of its head and members."[1] Needless to say, this definition is comprehensive and calls for some explanation.

Public Worship. It is unquestionably a fundamental duty of man to direct his whole life and activity toward God. Man does so when he responds freely to the divine being in those postures of the human heart that God expects of his creatures—in a word, when he practices religion, which is simply but sublimely the virtue of justice toward God.

This responsibility is first of all incumbent on us as individuals, each being bound to render homage to God according to our native capacity and the gifts of grace we have received. But the duty also binds the community of the human race, grouped as we are by mutual social ties. Not only man but also mankind is to worship God.

The Old Testament bears eloquent witness to the communal worship that Yahweh expected of his people. He made extensive provision for sacred rites and determined the regulations to be observed by the Israelites in rendering him the honor he ordained. He established a variety of sacrifices and designated the exact ceremonies with which they were to be offered him. His prescriptions on such matters as the Ark of the Covenant, the Temple, and the holy days were minute and very clear. He established a sacerdotal tribe with its high priest, and specified and described the vestments with which the sacred ministers were to be clothed (Lv. 24:1–8).

All of this, however, was a foreshadowing of the worship that the high priest of the New Covenant was to render to his heavenly

Father and in which he wished those who believe in his name to join as members of the Christian community.

During his stay on earth, Christ spent his mortal life in the exercise of his priestly ministry, from the moment of the Incarnation, when he came into the world to do the will of the Father, to the moment when he expired on the cross and commended his soul into the hands of the same Father, after he had finished the work he was sent to perform.

But this was not all. As Roman Catholicism understands the liturgy, it is God's will that the worship that Christ instituted and practiced during his stay on earth shall continue ever afterward without any intermission. As he told the apostles at the Last Supper, he would not leave mankind orphans. He continues to give us the support of his powerful and unfailing intercession as our advocate with the Father. He continues to give us the outpouring of his grace through the Church which, "by his sacrifice on the cross, he founded, consecrated, and confirmed forever."[2]

Christian liturgical practice began with the very founding of the Church. The believers "remained faithful to the teaching of the Apostles, to the brotherhood, to the breaking of bread, and to the prayers" (Ac. 2:42). Whenever their pastors could summon a group together, the faithful set up an altar on which they proceeded to offer the sacrifice and around which were ranged all the other rites appropriate for giving honor to God and the sanctification of souls.

The description in the early verses of the Acts of the Apostles indicates that, side by side with the Eucharist, a common meal was also celebrated. This meal was certainly the custom at Corinth, but there it led to abuses that St. Paul had to correct. "When you hold these meetings," he told them, "it is not the Lord's Supper that you are eating, since when the time comes to eat everyone is in such a hurry to start his own supper that one person goes hungry while another is getting drunk" (1 Co. 11:20–21).

Again, we know that the Lord's Supper was celebrated at Troas by St. Paul. It was the first day of the week (Sunday) when the faithful were gathered together for the breaking of bread. Paul, who was the first to depart the next day, was speaking to the brethren and continued his discourse until midnight. In the upper room in which the meeting was taking place, many lamps were lit. In the course of the apostle's long sermon, a young man named Eutyches went to sleep. He fell from the third floor to the ground and was picked up dead. Paul went down, took him in his arms, and brought him back to life. Then Paul returned, broke bread, ate, and conversed with the brethren until daybreak.

The vigil was unusually prolonged on that occasion because of the imminent departure of St. Paul, but this fact did not make any change in the character of the liturgical assembly. The breaking of bread was its central feature; it took place on Sunday, the day specially assigned for the celebration of the Eucharist (Ac. 20:5–12).

These and similar texts enable us to see how from the time of the apostles the command of the Lord, "Do this in memory of me," was carried out, and already we see here the outline of the liturgy that was very shortly to develop. Some writers have endeavored to distinguish between two different types of apostolic Eucharist. They suggest that in the accounts of the Acts concerning Jerusalem and Troas, we have a brotherly meal, a symbol of the union of Christians with each other and with Jesus; in the letter to the Corinthians we have a sacrificial meal, wholly penetrated with the memory of the death of the Lord. This hypothesis, which would divide the Eucharist, is not favored by the numerous documents of the Church, whether conciliar or papal, that treat of the apostolic liturgy.

St. Paul did not invent the twofold aspect of the Eucharistic liturgy, as the sacrifice in which Christ's sacrifice is renewed, and as the mystery of union by which the faithful grow in their love of Christ and, through him, in their love of one another. He received this, as he said, from the Lord (1 Co. 11:23–27).

Although from the beginning we see only one Eucharist, we can already distinguish in the liturgy the two great dogmas of the Incarnation and the Redemption. The Son of God present in us, uniting us to himself and to others, is one of the main themes of St. John, brought out with striking clarity in the two discourses of Christ at Capernaum and after the Last Supper. St. Paul, on the other hand, chiefly dwells on the fact that the Son of God died for us and, in the Eucharist, unites us to his sacrifice.

From apostolic times on, in the whole history of the liturgy, we can follow these two doctrinal currents. They will never be isolated from each other, but they will lead the Church's mystics and saints to contemplate by preference either our life-giving union with the "bread which has come down from heaven," or else our participation in his death, in the communion of our sufferings with the "blood of the Covenant."

As circumstances and the needs of the faithful required, public worship was organized, developed, and enriched by new rites, ceremonies, and regulations. But always there was a single end in view, as stated by St. Augustine, "that we may use the external signs to keep us alert, learn from them what distance we have come along the road, and by them be heartened to go on further with more eager step; for the effect will be more precious the warmer the affection which precedes it."[3]

As the Church's life and ecclesiastical forms expanded and accommodated to different cultures and times, there remained this one dominant fact: "The priesthood of Jesus Christ is a living and continuous reality through all the ages and to the end of time, since the liturgy is nothing more nor less than the exercise of this priestly ministry" of the Savior.[4]

United with its divine head and animated by his priestly Spirit, the Church is forever present among the faithful ministering to their needs. This ministration through the sacraments comes in seven stages, whose essential nature and number Catholics believe was determined by the Savior during his visible stay on earth.

They begin by entering what the councils call "the door of the Church," whose name was derived from the fact that the more common manner of administration was by immersion (Greek *baptizein,* to dip in water). Thus "the faithful are incorporated into the Church by baptism. They are assigned by its character a place in the worship of the Christian religion. They are reborn as children of God and obliged to profess before men the faith which they have received from God through the Church."

From apostolic times, Christians were further strengthened in their union with Christ and his Church; hence it was "made more complete by the sacrament of confirmation." Its function is to "enrich them with the special strength of the Holy Spirit and gives them a stricter obligation to act as true witnesses of Christ by spreading and defending the faith by word and deed."

At the apex of the liturgy has always been the Eucharist. "When they share the Eucharistic sacrifice, the source and culmination of all Christian life, they offer the divine victim to God and themselves with him." Yet, always too the faithful were reminded that this is a liturgy, hence a public act of worship that is to be performed together. "Thus with no confusion, but each in his own way, they all serve their own part in the liturgical action at the sacrificial offering and communion. Moreover, when they have had Christ's body for their refreshment at the sacred gathering, they are a concrete demonstration of the union of God's people, of which this august sacrament is the appropriate sign and the marvelously effective instrument."

Christ provided for the Church to continue his own ministry of forgiveness through the sacrament that was once called a "second baptism," for those who had sinned grievously after their baptism with water. Since earliest times, "those who approach the sacrament of penance win, by God's mercy, pardon for the offense done to him. At the same time they are reconciled with the Church, which their sin had injured and which, with charity, good example, and prayers, is working for their conversion."

What until recent years was known as extreme unction, is now appropriately called the holy anointing of the sick. In this sacrament, "with the prayer of the priests, the whole Church recommends the sick to the Lord, who suffered and has been glorified, asking him to give them relief and salvation. It goes further and calls upon them to associate themselves freely with the passion and death of Christ and in this way to make their contribution to the good of God's people."

No less than in the Old Testament, so in the New, not all are called to the priestly state. But "those among the faithful who are marked by holy order are appointed in the name of Christ to feed the Church with God's word and his grace," through the sacraments that they are empowered by Christ to administer in his name.

Roman Catholicism conspicuously maintains that marriage is not only a state of life pleasing to God but that Christ, before the Ascension, established it as a sacrament of the New Law. In this way, "the sacrament of matrimony makes Christian couples the sign of the mystery of the unity and fertile love existing between Christ and the Church, and gives them a share in this mystery. By its power they are a help to each other in the married life, in the acceptance of children and giving them an education in holiness. Thus they have their special gift among the people of God in their station of life and their own rank. This married life is the start of the family. In the family, human society's new citizens are born, whom baptism, by the power of the Holy Spirit, makes into children of God to provide for the perpetuation of God's people throughout the ages."[5]

With the assistance of all these sacramental means, the faithful are able to grow in holiness no matter what their vocation in life, even as they are giving to God the worship he requires. Their share in this bifocal function is, indeed, a liturgy because it is a "service of the people," in which the Church is publicly involved as the believing community.

Exterior and Interior Worship. It might seem needless for the Church to insist that the worship of God rendered by the Church should be both interior and exterior. But historically there are good reasons for the stress, especially in our day.

There has been an ebb and flow in the Church's long lifetime in the way people responded to the liturgy. At one time circumstances would arise when the external, i.e., sensibly perceptible, side of Catholic worship was emphasized, as happened in the sixteenth century, when the Council of Trent safeguarded the objective validity of the Mass and sacraments as divinely instituted channels of grace. At another time, the interior dispositions were emphasized in order to bring home to the faithful that the liturgy is not some magical ritual that confers divine blessings irrespective of the faith or virtue of those who participate. It was this latter aspect of the liturgy that came under such close scrutiny at the Second Vatican Council.

It would be a mistake, however, to undervalue the "external" side of the liturgy. Since the nature of man is a composition of body and soul, we should expect Christ to provide for man's worship of God and sanctification by God through such media as correspond to man's bodily nature. Likewise, we know from revelation that while we recognize God visibly, we are drawn by him to the love of things unseen. Then, too, every impulse of the human heart expresses itself naturally through the senses. It is only proper therefore that, since the worship of God concerns not only individuals but the whole community of mankind, it should be social; but this would be impossible unless religious activity is also organized and manifested outwardly. Finally, exterior worship reveals and emphasizes the unity of the Mystical Body, feeds as it were new fuel to its holy zeal, fortifies its energy, and intensifies its action day by day. Although it is true enough that "the ceremonies themselves can claim no perfection or sanctity in their own right, they are, nevertheless, the outward acts of religion, designed to rouse the heart, like so many signals, to veneration of the sacred realities, and to raise the mind to meditation on the supernatural. They serve to foster piety, to kindle the flame of charity, to increase our faith and deepen our devotion. They provide instruction for ordinary people, an appealing beauty for divine worship, continuity of religious practice. They make it possible to tell genuine Christians from their false or heretical counterparts."[6]

It we keep in mind that worship is external because it is visible and, unless it were visible, it could not be either corporate or communal, we begin to see how indispensable are the so-called externals of the liturgy. They are exterior only in the profoundly mysterious sense that they are perceptible by the senses; but they are not for that reason peripheral to man's approach to God or to God's communication to man, no more than Christ's very "external" body was peripheral to the redemptive work of the Son of God.

Nevertheless, the chief element of divine worship must be interior. Christ made this plain on several occasions, but never more pointedly than when the Pharisees and scribes complained about the disciples who were eating with unclean hands, contrary to the customs devised by certain ritual extremists. Christ not only defended his disciples but quoted the Old Testament to show how much more important are the interior dispositions than preoccupation with details and, in this case, unwarranted minutiae of external rites (Mk. 7:6–8).

Christ was not criticizing adherence to external liturgical forms, which he personally observed according to the Mosaic code. He castigated those who add to the divinely authorized prescriptions of worship their own human inventions and, with vehemence, those who pretend to honor God with nothing but neat and well-turned phrases, like actors in a theater, and consider themselves perfectly able to reach heaven without plucking such inveterate vices as envy, pride, and injustice from their hearts. It is consequently "essential that the faithful should come to the liturgy in the right frame of mind, suiting their thoughts to their voices and co-operating with the grace from on high, lest they receive in vain."[7]

Under the Hierarchy of the Church. While implicit in the fact that the liturgy is public worship, its dependence on the Church's hierarchy is so distinctively Catholic as almost to define its essence. This is more than a dependence on regulation or surveillance. It means that the liturgy is bound up with the apostolic hierarchy established by Christ in such a way that, except for the hierarchy, there would be no public worship as Catholicism understands the liturgy.

> Only to the Apostles, and thenceforth to those on whom their successors imposed hands, is granted the power of the priesthood, in virtue of which they represent the person of Jesus Christ before their people, acting at the same time as representatives of their people before God.
>
> This priesthood is not transmitted by heredity or human descent. It does not emanate from the Christian community. It is not a delegation from the people. Prior to acting as representative of the community before the throne of God, the priest is the ambassador of the divine Redeemer. He is God's vicegerent in the midst of the flock precisely because Jesus Christ is head of that body of which Christians are members. The power entrusted to him, therefore, bears no resemblance to anything human.[8]

Given this postulate of the faith, it is evident why the visible, earthly priesthood of the Savior is not handed down indiscriminately to all members of the Church but is conferred on designated men, through what has been appropriately called the spiritual generation of holy orders. As one of the seven sacraments, it not only imparts the grace suitable for the clerical ministry and state of life, but also confers an indelible "character" besides. The sacred minister is thus conformed to Jesus Christ the priest and uniquely qualified to perform those official acts of religion by which the faithful are sanctified and God is duly glorified in keeping with the divine laws and regulations.

Since the priest is so inextricably bound up with the ecclesiastical hierarchy, from whom his ordination is derived and on whom the exercise of his ministry relies, it is no wonder that the priestly functions of the liturgy are said to depend on the Church's authority. Nothing could be clearer than the statement of Ignatius of Antioch, at the turn of the first century. "Let no one," he warned, "do anything touching the Church, apart from the bishop. Let that celebration of the Eucharist be considered valid which is held under the bishop or anyone to whom he has committed it. Where the bishop appears, there let the people be, just as where Jesus Christ is, there is the Catholic Church."[9]

But there is another reason why the liturgy depends on ecclesiastical authority. The worship of God is a continuous profession of Catholic faith and a continuous exercise of hope and charity. In the sacred liturgy, the participants profess the Catholic faith explicitly and openly, not only in the actual celebration of the Eucharist and administration of the sacraments, but also by the recitation or singing of the Creed, the reading of the Scriptures, and by listening to the explanation of the word of God. The whole liturgical ensemble, therefore, has the Catholic faith for its content, which the Church believes has been entrusted for preservation and interpretation to the successors of the apostles under the bishop of Rome.

ADAPTATION AND DEVELOPMENT

The Church's authority in divine worship has not only organized or regulated the liturgy. As was less obvious before Vatican II, the hierarchy can also modify what is considered less relevant, remove what may have become outmoded, and add what the bishops in union with Rome believe will increase the honor paid to Christ and the Holy Trinity or instruct and better inspire the Christian people in their service of God.

Trent and Second Vatican. The two principal large-scale changes in ritual legislation that reflected liturgical development took place in the sixteenth century at the time of the Council of Trent and in the twentieth century at the Second Council of the Vatican. Both developments illustrate the Church's organic vitality, since it is able to make extraordinary adjustments in external practice and discipline while keeping intact the substance of divine worship as revealed by Jesus Christ.

In the sixteenth century the grave need was to produce some semblance of liturgical unity in a forest of competing multiplicity. There were literally scores of different rites, numerous prefaces, countless feasts, and a bewildering complexity of diocesan and national customs that at least partially occasioned the Protestant Reformation. These were gradually coalesced and unified, and for the next four hundred years greatly contributed to strengthening the unity of Catholic Christendom.

In the twentieth century the felt need was to expand and diversify what the Church recognized as an existing unity. The resulting changes covered a broad variety of adaptations to modern times.

The ecumenical movement helped Catholics to rediscover the

Bible and use it in the liturgy in a way comparable to pre-Reformation times. Consequently the main focus of the liturgy of the future is to be biblical, "for it is from the Scriptures that lessons are read, that actions and signs derive their meaning," and from which most of the ritual prayers and sayings have come.

Catholic worship should correspond to the communitarian age in which we live. No doubt the Church's rites are, in a sense, public and social by nature. But this fact should now be more actually manifest. Therefore, whenever the rites in question make "provision for communal celebration, involving the presence and active participation of the faithful, this way of celebrating them is to be preferred, as far as possible, to a celebration that is individual and quasi-private." Both factors are necessary to make the ritual communal: physical presence of an assembly, and the audiovisual involvement of the people.

The meaning of the word "hierarchical" that should apply to the liturgy as the faithful more actively participate is harmonious co-operation. Unlike other forms of prayer, even though organized, the liturgy should include persons who are exercising different functions on diversified levels—something like the combined melody in a musical symphony, where each member has a share in the production of a masterful whole. Everyone does his part, but no more. So, too, "in liturgical celebrations each person, minister or layman, in the performance of his office, is to do all that and only that which belongs to him from the nature of things and the rules of liturgy." If beauty is that which appeals on being seen, and if orderly functions are spontaneously appealing, public worship becomes more beautiful as more people contribute their part in a co-ordinated praise of the divine majesty.

No doubt the primary purpose of the liturgy is to worship God and thereby sanctify those who participate. But the faithful are also to learn from the Church's ritual, "for in the liturgy God speaks to his people and Christ is still proclaiming his Gospel." A variety of corollaries follow. Ritual prayers and symbols should be marked by a "noble simplicity" and normally should not require much explanation. Since the Bible is the best source of instruction, "there is to be more reading from Holy Scripture," and that more varied and suitable for different circumstances and times. The sermon must become an essential "part of the liturgical service," and its contents should draw "mainly from scriptural and liturgical sources."[10]

Vernacular was introduced into the liturgy on an unprecedented scale. Since language is one of the principal expressions of a society's culture, the Church decided to permit the use of the native language of the people alongside the Latin in the Roman rites. It is instructive in this connection to compare the teaching of Trent with that of Vatican II. In their declaration on the Eucharistic liturgy, the bishops at Trent stated, "Although the Mass contains much instruction for the faithful, it has nevertheless not seemed expedient to the Fathers that it be celebrated everywhere in the vernacular." They even condemned "anyone who says that the Mass ought to be celebrated in the vernacular only."[11] This attitude was understandable in the circumstances of those days, when Latin in the liturgy became the target of spirited opposition on the part of those who charged Rome with keeping the word of God closed within clerical circles and unavailable to the people. The decision to make Latin universally mandatory in the Roman rite was a wise one. It helped to preserve the Church's unity of faith and gave Catholics a sense of solidarity with their coreligionists throughout the world.

By the twentieth century, the situation had sufficiently altered to warrant the twenty-first ecumenical council's stress on the vernacular. First a general principle: "The use of Latin is to be maintained in the Latin rites, except where some special law obtains." Then a change:

> However, in the Mass, the administration of the sacraments, and other parts of the liturgy, the use of the vernacular cannot infrequently be very useful for the people. Therefore, it would be well to grant it some considerable place. . . . The decision about the use of the vernacular rests with the competent territorial authority of the Church.[12]

Always, of course, the translation of the official Latin text has to be finally approved by the Holy See. Moreover, even while giving wide scope to the use of the vernacular, "provision should be made to see that the faithful can say or sing together in Latin those parts of the Ordinary of the Mass that concerns them."

Allowing the use of the native language was really part of a larger decision made by the Church to adapt the liturgy to the culture and traditions of different people. The general principle from now on would be that "the Church has no wish to impose a rigid uniformity in matters that do not implicate the faith or the good of the whole community." This was not a new idea, as testified by the number of different rites in the Catholic Church, e.g., the Alexandrian used in Egypt and Ethiopia or the Byzantine among the Greeks, Russians, and Ukrainians.

Actually, the Council was looking into the future with the prospect of new nations and peoples being evangelized and entering the Church. Whenever possible, their "genius and talents" (culture) and "way of life" (tradition) are to remain unchanged and even admitted into the liturgy, provided they are "not indissolubly bound up with superstition and error" and "harmonize with the true and authentic spirit" of Catholic Christianity.[13] New rites were envisioned as the work of evangelization of peoples gained momentum in the Church's missionary outreach to the world.

Development of Doctrine.   Changes in the Church's liturgical customs are not only the result of prudent adaptation to the times or modification of external practices in order to increase the people's devotion and vitalize their active participation in divine worship; they are also sometimes the logical outgrowth of a genuine development of doctrine that calls for corresponding expression in appropriate liturgical forms.

The number of these developments has not been large, if we were to "count" the respective dogmas of faith. But then it is more accurate to speak of general areas of revealed truth and, in this sense, the progress has been considerable. Five major areas of the faith have shown such development:

> As Catholic doctrine on the Incarnate Word of God, the Eucharistic sacrament and sacrifice, and Mary the Mother of God came to be determined with greater certitude and clarity, new ritual forms were introduced through which the acts of the liturgy proceeded to reproduce this brighter light from the decrees of the teaching authority of the Church, and so to reflect this light that it might reach the hearts and minds of Christ's people more effectively.[14]

Through a series of seven councils, the doctrine of the Incarnate Word took on a depth and clarity of understanding that has ever since been reflected in the liturgy. Thus if we compare the earliest creeds used in Eucharistic worship before the fourth-century Councils of Nicea and Constantinople with the Creed we now profess at Mass, the contrast is startling. The divinity of Christ, his oneness with the Father, and that the Holy Spirit proceeds from both him and the Father are typical additions, deriving from doctrinal development, which the liturgy inherited because the Church's understanding of its founder had been deepened through struggle with heresy.

Equally remarkable was the gradual change that took place in the concluding words of the orations at Mass. The orations of the Roman ritual were originally so constructed that they concluded, without exception, "through Christ our Lord" or some equivalent. They were directed to God the Father and would come to a close with the well-known mediation formula. In the meantime, however, the influence of the French conflict with Arianism came to be felt. In order to bring out more strongly Christ's divine nature and exclude any semblance of subordinating him to the Father, one diocese after another began to fill out the concluding prayer with the phrase, "through Christ our Lord who lives and reigns with you in the unity of the Holy Spirit, God for ever and ever," or again, its equivalent.

Similarly, a deeper understanding of the Holy Trinity, arising from the contest with those who were embarrassed with a plurality of persons in God or who wished to explain these persons as merely three manifestations, gave a notable trinitarian emphasis to the Eucharistic liturgy in all the rites of the Catholic Church. If the stress has been greater in the East than the West, this too can be partly explained by the presence of Islam, with its positive denial that God could have any offspring and therefore the Trinity is a form of pagan mythology.

The Eucharist as permanent sacrament was certainly known from New Testament times. But the rationalizing tendencies in the early Middle Ages, which tried to explain the Real Presence more or less symbolically, produced a reaction in the Church in favor of venerating the reserved sacrament and adoring it ritually during Mass. Both of these practices are now an integral part of the Eucharistic liturgy.

Out of the challenges of the Reformation, the Catholic belief that the Mass is an expiatory sacrifice became ritualized in a stress on its propitiatory role to obtain mercy for sinners.

So, too, in our day there has been a renewed understanding of the Mass as sacrifice, indeed, but a sacrifice of praise and gratitude, of petition and love. It is not only, though necessarily, a sacrifice

of expiation. This is partly due to the increased awareness that
worship must be more than ever centered on God in an age that
is so preoccupied with man.

Devotion to Mary has been present in the Church since her departure from this earth, after she had helped to mother the nascent
Christian community. The definition of her divine motherhood by the
Council of Ephesus shows how firmly her position was established in
the people's faith and piety. Moreover, in Eastern Christianity her
place in the liturgy has for long been so prominent that it would be
hard to speak of a recent development. Nevertheless, two solemn
definitions in less than one hundred years, of Mary's Immaculate
Conception and bodily Assumption into heaven, have deeply affected
the liturgical practices of the Catholic Church everywhere. The influence corresponds, as more than one papal statement declared, to
the Church's recognition of woman's indispensable role in the up-
building of the Mystical Body of Christ.

XIII. SACRAMENTS OF THE CHURCH

Sustenance and Reconciliation

EUCHARIST

If there is one mystery of faith around which revolves the whole Catholic liturgy, it is the Eucharist. Christian piety has been lavish in the titles it gives to this mystery, believing it is impossible to exhaust its depth of meaning. The name "Eucharist," or thanksgiving, is to be explained either by the fact that at its institution Christ "gave thanks," or by the fact that this is the supreme act of Christian gratitude to God. Early instances of this title occur in the *Teaching of the Twelve Apostles,* in the letters of St. Ignatius of Antioch, and in the Apologies of St. Justin. Other familiar names are the Lord's Supper, the Table of the Lord, the Holy Sacrifice, the Holy of Holies, the Blessed Sacrament, or simply the Liturgy. Each of these and similar names concentrate on one or another of the three main aspects of the Eucharistic mystery, as Real Presence, as the Sacrifice of the Altar, or as the sacrament of Holy Communion.

In the New Testament there are four accounts of its institution, one by St. Paul in his letter to the Corinthians and three in the Synoptic Gospels of Matthew, Mark, and Luke. We have already seen how it was celebrated by the early Christian communities and from the beginning was a regular part of Christian worship.

While there is no institution narrative in John's Gospel, this is explainable by the fact that John wrote his Gospel to supplement what the other evangelists had already told. Moreover, his account of Christ's promise of the Eucharist is our most telling witness to the real bodily presence of Christ in the Blessed Sacrament.

Building on the biblical foundation, the Church has ever kept the faithful mindful of their great privilege in possessing the Holy Eucharist and their duty to avail themselves of the graces that Christ intends to confer through this treasury of his mercy. Different responsibilities have been of prime importance during various periods of Christian history. But, in our day, the Church's emphasis is on active participation in the Eucharistic liturgy.

The Church earnestly desires that Christ's faithful should not be there as strangers or silent spectators. On the contrary, through a good understanding of the rites and prayers, they should take part in the sacred action as persons who are conscious of what they are doing, with devotion and full collaboration. They should be instructed by God's word and be nourished at the table of the Lord's body. They should give thanks to God. By offering the Immaculate Victim, not only through the hands of the priest but also with him, they should learn also to offer themselves. Through Christ the Mediator, they should be drawn day by day into ever more perfect union with God and with each other, so that finally God may be all in all.[1]

Active and effective participation in the Eucharist, however, presumes some understanding of the mystery, as far as this is possible from the frequent teaching of the Church, from a comparison of this mystery with things that are naturally open to human reason and, as the saints have been the first to testify, from the experience that comes to those who "taste and see" that the Eucharist is, indeed, "a sacrament of love in which Christ is eaten, the mind is filled with grace, and a pledge is given to us of future glory."

REAL PRESENCE

When Catholic Christianity affirms, without qualification, that "in the nourishing sacrament of the Holy Eucharist, after the consecration of the bread and wine, our Lord Jesus Christ, true God and true man," is present "under the appearances of those sensible things," it rests its faith on the words of Scripture and the evidence of Sacred Tradition.[2]

The beginning of this faith comes from the discourse recorded by St. John, writing toward the end of the first century. Christ had already worked the miracle of multiplying the loaves and fishes. He had also spoken at length about the need for faith in him and his words as a condition for salvation. Then he continued:

> I am the bread of life. Your fathers ate the manna in the desert and they are dead; but this is the bread that comes down from heaven, so that a man may eat and not die. I am the living bread which has come down from heaven. Anyone who eats this bread will live for ever; and the bread that I shall give is my flesh, for the life of the world.

Then the Jews started arguing with one another. Did they understand him correctly? Was he actually telling them he would give his own flesh for food? "How can this man give us his flesh to eat?" they asked. Instead of reassuring them that he did not mean to be taken literally, Christ went on:

> I tell you most solemnly, if you do not eat the flesh of the Son of Man and drink his blood, you will not have life in you. Anyone who does eat my flesh and drink my blood has eternal life, and I shall raise him up on the last day. For my flesh is real food and my blood is real drink. He who eats my flesh and drinks my blood lives in me and I live in him. As I, who am sent by the living Father, myself draw life from the Father, so whoever eats me will draw life from me. This is the bread that came down from heaven; not like the bread that your ancestors ate; they are dead, but anyone who eats this bread will live for ever (Jn. 6:48–58).

The evangelist explains that Christ taught this doctrine in the synagogue, but that hearing it "many of his followers said, 'This is intolerable language. How could anyone accept it?'" Jesus was fully aware that his followers were complaining and, in fact, asked them, "Does this upset you?" But he took nothing back. Rather he insisted, "The words I have spoken to you are spirit and they are life. But there are some of you who do not believe." At the same time he explained that such faith is not of man's making, since "no one could come to me unless the Father allows him."

Following this animated dialogue, we are prepared for the statement, "After this, many of his disciples left him and stopped going with him." Then, to make absolutely certain there was no mistaking what he was saying, Jesus said to the Twelve, "What about you, do you want to go away too?" To which Simon Peter replied, "Lord, who shall we go to? You have the message of eternal life, and we believe" (Jn. 6:59–68).

The Church's decisive revelation on the Real Presence is in the words of the consecration, "This is my body; this is my blood," whose literal meaning has been defended through the ages. They were thus understood by St. Paul when he told the first Christians that those who approached the Eucharist unworthily would be guilty of the body and blood of the Lord. There could be no question of a grievous offense against Christ himself, unless Paul assumed that the true body and the true blood of Christ are really present in the Eucharist.

Moreover, the necessity of the natural sense of Christ's words is based upon the evident requirements in the circumstances when he spoke. They demanded that he would not, in a matter of such paramount importance, have recourse to meaningless and (worse still) deceptive figures of speech. Figures of speech enhance a discourse only when the figurative meaning is clear either from the nature of the case or from common usage, neither of which could be invoked to claim that Christ was talking figuratively at the Last Supper. On the contrary, what he said was the literal fulfillment of what he had promised at Capernaum. It is noteworthy, too, that the evangelist John referred to the betrayer as foreseen by Christ at the time he foretold the Eucharist, even as the predicted traitor went off to sell his Master after the Eucharist was instituted.

The faith of the early Church in Christ's real bodily presence in the Eucharist was incontestable. Ignatius of Antioch urged the Christians to "partake of one Eucharist, for one is the flesh of our Lord Jesus Christ, and one the cup to unite us with his blood."[3] Talking of the Eucharistic body of Christ, John Chrysostom told the faithful, "When you see it exposed, say to yourself: Thanks to this body, I am no longer dust and ashes, I am no more captive but a free man. Hence I hope to obtain heaven and the good things that are there in store for me, eternal life, the heritage of the angels, companionship with Christ. Death has not destroyed this body, which was pierced by nails and scourged." Indeed, "this is that body which was once covered with blood, pierced by a lance, from which issued saving fountains upon the world, one of blood and the other of water." Then to make the identity still more clear between the Eucharistic body and the historical body of Christ, the believer should say, "This body he gave us to keep and eat, as a mark of his intense love."[4]

In order to describe what takes place at the consecration, the Eastern Church used the term *meta-ousiosis,* literally "change of being," since that was the momentous transformation that was believed to take place whenever a duly ordained priest pronounced the words of institution at the sacrifice of the Mass.

The first serious ripples of controversy came in the ninth century, when a monk from the French Abbey of Corbie wrote against his abbot, St. Paschasius (785–860). Ratramnus (d. 868) held that Christ's body in the Eucharist cannot be the same as Christ's historical body once on earth and now in heaven because the Eucharistic body is invisible, impalpable, and spiritual. He wanted to hold on to the Real Presence but stressed the Eucharist as symbolic rather than corporeal. His book on the subject was condemned by the Synod of Vercelli, and his ideas, it is held, influenced all subsequent theories that contradicted the traditional teaching of the Church.

Within two centuries the issue had reached such a point of gravity that a formal declaration was evoked from the Holy See. In 1079, Archdeacon Berengar of Tours who favored Ratramnus' position and wrote against what he considered the excessive realism of Paschasius, was required by Gregory VII to accept the following declaration of faith in the Eucharistic presence:

> I believe in my heart and openly profess that the bread and wine placed upon the altar are, by the mystery of the sacred prayer and the words of the Redeemer, substantially changed into the true and life-giving flesh and blood of Jesus Christ our Lord, and that after the consecration, there is present the true body of Christ which was born of the Virgin and, offered up for the salvation of the world, hung on the cross and now sits at the right hand of the Father, and that there is present the true blood of Christ which flowed from his side. They are present not only by means of a sign and of the efficacy of the sacrament, but also in the very reality and truth of their nature and substance.[5]

In the sixteenth century, the controversy over the Church's traditional teaching was revived. But this time the variety of opinions became multiplied to such a degree that in 1577, at Ingolstadt in Germany, the book *Two Hundred Interpretations of the Words, "This Is My Body"* was published. Theories ranged from complete symbolism to some kind of spiritual presence. It was to meet this new and more serious challenge to the historic faith that the Council of Trent defined the Real Presence in a series of four canons, which covered the major aspects of the faith that were being called into question.

1. Responding to the claims of merely symbolic or spiritual presence, the Church condemned "anyone who denies that the body and blood, together with the soul and divinity, of our Lord Jesus Christ and, therefore, the whole Christ is truly, really, and substantially contained in the sacrament of the Holy Eucharist, but says that Christ is present in the sacrament only as a sign, or figure, or by his power."

The expression "whole Christ" proved to be decisive. Since the whole Christ is present in the fullness of his divine and human natures, this implies that he is present under the sacramental appearances with the totality of his divine attributes as well as his human properties. He is therefore in the Eucharist also with the essence of those dimensional features that we commonly associate with a living human being. The explanation of how these physical properties are possible is part of theological speculation, but the fact is a matter of faith.

2. By the thirteenth century the term "transubstantiation" had come to be used to identify the change that occurs at the time of the consecration of the Eucharistic elements. At the Fourth Lateran Council, this term was part of the conciliar creed professing belief in the Eucharist. But Trent went a step farther. It not only used the term, but also declared the fitness of the expression. The reason was that some were ready to admit a real presence, even a corporeal one, but claimed that Christ was present along with the elements of bread and wine. Not so, the Council held, as though "the substance of bread and wine remains in the holy sacrament of the Eucharist together with the body and blood of our Lord Jesus Christ." This would be to deny "that wonderful and extraordinary change of the whole substance of the bread into Christ's body and the whole substance of the wine into his blood, while only the species of bread and wine remain, a change that the Catholic Church has most fittingly called transubstantiation."

There was no dependence on Aristotelian philosophy in the Church's use of words like "substance" or "transubstantiation." Long before either term had become commonplace in the West, the East spoke regularly of the *ousia* or being of the bread and wine, which were changed into the *ousia* or being of Christ. That which constitutes bread and wine, in virtue of the sacramental consecration, ceased to be bread and wine and became the reality of the whole Christ. What alone remained were the species, i.e., appearances or external properties of what looked and tasted like bread and wine but were now the living body and blood of the Savior.

3. Again what may seem to have been a refinement actually touched on the essence of the sacrament, namely, the double question of whether Christ was entirely present under the form of bread or wine, and to what extent. Hence the Church's affirmation that "in the venerable sacrament of the Eucharist the whole Christ is contained under each species and under each and every portion of either species when it is divided up." Communion under both species had been customary everywhere, and was then the practice in the Eastern rites. But in the sixteenth century, the strong insistence that the chalice be given to everyone occasioned this definition, which was also the doctrinal foundation for receiving only under the form of bread.

4. Still another theory was the notion that the Real Presence is to be identified with the liturgical action. This was explained with different nuances, but at their center was the denial of an objective reality that is independent of the faith or piety or devotion of the participants. The Church countered from every angle. Thus one cannot say that the body and blood of our Lord Jesus Christ are "present only in the use of the sacrament while it is being received, and not before or after, and that the true body of the Lord does not remain in the consecrated hosts or particles that are left over after Communion."

Given this perdurance of Christ's presence as long as the species remain, it was only logical for the Church to worship the Blessed Sacrament as it would the person of Jesus himself. As a result, he is to be adored "in the holy sacrament of the Eucharist with the worship of latria, including the external worship." Concretely this means that the Blessed Sacrament is to be "honored with extraordinary festive celebrations" and "solemnly carried from place to place" and "is to be publicly exposed for the people's adoration."[6]

The teachings of Trent ushered in a renascence of faith in the Real Presence that affected many facets of the Catholic liturgy. Notable among these was the renewed impetus it gave to the worship of the Blessed Sacrament reserved in the tabernacle or exposed in a monstrance on the altar.

Names like St. Margaret Mary Alacoque (1647–90) and St. Peter Julian Eymard (1811–68) are typical of one phase of this renascence. Margaret Mary's revelations, which helped to promote the modern

devotion to the Sacred Heart, occurred while she was in adoration before the Blessed Sacrament. Peter Julian Eymard founded the Priests
of the Blessed Sacrament, with a special emphasis on devotion to
the Real Presence.

There the matter stood at the opening of the Second Vatican
Council. In the meantime, new theories arose that the Church felt
were endangering the unqualified faith in the Eucharistic presence
and how it was brought about. These theories centered around the
psychological notion of presence and the ritual notion of sign. The
two were closely associated and, in order to forestall any further
crisis, Paul VI took the unprecedented step of publishing a major
doctrinal encyclical between the third and final sessions of the Council.

The Pope distinguished no less than eight ways in which we may
speak of Christ being somewhere present. He is present in the
Church when it prays, since it is Christ who prays for us and in us
and to whom we pray as to our God. This is the sense in which we
believe that where two or three are gathered together in Christ's
name, he is there in the midst of them. He is present in the Church
when it performs its works of mercy, not only because we do to
Christ whatever good we do to his brethren, but also because it is
Christ, performing these works through the Church, who continually assists the faithful with his divine love. He is present in the
Church on its pilgrimage of struggle to reach the harbor of eternal
life, since it is he who through faith dwells in our hearts and, through
the Holy Spirit, whom he gives, pours his love into our hearts.

Christ is also present, in another way, in the Church as it
preaches his Gospel, since the Gospel that the Church proclaims is
the word of God. It is preached in his name, by his authority, and
with the assistance of his grace. He is no less present in the Church
as it governs the people of God, since the sacred power inherent in
the Mystical Body comes from him. As shepherd of shepherds, he is
present in the pastors who exercise the power conferred on them as
successors of the apostles. Still more sublimely, Christ is present in
the Church when it offers in his name the sacrifice of the Mass, and
he is intimately present to the Church whenever it administers the
sacraments.

All of these presences are, in their way, authentic, and they verify
the basic concept we have when we speak of someone being present to us. He is present in all these ways because he is active in our

regard, and his influence is experienced by those to whom he is present.

But the Real Presence is not only different from all the foregoing. It is also unique. It is the physical presence of Christ in our midst, no less truly than he is now present at the right hand of his Father. Consequently "this presence is called *real*—by which it is not intended to exclude all other types of presence as if they could not be 'real' too, but because it is presence in the fullest sense. It is a substantial presence by which Christ, the God-man, is wholly and entirely present."[7] If we would make a graphic comparison, there is as much difference between Christ's presence in the Blessed Sacrament and his presence elsewhere on earth as there was between his presence among the disciples when he appeared to them on Easter Sunday night and his presence in their midst before and after the appearance.

SACRIFICE OF THE MASS

Already at the Last Supper, Christ made it plain to the apostles that what he was there enacting and what he would complete on Calvary was a sacrifice, which he wanted them to continue in his memory. In Judaism, bread and wine were familiar sacrificial elements. The words Jesus used at the institution, when he spoke of the New Covenant, of his body that would be given up, of his blood that would be poured out, of doing this in memory of him—all have deep sacrificial implications.

In apostolic times the Church had no doubt that, while the sacrifice of the cross was certainly adequate for the redemption of the world, Christ intended to have this sacrifice perpetuated in a ritual manner until the end of time. This was one of the principal themes of the letter to the Hebrews, which assumed that Christ had offered himself once to God the Father upon the altar of the cross, but went on to affirm that his redemption was an enduring event. Christ's priesthood "remains forever." It continues "since he is living forever to intercede for all who come to God through him" (Heb. 7:24–25).

Renewal of Calvary. Christ's own association of what he did at the Last Supper with what he was to do on Good Friday has been the Church's own norm for intimately relating the two. The sacrifice of the altar, then, is no mere empty commemoration of Calvary, but a true and proper act of sacrifice, whereby Christ the high priest by an unbloody immolation offers himself a most acceptable victim to the eternal Father, as he did on the cross. "It is one and the same victim; the same person now offers it by the ministry of his priests, who then offered himself on the cross. Only the manner of offering is different."

The priest is the same, namely, Jesus Christ, whose divine person the human minister represents at the altar. "By reason of his ordination, he is made like the high priest and possesses the power of performing actions in virtue of Christ's very person."[8]

The victim is also the same, namely, the Savior in his human nature with his true body and blood. Worth stressing is that what makes the Mass a sacrifice is that Christ is a living human being with a human will, still capable of offering (hence priest) and being offered (hence victim), no less truly today than occurred on the cross.

However, the critical question still remains: Just how are the Mass and Calvary related? They are interrelated in three ways: as re-presentation, as memorial, and as effective application of the merits gained by Christ by his death on the cross.

1. The re-presentation means that on the cross, Jesus offered himself and all his sufferings to God by an immolation of himself that brought on his physical death, but an immolation that he freely offered to his heavenly Father. On the altar, by reason of the glorified state of his human nature, "death has no more power over him" (Rm. 6:9). Consequently, the shedding of his blood is impossible. Nevertheless, according to the plan of divine providence, the continued sacrifice of Christ is manifested in the Mass by external signs that are symbols of his death. How so? "By the transubstantiation of bread into the body of Christ and of wine into his blood, his body and blood are both really present." But that is not all. Their separation in consecration "symbolizes the actual separation of his body and blood. Thus the commemorative re-presentation of his death, which actually took place on Calvary, is symbolically shown by separate symbols to be in a state of victimhood."

Catholicism, therefore, affirms that because Christ is really present in his humanity in heaven and on the altar he is capable now, as he was on Good Friday, of freely offering himself to the Father. He can no longer die since he is now in a glorified body, but the essence of his oblation remains the same. It is the continued willing surrender of himself to the will of the Father.

2. The Mass is a memorial of Christ's passion and death throughout the Eucharistic liturgy, as described already in a ritual from the second century.

> The Apostles in their memoirs, which are called Gospels, have handed down what Jesus ordered them to do; that he took bread and, after giving thanks, said: "Do this in remembrance of me; this is my body." In like manner, he took also the chalice, gave thanks, and said, "This is my blood." And to them only did he give it.[9]

Is it only the death of Christ that is commemorated? The Church teaches it is "a memorial of his death and Resurrection," though obviously in different ways. When we say that the Mass commemorates Christ's death, we mean that in a mysterious way Christ really offers himself as the eternal priest and that his oblation is not only a psychological remembrance but a mystical reality. When we say that the Mass is a memorial of his resurrection, this too is not merely a mental recollection. After all, the Christ who is now in heaven and the principal priest at the altar is the risen Savior. His resurrection is not only an event that took place once, but a continuing fact of salvation history. To call the Mass a memorial of the resurrection may conjure up the image of a pleasant memory that swiftly crosses the mind. It should rather tell us that in the Mass the risen Lord is present and in our midst and bids us unite ourselves, still mortal, with him who is our resurrection.

3. The Holy Sacrifice is the divinely ordained means of applying the merits of Calvary. At this point it will be useful to clarify an otherwise complicated question: How does the Mass apply the merits of Christ's passion and death? During the period of the Reformation, this was one of the most vexing issues that faced the Church, whose priests were told they were wrong to claim that Masses were a source of divine grace. Either they were wrong, or St. Paul was mistaken when he wrote that when Christ died, "He, on the other hand, has offered one single sacrifice for sins, and then taken his place forever, at the right hand of God" (Heb. 6:10). The dilemma seemed insoluble: Either Christ died once for all and his death is sufficient for the redemption of mankind, or in spite of his death, Masses must be said to somehow shore up what was presumably inadequate in the passion of the Savior.

The Council of Trent addressed itself to the issue in a memorable paragraph that summarizes fifteen centuries of Catholic belief on the efficacy of the Mass, but an efficacy that depends entirely on Calvary:

> This sacrifice [of the Mass] is truly propitiatory, so that if we draw near to God with an upright heart and true faith, with fear and reverence, with sorrow and repentance, through the Mass we may obtain mercy and find grace to help in time of need. For by this oblation the Lord is appeased, he grants grace and the gift of repentance, and he pardons wrongdoing and sins, even grave ones.
>
> The benefits of this oblation (the bloody one, that is) are received in abundance through this unbloody oblation. By no means, then, does the sacrifice of the Mass detract from the sacrifice of the cross.
>
> Therefore, the Mass may properly be offered according to apostolic tradition for the sins, punishments, satisfaction, and other necessities of the faithful on earth, as well as for those who have died in Christ and are not yet wholly cleansed.[10]

What the Church teaches is that, while the blessings of salvation were merited for mankind on the cross, they are still to be applied to us, principally through the Mass. Between the two ideas of merit and application stand the towering facts of faith and human freedom: faith to believe that God wants us to use such channels as the Mass, and freedom to humbly unite ourselves in spirit with Christ's self-immolation—he on the cross, which he endured, and we on our cross, which he bade us to carry daily if we wish to be his disciples.

Participation by the Faithful. If there is anything that Catholics are being insistently reminded to do liturgically it is to participate actively in the Mass. They are told that "to participate in the Eucharistic sacrifice is their chief duty and supreme dignity," and they are urged to do so "with such earnestness and concentration that they may be united as closely as possible with the high priest, according to the apostle, 'In your minds you must be the same as Christ Jesus' (Ph. 2:5). And together with him and through him let them make their oblation, and in union with him let them offer up themselves."[11]

Participation in the Mass by the faithful has a high dignity, and the Church wants to impress this on the people. It also has its doctrinal limits, as the magisterium is not slow to point out. Writing to the bishops of the Catholic world, Pius XII told them that "there are today those who, approximating errors long since condemned, teach that in the New Testament by the word 'priesthood' is meant only that priesthood which applies to all who have been baptized; and hold that the command by which Christ gave power to his apostles at the Last Supper to do what he himself had done, applies directly to the entire Christian Church."[12]

This touches on the heart of the Catholic faith, which does not hold that all Christians are equally possessed of priestly power, so that the priest at the altar acts only in virtue of an office committed to him by the community.

Accepting this, however, as basic to a Catholic understanding of the priesthood, in what sense do all the faithful actively participate in the Eucharistic liturgy? They do so by uniting themselves in spirit with the priest, who represents Christ and the Church, and by offering themselves together with Christ as victims to the heavenly Father.

Since the time of the earliest liturgies in the East and West, this bilateral aspect of the Mass has been expressed in the ritual words and actions. In the first century the faithful were told to address the Father as a group in the plural.

> Regarding the Eucharist. Give thanks as follows: First, concerning the cup: "We give Thee thanks, our Father, for the Holy Vine of David Thy servant, which Thou has made known to us through Jesus, Thy servant. To Thee be the glory for evermore."
>
> Next, concerning the broken Bread: "We give Thee thanks, our Father, for the life and knowledge which Thou hast made known to us through Jesus, Thy servant. To Thee be the glory for evermore."[13]

In the Roman Sacramentaries going back to the sixth century and still present substantially in the liturgy of the Latin rite, we find the same duality, sometimes brought out in the strongest possible terms. Thus in the *Orate Fratres,* which remains intact in the revised postconciliar liturgy, the priest turns to the people and says: "Pray, brethren, that my sacrifice and yours may be acceptable before God the Father almighty." And in the *Hanc igitur,* just before the consecration, the priest addressed God: "We beseech you, Lord, that being appeased you may therefore receive this offering of our services and of your whole family."

In the new offertory prayers of the revised *Roman Missal,* the priest says: "Blessed are you, Lord, God of the universe, because we have received bread (wine) from your bounty. We offer you this fruit on the earth (vine) and the work of human hands, from which we shall receive the bread of life (spiritual drink)." And in one of the new canons of the Mass, the celebrant asks the Lord, "We beseech you to look upon the offering of your Church."

What does it mean to say that the people, and not only the priest, *offer* the holy sacrifice? They do so first of all from the fact that the minister at the altar is offering Mass in the name of all of Christ's members, since he represents Christ in the fullness of Christ's mystical membership, which now includes all who belong to the Mystical Body. The ordained priest represents the Savior, who is head of the Church. The people unite their sentiments of praise and petition, of expiation and gratitude with the prayers and intentions of the priest, who is acting in the name of Christ.

The function of the external ritual is to give expression to these sentiments, and active participation means active togetherness of heart between the high priest who is the principal celebrant of the Mass and the faithful who join their worship of the Father in union with his.

It also means that the people offer themselves as victims together with the Christ who continues to sacrifice himself to God in every Mass. Evidently this kind of self-immolation is not confined to the actual celebration of the liturgy. A better way of viewing the oblation is to see it as an ongoing self-surrender to the will of God, of which St. Peter spoke when he told the Christians to set themselves close to the Savior, "so that you too, the holy priesthood that offers the spiritual sacrifices which Jesus Christ made acceptable to God, may be living stones making a spiritual house" (1 P. 2:4–5). No doubt this manner of immolation reaches a peak during the actual celebration of Mass, no less than did Christ's self-giving when he actually died on the cross. Yet, like his, the surrender of self to the will of the Father is meant to go on in a kind of lifelong liturgy.

The Christian Community. Although implicit in this concept of participation by the faithful, one feature that has been specially clarified since Vatican II is the community character of the people's involvement in the liturgy. Some would say this feature had been strongly present in earlier days but was overshadowed by the aftermath of the Reformation. Others again believe it is simply the providential adaptation of Catholic worship to the communitarian character of the age. In any case, when the liturgy is being enacted, the end in view is that all those who participate have a sense of sharing in what is being done and not only feel they are watching what someone else is saying to them or doing in their stead.

This represents a major development in the Church's contemporary understanding of sacramental (especially Eucharistic) worship. Man's collective consciousness, his cultivated pragmatism and awareness of power as a human being to do things and produce effects that truly emanate from inside his own mind and will, are reflected in the active communal participation that Roman Catholicism advocates in the modern world. The faithful are to see themselves as coproducers and not merely onlookers, in every enterprise, including that which pertains to the spirit.

Moreover, their sense of active contribution is to be made manifest in such a way that those who participate come to realize that the Mass is the sacrifice of the Church. It is true, of course, that the simple willing presence of a congregation at Mass is already symbolic of their union of charity and their united offering to God. But this symbolism can be heightened, and it is this heightening that the Church has so much encouraged in these days.

The degree of this external symbolization will depend on circumstances. And more than one instruction from Rome cautions against doing things hastily, or ignoring the universal prescriptions governing the liturgy, or taking the notion of community too narrowly as this congregation only and not the whole community of believers in Christ.

Nevertheless, admitting all these reservations, the people are to realize that "the celebration of the Eucharist that takes place at Mass is the action not only of Christ, but also of the Church." They should come to experience that "no Mass, indeed, no liturgical action, is a purely private action, but rather a celebration of the Church as a society composed of different orders and ministries, in which each member acts according to his own order and role."[14]

Naturally this demands considerable adjustment to what some perhaps believe is a departure from authentic Catholicity. So far from being a departure, provided what is done conforms to the directives of the Holy See, it is rather a cleansing of liturgical forms and accommodating them to the needs of the people of God.

HOLY COMMUNION

There exist two dimensions to the Eucharistic liturgy that Catholic tradition has commonly recognized. The more familiar approach is to distinguish the Real Presence, the sacrifice of the Mass, and the Sacrament of the Altar. On this level, then, we look upon the Eucharist as simultaneously three things: the continued Immanuel or God-with-us in the person of Christ who really and truly dwells among us under the sacramental veils; the oblation of Christ in union with his Church, whereby he offers himself and us along with him to the heavenly Father and bids us join our self-surrender with his; and Holy Communion, in which Christ is received as the pledge of our future immortality.

The second approach, which may be called postconciliar because it has been specially developed since the twenty-first ecumenical council, is somewhat different. It rests on the former and presupposes it but goes a bit farther. Here the stress is on the Eucharist as a sacrifice in which the sacrifice of the cross is perpetuated; a memorial of the death and resurrection of the Lord; and a sacred banquet in which, through the communion of the body and blood of Christ, the faithful share the benefits of the paschal sacrifice, renew the New Covenant, which God has made with man once for all through the blood of Jesus, and in faith and hope foreshadow and anticipate the eternal banquet in the kingdom of the Father, proclaiming the Lord's death "until he comes."

In both approaches, the consummation of the Eucharistic liturgy is the reception of Holy Communion, in which the body and blood of Christ are received and by which we are intimately united with the incarnate Son of God.

The subject is so important and has such practical implications for the spiritual life of all the faithful that it should be treated at some length, from the vantage point of history and of pastoral practice.

Early Christianity to the Council of Trent.   Weekly reception of the Eucharist was customary already in apostolic times. In the *Didache,* the faithful are admonished that, "having come together on the Lord's Day, you are to break bread and give thanks, after you have confessed your sins, so that your sacrifice might be undefiled. But anyone who is estranged from his friend should not join us, until both have become reconciled, lest your sacrifice be polluted."[15] Equally clear is the description of the Sunday morning service given by St. Justin during the middle of the second century: "On the day which is called Sunday, we have a common assembly. . . . The Eucharistic elements are distributed and consumed. . . ."[16]

From the end of the second century there are numerous indications that priests and laity received Holy Communion every day. Tertullian mentions that Christians daily extend their hands, according to the prevalent custom, to receive the body of Christ.[17] St. Cyprian states that in Africa "we who are in Christ, daily receive the Eucharist as the food of salvation."[18] From Egypt we have the witness of Clement of Alexandria, and also of Origen, who says that "the Lord hates those who think that only one day is a festival of the Lord. Christians partake of the Lamb every day, that is, they daily receive the flesh of the Word of God."[19] St. Basil in Asia Minor writes that "it is commendable and most beneficial to communicate and partake of the body and blood of Christ every single day."[20]

Regarding the European practice, St. Ambrose wrote of northern Italy that Mass was celebrated every day, at which priest and people received of the "food of saints." Jerome says the same for Spain. The custom in France, at least among the hermits, was "to feed daily on the most pure flesh of the Lamb." Likewise at Rome, besides other witnesses, there is the well-authenticated story of St. Melania, who "never took bodily food until she had first communicated the body of the Lord."

As might be expected, the practice varied among the different churches. St. Augustine noted that while in some localities the faithful receive Holy Communion every day, in others they communicate only on Saturday and Sunday, and in still others on Sunday alone. Even among the Christians of one locality there were considerable differences. St. John Chrysostom complained that some of the faithful approached the sacred banquet not more than once or twice a year, while others received frequently. He deplored the fact that while Mass is celebrated every day, yet people will assist at the sacrifice without partaking of the sacrament. At Milan, too, Ambrose rebuked the Christians for allowing laxity to creep into the diocese: "If this is the daily bread," he asked, "how is it you wait a full year before receiving it, as the oriental Greeks are in the habit of doing? You should receive daily what is to your benefit. So live that you may deserve to communicate every day."[21]

From the beginning of the ninth century we see a notable decline in the frequentation of the sacraments. Thus the Council of Tours, in 813, had to make this decree: "If not more often, at least three times each year the laity must receive Holy Communion, unless someone be prevented by reason of a major crime."[22]

Instead of improving, however, the situation became worse, until finally in 1215 the Fourth Lateran Council enjoined at least annual Communion at Eastertime: "Everyone of the faithful of both sexes, after reaching the age of reason, should in private faithfully confess all his sins at least once a year . . . reverently receiving the sacrament of the Eucharist at least at Eastertime. . . . Otherwise, while living he shall be forbidden entrance into the Church, and at death shall be deprived of Christian burial. Let this salutary decree be published frequently, lest anyone try to excuse himself on the score of complete ignorance."[23]

During the four centuries following the Lateran Council spiritual writers strongly recommended the practice of frequent Communion, even, on occasion, its daily reception. Moreover, popular preachers among the Franciscans and Dominicans helped to promote the frequentation of the sacraments. Nevertheless, the response that this evoked among the clergy, and consequently among the laity, was in general very slight. For the most part they succeeded in bringing the people to receive at least on the three major feasts of Christmas, Easter, and Pentecost. In order to understand this anomaly it is necessary to glance at the ascetical principles that were currently in vogue, from the early thirteenth century to the Council of Trent.

St. Thomas praised daily Communion, but only for those in whom frequency of reception increases the fervor of charity without decreasing reverence and respect. He proposed the question of "whether it is lawful to receive this Sacrament daily," and answered in the affirmative, quoting St. Augustine: "This is our daily bread; take it daily, that it may profit you daily." In practice, however, he believed that few people satisfy these requirements.[24]

St. Thomas' friend and contemporary, St. Bonaventure, likewise extolled the practice of frequent Communion. Yet the conditions he set down would make daily reception something of a rarity. He recalled the three stages in the Church's discipline: daily, triannual, and annual Communion, and allowed each person to judge for himself how often he should approach the altar.[25]

It was in this spirit that the author of the *Imitation,* writing in the early fifteenth century, described the ideal Christian as one "who so lives and keeps his conscience in such purity as to be prepared and well disposed to communicate every day." Yet only provisionally, "if it is permitted to him and he might pass without observation."[26]

Not until the middle 1500s do we find what may properly be called a renascence of Eucharistic piety. Moreover, it is possible to identify the main source of this resurgence, and even the persons who brought it about. It was in Spain that the greatest impetus was given to promoting frequent reception of Holy Communion; in Spain too the first signs appeared of a theological defense of the devotional practice. Spanish bishops were among the most outspoken for a return to the practice of the early Church.

Finally, in 1551 the Council of Trent passed a decree on the Holy Eucharist, urging "all who bear the Christian name . . . mindful of the boundless love of our Lord Jesus Christ . . . that they may believe and venerate these sacred mysteries of his body and blood, with such constancy and firmness of faith, with such piety and worship, that they may be able to receive frequently that supersubstantial bread." It went on to specify that this meant "at every Mass they attend."[27]

These documents placed in the hands of the Church's pastors the authority they needed to propagate frequent Communion among the faithful, not only in private correspondence but officially, on as wide a scale as their resources permitted.

Among others, St. Robert Bellarmine wrote a treatise on frequent Communion, in which he listed and answered all the current objections against the practice. "Experience bears out," he stated, "that those who receive frequently with a desire to grow in holiness make wonderful progress in the spiritual life." It was his conviction that "this is the unique and infallible way of reforming the Church of Christ." To the objection that "it is more respectful to Christ not to receive him so often," he replied: "It is precisely in receiving the Holy Eucharist even daily that we show forth the reverence which the Lord expects of us."[28]

Jansenism to the Second Vatican Council. As so often happens in the history of the Church, there was a strong reaction, with Jansenism presenting the best-organized opposition.

The cofounder of Jansenism was Antoine Arnauld, friend of Jansenius' disciple the abbot of St. Cyran. Where Jansenius was heavy and speculative, Arnauld had a consummate mastery of his native tongue and was eminently practical. But he was at one with the master in his attitude toward man's sinfulness and therefore of his unworthiness. He crystallized all the essentials of Jansenistic theory in his

Frequent Communion, first published in 1643 and destined to become, with Jansenius' book *Augustinus,* the main arsenal of this particular theology for subsequent centuries.

In the first part of his book, Arnauld discussed the teaching of the Fathers, and in the third part the requisite preparation for Holy Communion. Between the two sections he inserts a lengthy dissertation on the penitential system of the early Church. His real aim, to check frequent Communion, is nowhere expressly stated by the author.

Typical of Arnauld's expectations for receiving Holy Communion was his commentary on a passage from St. Augustine, exalting the dignity of the Eucharist. Arnauld used the reference to suit his own purpose. In context Augustine was talking about reverence for the Blessed Sacrament because the same Jesus is present in heaven and in the Eucharist. Arnauld shifted the words to mean that communicants on earth must have the same detachment from creatures that the angels and saints possess in heavenly glory.[29]

In the judgment of contemporary observers, Arnauld's book came to be looked upon as a fifth gospel. To many people it was a welcome excuse for delaying the irksome duty of confession; in fact, abstention from the sacraments became invested with the halo of a higher perfection. St. Vincent de Paul reported that in one parish alone, St. Sulpice in Paris, the number of Communions decreased by hundreds shortly after the appearance of *Frequent Communion.* Even in the first period of Jansenism, people were so influenced by this book that they omitted their Easter duty and refused Viaticum because they were not sufficiently detached from creatures. Jansenistic priests were known never to say Mass; others considered it a matter of principle to reduce the reception of the sacraments to a minimum, so that Catholics were found who had not made their first Communion by the age of thirty.

The delicate political situation, involving both the Crown and those prelates who had supported Jansenism, contributed to the fact that Arnauld was not censured by the Church for many years. Not until fifty years later did the Holy See feel free to condemn his teaching. In 1690, Alexander VIII, through the Holy Office, proscribed a list of thirty-one propositions, two of which deal immediately with the reception of the Eucharist:

> Those who pretend they have a right to Communion before having done fully adequate penance for their sins are to be regarded guilty of sacrilege.

In like manner, those are to be forbidden Holy Communion in whom there is not yet the purest love of God, unmixed with any lesser affection.[30]

The condemnation of Jansenistic rigorism did not make an appreciable difference in the general practices of the people, except for putting a check on the extremists. For the next century, Rome kept encouraging bishops and priests to permit more frequent Communion, but the seeds of Jansenism had taken too deep a root in Catholic piety to be eradicated easily. Credit for the final eradication is due to Pius X.

Several factors conspired to give to the world, under Pius X, the famous decree on frequent Communion. The Pope's own antecedents, his years of experience as a parish priest, and above all his personal devotion to the Eucharist, made him painfully conscious of the harm done to souls who only seldom approached the holy table. Furthermore, he realized that the root of the problem lay not among the faithful but among those who were to guide the people in the way of salvation. Theologians were undecided on what precise conditions were required for frequent reception. In principle they agreed on the value of the Blessed Sacrament as a means of sanctification; but in practice they were divided on the proper dispositions that were needed. The majority held for stringent conditions, not excluding the conquest of inordinate affections. When occasionally an author would modify these conditions, he was accused of teaching "erroneous doctrine."

The decree of St. Pius X was appropriately entitled *The Holy Synod of Trent.* Eminently practical, it posed four specific problems that had vexed theologians for centuries, and answered them with unambiguous clarity:

1. At the outset, in the very subtitle of the decree, *On Daily Reception,* the question is settled, what exactly "frequent" Communion means. Without qualification, the Pope explains that "frequent" means daily reception of the Blessed Sacrament. Arguing from the analogy of food used by Christ himself, and the "all but unanimous interpretation of the Fathers" that daily bread in the Lord's Prayer means daily Communion, he concluded that "the Eucharistic bread should be our daily bread."

2. But this is not enough. Granted that daily Communion is permissible, is it commendable to all classes of persons—priests and religious, lay people and children? Unequivocally, "the desire of Jesus Christ and of the Church [is] that all the faithful should daily

approach the sacred banquet." This is directly contrary to the rigorism that excluded the majority of people from the holy table. Although implicit in the decree of 1905, frequent Communion for children had to be explicitly promulgated in subsequent decrees: twice in 1906 to urge "frequent reception even for children," and in 1910 to order that they might be admitted to first Communion "as soon as they begin to have a certain use of reason."

3. Still further, the question of necessary dispositions had to be settled. And the Pope in this case bypassed the more common opinion current for centuries to decide in favor of the minority school, which required only the state of grace and a right intention. The two paragraphs on this point represent the heart of the decree.

> Frequent and daily Communion, as a thing most earnestly desired by Christ our Lord and by the Catholic Church, should be open to all the faithful, of whatever rank and condition of life; so that no one who is in the state of grace, and who approaches the holy table with a right and devout intention, can lawfully be hindered therefrom.
>
> A right intention consists in this: that he who approaches the holy table should do so, not out of routine or vainglory or human respect, but for the purpose of pleasing God, of being more closely united with him by charity, and of seeking this divine remedy for his weaknesses and defects.

4. Finally the crucial distinction is drawn between dispositions that are strictly necessary and those that are only praiseworthy. Those who had opposed frequent Communion for all the faithful had failed to make the distinction.

> Although it is most expedient that those who communicate frequently or daily should be free from venial sins, especially such as are fully deliberate, and from any affection thereto, nevertheless it is sufficient that they be free from mortal sin, with the purpose of never sinning mortally in the future; and if they have this sincere purpose, it is impossible but that daily communicants should gradually emancipate themselves even from venial sins, and from all affection for them.

Obviously, "since the sacraments of the New Law . . . produce a greater effect in proportion as the dispositions of the recipient are better," the faithful should be encouraged that "Holy Communion be preceded by serious preparation, and followed by a suitable thanksgiving according to each one's strength, circumstances, and duties." Nevertheless, while exhorting the people to cultivate the best possible dispositions, "confessors must take care not to dissuade anyone from frequent and daily Communion, provided he is in the state of grace and approaches with a right intention."

St. Pius X drew on the teachings of the Council of Trent to bring out the fact that the Eucharist is by divine intention the food of which Christ spoke in the Gospel of John and that he instituted at the Last Supper as the sacrament of unity, because its special purpose is to increase the practice of charity:

> The desire of Jesus Christ and of the Church that all the faithful should daily approach the sacred banquet is directed chiefly to this end, that the faithful, being united to God by means of this sacrament, may thence derive strength to resist their sensual passions, to cleanse themselves from the stains of daily faults, and to avoid those graver sins to which human frailty is liable.[31]

The stress on the Eucharist as a sacred banquet, or in more prosaic terms, a holy meal, has been popularized since the Second Vatican Council. Its foundations are biblical and its purpose is precisely that, functional. No less than ordinary food is meant to nourish the body, give it strength, and bring a certain amount of pleasure, so partaking of Christ's body and blood has been given to us as nourishment for the spirit, through the infusion of divine love; as source of strength to cope with our weakness, especially our proneness to selfishness and greed; and as cause of our joy in the service of the Lord, by giving us satisfaction in the performance of what human nature (without this grace) would consider burdensome duties.

But the word "banquet" has one more implication today that was not so obvious even in the days of Pius X, namely, the notion of togetherness, which our lonely urban civilization makes us realize we so desperately want. It is not too much to say that, in an age when family meals are becoming increasingly rare because family life has been gravely impaired, Holy Communion will obtain the grace for communities everywhere to recover their identity through the reception of him who prayed, "May they all be one, Father, may they be one in us" (Jn. 17:21).

WORSHIP OF THE HOLY EUCHARIST

One of the surprises of the Church's teaching since the Second Vatican Council is her strong emphasis on devotion to the Real Presence. Worship of the Holy Eucharist, not only during Mass or when receiving Communion but as reserved on the altar, has been part of Catholic life and practice since the earliest centuries. With the renewed stress on active participation in the liturgy, however, some had difficulty reconciling what seemed to be private exercises of piety with authentic liturgical theology. As a result, in some sectors of the Church such customs as exposition of the Blessed Sacrament, Benediction, and Forty Hours were eclipsed in favor of a more "dynamic" and "involved" Eucharistic liturgy.

The basic issue at stake was to maintain a balance between what had come to be called the horizontal aspect of the liturgy, concerned with people, and its vertical dimension, concerned with God.

In order to redress this balance and at the same time reinvigorate devotion to Christ's abiding presence in the Eucharist, the faithful were first of all reminded that such devotion "has a valid and firm foundation, especially since belief in the real presence of the Lord has as its natural consequence the external and public manifestation of that belief."[32] As social beings we profess to others what we possess within ourselves.

What was further needed, though, was for the Church to establish the precise relationship between prayer before the Blessed Sacrament and the Eucharist as liturgy. This was done by first stating a principle and then explaining its application. The principle declares that, "When the faithful adore Christ present in the sacrament, they should remember that this presence derives from the Sacrifice and is directed toward both sacramental and spiritual Communion." Except for the Sacrifice of the Mass there would be no Eucharistic Presence to adore, and through devotion to this Presence between Masses attended the faithful are better disposed to profit from their participation in the Liturgy and reception of Holy Communion. The application opens the door to a Eucharistic renascence which integrates every facet of Eucharistic piety:

> The devotion which leads the faithful to visit the Blessed Sacrament draws them into an ever deeper participation in the Paschal Mystery. It leads them to respond gratefully to the gift of him who through his humanity constantly pours divine life into the members of his body. Dwelling with Christ our Lord, they enjoy his intimate friendship and pour out their hearts before him for themselves and their dear ones, and pray for the peace and salvation of the world. They offer their entire lives with Christ to the Father in the Holy

Spirit, and receive in this wonderful exchange an increase of faith, hope and charity. Thus they nourish those right dispositions which enable them with all due devotion to celebrate the memorial of the Lord and receive frequently the Bread given us by the Father.

The faithful should strive to worship Christ our Lord in the Blessed Sacrament in harmony with their way of life. Pastors should exhort them to this, and set them a good example.[33]

The closing observations are revealing. While all the faithful should make devotion to Christ's abiding presence part of their daily lives, those in Church authority are to set the pattern and teach the people accordingly.

PENANCE

Throughout his public life, Christ proclaimed the mercy of God toward sinners. He had come, he said, to preach the good news of salvation and deliverance from sin. Publicans and prostitutes will reach the kingdom of God before high priests and elders of the people. There is more joy in heaven over one sinner who repents than over the ninety-nine just who have no need of repentance. Three whole parables—of the lost sheep, of the lost drachma, and of the prodigal son—tell of God's fatherly love and of his divine solicitude for those who invoke his mercy.

Almost everything he said and all the wonders he worked spoke of the mission that he was sent into the world to accomplish and that verified his name of Jesus, Savior from sin.

Consistent with his words and actions until the moment of his death, forgiving those who crucified him, the risen Christ instituted the sacrament of mercy as his first gift to the Church on Easter Sunday night. The scene of his appearance to the disciples is recorded by St. John:

> He said to them, "Peace be with you," and showed them his hands and his side. The disciples were filled with joy when they saw the Lord, and he said to them again, "Peace be with you. As the Father sent me, so am I sending you." After saying this he breathed on them and said: "Receive the Holy Spirit. For those whose sins you forgive, they are forgiven; for those whose sins you retain, they are retained" (Jn. 20:20–23).

The Catholic Church considers these words to imply that Christ conferred on the apostles and their successors not merely the right to declare that a person's sins are forgiven—this would have been meaningless under the circumstances; rather he gave them the power of forgiving in his name those who are judged worthy of remission and of withholding absolution from those who are not disposed to be absolved.

THE EARLY CHURCH

In order to have an accurate picture of the practice of the sacrament of penance in the early Church, we must keep in mind the high expectations demanded of the Christians in those days. We get some idea of what this meant from the letters of St. Paul and the Acts of the Apostles, where believers were subjected, from Pentecost on, to persecution for their faith and among whom, we are told, the Spirit of God was miraculously active in producing heroic virtue that converted thousands to Jesus Christ.

Those who sinned grievously were at first not numerous. And when they sinned they could be reconciled with God and with the Church through what has come to be known as solemn penance. Its liturgical form was not unlike that of baptism, and was designed only for those who had committed the gravest sins. Most of the extant literature on the subject describes this type of sacramental reconciliation and has naturally received most attention.

But there was also a private administration of the sacrament of penance, from the beginning, as attested by a severe letter of Pope Leo I in 459 censuring those who presume to act "against the apostolic regulations" by demanding public manifestation of sins. "It is sufficient," he affirmed, "that the guilt which people have on their consciences be made known to the priests alone in secret confession."[1]

These two traditions were not strictly parallel, since we know that in some countries well into the early Middle Ages the practice of solemn penance was so widespread we may presume that this eclipsed the private form. In fact, there is a series of Roman documents from the third century on that sought to mitigate the tendency toward rigorism in specific dioceses. Sometimes, as with Leo I, Rome would recall the "apostolic regulations" that did not require public exposure of one's misdeeds. At other times, it would seek to lessen the heavy penalties exacted of sinners either as a condition for reconciliation with the Church or admission to full communion with the faithful.

The well-known Penitential Books belong in this part of the history of the sacrament of penance. These were sets of books containing directions to confessors in the form of prayers, questions to be asked, and exhaustive lists of sins with the appropriate penance prescribed. They were of Celtic origin, of which the earliest are two sets of canons ascribed to St. Patrick and dating from the fifth century. In time they spread with the Celtic and Anglo-Saxon missions all over Europe, the most famous ascribed to St. Theodore, archbishop of Canterbury (620-90).

Depending on the gravity of a sin, the works of satisfaction would be prescribed accordingly. For the graver crimes—parricide, perjury, adultery, and abortion—they prescribed such penances as exile, going on a distant pilgrimage, or seclusion in a monastery for life or for ten or seven or three years. For lesser sins the satisfaction might consist in fasting either for a long period or periodically, or again in certain prayers, scourging oneself with knotted cords, or almsgiving.

The wide use of the Penitential Books with the specified directives to priests indicates the corresponding regularity of private penance in the Church from patristic times. But this in turn tells us that we should distinguish the terms "private penance" and "public penance" very carefully; to be exact we must see here not two but four types of sacramental confession and absolution, used in the Church in varying degrees in different places until the Middle Ages.

1. There was first of all the private confession of secret sins, which the Church approved and which Rome insisted was of apostolic origin. Consequently, in spite of abuses to the contrary, the Church's official position has always been that secret sins, no matter how grave, could and should be confessed privately and expiated privately. If the penance imposed for grave secret sins in earlier days was more severe than later on, this is partly explained by the development of doctrine on the nature of penance in Catholic thought and partly by the gradual practice of indulgences, one purpose of which was precisely to mitigate the need for extraordinary external acts of satisfaction.

2. Another form of private confession, going back to the earliest days of sacramental liturgy, covered sins that were not mortal and

that the Fathers of the Church called "daily" or "ordinary." Two
streams of tradition, however, must be distinguished: among the laity
and clergy in general, and among men and women living a monastic
or religious life. The two currents mutually affected one another, but
they were not the same.

Among people in the world, the practice of confessions of devotion as distinct from those of obligation because only venial sins
were confessed is certain from scattered statements among the
Fathers reminding the people that such sins can also be remitted by
other means than sacramental absolution, e.g., attendance at Mass,
works of charity, earnest prayer, and the practice of virtues contrary
to their sinful tendencies. It is further confirmed by the Penitential
Books which, though mainly concerned with grave sins, also took
stock of the many lesser faults to which people are prone and with
which the priests may deal in the sacrament of penance.

Among religious, who often became solitaries or entered monasteries because they wished to practice a higher virtue than they
thought possible in the growing secularization of the post-Constan-
tinian era, confession of one's failings was not only practiced but
formally prescribed. A brief look at the Rule composed by St.
Benedict (480–550) will show what this meant. His prescription on
the subject occurs as the fifth degree of Benedict's twelve degrees
of humility:

> The fifth degree of humility is to hide from one's abbot none of
> the evil thoughts that beset one's heart, nor the sins committed in
> secret, but to manifest them in humble confession. To this the Scrip-
> ture exhorts us, saying, "Make known thy way to the Lord, and
> hope in him." And again, "Confess to the Lord for he is good, and
> his mercy endures forever."

This kind of confession was expected often from religious. And
the manifestation of conscience was considered so valuable, it
was to be made (apart from the sacrament) even when the abbot
was not a priest. We know that St. Benedict inherited the practice
from St. Basil, who repeatedly stressed the importance for a religious
to humbly avow his secret failings, not just to anyone, but to those
who had the grace of state and the gift of wise discretion.

From Basil and Benedict on, the custom of voluntary manifestation
of conscience and, when a priest was available, of sacramental confession entered the whole fabric of religious life, in the East and

West, among men and women, in monasteries and communities for the active apostolate.

3. Public penance could be either solemn or not, depending on the gravity of the offense committed and the amount of scandal given. The literature on public penance in the Church, up to the time of St. Thomas Aquinas, is so large that it has received a great deal of attention. Unfortunately, this attention may give the mistaken impression that such dramatic practices were either the rule and not the exception, or that private penance was a late innovation, or that the Church has changed the very substance and not merely the exterior features of the sacrament of Christ's mercy.

When public penance was also solemn, the reason had to be an unusual one. Already in the third century, Origen cautioned that such solemn admission of guilt and later reconciliation should be done only exceptionally. "If after much deliberation," he writes, speaking of the bishop or priest to whom the confession was made, "he has understood the nature of your illness, and judges that to be cured it must be exposed in the assembly of the whole Church, follow the advice of that expert physician, and thereby others may perhaps be able to be edified, while you yourself are the more easily healed."[2]

Among the public crimes that might be subjected to solemn penance, those that appear most often in the records are adultery, apostasy, fornication, and murder. The liturgical discipline varied, with a tendency toward greater strictness (demanding solemn expiation and reconciliation) in the West and in those places that were less responsive to Rome's directives. The complaint of Tertullian, by then become a Montanist, against "the sovereign Pontiff, otherwise called the bishop of bishops," is historic. He accused the Pope of saying: "I remit the sins of adultery and fornication to those who have done penance."[3]

The more common and approved practice was to limit solemn penance to those crimes that gave such scandal as seemed to call for proportionate expiation. Writing in the thirteenth century, Thomas Aquinas said that the crime must have "aroused the whole city." But even then, he made an exception for certain public sinners, like clerics, who had to perform penance, of course, but not in a solemn way, lest greater harm than good be done by the degradation.

There were two phases to solemn penance. The first stage was the liturgical entry into the state of penance, which might include receiving a garment of sackcloth and being sprinkled with ashes. Later an act of symbolic importance was added. The penitent was "expelled" from the church building while antiphons were sung recalling Adam's expulsion from Eden. "See," said the bishop, "how you are driven away from the threshold of holy Mother Church because of your sins and your crimes, as Adam the first man was driven out of paradise because of his disobedience."

The reconciliation of the penitents was normally reserved for Holy Thursday, and was a long ceremony as presented in the texts of the eighth century. Besides other prayers, the presiding priest or bishop asked God to restore the sinners to full communion with the Church:

> Most kind Lord, call back with your accustomed goodness these your servants whose sins have separated them from you. For you did not disdain the humiliation of the wicked Achab, but spared him his due punishment. You heard Peter's weeping and then entrusted him with the keys of the kingdom of heaven. And to the thief who confessed his sins, you promised the rewards of that same kingdom.
>
> Welcome back, then, most kind Lord, these persons for whom we offer our prayers, and give them back to the bosom of your Church, so that the enemy can in no way triumph over them. Rather may your Son, who is equal to you, reconcile them with you and purify them of all sin, so that they may be worthy to be admitted to the Eucharistic banquet. Thus may he restore them to his flesh and blood, and so lead them, after this life, to the kingdom of heaven.[4]

Not infrequently people would postpone their reconciliation with the Church for grave crimes until shortly before death. In such cases, a shortened form of absolution and reinstatement was used.

It should be noted, however, that even where solemn liturgical penance was practiced, this did not mean that absolution from guilt had to wait until full satisfaction was performed. The contrary practice was more than once censured as an abuse.

4. Finally, there was a form of public penance that the Church did not consider solemn. The person would secretly confess some grave sin from which he was absolved and for which he was given an external work of satisfaction to perform. Others might easily conclude from what the person was doing that this had been imposed by the confessor, but he was spared the humiliation of being formally identified as a penitent.

The legislation of sacramental confession for all the faithful by the Fourth Lateran Council may seem to have been the final step in a long process of liturgical development, especially if we think that public penance was the rule for the first millennium of the Church's history. Actually, the Lateran decree was more disciplinary than anything else. It specified who was expected to go to confession, how often, and under what conditions.

> Let everyone of the faithful of both sexes, after he has reached the age of discretion, devotedly confess in private all his sins at least once a year to his own priest, and let him strive to fulfill to the best of his ability penance enjoined upon him.[5]

This conciliar teaching has ever since been incorporated into the Church's practice, with certain obvious distinctions that are common knowledge. Thus the Church assumes that children are also to receive the sacrament of penance when they reach the age of reason, even though at that age they would not have committed any grave sins. Moreover, the gravity of annual confession naturally rests on the gravity of the sins a person has committed. If there have been no mortal sins, the duty of annual confession is not strictly binding.

But if we turn from the letter of the legislation to its spirit, what the Council sought was to encourage more frequent confession. It laid down the absolute minimum requirements, seeing that so many people were neglecting the essentials. It had no intention, as we know from the history of those times, to limit the frequentation of the sacraments.

COUNCIL OF TRENT TO MODERN TIMES

Since the sacrament of confession was challenged on many fronts by the Reformers, the Council of Trent defended the Catholic Tradition on every count. The resulting assembly of doctrine is among the most detailed in the history of conciliar teaching.

Christ instituted the sacrament of penance "to reconcile the faithful with God as often as they fall into sin after baptism."[6] For the entire and perfect remission of these sins there are three acts required of the penitent, namely: "contrition, confession, and satisfaction." The sinner must be truly sorry for having offended God, tell his sins to the priest, and make reparation for the evil he committed. The last two of these necessary acts have come to identify the sacrament as either auricular confession or expiatory penance. It is insufficient simply to have one's "conscience stricken by the realization of sin, and the faith derived from the Gospel or from absolution, by which a person believes that his personal sins are remitted through Christ."[7] The point is that by divine law there must be a manifestation to the priest of what the sinner did wrong, and not just a subjective sense of guilt or even merely a trustful confidence in God's mercy.

Doctrinal Issues. The Church is specially concerned to vindicate the judgmental character of confession, so that "the sacramental absolution of the priest" is "a judicial act." What the priest does is not "the mere ministry of pronouncing and declaring that the sins of the person confessing are remitted, provided only that he believes himself absolved," as though "the confession of the penitent is not required so that the priest can absolve him."[8]

Two issues that had a long background but reached a peak in the sixteenth century were the relationship of a priest's own holiness and his ability to absolve, and who alone has the power from Christ to give sacramental absolution. On both issues the Catholic doctrine is unmistakable. It is therefore untenable to say that "priests who are in the state of mortal sin do not have the power of binding and loosing; or that priests are not the only ministers of absolution, but that to everyone of Christ's faithful it was said: 'Whatever you bind on earth shall be bound in heaven; and whatever you loose on earth shall be loosed also in heaven,' and 'Whose sins you shall forgive, they are forgiven them; and whose sins you shall retain, they are retained' "—as though anyone can absolve sins, by correcting the public sinner and by hearing the secret faults of those who wish to confide in their fellow Christian.[9]

While every priest and bishop has the power to absolve sins, the Church reserves the right to determine when he may use it, so that without such authorization his absolution would be invalid. The same applies to removing any ecclesiastical censures or penalties, like excommunication. Nevertheless, "this same Church of God has always devoutly upheld that there is no reservation at the hour of death, lest this reservation be the occasion of anyone's damnation; and therefore any priest can absolve any penitent from all sins and censures" when he is in danger of death.[10] This includes priests who have been laicized, i.e., dispensed from their active priestly duties and, in fact, even those who have left the active service of the priesthood without dispensation of the Holy See.

One of the gravest questions that were controverted, and on which a definitive decision had to be made, was the quality of the sorrow required for receiving valid absolution. Those who held out for perfect contrition, animated by the love of God, practically reduced confessions to a needless burden, since the Church has always held that even mortal sins are remitted by an act of perfect sorrow, provided the person intends later on to tell his sins in confession. The technical term "attrition" has come to be used to describe that sorrow for sins that is not motivated by the perfect love of God, and yet is sufficient for the remission of guilt provided the person also confesses to a priest. This kind of lesser contrition is "engendered by the examination, consideration, and detestation of sins, as a person reviews all his years (or lesser periods) in bitterness of soul, meditating on the seriousness of his sins, their number and heinousness, the loss of eternal happiness and the eternal damnation incurred, and so proposes to lead a better life." Although clearly not as sublime as the sorrow for having offended God, who is all good and deserving of all my love, yet attrition is "a true and very beneficial sorrow" that "prepares a person for the reception of grace."[11]

The practical value of this teaching is incalculable. It implies what is common knowledge, that people steeped in sin are psychologically not ready to rise to such high motivation as the perfect act of contrition demands. Nevertheless, and this is one of the great blessings of the sacrament, provided they fear God because of what they believe they deserve for having sinned, and confess their sins, they are restored to divine friendship.

What sins must be confessed? To obtain remission of sins in the sacrament of penance, it is necessary "according to divine law to confess each and every mortal sin that is remembered after proper and diligent examination, even secret sins, and sins against the last two commandments, and those circumstances which change the species of a sin." Consequently it is no mere ecclesiastical precept but a divine mandate, and it covers even internal mortal sins, say of lust or envy, along with such details as would substantially affect the nature of the sin.

Though conciliar documents seldom do this, in this case the

doctrine about the necessary matter for confession states that the reason for such explicit declaration is not only pragmatic, "to instruct and console the penitent," nor a vestige from the past when "it was formerly observed only for the purpose of imposing canonical penance." Moreover, besides mortal sins it is also "permissible to confess venial sins" and indeed praiseworthy to do so.[12]

One of the distinctive features of Catholic Christianity is its notion of temporal punishment due to sin. Behind the notion is the belief that a person's guilt before God may be remitted without necessarily removing all the debt of penalty for having broken a divine law. Venial sins carry with them only temporal punishment, either in this life or in purgatory; mortal sins carry the penalty of eternal punishment, which is always remitted with the remission of guilt, but unexpiated temporal punishment may still be due. Satisfaction for such temporal punishment is one of the keystones of Catholic penitential worship. It is made to God through the merits of Christ "by the penances sent from God and patiently endured, or those imposed by the priest, or by the penances voluntarily undertaken, such as fasts, prayers, almsgiving, or other works of piety."[13] There is more to obtaining forgiveness than simply avoiding past sins; it also includes the practice of reparation, on the premise that by sinning we offend God and the Church (and so need to be reconciled) and bring disorder into the world (and so need to expiate).

Frequent and Early Confession. As new scholarly evidence accumulates, it becomes clear that reception of the sacrament of penance was not a rare practice for those Christians who wished to avail themselves of its salutary blessings. The monastic record is plain enough, and since the days of Basil and Benedict conclusive, that men and women religious went to confession quite often. This was so true that on several occasions the Church had to intervene to insist that such confessions be made to a priest, and that absolution by a fellow religious who was not ordained would not be valid.

Also among the faithful, however, along with the dramatic public penances for grave scandals, the practice of receiving sacramental absolution and the corresponding graces was recognized. Already in the early fourth century, the writer Lactantius pointed to the regular reception of this sacrament as a mark of Catholicism,

as distinct from heretical, Christianity. "That is the true Church,"
he said, "in which there is confession and penance, which supplies
a wholesome remedy to the sins and wounds to which the weakness
of the flesh is subject."[14] As the practice of more frequent confession developed, still in the patristic age, it assumed that people
would approach the sacrament, not only to obtain remission of grave
sins, but to receive "a wholesome remedy" for their weaknesses.

But no less than frequent Communion, regular confession among
the faithful in general died down to such an extent that the Fourth
Lateran Council had to legislate at least annual reception of both
sacraments. If it seems strange to us that in 1215 the Church would
require even children who had reached the age of discretion to
confess all their sins, this can be explained in several ways. The
position of the Church has never been tied to any psychological
theory that excludes, on principle, the capacity for grave sin once
a person has reached the age of discretion. Discretion, it should be
noted, means the ability to make moral judgments that affect one's
relationship to God. Moreover, since the immediate focus of confession is the objective sins a person has committed, the subjective
degree of responsibility should be left for God to decide. The
Church wisely omits theorizing about when a person's mind (and
will) are sufficiently developed to make it possible for him to
perform an action that is both objectively grave and for which
he is fully responsible. Sacramental confession is valuable spiritually
for everyone who receives it, even in the absence of grave guilt.
Hence the sweeping legislation, whose wisdom has been proved
from experience, to require all the faithful from early childhood on
to benefit supernaturally from sacramental absolution and the
Holy Eucharist.

We know that the Lateran decree did not make a serious impact
on the frequentation of the sacraments, and the Council of Trent
had to return to the same theme. Along with urging a restoration
of the pristine practice of receiving the Eucharist at every Mass
attended, Trent repeated the Lateran directive. But it also did more.
It leveled a formal anathema against anyone who "denies that each
and every one of Christ's faithful of both sexes is bound to confess
once a year according to the regulation of the great Lateran Council."[15]

Trent made a lasting impression on the liturgical life of the
people, and both sacraments began to be used more regularly,

thanks partly to the reforming zeal of men like St. Charles Bor-
romeo (1538–84) and partly to the preaching and teaching efforts
of men and women religious who had learned from their own spiritual lives that reformation of morals is inseparable from the sacramental graces received in the sacraments of love and reconciliation.

Then came the Jansenist interlude. Its impact on confession was
not unlike that which affected reception of the Eucharist. In fact,
on the basis of its own logic, Jansenism was so immersed in the idea
of man's sinfulness that the first effect of its principles came to be
felt on the level of the sacrament of penance and only then also on
the question of Holy Communion.

The same Antoine Arnauld whose book caused such turmoil with
regard to frequent Communion also militated against frequent and
early confession. His volume was aimed to discredit both—on the
grounds that the Church had departed from the hardy vigor of ancient times when sinners had to perform long and severe penances
before they could be absolved. Arnauld's most famous critic before
the Church made final judgment was St. Vincent de Paul (1580–
1660), who challenged the Jansenistic theory that sacramental absolution is merely declaratory. In the view of Jansenism, actual
remission of sins does not take place until after, and is conditioned
upon, the performance of extraordinary penances in vogue in the
early Church. Vincent countered with a concession and then a
theological conclusion. What if, for the sake of argument, it were
granted that the Church in the early centuries required the observance of public penance? Does it follow that the Church must
do the same now? What are the Jansenists talking about when
they claim that unless the ancient practice is restored, the Church
"would not be the pillar of truth, ever consistent with itself,
but a synagogue of errors; is not that statement baseless?" Must
we not distinguish between things that the Church cannot change
because they are part of revelation, and things which, under the
Church's direction, are subject to change?

> Cannot the Church, which never alters where matters of faith are
> in question, make changes in matters of discipline, and has not God,
> who is immutable in himself, altered his way in regard to men? Did
> not his Son, our Lord, sometimes act differently toward his own
> followers, and the Apostles toward theirs? What, then, does this man
> [Arnauld] mean when he says that the Church would err if she did
> not hold fast to a desire to re-establish those forms of penance which
> she employed in the past? Is that orthodox teaching?[16]

Jansenists were saying that "there had been no Church for the last five hundred years," i.e., ever since reconciliation was available on such easy terms. As they read the practices of the early Church, only public penance was recognized, and only long and arduous works of satisfaction were accepted as necessary preconditions for priestly absolution, which, in fact, was simply a declaration that the sins were remitted by the previous penance already performed.

Vincent de Paul admitted that the errors of Jansenism were frequently mixed in with orthodox statements of Catholic teaching. All innovators do the same. "They sow contradictory statements through their books, so that, if found fault with on any point, they can escape by saying that they had said the contrary in other places."[17] This was one reason why the decisive censure from Rome of Jansenist positions on the sacrament of confession waited so long. When Rome finally took issue with the Jansenists, it denied the following four propositions:

1. It is the will of Christ that adequate satisfaction for sins should precede sacramental absolution.

2. The practice of immediate and easy absolution of sins is contrary to the purpose of the sacrament of penance.

3. The current practice in the administration of the sacrament of penance, although confirmed by long-established custom, is clearly an abuse and against the true mind of the Church.

4. Those who claim they have a right to Communion before having done sufficient penance for their sins are guilty of sacrilege.[18]

Contemporary historians observed that the real issue of Jansenism was not the conditions for receiving the sacraments but the authority of Rome to determine the dispositions necessary for valid absolution before Holy Communion.

Through the eighteenth and nineteenth centuries the seeds planted by the Jansenists took deeper root than is commonly supposed. A memorable synod of Jansenists, we recall, met under Scippione de Ricci; the net result was to have no less than eighty-five of its decisions outlawed by Rome. Fifteen of these dealt immediately with confession, including the claim that no one should be admitted to the tribunal of penance until his sorrow for sin was animated by the perfect love of God. There was also the idea that some persons might have to wait a lifetime before reaching this necessary degree of supernatural charity. It was further said that people should drastically reduce their frequentation of the sacrament of penance, involving the confession of venial sins; otherwise confession becomes routine and despised by the faithful.[19]

By the time of St. Pius X, the custom of frequent and early sacramental confession had suffered the same fate as reception of Holy Communion. He literally reversed the trend set in motion by Jansenism and restored the custom that the Church had urged on the faithful for centuries: everyone should have early and ready access to both sacraments as powerful means of grace given to the Church by Christ.

Five years after his decree on frequent Communion, Pius X published another document, this time on first confession and Communion, in which he sought to undo the harm caused by "the errors of Jansenism" and bring to a new height of development the Church's teaching on the importance of these sacraments for all who have reached the age of reason.

He recalled the long history of the Church's solicitude for the young. Regarding Communion, he noted that in ancient times the remaining particles of the sacred species were given to nursing infants. Why, then, should extraordinary preparation now be demanded of children who are living in the midst of so "many dangers and seductions" and therefore "have a special need of this heavenly food"? The same with confession. Children need the graces of this sacrament.

The Pontiff deplored the misguided zeal of those who delayed the reception of the Eucharist. But he was equally outspoken about depriving the young of the graces of early confession. "No less worthy of condemnation," he said, "is that practice which prevails in many places of keeping from sacramental confession children who have not yet made their first Holy Communion, or of not giving them absolution." This is contrary to the mind of the Church. "The Lateran Council required one and the same age for reception of either sacrament when it imposed the one obligation of confession and Communion. Therefore, the age of discretion for confession is the time when one can distinguish right from wrong, that is, when one arrives at a certain use of reason."

The Pope then went on to specify the implications of this teaching, as affecting both sacraments. He made a studied effort to prevent separating the two.

1. The age of discretion both for confession and for Holy Communion is the time when a child begins to reason, i.e., about the

seventh year, more or less. From that time on begins the obligation of fulfilling the precept of both confession and Communion.

2. A full and perfect knowledge of Christian doctrine is not necessary either for first confession or first Communion. Afterward, however, the child will be expected to learn gradually the entire catechism according to his ability.

3. The obligation of the precept of confession and Communion which binds the child particularly affects those who have charge of him, namely, parents, confessor, teachers, and the pastor.

4. The custom of not admitting children to confession or not giving them absolution when they have already attained the use of reason must be entirely abandoned. The Ordinary shall see to it that this condition ceases absolutely, and he may if necessary use legal measures accordingly.[20]

There the matter stood until the Second World War. First confession before Communion at an early age, and frequent reception of both sacraments was common throughout the Catholic world. Then began, first in Europe and later elsewhere, a trend away from "confessions of devotion," which included children's confessions from the age of discretion.

By 1943, Pius XII had to show a firm hand to writers who argued against these "endless lines of penitents," most of whom had no more to confess than occasional faults against charity or, the children, disobedience to their parents. The Pope called the critics purveyors of "false doctrines," which are "not directed to the spiritual advancement of the faithful but turned to their deplorable ruin." Their position was essentially negative, asserting that "little importance should be given to the frequent confession of venial sins. Far more important, they say, is that general confession which the spouse of Christ, surrounded by her children in the Lord, makes each day by the mouth of the priest as he approaches the altar of God."

The Pope admitted the value of penitential formulas in the Mass. But a sacrament is an effective sign of grace, here of assistance to deal with human sinfulness. What follows is at once a clear statement of Catholic belief in the confession of venial sins and a defense of the Church's encouragement of the earliest possible reception of the one sacrament specially instituted by Christ for healing the frailties of our nature.

It is true that venial sins may be expiated in many ways which are to be highly commended. But to ensure more rapid progress day by

day in the practice of virtue, we will that the pious practice of frequent Confession, which was introduced into the Church by the inspiration of the Holy Spirit, should be earnestly advocated.

By it genuine self-knowledge is increased, Christian humility grows,
bad habits are corrected, spiritual neglect and tepidity are resisted,
the conscience is purified, the will strengthened, a salutary self-control is attained, and grace is increased in virtue of the sacrament
itself. Let those, therefore, among the younger clergy who make
light of or lessen esteem for frequent confession realize that what
they are doing is alien to the Spirit of Christ and disastrous for the
Mystical Body of Christ.[21]

In 1947, the Pope returned to the same theme, using stronger
words against those who discouraged confessing venial sins. He
recalled "with sorrow" the consequence of such an attitude, which
is "most dangerous to the spiritual life," and pleaded with bishops
to propose this teaching "for the serious consideration and dutiful
obedience of your flock, especially to students for the priesthood
and young clergy."[22]

After the Second Vatican Council the scene shifted in certain
countries to preoccupation with the optimum age for first confession.
Relying on the findings of the psychological sciences, some writers
concluded that the human conscience is not sufficiently developed at
"the age of discretion" to allow children to confess their sins and
receive absolution until much later, say, around the age of puberty.

When Paul VI approved the *General Catechetical Directory* in
1971, he took stock of the new challenge and authorized a special
section dealing with this very subject. The reasons offered for de-
ferring confession were given due attention:

> So that the Communion of children may be appropriately received
> early, and so that psychological disturbances in the future Christian
> life which can result from a too early use of confession may be
> avoided, and so that better education for the spirit of penance and a
> more valid catechetical preparation may be fostered, it has seemed
> to some that children should be admitted to first Communion with-
> out first receiving the sacrament of penance.[23]

These reasons for deferral of confession were duly weighed.
Nevertheless, "having heard the conferences of bishops," the Holy
See concluded that the common and general practice should be re-
tained.

Two years later, Rome took another look at the situation and decided that "an end must be put to these experiments" that inverted the order of the sacraments. The Church has had centuries of experience since the Lateran Council "ordered that children from the age of discretion should receive the sacraments of penance and Holy Eucharist. This precept, accepted into practice throughout the universal Church, brought, and continues to bring, much fruit for the Christian life and perfection of the spirit."[24]

During the controversy about the best age for admitting children to first confession, ecclesiastical documents readily admitted that modern times make it more difficult for the average child to develop clear values of his own. For one thing, he sees the inconsistency of behavior in the adult world that is mainly responsible for his upbringing. There is so much confusion surrounding him and so little attention paid to the child's dilemma, so few persons with time and patience to listen to him and to help him untangle some of the confusion. No wonder some children remain without sufficient clarity of beliefs or purpose. But for that very reason, along with improved pedagogy and the need for tender and loving care, the child today needs at a very early age the inflow of grace that comes from the divinely instituted means of growing through the Eucharist, in the love of God and of neighbor; and of coping, through Christ's own sacrament of peace, with the temptations that assail him on every side.

Ritual Changes. Consistent with the spirit of the Second Vatican Council, the Holy See has also revised the liturgical administration and reception of the sacrament of penance. Its directives, of over a hundred pages in the official text, are in two parts. The first contains a doctrinal section, pastoral and liturgical norms, and the revised rites for the different forms of celebration of the sacrament. The second part is offered as a help to episcopal conferences and liturgical commissions and contains eight models for nonsacramental penitential services.

The term "penance" is chosen in preference to the term "confession," which has been more customary up to now. It was felt that the word "confession" does not convey "the full significance of this sacrament in the life of the Church. For this reason, the newer terminology is a better indication" of the deeper understanding of what the sacrament means. As a rule, the term "penance" has a more general connotation, to cover not only the sacramental rites but also the penitential services that do not include sacramental absolution.

More specifically, the term "reconciliation" is used to describe the liturgical action, to convey the fact that sacramental penance is an encounter between God and man. "Penance," on the other hand, puts the accent rather on what man does. "The term 'reconciliation,' which was in use from primitive times and since the Council of Trent, will serve to set in relief a fundamental aspect of the renewal of penance, that of the encounter between a son and his Father."

What were the main lines of liturgical development intended by the new ritual? In particular, the communal and ecclesial character of penance are set more clearly in evidence in the new rite; sin is an offense against God and also an offense against one's brothers; penance is likewise reconciliation with God and with the Church, which plays a part in the penitent's conversion, by charity, example, and prayer.

The sacrament of penance may be administered in three ways or, really, four, since the first way has a longer and a shorter form. The purpose of the variety is better to emphasize the various aspects of penance and to meet the needs of the faithful.

1. The key element in the first form is individual confession. "If it is true that the sacrament of penance . . . ought to go hand in hand with the renewal of life, it ought to be administered in the form of a serene and tranquil dialogue between the priest and penitent, in the framework of prayer and, when possible, of the word of God, in a suitable setting and with no pressure of time."

In the ordinary rite, it is presumed that enough confessors are available, that there is enough time and a suitable setting. The ritual proceeds as follows: the priest greets the penitent; they pray together and, if there is time, a passage of scripture is read; the penitent confesses his sins, and the priest offers encouragement and advice; the penitent expresses his sorrow, using a suitable formula; absolution is then given.

The shorter form uses as much of what is optional in the ordinary rite as time will allow.

2. There are three parts to the second form, which is a combination of common celebration and individual confession of sins with absolution. In the first part is a liturgy of the word and prayer, in common. There follows confession and absolution. Lastly, again

together, there is a thanksgiving and expression of joy at being reconciled with God.

3. The final form is entirely communal, including collective absolution. However, this way of administering the sacrament of penance is limited to exceptional circumstances, since "individual and integral confession and absolution remains the only ordinary way by which the faithful may be reconciled with God and with the Church, except when this is physically or morally impossible." When would this be verified? "It can happen when the number of penitents is too great for the number of confessors present to hear their confessions properly, individually, in the time available, with the result that the penitents through no fault of their own would be compelled to remain without sacramental grace or Holy Communion for a long time." Nevertheless, "if enough confessors are available, the mere presence of a large crowd of penitents—as on a great festival or at a pilgrimage—does not justify communal confession and absolution."

Who decides when individual confession and absolution would be physically or morally impossible? The judgment on this critical issue is reserved to the local ordinary after he has duly conferred with the other members of the national episcopal conference.

One more important proviso: Persons "whose grave sins are forgiven by communal absolution should make an auricular confession before they receive another absolution, unless a just cause prevent them. They should certainly, unless it be morally impossible, go to confession within the year. They too are subject to the precept which obliges all the faithful to confess, individually, to a priest, at least once a year all the sins, certainly their grave sins, which they have not hitherto confessed singly."

The new formula of absolution concludes with the historic words by which the sinner is reconciled, but includes sentiments that are unfamiliar in the Roman Rite. The priest, with his hands extended over the penitent's head, or at least with his right hand extended, says:

> God, the Father of mercy, reconciled the world to himself through the death and resurrection of his Son and gave the Holy Spirit in abundance for the forgiveness of sins. May he grant you pardon and peace through the ministry of the Church. And I absolve you from your sins in the name of the Father, and of the Son, and of the Holy Spirit.

The penitent replies, "Amen." After the absolution, the priest says, "Give thanks to the Lord, for he is good," to which the penitent replies, "For his steadfast love endures forever." Then the priest dismisses the reconciled penitent with the words, "The Lord has forgiven your sins. Go in peace." Four alternate formulas are given for the final dismissal, five different texts are available for greeting the penitent, and no less than eight forms of contrition are offered for use in the sacrament. What remains constant is the formula of absolution.

While recognizing that the immediate purpose of the sacrament is to remit grave sins, the new ritual emphasizes its salutary function also when mortal offenses against God have not been committed:

> Frequent and reverent recourse to this sacrament, even when only venial sins are in question, is of great value. Frequent confession is not mere ritual repetition, nor is it merely a psychological exercise. Rather is it a constant effort to bring to perfection the grace of our baptism, so that, as we carry about in our bodies the death that Jesus Christ died, the life that Jesus Christ lives may be more and more manifested in us. In such confessions, penitents, while indeed confessing venial sins, should be mainly concerned with becoming more deeply conformed to Christ and more submissive to the voice of the Spirit.[25]

With the publication of *The Order of Penance,* the last major implementation of the late Council's decisions on the rite of the sacraments was completed. It was a fitting capstone to the Church's liturgical adaptation to the needs of our times.

Permanent Character

If we were to divide the sacraments according to their frequency of reception, we should immediately say that the Eucharist and penance are received often, whereas the other sacraments are received only once or very seldom. In popular language, when we speak of "going to the sacraments," we mean assisting at the sacrifice of the Mass at which Holy Communion is received and confessing our sins, whether grave or venial, and obtaining sacramental absolution from the priest.

In this sense, the liturgical life of the faithful mainly centers around the Eucharist and Christ's sacrament of peace. And most of the Church's hierarchical teaching on the liturgy concerns divine worship and sanctification in these two ways.

But there are five other sacraments in the Catholic Church. How do they differ from the Eucharist and the sacrament of reconciliation? On the level of our reflection, they differ mainly in the fact that these sacraments have a more or less lasting effect they produce in the person who receives them. The expression "more or less" is important, because three of the sacraments have an utterly lasting effect that perdures until death and, Catholic theologians further hold, even into eternity. The other two have a relatively lasting effect, in one case as long as the other partner in marriage remains alive, and in the other case, as long as the grave illness or infirmity that occasioned the sacrament continues.

The sacraments of baptism, confirmation, and holy orders are believed by the Catholic Church to confer what is called a sacramental character. Although the issue had been raised many times before, it became critical at the time of the Council of Trent, which declared that "in these three sacraments a character is imprinted on the soul, that is, an indelible spiritual sign which makes their repetition impossible."[1]

During the first centuries of the Church's history, such schisms as Donatism and heresies as Pelagianism served to bring out more clearly that once a person had been baptized, confirmed, or ordained he could never be rebaptized, reconfirmed, or reordained. Actually, the disputes of those days centered on the value of the sacraments when administered or received by a schismatic or heretic, or, for that matter, a grave sinner. Even in the well-known rebaptism controversy of the third century, when St. Cyprian maintained that baptism received in heresy had to be repeated, he had no doubt that once valid baptism had been received, it could not be received again. His problem was that he thought heretical baptism was null and void. Later on, others had the same difficulty who tried to oblige bishops and priests who had been ordained by Arians or similar heretics to be ordained a second time; they considered the first ordinations invalid. Rome had to step into the controversies and settle the issue by deciding that for the valid dispensing of the sacraments, it is necessary and sufficient that the one who administers them perform the sacramental rite in the proper manner and that he have the intention, at least, of doing what the Church does. With the passing years, still further clarity came regarding the validity and efficacy of the sacraments as independent of the orthodoxy and state of grace of the one who administers a sacrament.[2]

All the while, however, there was never any doubt that a baptism, confirmation, or ordination that had once been validly received could not be validly received again. A baptized person who had fallen from baptismal innocence might be excluded from communion with other Christians or deprived for a time of the right to approach the Eucharist, until he had been reconciled by absolution and suitable penance. But the Church did not rebaptize or reconfirm him. In the same way, a bishop or priest could be deposed from the active ministry but, if he were later reinstated in office, he would take up his functions without any renewal of the rites of episcopal or priestly ordination. The few instances of reordination to be found in such disturbed periods as the tenth century are explainable by the suspicion that the first ordination had been null and void, not by the fear that a valid ordination could later be nullified.

These three sacraments, therefore, have an unlosable, permanent effect that remains even when the person who receives them falls into grave sin, loses his faith, or leaves the Church. This ineffaceable effect is, then, distinct from the grace of holiness, since it can endure without it. The Church has come to call this effect the character.

The word "character" is not to be taken in the sense in which we commonly understand it, i.e., the estimate placed upon a person or thing, its reputation or value. Its meaning is rather derived from the ancient Greek term *charassein,* used in the Bible to describe an image or inscription engraved in a permanent way on a medal, coin, or piece of stone. The letter to the Hebrews uses this expression to speak of Christ as "the radiant light of God's glory and the perfect copy (character) of his nature" (Heb. 1:3). Here the meaning is not only of an indelible portrait but of an essential likeness. In the Apocalypse, on the other hand, the same term recalls the practice in certain cities of marking slaves with an indelible brand. Those are cursed who let themselves be marked on the forehead with the sign of the beast. But the faithful are marked with the sign of Christ's servants.

Our most explicit references to the sacramental character occur in St. Paul, where he is speaking of the effects of baptism and

confirmation on the followers of Christ. The Pauline figure is that of
a seal.

> Remember it is God himself who assures all of us and you, of our
> standing in Christ, and has anointed us, marking us with his seal and
> giving us the pledge, the Spirit, that we carry in our hearts (2 Cor.
> 1:21–22).
>
> Now you too, in him, have heard the message of the truth and
> the good news of your salvation, and have believed it; and you have
> been stamped with the seal of the Holy Spirit of the Promise (Ep.
> 1:13).
>
> Guard against foul talk; let your words be for the improvement of
> others as occasion offers, and do good to your listeners, otherwise
> you will only be grieving the Holy Spirit of God who has marked
> you with his seal for you to be set free when the day comes (Ep. 4:
> 30).

In the letter to the Corinthians, the theme of the anointing also
recalls the notion of an irrevocable consecration. Saul remained
the anointed of the Lord even when, because of his sins, he had
fallen from his royal state and was replaced by David. It was
forbidden to lay hands on him, and the man who killed Saul was
instantly punished.

But there is more to the meaning of character than either permanence or assimilation. Since the one to whom a person is permanently assimilated is Jesus Christ, the sacramental character imprints on the soul of the one who receives it a likeness to that
attribute of Christ with which the sacraments of baptism, confirmation, and ordination are mainly concerned, namely, Christ's priesthood.

The classic explanation of how this occurs is to say that the
sacramental character makes us participate in the priesthood of
Christ by conferring on the faithful the supernatural power of
offering the sacrifice of the New Testament and of imparting grace
through the administration of the sacraments. This power is received
initially in baptism, more developed in confirmation, and perfected
in the sacrament of holy orders.

On further reflection, we see that this power gives those who
possess it the ability to become reconcilers of men with God by
means of the sacrifice of Calvary. It is sometimes called ascending or
upward mediation. At the same time, it enables them (in varying
degrees) to become sanctifiers or dispensers of God's grace by means

of the sacraments, which is also known as descending mediation. That is why baptized Christians who offer the sacrifice of the Mass are, in their way, mediators of intercession for a sinful humanity. That is why only baptized persons can confer on one another the sacrament of matrimony. That is why also only priests can validly administer certain sacraments, like penance, and only those who have received the fullness of the priesthood can ordain others to the priestly state.

Implicit in the Church's doctrine on the character is the carefully nuanced distinction between the sacraments as such, and the grace with which the sacraments are commonly associated. There is something so mysteriously transcendent about three of the sacraments that they radically and permanently change the person who receives them by an immutable participation in Christ's priesthood. He remains unalterably baptized, or confirmed, or ordained, no matter what else may happen to his holiness in the sight of God. He thus retains an enduring substratum of union with God that needs only to be activated to rise from its dormant state.[3]

Since the time of Trent, the doctrine of the sacramental character has been greatly developed in the Church's teaching in two main directions: to bring out the likeness to Christ that the character imparts, and to show how the character unites the members of the Mystical Body of the Savior.

On the first level of development, the implications are breathtaking. In virtue of the character that Christians possess, they are anointed with something similar to what occurred in Christ's humanity when it was assumed by the divinity. In Christ the hypostatic union was the root from which the grace sprang; it imparted an infinite dignity to the humanity and guaranteed the enduring existence of this dignity.

In Christians, the character they possess is something like the source of grace, inasmuch as it places them in contact with Christ. He is the heavenly vine whose branches we are through the character, which gives us a right actually to possess grace if we place no obstacle in the way.

Since it is the same Christ whose character is imprinted on all who are baptized, they are united with one another in a mystical union that defies explanation but is no less real. Their likeness to him produces a likeness among themselves that is grounded on the unity of which he spoke at the Last Supper. It is a unity patterned on the union between Christ and his Father. The priestly prayer of the Savior before he died was that this union in the Godhead would be imitated in mankind. Its foundation is in the character that all Christians possess, but its development depends upon their co-operation with the graces, especially of the Eucharist, that they receive.

BAPTISM

Baptism is the sacrament of spiritual rebirth. Through the symbolic action of washing with water and the use of appropriate ritual words, the baptized person is cleansed of all his sins and incorporated into Christ. He becomes a member of the Mystical Body and receives the graces of the supernatural life.

The sacrament of baptism is conferred by infusion (pouring) or aspersion (sprinkling) of water or by immersion in water while the one who baptizes pronounces the words, "I baptize you in the name of the Father and of the Son and of the Holy Spirit."

Catholic Christianity distinguishes between solemn and emergency baptism. The ordinary minister of solemn baptism is a priest or deacon but in case of emergency anyone, even though not a Catholic, can validly baptize. The one baptizing (in infusion) pours water on the forehead of the person being baptized and says the ritual words while the water is flowing. In solemn baptism the water is specially blessed during the ceremony.

The Catholic Church also recognizes as valid baptism the ceremony properly performed by ministers who are not Roman Catholic. Unlike some denominations in the Protestant tradition, however, the Catholic Church has always considered the baptism of infants to be valid. In fact, she requires infants to be solemnly baptized as soon after birth as conveniently possible. When there is danger of death, anyone may baptize an infant. If the child survives the ceremonies of solemn baptism should be supplied. Baptism is conferred conditionally when there is doubt about the validity of a previous baptism. This pertains especially to adults who are being received into the Church.

Sponsors or godparents are required, at least one, although they are not necessary for valid conferral of the sacrament. They are to be Catholics whose role, of course, is secondary to that of the parents. Nevertheless, they are important. They serve as official representatives of the community of faith and, with the parents, request baptism for the child. Their function after baptism is to serve as proxies for the parents if the parents should be unable or fail to provide for the religious training of the child.

At baptism, the Church expects the child to be given a name with Christian significance, usually the name of a saint, to symbolize newness of life in Christ and entrance into the Christian community.

SACRAMENTAL EFFECTS

The many ritual changes introduced by the Second Vatican Council may lead one to suppose that this reflects also a substantial change in the Church's faith or even a reversal of Catholic doctrine. Not at all. Thus the changes in the liturgical celebration of baptism, though considerable, are only modifications introduced by the Church to make the reception of the sacrament more meaningful to all who participate and, in the case of adults, to better dispose them for the blessings that are conferred. The better their dispositions, the more fruitful the benefits they receive.

All the while, however, there has been no alteration but only a deeper realization of the supernatural effects of baptism in everyone who is validly baptized. Some of these effects are explicitly taught in the New Testament and the ancient Fathers, others are described in the liturgical prayers and instructions of the baptismal rite that have come down through the centuries, and still others are the result of prayerful study and reflection that the Church has incorporated into her official teaching of the faithful.

Remission of Sins. Commonly listed first among the effects of baptism is its efficacy to remit original sin and actual guilt, no matter how grave the offenses against God may have been. St. Paul, after narrating a series of crimes, including idolatry, adultery, and sodomy, told the Christians, "These are the sort of people some of you were once, but now you have been washed clean, and sanctified, and justified through the name of the Lord Jesus Christ and through the Spirit of our God" (1 Co. 6:11). According to St. Augustine, "By the generation of the flesh, we contract original sin only. By the regeneration of the Spirit, we obtain forgiveness not only of original, but also of actual sins."[4] And in one comprehensive statement, St. Jerome wrote that "All sins are forgiven in baptism."[5]

During the heat of controversy in Pelagian times, the Church defined that all sin is fully removed with baptism. Then the Council of Trent restated what is universal Catholic doctrine, that "God hates nothing in those who are regenerated. For there remains nothing deserving of condemnation in those who are truly buried with Christ by baptism unto death, who walk not according to the flesh." They become "innocent, spotless, pure, upright, and beloved of God."[6]

While all guilt of sin is removed, the infirmity of our fallen human nature remains after baptism. Thus we retain concupiscence, which is our unreasoning appetite that can lead to sin, but as long as we do not consent to wrong desires or impulses, so far from sinning we gain merit in the sight of God. Indeed, the struggle with these unruly drives is part of our earthly probation. But the drives are not sins, no matter how urgent they may be.

Remission of All Punishment Due to Sin. Not only does baptism remove the guilt of sin and reinstate the sinner in God's friendship, but with it all the punishment due to sin is also mercifully forgiven. To communicate the merits of Christ's passion and death is common to all the sacraments, but of baptism alone does St. Paul say that by it we die and are buried together with Christ.

The Church has always understood this to mean, among other things, that once a person is baptized he is completely "with Christ." No matter what he may have done before, he is not required to perform any penance or works of satisfaction for his past. To require such expiation, it has always been held, would be an indignity to baptism and contrary to Christian Tradition.

It may be asked why, if all penalties due to sin are removed, we should still have to suffer so much from infancy through life until death. Two reasons are commonly given. Since by baptism we have become united to Christ, we should also become likened to him. Christ we know, though clothed from conception with the fullness of grace and truth, was not spared the human infirmity that he assumed until, having suffered and died on the cross, he rose to the glory of immortality. Moreover, our bodily infirmities, the capacity for pain in body and spirit, and the sufferings we experience because of our unruly passions, have within them the "seed and material of virtue" from which we shall eventually receive a more abundant harvest of glory and ample rewards. When, with patient resignation to providence, we bear all the trials of life and, aided by the divine assistance, subject to the dominion of reason the rebellious desires of our heart, we should cherish an assured hope that, like St. Paul, after we have fought the good fight, finished the course, and kept the faith, our Lord, the just Judge, will render to us the crown of justice that is laid up for us.

Grace of Regeneration.   Baptism does more than remove the guilt and penalty due to sin. It infuses into our souls the life of grace that Christ won for us by his death and Resurrection. The New Testament is filled with terms that bring out what this means. Christ in his conversation with Nicodemus spoke of the need for being born again, and did not contradict the cautious Pharisee who could not understand how a man could enter his mother's womb a second time. It was in this context that Christ foretold the necessity of baptism for salvation. Besides a rebirth, baptism is also a regeneration, inasmuch as we have a second genealogy besides our natural one. As baptized Christians we are, in the words of the evangelist, procreated not of human stock, nor of the will of man, but of God himself. St. Paul exhausts the figures of speech to make clear the newness of life that baptism brings to those who have received the "laver of redemption." The Corinthians were told that they had become "a completely new batch of bread," the Galatians that they were now "a new creature," the Ephesians that they had "put on the new man," the Colossians that they had "stripped off your old behavior with your old self, and you have put on a new self, which will progress toward true knowledge the more it is renewed in the image of its Creator" (Col. 3:9–10). Baptism is the second Genesis for those who have been called to this vocation.

Virtues Infused.   The new life conferred in baptism is an objective reality, which St. Augustine called the "soul of the soul," and which therefore has capacities that are as much beyond the powers of mere nature as the ability to think or choose is above the capacity of irrational beasts. Faith, hope, and charity are said to be infused, i.e., poured into, the one baptized, long before he reaches the age of reason if the sacrament is conferred in infancy. All, whether infants or adults, receive this infusion as a sheer gift of God (Tt. 3:3–5).

Among the gifts of grace infused at baptism are the peace and joy of the Holy Spirit, which make possible the practice of the Beatitudes, even to loving the cross in suffering for Christ, and the practice of the counsels, even to making a lifetime sacrifice of earthly possessions in imitation of Christ.

Incorporation into Christ. Through baptism we become united to Christ as head of the Mystical Body. This is the dominant theme of the Pauline letters, which remind the faithful of their organic union with Christ in the one body, which is the Church, and of which they are truly members, comparable to the limbs of a human body, whose direction depends on the head and whose animation derives from the same soul.

This is also thematic in the new baptismal liturgy, which reminds parents, godparents, and the neophytes (or children) that through baptism we are incorporated twice over, once into Christ and once again into his Church, although both are really two aspects of the same incorporation. He has identified himself with the body, which is the Church, so that in becoming members of the latter we are joined with him in that mystical union of which the baptismal character is the indelible sign.

It is here, too, that the ecumenical movement finds its most solid doctrinal foundation. Catholics can now affirm with full security that they are closely joined "with those who are baptized and have the honor of the name Christian, yet do not profess the faith in its entirety." Why so? Because they are "marked by baptism and thereby joined to Christ." Because, since they are incorporated into Christ, they have "a real union in the Holy Spirit, for he is at work among them too with the power of sanctification in gifts and graces; he has given some of them strength to the extent of shedding their blood." Consequently, it is the same Spirit of Christ, dwelling in the hearts of all Christians, in those who profess Roman Catholicism and in those who do not. He is "rousing in all Christ's disciples desire and action, in the hope that all men may be united peacefully, in the manner that Christ appointed, in one flock under one shepherd."[7]

There is an ecumenical movement in Christendom today only because one and the same Christ already mysteriously unites all who have been baptized in his name. He is active in his members and is urging them to become more fully united among themselves.

Right to Heaven. Since baptism confers the life of grace in the soul, it carries the promise of salvation. In the new liturgy, when the person has been baptized, he is clothed with a white garment. The celebrant then says: "You have become a new creation, and have clothed yourself in Christ. See in this white garment the outward sign of your Christian dignity. With your family and friends to help you by word and example, bring that dignity unstained into the everlasting life of heaven." The Church's commentators on the Gospels have always seen in the parable of the wedding garment the symbol of sanctifying grace received at baptism, without which no one is admitted to the banquet of the heavenly kingdom.

A more delicate question is the lot of those children who die without receiving baptism. According to God's universal salvific will, we believe that somehow he gives all persons the opportunity of reaching heaven. There is such a thing as baptism of desire, defined by the Council of Trent, but this assumes sufficient mental maturity to make an act of faith and love of God.

We must, however, say with the Church that "There are people who are in ignorance of Christ's Gospel and of his Church through no fault of their own, and who search for God in sincerity of heart; they attempt to put into practice the recognition of his will that they have reached through the dictate of conscience. They do so under the influence of divine grace; they can attain everlasting salvation."[8] By implication, their children who die before the age of reason can also be saved.

Saying this does not deny what the Church also teaches through two ecumenical councils, that even those who die with only original sin on their souls cannot reach the beatific vision.[9] There is also the condemnation of the Jansenists, as teaching something "false, rash, and injurious to Catholic education," who claimed it was a Pelagian fable to hold that there is a place "which the faithful generally designate by the name of the limbo of children," for the souls of those who depart this life with the sole guilt of original sin.[10] St. Thomas taught that limbo is a place of perfect natural happiness, but minus the supernatural vision of God to which, of course, no creature has a natural right.

The Church today reflects the same basic concern in its baptismal liturgy. "As for the time of baptism," the Roman Ritual states, "the first consideration is the welfare of the child, that it may not be deprived of the benefit of the sacrament." Therefore, "if the child is in danger of death, it is to be baptized without delay." Under these circumstances, anyone can baptize, even a person who is not a Christian, provided he carries out the wishes of a Christian believer and performs the correct baptismal ritual.

CONCILIAR CHANGES

When the Second Vatican Council treated the sacrament of baptism in its various documents, it carefully distinguished between the unchangeable faith of which the sacrament is the visible expression, and certain ritual changes to be made in its administration.

We know from the Gospels that baptism was conferred by water and words, where the words pronounced were those recorded by St. Matthew, i.e., "in the name of the Father, and of the Son, and of the Holy Spirit." The trinitarian formula is specified in the first-century *Didache,* which indicates that at least by the year A.D. 100 this was the common usage, whatever may be said about baptizing "in the name of the Lord Jesus" recorded in the Acts of the Apostles.

We also know that although immersion was the earliest practice, people were also baptized by pouring of the water already in apostolic times.[11] Catholicism has never been vexed over the question of when exactly Christ instituted the first sacrament, except to suggest that a most likely time was when Christ was himself baptized by John the Baptist in the Jordan, but the obligation to baptize was not promulgated by the Savior until shortly before his Ascension.

In keeping with its spirit of renewal and adaption, Vatican II mandated a variety of changes in the ceremonies of baptism and in the preparation of catechumens for their admission to the Church.

The baptism of infants remained substantially intact. "From earliest times, the Church, to which the mission of the preaching of the Gospel and of baptizing was entrusted, has baptized children as well as adults. Our Lord said, 'Unless a man is reborn of water and the Holy Spirit, he cannot enter the kingdom of God' (Jn. 3:5). The Church has always understood these words to mean that children should not be deprived of baptism, because they are baptized in the faith of the Church."[12]

But the baptismal ceremonies were considerably changed. They are to bring out the fact that those being baptized are infants, and also the specific roles of parents and godparents. One exhortation addressed to parents at the baptism of several children illustrates the new emphasis:

> You have asked to have your children baptized. In doing so you are accepting the responsibility of training them in the practice of the faith. It will be your duty to bring them up to keep God's commandments as Christ taught us, by loving God and our neighbor. Do you clearly understand what you are undertaking?

The new baptismal rite contains variants, to be used at the discretion of the bishop of the diocese, for occasions when a large number are to be baptized together. Moreover, a shorter rite is available for mission lands, to be used by catechists, but also by the faithful in general when there is danger of death and neither priest nor deacon are available.

In place of the former rite called the "order of supplying what was omitted in the baptism of an infant," a new rite has been drawn up. This shows very clearly that the infant, baptized by the short ritual for emergency reasons, has already been received into the Church.

But the most dramatic change affected the preparation of catechumens in missionary lands. In the early Church, the title catechumens (from the Greek *catechoumenoi,* those being instructed) was given to adults preparing for baptism. They were assigned a place in the Church but were solemnly dismissed before the Eucharist proper began. Only those who had reached the immediate stage of awaiting baptism at the coming Easter formed a separate group, the enlightened ones. There was an elaborate ritual of preparation, with a succession of scrutinies, in the preceding Lent, the candidates being finally admitted at the Paschal Mass.

The Church's experience in recent centuries pointed to the need for restoring the catechumenate. It is not to be a "bare explanation of dogmas and commandments, but a training period and apprenticeship of adequate duration for the whole of the Christian life." This means that "catechumens should be properly initiated into the mystery of salvation and, through the practice of evangelical morality and with sacred ceremonies held at successive intervals of time, they should be introduced into the life of faith, of the liturgy and the charity of the people of God."[13]

One of the lessons the Church has learned since the missionary enterprises of the early Middle Ages and the sixteenth century is that Catholic Christianity is a demanding religion. Too many people in many lands had been converted to the faith but without adequate preparation of mind and heart, and with sad consequences as a result. Lacking in depth of understanding or commitment, or injudiciously baptized in large numbers, the neophytes later drifted back into their superstitions or fell into a curious mixture of Christianity, animism, and moral customs that were incompatible with the high ethical requirements of the Gospel.

Mindful, however, of the biblical case of Cornelius the Roman centurion, the Church has been careful to note that catechumens "are already linked to the Church, belong to the household of Christ, and not infrequently already lead a life of faith, hope, and charity."[14] These persons, not yet baptized, are already the objects of God's special providence and may be (as Augustine pointed out) more holy than certain unworthy Christians. Once baptized, they receive an infusion of divine grace and a title to divine assistance that only those who have been reborn of water and the Holy Spirit can expect from God's mercy.

CONFIRMATION

In order to appreciate the importance of confirmation in the Catholic liturgy, we should see it as a stage in the sacramental progress of the Christian, comparable to the origin, development, and nourishing of natural life. The faithful are reborn to a share in the divine nature by baptism, are strengthened by the sacrament of confirmation, and finally are sustained by the food of eternal life through the Holy Eucharist.

By means of these sacraments of initiation, Christians receive in increasing measure the treasures of divine grace and advance toward the perfection of charity in their love of God and of neighbor. Always confirmation was associated with baptism, as its name implies, to confirm the supernatural life already received, and with the Eucharist as the means by which the fully confirmed believer might be often fortified.

HISTORICAL DEVELOPMENT

Throughout the Gospel narratives we see how the Holy Spirit assisted Christ in fulfilling his messianic mission. On receiving the baptism of John, Jesus saw the Spirit descending on him and remaining with him. He was led by the Spirit to undertake his public ministry as the Messiah foretold by the prophets, and relied on the constant presence and assistance of the same Spirit. While teaching the people of his own native Nazareth, he intimated that the words of Isaiah referred to himself, namely, "the Spirit of the Lord is upon me."

He promised the disciples that the Holy Spirit would help them also to bear fearless witness to their faith even before persecutors. The day before he died, he assured the apostles that he would send the Spirit of truth from his Father, who would stay with them forever. And after the Resurrection, Christ promised the coming descent of the Holy Spirit, from whom his followers would receive power to testify before the world to the mystery of salvation.

On the feast of Pentecost, the Holy Spirit came down in an extraordinary way on the apostles as they were gathered together with Mary the Mother of Jesus and the group of men and women disciples. They were so filled with the Holy Spirit that by divine inspiration they began courageously to proclaim "the mighty works of God." Peter openly regarded the Spirit who had thus come down upon the apostles as the first gift of the messianic age. Those who believed the apostles' teaching were then baptized, and they too received "the gift of the Holy Spirit."

From that time on, the apostles carried out the wishes of Christ by imparting to the newly baptized the gift of the Spirit by the laying on of hands. They looked upon this as a completion of the grace of baptism. That is why the letter to the Hebrews lists among the first elements of Christian instruction the teaching about baptisms (plural) and the laying on of hands. This laying on of hands is considered by Catholic Tradition the beginning of the sacrament of confirmation, which in a certain way perpetuates the pentecostal grace in the Church.

This makes clear the special importance of confirmation for sacramental initiation by which the faithful "as members of the living Christ are incorporated into him and made like him through baptism and through confirmation and the Eucharist."[15]

From apostolic times, communicating the gift of the Holy Spirit has been carried out in the Church with a variety of ritual forms. These forms underwent many changes in the East and West, but always preserving the essential feature of conferring the Holy Spirit.

Washing with water, anointing with oil, and the laying on of hands all came to be associated with entrance into the fullness of Christian life, and the aggregate spiritual effect that flowed from these outward observances was held to include the removal of sin, admission to the Church of the redeemed, "sealing" to eternal life, and imparting of the Spirit. But practices differed. While at one place washing, anointing, and imposition of hands might be considered different parts or aspects of a single rite, elsewhere they could be regarded as connected with two, or possibly even more, stages in the Christian's progress into the fullness of sacramental life.

Confirmation, without the precise name, appears as a rite clearly separate from baptism by the end of the second century. The same clear distinction was made by Pope Cornelius in the middle of the third century. By the fourth century, confirmation, whether conferred by anointing or laying on of hands, was everywhere a separate rite.

With the liberation of the Church after Constantine, a new factor entered the picture. Previously the bishop was able to take a personal interest in all the candidates for baptism. Now he found that he could not baptize everyone in person, and the functions of the parish priest (immersion or ablution) and bishop (anointing), which had been closely associated, gradually became distinct. What had often been scarcely distinguishable elements in the single baptism-confirmation rite were now performed by different ministers.

Before long, however, the respective customs in the East and West became settled. In the Eastern Church the primitive custom of administering confirmation in immediate relation to baptism was retained. This was done by confining the bishop's part to the consecration of the oil used for the anointing. This was taken to the parish priest, who performed the actual rite of confirmation as occasion required. After anointing, it became a regular practice in the East to dispense Holy Communion at once, so that the infant received all three sacraments in a single service. Such has remained the Eastern custom down to the present day.

In the West, on the other hand, the bishop retained the function as regular minister of the rite, as he had also been originally of baptism. Confirmation was therefore deferred until an opportunity arose of presenting the candidate to the bishop in person. One result was that, owing to the difficulties of communication and the many duties of a bishop, confirmation became very irregular in the Middle Ages.

RITE OF ADMINISTRATION

The practice in the Latin rite had remained substantially the same over the centuries. The bishop of the diocese or one of his auxiliaries was the ordinary minister of confirmation and the priest rarely, if ever, administered the sacrament. Already before the Second Vatican Council, however, priests were authorized to confirm under certain restricted circumstances. Since the Council, this authorization has been greatly extended.

One of the conciliar provisions was very specific: "The rite of confirmation is to be revised and the intimate connection which this sacrament has with the whole of Christian initiation is to be more clearly set forth."[16] As a result a number of significant changes was made in the ritual administration of the sacrament, all consistent with the general idea of bringing out the role of confirmation in the total entrance into sacramental life. Two facets of this change are specially pertinent: Confirmation is now preceded by the formal renewal of baptismal promises which, in most cases, had originally been made by the child's sponsors; and the conferral of confirmation is to be done during the sacrifice of the Mass, at which Holy Communion is received.

But more important than these liturgical modifications was the decision in 1971 of Paul VI to make the essence of confirmation consist in the anointing with chrism, which is a mixture of olive oil and balsam consecrated by the bishop on Holy Thursday; along with laying on of hands; and the pronunciation of a new formula for conferring the sacrament. The Pope first noted that until now, in the Latin rite, the formula commonly used dated from the twelfth century. It said: "I sign you with the sign of the cross and confirm you with the chrism of salvation. In the name of the Father and of the Son and of the Holy Spirit." He then explained why a change was being made and what the new confirmation rite would be:

> It is clear that in the administration of confirmation in the East and the West, though in different ways, the most important ritual action was the anointing, which in a certain way represents the apostolic laying on of hands. Since this anointing with chrism appropriately signifies the spiritual anointing of the Holy Spirit, who is given to the faithful, we want to confirm its importance and continuance.
>
> Regarding the words pronounced in confirmation, we have examined with due consideration the dignity of the venerable formula used in the Latin Church. However, we judge preferable the very ancient formula of the Byzantine rite, by which the Gift of the Holy Spirit himself is expressed and the outpouring of the Spirit which took place on the day of Pentecost is recalled. We therefore adopt this formula, rendering it almost word for word.
>
> Therefore, in order that the revision of the rite of confirmation may fittingly embrace also the essence of the sacramental rite, by our supreme apostolic authority we decree and lay down that in the Latin Church the following should be observed in the future: The sacrament of confirmation is conferred through the anointing with chrism on the forehead, which is done by the laying on of the hand, and through the words, "Receive the seal of the Gift of the Holy Spirit."[17]

By way of conclusion, Pope Paul added that the laying of hands on the candidates, which is done with the prescribed prayer before the anointing, does not belong to the essence of the sacramental rite. Nevertheless, it is to be held in high esteem, in that it contributes to the integral perfection of the confirmation ritual and affords a better understanding of the sacrament. So there is a double laying on of hands, but only the second—at which the forehead is anointed—is strictly essential for conferring the sacrament. What the Church wishes clearly to manifest is the transmission of the Holy Spirit, by apostolic genealogy going back to Pentecost, through the symbolism of consecrated hands being laid on the head of one receiving the Gift of God.

SACRAMENTAL EFFECTS

It is predictable that the sacrament of confirmation will receive more than ordinary attention in the modern Catholic world. Its need becomes more obvious as we reflect on the call to witness to Christ and the faith, of which the Church so earnestly reminds the faithful today.

We may in general define confirmation as the sacrament of spiritual strengthening, as distinct from baptism, which is the sacrament of spiritual regeneration. Confirmation assumes that the person has already been baptized and, in fact, the confirming ritual would be invalid if inadvertently performed on someone who is not baptized.

In keeping with all sacraments of the living, i.e., those to be received in the state of grace, confirmation increases the person's possession of divine life; it confers actual graces and what is called the special sacramental grace peculiar to this sacrament; and, in this case, it also gives a unique sacramental character.

1. The person who is confirmed receives a deepening of God's friendship and, as we commonly say, an increase of sanctifying grace. Since the state of grace means a share in the life of God, we should expect this sacrament to affect that area of the divine life which has to do with its capacity to survive. Thus the supernatural life becomes more resilient, more capable of resisting dangers to its continued existence and growth, and more alert to protecting itself against what might threaten its well-being.

Associated with sanctifying grace are the infused virtues and gifts of the Holy Spirit. Among the latter, the gift of fortitude or courage best identifies the purpose of confirmation, which immeasurably strengthens this gift and enables the person "to do battle against the enemies of salvation," if necessary by suffering martyrdom.

2. Actual graces, as illuminations of the mind and inspirations of the will to meet the needs of the spiritual life, are also received. The sacrament confers these graces "by title," for those who are confirmed before the age of reason, and both actually and "by title" for persons who receive the sacrament after the age of discretion. The difference between these two forms of obtaining grace is simply that the confirmed Christian is gifted with additional helps from God to live out his faith courageously, and he receives the help not only at the moment of confirmation, but also acquires a claim or title to such divine assistance for the rest of his life, as occasion and circumstances require.

These graces are always deeply interior aids, which only God, who dwells in the souls of the confirmed, can supply. But they are also those myriad external graces, as persons, places, and things, that divine providence arranges to protect his chosen ones from extreme dangers and afford them the support they need to live up to the demands of their calling.

3. The special sacramental grace is to perfect, in the sense of complete, the effects of baptism. It brings to perfection the supernatural life infused at baptism by giving it the power to withstand opposition from within, which is human respect and fear, and from without, which is physical or psychological coercion to deny or compromise what the faith demands. The Church's own definition on the effects of confirmation brings out both aspects in terms of the ritual performed:

> The effect of this sacrament is that the Holy Spirit is given in it for strength just as he was given to the Apostles on Pentecost, in order that the Christian may courageously confess the name of Christ. And therefore, the one to be confirmed is anointed on the forehead, where shame shows itself, lest he be ashamed to confess the name of Christ and especially his cross which was, indeed, according to the Apostle, a stumbling block to the Jew and to the Gentiles foolishness. For this reason the recipient is signed with the sign of the cross.[18]

We might say that the sacrament of confirmation enables the Christian to live up to Christ's mandate of taking up one's cross daily and following him faithfully, in spite of one's personal feelings and in the face of criticism or contradiction from others.

4. But confirmation also imprints a character on the soul of the Christian. This character means assimilation to Christ the priest, in the twofold sense of having the strength to bear suffering (passively) in union with him and the courage to sacrifice pleasant things (actively) out of love for him.

It also means assimilation to Christ the teacher, by the acquisition of a strong will in adhering to the faith in the face of obstacles, a strong mind in not doubting the articles of faith, a strong humility of spirit in professing the faith, and a strong wisdom that knows how to communicate the faith to others effectively.

It finally means assimilation to Christ the king, by infusion of a strong leadership that can direct others on the path to salvation, of a strong character that can withstand the ravages of bad example or the snares of seduction, and a strong personality that will attract even the enemies of Christ to his standard.

We might summarily describe the sacramental character of confirmation by saying that it is the sacrament of witness to Christ, in the Church, before the world—where each phrase carries with it profound implications for the Catholic apostolate. The character that this sacrament imprints on the soul empowers it to testify publicly to one's faith in Christ—hence the patristic expression "sacrament of martyrdom." The witness is to Christ, by the fearless profession of loyalty to him and his cause, fidelity to his teachings, and absolute trust in his love. Yet this character is also social by nature. The strength it confers is to a task that is to be done with others as a collective witness, and for others as a service to their spiritual needs. It thus testifies to Christ's continued presence and activity today and verifies his promise to be with his Church all days, even to the end of time. The object of this witness is the world, which includes all those who profit from the evidence of unswerving loyalty to Christ and his Church, whether they are Christians or not, since everyone admires moral courage, which consists not in blindly overlooking danger but seeing it and conquering it—in this case through confidence in God.

Confirmation has been rightly called the sacrament of Catholic Action, as the Church's conciliar teaching explains: "The faithful derive the right and duty to the apostolate from their union with Christ their head. Incorporated into Christ's Mystical Body through baptism, and strengthened by the power of the Holy Spirit through confirmation, they are assigned to the apostolate by the Lord himself."[19] Every baptized person, confirmed by the Spirit of God, has a mission to bring others to Christ because he has the grace of zeal that these sacraments confer.

ORDINATION

The sacrament of orders is so closely associated with the sacraments of the Eucharist and penance that everything pertaining to these unique gifts of Christ to his Church also pertains to the unique powers that only those specially ordained to the priestly office possess.

Yet in our day, as in other significant eras of Catholic Christianity, certain aspects of the priesthood have come under special scrutiny or face extraordinary challenges. In the process of undergoing the reflection and self-understanding that these occasion, the Church has become more aware of what the priesthood really means, and its teaching has taken on a clarity that promises to make this mystery of the faith particularly vital in the years to come.

The ultimate basis for the sacrament of orders is Christ's own priestly ministry on earth, coupled with the historical fact that he went out of his way to associate others with him to learn his teachings, acquire his spirit, receive his powers, and thus continue his saving work for the human race.

If we look for precedents to this communicated ministry of Jesus, we find it in the ancient prophets who passed on their prophetic powers to those who would follow them as teachers in Israel. We find it in the priestly castes of the family of Aaron, which by divine legislation passed on its sacerdotal privileges from father to son. We find it in the royal family of David and his descendants, of whom the Messiah was to be born.

Christ made sure that this concept of succession from the past to his time, and from him into the future, was clear in everything he did. His choice of the twelve apostles, who would judge the twelve tribes of Israel, and the very name of "apostles," as men whom he was sending, became the keystone of the messianic community after his Ascension and the descent of the Holy Spirit. Time and again he told the apostles that he was sending them into the world to teach and preach, to baptize and sanctify, to go into the whole world and make disciples of all nations. What he did at the Last Supper, when he told the twelve to continue what he had just performed, and on Easter Sunday night, when he told them to forgive sins in his name, were only the culmination of his entire public life and the logical outcome of what he had been promising to confer since he first called them, one by one, to follow him and he would make them fishers of men.

DOCTRINAL PRINCIPLES

While there had been questions raised at various times about the nature and functions of the priesthood before the sixteenth century, they were not so sweeping or incisive as occurred during the Reformation. It is not surprising, then, that the Council of Trent should

have faced the issues raised and left the Church an extensive presentation of Catholic doctrine on the sacrament of orders. What is
more surprising perhaps is that the Second Vatican Council, four
centuries later, went over the same ground covered by Trent and
consciously restated the same doctrine, while adding nuances and
highlighting certain features that will call for special emphasis today.

Holy Orders is "truly and properly a sacrament instituted by
Christ our Lord." It is not a mere "human invention thought up by
men, a kind of rite of choosing ministers of the word of God and
the sacraments."[20] Ordination is not simply an installation of
Church leaders or administrators of the sacraments.

When the bishop pronounces the words "receive the Holy Spirit,"
there is a special conferral of divine gifts, in such a way that the
sacramental "character is imprinted by ordination." As a consequence, it is impossible that a man "who was once a priest can become a layman again."[21] The process of laicization, as it is called,
whereby a priest is dispensed from certain priestly duties and, if he
had been a celibate, may even be allowed to marry, does not mean
that he is literally reduced to the lay state. This cannot happen because the Catholic Church believes that the priestly character is
indelible and therefore unchangeable. One of two things may occur,
however, depending on circumstances. More commonly the still
remaining priest is given a dispensation from priestly obligations if
he agrees to not exercise his priestly ministry, and may thus publicly
not be recognized for what he really is. Or more rarely his ordination
ritual may be declared null and void, for extraordinary reasons—
not easily provable—such as the absence of genuine intention to
become a priest.

The basis of sacramental orders is its divine origin, not only
that somehow God inspired the Church to create the sacrament,
but that the priesthood is truly a revelation of the New Testament.
The Catholic faith, therefore, excludes any such explanation as the
following:

> That there is not a visible and external priesthood in the New
> Testament, or that there is no power of consecrating and offering
> the body and blood of the Lord, and of remitting and of retaining
> sins, but says that there is only the office and simple ministry of
> preaching the Gospel, or says that those who do not preach are not
> priests at all.[22]

In the Catholic understanding of the priesthood, the "cultic" or liturgical elements are so fundamental that they constitute the essential difference between those who are and those who are not possessed of sacerdotal powers.

One more feature of holy orders, which at least partially accounts for the name "orders," is the different levels or grades of ordination recognized in the Church. At this point, the Second Vatican Council introduced a number of clarifications and also innovations that typify a doctrinal development of the faith.

GRADATION IN THE MINISTRY

In the New Testament we discover several grades of ministry coexisting. A broad distinction might be made, on the one side, between a "missionary" or "itinerant," an "apostolic" or "charismatic" ministry, although the latter term is misleading; and, on the other hand, of a "local" or "settled" ministry. The former is represented by the apostles, which included also men like Barnabas. The latter is represented by bishops (*episcopoi*), which literally means "overseers"; presbyters (*presbyteroi*), meaning "elders," from which the term "priest" is derived; and deacons (*diakonoi*), which means servants, messengers, or ministers.

This second group in the New Testament is the nucleus of the traditional threefold ministry, which the Catholic Church identifies with the sacrament of orders. Except for the semantic problem that the terms "bishop" and "presbyter" are sometimes used interchangeably in the Scriptures, the distinctive existence of these three grades is a matter of biblical record.

As time went on, we find still other classifications appearing. At Rome, under Pope Cornelius in the middle of the third century, there were, besides the bishop, forty-six presbyters, seven deacons, seven subdeacons, forty-two acolytes, and fifty-two exorcists, readers, and doorkeepers. By the later Middle Ages it was the prevalent view that there were seven orders, of which three were major—namely, priest, deacon, and subdeacon—and the other four were minor, i.e., acolyte, exorcist, reader, and doorkeeper. Significantly, the later distinction between "consecration" for a bishop and "ordination" for the others was unknown in early times.

The Council of Trent bypassed the issue except to make plain that there is in the Church a "divinely instituted hierarchy consisting of bishops, priests, and ministers."[23] The word "other" before "ministers" was dropped only the day before this definition of Trent was finalized.

That was the situation up to the eve of the Second Vatican Council. Regularly a young man entered the clerical state by receiving tonsure, so named because ritual called for the shaving of part or all of the hair of the head. Exceptions were made in certain countries, like the United States and England, where this was not in accordance with popular usage. A token cutting of some strands of hair was done instead.

Then, depending on the prudent judgment of the bishop, various times had to elapse before the cleric was admitted to the minor orders. Acolytes had to wait at least a year before being promoted to the subdiaconate; subdeacons and deacons, at least three months in their respective orders before being promoted to the diaconate and priesthood, respectively, unless in the judgment of the bishop the need or advantage of the Church demanded otherwise.

Conciliar Changes. While the *Constitution on the Liturgy* of the Second Vatican Council merely stated that "Both the ceremonies and texts or the ordination rites are to be revised," the actual revision went far beyond this simple directive. Three principal documents of Paul VI deal with the subject of ordination: an apostolic constitution on the new rite for the ordination of deacons, priests, and bishops; and two apostolic letters, one setting down certain norms for the diaconate, and another in which tonsure, the minor orders, and the subdiaconate were reformed.

The papal declaration on the ordination of deacons, priests, and bishops begins with the solemn words, "By our supreme apostolic authority we decree and establish the following with regard to the matter (materials and actions) and form (words) in the conferral of each order." Then follow three paragraphs, one for each of the orders, in sequence, to remove every ambiguity and clarify the essence of each conferral of the sacrament:

> In the ordination of deacons, the matter is the imposition of the bishop's hands upon the individual candidates, which is done in silence before the consecratory prayer; the form consists of the words of the consecratory prayer, of which the following pertain to the na-

ture of the Order and therefore are required for the validity of the act: "Lord, we pray, send forth upon them the Holy Spirit so that by the grace of your seven gifts they may be strengthened by him to carry out faithfully the work of the ministry."

In the ordination of priests, the matter is likewise the imposition of the bishop's hands upon the individual candidates, which is done in silence before the consecratory prayer, the form consists of the words of the consecratory prayer, of which the following pertain to the nature of the Order and therefore are required for the validity of the act: "We ask you, all-powerful Father, give these servants of yours the dignity of the presbyterate. Renew the Spirit of holiness within them. By your divine gift may they attain the second order in the hierarchy and exemplify right conduct in their lives."

Finally, in the ordination of a bishop, the matter is the imposition of hands on the head of the bishop-elect by the consecrating bishops, or at least by the principal consecrator, which is done in silence before the consecratory prayer; the form consists of the words of the consecratory prayer, of which the following pertain to the nature of the Order and therefore are required for the validity of the act: "Now pour out upon this chosen one that power which flows from you, the perfect Spirit whom he gave to the Apostles, who established the Church in every place as the sanctuary where your name would always be praised and glorified."[24]

The provisions of Pope Paul clarified many things, notably the fact that the diaconate is essentially a ministry, that the presbyterate is the second order in the Catholic hierarchy, with stress on the holiness of life expected of priests, and that the episcopate is derived from the apostles and places bishops into hierarchical communion with the head and members of the episcopal college. Thus collegiality is founded on the apostolic succession and on corporate union among the bishops in union with the see of Peter.

Permanent Diaconate.   The new ceremony for the ordination of deacons was only a prelude to the new importance the diaconate will assume in the Catholic Church. Three years after the ordination rites were established, the Pope issued a lengthy declaration that traced the history of the diaconate from biblical times, and re-established this order as a permanent order in the Church, and not merely (as it had become in the West) a temporary stage on the way to the priesthood. Its most salient features are the following:

1. Two forms of the diaconate are hereby recognized in the Latin

Church, a permanent form, which remains for life, and a transitional form, which precedes ordination to the priesthood.

2. Before ordination, candidates for the diaconate make out a formal statement indicating which form of diaconate they wish to enter and testifying that they are doing so "freely and of their own accord."

3. Two forms of the permanent diaconate are approved, one that includes the lifetime of celibacy and another that confers the order on married men. Regarding celibacy, the papal document states that "its obligation for candidates to the priesthood and for unmarried candidates to the diaconate are indeed linked with the diaconate. The public commitment to holy celibacy before God and Church is to be celebrated in a particular rite, even by religious, and it is to precede ordination to the diaconate. Celibacy taken on in this way is a diriment (invalidating) impediment to entering marriage. In accordance with the traditional discipline of the Church, a married deacon who has lost his wife cannot enter a new marriage."

4. Correspondingly, two kinds of theological education are prescribed by the norms of the apostolic see. Those planning to become permanent deacons are to follow a course of studies designed by the episcopal conferences and approved by Rome.

5. Regarding the recitation of the Divine Office, deacons who are called to the priesthood "are bound by their sacred ordination to the duty of celebrating the liturgy of the hours," whereas "it is most fitting that permanent deacons should recite daily at least a part of the liturgy of the hours, to be determined by the episcopal conference."

6. The law used to be that a person became a cleric when he received his first tonsure. At the same time he became "incardinated" in a diocese, if he belonged to the diocesan clergy; this meant that he was subject to the bishop of that diocese as a member of his clergy. From now on "entrance into the clerical state and incardination into a diocese are brought about by ordination to the diaconate."[25] This has far-reaching practical implications as regards the personal responsibility of candidates for the diaconate and the relative freedom of the bishops until a mutual understanding is reached with those who are to be incardinated in their dioceses.

Institution of the Ministries. The third major decision of Paul VI affected the subdiaconate and what had been called minor orders.

For numerous reasons, but mainly because the whole spectrum of clerical states from tonsure through the subdiaconate had become more symbolic than real, the Pope decided to completely abolish tonsure and to realign the other orders in such a way that they would be truly practicable in the Church today.

1. What up to now had been called minor orders are henceforth called ministries. These may be committed to lay Christians. Hence they are no longer to be considered as reserved to candidates for the sacrament of orders.

2. Two ministries, adapted to present-day needs, are to be preserved in the whole Latin Church, namely those of readers and acolytes. The functions heretofore committed to the subdeacon are entrusted to the reader and acolyte. Consequently "the major order of subdiaconate no longer exists in the Latin Church. There is nothing, however, to prevent the acolyte being also called a sub-deacon in some places, if the episcopal conference judges it opportune."

3. The reader is appointed for a function proper to him, that of reading the word of God in the liturgical assembly. Accordingly, he is to read the lessons from sacred Scripture, except for the Gospel, in the Mass and other sacred celebrations. He is to recite the psalms between the readings when there is no psalmist. He is to present the intentions for the general intercessions in the absence of a deacon or cantor. He is to direct the singing and the participation by the faithful. He is to instruct the faithful for the worthy reception of the sacraments. He may also, insofar as necessary, take care of preparing the faithful who by a temporary appointment are to read the Scriptures in liturgical celebrations. In order that he might "more fittingly and perfectly fulfill these functions, let him meditate assiduously on sacred Scripture."

4. The acolyte is appointed in order to aid the deacon and to minister to the priest. It is therefore his duty to attend to the service of the altar and to assist the deacon and the priest in liturgical celebrations, especially in the celebration of Mass. He may also distribute Holy Communion as an auxiliary minister at the Eucharistic liturgy and to the sick.

In the same extraordinary circumstances, the acolyte may be entrusted with publicly exposing the Blessed Sacrament for adoration by the faithful and afterward replacing it, but not with giving benediction. He may also, to the extent needed, take care of instructing other faithful who by appointment assist the priest or deacon by carrying the missal, cross, candles, and similar functions.

5. "In accordance with the venerable tradition of the Church, institution in the ministries of readers and acolytes is reserved to men." The ministries are conferred by the bishop of the diocese and, in clerical religious institutes, by the major superior, according to the liturgical rites composed for this purpose by the Church. Women may perform these ministries to the degree that they are delegated to do so.

6. Candidates for the diaconate and the priesthood are to receive the ministries of reader and acolyte in order to better dispose themselves for the future service of the word and of the altar. The conferring of these ministries, however, does not imply the right to sustenance or salary from the Church.[26]

Typical of the seriousness with which the Church takes the newly created ministry of reader is the ritual for their institution. It consists of seven parts, of which the sixth and last are a prayer of invocation and the actual conferring of the ministry. The bishop prays:

> God, source of all goodness and light, you sent your only Son, the Word of life, to make known the mystery of your love. In your kindness bless our brothers who have been chosen for the ministry of readers. As they meditate on your Word, help them to understand it better and to proclaim it faithfully to your people. We ask this through Christ our Lord.

Each candidate then goes to the bishop, who gives him a Bible to hold. While handing the Bible to the person, the bishop says: "Receive this book of Holy Scripture and announce the word of God faithfully, so that it may grow in the hearts of men." The reader answers, "Amen."[27]

CLERICAL CELIBACY

Early Church discipline on clerical celibacy varied in the East and West and sometimes from province to province. During the first three centuries, although practiced by a considerable number of the clergy, it was not of general obligation throughout the Church. The requirement for all the clergy of Spain at the Council of Elvira about the year 305 marked the beginning of official divergence in the practice of Eastern and Western Christianity.

In 315, two local councils in Galatia and Cappadocia forbade priests to marry. At the First Council of Nicea, a vigorous discussion took place over the proposal to forbid married bishops, priests, and deacons to live with their wives. Paphnutius, a bishop of Upper Egypt, settled the dispute by persuading the Council to follow the ancient tradition that prohibited marriage after ordination.

Gradually the law of celibacy in the Western Church became more definite and strict. A council held at Rome under Pope Siricius in 386 and two councils held at Carthage a little later imposed continence on all bishops, priests, and deacons. This decree was enforced to a certain extent throughout the West and was strongly favored by such Fathers of the Church as Augustine and Jerome.

It was not until the eleventh century, however, that clerical celibacy became effectively obligatory. Significantly, it was part of a general reformation of the Church after centuries of conflict and turmoil. The three essential objectives of the reform movement, which culminated under Gregory VII (1020–85), were freedom of papal elections, observance of clerical celibacy, and liberation from political control of ecclesiastical offices. Although unlike in many ways, the three objectives had one feature in common: They were all directed to give the Church freedom from secular powers to exercise her divinely instituted mission for souls.

The Roman synod of 1074, under Gregory VII, forbade married men to be ordained and, if ordained, to exercise their priestly functions. The laity were forbidden to receive ministrations from married clergy. The decrees of the synod were delivered to various countries by papal legates, but the decrees received mixed acceptance. As he faced the frightful difficulties of his task of reform, Gregory asked for prayers to obtain the courage he needed. In more than one diocese, when the clergy heard that the papal legates intended to hold a reform council, they rose up in opposition, often with the support of their bishops. As he lay dying in exile in Salerno, the Pope was heard to say, "I have loved justice and hated iniquity; therefore I die in exile."

With the death of Gregory VII, the tide had turned. From then on, in spite of severe pressures to relax the law, the Western Church has not wavered in its celibate requirements for the clergy. This was one of the main controverted issues in the sixteenth century, which prompted a special anathema at the Council of Trent of anyone who claimed that clerics in sacred orders "can contract marriage, and that such marriage is valid, notwithstanding the ecclesiastical law or vow, and that the contrary is nothing else than a condemnation of marriage, and that all who feel they have not the gift of chastity—even though they have vowed it—can contract marriage."[28]

The Second Vatican Council, in its extensive treatment of the sacrament of orders, went into detail on the matter of celibacy because of the demands in some quarters to make it optional. Recognizing the grave shortage of priests in many countries compared to the number of professed Catholics, the Council authorized the permanent diaconate and allowed these permanent deacons to be ordained as married men. But it remained inflexible on priestly celibacy.

It conceded the fact that celibacy is not required by the nature of the priesthood itself. This is clear from the custom in the early Church and the traditions of the Eastern Churches. These traditions the Council had no intention of changing, and it encouraged those who became priests after marriage to persevere in their sacred calling and continue to devote their lives in the service of the people.

Nevertheless, celibacy is in many ways particularly suited to the priesthood. Each reason is intimately related to the worship of God and the more effective ministry of the faithful:

> The priestly mission is directed entirely to the service of the new humanity which Christ, victorious over death, creates anew in the world through his Spirit. It has its origin "not from human stock, not from nature's will or man's, but from God" (Jn. 1:13). Priests, moreover, through virginity or celibacy undertaken for the sake of the kingdom of heaven, are consecrated to Christ anew in a new and exalted sense. It is easier for them to keep close to him with undivided love. They are more free, in him and through him, to devote themselves to the service of God and man. They are less encumbered in the ministry of the kingdom of Christ and in the divine work of regeneration.

> Their fatherhood, which is in Christ, makes them more suited for work. Priests proclaim by the state of celibacy their determination to give themselves completely to the sacred task of pledging the faithful to one spouse, that is, of presenting the Church of Christ as his spotless bride. Thus they recall the mystic nuptials, established by God and later to be fully revealed, whereby the Church claims Christ as her one true spouse.

Inevitably, then, the Council declared itself committed to a practice "based on the mystery of Christ and his mission." Admitting that celibacy was at first "recommended to priests" and only later "imposed on all who were to be promoted to sacred orders," it saw here an authentic development of doctrine-become-practice. Hence it concluded that "this legislation, pertaining to those who are destined for the priesthood, this holy synod again approves and confirms."[29]

Hidden in the Church's insistence that celibacy remain unchanged and that it should be kept even more perfectly is the experience of the ages. As costly as its demands on human nature may be and as tempting as concessions may seem, its value has been proved in the supernatural order, where alone the Catholic priesthood has meaning. It draws heavenly blessings not only on the priest himself to make him more holy, but in the graces that his sacrifice merits before God in favor of the people to whom he ministers by his life and liturgy.

Enduring Grace

MARRIAGE

The liturgical side of marriage begins with the assumption that marriage among Christians is simultaneously a contract, an institution, and a sacrament. While all three aspects are closely related, and one flows into the others, they are not the same.

Marriage among all peoples is always, by its very nature, a contract. This does not mean that it is merely a civil contract, even though in many countries the State exercises considerable authority over the marriage agreement. It is by nature a sacred contract or covenant, in that God established marriage as the natural means of procreating and educating his choicest earthly creatures. It is, moreover, sacred, because it is the means of mutual help for husband and wife, not only for their material and temporal well-being, but to lead them to their eternal destiny, which is God. It is finally sacred because faith assures us it mystically represents the union of the divine and human natures in the Incarnation of the Son of God.

Catholicism believes that when it is between two baptized persons, the very contract of marriage becomes a sacrament. As defined by the Church, matrimony is "truly and properly one of the seven sacraments of the law of the Gospel." It was "instituted by Christ" and not merely "introduced into the Church by men."[30] In other words, "because of the grace given through Christ, it is superior to the marriage unions of earlier times," and as "our holy Fathers, the councils, and the tradition of the universal Church have always rightly taught, matrimony should be included among the sacraments of the New Law."[31]

Marriage is also an institution. A contract can be made where two or more people agree on a course of action, but there the matter may end. Not so with marriage. The marrying partners not only agree to take each other as husband and wife but also to continue taking each other until death, to begin to live with one another in the most intimate union possible between two people and to share their respective lives with one another (and with whatever children God may send them) by forming a family. If all institutions worthy of the name are established societies—especially those of a public character, which affect the welfare of the community—marriage is not only an institution; it is the basic institution of human society on which all other corporate establishments somehow depend.

LITURGICAL HISTORY

The sacrament of marriage has a ritual history all its own. Its celebration among Christians has always been associated with the liturgy, but also with local customs and practices to a much greater extent than any of the other sacraments. The doctrinal reason for this is that matrimony, unlike the other sacraments, is conferred by the marrying partners on one another. The essence of the contract, and therefore of the sacrament, consists in the mutual consent. Other features of the ceremony, even when prescriptive or ritually elaborate, are adaptable to different times and circumstances, and the Church's regulations in this matter have correspondingly varied over the centuries.

The early Christians followed the customary family rites of their city or province, while making a serious effort to Christianize these rites and, as far as possible, to break with anything that was idola-

trous or licentious. More important, however, than liturgical forms
was that marriages were approved by the Church's authority. Ignatius of Antioch's letter to St. Polycarp (A.D. 107) is very explicit:

> Tell my sisters to love the Lord and to be satisfied with their hus-
> bands in flesh and spirit. In the same way tell my brothers in the
> name of Jesus Christ to love their wives as the Lord does the
> Church. If anyone is able to persevere in chastity to the honor of the
> flesh of the Lord, let him do so in all humility. If he is boastful about
> it, he is lost. If he should marry, the union should be made with the
> consent of the bishop, so that the marriage may be according to the
> Lord and not merely of lust. Let all be done to the glory of God.[32]

The "consent of the bishop" or his representative did not mean
that the Church's universal practice in the early centuries was to
require the physical presence of a bishop or priest for a sacramental
marriage. Saying this, however, is not the same as questioning that
the Church always considered Christian marriages uniquely sacred
and, indeed, sacramental. Thus by the end of the fourth century,
St. Ambrose could say that "Marriage should be sanctified by the
priestly veil and blessing."[33]

We have evidence of a nuptial Mass with priestly solemnization
from the fourth and fifth centuries. The papal decrees of the fourth
century laid down that the lower orders of the clergy were bound to
have their marriages solemnized by a priest. For the laity, the
priest's presence and blessing was looked upon in the nature of the
Church's approval of the contract.

The first evidence in Rome and Italy of a truly liturgical celebration of marriage dates from the time of Pope Damasus (366–
84). The ritual applied only to the first marriage which, it was said,
was celebrated by God himself in heaven. The marriage blessing was
accompanied by ritual actions, which took the form of the veiling
of the bride by the priest, with the result that "veiling by the priest"
and the "marriage blessing" became almost synonymous. This ceremony was extended to form an entire liturgy. It took place in the
church. The father led the wedding guests to the altar, where the
bishop celebrated the marriage with an improvised prayer, covering
the bride and bridegroom with a veil.

According to Pope Nicholas I (858–67), gifts were offered by
bride and groom during the nuptial Mass. Both bride and groom
received the Eucharist. The practice of placing wreaths on the bride
and groom, the crowning ceremony, originated in the East and was

gradually adopted in Rome and elsewhere. The ceremony took place on the day on which the bride was solemnly brought from the bridegroom's house, although customs differed about the time for the crowning. The classic explanation of the crowning was given by St. John Chrysostom: "A crown is placed on the heads of the bridegroom and the bride as a symbol of victory, for they are advancing unconquered toward the haven of marriage, they who have not been conquered by pleasure."[34]

In the Western Church, the exchange of vows often took place outside the church building and without the assistance of a priest. Then the act of making the contract was brought into the sanctuary and surrounded with liturgical prayers. By the Middle Ages, however, the exchange of vows had to take place, under pain of nullity, in the presence of the pastor or his delegate, who questioned the bridal couple as to their mutual consent, and in the presence of two other witnesses. Also, the whole ceremony took place in the church and was preceded by an instruction given by the priest.

Aware of its divine right to guide the faithful in their marital plans and commitments, the Church enacted laws dealing with marriage from the time of its liberation under Constantine. The Council of Elvira in Spain (325) already passed a series of canons on the subject.

By the sixteenth century, however, there were some who questioned the Church's right to make such legislation. The Church's function, they claimed, was only to encourage and exhort, never to prescribe, especially in such vital matters as who could marry validly under what circumstances and, if dispensations were needed, who had the right to make exceptions even as a condition for the validity of the marriage contract. The Council of Trent countered by defining that it was not only those grades of relationship mentioned in Leviticus (18:6–16) that can be an impediment of marriage, or that "the Church does not have the power of dispensation over some of these grades or the power to determine more grades prohibiting or invalidating impediments." Concretely, too, the Church has a right to declare that the bond of a marriage cannot be dissolved "by reason of heresy, domestic incompatibility, or willful desertion by one of the parties."[35] It is, therefore, Catholic doctrine that the Church has been divinely authorized to set the conditions for the valid and licit reception of the sacrament of marriage.

Nevertheless, before the Council of Trent there was no universal law of the Church on what is called the form of marriage, i.e., under what ecclesiastical conditions the contract would be valid. The first such invalidating law was enacted in 1563 and was known from its initial word as Tametsi. It required for the validity of marriage the presence of the pastor or local bishop of one of the parties, according to their residence. There were two difficulties in the application of this law: first, the problem of determining residence; and second, the fact that the law was not promulgated everywhere.

Various adjustments were made, but there was no radical solution until St. Pius X in 1908 authorized a sweeping decree that remedied the two main weaknesses of the sixteenth-century legislation. It was later on substantially incorporated into the Church's canon law. Essentially it required for validity the presence of the pastor or bishop of the place where the marriage was celebrated, if this occurred outside the parochial limits of the contracting parties; and the new decree was promulgated throughout the Catholic world. Exceptions were also provided for situations where a priest was not easily available.

SINCE THE COUNCIL

The experience of four centuries since the Council of Trent made it comparatively easy for the Church's leaders in our day to provide for adaptation to the times while safeguarding the essentials of Catholic faith and worship. There was first the conciliar provision that "the marriage rite now found in the Roman Ritual be revised and enriched in such a way that the grace of the sacrament is more clearly signified and the duties of the spouses are taught." Then, dipping back to the sixteenth century, the Second Vatican Council quoted a little-known passage from Trent to the effect that as far as possible "praiseworthy customs and ceremonies" of the particular region be retained. In line with this openness, ecclesiastical authorities are "free to draw up their own rite suited to the usages of place and people," always subject to Roman approval. However, "the rite must always conform to the law that the priest assisting at the marriage must ask for and obtain the consent of the contracting parties." Finally, marriage is normally to be celebrated with the offering of the Eucharistic sacrifice.[36]

New Ritual. The new marriage rite fulfills the provision that the sacramental grace and duties of the marrying partners be clearly signified. Three forms of the nuptial blessing are offered for the priest's choice, of which the first is the longest and most expressive. The words in brackets are editorial introductions to indicate the focus of each petition in the nuptial prayer:

[*Marital exclusiveness and indissolubility*] Father, by your power you have made everything out of nothing. In the beginning you created the universe and made mankind in your own likeness. You gave man the constant help of woman so that man and woman should no longer be two, but one flesh, and you teach us that what you have united may never be divided.

[*Symbol of Christ's union with the Church*] Father, you have made the union of man and woman so holy a mystery that it symbolizes the marriage of Christ and his Church.

[*Marriage, a holy institution*] Father, by your plan man and woman are united, and marriage has been established as the one blessing that was not forfeited by original sin or washed away in the flood.

[*Love and peace for the wife*] Look with love upon this woman, your daughter, now joined to her husband in marriage. She asks your blessing. Give her the grace of love and peace. May she always follow the example of the holy woman whose praises are sung in the Scriptures.

[*Honor and love in the husband*] May the husband put his trust in her and recognize that she is his equal and the heir with him in the life of grace. May he always honor her and love her as Christ loves his bride, the Church.

[*Mutual fidelity and children*] Father, keep them always true to your Commandments. Keep them faithful in marriage and let them be living examples of Christian life. Give them the strength which comes from the Gospel so that they may be witnesses of Christ to others. Bless them with children and help them to be good parents. May they live to see their children's children. And, after a happy old age, grant them fullness of life with the saints in the kingdom of heaven.

Throughout the ceremony, which is celebrated during Mass, the couple are told that their marriage is "for the rest of your lives," that they are to "accept children lovingly from God, and bring them up according to the law of Christ and his Church," that the rings they exchange are to be symbols "of true faith in each other and always remind them of their love," and that the Lord will "strengthen your consent and fill you both with his blessings."

Moreover, for the first time in Catholic liturgical history, the universal Church is provided with distinctive rituals for celebrating marriage between a Catholic and unbaptized person, whether the latter is a catechumen preparing to enter the Church or a non-Christian. In either case, the marriage may be performed in the church or some other suitable place.

Mixed Marriages. More than almost anything else in the Church's liturgical transformation is the attitude toward mixed marriages in which one spouse is a Roman Catholic and the partner is either a baptized person from another Christian tradition or is not a Christian.

Stemming from the ecumenical movement, and also from the new sense of identity among the non-Christian religions of the world, first the Council paved the way and then the Pope determined the norms that are to govern these mixed marital unions. As a Catholic reflects on their import, he may at first be scandalized at what perhaps appears to him a compromise with the integrity of the faith, or certainly an about-face in what had been the Church's practice regarding such marriages in the past.

In order to appreciate the significance of what has happened, and to place the matter into perspective, two things should be done. The reasons that led up to the changed posture should be examined; then the norms themselves can be stated, along with some crucial explanations.

Mixed marriages have always been a vital concern of the Church. But today she is constrained to give even greater attention to them, owing to the conditions of the modern age. In the past, Catholics were separated from members of other Christian confessions and from non-Christians, by their situation in the community or even by physical boundaries. But all of this is changing. Not only has the separation been reduced, but communication between and among people of different regions and religions has greatly developed, and as a result there has been a great increase in the number of mixed marriages in every country of the world. A contributing factor has been the growth and spread of civilization and industry, urbanization and consequent rural depopulation, migrations in great numbers, and the increase of exiles, as we might call them, everywhere.

What is the Church's position on mixed marriages in general? It has not essentially changed since biblical times:

> The Church is aware that mixed marriages, precisely because they admit differences of religion and are a consequence of the division among Christians, do not, except in some cases, help in re-establishing unity among Christians. There are many difficulties inherent in a mixed marriage, since a certain division is introduced into the living cell of the Church, as the Christian family is rightly called. Moreover, in the family itself the fulfillment of the Gospel teachings is more difficult because of diversities in matters of religion, especially with regard to those matters which concern worship and the education of children.

Having said all of this, however, the Church is also conscious that people have a natural right to marry and beget children—hence the dilemma that needs to be resolved. The Church seeks to make such arrangements that "on the one hand the principles of divine law are scrupulously observed and on the other hand the recognized right to contract marriage is respected."

Accordingly, the new provisions regarding mixed marriages are at once a tribute to the Church's pastoral care of the faithful and a witness of her fidelity to the revelation bequeathed by the Savior.

1. A marriage between two baptized persons, of whom one is a Catholic, while the other is a non-Catholic, may not licitly be contracted without the previous dispensation of the local Ordinary, since such a marriage is by its nature an obstacle to the full spiritual communion of the married parties.

2. A marriage between two persons, of whom one has been baptized in the Catholic Church or received into it, while the other is unbaptized, entered into without previous dispensation by the local bishop, is invalid.

3. The Church, taking into account the nature and circumstances of times, places, and persons, is prepared to dispense from both impediments, provided there is just cause.

4. To obtain from the local bishop dispensation from an impediment, the Catholic party shall declare that he or she is ready to remove all dangers of falling away from the faith. He or she is also gravely bound to make a sincere promise to do all in his power to have all the children baptized and brought up in the Catholic Church.

5. At the opportune time, the non-Catholic party must be informed of these promises that the Catholic party has to make, so that it is clear that he or she is cognizant of the promise and obligation on the part of the Catholic.

6. Both parties are to be clearly instructed on the ends and essential properties of marriage, not to be excluded by either party.

7. The canonical form (priest and witnesses) is to be used for contracting mixed marriages and is required for validity. If serious difficulties stand in the way, local bishops have the right to dispense from the canonical form in any mixed marriage.

8. The celebration of marriage before a Catholic priest or deacon and a non-Catholic minister performing their respective rites together is forbidden; nor is it permitted to have another religious marriage ceremony before or after the Catholic ceremony, for the purpose of giving or renewing matrimonial consent.

9. Local bishops and parish priests shall see to it that the Catholic husband or wife and the children born of a mixed marriage do not lack spiritual assistance in fulfilling their duties of conscience. They shall encourage the Catholic husband or wife to keep ever in mind the divine gift of the Catholic faith and to bear witness to it with gentleness and reverence, and with a clear conscience. They are to aid the married couple to foster the unity of their conjugal and family life, a unity that, in the case of Christians, is based on their baptism too. To these ends it is to be desired that those pastors should establish relationships of sincere openness and enlightened confidence with ministers of other religious communities.[37]

Since the percentage of mixed marriages in some countries is exceptionally high, approaching one half of all the marriages that Catholics enter, these directives of the Church are bound to have widespread implications. Doctrinally there is no problem. The essence of a matrimonial contract is the mutual exchange of consent between the contracting parties. If they are both baptized, whether professed Catholics or not, they certainly receive the sacrament of marriage and with it the title to all the graces that Christ confers on those who marry in his name. Since marriage is a "sacrament of the living," the graces of the sacrament demand the right disposition of soul. A person must be in the state of grace to receive the sacrament fruitfully.

A couple, therefore, preparing for an interfaith marriage need to know the difference between receiving a sacrament only, and receiving also the extraordinary blessings that Catholics believe are attached to the sacrament. Hence the value of both parties to such a marriage making their peace with God, by whatever means each believes are effective, before pronouncing the marriage vows.

Mixed marriages are generally frowned upon by churchmen who are not Catholic. The heart of the matter is concern about the encroachment of an "authoritarian" Church into the lives of their people. Responsive to this concern, the Catholic Church sincerely wishes to avoid giving needless offense to those who are Christians, indeed, but not Roman Catholic. Thus the new approach is to place the burden of responsibility on the shoulders of the Catholic partner to the marriage. He or she declares the readiness "to remove all dangers of falling away from the faith," and is "also gravely bound to make a sincere promise to do all in his power to have all the children baptized and brought up in the Catholic Church."

What the Church cannot dispense from is the obligations of the divine law affecting the Catholic party and his or her children. No one can give a dispensation from the duty of remaining loyal to the Catholic faith or the correlative duty of sharing this faith with flesh-and-blood offspring. Enlightened charity never has to compromise with the truth.

ANOINTING

Sacred anointing of the sick is a sacrament of the New Law instituted by Christ to give spiritual aid and strength and perfect spiritual health, including, if need be, the remission of sins. Conditionally it also restores bodily health to Christians who are seriously ill. It consists essentially in the anointing by a priest of the body of the sick person, accompanied by a suitable form of words.

The Catholic Church professes and teaches, therefore, that the anointing of the sick is one of the seven sacraments that Christ personally gave to the Church. Two passages in the New Testament are commonly used in conciliar and papal documents as referring to this sacrament. One is in the Gospels, and the other is in the letter of James.

BIBLE AND TRADITION

The evangelist Mark describes the meeting that Jesus had on one occasion with the twelve apostles, in which he instructed them to go out to neighboring towns, preaching and healing the sick. He told them that "if any place does not welcome you and people refuse to listen to you," they should shake off the dust of their feet and leave the place. "So they set off to preach repentance; and they cast out many devils, and anointed many sick people with oil and cured them" (Mk. 6:11–13).

Although the Church has not declared that this passage treats explicitly of the sacrament of anointing, she has said that the "holy anointing of the sick as a true and proper sacrament is implied in Mark's Gospel."[38] This guarded statement was occasioned by the fact that, in context, Mark speaks only of bodily healing, the apostles had not yet been ordained priests, and it was not likely that many of those anointed had first been baptized. Yet some eminent Church authorities, including St. Bede the Venerable (673–735), saw here a direct reference to holy anointing as a sacrament, either because Christ instituted it on that occasion, or at least it shows he promised or intended to institute it.

The classic biblical text adduced in favor of anointing occurs in the letter of James. According to the Council of Trent, the sacrament of holy anointing "is commended to the faithful and promulgated by the apostle James, the brother of the Lord: 'Is anyone among you sick? Let him bring in the presbyters of the Church, and let them pray over him, anointing him with oil in the name of the Lord. And the prayer of faith will save the sick man, and the Lord will raise him up, and, if he be in sins, they shall be forgiven him' " (Jm. 5:14–15). In these words, as the Church has learned from the apostolic Tradition transmitted to her, he teaches the matter, the form, the proper minister, and the effects of this salutary sacrament. For the Church has understood that the matter is oil, blessed by a bishop; for the anointing very fittingly represents the grace of the Holy Spirit which anoints the soul of the sick person in an invisible manner. The following words are the form: 'By this anointing,' etc."[39]

It may seem unusual that Trent actually left the "etc." dangling after the words, "By this anointing." The historical reason was that different verbal forms were used in the Church, in the East and West, for the administration of what came to be known as extreme unction. The most common form in the Latin rite was then, "By this holy anointing and his most gracious mercy, may the Lord pardon you whatever sins you have committed by your sight, hearing, smell, taste and speech, touch, and walk. Amen." The custom was to anoint, in sequence, the eyes, ears, lips, hands, and feet, while pronouncing the appropriate words. In case of emergency, a single anointing on the forehead was sufficient.

Who can administer the anointing of the sick? Relying on the words of St. James, the Church declares that "the proper ministers of this are the presbyters of the Church. This does not refer to the older men nor to the more influential men in the community, but to the bishops or the priests duly ordained by the bishops through the laying on of hands of the presbyterate."[40]

What are the effects of this sacrament? A cluster of effects is recognized by the Catholic Church, all flowing from the basic gift of the Holy Spirit. His anointing "takes away sins, if there are any still to be expiated, and removes the traces of sin. It alleviates and strengthens the soul of the sick person. It gives him great confidence in the divine mercy. Encouraged by this, the sick person more easily resists the temptations of the devil who lies in wait for his heel. This anointing occasionally restores health to the body if health would be of advantage to the salvation of the soul."[41]

Summarily, then, there are six effects of anointing, namely: forgiveness of the guilt of unremitted sin, even grave sin for which the person had at least imperfect sorrow, i.e., faith that motivated the fear of God; remission of the temporal punishment still due for remitted sin, to such a degree that the expiation can be complete; supernatural patience to bear with the sufferings of one's illness; extraordinary confidence in God's mercy, which a person certainly needs as he perhaps faces eternity; special infusion of moral courage to resist the temptations of the devil, who is particularly active at such times; and the restoration of bodily health if, as God foresees it, the cure would be good for the person's spiritual welfare.

These effects of the sacrament continue as long as the one who receives it remains in the same infirm condition that occasioned the reception. One word in the teaching of Trent on this matter opened the door for what has more recently become a changed attitude toward anointing of the sick. The sixteenth-century Council stated that "this anointing is to be used on the sick, *especially* [author's emphasis] on those who are so dangerously ill that they are thought to be departing this life. Hence the name, the sacrament of the departing." The point is that the Church does not wish to restrict the sacrament exclusively to those who are actually dying. Should they recover after being anointed, "they can again receive the help of this sacrament when their life is again in similar danger."[42] Anointing of the sick is, therefore, unique in that the benefit perdures until the need for its sacramental efficacy has passed.

RITUAL CHANGES

Some believe that the ritual changes for the anointing of the sick, mandated by the Second Vatican Council, are more far-reaching than those for any other sacrament of the Catholic liturgy. The structural changes, though considerable, are less significant than those pertaining to the persons for whom the anointing is intended and the circumstances under which the rite is to be administered.

While other factors were also operative, one of the reasons for the revised anointing liturgy was the remarkable development in medical care in all countries and the corresponding increase in the life expectancy everywhere. Homes for the aged were almost an innovation of organized Catholic charity when the Little Sisters of the Poor were founded in France in 1839. Today the institutional care of the aging is a major apostolate of the Church.

The conciliar *Constitution on the Liturgy* opened the way for change by noting that this sacrament should acquire a new name. It went on to decree certain appropriate modifications:

"Extreme unction," which may also and more fittingly be called "anointing of the sick," is not a sacrament for those only who are at the point of death. Hence, as soon as any one of the faithful begins to be in danger of death from sickness or old age, the fitting time for him to receive this sacrament has certainly already arrived.

In addition to the separate rites for anointing of the sick and for Viaticum, a continuous rite shall be prepared according to which the sick person is anointed after he has made his confession and before he receives Viaticum.

The number of anointings is to be adapted to the occasion, and the prayers which belong to the rite of anointing are to be revised so as to correspond with the varying conditions of the sick who receive the sacrament.[43]

Nine years later, Paul VI issued an apostolic constitution on the sacrament of the anointing of the sick, in which he implemented the Council's directives. He began by noting that, besides the liturgical features, he was also concerned that the spiritual purpose of the sacrament would be insured. He recalled that the Church looks to the sick to "contribute to the welfare of the whole people of God by associating themselves freely with the passion and death of Christ," as urged by Peter and Paul in their letters to the first Christians.

"We thought fit," he said, "to modify the sacramental formula in such a way that, in view of the words of James, the effects of the sacrament might be fully expressed." Accordingly, the new formula for conferring the sacrament is: "Through this holy anointing and his most loving mercy, may the Lord assist you by the grace of the Holy Spirit, so that, freed from your sins, he may save you and in his goodness raise you up."

Moreover, instead of five senses, only two are to be anointed: the forehead and the hands. But in case of necessity, "it is sufficient that a single anointing be given on the forehead or, because of the particular condition of the sick person, on another more suitable part of the body, the whole formula being pronounced."

Someone may wonder why the words are in the form of a prayer, since sacraments produce their effect in virtue of the rite performed and are not conditioned on a prayerful request for God's blessing. The theological explanation is that, although the spiritual effects are indeed produced, as it were automatically, provided the person is rightly disposed, the bodily effect of healing is conditional and therefore consistent with a petition to be granted. Then, too, St. James expressly says that the sacrament is to be so received that "the presbyters are to pray over" the sick person.

Until now, olive oil was prescribed for the valid administration of the sacrament. This is no longer necessary. As stated by the Pope, "since olive oil is unobtainable or difficult to obtain in some parts of the world, we decreed, at the request of numerous bishops, that in the future, according to the circumstances, another kind of oil could also be used, provided that it be obtained from plants, inasmuch as it is similar to olive oil."[44]

At the same time as the papal constitution, the Holy See issued the provisions of the new ritual "for the anointing of the sick and their pastoral care." They are of universal import for the faithful who follow the Roman Rite.

1. How may one judge the gravity of the illness that permits the conferring of this sacrament? "It is sufficient to have a prudent or probable judgment about its seriousness. All anxiety about the matter should be put aside and, if necessary, the physician might be consulted."

2. How often may the sacrament of anointing be administered? "This sacrament can be repeated if the sick person had recovered after his previous reception of anointing. It can also be conferred again if, during the same illness, his dangerous condition becomes more serious."

3. What about receiving the sacrament before undergoing surgery? "Before a surgical section (popularly 'operation'), holy anointing can be given to the sick person as often as the dangerous illness is the cause of this surgery." Evidently the Church distinguishes between an illness that might not of itself warrant reception of the sacrament, and the same illness preceding surgery. In the latter case, anointing becomes warranted.

4. What about the anointing of old people? "Anointing can be conferred on the aged who are greatly weakened in strength, even though there is no sign of a dangerous illness." This is a major development in the concept of the sacrament of the sick. Old age of itself, provided there is notable debility of one's native powers, is enough to allow the valid reception of holy anointing.

5. Can the sacrament be conferred on children? "Holy anointing can also be administered to children already from the time they have reached the use of reason, so that they can be strengthened by this sacrament." Consequently the motive for conferring the sacrament is not (though it may include) remission of their personal sins, but to obtain the strength they may need either for bearing their sufferings, or to overcome discouragement or, if it is God's will, to be restored to health.

6. What aspects of the Church's teaching on the subject should be stressed in catechetical instruction? "The faithful should be so taught,

in classes and at home, that they will themselves ask to receive the anointing and receive it as soon as the opportunity presents itself; and that they will not give in to the bad practice of postponing the reception of the sacrament. Moreover, all those who take care of the sick should be educated in the nature of this sacrament."

7. Can the sacrament be conferred on people who are unconscious? "The sacrament can be conferred on the sick, even though they have lost the use of their senses or their reason, if as believers they would likely have asked for the holy anointing while they were in possession of their faculties." This is a broad concession that may be applied to most baptized persons, who would even probably have wanted to be anointed before they lapsed into unconsciousness.

8. Should a priest anoint a person who is apparently dead? "When a priest is called to a sick person who is already dead, he should ask God to assist him to be delivered from his sins and mercifully receive him into his kingdom. But if he is in doubt whether the sick person is really dead, he can give him the sacrament conditionally." This single provision will relieve many pastoral problems that had arisen in the past. If there is any doubt whether a person is dead, he may (and should) be anointed.

9. Eastern Churches have a concelebrated anointing. Is there anything like this now possible in the Latin Rite? "When two or more priests are with a single sick person, there is nothing to prevent one of them to say the prayers and perform the anointing with its proper formula, while the others share among themselves other individual parts of the ritual, such as the initial rites, reading the word of God, the invocations or exhortations. Moreover, each of them can impose hands."

10. Must the oil always be blessed by the bishop for a valid anointing? "The proper matter for the sacrament is the oil of olives or, as needed, another oil made from plants. The oil to be used in the anointing of the sick must have been blessed for this purpose by the bishop or by a priest who, either by law, or by a special grant of the apostolic see, has the faculty to do this. Besides the bishop, the law itself provides that the oil necessary for the anointing of the sick can be blessed (1) by the person whose authority is equivalent to the bishop of the diocese, and (2) in case of real necessity, by any priest." It is impossible to exaggerate the value of this new concession, since it allows any priest to bless any vegetable oil

and then use it for sacramental anointing in case of emergency, as can easily arise in times of accident or sudden disaster.

11. Are any adaptations of the prescribed ritual permissible? "The anointing is conferred on the sick person's forehead and hands. The formula is conveniently divided in such a way that the first part is recited while anointing the forehead, and the second part while anointing the hands. There is no objection, however, depending on the culture and customs of a people, to having the number of anointings increased or the place of anointing changed. This will have to be provided in drawing up the particular ritual books." Here we see a completely new approach to adapting the essentials of a sacrament to the broad variety of nations and cultural situations. It has special relevance in the countries of Africa and the Far East, where traditions are so strong and the Church is ready to adjust, within doctrinal limits, to the legitimate expectations of different peoples.

12. Should the anointing of the sick be done with public solemnity? "The one who administers the sacrament should first keep in mind the circumstances and other needs, notably the desires of the sick persons and the rest of the faithful." For example, "his first concern should be about the fatigue of those who are ill, and the changes in their physical condition during the day or even at a given hour. For this reason, he can, if need be, shorten the celebration." But saying all of this, the mind of the Church is to favor a more solemn liturgy of anointing, when this can prudently be done. Accordingly, the anointing should take place, when feasible, in the presence of relatives and friends who can participate in the ceremony and in so doing represent the whole Church of God. They can make the prayer responses within the rite and even participate with appropriate music. Where the anointing is part of a continuous rite that includes reception of Holy Communion, "if possible Viaticum should be received during Mass, so that the sick person can communicate under both species."[45] In fact, the Church's pastoral care reflected in the postconciliar ritual for the sick and dying is to make sure they receive all the sacraments they may need, anointing and the Eucharist, penance, and even confirmation. They should be fortified with every sacramental grace on their journey to eternity, or to continued suffering, or to a renewed state of health —according to the dispositions of providence.

XIV. SACRAMENTALS

Besides the seven sacraments, the Catholic Church has a variety of what are called sacramentals. Although the term "sacramentals" did not come into common usage until the early Middle Ages, the practice dates from the early days of Christianity and had its anticipation in the religious customs of ancient Israel.

A technical definition of sacramentals would say that they are things or actions the Church uses after the manner of sacraments, in order to achieve through the merits of the faithful certain effects—above all, those of a spiritual nature. Some writers speak of the sacramentals as lesser sacraments, to distinguish them from the principal sacraments of the New Law.

Since so much of Catholic piety is associated with sacramentals, it will be useful to see how the Church understands them on two levels: by comparison with the sacraments, and in contrast with other sacred elements of Roman Catholicism.

Sacramentals differ from the sacraments in not having been instituted by Christ in order to be perpetuated within the Church as divinely established means of conferring grace. For the most part, sacramentals are instituted by the Church, and even where we know that Christ practiced what is now considered a sacramental (such as the washing of feet at the Last Supper), the ritual was not intended by him as essentially related to the salvation or sanctification of the world.

They further differ from the sacraments in their efficacy. Sacraments confer grace as instrumental causes in such a way that, provided no obstacle interferes, the grace they signify they also produce by the power of God, who works through them. A newborn child is baptized, and the gifts of the Holy Spirit are infused. Not so the sacramentals. Their efficacy does not come from the ritual performed but partly from the dispositions of the person who uses them and partly from the intercessory prayer of the whole Church, to which there belongs a particularly effective power because she is the holy and immaculate bride of Christ. This latter influence is what makes the sacramentals different from other religious practices (outside the sacraments), whose efficacy depends on the sanctity and fervor of the single person. Sacramentals are forms of ecclesial, as distinct from merely individual, piety. Built into the efficacy of the sacraments is an infallibility that God himself assures. Sacramentals lack this kind of inevitable effectiveness; they depend on the influence of prayerful petition: the person's who uses them, and the Church's in approving their practice.

The sacramentals finally differ from sacraments in the effects they produce. Unlike the sacraments, they do not confer sanctifying grace directly but merely dispose a person to its reception. This can occur in different ways, depending on the nature of the sacramental. A blessed article, like a crucifix or medal, acquires an objective holiness in virtue of the benediction placed upon it. Aware of this fact, the believer treats it accordingly and is thus prepared in heart to receive whatever grace God intends to confer on him. So, too, with verbal blessings and other sacramentals. They stimulate the faith of the one who reverently hears or uses them and thus indirectly are occasions for the reception of divine favors.

VARIETIES

There is no agreed way of classifying the sacramentals of the Catholic Church; they are too numerous, and they tend to overlap in practice. Yet some analysis of this aspect of the Church's worship is important, both because it is so distinctively Catholic and because in most cases it closely integrates with the Eucharist and the major sacraments of the liturgy. In fact, when we speak about the liturgy, we generally include the whole ensemble of sacraments, sacrifice, and sacramentals by which the faithful pray to God and receive his blessings in return.

Time and Place. We are not accustomed to thinking of sacramentals in connection with what is known as sacred time. But the first and, in its way, most comprehensive type of sacramental concerns the liturgical seasons, feasts, and fasts of the Catholic Church. They qualify as sacramentals in that they are established by the Church in order to stimulate the faith of the people and dispose them to a regular and more generous service of God.

Essential to the notion of sacred time is the idea of commemoration with a view to appreciation, i.e., periodic reminder in order to keep alive and deepen one's realization of the truths of faith.

> Holy Mother Church is conscious that she must celebrate the saving work of her divine Spouse by devoutly recalling it on certain days throughout the course of the year. Every week, on the day which she has called the Lord's day, she keeps memory of the Lord's Resurrection, which she also celebrates once in the year, together with his blessed passion, in the most solemn festival of Easter.
>
> Within the cycle of a year, moreover, she unfolds the whole mystery of Christ, from the Incarnation and the birth until the Ascension, the day of Pentecost, and expectation of blessed hope and of the coming of the Lord.
>
> Recalling thus the mysteries of redemption, the Church opens to the faithful the riches of her Lord's powers and merits, so that these are in some way made present for all time, and the faithful are enabled to lay hold upon them and become filled with saving grace.[1]

One of the directives of the late Council was to make sure that the minds of the faithful are "primarily directed toward the feasts of the Lord whereby the mysteries of salvation are celebrated in the course of the year." The result is that the new liturgical calendar gives preference to these commemorations "over the feasts of the saints, so that the entire cycle of the mysteries of salvation may be suitably recalled."[2]

Five such seasons now form the ecclesiastical year. In Advent the coming of the Lord is anticipated, looking back historically to the age of prophecy foretelling the birth of the Messiah and looking forward prophetically to his coming at the dawn of each person's eternity and his majestic coming on the last day of the present world. In the Christmas season the earthly birth of the Savior is remembered, his infancy and hidden years at Nazareth. During the Lenten period the passion and death of Christ are dwelled upon, with daily biblical reminders of the need to follow Christ in carrying one's daily cross. The Easter season relives the Resurrection and Ascension of Christ, and closes with commemoration of Pentecost; with special reference to the sacraments of baptism and confirmation, along with the Eucharist, to remind the faithful of their responsibility as witnesses of the Savior. The long series of weeks from Pentecost to Advent have salvation history as their basic theme, to bring out the essential continuity of God's providence toward his Chosen People from Abraham to Jesus Christ. The stress is on the covenant relationship that exists between the Lord who calls and the generous self-giving he expects of those who are called to be his.

Besides the seasons, there are saints' days in the Catholic understanding of sacred time. "The saints have been traditionally honored in the Church and their authentic relics and images held in veneration. For the feasts of the saints proclaim the wonderful works of Christ in his servants, and display to the faithful fitting examples for their imitation." The sanctification of his servants also partakes of the mystery of Christ, now in his mystical existence among the faithful.

But good things can also get out of hand. The legitimate and necessary worship of saints had to be kept within the bounds of authentic Catholic piety. Hence the call for revision that in some quarters caused a great deal of needless worry:

> Lest the feasts of the saints should take precedence over the feasts which commemorate the very mysteries of salvation, many of them should be celebrated by a particular Church or nation or family of religious. Only those should be extended to the universal Church which commemorate saints who are truly of universal importance.[3]

When the revision of the ecclesiastical calendar was made, about forty feasts of saints were eliminated, almost a hundred were made optional for particular places, e.g., the diocese or country where the saint lived, and some sixty remained for general observance in the Roman Rite.

Besides sacred time, there is such a thing as sacred place. The very word "temple" (from the Latin *templum*) originally meant "a part cut off" from the rest of a given area to mark a consecrated piece of ground. It had the same general meaning as sanctuary. In Catholic Christianity the sacred place par excellence is the church or chapel where the Eucharistic sacrifice is offered and the Blessed Sacrament is reserved. It is also the normal place for the celebration of other sacraments and the customary scene for the assembly of the faithful to worship God.

There are other sacred places or spaces, too, which are characteristically Catholic. They are the numerous shrines in different parts of the world, where it is believed that God bestows special favors on those who come to pray there. Lourdes in France, Fatima in Portugal, Montserrat in Spain, Assisi in Italy, St. Anne de Beaupré in Canada, the Martyrs' Shrine in the United States and Canada,

Guadalupe in Mexico, Knock in Ireland, Banneux in Belgium, Czestochowa in Poland, and the holy places in Palestine are only some of the best known. Many shrines were reportedly the scene of some apparition, generally of Christ or the Blessed Virgin, and before approval by Church authorities had to be carefully examined. As a matter of record, most purported apparitions are disapproved and therefore the places do not become Catholic shrines. In some countries, the shrines become national symbols of the people's faith.

Actions, Words, and Objects. The widest variety of what are usually called sacramentals are sacred actions, words, and objects, to which the Church either attaches a ritual blessing or by which she teaches the faithful that they can obtain certain graces from God.

Sacramental actions are first and most prominently the gestures, postures, and bodily movements that the Church officially associates with the Eucharist and administration of the sacraments. Typical of the simplification process in recent years, the number of signs of the cross to be made by the priest during Mass has been reduced from a maximum of fifty-four to a present limit of less than ten.

But not only in public assembly, action sacramentals are of the essence of Catholic devotional practice. Genuflecting and kneeling, folding one's hands in prayer, making the sign of the cross over oneself or another person or some object, bowing the head and sprinkling with holy water—all are commonplace. They testify to the faith that inspires them and, on the Church's authority, carry with them the promise of God's help, always in spirit and often also temporally and in body.

Words, too, can be sacred, and they become sacramentals when what is said or sung, or the time it is done, or the manner of doing it has been "sacramentalized" by the Church. Indulgenced prayers belong to this category. But precisely here we should distinguish between private prayers, which are certainly pleasing to God, and word sacramentals in the technical sense. The latter may, of course, be said privately by a single person, but they are really ecclesial, because they draw on the total intercessory power of the Church, and to that extent they have a special meritorious value before God.

Sacred articles or object sacramentals span just about every conceivable thing for which the Church has provided an appropriate blessing. The expression "blessed object" can refer to persons or physical buildings, things that are eaten or taken as drink, articles of clothing or medals that are worn, vestments of the priest at the altar, the distinctive habits of men and women religious, or the rings exchanged by a couple at marriage.

As might be expected, sacramentals are never divorced from the person who uses them. To make sure this cardinal principle of Christian worship was not forgotten, in its reformation of the liturgy the Church decreed that "The sacramentals are to undergo a revision which takes into account the primary principle of enabling the faithful to participate intelligently, actively, and easily. The circumstances of our own days must also be considered." Concretely this has meant that, while sacramentals remain an integral part of Catholic life and worship, they should be so taught to the people that their own personal role becomes primary. Intelligent participation presumes understanding of what a sacramental is intended to do. Active participation indicates that sacramentals are not some kind of fetishes that work magically by just being had or worn or said. It requires voluntary effort based on faith in order to achieve the purpose for which they were instituted. This in turn calls for supernatural trust that what the Church approves and encourages, Christ also confirms with his heavenly grace. Easy participation intimates that sacramentals are to be aids, not hindrances, to living out one's service of God. Two directives of Catholic liturgical reform are to facilitate access to the rich treasury of the Church's sacramentals: "Reserved blessings shall be very few," and "Let provision be made that some sacramentals, at least in special circumstances and at the discretion of the bishop, may be administered by qualified lay persons."[4]

Reserved blessings are those that only certain priests, with special faculties, can confer or, in some cases, only the bishop. Reducing these to a minimum increases the prospects of more such blessings becoming available. Giving the laity the right to administer certain sacramentals has the same end in view, besides revealing what is already part of the Church's faith, that those who are baptized have certain privileges as sharers in the royal priesthood of Christ.

Liturgy of the Hours. In a class by itself is the Liturgy of the Hours (Divine Office), which is the public prayer of the Church for sanctifying the day by praising God. Its daily recitation, or celebration, is a sacred duty of men in holy orders and of men and women religious according to their rule of life. It is highly recommended to all the faithful.

By tradition going back to early Christian times, the faithful devoted themselves to prayer at certain hours. Gradually the practice developed of praying together not only in the morning and at sundown but at regular intervals during the day. It was not long before the custom arose of arranging the whole course of the day and night in such a way that somewhere in the Church the praises of God would be sung and his name would be hallowed by those who believe.

Since the Second Vatican Council, the Liturgy of the Hours has been thoroughly revised in its structure and form. At the same time its indispensable function in the Church's life and activity has been emphasized.

> In the Liturgy of the Hours, the Church exercises the priestly office of her head and constantly offers God a sacrifice of praise, a verbal sacrifice that is offered every time we acknowledge his name.
>
> By offering praise to God in the Hours, the Church joins in singing that canticle of praise which is sung throughout all ages in the halls of heaven; it is a foretaste of the heavenly praise sung unceasingly before the throne of God and the Lamb, as described by John in the Apocalypse.
>
> As well as praising God, the Church's liturgy expresses the hopes and prayers of all the Christian faithful and intercedes before Christ and through him before the Father for the salvation of the whole world. This voice is not only of the Church but of Christ.
>
> Whoever participates in the Liturgy of the Hours makes the Lord's people grow by imparting to them a hidden apostolic fruitfulness. For the goal of apostolic works is that all who are made children of God by faith and baptism should come together to praise God in the midst of his Church, to take part in her sacrifice, and to eat the Lord's Supper.
>
> The readings and prayers of the Liturgy of the Hours constitute in turn a wellspring of the Christian life. From the table of Sacred Scripture and the words of the saints this life is nourished, and by prayer it is strengthened. The Lord alone, without whom we can do nothing, can if we ask him give fruitfulness and increase to the works in which we are engaged.[5]

The revised Liturgy of the Hours now consists of Lauds and Vespers, the morning and evening prayers called "the hinges" of the Office; Matins, to be said at any time of the day, which retains the form of a nocturnal vigil service and is called the Office of Readings; Terce, Sext and None, any one of which may be chosen for prayer at an appropriate time of the day, approximately mid-morning, noon, or mid-afternoon; and Compline, which is the night prayer.

In the new Office, the hours are shorter than they had been, with more textual variety, meditation aids, and provisions for silence and reflection. The psalms are distributed over a four-week period instead of a week. Readings include some of the best material from the Fathers of the Church and authors with a reputation for sanctity and orthodoxy. Biographies of the saints are drawn from scholarly sources.

FAST AND ABSTINENCE

In a category of its own is the Catholic practice of fast and abstinence. While it partakes of the essentials of sacred time and place, it is unique in the sense that its foundation lies deep in Christian revelation, and throughout the Church's history it was assumed that doing penance was a necessary condition for salvation. What the Church did, therefore, was not to create the notion of penance but merely specify at different times the manner of its practice and exhort the people to its faithful observance.

Fasting, which was rigorously practiced in Judaism and by the disciples of John the Baptist, was taught by Christ in word and example. It was observed by the apostles (Ac. 13:2, 14:23; 2 Co. 11:27); and in the early Church, weekly fast days soon developed, Wednesday and Friday being mentioned in the first century.

In the West, Saturday was later substituted for Wednesday (about A.D. 400), but was again abolished in more recent times. The fast of Lent, which was from the beginning connected with the feast of Easter, lasted originally only two days, but it had been extended at least in many places to forty by the fourth century. The Eastern Church added three further periods of fasting: Advent (from November 15); from Trinity Sunday to the feast of St. Peter and Paul; and the two weeks before the Assumption. The West only developed the vigil fasts before the great feasts and the fasts of the ember days at the beginning of each of the four seasons of the year.

In early times, fasting meant entire abstinence from food for the whole or part of the fast day. The only complete fast still retained until recent times was the Eucharistic fast lasting from the previous midnight.

Among the changes in Catholic practice in the twentieth century, those affecting fast and abstinence have had the most obvious influence not only on the faithful but on the whole culture in which they live. The changes came in two stages: first regarding the Eucharistic fast, and then for all penitential customs in the Church.

The fast before Communion shows the rapid pace in Catholic liturgical practice. Complete fast from food and drink, from midnight, was widespread in the fourth century, and by the Middle Ages it was mandatory everywhere. Within ten years all this was changed. In 1953 the obligation was reduced to complete abstinence from solid food, but permission for water at any time and for liquids (except alcoholic) up to one hour before Communion was granted. Four years later the permission was extended to solid food and alcoholic beverages up to three hours before receiving. And in 1964, at the close of the third session of the Vatican Council, Paul VI reduced the precept to complete abstinence from everything except water and medicine for only the last hour.

The reasons behind the change were more than a shift of legislative posture. They typified the Church's ability to adapt to changing circumstances, provided the alteration of a divine law is not involved. Some of the reasons given by the Popes were historical (new conditions of time), psychological (grave difficulties apt to deter people), humanitarian (travel, health, labors, missionaries, late hour), sociological (working people in factories, transportation, shipping, mothers, children), and especially sacramental (to promote the reawakened devotion toward the Eucharist). An unprecedented growth in the reception of the sacrament among Catholics was the immediate result of this adjustment to the times.

Two years after the change in the Eucharistic fast, Paul VI issued another document on the whole spectrum of the Church's laws of fast and abstinence. In the apostolic constitution *Paenitemini* (Be Converted), the Pope first explained how penance belongs to the heart of Christianity; then he pointed out how different times call for different forms of penance; and finally, he delineated the new norms to be observed in the practice of penitence in our day.

Following in the footsteps of the Master, Catholics were told, every Christian must renounce himself, take up his own cross, and participate in the sufferings of Christ. Thus transformed into the image of Christ's death, he is made capable of meditating on the glory of the resurrection. Following the Master, a Christian should no longer live for himself, but must live for the God who loves him and gave himself up for the redemption of the world. He will also have to live for his brethren, completing as far as he can in his own body "to make up all that has still to be undergone by Christ for the sake of his body, the Church" (Col. 1:24).

Furthermore, since the Church is closely linked to Christ, the penance of the individual Christian also has an intimate relationship with the whole ecclesial community. In baptism he receives the fundamental gift of conversion (*metanoia*) which, if lost through sin after baptism, is restored and reinvigorated in those who avail themselves of the sacrament of mercy.

Against this background of the perennial faith, the Church in our day wants to make sure that the spirit of penance not only survives but will thrive. This poses the urgent need "to seek, beyond fast and abstinence, new expressions of the precise goal of penance that are both more suitable for its practice and truly in accordance with the changing times." Always to be kept in view are the need for physical asceticism of the body, and the performance of penance "by participation in the sufferings of Christ." The first without the second could become a form of stoicism; the second without the first could be suspect, since we know that a true follower of Christ is not only willing to suffer but actually undergoes suffering, to be more like the Savior and, unlike the Savior, to help control his passions and expiate his sins.

On the practical level of how the new approach to penance is to be followed, certain postulates of the Catholic religion are first made clear.

1. Penance is a virtue. It is mainly exercised in persevering faithfulness to the duties of one's state in life, in the acceptance of the difficulties arising from one's work and from living with others in society, in a patient bearing of the trials of earthly life and of the utter insecurity that pervades it.

2. Those Christians who are afflicted with infirmities, illness, poverty, or misfortune, or who are persecuted for the love of justice, are to unite their sorrows to the sufferings of Christ. In this way, they not only satisfy more perfectly the precept of penance but also obtain divine grace for others, while assuring themselves the Beatitude that Christ promised for those who suffer.

3. The duty of penance must be satisfied in a special way by priests, who are more closely linked to Christ by sacramental character. The same special obligation applies to those who have entered

the religious life or secular institutes, since one of the reasons for their vocation is "to follow more closely the abnegation of the Lord and to find a more ready and efficacious path to perfect charity."

But that is not all. The Church wants all the people of God to do penance, and not only passively in accepting from God's hands the hard things of life. She therefore "exhorts all Christians without distinction to respond to the divine precept of penance by certain voluntary acts which go beyond the renunciation imposed by the burdens of everyday life."

This response can take on various forms, and one of the principal adjustments that will have to be made is to realize that penance is not only fast and abstinence. There are other ways besides.

> Although Mother Church has always observed in a special way abstinence from meat and fasting, it wants to indicate in the traditional triad of prayer, fasting, and charity, the fundamental means of complying with the divine precept of penance.
>
> These means have been the same throughout the centuries, but in our day there are special reasons, depending on different needs in different places, why one form of penance should take precedence over others. Thus where the economic conditions are higher, Christ's faithful should give a greater witness of asceticism in order to avoid becoming enmeshed in the spirit of the world. They will also have the opportunity to give the witness of charity toward their brethren who suffer poverty and hunger beyond any border of nation or continent. But in places where the standard of living is lower, it will be more pleasing to God the Father and more useful to the members of the body of Christ if Christians offer their suffering in prayer to the Lord in union with the cross of Christ. All the while, of course, they are to promote the better practice of social justice.[6]

What about the traditional days and seasons of penance? The general principle that the Church now wishes to follow is that those times be chosen "which in the course of the liturgical year are closer to the paschal mystery of Christ, or which may be required by the special needs of the ecclesial community." This means that "the time of Lent preserves its penitential character," in the universal Church, along with specific fast and abstinence regulations. Other days of penance are to be decided by the bishops of the various countries.

As revolutionary as these changes may seem, they are not really so drastic. There is no question of mitigating the necessity for penance or of compromising on the laws of God. Emphatically, "by divine law all the faithful are required to do penance." The only difference is in "the prescriptions of the ecclesiastical law." The Church wishes to preserve, where it can be more readily observed, the custom of practicing penance also through abstinence from meat and fasting. At the same time, "she intends to ratify with her prescriptions other forms of penance as well, according as they seem opportune to episcopal conferences." The bishops have the responsibility of explaining to their people what these penitential forms consist in and how they are to be observed.

Fridays do not disappear as days of penance, and the faithful may continue to practice abstinence if they so desire or, if the bishops decide, abstinence can be prescribed. But other means are now available to make the Friday of each week something of what Lent is in the entire year.

Since fasting (along with abstinence) is only one of three recognized forms of penance in the Church, the other two need to be better known. Prayer can be penitential, both private and liturgical. This includes "the more frequent use of the sacrament of penance."[7] Charity toward the neighbor calls for surrender of self-love and the sharing of one's possessions.

Looking into the future, the great hope of Christ's Church is to protect the faithful from the ever-recurring danger of formalism and pharisaism, i.e., from feeling satisfied with any form of penance that is purely external. The essence of true penance is interior change of heart, from unruly attachment to creatures to a love of the Creator. Whatever helps in this conversion is penitential and truly pleasing to God.

XV. INDULGENCES

An indulgence, as understood by Catholic Christianity, is the remission of the temporal punishment due to forgiven sins, in virtue of the merits of Christ and his Church. This preliminary description is based on certain premises of faith that at different times in Christian history had to be reaffirmed and their implications re-examined, as happened in the sixteenth century at the time of the Reformation and in the twentieth century at the Second Council of the Vatican.

DOCTRINAL PRINCIPLES

The premises are easily stated. It is a divinely revealed truth that sins bring punishments inflicted by God's sanctity and justice. These must be expiated either on this earth through the sorrows, miseries, and trials of life, and above all through death, or else through purifying penalties in the life beyond. Moreover, they are to be expiated either by the sinner himself or also by others who make reparation, as far as possible, in his stead.

The just and merciful God imposes these punishments for the purification of souls, the defense of the sanctity of the moral order, and the restoration of his glory to its full majesty. Every sin, we believe, causes a disturbance in the order established by God, along with the destruction of precious values within the sinner and in the human community. Christians have always regarded sin not only as a transgression of the divine law, which it is; they have also seen it as disregard for the friendship between God and man, an offense against the Creator, and an ungrateful rejection of the love of God shown us in so many ways but especially in the person of Jesus Christ.

To obtain full remission of sins, therefore, two things are necessary. Friendship with God must be re-established by a sincere conversion of heart, and amends must be made for the injustice committed against his goodness. In addition, however, all the personal and social values and even those of the universal nature that have been diminished or destroyed by sin, must somehow be repaired. Call this reparation or reintegration. The important thing is that the restoration be done either by voluntarily "making up" for the wrong done or freely accepting the punishments demanded by an all-wise and holy Lord. As the Scriptures so eloquently declare, the very existence and gravity of the punishment should impress us with the folly and gravity of sin and its harmful consequences to mankind.

One more item of faith needs to be mentioned: The guilt of sin can be completely removed, but the vestiges of sin, or the temporal penalties still due, "may remain to be expiated or cleansed and, in fact, frequently do remain even after the remission of guilt."[1] The prayers of the Eucharistic liturgy reflect this belief, often asking God that "we, who are justly subjected to afflictions for our sins, may be mercifully set free from them for the glory of your name."

How does this doctrine affect the existence and meaning of indulgences? Indulgences are intelligible once it is seen that this work of reparation calls on the resources of the whole Church, and not only of the individual sinner, nor only of an individual helper in the expiation.

Given this constant belief of the Church, it was not surprising that already the Church of the Fathers should have looked upon the work of satisfaction as a community enterprise and that, within the Church, her pastors were charged with guiding the faithful in their co-operative reparation. "The bishops, therefore, prudently assessing these matters, established the manner and the measure of the satisfaction to be made and indeed permitted canonical penances to be replaced by other possibly easier works, which would be useful to the common good and suitable for fostering piety, to be performed by the penitents themselves and sometimes by others among the faithful."[2]

As we approach the history and current practice of indulgences, we might recapitulate the doctrinal premises, which have not changed over the centuries, although the application of the doctrine has notably changed, especially in recent years.

Indulgences presuppose (1) a retributive basis for divine justice, i.e., that sins must have a penalty either on earth or in purgatory, even (it may be) after the sinner has been reconciled with God by sacramental absolution; (2) the existence of the "treasury of merits," i.e., the infinite merits of Christ, together with the merits of the Blessed Virgin Mary and the saints, which the Church possesses in virtue of the communion of saints; (3) the belief that the Church, by her power of jurisdiction, has the right of administering the benefit of these merits in consideration of the prayers or other pious works undertaken by the faithful.

HISTORICAL DEVELOPMENT

In the early Church, certainly from the third century, the intercession of confessors and those awaiting martyrdom was allowed by the ecclesiastical authorities to shorten the canonical discipline of those under penance. Yet the general relaxation of the penitential discipline, in vogue up to the Middle Ages, came only later. There is consequently no certain evidence for general indulgences before the eleventh century.

To appreciate what the indulgence meant, we should recall how severe the previous canonical penances were. They were called canonical because they were prescribed according to specific rule (canon) and very detailed in their description. Sample penances, which assumed sacramental confession and therefore remission, illustrate the severity:

> If any layman defiles his neighbor's wife or virgin daughter, he shall do penance for an entire year on an allowance of bread and water, and he shall not have intercourse with his own wife. After a year of penance, he shall be admitted to Communion, and shall give alms for his soul.[3]
>
> Anyone who curses his neighbor, let him beg pardon, and let him undergo a week's strict penance.[4]
>
> Whoever knowingly commits perjury, shall do penance for forty days on bread and water, and seven succeeding years; and he shall never be accepted as a witness; and after these things he shall receive Communion.[5]
>
> If anyone publicly blasphemes God or the Blessed Virgin or any saint, he shall stand in the open in front of the doors of the church on seven Sundays, while the solemnities of the Masses are being performed, and on the last of these days without robe and shoes, with a cord about his neck. And on the seven preceding Fridays he shall fast on bread and water; and he shall then by no means enter the church. Moreover, on each of these seven Sundays he shall feed three or two people or one person, if he is able. Otherwise he shall do

another penance; if he refuses, he shall be forbidden to enter the church; in case of death, he shall be denied public burial.[6]

As the Church began to mitigate the rigors of these penitential exercises, two factors entered the change of policy. One was the practical difficulty of implementing the canonical penances, with the increased size of Church membership; and the other was a clearer awareness that expiation could be performed with less external severity on the part of the individual because the Church's prayers of intercession were also available.

We know that plenary indulgences were offered to those who took part in the Crusades, and bishops were authorized to give limited indulgences at the dedication of churches and their anniversaries, one of the most famous of these being the Portiuncula Indulgence, named after the Umbrian village about two miles from Assisi where St. Francis received his vocation in 1208. Also known as the Pardon of Assisi, the indulgence was decreed by Pope Honorius III in 1221 and originally could be gained for the souls in purgatory only in St. Francis' own Chapel of our Lady of the Angels.

The practice of allowing other acts of piety to substitute for the canonical penances gradually acquired various names. It was called a "grant," or "dispensation," or "remission," or "concession," or "mitigation." But the most common was *indulgentia,* which literally meant "forbearance," or kindness in not exacting the full measure of what is due, in the Gospel spirit of the one whose heavy debt was forgiven with the implicit understanding that he would remit the lesser amount that another man owed him.

The term "indulgence" remained even after severe canonical penances were discontinued and the original meaning of the word had changed. Thus we have here a real development of the doctrine of vicarious merit. The prayers and good works of the whole Church, and not only of the individual sinner for himself, came to be more clearly seen as effective reparation for the temporal penalty due to remitted sins.

As the Church extended the mitigation, i.e., indulgence, in the form of equivalent prayers and good works, abuses crept in, and by the sixteenth century they had become the focus of justifiable criticism. "Unfortunately," admitted Paul VI, "the practice of indulgences has at times been improperly used either through 'untimely and superfluous indulgences' by which the power of the keys was hu-

miliated and penitential satisfaction weakened, or through the collection of 'illicit profits' by which indulgences were blasphemously
defamed."[7] The twentieth-century Pontiff was paraphrasing the
Council of Trent in its own denunciation of the "traffic in indulgences" that helped provoke the Reformation.

Trent was outspoken in its condemnation of those who disgraced
the faith by their "improper use" of indulgences. At the same time,
it insisted that the Church, while deploring the abuse, "teaches and
establishes the fact that the use of indulgences must be preserved because it is supremely salutary for the Christian people and authoritatively approved by the sacred councils; and it condemns with anathema those who maintain the uselessness of indulgences or deny the
power of the Church to grant them."[8]

Trent was repeating what the Fourth Lateran Council had said
three centuries earlier, censuring the practice of granting "indiscreet
and superfluous indulgences," which tend to bring the Church's authority and penitential satisfaction into disrepute.[9]

During the four centuries before the Second Vatican Council, the
use of indulgences in the Church became widespread. As a result,
systematic classifications came to be made, which the Church recognized in granting various indulgences to the people.

Indulgences were first of all distinguished as either plenary or
partial. Plenary was one that so far as the intention of the authority
granting it was concerned, remitted all the temporal punishment
due to sin; partial was one that remitted only part of it. The reason
for the qualification in the definition of plenary indulgence was
that it might be only partially gained. Partial indulgences were expressed in periods of time that designated the equivalent of the temporal punishment remitted, in terms of the canonical penances
formerly practiced by the Church. Thus an indulgence of seven
years was a remission of the temporal punishment equivalent to the
canonical penances performed for seven full years (including Lent).
At one time, the addition of "seven quarantines" indicated an additional remission equivalent to that of the canonical penances performed during seven periods of Lent, during which they were more
severe.

Another division was into personal, real, mixed, and local indulgences. An indulgence was personal if granted directly to persons
(individuals or communities) independently of any particular place
or thing. It was real if attached to some object or thing that

had to be used by a person gaining the indulgence. It was mixed if it could be gained only by a designated class or quality of person (e.g., one enrolled in a certain confraternity) or by the use of a certain thing (e.g., a blessed scapular). It was local if directly attached to a place (e.g., church, shrine, or image located there) that had to be visited to gain the indulgence.

Indulgences were said to be perpetual if their concession was without limit of time; they were said to be temporary if limited in time (e.g., during the year of the jubilee).

Again, indulgences might be applicable to the deceased only, or to the living only, or to both the living and the departed, i.e., to either the one or the other. Thus the indulgence for visiting a cemetery and offering prayers for the dead during the octave of All Souls' Day was for the deceased only. An indulgence for the living could not be applied to any other living person than the one who gained it. Nevertheless, the indulgence of a privileged altar for the dying was applicable to the dying person for whom the Mass was offered; but such an indulgence was said to be for the living by way of absolution, effective at the moment of death. All indulgences granted by the Holy Father were applicable to the deceased, unless the contrary were stated.

Finally some indulgences were called "toties quoties," meaning "as often as." They could be gained anew each time the prescribed work of piety was performed.

Besides these categories, Church law covered no less than fourteen canons on such subjects as the power to grant indulgences, their publication, transfer of indulgences with transfer of feast, conditions for gaining indulgences, and their cessation.

POSTCONCILIAR CHANGES

Since indulgences may correctly be regarded as types of sacramentals, the directives of the Second Vatican Council on revising sacramentals applied also to indulgences. This becomes all the more obvious on reflection that indulgences are commonly attached to the use of sacramentals.

When Paul VI published his apostolic constitution on indulgences, he first made sure that the doctrinal presuppositions were clearly stated. No doubt many Catholics today do not give the same attention to indulgences as in other days, although cultures and individuals differ immensely, and it is impossible to generalize. Nevertheless, objectively the granting of indulgences by the Church belongs to the heart of its penitential discipline, and the more keen the realization of sin, the more eagerly will people avail themselves of this effective means of having the punishment due to sin remitted.

As a general statement, "the rulings of the Code of Canon Law and of the decrees of the Holy See concerning indulgences which do not go counter to the new norms remain unchanged."

Three principal considerations were kept in mind as the new norms were established: to establish a new measurement for partial indulgences; to reduce the number of plenary indulgences; and to re-examine and reformulate the so-called "real" and "local" indulgences attached to objects and places.

Definition. The new and amplified definition states that "an indulgence is the remission before God of the temporal punishment due to sins forgiven as far as their guilt is concerned, which the follower of Christ with the proper dispositions and under certain determined conditions acquires through the intervention of the Church, which, as minister of the redemption, authoritatively dispenses and applies the treasury of the satisfaction won by Christ and the saints."

Indulgences therefore apply only to forgiven sins, where the forgiveness refers to guilt before God, whereas the penance to be expiated refers to the disorder that sin produces in the world.

Indulgences can be gained by Christians who are rightly disposed but who also fulfill the requirements the Church sets down as the dispenser of Christ's redemptive merits.

Plenary and Partial. The traditional distinction between plenary and partial indulgences remains, in such a way that "an indulgence is partial or plenary as it removes either part or all of the temporal punishment due to sin." However, a new concession: "Partial as well as plenary indulgences can *always* be applied to the dead by way of suffrage." This is a change from the former restriction, which selectively reserved the application of indulgences for the souls in purgatory.

All particularities in terms of days, months, or years are now removed from partial indulgences. With the abolishment of this long-standing designation, a new norm has been established. This takes into consideration the specific action of the faithful Christian who performs a work to which an indulgence is attached.

> By their acts, the faithful can obtain, in addition to the merit which is the principal fruit of the act, a further remission of temporal punishment in proportion to the degree to which the charity of the one performing the act is greater, and in proportion to the degree to which the act itself is performed. It has therefore been considered fitting that this remission of temporal punishment which the Christian faithful acquire through an action should serve as the measurement for the remission of punishment which the ecclesiastical authority bountifully adds by way of partial indulgence.[10]

Concretely, this means that the old norm based on the ancient canonical penances no longer holds. From now on, the measure of how efficacious an indulgenced work is will depend on two things: the supernatural charity, love of God and neighbor, with which the indulgenced task is done; and the perfection or sublimity of the indulgenced task itself, since there are depths of perfection with which we do things and heights of sublimity in what we perform.

Corresponding to this momentous change, the Church has also reduced the number of plenary indulgences in order that the faithful might hold them in greater esteem and may, as a result, acquire them with proper dispositions. What happened was that "the greater proliferation of indulgences, the less attention is given to them; what is offered in abundance is not greatly appreciated. Besides, many of the faithful need considerable time to prepare themselves properly for acquisition of a plenary indulgence." We may, then, look upon partial indulgences as preparatory to gaining plenary ones, on the assumption that the dispositions needed to gain a plenary indulgence are above ordinary.

Although no one but God knows for certain when a plenary indulgence is actually gained, because only he knows whether a person's dispositions are adequate, one criterion for such dispositions is that "all attachment to sin, even venial sin, be absent." If these dispositions are in any way less than complete, the indulgence will be only partial. The same proviso applies to the three external conditions necessary to gain a plenary indulgence: sacramental confession, Eucharistic Communion, and prayer for the intentions of the Pope. If these conditions are not satisfied, an otherwise plenary indulgence becomes only partial.

These conditions may be fulfilled "several days before or after the performance of the prescribed work; nevertheless, it is fitting that Communion be received and the prayers for the intention of the Supreme Pontiff be said the same day the work is performed." Moreover, a single sacramental confession suffices for gaining several plenary indulgences, but Communion must be received and the prayers for the Pope's intentions said to gain each plenary indulgence. Praying for the Pope's intentions is fully satisfied by the recitation of one Our Father and one Hail Mary, but the people are free to recite any other prayers according to their own piety and devotion to the Vicar of Christ.

A plenary indulgence can be gained only once a day, except by those who are on the point of death. Partial indulgences can be acquired more than once a day, unless there is an explicit indication to the contrary.

Where the work prescribed for gaining a plenary indulgence is connected with a devout visit to church or oratory, it is enough to recite the Our Father and the Creed. Where an object of piety (crucifix, cross, rosary, scapular, or medal) has been blessed by the Pope or any bishop, those who devoutly use it can acquire a plenary indulgence on the feast of the apostles Peter and Paul, provided they also make a profession of faith using any legitimate formula. In general, however, using objects blessed by any priest allows a person to gain a partial indulgence.

Anticipating the situation of those who cannot be assisted by a priest to bring them the last sacraments and impart the apostolic blessing, "Holy Mother Church nevertheless grants a plenary indulgence to be acquired at the point of death, provided they are properly disposed and have been in the habit of reciting some prayers during their lifetime. To use a crucifix in connection with the acquisition of this plenary indulgence is a laudable practice."[11] Implicit in this extraordinary grant is the person's intention, at least habitual, to gain such a final remission of all temporal punishment due to sin. Depending on his dispositions, he can be ready for immediate entrance into heaven without suffering the pains of purgatory.

Concerning Masses offered for the souls in purgatory, another major development was a sweeping simplification: "Holy Mother Church, extremely solicitous for the faithful departed, has decided that suffrages can be applied to them to the widest possible extent

at any sacrifice of the Mass whatsoever, abolishing all special privileges in this regard."[12]

Actions of the Faithful. Consistent with the Church's new outlook
on the way indulgences are to be acquired, it was only natural that
certain long-familiar classifications would be revised and, in this
case, disappear. Thus "the division of indulgences into 'personal,'
'real,' and 'local' is abolished, so as to make it clear that indulgences are attached to the actions of the faithful even though at
times they may be linked with some object or place."[13]

This provision needs to be explained. It does not mean that sacred
objects like rosaries, medals, statues, or crucifixes are no longer to
be blessed, nor that sacred places like church buildings will not be
consecrated. The Church's sacramentals remain intact. What it does
mean is that the whole attitude of the faithful ought to be directed
to where it belongs, toward the person who is gaining the indulgence
and his suitable dispositions. The new approach toward "so-called
'real' and 'local' indulgences is to reduce them and give them a sim-
pler and more dignified formulation."[14] The purpose behind this
injunction is to remove any vestige of animism from the Catholic
belief in indulgences, as though blessed articles and places had an
inherent quality of remitting the penalties due to sin independent
of the sorrow and desire for amendment of the sinner.

Soon after Pope Paul's document on indulgences, he authorized
the publication of a *Handbook of Indulgences* that, quite alone,
would deserve a place in the Church's history. It is a model of simplicity, minus the elaborate numerical data that for centuries had
been associated with indulgences. What is most remarkable, however, is that the new synthesis on this vitally practical aspect of
Catholic piety begins with "Three General Grants," followed by
scores of indulgenced exercises. These grants are offered in order
that "Christ's faithful might, as it were, weave their daily life with
the Christian spirit and, according to their state, grow in the perfection of charity."

A partial indulgence is granted to any of Christ's faithful who, in
the performance of his duties and bearing the trials of life, raises his
mind to God in humble confidence and adds, even mentally, some
pious invocation.

A partial indulgence is granted to any of Christ's faithful who, in the spirit of penance, freely abstains from something which is permissible and pleasing to him.

A partial indulgence is granted to any of Christ's faithful who, led by the spirit of faith, with a kindly heart expends himself or some of his possessions in the service of his brethren who are in need.[15]

Each of these newly created, all-purpose indulgences is supported by biblical texts to show how readily and almost constantly we can "offer up" to God in reparation for our sins. Faith tells us that anything in life that costs us any sacrifice is an effective means of making satisfaction. Experience tells us that there are few things in life that do not call for some self-surrender. The Church's hope is that, by enriching these myriad acts of self-denial from the treasury of the communion of saints, what are called indulgences will become divinely fruitful instruments of sanctification. After all, in the providence of God, one reason he permits sin is that repentant sinners might be sanctified.

EPILOGUE

The foregoing pages of the Catechism are so obviously addressed to the mind that it is possible to overlook the corresponding importance of the heart in learning and teaching Catholic Christianity. All that Christ taught during his visible stay on earth brings out clearly the need for something more than mere knowledge to please God and something more necessary than just faith to attain the destiny he has in store for those who please him.

Thus, as we began so we end this compendium of the Catholic religion by pointing out that salvation does not depend on either faith *or* charity but on faith *and* charity. It is not enough to believe, even with a faith that moves mountains or that works miracles. We must also have charity, which is based on faith indeed but goes beyond faith to reach out to the One in whom we believe, and from this love for God reaches out to all whom his providence places, though casually, into our lives.

The Second Vatican Council clarified many things for the faithful. Not the least of these is the absolute need for honesty in the Church. We are to practice what we profess and live our faith by loving the God we believe in. For his sake we are to love our neighbor as he, the God-man, has been loving us, i.e., generously, effectively and selflessly, if need be through the sacrifice of our lives for those whom he identifies with himself.

This is not to minimize the value of knowing what God has revealed and what the Church he founded understands this revelation to mean. The mind must be enlightened in order to motivate the will to action and animate the affections to love. But, once enlightened, the believer cannot rest in his own reflections or remain sterile with the insights he has received. Otherwise his faith without good works is dead and the exalted lights from God will go unrewarded in time and eternity. "If you love me," Jesus said, "keep my commandments." This certainly means that our minds have first accepted Christ who is the Truth. But then our hearts must also follow him who is the Way, so that our whole being may become filled with him who is our Life.

REFERENCES

I. THE WORD OF GOD

1. Second Vatican Council, *Dogmatic Constitution on Divine Revelation*, I, 2.
2. Ibid.
3. First Vatican Council, *Dogmatic Constitution on the Catholic Faith*, 2: Denzinger 1786 (3005).
4. Second Vatican Council, *Dogmatic Constitution on Divine Revelation*, I, 6.
5. Ibid., I, 4.
6. Ibid.
7. St. John Damascene, *Exposition of the Orthodox Faith*, III, 12.
8. Koran, Surah 112:3.
9. First Vatican Council, *Dogmatic Constitution on the Catholic Faith*, 3: Denzinger 1789 (3008); Second Vatican Council, *Dogmatic Constitution on Divine Revelation*, I, 5.
10. St. Thomas Aquinas, *De Virtutibus in Communi*, 12.
11. Council of Trent, *Canons on the Sacrament of Baptism*, Canon 13: Denzinger 869 (1626).
12. Second Vatican Council, *Declaration on Christian Education*, 2.
13. Ibid., 3.
14. Ibid.
15. Friedrich W. Nietzsche, *The Antichrist*, I, 15.
16. St. Pius X, encyclical *Pascendi* (September 8, 1907): Denzinger 2081–85 (3484–86).
17. First Vatican Council, *Dogmatic Constitution on the Catholic Faith*, 3: Denzinger 1789 (3008).
18. Ibid.
19. Ibid., Denzinger 1791 (3010).
20. St. Augustine, *De Utilitate Credendi*, passim.
21. First Vatican Council, *Dogmatic Constitution on the Catholic Faith*, 3: Denzinger 1791 (3010).
22. Ibid.
23. Ibid., Denzinger 1792 (3011).
24. Fifth Lateran Council, *Apostolici Regiminis*: Denzinger 738 (1441).

25. First Vatican Council, *Dogmatic Constitution on the Catholic Faith,* 3: Denzinger 1794 (3014).

26. Ibid., Denzinger 1794 (3013–14).

27. Ibid., 3–4: Denzinger 1790 (3009), 1796 (3016).

28. St. Clement I, *Letter to the Corinthians,* 24.

29. First Vatican Council, *Dogmatic Constitution on the Catholic Faith,* 3: Denzinger 1794 (3013–14).

30. Ibid., Denzinger 1794 (3013); Second Vatican Council, *Dogmatic Constitution on the Church,* VII, 50.

31. Second Vatican Council, *Decree on the Mission Activity of the Church,* II, 10.

32. First Vatican Council, *Dogmatic Constitution on the Catholic Faith,* 4: Denzinger 1816 (3041).

33. Second Vatican Council, *Dogmatic Constitution on Divine Revelation,* II, 7.

34. Ibid.

35. Ibid.

36. Ibid., II, 8.

37. Ibid.

38. St. Pius X (Biblical Commission), *Mosaic Authenticity of the Pentateuch:* Denzinger 1997, 2000 (3394, 3397).

39. Ibid., Denzinger 1999 (3396).

40. Second Vatican Council, *Dogmatic Constitution on Divine Revelation,* IV, 15.

41. St. Damasus I, *Decretum Damasi:* Denzinger 84 (179).

42. Council of Trent, *Decree on Sacred Scripture and Tradition:* Denzinger 783 (1501).

43. Second Vatican Council, *Dogmatic Constitution on Divine Revelation,* II, 9.

44. Ibid., II, 10.

45. Ibid., II, 8.

46. First Vatican Council, *Dogmatic Constitution on the Catholic Faith,* 4: Denzinger 1817, 1818 (3042, 3043).

47. Second Vatican Council, *Dogmatic Constitution on Divine Revelation,* V, 19.

II. THE LIVING GOD

1. Pius IX, encyclical *Qui Pluribus* (November 9, 1846), included an analysis and condemnation of communism: Denzinger (2786).

2. Leo XIII defined Marxism in the encyclical *Quod Apostolici Muneris* (December 28, 1878): Denzinger 1851 (3133).

3. First Vatican Council, *Dogmatic Constitution on the Catholic Faith*, 1: Denzinger 1782 (3001).

4. First Council of Constantinople: Denzinger 86 (150); Fourth Lateran Council: Denzinger 428 (800); Council of Florence: Denzinger 706 (1333); Council of Trent: Denzinger 994 (1862).

5. Ludwig Feuerbach, *The Essence of Christianity*, passim.

6. St. Augustine, *Expositions on the Psalms*, 101:2, 10.

7. *Pastor Hermae*, Mandate 1:1.

8. St. Gregory of Nyssa, *Contra Eunomium*, 3.

9. Tertullian, *Adversus Marcionem*, I, 3.

10. First Vatican Council, *Dogmatic Constitution on the Catholic Faith*, 1: Denzinger 1802–4 (3022–24).

11. Georg Hegel, *Encyclopedia* (notably second edition), passim.

12. Pius XI, encyclical *Divini Redemptoris*, II, 9.

13. Second Vatican Council, *Pastoral Constitution on the Church in the Modern World*, I, 19.

14. Ibid.

15. Ibid., II, 26.

16. *The Nicene Creed:* Denzinger 54 (125).

17. *The Constantinople Creed:* Denzinger 86 (150).

18. First Council of Nicea, First Council of Constantinople, Council of Ephesus, and especially the Council of Chalcedon: Denzinger 148 (301–2), treat expressly of the meaning of "nature" and "person" in God.

19. Paul VI, *Credo of the People of God*, proclaimed at the close of the Year of Faith (June 30, 1968).

III. GOD, MAN, AND THE UNIVERSE

1. First Vatican Council, *Dogmatic Constitution on the Catholic Faith*, 2: Denzinger 1785 (3004).

2. Ibid., Denzinger 1806 (3026).

3. Ibid., Denzinger 1805 (3025).

4. Fourth Lateran Council, *On the Catholic Faith:* Denzinger 428 (800); First Vatican Council, *Dogmatic Constitution on the Catholic Faith*, 1: Denzinger 1782–83 (3001–2).

5. St. Thomas Aquinas, *Summa Theologica*, Pars Prima, 46, 2.

6. Fourth Lateran Council, *On the Catholic Faith:* Denzinger 428 (800).

7. Julian Huxley, *Religion Without Revelation*, passim.

8. First Vatican Council, *Dogmatic Constitution of the Catholic Faith*, 1: Denzinger 1783 (3002).

9. Ibid., Denzinger 1805 (3025).

10. St. Augustine, *Expositions on the Psalms:* 134, 10.

11. Council of Sens, *The Errors of Peter Abelard,* Proposition 7: Denzinger 374 (726).

12. Council of Florence, *Decree on Behalf of the Jacobites:* Denzinger 703, 706 (1330, 1333).

13. Council of Trent, *Canons on Justification,* 6: Denzinger 816 (1556).

14. Second Vatican Council, *Pastoral Constitution on the Church in the Modern World,* III, 39.

15. St. Thomas Aquinas, *Summa Theologica,* Pars Prima, 43, 1: *Summa Contra Gentiles,* II, 45.

16. St. Augustine, *De Genesi ad Litteram,* V, 20, 40.

17. St. Thomas Aquinas, *Summa Theologica,* Pars Prima, 6, 3; 104, 1; *De Potentia,* 1.

18. St. Ignatius Loyola, *Spiritual Exercises,* "Contemplation for Obtaining Love."

19. First Vatican Council, *Dogmatic Constitution on the Catholic Faith,* 1: Denzinger 1784 (3003).

20. St. Thomas Aquinas, Exposition, *Perihermenias,* I, 14.

21. St. Thomas Aquinas, *Compendium Theologiae,* 142.

22. First Vatican Council, *Dogmatic Constitution on the Catholic Faith,* 1: Denzinger 1783 (3002), 1805 (3025).

23. Doctrine on the angels explicitly taught by ecumenical councils before the Second Vatican: Fourth Lateran Council, *On the Catholic Faith:* Denzinger 428 (800); Second Council of Lyons, *The Profession of Faith of Michael Palaeologus:* Denzinger 461 (851); Council of Florence, *Decree on Behalf of the Jacobites:* Denzinger 706 (1333); Council of Trent, *The Profession of Faith of the Council of Trent:* Denzinger 994 (1862); First Vatican Council, *Dogmatic Constitution in the Catholic Faith,* 1: Denzinger 1783 (3002), 1802, 1804–5 (3022, 3024–25).

24. Pius XII, encyclical *Humani Generis:* Denzinger 2318 (3891).

25. St. Basil, *Adversus Eunomium,* III, 1.

26. Confer the Letters of Bl. Peter Fabre and St. Aloysius Gonzaga on devotion to the guardian angels of individuals and communities.

27. *Catechism of the Council of Trent,* "First Commandment."

28. *Roman Breviary* (Approved by St. Pius X), Feast of the Guardian Angels.

29. Council of Trent, *Decree on Original Sin:* Denzinger 788 (1511).

30. St. Ignatius Loyola, *Spiritual Exercises,* "The Two Standards."

31. Paul VI, *Address to General Audience* (Nov. 15, 1972).

32. Fourth Lateran Council, *On the Catholic Faith:* Denzinger 428 (800); First Vatican Council, *Dogmatic Constitution on the Catholic Faith,* 1: Denzinger 1783 (3002).

33. Pius XII, *Address to the Pontifical Academy of Sciences* (Nov. 30, 1941): Denzinger 2285; Pius XII, encyclical *Humani Generis:* Denzinger 2327 (3896).

34. Pius XII, *Address to the Pontifical Academy of Sciences* (Nov. 30, 1941).
35. Pius XII, encyclical *Humani Generis:* Denzinger 2327 (3896).
36. First Vatican Council, *Dogmatic Constitution on the Catholic Faith,* 4: Denzinger 1797 (3017).
37. *Evolution After Darwin,* ed. Sol Tax (University of Chicago Press, 1960), Vol. I, 45.
38. Charles Darwin, *The Descent of Man,* III, 21.
39. Ibid.
40. Pius XII, encyclical *Humani Generis:* Denzinger 2328 (3897).
41. St. Gregory of Nyssa, *De Opificio Hominis,* 8.
42. St. Augustine, *De Genesi ad Litteram,* VI, 3.
43. Paul Tillich, *Systematic Theology,* II, *passim.*
44. Second Council of Orange, Canons 1–2: Denzinger 174–75 (371–72).
45. Council of Trent, *Decree on Original Sin,* 1: Denzinger 788 (1511).
46. Ibid., 5: Denzinger 792 (1515).
47. Ibid., 1: Denzinger 788 (1511).
48. Second Council of Orange, Canon 2: Denzinger 175 (372); Council of Trent, *Decree on Original Sin,* 2: Denzinger 789 (1512).
49. Fourth Lateran Council, *On the Catholic Faith:* Denzinger 428 (800).
50. St. Augustine, *Confessions,* XII, 7.
51. Fifth Lateran Council, *Apostolici Regiminis:* Denzinger 738 (1440).
52. Synod of Constantinople, confirmed by Pope Vigilius I, *Anathemas Against Origenism,* Canon 1: Denzinger 203 (403).
53. St. Augustine, *Letter 166,* 2, 3.
54. First Vatican Council, *Dogmatic Constitution on the Catholic Faith,* 1: Denzinger 1804 (3024).
55. St. Thomas Aquinas, *De Malo,* 2.
56. Benedict XII, *Libellus "cum Dudum" ad Armenios:* Denzinger 532 (1006).
57. Pius XII, encyclical *Humani Generis:* Denzinger 2327 (3896).
58. Leo XIII, encyclical *Libertas Praestantissimum,* 30.
59. John XXIII, encyclical *Pacem in Terris,* V, 167.
60. Second Vatican Council, *Pastoral Constitution on the Church in the Modern World,* introduction, 9.

IV. JESUS CHRIST   Testimony of the Church

1. The text of the original Nicene Creed is preserved in many sources, e.g., Socrates, *Historia Ecclesiastica,* I, 8; and Theodoret, *Historia Ecclesiastica,* I, 11.
2. First Council of Constantinople, Canon 3, *Mansi,* III, 557–66.

3. Nestorius, in Hefele, *History of the Councils*, III, 12.
4. Council of Ephesus, *On the Incarnation of the Son of God:* Denzinger 111a (250–51).
5. St. Cyril of Alexandria, *Acta Conciliorum Oecumenicorum*, I, 4, 15–20.
6. Eutyches, *Mansi*, VI, 744.
7. Council of Chalcedon, *Acta Conciliorum Oecumenicorum*, II, 1, 277.
8. Council of Chalcedon, *The Chalcedonian Creed:* Denzinger 148 (301–2).
9. Pius VI, constitution *Auctorem Fidei*, 61: Denzinger 1561 (2661).
10. Ibid., 62: Denzinger 1562 (2662).
11. Ibid., 63: Denzinger 1563 (2663).
12. St. Pius X (Holy Office), Decree *Lamentabili:* Denzinger 2027–35 (3427–35).
13. Second Vatican Council, *Dogmatic Constitution on Divine Revelation*, V, 19.
14. Paul VI (Biblical Commission), Instruction *Sancta Mater Ecclesia*, April 21, 1964, *passim*.
15. Benedict XV (Holy Office), *Decree on the Knowledge in the Soul of Christ:* Denzinger 2183–85 (3645–47).
16. St. Gregory, I, *Letter to Eulogius:* Denzinger 248 (474–76).
17. Pius XII, encyclical *Sempiternus Rex:* Denzinger 2334 (3905).

V. BLESSED VIRGIN MARY

1. Few doctrines of Christianity have been more often explicitly taught by the ecumenical councils than Mary's divine maternity. Thus Ephesus, *The Incarnation:* Denzinger 111a and *The Anathemas of the Chapter of Cyril*, Canon 1: Denzinger 113; Chalcedon, *Definition of the Two Natures of Christ:* Denzinger 148; Second Constantinople, *Anathemas Concerning the Three Chapters*, Canons 2, 6: Denzinger 214, 218 (422, 427); First Lateran Council, *The Trinity, the Incarnation*, Canon 3: Denzinger 256 (503); and Third Constantinople, *Definition of the Two Wills of Christ:* Denzinger (554). Her virginity was defined almost as often, e.g., Chalcedon, *The Incarnation* (*against Eutyches*): Denzinger 144 (294); Second Constantinople, *Anathemas Concerning the Three Chapters*, Canons 2, 6, 14: Denzinger 214, 218, 227 (422, 427, 437); First Lateran, *The Trinity, the Incarnation*, Canon 3: Denzinger 256 (503); and Fourth Lateran, *The Trinity, Sacraments, Canonical Mission*, I: Denzinger 429 (801).

2. St. Augustine, *Sermon 186*.

3. Paschasius Radbertus, *De Partu Virginis*, 1.

4. St. Bernard, *Letter to the Canons of Lyons*, 5, 7.

5. St. Albertus Magnus, *In Librum Tertium*, 4, 4.

6. Duns Scotus, *Commentarium in Sententiarum*, III, 3, 1, 4.

7. Ibid., III, 3, 1, 2.

8. Council of Trent, *Decree on Original Sin:* Denzinger 787–92 (1510–16).

9. St. Pius V, *Errors of Michael du Bay*, Proposition 73: Denzinger 1073 (1973).

10. St. Gregory of Tours, *Miracula*, I, 4.

11. Pius IX, *Ineffabilis Deus:* Denzinger 1641 (2803–4).

12. Pius XII, constitution *Munificentissimus Deus*, III, 44.

13. Pius XII, encyclical *Humani Generis*, 21.

14. Pius XII, encyclical *Fulgens Corona*, 21.

15. Pius XII, encyclical *Fulgens Corona*, 3–4.

16. Second Vatican Council, *Dogmatic Constitution on the Church*, VIII, 60.

17. Ibid., VIII, 56.

18. Ibid., VIII, 62.

19. Ibid.

20. The Council of Ephesus condemned anyone who said that Christ "offered oblation for himself, and not rather solely for us": Denzinger 122; also the Council of Trent: Denzinger 799 (1528–29).

21. Second Vatican Council, *Dogmatic Constitution of the Church*, VIII, 58.

22. Ibid., VIII, 60.

23. Ibid., VIII, 67.

VI. THE GRACE OF GOD Supernatural Life

1. St. Thomas Aquinas, *Summa Contra Gentiles*, IV, 11.

2. Second Vatican Council, *Decree on the Missionary Activity of the Church*, VI, 36.

3. Leo XIII, encyclical *Exeunte Jam Anno*.

4. Council of Trent, *Decree on Justification*, 7: Denzinger 799 (1528).

5. St. Francis de Sales, *The Love of God*, II, 11.

6. St. Thomas Aquinas, *Summa Contra Gentiles*, I–II, 72, 5.

7. Ibid.

8. St. Augustine, *In Joannis Evangelium*, 49.

VI. THE GRACE OF GOD   Indwelling Spirit

1. *Creed of Epiphanius* (longer form): Denzinger 13 (44).
2. St. Augustine, *Epistola ad Dardanum,* IV, 17.
3. Council of Trent, *Doctrine on the Sacrament of Penance,* 8: Denzinger 904 (1689).
4. Pius XII, encyclical *Mystici Corporis Christi,* II, 79.
5. St. Theresa of Avila, *Autobiography,* XXIX, 17–18.
6. St. Thomas Aquinas, *Summa Theologica,* Pars Prima, 43, 3.
7. St. Augustine, *De Vita Beata,* IV, 35.
8. St. Augustine, *De Civitate Dei,* XII, 1.
9. St. Augustine, *In Joannis Evangelium,* 76.
10. St. Thomas Aquinas, *Summa Theologica,* Pars Prima, 38, 2.

VI. THE GRACE OF GOD   Actual Graces

1. Pelagius, quoted by St. Augustine, *De Gratia Christi,* I, 2, 41.
2. St. Augustine, *De Diversis Quaestionibus, ad Simplicianum,* I, 12, 22.
3. St. Augustine, *De Peccatorum Meritis et Remissione,* II, 32–33.
4. Council of Carthage, *On Grace* (approved by Pope St. Zosimus), Canon 4: Denzinger 104 (226).
5. St. Prosper of Aquitaine, *Indiculus,* 6: Denzinger 135 (244).
6. Second Council of Orange, *Original Sin, Grace and Predestination,* Canon 7: Denzinger 180 (377).
7. St. Thomas Aquinas, *Summa Theologica,* I, II, 109; III, 2.
8. Council of Trent, *Decree on Justification,* 5: Denzinger 797 (1525).
9. Council of Trent, *Doctrine on the Sacrament of Penance,* 4: Denzinger 898 (1677).

VI. THE GRACE OF GOD   Infused Virtues and Gifts

1. Virtue as moral goodness (Wis. 4:1, 5:13; 2 M. 6:13), and as particular moral quality (Wis. 8:7).
2. Divine powers (1 P. 2:9; 2 P. 1:3), moral vigor (2 P. 1:5), and moral virtue (Ph. 4:8).
3. St. Thomas Aquinas, *Summa Theologica,* I, II, 64, 4.
4. Innocent III, letter *Maiores Ecclesiae Causas* to Ymbertus, bishop of Arles: Denzinger 410 (780).
5. Leo XIII, encyclical *Testem Benevolentiae* (Jan. 22, 1899).

6. St. Thomas Aquinas, *Summa Theologica*, II–II, 8, 7.
7. St. Augustine, *De Magistro*, 38.
8. St. Augustine, *De Sermone Domini in Monte*, 1.
9. St. Thomas Aquinas, *Summa Theologica*, II–II, 121, 1.
10. Ibid., II–II, 140, 1.
11. St. Augustine, *Sermon 88*.

VII. THE CHURCH

1. Second Vatican Council, *Dogmatic Constitution on the Church*, II, 9.
2. Pius XII, encyclical *Mystici Corporis Christi*, I, 26.
3. St. Leo, *Sermon LXVIII*, 3.
4. Pius XII, encyclical *Mystici Corporis Christi*, I, 33.
5. Second Vatican Council, *Dogmatic Constitution on the Church*, I, 6.
6. First Vatican Council, *Dogmatic Constitution I on the Church of Christ:* Denzinger 1821 (3051).
7. Second Vatican Council, *Dogmatic Constitution on the Church*, I, 8.
8. Paul VI (Congregation for the Doctrine of the Faith), *Mysterium Ecclesiae*, Part 1.
9. Second Vatican Council, *Dogmatic Constitution on the Church*, V, 40.
10. Origen, *Against Celsus*, III, 29.
11. Council of Arles, *The Baptism of Heretics*, Canon 9: Denzinger 53 (123).
12. Innocent III, *Profession of Faith Prescribed for Durand of Osca and His Waldensian Companions:* Denzinger 424 (793).
13. Council of Constance, *Errors of John Wycliffe*, Propositions 4, 8, 15: Denzinger 584, 588, 595 (1154, 1158, 1165); *Errors of John Hus*, Propositions 8, 12, 20, 30: Denzinger 634, 638, 646, 656 (1208, 1212, 1220, 1230).
14. Clement XI, *Errors of Paschasius Quesnel*, Propositions 74, 76: Denzinger 1424, 1426 (2474, 2476).
15. Pius XII, encyclical *Mystici Corporus Christi* (Jun. 29, 1943).
16. *Code of Canon Law*, Canon 1325, n. 2.
17. St. Ignatius, *Letter to the Smyrneans*, 8, 2.
18. Second Vatican Council, *Decree on the Missionary Activity of the Church*, I, 5.
19. Ibid., IV, 26.
20. John XXIII, *Opening Address to the Second Vatican Council* (Oct. 11, 1962).
21. Council of Trent, *Canons on the Sacrament of Order*, Canons 1–7:

Denzinger 961–67 (1771–77): Second Vatican Council, *Dogmatic Constitution on the Church*, III, 21.

22. Second Vatican Council, *Dogmatic Constitution on the Church*, III, 22.

23. Ibid., III, 21.

24. Ibid., III, 22.

25. Paul VI, *Mysterium Ecclesiae*, Part 2.

26. Second Vatican Council, *Dogmatic Constitution on the Church*, II, 12.

27. Paul VI, *Mysterium Ecclesiae*, Part 2.

28. Second Vatican Council, *Dogmatic Constitution on Divine Revelation*, II, 8.

29. Paul VI, *Mysterium Ecclesiae*, Part 2.

30. Council of Ephesus, *The Primacy of the Roman Pontiff:* Denzinger 112 (237).

31. Council of Trent, *Doctrine on the Sacrament of Orders*, IV: Denzinger 960 (1767).

32. First Vatican Council, *Dogmatic Constitution I on the Church of Christ*, IV: Denzinger 1839 (3073).

33. *Acta Concilii Vaticani*, Mansi, LIII, col. 326.

34. Second Vatican Council, *Dogmatic Constitution on the Church*, III, 25.

35. St. Ireneus, *Adversus Haereses*, II, 24, 1.

36. Origen, *Homilia In Jesu Nave*, 3, 5.

37. Lactantius, *Divinae Institutiones*, IV, 30, 1.

38. Second Vatican Council, *Dogmatic Constitution on the Church*, II, 14.

39. Second Vatican Council, *Decree on the Missionary Activity of the Church*, I, 5.

40. Second Vatican Council, *Declaration on the Relation of the Church to Non-Christian Religions*, 2.

41. Paul VI (Congregation for the Clergy), *General Catechetical Directory*, II, 18.

42. Paul VI, *Homily at the Canonization of the Forty Martyrs of England and Wales* (Oct. 25, 1970); citation from the *Dogmatic Constitution on the Church*, V, 42.

43. Clement I, *Letter to the Corinthians*, 46, 6.

44. Letter of Monsignor Bonomelli, *World Missionary Conference, 1910*, Vol. VIII, p. 221.

45. Pius XI, encyclical *Mortalium Animos* (Jan. 6, 1928).

46. Pius XII, address to the German Conference at Mainz, *L'Osservatore Romano* (Nov. 9, 1948).

47. John XXIII, *Unitas*, XIV, 2.

48. Second Vatican Council, *Decree on Ecumenism,* I, 3.
49. Ibid., I, 4.
50. Gelasius I, *De Duplici Suprema Potestate in Terris:* Denzinger (347).
51. Boniface VIII, *Unam Sanctam:* Denzinger 469 (873).
52. Boniface VIII, *De Consideratione ad Eugenium III,* IV, 3.
53. Pius XI, encyclical *Divini Redemptoris,* II, 10–11.
54. Second Vatican Council, *Dogmatic Constitution on the Church,* IV, 36.
55. Leo XIII, encyclical *Immortale Dei,* 22 (citation from letter of Ivo of Chartres to Pope Paschal II, *Epistola 238*).
56. Leo XIII, encyclical *Immortale Dei,* 36.
57. Second Vatican Council, *Declaration on Religious Liberty,* II, 13.
58. Second Vatican Council, *Declaration on Christian Education,* 5.

VIII. HUMAN DESTINY

1. Justinian, edict to Menna, patriarch of Constantinople, published in the synod of Constantinople, confirmed by Pope Vigilius, *Canons Against Origen,* Canon 9: Denzinger 211 (411).
2. Benedict XII, constitution *Benedictus Deus:* Denzinger 530–31 (1000–2).
3. Paul VI, homily *Precious Time of Penitence* (Feb. 24, 1971).
4. Benedict XII, constitution *Benedictus Deus:* Denzinger 530 (1000–1).
5. Council of Florence, bull *Laetentur Caeli:* Denzinger 693 (1304–6).
6. St. John Chrysostom, *Homilia in Hebraeos,* 6, 4.
7. *Catechism of the Council of Trent,* Article XII, "Life Everlasting."
8. St. Anselm, *Proslogion,* XXV, 4.
9. Second Vatican Council, *Dogmatic Constitution on the Church,* VII, 50.
10. John XXIII, *Journal of a Soul,* Appendix 6.
11. St. Ignatius, *Letter to the Ephesians,* 16, 1.
12. St. Ireneus, *Adversus Haereses,* IV, 28, 2.
13. St. Augustine, *The City of God,* XXI, 23.
14. *Symbolum "Quicumque,"* Athanasian Creed, 1, 40, 41.
15. Fourth Lateran Council, *The Trinity, Sacraments, Canonical Mission,* I: Denzinger 429 (801).
16. Benedict XII, constitution *Benedictus Deus:* Denzinger 530–31 (1000–2).
17. Council of Trent, *Canons on Justification,* Canons 25, 30: Denzinger 835, 840 (1575, 1580); *Canons on the Sacrament of Penance,* Canon 5: Denzinger 915 (1705).
18. Second Vatican Council, *Dogmatic Constitution on the Church,* VII, 48.

19. Innocent IV, letter *Sub Catholicae* (Mar. 6, 1254).
20. Second Council of Lyons, *Profession of Faith of Michael Palaeologus:* Denzinger 464 (856).
21. Council of Florence, bull *Laetentur Caeli:* Denzinger 693 (1304–6).
22. Council of Trent, *Decree Concerning Purgatory:* Denzinger 983 (1820).
23. Second Vatican Council, *Dogmatic Constitution on the Church,* VII, 51.
24. Paul VI (Congregation of Rites), *Instruction on the Liturgy,* VIII, 35 (Oct. 16, 1964).

IX. NORMS AND POSTULATES

1. Pius XII (Holy Office), Instruction *De Ethica Situationis:* Denzinger 3918.
2. Paul VI (Congregation for the Clergy), *General Catechetical Directory,* II, 63.

X. COMMANDMENTS OF GOD

1. Second Council of Nicea, *Definition on Sacred Images:* Denzinger 302 (600).
2. Council of Trent, *Invocation, Veneration and Relics of Saints:* Denzinger 984 (1821).
3. Second Vatican Council, *Dogmatic Constitution on the Church,* VII, 50.
4. Ibid., VII, 51.
5. Benedict XV, *Response of the Holy Office:* Denzinger 2182 (3642).
6. Second Vatican Council, *Dogmatic Constitution on the Church,* VII, 51.
7. Second Vatican Council, *Decree on the Pastoral Office of Bishops,* II, 20.
8. Third Council of Baltimore (1884), n. 292.
9. Second Vatican Council, *Decree on the Priestly Ministry and Life,* II, 6.
10. St. Ignatius of Antioch, *Letter to the Magnesians,* 8, 1.
11. *Didache,* XIV, 1.
12. St. Justin Martyr, *First Apology,* 67.
13. *Code of Canon Law,* Canon 1248.
14. Second Vatican Council, *Constitution on the Liturgy,* V, 106.
15. John XXIII, encyclical *Mater et Magistra,* 252–53.
16. *Letter to Diognetus,* 5, 1.

17. Pius XII, *Decree of the Holy Office* (Dec. 2, 1940).
18. Second Vatican Council, *Pastoral Constitution on the Church in the Modern World*, II, 27.
19. Ibid., III, 64.
20. Seneca, *De Ira*, I, 15.
21. *Didache*, II, 2.
22. *Epistle of Barnabas*, II, 19.
23. Tertullian, *Apologia*, IX, 6–7.
24. St. Ignatius Loyola, *Spiritual Exercises*, "Rules for Thinking with the Church," Rule 1.
25. St. Basil, *Three Canonical Letters*.
26. Athenagoras, *Presbeia peri Christianon*, 35.
27. Origen, *Contra Haereses*, 9.
28. Epiphanius, *Panarion*, PG 41, 339.
29. St. Jerome, *Letter 22* (to Eustochium), 13.
30. Second Council of Braga, Canon 77.
31. Pius XI, encyclical *Casti Connubii*, I, 63–7 I, 63–67.
32. Pius XII, allocution to the Association of Large Families, *Acta Apostolicae Sedis* (1951), XLIII, p. 855.
33. John XXIII, encyclical *Mater et Magistra*, III, 194.
34. Second Vatican Council, *Pastoral Constitution on the Church in the Modern World*, IV, 51; Paul VI (Congregation for the Doctrine of the Faith), *Declaration on Procured Abortion*, III, 12 (Dec. 5, 1974).
35. Piux XI, encyclical *Casti Connubii*, II, 68–70.
36. Second Vatican Council, *Pastoral Constitution on the Church in the Modern World*, V, 80.
37. Ibid., V, 83.
38. St. Clement I, *Letter to the Corinthians*, 2–3.
39. Pius XI, encyclical *Casti Connubii*, II, 22.
40. Second Vatican Council, *Pastoral Constitution on the Church in the Modern World*, V, 87.
41. Ibid., V, 89.
42. Ibid., II, 49.
43. Confer documents on masturbation or homosexuality, issued by Leo IX (A.D. 1054), Alexander VII (A.D. 1665–66), Innocent XI (A.D. 1679), Pius XI (A.D. 1929–30), Pius XII (A.D. 1955), and John XXIII (A.D. 1961).
44. Paul VI (Congregation for the Clergy), *General Catechetical Directory*, V, 86.
45. Paul VI, address *To Live the Paschal Mystery*, May 31, 1971.
46. Council of Trent, *Doctrine on the Sacrament of Matrimony*, Canon 7: Denzinger 977 (1807).

47. Pius VI, rescript to the bishop of Agria (Jul. 11, 1789); quoted by Pius XI.
48. Council of Trent, *Doctrine on the Sacrament of Matrimony*, Canon 2: Denzinger 972 (1802).
49. Pius XI, encyclical *Casti Connubii*, I, 20.
50. Ibid., 1, 23.
51. *Didache*, II, 2.
52. St. Clement of Alexandria, *Paidagogos*, II, 9–10.
53. St. Augustine, *De Conjugiis Adulterinis*, II, 12.
54. Gregory IX, *Decretals*, V, 12, 5.
55. Sixtus V, *Effrenatum* (Oct. 27, 1588).
56. Pius IX, *Decision of the Holy Office* (May 21, 1851).
57. Pius XI, encyclical *Casti Connubii*, II, 54, 56.
58. Paul VI, encyclical *Humanae Vitae*, I, 6.
59. Ibid., I, 14.
60. Ibid., 1, 4.
61. Ibid., III, 25.
62. Pius XI, encyclical *Casti Connubii*, II, 59.
63. Pius XII, *Allocution on Moral Questions Affecting Married Life* (Oct. 29, 1951).
64. Paul VI, encyclical *Humanae Vitae*, II, 16.
65. Ibid., II, 24; Second Vatican Council, *Pastoral Constitution on the Church in the Modern World*, II, 51.
66. Paul VI, address *We Had No Doubt About Our Decision* (Jul. 31, 1968).
67. Tertullian, *De Pudicitia*, I: Denzinger 43 (105).
68. Council of Lyons, *The Rites of the Greeks*, XVIII: Denzinger 453 (835); Council of Vienne, *The Errors of the Beghards and the Beguines* (*the State of Perfection*), Proposition 7: Denzinger 477 (897); Alexander VII, *Various Errors on Moral Matters*, Proposition 25: Denzinger 1125 (2045); Innocent XI, *Various Errors on Moral Subjects*, II, Proposition 48: Denzinger 1198 (2148).
69. Second Vatican Council, *Pastoral Constitution on the Church in the Modern World*, II, 49.
70. Pius XI, encyclical *Quadragesimo Anno*, II, 47.
71. Second Vatican Council, *Pastoral Constitution on the Church in the Modern World*, III, 69.
72. Paul VI, encyclical *Populorum Progressio*, I, 22–24.
73. Second Vatican Council, *Pastoral Constitution on the Church in the Modern World*, III, 72.
74. Pius XI, encyclical *Quadragesimo Anno*, I, 31.
75. Pius XII, address to the International Congress on Human Relations in Industry (Oct. 5, 1953).

76. Second Vatican Council, *Pastoral Constitution on the Church in the Modern World*, III, 67–68.
77. St. Augustine, *De Mendacio, passim.*
78. Fourth Lateran Council, *The Trinity, Sacraments, Canonical Mission*, XXI: Denzinger 438 (814).
79. Paul VI (Pontifical Commission for the Means of Social Communication), *Pastoral Instruction* (May 23, 1971), II, 41.
80. Second Vatican Council, *Decree on the Media of Social Communication*, II, 13.
81. Paul VI, *Pastoral Instruction*, II, 52–53.
82. Ibid., II, 60.
83. Ibid.
84. Pius XII, allocution to Catholic journalists (Feb. 17, 1959).
85. Second Vatican Council, *Decree on the Media of Social Communication*, I, 3.
86. Paul VI, *Pastoral Instruction*, II, 30–31.

XI. GROWTH IN HOLINESS

1. Second Vatican Council, *Dogmatic Constitution on the Church*, V, 41–42.
2. Ibid., VI, 44.
3. Paul VI, apostolic exhortation *Evangelica Testificatio*, 2.
4. Second Vatican Council, *Dogmatic Constitution on the Church*, VI, 46; Council of Trent, *Canons on the Sacrament of Matrimony:* Denzinger 980 (1810).
5. Second Vatican Council, *Dogmatic Constitution on the Church*, VII, 50.
6. St. Ignatius Loyola, *Spiritual Exercises*, "First Principle and Foundation."
7. St. Thomas Aquinas, *Summa Theologica*, I, II, 108, 4.
8. Pius XI, encyclical *Miserentissimus Redemptor*, II, 11.
9. Pius XII, encyclical *Mystici Corporis Christi*, III, 103–5.
10. St. Francis de Sales, *Introduction to a Devout Life*, I, 3.
11. Ibid., II, 13.
12. Pius XII, apostolic exhortation *Menti Nostrae*, I, 51.
13. Paul VI, address *Need of Conscience for the Man of Today*, Aug. 2, 1972.
14. Second Vatican Council, *Decree on the Apostolate of the Laity*, I, 2.

588   SACRAMENTS OF THE CHURCH

XII. THE LITURGY

1. Pius XII, encyclical *Mediator Dei*, I, 20.
2. Innocent XI, *Triumphus Pastor* (Oct. 3, 1678).
3. St. Augustine, *Epistola ad Probam*, 18.
4. Pius XII, encyclical *Mediator Dei*, I, 22.
5. Second Vatican Council, *Dogmatic Constitution on the Church*, II, 11.
6. Pius XII, encyclical *Mediator Dei*, I, 23.
7. Second Vatican Council, *Constitution on the Sacred Liturgy*, I, 11.
8. Pius XII, encyclical *Mediator Dei*, I, 40.
9. St. Ignatius of Antioch, *Letter to the Smyrneans*, 8.
10. Second Vatican Council, *Constitution on the Sacred Liturgy*, I, 24, 27, 28, 33.
11. Council of Trent, *The Doctrine on the Most Holy Sacrifice of the Mass*, VIII: Denzinger 946 (1749); Council of Trent, *Canons on the Most Holy Sacrifice of the Mass*, Canon 9: Denzinger 956 (1759).
12. Second Vatican Council, *Constitution on the Sacred Liturgy*, I, 36.
13. Ibid., I, 37.
14. Pius XII, encyclical *Mediator Dei*, I, 52.

XIII. SACRAMENTS OF THE CHURCH   Eucharist

1. Second Vatican Council, *Constitution on the Sacred Liturgy*, II, 48.
2. Council of Trent, *Decree on the Most Holy Sacrament of the Eucharist*, I: Denzinger 874 (1636).
3. St. Ignatius of Antioch, *Letter to the Philadelphians*, 4.
4. St. John Chrysostom, *Commentary on Corinthians*, 24, 4.
5. Fourth Roman Council, *The Most Holy Eucharist:* Denzinger 355 (700).
6. Council of Trent, *Canons on the Most Holy Sacrament of the Eucharist*, Canons 1–6: Denzinger 883–88 (1651–56).
7. Paul VI, *Mysterium Fidei*, IV, 35–39.
8. Pius XII, encyclical *Mediator Dei*, II, 68–69.
9. St. Justin Martyr, *First Apology*, 66.
10. Council of Trent, *The Doctrine on the Most Holy Sacrifice of the Mass*, II: Denzinger 940 (1743).
11. Pius XII, encyclical *Mediator Dei*, II, 80.
12. Ibid., II, 83.
13. *Didache*, IX, 1–3.

14. Paul VI (Sacred Congregation of Rites), *Instruction on Worship of the Eucharistic Mystery* (May 25, 1967), Introduction, 3.
15. *Didache*, XIV, 1.
16. St. Justin, *First Apology*, 67.
17. Tertullian, *De Idololatria*, 7.
18. St. Cyprian, *De Dominica Oratione*, 18.
19. Origen, *Quis Dives Salvetur*, 23.
20. St. Basil, *Epistula*, 93.
21. St. Ambrose, *De Sacramentis*, 5, 24.
22. Council of Tours (Decrees), *Sacrorum Conciliorum Nova Collectio* (Mansi), XIV, 91.
23. Fourth Lateran Council, *The Trinity, Sacraments, Canonical Mission*, V: Denzinger 437 (812).
24. St. Thomas Aquinas, *Summa Theologica*, III, 80.
25. St. Bonaventure, *In Quartum Librum Sententiarum*, XII, 2, 2, 2.
26. Thomas à Kempis, *Imitation of Christ*, IV, 10.
27. Council of Trent, *Decree on the Most Holy Sacrament of the Eucharist*, VIII; Denzinger 882 (1649); Council of Trent, *Doctrine on the Sacrifice of the Mass*, VI: Denzinger 944 (1747).
28. St. Robert Bellarmine, *Opera Oratoria Postuma*, Vol. IV (Rome, 1943), pp. 247, 249.
29. Antoine Arnauld, *De la fréquente communion* (Lyon, 1683), p. 729.
30. Alexander VIII, *Errors of the Jansenists*, Propositions 22–23: Denzinger 1312–13 (2322–23).
31. St. Pius X, Decree *Sacra Tridentina Synodus:* Denzinger 1981–90 (3375–83).
32. Paul VI (Congregation of Rites) Instruction *Eucharisticum Mysterium*, III, 49.
33. Ibid., III, 50.

XIII. SACRAMENTS OF THE CHURCH Penance

1. St. Leo I, *Secret Confession:* Denzinger 145 (323).
2. Origen, *Homily on Psalm 37*, 6.
3. Tertullian, *De Pudicitia*, I, 6.
4. *Pontificale Romanum*.
5. Fourth Lateran Council, *The Trinity, Sacraments, Canonical Mission*, XXI: Denzinger 437 (812).
6. Council of Trent, *Canons on the Sacrament of Penance*, Canons 1 and 3: Denzinger 911, 913 (1701, 1703).
7. Ibid., Canon 4: Denzinger 914 (1704).
8. Ibid., Canon 9: Denzinger 919 (1709).
9. Ibid., Canon 10: Denzinger 920 (1710).

10. Council of Trent, *Doctrine on the Most Holy Sacrament of Penance,* VII: Denzinger 903 (1686).
11. Council of Trent, *Canons on the Sacrament of Penance,* Canon 5: Denzinger 915 (1705).
12. Ibid., Canon 7: Denzinger 917 (1707).
13. Ibid., Canon 13: Denzinger 923 (1713).
14. Lactantius, *De Divinis Institutionibus,* IV, 30.
15. Council of Trent, *Canons of the Sacrament of Penance,* Canon 8: Denzinger 918 (1708).
16. St. Vincent de Paul, *Correspondance, entretiens, documents,* Vol. III (Paris, 1921), p. 323.
17. Ibid., p. 366.
18. Alexander VIII, *Errors of the Jansenists,* Propositions 16, 17, 18, 22: Denzinger 1306, 1307, 1308, 1312 (2316, 2317, 2318, 2322).
19. Pius VI, *Errors of the Synod of Pistoia* (Aug. 28, 1794).
20. St. Pius X, *Quam Singulari* (Aug. 8, 1910).
21. Pius XII, encyclical *Mystici Corporis Christi,* 88.
22. Pius XII, encyclical *Mediator Dei,* 177.
23. Paul VI (Congregation for the Clergy), *General Catechetical Directory,* Addendum, 4.
24. Paul VI (Congregation for Discipline of the Sacraments, Congregation for the Clergy) (May 24, 1973).
25. Paul VI (Congregation of Divine Worship) (Dec. 2, 1973).

XIII. SACRAMENTS OF THE CHURCH Baptism— Confirmation—Priesthood—Marriage—Anointing

1. Council of Trent, *Canons on the Sacraments in General,* Canon 9: Denzinger 852 (1609).
2. St. Stephen I, *The Baptism of Heretics:* Denzinger 46 (110); Pope Innocent III, *Profession of Faith Prescribed for Durand of Osca and His Waldensian Companions:* Denzinger 424 (793); Council of Constance, *Questions to be Proposed to the Wycliffites and Hussites,* Proposition 22: Denzinger 672 (1262); Council of Florence, *Decree for the Armenians:* Denzinger 695 (1310–13); Council of Trent, *Canons on the Sacraments in General,* Canon 11: Denzinger 854 (1611); Council of Trent, *Canons on the Sacrament of Baptism,* Canon 4: Denzinger 860 (1617).
3. *Catechism of the Council of Trent,* II, "Effects of the Sacraments," 2.
4. St. Augustine, *De Baptismo,* I, 15, 20.
5. St. Jerome, *Letter 69,* 4.
6. Council of Trent, *Decree on Original Sin:* Denzinger 792 (1515–16).
7. Second Vatican Council, *Decree on Ecumenism,* I, 3.
8. Second Vatican Council, *Dogmatic Constitution on the Church,* II, 16.

9. Second Council of Lyons (A.D. 1274), *Profession of Faith:* Denzinger 464 (858); Council of Florence (A.D. 1439), *Decree for the Greeks:* Denzinger 693 (1306).

10. Pius VI, *Errors of the Synod of Pistoia*, Proposition 26: Denzinger 1526 (2626).

11. *Didache*, VII, 1.

12. *Rite of Baptism for Children*, Revised by Decree of the Second Vatican Council and Published by Authority of Pope Paul VI, Introduction, 2.

13. Second Vatican Council, *Decree on the Missionary Activity of the Church*, II, 14.

14. Ibid.

15. Second Vatican Council, *Decree on the Missionary Activity of the Church*, VI, 36.

16. Second Vatican Council, *Constitution on the Sacred Liturgy*, III, 21.

17. Paul VI, *Apostolic Constitution on the Sacrament of Confirmation* (Aug. 15, 1971).

18. Council of Florence, *Decree for the Armenians:* Denzinger 697 (1319).

19. Second Vatican Council, *Decree on the Apostolate of the Laity*, I, 3.

20. Council of Trent, *Canons on the Sacrament of Orders*, Canon 3: Denzinger 963 (1773).

21. Ibid., Canon 4: Denzinger 964 (1774).

22. Ibid., Canon 1: Denzinger 961 (1771).

23. Ibid., Canon 6: Denzinger 966 (1776).

24. Paul VI, apostolic constitution *Pontificalis Romani Recognitio* (Apr. 6, 1969).

25. Paul VI, apostolic letter *Ministeria Quaedam* (Jan. 1, 1973).

26. Paul VI, apostolic letter *On the Reformation of First Tonsure, Minor Orders and Subdiaconate* (Jan. 1, 1973).

27. *De Institutione Lectoris*, 6, 7.

28. Council of Trent, *Canons on the Sacrament of Matrimony*, Canon 9: Denzinger 979 (1809).

29. Second Vatican Council, *Decree on the Ministry and Life of Priests*, III, 16.

30. Council of Trent, *Canons on the Sacrament of Matrimony*, Canon 1: Denzinger 971 (1801).

31. Council of Trent, *Doctrine on the Sacrament of Matrimony:* Denzinger 970 (1800).

32. St. Ignatius of Antioch, *Letter to Polycarp*, 5, 2.

33. St. Ambrose, *Letter 19*, 7.

34. St. John Chrysostom, *Homily on First Timothy*, 9.

35. Council of Trent, *Canons on the Sacrament of Matrimony*, Canon 3, 5; Denzinger 973, 975 (1803, 1805).

36. Second Vatican Council, *Constitution on the Sacred Liturgy*, III, 77.
37. Paul VI, apostolic letter *Matrimonia Mixta* (Mar. 31, 1970).
38. Council of Trent, *Doctrine on the Sacrament of Extreme Unction*, I: Denzinger 908 (1695).
39. Ibid.
40. Ibid., III: Denzinger 910 (1697).
41. Ibid., II: Denzinger 909 (1696).
42. Ibid., III: Denzinger 910 (1698).
43. Second Vatican Council, *Constitution on the Sacred Liturgy*, III, 73–75.
44. Paul VI, apostolic constitution *Sacram Unctionem Infirmorum* (Jan. 1, 1974).
45. Paul VI (Congregation for Divine Worship), *Ordo Unctionis Infirmorum Eorumque Pastoralis Curae* (Jan. 1, 1974).

XIV. SACRAMENTALS

1. Second Vatican Council, *Constitution on the Sacred Liturgy*, V, 102.
2. Ibid., V, 108.
3. Ibid., V, 111.
4. Ibid., V, 79.
5. Paul VI (Congregation for Divine Worship), *Instruction on the Liturgy of the Hours*, I, 15–8.
6. Paul VI, apostolic constitution *Paenitemini*, III.
7. Ibid., III, Norm IX, 1.

XV. INDULGENCES

1. Paul VI, apostolic constitution *On Indulgences*, I, 3.
2. Ibid., III, 6.
3. *The Penitential of Finnian* (sixth century), 36.
4. *Old Irish Penitential* (ninth century), 13.
5. *The Milan Penitential* (based on eleventh-century sources), Second Commandment, 1.
6. *The Milan Penitential*, Second Commandment, 3.
7. Paul VI, apostolic constitution *On Indulgences*, IV, 8.
8. Council of Trent, *Decree Concerning Indulgences:* Denzinger 989 (1835).
9. Fourth Lateran Council, *On Abuse in Granting Indulgences*, 440 (819).
10. Paul VI, apostolic constitution *On Indulgences*, V, 12.
11. Ibid., Norms, 18.

12. Ibid., Norms, 20.
13. Ibid.
14. Ibid., V, 12.
15. Paul VI (Apostolic Penitentiary), *Enchiridion Indulgentiarum,* "Concessiones Generaliores," 1–3.

INDEX

Abel, slain by Cain, 324
Abelard, Peter, optimism of, 74
Ablution, baptism by, 511–12
Abnegation: holiness through, 428–30
penance as, 557–58
Abortion: Church's authority and, 247, 370
condemned by Church Fathers, 334–40
early history of, 334–35
legalized, 337–38, 340–41
Pope Paul VI condemns, 341
relation to origin of soul, 106
therapeutic, 337–38
Abraham: biblical origins, 44
Church began with, 206
Absolution: Council of Trent on sacramental, 488–89
formula of sacramental, 499–500
Abstinence: Friday, 558–59
indulgence for voluntary, 569–70
penance through, 555–59
temperance as, 198
Academic freedom, religious liberty and, 252
Acolyte, ministry of, 526–28
Action, justice as, 198
Action sacramentals, 552–53
Active mortification, penance as, 558
Act of charity, indulgence for performing any, 569–70
Acts of man, meaning of, 283–84
Acts of the Apostles, doctrine on angels, 85
Actual grace: Catholic doctrine on, 189–93
confirmation confers, 517–19
light and strength from, 189–90
Adam: Church's teaching on fall, 100–1
origin of, 91–93
sin affected mankind, 119–20, 485–86
special creation of, 91–92
Admonition, duty of parents, 321–22
Adultery: Montanist rigorism, 485
Mosaic law on, 351–52
Advent: Eastern Church fast during, 555
liturgy of, 550
Advertising, morality of, 415–17
Against Heresies, Ireneus, 212
Agape, Christian love as, 289
Aged, Church's care of, 543
Age of discretion, meaning of, 490–91
Agility, quality of glorified body, 265–66
Agnoetes, error about Christ's human knowledge, 147
Aionios, eternal, 268–69
Akatharsia, uncleanness, 366–67
Alacoque, St. Margaret Mary, devotion to Eucharist, 463–64

Albertus Magnus, St., objection to Immaculate Conception, 153
Albigensianism, condemned by Innocent III, 199
Albigensians, problem of evil, 71–72
Alcoholic beverages, prohibition of, 387–88
Aletheia, truth, 401
Alexander VII, Pope, premarital relations condemned, 382
Alexander VIII, Pope: Jansenism condemned by, 476–77
teaching on Holy Communion, 476–77
Alexandrian Rite, 454
Alfred the Great, Sunday Mass obligation, 314–15
Alphabetical writing, Bible origins and, 43–44
Ambrose, St.: on actual grace, 178
contraception condemned, 368
Holy Communion, 473
role of angels, 86–87
sacrament of marriage, 532–33
salvation of non-Catholics, 234–35
taint of Origenism in, 270
Americanism, supernatural virtue underestimated, 199–200
Anastasius, spokesman for Nestorius, 133
Anastasius I, Emperor, Church conflict with, 245–46
Andrew of Crete, St.: conception of Mary, 152
teaching on Mary's assumption, 154
Angelos, messenger of God, 85–86
Angels: choirs of, 85
development of revelation, 84
good and bad, 83–90
Old and New Testament faith in, 84–85
veneration with *dulia,* 442
Anger, Christ's prohibition of, 325
Anne, St., Mother of Mary, 152
Annunciation of Mary, 84, 167
Anointing, sacrament of: biblical foundation, 540–42
children may receive, 545
concelebrated, 546
effects of, 542–43
gravity of illness for, 545
instruction for, 545–46
liturgical history of, 541–43
new formula of, 544
prior to surgery, 545
public solemnity of, 547
repetition of, 545
ritual changes in, 543–47
union with Christ's passion, 447
Anselm, St., teaching on love in heaven, 266
Anthony of Egypt, St., early ascetic, 215